Spirit of the Somerset & Dorset Railway

*To John
my very best
wishes*

[signature]

This edition
has been limited to
2,500 numbered copies
of which this is
No.

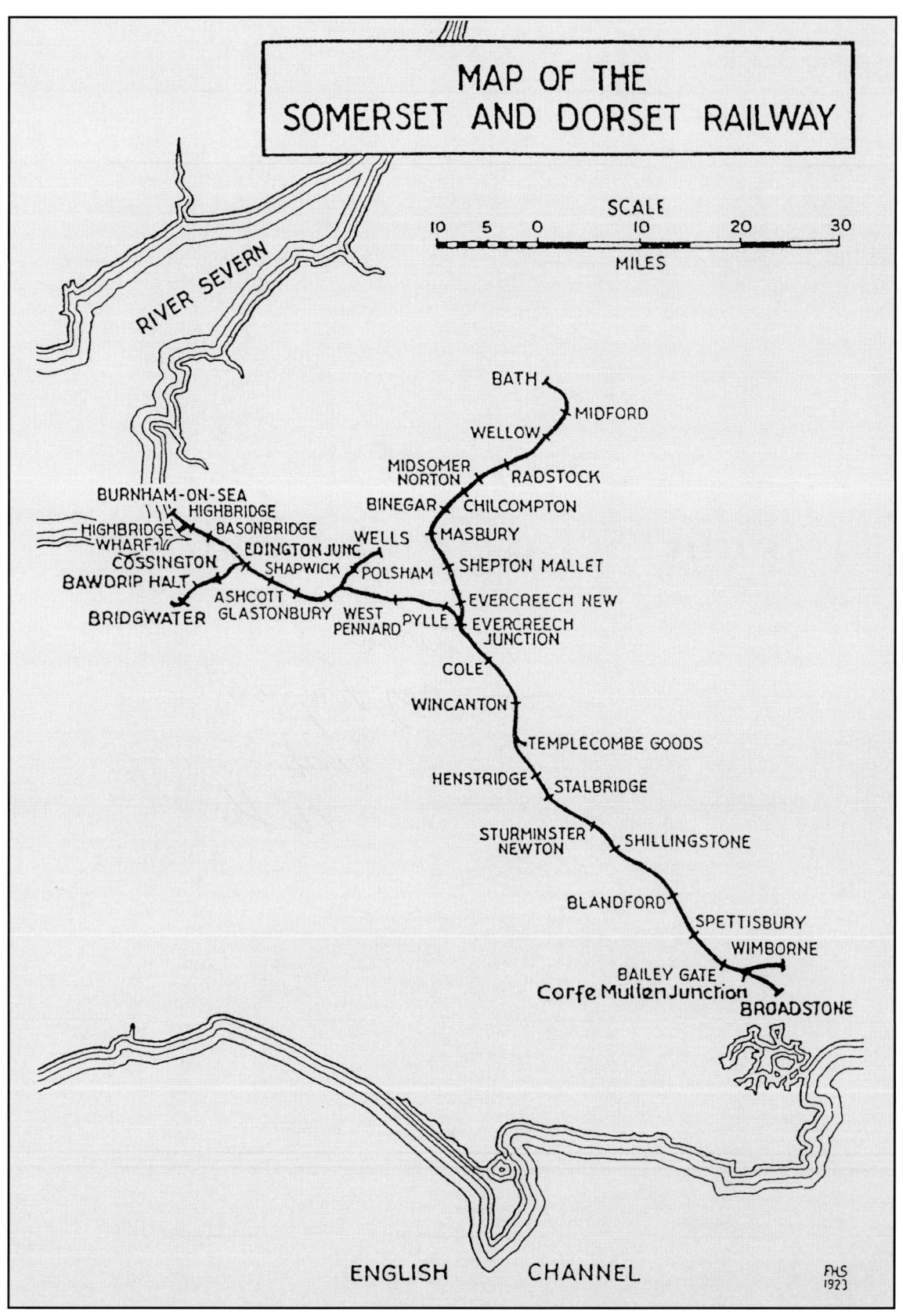

This 1923 map of the Somerset & Dorset Railway shows all stations except the halts of Stourpaine & Durweston, Charlton Marshall, Corfe Mullen, which all opened in 1928, and Shoscombe & Single Hill, which opened in 1929. (*by courtesy of the Somerset & Dorset Railway Trust*)

Spirit of the Somerset & Dorset Railway

Alan Hammond

Millstream Books

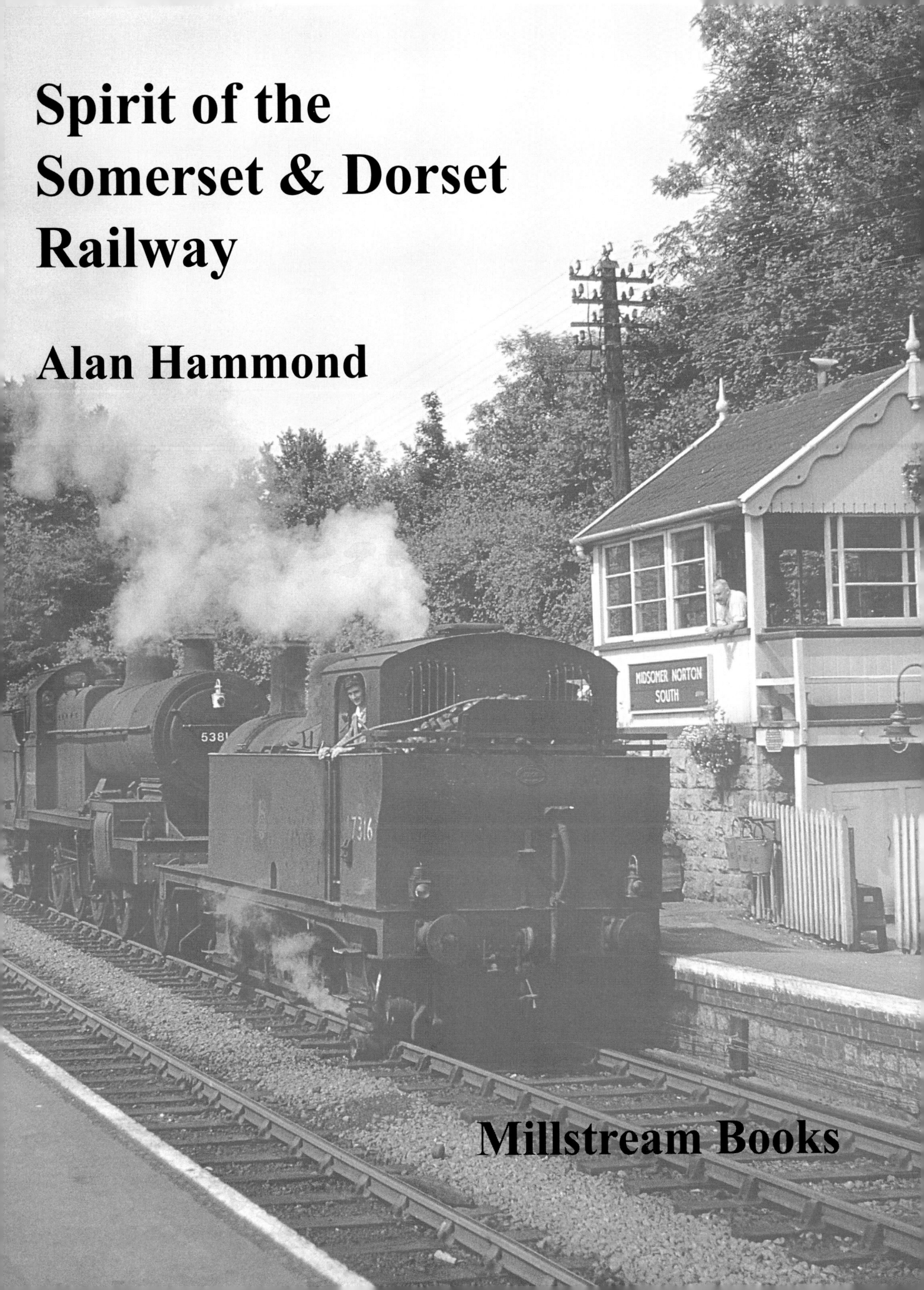

This book is dedicated to
Roy Miles
who passed away on 19 November 2001.
Roy was a guard on the old S&D and was passionate about this railway.
He was a kind man who would help anybody.
Enthusiasts from all around the country sought Roy's knowledge about the S&D and other railways.
He wrote a super book about his working life on the railway, called Right away with the Pines.
Roy will be remembered as a smashing fellow and it was a privilege to have known him.

First published in 2003 by
Millstream Books, 18 The Tyning, Bath BA2 6AL

Set in Times New Roman and printed in Great Britain by
The Amadeus Press, Cleckheaton, West Yorkshire

© Alan Hammond 2003

ISBN 0 948975 66 0

British Library Cataloguing-in-Publication Data:
a catalogue record for this book is available from the British Library

All rights reserved. No part of this publication may be reproduced, stored in a retrieval system, or transmitted in any form or by any means, electronic, mechanical, photocopying, recording or otherwise, without the prior permission of Millstream Books.

Foreword

I am very pleased to be able to write the foreword for Alan Hammond's new book.

One of the nearest stations to where I lived in my childhood had the wonderful name of Bramley and Wonersh on the Guildford to Horsham branch. It was an idyllic setting on the edge of the Surrey and Sussex border. In some way it probably mirrors the stations of Wellow and Sturminster Newton on the Somerset & Dorset.

Transport has been a very important part of my life, firstly with the launch of my company Virgin Atlantic Airways and Virgin Cargo in 1984. Our first plane, a Boeing 747, was aptly named *Maiden Voyager* and on her first trip we flew to New York. In 1996 Virgin Rail Group Ltd was born and in 1997 Intercity West Coast was introduced. Each time I get caught in traffic leaving London or trying to get round the M25 or Birmingham, my confidence in the long-term prospects of the railways is refuelled.

Alan Hammond's affinity with the Somerset & Dorset Railway is self-evident in his new book. It is full of fascinating memories of staff and passengers, with a superb array of photographs, which takes us back in time to the days of steam on the old S&D. *Spirit of the Somerset & Dorset Railway* certainly complements his previous five books on this much-loved railway.

I am very positive that Virgin Rail Group will be an important part of a new modern railway that will take us through the twenty-first century, but let us not forget the pioneers of the railways who made it all happen in the first place.

Sir Richard Branson, 2003

Introduction & Acknowledgements

As I continue my adventures over the Somerset & Dorset Railway I have come in contact with many people who have fond memories of the line. I have interviewed over 200 S&D members of staff and have in excess of 130 hours of audiotape of their memories. I have also spoken to many enthusiasts and numerous people who travelled over the railway and others who came in contact with the S&D through their work. They all have one thing in common with this special railway: they have a genuine interest in the Somerset & Dorset. Through their kindness I have been allowed to use many of their personal stories and photographs in my five previous books on the line. Now more memories and photographs have come to light and with this in mind I have brought out this new book. Like all books of this nature many people have contributed in different ways.

A special thank you to Sir Richard Branson for writing the foreword. I would also like to express my gratitude to railway television presenter Mike Arlett for his childhood memories of the Midford area, which I am sure will rekindle those schooldays for many of you. To Tim Graham, my publisher, for his design skills and support on our sixth book together.

A really big thank-you must go to Keith Barrett who has given me vast amounts of help in all aspects of the book and has also, together with Cliff Smith, tracked down many names of staff in the photographs. To Andy Moon who has given me help and advice on all my other previous books on the S&D. I am most grateful to Roy Pitman who has been a great support and friend to me, especially with proof reading of the book, as have Christine and Irene Hammond, Richard Derry, John Simms, Keith Barrett, and Cliff Smith.

My sincere thanks go to all the contributors of memories and photographs. Rod Blencowe has helped enormously with his collection of photographs, also Len Taylor for his excellent photos of the Wincanton area. The Somerset & Dorset Railway Trust have always supported me with their archive of photographs with the help of Jason Baker, who has done a first-class job in collating many hundreds of their photographs. Tim Deacon has been a real help with his list of S&D staff names.

Many others have helped in different ways. I would like to say thanks to Lesley Miles, Mona Pitman, Bob Downes, Roy White, Ivor Ridout, Stan & Kate Blacker, Percy Parsons, Gordon Hatcher, George Judd, Arthur King, Dennis Ashill, Vic Freak, Gordon Lee, John Mansfield, Jim Milton, Terry Loader, Jim Jewell, Paul Fry, John Stamp, Laurie Poulton, Bernard Andrews, Graham Moore, Bill Harford, David Milton, Joan, Fred and Andrew Fisher, Betty Spiller, Ted Drew, Chris Handley, Fred Lester, John Lancastle, Nigel Pass, Richard Dagger, Bernard Martin, Barbara Burdge, Frank Staddon, Joan & Alan Gregory, Zoe Stowe, John Dray, Rose Ware, Robin Gould, Ken Padfield and Tony Haggett.

As many photographs are from the collections of S&D staff, a reader may well recognize a photograph that he or she took. In this case, I offer my apologies in advance for not being able to credit you in person.

Since my last S&D book we have sadly lost some more staff; our thoughts are with the families of Roy Miles, Geoff Moxey, Bill Goodland, Dennis Thorne, Jim Maidment, Peter Pike, Phil Hatcher, Bill Parsons and Dennis Nettley.

My special thanks and love go to my wife and best friend Christine, who has been a pillar of strength and support to me and is an important member of the team.

Alan Hammond
Minehead, 2003

(*above*) Two thirsty S&D crews enjoy a cup of tea at the station buffet. In the picture are Doug Holden, Ted Paulley, Graham Toghill and Harold Burford. (*Jim Jewell collection*)

BR Standard class 3 Tank No.82004 waits in the gloom of Bath Green Park station with a single-coach evening train to Binegar in 1965. (*SDRT collection*)

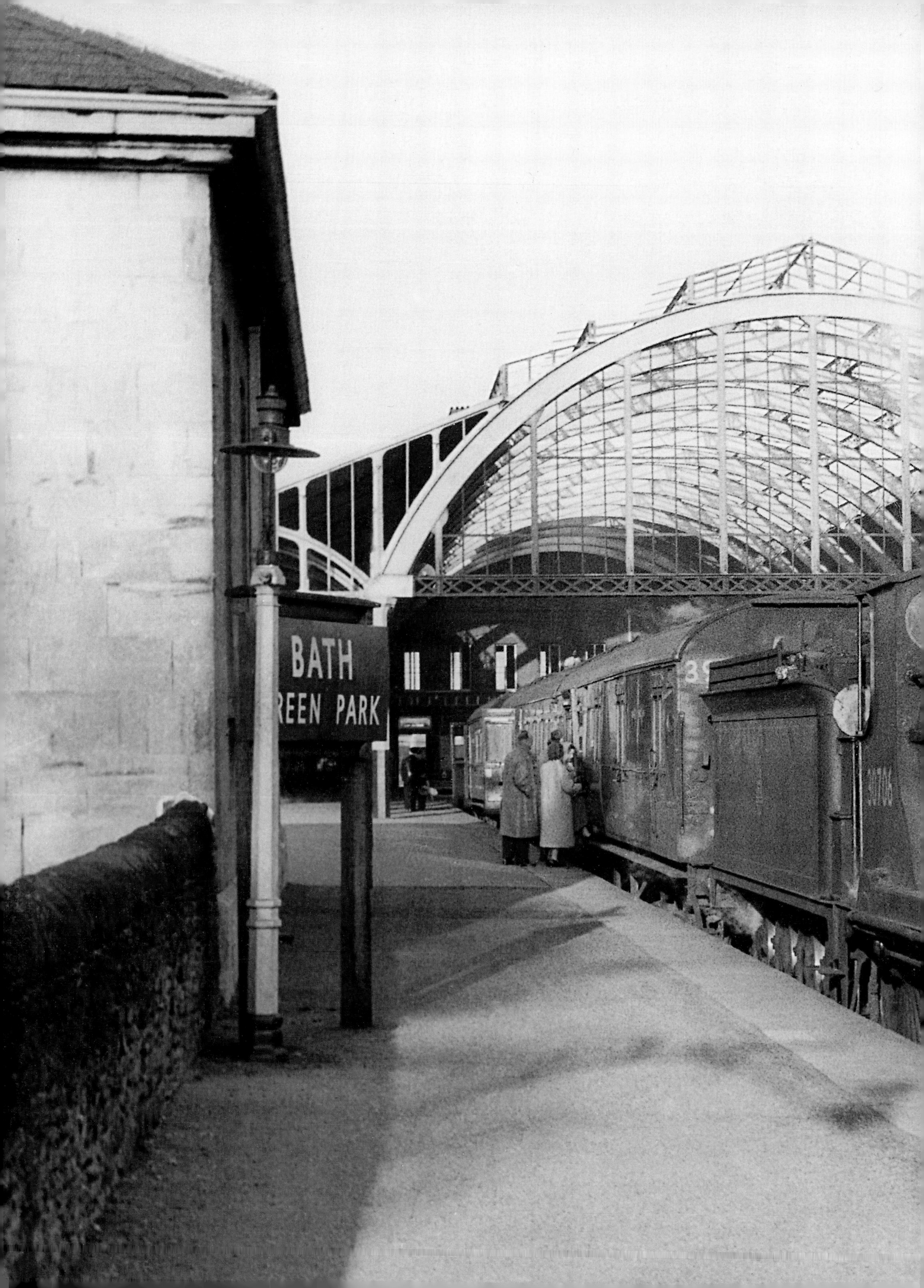
BATH
REEN PARK

An unusual visitor to Bath Green Park, class T9 No.30706, which was covering for a failure at Bournemouth. The shadows on the platform and locomotive tell us that it is early evening, so the train would be the 19.05 to Bournemouth West, c.1958. (*R.E.Toop*)

Arthur King

It is 64 years since I started on the S&D as a cleaner at Bath Green Park. My memories of the S&D are that it was a happy line; the staff rarely had any differences and got on well with each other. You could always get plants for your garden or a rabbit or two from any station down the line. The work varied greatly and there was never a dull moment. Many families at Bath worked on the S&D including my father Arthur and brother Gordon; Archie, Bill and Tom Gunning; Frank and Reg Staddon; Oscar and Tony Pitt; Doug and Ralph Holden; Edgar and Ron Gray; and Ernie and Fred Hemmings.

One Saturday morning during the summer workings I had just returned to Bath loco after an assisting turn to Evercreech Junction. I had to clean the fire for another turn but could not get back on the pit. I was waiting on No.5 road for one to become available. The foreman Arthur Elliott came along and said they were waiting for the engine. I said I was waiting for a pit. "Throw it out here," he said. I passed comment that someone may come along; he said: "Shout out before throwing it". I did this a minute or two later and the first person to come by was foreman Elliott. I threw the first shovel-full of red-hot clinker all over him catching his suit alight. He had to send home for another suit; I don't think he asked anyone else to throw it out there again.

One day I worked the 11.20 goods from Bath to Evercreech. On the return journey I had a light load, which meant I could go faster up the bank. Before we could leave the Junction we had to wait for another freight to clear Shepton Mallet distant signal; it was heavier than ours. When it cleared, we left the Junction at a fair speed. When we got to Shepton Mallet distant signal, to our surprise it was in the off position. I said to my fireman, "Blimey, he cleared Masbury quick", so away we went with all signals off to Winsor Hill. When we got through the tunnel there in front of us was the other train. I kept going behind it until we got to Masbury signalbox where I stopped and asked the signalman Les Willsher what was going on; he was surprised to see me. He got in touch with the Shepton Mallet signalbox and apparently the signalman had gone to the toilet and forgot to put the signals back. Being good S&D men we squared it up between us and nobody knew.

One of my hardest driving turns at Bath was when I had to work to Bournemouth on a summer Saturday and work another train back to Bath. The engine for the return was a Battle of Britain class engine, which was prepared at Bournemouth Central and brought over to us at Branksome. I left Bournemouth West with 10 coaches on and everything was all right until we got to Blandford Forum where I had to stop as booked. By now it had started to rain making the rails very slippery, which I soon found out on getting the right away. I had not gone far up the bank when the engine started to slip. I opened the sand lever to check this but it had no effect and the engine kept slipping and we came to a standstill. I found that the engine would go 2 beats each time the regulator was opened before it started to slip. I then opened the regulator, let it have 2 beats then closed it down and it didn't slip. I kept doing this until we got to the top of the bank; did my arm ache by then. At Evercreech Junction we had a pilot engine on the front so it was all right up the bank to Bath. I reported this to the shed foreman at Bath loco and he had the engine examined. It was found that the sand boxes had not been filled at Bournemouth Central where the engine was prepared. Another incident I recall was in 1948 when I was disposing of an engine on No.3 road at Bath shed. I was breaking up the clinker with the bar and was leaning on it because the clinker was that bad. All of a sudden it broke and I fell on the footplate hurting my back; it was very painful and I could not move. An engine was taking on water on the coal stage; Charlie Morris was standing by the water valve and I called out for him to get help and he replied that he could not go, as his tank was nearly full. Help eventually came along and I was sent to hospital and had an operation on my back – I had slipped a disc. I was in plaster from my chest to my thighs for over four months, then put into a steel and leather brace to stop my spine moving.

After some time I went back to work on light duties, which began with the 07.00 loco shunt on shed with Lou Ricketts. When we had finished for the day we would book off and take a short-cut across the main line, going down the steps by the up-side shunters' cabin to the main road (Albert Terrace). One day I noticed the signal was off for an approaching train, it was for the Pines Express from the north running 15 minutes late. I saw it coming and stopped, but Lou kept walking across. The train was almost on top of us when I grabbed hold of his arm and pulled him back, it was a near thing. Lou went as white as a sheet and was

shaking; we went back to our cabin, sat down and had a cup of tea to get over the shock. Lou could never thank me enough and commented later that I had saved his life.

One day we were working the return of the 02.40 mail from Bournemouth West to Bath; we changed tablets at Shillingstone all right. At the distant signal for Sturminster Newton I put the tablet in the catcher for changing at the signalbox. I held the hand lamp and shone the light on the catcher to see the exchange. When we got to Stalbridge we were stopped at the box and told we did not give up the tablet at Sturminster. I told the signalman that I watched the exchange, his catcher must have knocked it out and it must be on the floor somewhere. He kept us there for some time while the Sturminster signalman searched for it. After a while I decided to go up in to the box and speak to the Sturminster signalman on the phone myself. I got off the engine and took my hand lamp with me. As I passed the rear of the tender my lamp shone on the step and there was the tablet. It must have got knocked out of our catcher, pitched on the rear step of our Black 5 and ridden all the way to Stalbridge without falling off. We had to uncouple our engine and take it back to Sturminster, taking with us the single-line tablet for us to return to Stalbridge and to work our train forward, very late.

Whilst working the same train back on a different day, I was then a fireman and was with driver Bert Reed. We left Branksome shed and went tender-first to Bournemouth West to pick up our train. The guard came up and gave the driver the load and got back into his van. The signal came off and the driver opened the regulator and we were away. I picked up the hand lamp to exchange signals with the guard and bang I was up in the tender. Bert had not put it in forward gear and we had gone backwards into the stop blocks. Luckily the guard was all right, he had seen what was happening and jumped off. The blocks were in a real mess, but the train was fine and away we went the right way this time.

My memories still go back to those days when I recall many railwaymen like Bill Appleby, Cliff West, Stan Bonfield, Sid White, Alfie Smith, Bernard Ware, Ron Merchant, Harold Moody, Ivor Willshire, Harry Starkey, Ray Adams, Bernard Kilmister, Lou Ricketts, George Tucker, John Stamp, Arthur Turner and many more.

Footplate crew Arthur King (left) and his son Arthur are seen at Bath coal stage (No.2 road). The two locos are 2P No.40568 (left) and 8F No.48672. Up above to the right are two members of the coal stage team. (*Arthur King collection*)

Bath Green Park in pre-nationalisation days. Black Five No.4844 with safety valves well lifted waits for the right away, c.1947. At the other end of the train an engine waits for release to return to the MPD; to the left a train for Bristol. In the right background can be seen the spire of Holy Trinity Church which was gutted during the German Baedeker raids of 1942. (*H.C.Casserley*)

Driver Dennis Norris and fireman Robin Gould in the cab of BR class 4 No.75009 at Bath Green Park. Quite a memorable event for both of them as they had just piloted the last assisted Pines Express northbound. (*Robin Gould collection*)

Class 2P No.40564 pilots West Country No.34106 *Lydford* into Bath Green Park station, c.1957. On the right of the picture is the water softening tower with the building of crane manufacturers, Stothert & Pitt's, behind. (*L.G.Marshall/R.K.Blencowe collection*)

7F No.53808 is moving off to Bath MPD, having uncoupled from a mixed freight train hauled from Evercreech Junction, c.1961. On the right there is a glimpse of the side of Stothert & Pitt's boiler shop. (*Martyn Burch*)

Railway policeman Gordon King looks up as 5700 class No.3681 driven by John Stamp and fired by Howard Reynolds is seen here at Bath Green Park on 5 March 1966. The Pannier will pull the train clear to allow the loco to come off the train, through the cross over and back into traffic. (*John Stamp*)

(*above*) Fireman Cliff Smith at Bath Green Park beside Jubilee 4-6-0 No.45564 *New South Wales*, waiting to back onto a train coming off the S&D to work to the north. (*John Stamp*)

A close up of Bath Green Park shunting engine 5700 class 0-6-0 PT No.3742 with Stan Shellard in charge. (*Nigel Pass collection*)

Young Nigel Pass in the cab of 7F No.53806 in 1964. Nigel was probably the last person to set foot onto the footplate of this engine, as later that day she was taken to J.Cashmore at Newport to be scrapped. (*Nigel Pass collection*)

A team photo at Bath Green Park shed. From left to right are David Massey, Harold Crossey, Eric Webber, Bev Reynolds and in the cab of 5700 class 0-6-0 PT No.3681 is Howard Reynolds. (*John Stamp*)

(*above*) Railwaymen of the 1920s. Behind the young girl is Alf Metcalfe who later worked on the S&D for many years. Note the gaiters on the gentleman on the left-hand side. (*Ray Metcalfe collection*)

Porter Joyce Ainsworth carries out a spot of weeding at Bath Green Park station gardens in the 1950s. (*Roy Miles*)

(*above*) Bath Junction signalbox on a wet day, with the Alfred Whitaker single-line tablet apparatus evident in front of the box either side of the line. Signalmen Dave Boston and Bernard Ware worked here for a number of years. Behind the signalbox, the line to Mangotsfield can be seen, also part of one of Bath Gas Works gasholders. (*SDRT collection*)

Shed foreman Arthur Elliott stands next to Jinty No.7316 complete with snow plough in the Boat Road at Bath in the 1940s. (*Jack Hobbs collection*)

Appearing supremely confident, BR Standard class 9 No.92001 effortlessly eases its train out of Bath Green Park bound for Bournemouth West. The trainspotter sitting on the bridge abutment has seen it all before. Anyway, there will be another one along presently, or will there? (*Martyn Burch*)

An extremely cold view of BR Standard 5 No.73052 about to enter Combe Down Tunnel in January 1963. Young Bath firemen John Sawyer, Mike Ryall, Ian Bunnett, Chris Holder, David Norman, Roger Eames, Brian Short, Chris Fell, Richard Kelson, Derek Coles, Wayne Mayo, Colin Powis and John Tooze will always remember the first time they went through this long and uninviting tunnel. (*Martyn Burch*)

BR class 4 No.75073 draws into an immaculate Midford station. What a beautiful view it must have been from the signalbox looking out over the Midford Valley. (*E.T.Gill/R.K.Blencowe collection*)

A photo such as this, is perhaps how most of us would like to remember the S&D, as class 2P No.40652 pilots an unidentified BR class 5 with a down express at Midford in 1959. (*E.T.Gill/R.K.Blencowe collection*)

BR class 4MT No.80013 makes a fine sight after passing Midford with a southbound train in July 1964. (*Dave Walden*)

Mike Arlett

Memories Of Twinhoe & The Spile Bank

On reflection, I think there was always an element of friendly rivalry between Midford signalman Charlie Eyre (who hailed from 'up North') and his two colleagues Harry Wiltshire and Percy Savage (both local S&D men, through and through)! Over the years, Charlie very occasionally allowed me to accompany him on the two-mile walk from his home in Wellow to the box at Midford. Officially, this should have been via the narrow lanes, which in addition to being very hilly provided a rather indirect route. How much better, therefore, to follow – at least in part – the trackside and, in so doing, discover much more about the delights of both the railway and the countryside as we headed past Lower Twinhoe. "Harry, Charlie showed me where the old canal used to run on this side of Wellow." "Did he" says Harry, "but I bet he didn't show you the Spile Bank." "What's the Spile Bank, Harry?" "Ask Charlie!" and I did, and Charlie didn't know … and I didn't think it prudent to ask Harry again!

My memories of the Somerset & Dorset before the start of the 'swinging sixties' (and the purchase of my first car) were, of necessity, mostly limited to the line between Bath and no further south than Wellow. The thought of cycling beyond the latter village never even crossed my mind! Only the occasional train journey – perhaps an excursion to Bournemouth – would take me further afield on the S&D. It was not until around 1958 that a small group of like-minded school friends tackled a 50-mile marathon to Evercreech Junction and back one hot summer Saturday. As one lad commented, "a long way to pedal to see a line-up of assisting locomotives, all of which were destined to pass through Midford later in the day!" The fact that we had witnessed something out of the ordinary was of no consequence – steam locomotives were 'ten-a-penny', an everyday sight.

Summer Saturdays, together with less frequent weekday visits to 'the Dorset' during the school holiday, were generally spent on the station platform at Midford or part-way up Primrose Hill, on the road leading towards Twinhoe; the steep hillside providing a wonderful vantage point from which to view the line across the viaduct to the station and beyond. These were trainspotting days; the interest lay in the variety and combinations of motive-power, coupled with the fascination of the single-line section towards Bath. Discovering new locations depended on how adventurous we felt; it didn't pay to stray too far from the immediate lineside for fear of missing just one of the many passing summer Saturday 'expresses' en route to Bournemouth from far away places like Nottingham, Walsall, Lincoln, Bradford, or even Cleethorpes. I had to use my father's AA handbook to find out the whereabouts of some of these towns!

One major deterrent to exploring the lineside beyond the immediate environs of Midford, was the fact that, unlike the route of the railway, the roads and lanes climbed steeply away from Midford station in all directions! This involved much foot slogging (whilst pushing the bike) up gradients which put to shame the mere 1 in 50 of the S&D! 1 in 5 would be more like it! Even the mile from Midford to the lineside at Lower Twinhoe involved such a climb up the hillside and then, of course, back down the other side. But, on reflection, it always seemed worth the effort.

Armed only with a notebook, two Ian Allan 'ABCs' (London Midland and Southern Regions!), some sandwiches and the inevitable bottle of Tizer, what better way to while away a few hours. Having clambered up Primrose Hill, the grade eventually eased to the stage where pedal power could be resumed. Here, whilst there were wide-sweeping views across the countryside, the railway was now hidden from view, far below. Onwards, a little further, to a left turn at a small junction in the lane, heralded the start of an equally steep descent. Soon, however, the metalled lane petered out to become a narrow stone and dirt track which tumbled on down the hillside towards a bridge (No.20) under the railway. Approaching the bridge, the lane (probably an old drove-road) descended into a narrow cutting; the near vertical banks on either side supporting the fields. Here I could scramble up the steep embankment and crawl under the fence to emerge back into sunlight at a point where there was an elevated mound of grass to the side of the line, close to the Midford 'up distant' signal. I had seen photographs taken from this very same spot – a sort of grandstand view of the line as it swept around the valley in a wide reverse curve.

Just imagine, if you can, a sunny midweek afternoon in July; the only sounds are of the countryside; perhaps the lowing of the cattle as they are herded towards the farm for afternoon milking, the clanging of milk churns and the distant drone of a petrol-driven generator used to power the milking machines. Hand milking still persisted on a few of the smaller farms but, generally, cattle were now milked by machine. Herringbone parlours, bulk milk tanks and the like were still of the future, so milk was still taken to the dairy or factory in churns. More than one local farmer around Midford and Wellow has since recounted to me how, when working out in the fields, the passing trains on the S&D acted as their clock; so perhaps it was the sound of the southbound 'Pines' that heralded the afternoon milking session! Both locomotives could be heard as they were opened up at the foot of the 1 in 60 from Midford for the short climb towards Twinhoe. They were out of sight until reaching the occupation overbridge (No.19) where the line skirted Rainbow Wood. Then sweeping around the curves, past my vantage point, an old Midland class 2P 4-4-0 assisting a modern BR class 5. Within a minute, they are gone, the long rake of coaching stock receding from view, around yet another bend; this time passing Hankley Wood. It is all over so soon, but no matter, for appearing around that same bend comes an 'up' freight train – the 1.05pm from Evercreech Junction, running about 10 minutes ahead of schedule. The Midford 'up distant' is 'on' and the train is already slowing in anticipation of being brought to a halt at the 'outer home' signal, half a mile further north. That means the 3.15pm stopper to Templecombe will be on its way out of Bath, on the single-line section to Midford. The freight is hauled by one of the S&D class 7F 2-8-0s, and as she drifts past, the crew give a wave – or shout something rude! Slowly, the train rattles by until finally, the rear guard's van passes from view. Right on cue, at 3.30pm, the stopper appears – a class 4F 0-6-0 with a train of three elderly coaches, chattering by at no great speed. This train will pause at all stations and halts (Masbury to set down only) to Templecombe; a further 32 miles to be completed in a leisurely hour and a half! Back in the direction of Midford, the sound of a whistle. Out of sight, the class 7F, having been given the road, can be heard restarting the up freight and quickly gathering some speed to attack the climb northwards from Midford viaduct, up the Park Bank, across Tucking Mill Viaduct and into Combe Down Tunnel. And that's probably all I watched before heading back. Just another pleasant little interlude; I had seen all four locomotives before, but no matter – next time it might be different. As far as I was concerned, there would always be 'a next time'.

Simple times; happy times and seemingly a million miles away from the insecurities of life today. I still count myself very fortunate that I grew up during the era when it was still possible to witness at first hand the final decade of this marvellous old line.

Looking back through my rose-tinted glasses at those far-off days, the sun always shone at Midford. "Well of course it did" retorts my wife; "that's because you would never have ventured there if it was raining!" Sandra is right, of course. I can't recall setting off on a twelve-mile bike ride if rain clouds were threatening. I mean, it didn't matter, it would all still be there the following Saturday, and the following summer. It would be there forever, wouldn't it!

Oh, by the way, it took me nearly 30 years to discover what Harry Wiltshire had been talking about when he referred to the 'Spile Bank'. About ten years ago (long after Harry had departed to that great signal-box in the sky), the S&D Railway Trust acquired some diary notes made by a Thomas Edmund Maidment. He had been employed in the Resident Engineer's Office of the S&DJR during the era when much of the main line north of Evercreech Junction had been doubled. Mr. Maidment's diary included several references to the widening of the Wellow to Midford section. One entry, dated 24th August 1892, read as follows "Made tracing shewing spoil bank at Twinhoe and took out quantities". The penny finally dropped. I had simply mistaken Harry's pronunciation of the word 'spoil' – and me a 'moonraker'! The location was a convenient place selected by the railway company to deposit an accumulation of surplus soil (spoil) dug out when it was widening this section of the line. What's more, the 'Spile Bank' turned out to be that very same grass-covered mound onto which I had clambered all those years ago to spend the occasional half-hour or so, just watching the trains go by!

London and South Western Ry.
787
From WATERLOO
TO
MIDFORD
Via TEMPLECOMBE.

Wellow station looking towards Midford with the signalbox visible in the distance. The whole scene looks neat and tidy; the permanent way gang are putting their kit away in the hut at the end of the platform. *(E.T.Gill/R.K.Blencowe collection)*

September 1959	BR.29621

W.R. TELEPHONE CIRCUIT NO. 744
WELLOW SIGNAL BOX - RADSTOCK
  NORTH "B" SIGNAL BOX

STATION	CALL
Wellow Signal Box	1 - 3
Shoscombe Halt	2 - 1
Writhlington	3
Radstock North "A" Box	2
Shunters	2 - 2
"B" Signal Box	1 - 2

(*above*) Fireman Albert Parsons looking out of the cab of a 5MT on the down road at Wellow in 1965. (*SDRT collection*)

(*below*) Young fireman Oliver Barnes taking a rest on the southbound Pines Express on 28 July 1939. (*S.C.Townroe/R.K.Blencowe collection*)

(*above*) The telephone circuit operating between Wellow and Radstock in 1959. (*Keith Barrett collection*)

(*below*) Taken on the footplate of a class 5 is driver Bill Amos on the southbound Pines Express on 28 July 1939. (*S.C.Townroe/R.K.Blencowe collection*)

LMS 7F No.13805 heads towards Shoscombe with a down freight in 1935. The permanent way looks immaculate. (*Jack Hobbs collection*)

LMS class 7F No.13809 speeds towards Shoscombe with a down freight in 1937. (*Jack Hobbs collection*)

Class 4 No.76057 passing Shoscombe and Single Hill Halt with the 13.10 Bournemouth West to Bristol Temple Meads train in 1965. (*C.L.Caddy*)

This early photograph shows a class 2P leaving Shoscombe and Single Hill Halt with a down train. (*SDRT collection*)

LMS class 7F No.13810 hauls a southbound freight near Radstock in 1935. (*Jack Hobbs collection*)

Class 2P No.700 and an unidentified class 4F 0-6-0 run past Writhlington Colliery sidings with a southbound train in 1949. (*R.K.Blencowe collection*)

(*above*) 0-4-0ST No.45A was built at Highbridge Works in 1895. It is seen here at Radstock in 1912. Note the grand old gentleman on the footplate. (*George Pitman*)

Somerset & Dorset Railway Trust engine 7F No.53808 is seen at Radstock with driver Jimmy Machin (left) and fireman Mike Lodder on board. (*Jim Jewell collection*)

West Country class No.34099 *Lynmouth* thunders past Radstock East box with a down express in 1958. (*R.C.Riley*)

A superb action shot of BR Standard class 4 No.76062 sweeping past Radstock goods yard with a short passenger train. (*E.T.Gill/R.K.Blencowe collection*)

Signalman Ken Evans leans out of Radstock West signalbox which later became North box. (*SDRT collection*)

(*below*) BR class 4 No.75023 is about to pass Radstock North B box, home to such signalmen as Bert Haines, Les Willsher, Walt Woods and Phil Crouchen. On the left can be seen a wonderful array of what would now be classic cars; on the far right is the Radstock Co-operative Bakery. (*E.T.Gill/R.K.Blencowe collection*)

A rare occurrence of a U1 class No.31906 on the S&D, approaching Midsomer Norton station in March 1954. (*Alan Newman*)

Caught hard at work in 1949 are LMS class 2P No.634 piloting an unidentified Black 5, about to pass Midsomer Norton with a heavy twelve-coach train for Bournemouth. (*R.K.Blencowe collection*)

Fireman Albert Parsons (left) and driver Vic Ball on the footplate in 1965. (*SDRT collection*)

(*below*) Fireman Eric Wilson (left) and driver Horace Clark on 3F 0-6-0T No.47544 at Norton Hill Colliery in 1965. (*Author's collection*)

(*above*) Midsomer Norton station staff photographed in the 1920s. From left to right are stationmaster Frank Franks, Joe Crouchen with his pipe, C.Lamb, H.Coombes, the stationmaster's son, Frank Packer and Fred Pearce.
(*Mrs M.Packer*)

Three young lads in the delightful gardens of Midsomer Norton station. Do you recognize yourself?
(*Ken Dando collection*)

A splendid panoramic view of Midsomer Norton station in 1962. The S&D Railway Heritage Trust is making giant steps to bring the good times back to the station. *(E.T.Gill/R.K.Blencowe collection)*

Midsomer Norton signalman Joe Crouchen enjoys a yarn on a glorious summer's day with the driver of class 3F No.47544. *(E.T.Gill/R.K.Blencowe collection)*

A somewhat grubby Standard class 4 No.76062 is about to leave Midsomer Norton station with a down local. (*E.T.Gill/R.K.Blencowe collection*)

Standard class 4 2-6-4T No.80059 stops at Chilcompton with a down local in 1964. (*E.T.Gill/R.K.Blencowe collection*)

Class 2P No.40569 heads away south from Chilcompton station. The train seems to consist of ex-LMS coaches. (*Lens of Sutton*)

7F No.53809 hauls a freight train through Chilcompton going south in 1959. The station site was open to cold winds during the winter and the water column needed to be well shrouded to prevent freezing. (*E.T.Gill/R.K.Blencowe collection*)

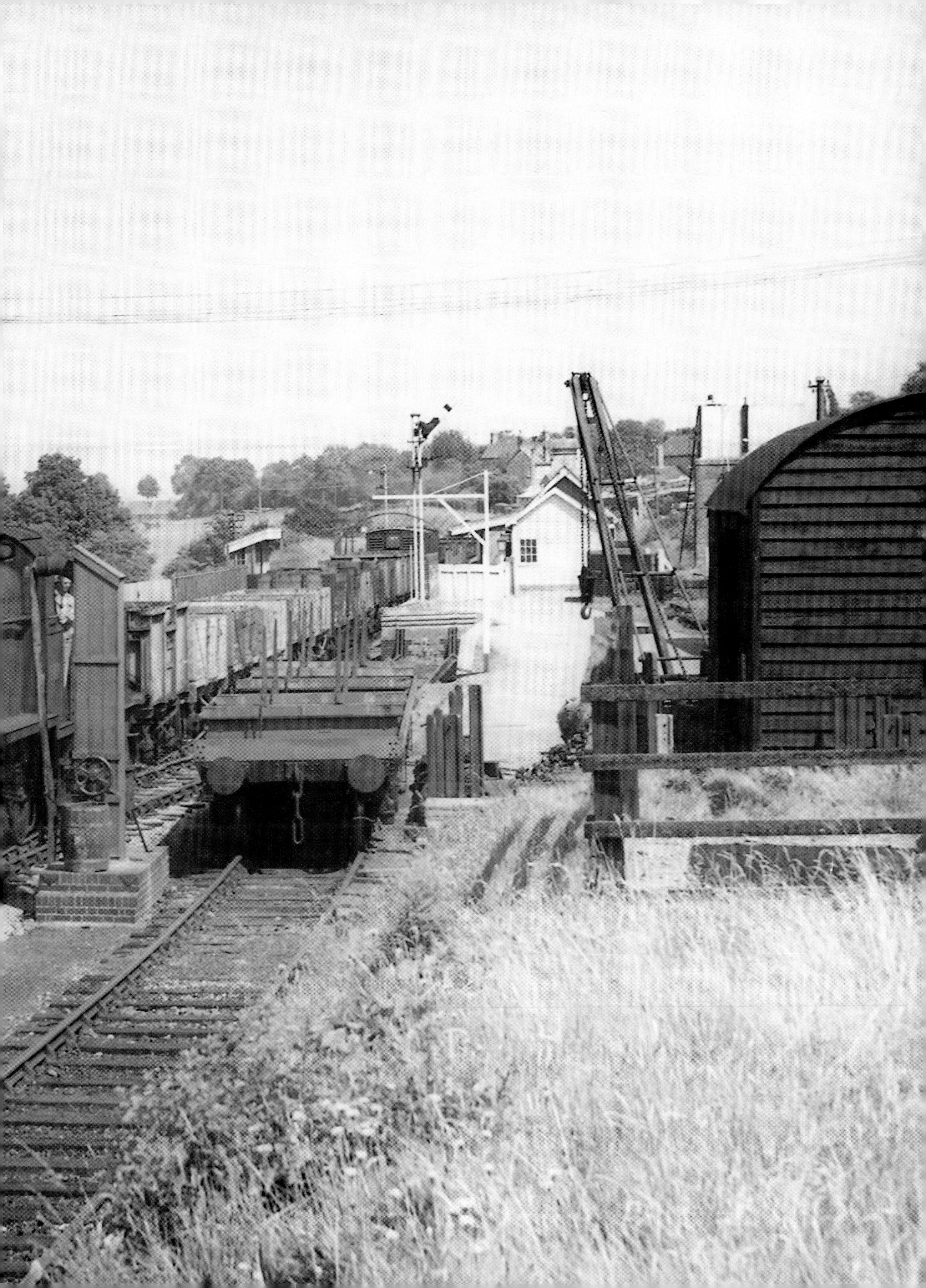

Stationmaster Stan Routley at Chilcompton station in 1952. He started his railway career at Weymouth, then went on to Highworth and Swindon. Stan took up his appointment at Chilcompton in 1951 where he remained until his early death in May 1953 at the age of 45. (*Joan & Alan Gregory collection*)

(*below*) Another shot of Stan with Chilcompton signalman Bill Coombes in the 13-lever box in 1952. Bill was a dab hand with the scissors and did many a haircut in the box. (*Joan & Alan Gregory collection*)

Driver Fred Hemmings placing the lamp on BR class 3 No.82004, after the loco has run around the train at Binegar on the 18.05 from Bath, ready to work back to the city. (*SDRT collection*)

(*below*) Class 2P No.40652 pilots a BR Standard class 5 through Binegar station towards Masbury in 1959. (*E.T.Gill/R.K.Blencowe collection*)

This photograph captures a sylvan scene as class 5 No.73050 with a southbound Bournemouth train is climbing the incline between Binegar and Masbury in 1954. (R.E.Toop)

Class 2P No.40563 with an unidentified WC class, climbs towards the summit of the line near Masbury with a down express. Looking out of the cab is Templecombe fireman Graham Cockerell. (*R.K.Blencowe collection*)

Working hard through Masbury Halt is BR class 4 No.75009 and an unidentified 9F with an up train for Bath. (*E.T.Gill/ R.K.Blencowe collection*)

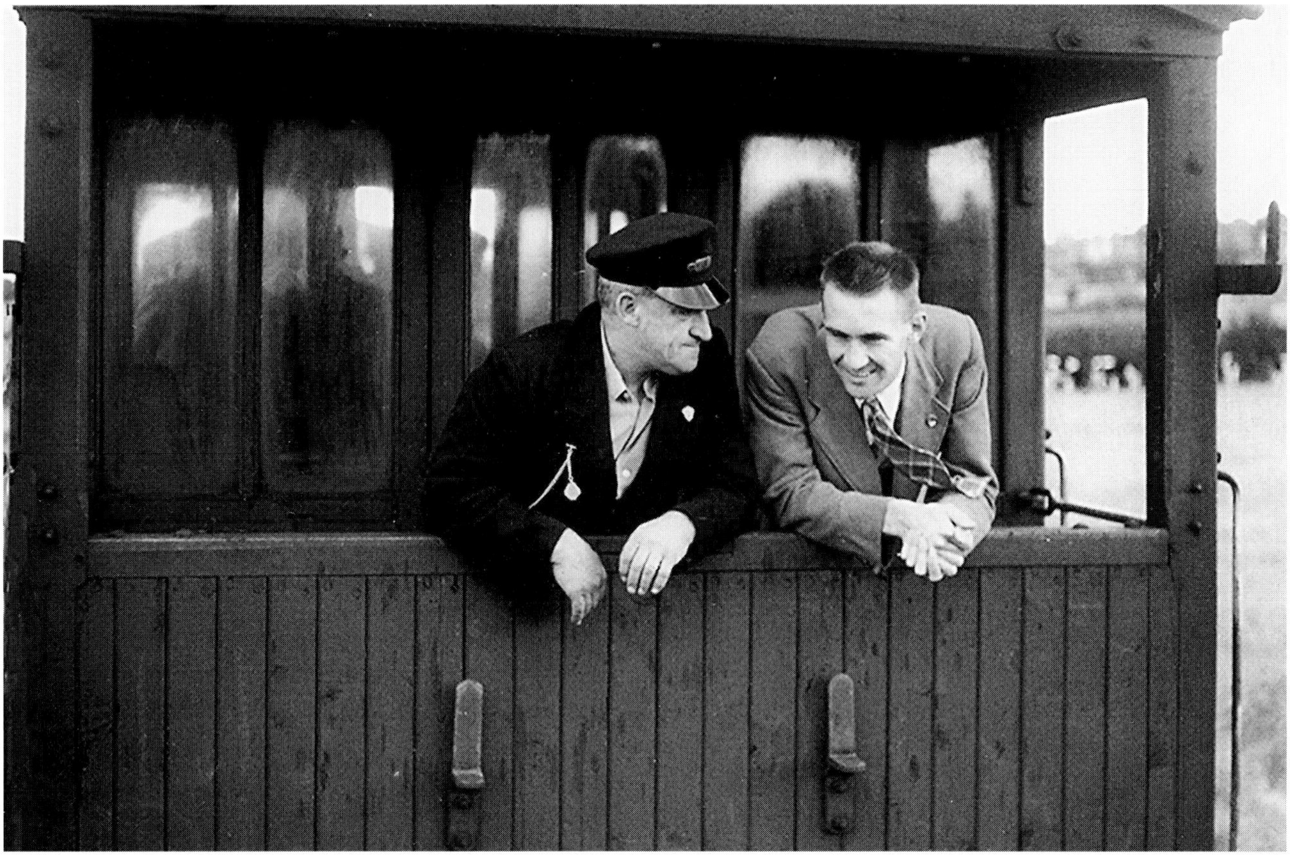

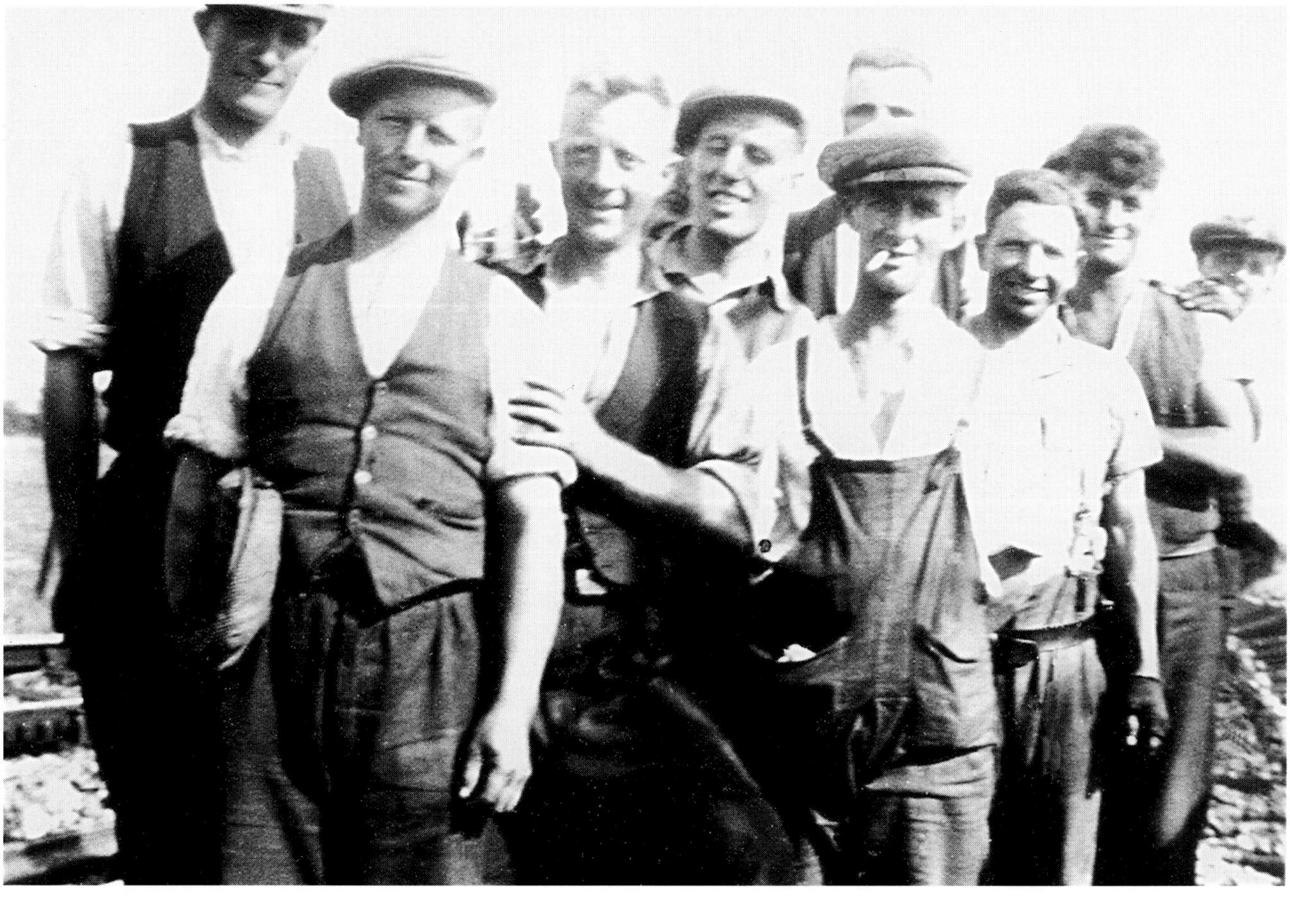

(*above*) A mother with her two children, one carrying a small dog, joins the signalman in watching an unidentified Black 5 and Standard class 5 climb past Masbury Halt with an up express. (*SDRT collection*)

(*left above*) S&D clerk Ken Padfield (right) enjoys a ride and a chat with guard Ivor Meader on the veranda of a brakevan between Binegar and Masbury in 1959. (*Ken Padfield collection*)

(*left below*) Permanent way gang working at Masbury in the 1930s. Among those in the photograph are Fred Bryant, Tom Paul, Dai Reakes, Albert Carter, Bill Flay, Ted Higgins, Fred Dunford and George Baker. (*Stan Blacker collection*)

(*right*) Class 4F No.44175 and WC class No.34095 *Brentor* pass under Oakhill Road Bridge (No.69) near Masbury Summit with the 07.35 (Sat) Nottingham to Bournemouth train. (*R.K.Blencowe collection*)

47

The collapse of Bath Road Viaduct looking north from Shepton Mallet in February 1946. Max Shore was a young junior porter at Shepton Mallet station at the time. He was chatting to Tom Corbin, a mason who was pointing some bricks at the viaduct. A train went over and some cement came out above them. Max remarked about this to Tom, who replied: "If it wasn't safe, son, I would not be here"; seven hours later the bridge collapsed. *(Stan Blacker collection)*

This regal photograph of Shepton Mallet stationmaster Ambrose Norris was taken on 28 October 1937, the day of his retirement. He was also stationmaster at Henstridge and Binegar and spent all his working life on the S&D.
(*Stan Blacker collection*)

S&D men seen here at Shepton Mallet, from right to left, are Harold Cummings, Ted Blacker, Len Brooks and an unknown railwayman.
(*Stan Blacker collection*)

On a fine spring day in 1962, BR class 5 No.73049 is about to leave Shepton Mallet station with a down local. (*E.T.Gill/R.K.Blencowe collection*)

Standard class 4 No.75007 runs into Shepton Mallet (Charlton Road) with an up local in 1962. *(E.T.Gill/R.K.Blencowe collection)*

Stan Blacker

In 1919 my father Edward (Teddy) Blacker became a porter at Charlton Road, Shepton Mallet station. On requesting details of his service from the local records office I found out that he had never missed a day's work in the 35 years service he gave to the S&D.

I remember an incident that helped confirm his loyalty to the railway. Before the days of refrigeration, a goods train used to arrive by 08.00 from Bath carrying 60lb blocks of ice. These would be delivered all down the line to the fish merchants who had ordered a block of ice. We had many fish merchants in and around Shepton Mallet, five in one street, so about a dozen blocks had to be unloaded at Charlton Road station. One morning when on early turn my father was unloading the blocks of ice when he dropped one on his foot. Such was his dedication to the railway that he went to work for three weeks with a slipper on the injured foot and a boot on the other.

On Sunday evenings each summer when the excursions were returning from Bournemouth, my father was only too pleased to be on duty to earn a few extra shillings for our family. I was taken with him each Sunday evening and had to sit in the signalbox with the signalman. I stayed there until the last excursion had gone through. The signalman always on duty on those Sundays for many years was Bill Franks. I spent many happy hours with him in the box watching all the trains go by.

During World War Two, employees were expected to join one or two of the home services to protect where they worked. My father joined the railway section of the Home Guard at Charlton Road station with another porter Bill Lintern. Both were given the same place to guard, which was the viaduct just outside the station. My father being only five feet tall could not look over the parapet of the viaduct, but Bill could, as he was over six feet. So when they spent their duty hours together, Bill always gave my father a running commentary on what was happening down below.

On reaching the retirement age of 65 he was asked to report to railway headquarters at Southampton. On arrival he was taken to the manager's office where the latter congratulated him and thanked him for his loyal and devoted service to the Somerset & Dorset Railway. He was told he did not qualify for a pension, but was entitled to a lorry-load of railway sleepers, which would be delivered to his home each year. He was not even given lunch, so he caught the next train back to Shepton Mallet. As for the railway sleepers, at 65 my father was in no condition to saw them up so my brother and I did it for him. After several years my father told the railway authorities he no longer wanted the sleepers.

In 1933 my father managed to get employment for my brother Bill with the telegraph and linesmen gang at Shepton Mallet. Both he and a friend, Jack Gane, were taken on for a few months only. It was a very hard winter on the Mendip Hills and the railway needed extra labour. The weather had caused extensive damage to the poles and wires. Other permanent way members of this gang were foreman Fred Gregory, Bill Harris, Hubert Boyce and Percy Hill. Bert Achilles who was the storeman and timekeeper at the depot based at Shepton Mallet tried to keep both of these newcomers on after the work had been carried out. But the S&D railway authorities would not have it, so it was back to unemployment. In 1935 father again got him a job on the S&D, this time with the railway gang relaying Combe Down Tunnel; this lasted three months. He lodged at Bath with the only Sheptonian Harry Newsome; all the others in the gang were outsiders. Some of the other members of the gang working at Combe Down were Mr.Barnes, Mark Lambert, Reg Chinock and Oliver Green. At about this time a ganger with the Shepton Mallet gang, Harry Lemon, was killed at Barren Down by the 10.53 down train.

My uncle Walter Gunning was a member of the Masbury gang and had to walk with his mate Harry Fear the three miles from Shepton Mallet to Masbury everyday to work, and back again, in all weathers. Other members of the gang at that time were Tom Russ, Fred Stock, Charlie Gilson and Roy Wollard. Another member of the gang was George Baker who started work in 1935. They were sent wherever they were required, from Bath to Sturminster Newton.

When going south to the Sturminster area members of the gang had to make their own way there. George used to leave his home at Croscombe on Monday mornings at 04.00 to cycle to lodgings at Wincanton

where he stayed the week. He would then catch an early train from Wincanton to Sturminster to start work at 07.00 until 17.00. On Saturday evenings George cycled back from his lodgings at Wincanton to his home at Croscombe to spend Sundays with his parents. His wages were about £2 a week and if he worked a Sunday it would be £3. At that time the practice on the Somerset & Dorset would be to employ the permanent way men for eleven months then stand them off for a month. By doing this they never had to pay holiday money. They would then re-employ them for another eleven months. The best effort of this gang at track laying was at Wincanton in 1937, when the gang formed part of 140 men from different gangs who re-laid ¾ of a mile of track on one Sunday.

There was one tragic event with the gang, which George remembers. They were relaying at Masbury and all the old sleepers were loaded on to railway trolleys to be taken back to Charlton Road. On one of the trips about eight of the gang were on top of the sleepers as they set off for Charlton Road. After a short distance, through the camber of the track, sleepers began to fall off, as did members of the gang. Because of how the sleepers were loaded the motor trolley driver Walter Gunning was unable to get to the brake. By the time the trolley arrived at Charlton Road there were only six sleepers and three of the gang left on the trolley. Albert Carter, a member of the gang, fell off with a couple of sleepers on the Kilver Street Viaduct and was killed. Enquiries went on for months, and all members of the gang were interviewed many times. On several occasions they were all taken to the start of their journey and the route retraced. In the end no blame was apportioned to anyone.

In the war years many women worked on the permanent way at Shepton Mallet; we had May Davies, Kath Cable, Rose Brooks, Mary Fraser, Joan Hughes and Mary Toose. Walter Gunning was the foreman of the gang.

Permanent way ladies at Shepton Mallet in the war years. From left to right are Kathleen Cable, Rose Brooks, Kathleen Hawkins, Joan Hughes and Mary Fraser. (*Rose Ware, née Brooks, collection*)

There were other ladies I recall who also carried out a fine job in those years. At Evercreech Junction there were porters Betty Spiller, Joyce and Dorothy Reakes and Betty Simms, known affectionately as 'The Firm'. At Evercreech New in the booking office were Edna Simms and Emily Poole. Down at Highbridge there was Norah Cook and Joyce Bell.

As a former postman my route took me to the S&D crossing keepers' cottages at Bruton Road where Fred and Freda Box and family lived, and at Lamyatt Road where Norman and Mary Lockwood and their children lived. It was the custom then, that if Norman ever wanted any coal he would place a stick with a large piece of white material on it. This would be placed at a safe distance from the house. The crew of any goods train travelling past during the night, on seeing the flag, would throw off some nice lumps of coal for Norman to collect in the morning. One evening Norman placed the flag at a safe distance from the house as a signal for coal. Now his children were full of mischief and before retiring for the night, and without Norman knowing, the eldest of the children moved the flag and stuck it in the ground right outside the house. During the night there was an almighty bang. Norman and Mary woke up in a fright and dashed downstairs to find the front door knocked right off its hinges and into the hallway, as was the coal. When I called in the morning there was no letterbox to put the mail in.

While speaking to a former S&D fireman Alan Mason, he recalled to me a couple of incidents which occurred on the branch. In the first one, Driver Clarence Rawles and Alan left Evercreech Junction on the 06.05 goods to Highbridge. They went through West Pennard at a fair rate of knots. They were nearing Pennard Lane Crossing where the keeper was known sometimes to be late in opening the gates. They came to the crossing and the light was against them, which of course meant the gates were closed. They tried to stop without success. Clarence said to Alan: "It's about time we woke this man up". Alan saw the keeper with his trousers around his ankles trying to pull them up as they went through the gates smashing them to matchwood. Clarence leant over the side of the cab and said to the keeper: "Good morning, Mr Griggs, you now have some firewood".

The other memory concerned a driver, Alan (Tankard) Jones. He had left Evercreech Junction for Highbridge with a goods train, shunted some wagons off at Glastonbury and then dropped off water at Shapwick and Catcott and arrived at Highbridge. He then took another goods from Highbridge back down the branch. Between Glastonbury and West Pennard, there was an almighty bang and the engine came to a grinding halt. The fireman protected the train with detonators and Alan Jones walked into West Pennard station and informed them of the problem. They sent out another engine from Evercreech to pull it back into the Junction and then on to Templecombe to be examined. It was found it had chucked a cotter pin. When the engine was examined more thoroughly they found it was not a cotter at all, it was a pickaxe handle used as a cotter and it had broken in two.

My wife Kate has strong S&D links. During her childhood the conversation was often about the Somerset & Dorset Railway. Living in the small village of Lamyatt, two miles from Evercreech Junction, there was little work, only farming or the railway. Her father Tom Russ left school at 14 and joined the S&D in 1902 at Evercreech Junction. He stayed there until the Great War in 1914 when he was enlisted into the Royal Horse Artillery. After four years in France he returned to Evercreech Junction permanent way. He was promoted to ganger at Glastonbury in 1935. He worked the length from the Junction to Glastonbury, then moved on to Shepton Mallet were he worked the line to Binegar. When the Bath Road Viaduct collapsed in 1946 the inspector and Tom were first at the scene. Walking from the station they found part of the bridge in the road below, a few more steps and they would have fallen down there as well. Tom retired in 1953 after giving 47 years service to the S&D. Other members of her family who worked on the S&D were guard Harry Goodland, his son Bill who was a porter, signalman Frank Padfield and his brothers Win, Reg and Ern.

The Somerset & Dorset Railway was an important part of our family's life. To us, and to the people of Shepton Mallet, it was a devastating blow when the line closed in 1966. Even now, after 37 years, many people still ask the question – why did they close the old Somerset & Dorset?

Taken at Shepton Mallet station in the 1940s are, from left to right, lorry driver Bill Cummings, porter Ted Blacker and an unknown railwayman. (*Stan Blacker collection*)

This picture was taken on 19 September 1935 at Shepton Mallet yard. The members of the Permanent Way gang have temporary laying-off cards in their hands. They would be re-employed when needed. From left to right are Ted Higgins, Ted Guppy, Vic Beeho, Eddie Hall, Dai Reakes, Tom Moulton, Harold Cummings, Harry Higgins, Frank Hurle and F. Doulting. (*Stan Blacker collection*)

This SLS special, seen here at Shepton Mallet, was one of the last trains to run over the S&D on 6 March 1966. Pilot engine 8F No.48706 was driven by Archie Gunning and his brother Bill drove the train engine, a BR Standard class 4 Tank No.80043. What a sad time it must have been for loyal station staff like Emily Poole, Roy Wollard, Bob Gilham, Frank Trott, George Coles and Reg Carter when the station closed. (*E.T.Gill/R.K.Blencowe collection*)

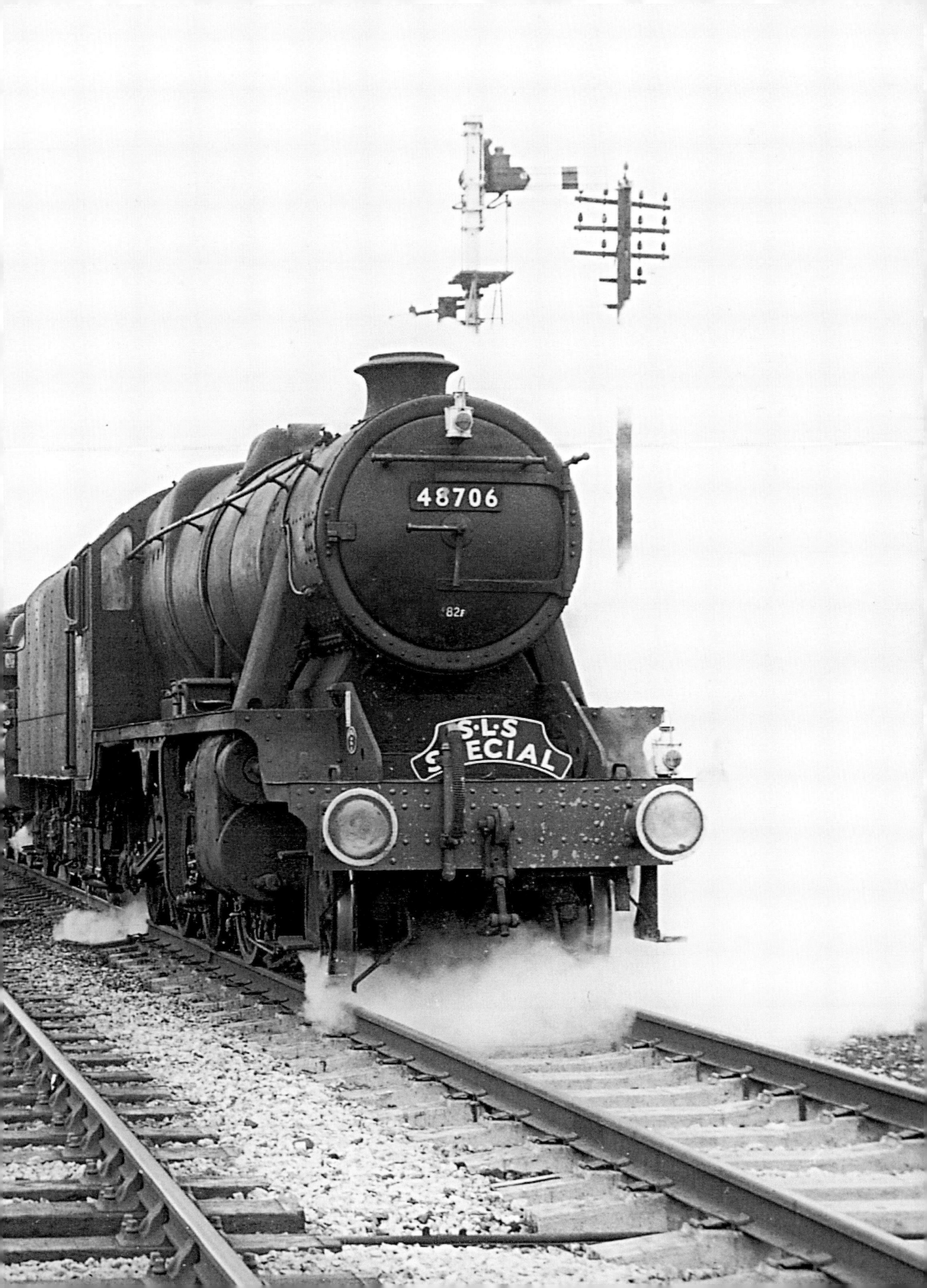
48706
S·L·S
SPECIAL

Evercreech New station, looking north; all seems clean and tidy. The profusion of roses interwoven with railings must have looked very colourful. The old lime kiln is seen behind the signalbox. *(E.T.Gill/R.K.Blencowe collection)*

The tall and attractive Evercreech New signalbox with its 20 levers. It was situated on the up platform. The original box was destroyed by fire in 1918. Signalmen who worked this box included Ted Lambert, Jim Gould, Basil Lay, Sid Pitt and Ted Simms. (*R.K.Blencowe*)

Ivatt class 2 No.41307 and Standard class 4 Tank No.80138 leave Evercreech New with the 14.00 Templecombe to Bath local. With closure only a day away, as many engines as possible were being worked north, so as to be on Bath depot when the end came. (*E.T.Gill/R.K.Blencowe collection*)

A hazy midday sun throws a shadow on the platform at Evercreech Junction in 1949. The driver of 2P No.40601 leans out of his cab as a little boy sitting on a trolley, with legs dangling, looks over to the engine. (*R.K.Blencowe collection*)

A similar view at Evercreech Junction in 1949. A double-headed express bound for Bournemouth with LMS class 2P No.634 and an unidentified 5MT (nicknamed Crab). (*R.K.Blencowe collection*)

(*above*) Driver Fritz Lawrence in the cab of a class 2 No.41307 at Evercreech Junction down platform. (*SDRT collection*)

Shunters at Evercreech Junction up sidings. From left to right are Ken Atkins, Eddie Riggs, Fred Hicks and on the running plate of the Collett, driver Clarence Rawles busy with the oil can. (*Ken Atkins collection*)

Passed fireman Bill Webb leans out of the cab of Collett 0-6-0 No. 3216 in the late 50s at Evercreech Junction. (*Bill Webb collection*)

(*below*) Driver John Dray oiling BR class 5 No.73049 at Evercreech Junction before working this engine to assist the Pines to Bath. (*John Dray collection*)

2P No.40634 piloting West Country class No.34040 *Crewkerne* at Evercreech Junction, c.1956. The train engine required water which meant that the pilot had to draw forward, thereby blocking the crossing gates. Road traffic waiting for the gates to open was held up a while longer. No doubt there were more than a few moans here. (*L.G.Marshall/R.K.Blencowe collection*)

The epitome of the S&D, as class 2P No.40697 pilots a Standard class 5 No.73052 out of Evercreech Junction with a northbound express in 1956. (*L.G.Marshall/R.K.Blencowe collection*)

(*above*) Class 4F No.44557 seen approaching Evercreech Junction with a local to Bath in 1956. (*L.G.Marshall/R.K.Blencowe collection*)

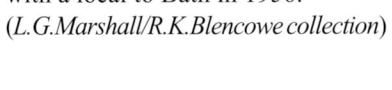

Fireman Ron (Runner) Bean looks out from the cab of 7F No.53800 at Evercreech Junction. Ron with driver Bill Rawles was on the footplate of the first 9F No.92204 to run on S&D metals in 1960. (*Pat Bean collection*)

Against a background of Evercreech Junction station gardens are, from left to right, stationmaster Alec Stowe, Bath Green Park shedmaster Harold Morris and photographer Ivo Peters. For me, and I am sure for many others, Ivo's superb films and photographs were inspirational in my passion for the S&D. (*Mrs. Zoe Stowe collection*)

Bath Railway Society members pose in front of 7F No.53805 in 1959. From left to right are B. Robbins, John Allan, Ken Padfield, Ron Hurst, D. Burt, S. White, Phil Williams, K. Tosio, Mr. Boase, Hugh Ballantyne, Dick Croft, guard Ivor Meader, Chris Hurford, Mr. Lee, inspector Skinner and shunters Charlie Vaughan and Oliver Pullen. The driver on the right in the cab is Davy Jones. (*Ken Padfield collection*)

(*right*) Stationmaster Jack Pike on duty at Evercreech Junction in the 1950s. (*Peter Pike*)

(*above*) Caricature of Bob Fry at Evercreech Junction station, drawn by stationmaster Reg Jeans. Bob was a shunter at the Junction and each morning he would cycle to work from Wells. As soon as he arrived he would get his own personal frying pan out and have a good fry up in the shunters cabin.

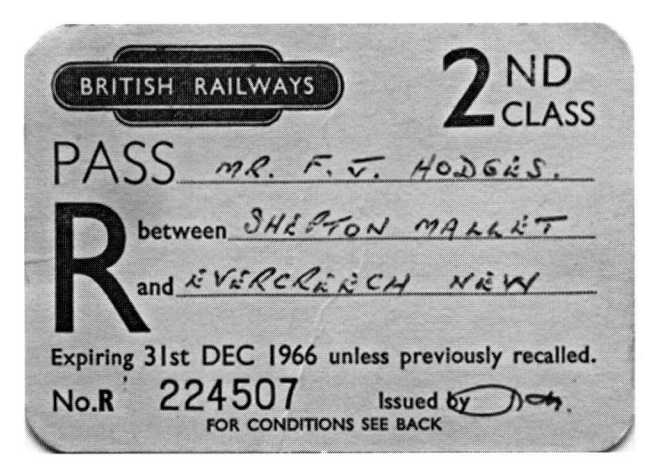

(*right*) Permanent way men Frank Hodges (left), with a ganger's track gauge, and Bryn Yeoman at Evercreech Junction in the 1950s. Above is Frank Hodges' rail pass. (*Martin Manship collection*)

(*right*) Evercreech Junction station staff in the 1950s. From left to right are Ern Phillips, Alf Russell, Vic Freak, Albert Taylor and Albert Attwood. (*Vic Freak collection*)

(*left*) Three characters at Evercreech Junction, from left to right, are shunter Charlie Vaughan, signalman Ted Simms and booking clerk Lew Hamer. (*Mrs. Zoe Stowe collection*)

(*right*) Class 8F No.48760 leaves Evercreech Junction with a down freight. The cans on the buffer beam are for supplying drinking water to crossing keepers Fred and Freda Box at Bruton Road. (*Mrs. Zoe Stowe collection*)

(*above*) Standing in front of Bruton Road Crossing in the 1890s are crossing keepers Mr. & Mrs. William Good. Another member of the family, James Good, was an S&D driver. (*SDRT collection*)

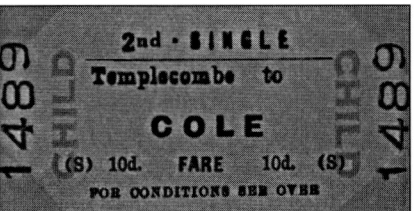

(*left*) Porter Alf Elliott with a lamp in each hand stands in front of the Cole station sign in the 1950s. Somebody has been busy with the white paint. (*Mick Elliott collection*)

Class 2 No.41242 makes a fine sight as it enters Cole for Bruton in 1962 with a short down local. (*E.T.Gill/R.K.Blencowe collection*)

Looking north at Cole station a two-coach train is heading south hauled by a class 2 Tank No.41241 in 1950. In the goods yard an old lorry can be seen, possibly a late twenties or early thirties Morris Commercial. (*Jack Hobbs collection*)

On the last Saturday on the S&D, un-rebuilt WC class No.34006 *Bude* and Battle of Britain class No.34057 *Biggin Hill* head the southbound LCGB 'The Somerset & Dorset Rail Tour' at Wincanton on 5 March 1966. (*Len Taylor*)

A more familiar sight as Standard class 4 No.75072 is seen leaving Wincanton with a down stopper in the 1960s. (*Len Taylor*)

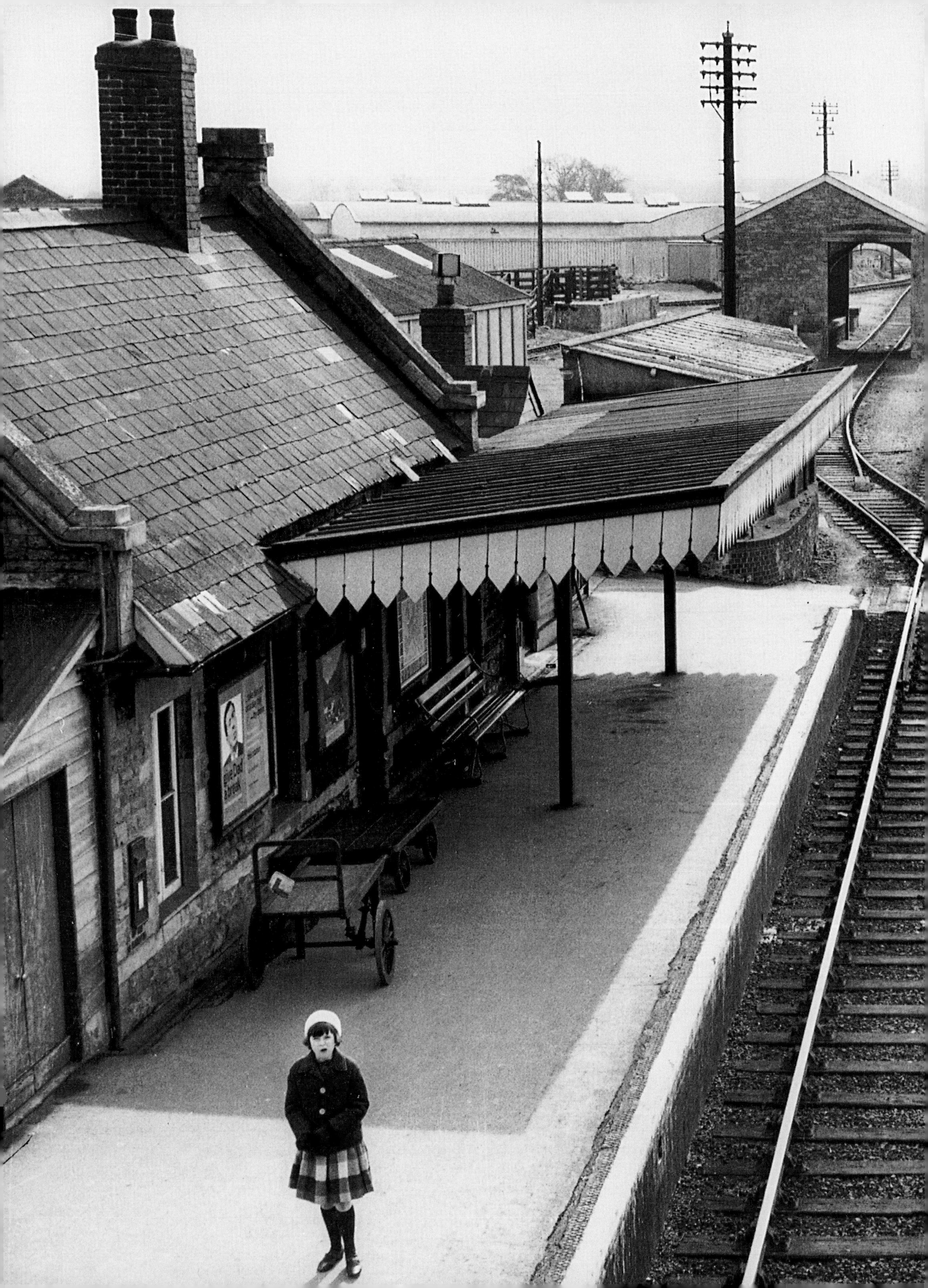

The excellent vista afforded from the footbridge gives a bird's eye view of Wincanton station. Young Marie Kiddle looks up at the photographer who has captured this evocative view of a once busy station. How local residents must wish it was still there. (*Len Taylor*)

George Judd

Living in Evercreech during the forties and fifties the railway was an important part of life; numerous families gained employment from it and of course used it to travel on the line. There were two coal merchants in the village, F&PR Brown and Alan Feaver, whose yard was next to my house. The milk factory of Prideaux's also used the railway facilities for their dried milk products. I remember during the summer holidays riding in a horse-drawn delivery dray with Jack Simms on some of his village deliveries of parcels; the dray still had S&DJR on its side. The horse, Prince, was kept in a stable opposite my home and had a wonderful array of railway brasses. In the late fifties, the deliveries and collections were motorised, first with a Scammell mechanical horse and then a GW Thornycroft Nippy, which had two or three different trailers for various needs. The driver of this vehicle was Clive Withers.

My use of the railway started in the forties when my mother would take me on holiday to relatives either in Bournemouth or Gloucester. The Gloucester holiday always appealed to me more as I would do some trainspotting at the Gloucester stations. We always used the Pines Express for this trip and had to get a taxi to and from Evercreech Junction. I used to spend a lot of time trainspotting at Evercreech New and was tolerated by the staff. Names I recall there were stationmaster Bob Hayes, porter Charlie Hartnell and signalman Sid Pitt. Summer Saturdays were my favourite time especially with all the different motive power on show like BR Standard class 4s and 5s and of course the old 7Fs. At Christmas time my mother and I would travel to Bath by train for the annual pantomime at the Theatre Royal. This also gave me a short spell of time at Bath Green Park to do some spotting and bunk the shed.

Alongside Evercreech New station was an old disused limekiln and quarry, which had a narrow-gauge rope-worked incline from the quarry to the station levels. This provided my friends and me with hours of fun riding down in an old truck, and then pushing it back up again. One day someone changed the points at the bottom so we had to jump off quickly just before the truck shot at high speed off the track and sank to the bottom of the quarry, which was full of water.

I started school at Sexey's in 1950; this allowed me a daily return trip, usually behind a 2P or 4F from Evercreech New to Cole. It was during this time I got to know S&D staff, mostly the guards like Reg Brewer, Len Rossiter, Dickie Bird and Roy Miles. Some of these, including Roy, were very friendly, others I think looked on us as a bit of a nuisance, which they had to put up with. The station at Cole had a lovely garden with a goldfish pond. The gardens were well looked after by the staff, which included porter Alf Elliott. Unfortunately the pond regularly became a place for first-year-boys' caps, much to the annoyance of the staff. One of the signalmen here was Fred Thick and the stationmaster was Bob Gould.

In later years if we had a free period in the afternoon, some of the girls from Sunny Hill School would catch the earlier afternoon train home with us. This would be the branch train consisting of two non-corridor coaches usually pulled by a 0-4-4T or a 2-6-2T which was much more conducive to amorous adventures than the usual train. It was a shorter journey so we had to walk from Evercreech Junction. One scary moment still sticks in my mind. One afternoon on this particular train, somebody thought it was a good idea to get out of the train and try to walk around the outside and back in the other side by hanging on to the door handles. Needless to say it didn't work and as the train pulled into Evercreech Junction one boy was still hanging on outside and another was just getting back in. The four of us were grabbed by the station staff headed by Bill Cornell (another wonderful character from Evercreech) and locked in the porter's room until our parents collected us. This of course resulted in a hiding from our parents and six of the best when we arrived at school the next day.

One day we missed the normal school train home, so two of us decided to go to Wincanton in order to catch the next train. We completely forgot that the train did not stop at Evercreech New and we ended up at Shepton Mallet. We now had no money, so we ran off the end of the platform across the yard and over the GWR line to reach the road. By this time Bill Cornell at the Junction had contacted my father to tell him he had seen us go past in the train. My father picked us up at Cannards Grave and my pocket money was stopped for the week.

In July 1955 I started work as a junior postman and still travelled daily by train from Evercreech New. My

duties involved a small delivery round, delivering telegrams and meeting trains at Wincanton station. I got to know the passenger guards quite well and struck up a friendship with Roy Miles. I well remember one Bath guard Harry Woolley, a very large man. One day when I was giving him some cheek, he picked up a large parcel in one hand and threw it at me, knocking me to the ground. After that I was careful what I said to him.

The station staff at that time were stationmaster Doug Colwell, booking clerk Fred James, checker Harry Light and porters Jock Nicol and Irving Whittle. Fred Bushrod drove the delivery lorry (later I lodged with him and his wife Nellie) and George James was one of the signalmen. Another duty at Wincanton involved spending time at the Cow & Gate milk factory packing large quantities of parcels. Harry Light and sometimes Irving Whittle would be present to load the daily train of larger parcels from the private siding in the factory. The amount of mail generated by the Cow & Gate factory made Wincanton a pretty busy office and sometimes it was a rush to catch the trains. A missed train was very much frowned upon by the Post Office management and questions would be asked. I recall loading one of our more elderly vans with mail. The driver Harry Nash was rushing to catch a train. He jumped into the cab and promptly sat on the road. The floor around the driver's side had rotted away. There was a frantic rush to transfer the mail into another van to catch the train, which we did. After passing my driving test I was let loose with a Morris 1000 and one of my duties was to meet the 02.40 down mail from Bath.

I met Margaret my future wife when I went to the cinema, as she was an usherette. I soon found out that her uncle Ernie Davis was one of the permanent way gang whom I had known for some time, together with other gang members Bob Foot, Maurice Hughes and Win Padfield.

In the summer of 1958 I was conscripted for National Service and after basic training I was sent to Cyprus. I rejoined the postal service in 1960. This was a bad time for the S&D as there had been a washout at Midford. All mail had to be despatched and received by road from Bath; this gave me some much-needed overtime. I settled back into the routine of postal work and one of the duties was despatching mail on the late train at Wincanton. This meant a lengthy wait at the station, which was usually spent in the signalbox drinking tea with George James or Jeff Martin and sometimes relief signalman Norman Rallison. Norman had been one of the officers in the army cadet force when I was a member. Sometimes this train, which arrived from the Bath direction, would have a cattle wagon on and this would be shunted into the cattle dock before the train continued. On one particular day an elderly postman on the late turn was on the lookout to make a few bob. He unloaded two calves from inside the mail train and delivered them to the appropriate farm before garaging the van. I was the unlucky one when at 05.00 the next day I got into the van to find this terrible smell and the vehicle full of cow's mess; he was not my favourite man that day.

One of the problems at Wincanton station was the staggered platforms, which meant that mail had to be taken across the foot crossing and down the ramp of the southbound platform. This of course was about midway down the northbound platform, so you had to stand in the foot crossing to load or unload the barrows. I remember many times just managing to get away as the train blew up as it was coming over Hawker's Bridge, just inside the distant signal. I wonder what health and safety would make of that now?

It is well known that the staff on the S&D were like one big family. I felt part of this, I seemed to know so many of them like Norman Ashfield, Jim Gould, Harry Steele, Paddy Smyth, Alf Elliott and Bill Fishleigh, who can be heard announcing trains at Templecombe on some of the audio recordings. My last journey on the S&D was a return trip from Wincanton to Bath on Thursday 3 March 1966. I spent most of Saturday and Sunday at Templecombe witnessing the end. The last steam engine I photographed on the S&D was No.77014 at Blandford Forum on a LCGB 'Dorset & Hants Rail Tour' on 16 October 1966. The last ever train I saw on the line was a demolition train at Horsington with class 22 No.D6340 in charge. I never worked on the S&D, but the memory of those wonderful days will stay with me forever.

SOUTHERN RAILWAY (South Western Section).

787

FROM WATERLOO TO WINCANTON

In bright sunshine in the 1960s BR class 5 No.73049 stands in the platform at Wincanton station. (*Len Taylor*)

Standard class 4 No.76026 restarts away from Wincanton with a down local. Who is John on the side of the tender? (*Len Taylor*)

Wincanton permanent way gang in the 1950s. From left to right are Ernie Davis, Bob Foot, Percy Hannam, Maurice Hughes, George Harding and Charlie Cook. (*George Judd collection*)

A dispiriting scene as Jock Nicol and Irving Whittle burn station papers at Wincanton station after closure in 1966. (*George Judd*)

(*above*) Another familiar S&D scene as BR Standard class 5 No.73054 hauls a southbound passenger train out of Wincanton. Note the churns on the right of the photograph, probably from the Cow & Gate milk factory. (*Len Taylor*)

A sad and sorry sight at Wincanton station. The signalbox is just about standing. The footbridge where station staff like Norman Ashfield, Norman Gould, Norris Kiddle, Bob Russ and Eric Hamblin crossed many times is still there. A discarded churn lies on the track bed and a red and white limited clearance sign is still fixed on the wall of the goods shed. Dr. Beeching has a lot to answer for. (*Len Taylor*)

Class 2P No.40509 with a Midland tender leaves Templecombe Junction (No.2) with a down train for Bournemouth. Note the tablet is placed in the catcher at the bottom of the signalbox steps ready for the crew to collect and proceed to Stalbridge, c.1952. (*S.C.Townroe/R.K.Blencowe collection*)

LMS 4-4-0 No.302 waits to pilot a Bournemouth train out to No.2 Junction from Templecombe station. (*Jack Hobbs collection*)

LMS 7F No.9677 at Templecombe Lower yard on 5 July 1930. Standing by the buffer is Walt Webb. (*H.C.Casserley*)

Driver Richard Rendle on the left and coalman Fred Filer are ready to turn an engine on the turntable at Templecombe shed. Standing behind in the yard is class 4F No.44411. Fred was one of many railwaymen that liked his quota of cider.
(*Andrew Fisher collection*)

Driver George Welch, with hands on hips, replenishes No.41296 with water at Templecombe in 1964.
(*Andrew Fisher collection*)

SR U class No.31632 has just been turned on Templecombe shed in 1960. It came off the 10.05 from Exmouth to Cleethorpes at Templecombe station, then ran light engine to the shed for servicing. It would later work the return trip.
(*Peter Pike*)

(*above left*) Passenger guard Percy Hamblin signs on for duty in the guards room at Templecombe. (*Roy Miles collection*)

(*above right*) Templecombe railwaymen, from left to right, are shunter Jim Cull, inspector Bert Day and carriage and wagon department Den Foot, c.1960. (*Keith Barrett collection*)

(*below*) Driver Alwyn Hannam relieving John Dray who is about to step off Standard 5 No.73019. (*John Dray collection*)

(*above*) Cleaner Tony Hicks looks out from the footplate of a Jinty Tank at Templecombe shed in 1959. (*Wally Arnott*)

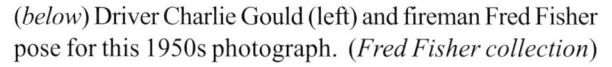

(*above*) Driver Bert Rendle (left) with fireman Rodney Scovell on BR class 5 No.73051. Note the small tablet in Rodney's hand. (*Rodney Scovell collection*)

(*below*) Driver Charlie Gould (left) and fireman Fred Fisher pose for this 1950s photograph. (*Fred Fisher collection*)

SOUTHERN RAILWAY.
(7/45)
TO
Stock 787
TEMPLECOMBE

(*above*) Driver John Dray is about to take out Standard class 5 No.73019, on the 13.15 freight from Templecombe Upper to Evercreech Junction. (*John Dray collection*)

S&D railwaymen enjoying a drink after work at the Royal Hotel, Templecombe. In the photo are Art Hatcher, Harry Hansford, Dave Rendle, Ted Candy, Len Counsell and Frank Ray. (*Gordon Hatcher collection*)

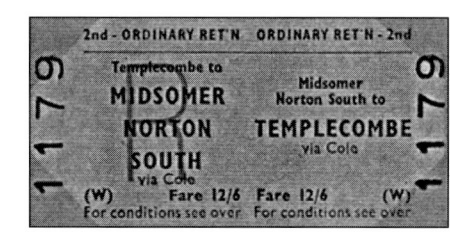

(*left*) Scottie class 3F No.2884 (ex No.61/38) is busy on Templecombe shed in 1930. This is a G5 rebuilt, having acquired not only the new boiler and firebox but also deeper frames visible in the picture. This locomotive was the last of the 28 Scotties to be built and one of the last to be withdrawn. (*H.C.Casserley*)

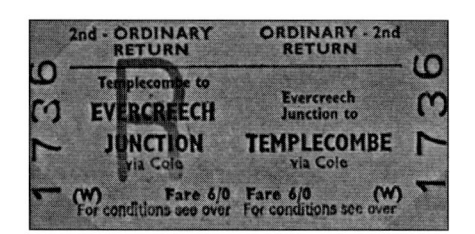

(*right*) The Templecombe skeleton – look who missed the last S&D train on 7 March 1966. Contrary to popular belief this is not Dr.Beeching. (*Robin Gould collection*)

3F No.43436 on Templecombe shed in 1957. On the left is fireman Trevor Nettley, walking away is foreman Doug Barnard and in the engine cab is driver Reg Darke. The locos are being shunted into the correct position ready to leave the shed early on Monday morning. (*L.G.Marshall/R.K.Blencowe collection*)

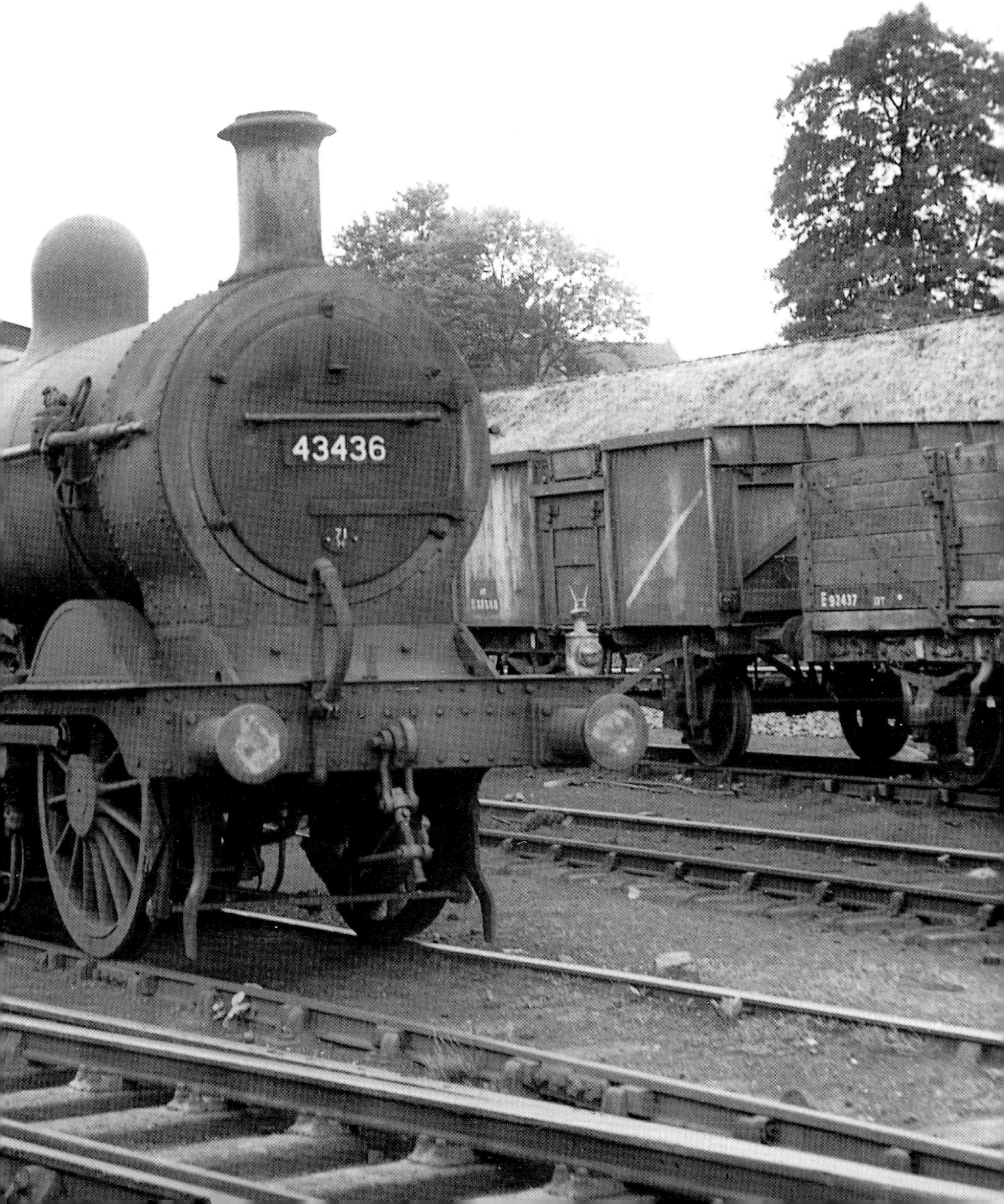
43436

(*above*) A view of Common Lane Crossing house, just south of Templecombe in 1951. In the left-hand bedroom Vera Fudge is busy cleaning the windows. With her husband Leonard they were in charge of the crossing. The house has been preserved and is now part of the Gartell Light Railway. (*S.C.Townroe/R.K.Blencowe collection*)

(*right*) Guard Hugh Berryman with his daughter Joan in front of Park Lane Crossing gates in the 1940s. Joan's mother Mabel was the crossing keeper here. Note the height of the crossing gate lamp; was this because of the brow in the road? (*Andrew Fisher collection*)

If you are a collector of vintage vehicles look away now. Looking towards Templecombe we see overbridge No.159. In the overgrown siding at Henstridge is a graveyard for three cars and one van. (*Eric Rimmer*)

The local people turn out to see class 8F No.48706 and class 4 No.80043 (out of view) pass Henstridge with the northbound SLS special on the very last day of service. (*SDRT collection*)

4F No.44422 pulls away with a cloud of smoke and steam from Henstridge with a local passenger train. (*Keith Barrett collection*)

Viewed from the track bed is Stalbridge station looking north. On the left can be seen the stationmaster's house and the station offices. (*Keith Barrett collection*)

On a bright sunny day BR class 4 No.75007 enters Stalbridge station. I wonder if the gentleman on the right wished he could see this scene now, 40 years on since this photo was taken. (*C.L.Caddy*)

From left to right, driver Lou Long and fireman Fred Fisher have their photograph taken at Stalbridge, before taking out a goods train, with class 4F No.44560 in charge. (*Andrew Fisher collection*)

BR class 5 No.73049 heads the 15.40 from Bournemouth West which is about to pull into Stalbridge station. On the right is signalman Robert (Jock) McKennie watching the exchange of the tablet from the tablet apparatus. (*Keith Barrett collection*)

BR class 5 No.73001 with its number painted on the smokebox is about to leave Stalbridge. The top lamp bracket is missing, so it ran with an incorrect head code. (*Keith Barrett collection*)

Looking along the up platform on a very cold January day, class 2 No.41208 enters Sturminster Newton. With only two months before closure, passengers at this station are still supporting the S&D, as can be seen on the down platform. (*C.L.Caddy*)

The porter looks on as Standard class 4 No.76057 is about to arrive at Sturminster Newton station in 1961. Note the dipped up platform. (*E.T.Gill/R.K.Blencowe collection*)

Graham Moore

I started work on the railways in the mid 1930s as a junior clerk. Wages were £55 a year rising to £80 at the age of 18. It was general practice at that time to allow staff in lodgings a free ticket every two weeks to travel home. My first position was at Montpelier then on to Clifton Down on the Bristol to Avonmouth line. I used to travel home to Child Okeford every other week getting off at Shillingstone.

On summer Saturdays many extra trains ran from the north of England to Bournemouth West and all trains stopped at Bath. I caught these extra trains at Bath on many occasions, getting off at Blandford and then back to Shillingstone on the waiting local train. One Saturday I was on a train which stopped at Stourpaine where there was a passing loop. The carriage I was on happened to stop right opposite the signalbox. I knew the signalman there and he knew I wanted to get to Shillingstone. He said the local train was on the other line waiting, and with his support I transferred from the Bournemouth train to the local one, which of course I normally would have caught at Blandford. On reflection, being much older now, it would appear a dangerous thing to do but neither train could move until given the token by the signalman.

I was transferred from Clifton Down to Shillingstone where George Coles was the stationmaster; Don Ridout and Bill Lintern were other staff I recall. I was then transferred to Blandford goods and on to Templecombe Lower yard to replace Stan Parfitt. It was not clear where the Derby staff office would send Stan. Stan travelled daily from Radstock.

After a period of time I was sent to the booking office at Blandford where I worked with Len Farley and Phil Newman. Blandford was the station for Bryanston public school. At the beginning and the end of each term the station became very busy with lots more baggage and trunks. I believe it was also the practice for two separate compartment coaches to be added to the train at Bournemouth West to enable pupils at Blandford Grammar School to travel home to Shillingstone and Sturminster Newton on Wednesdays and Saturdays. Why they could not travel on the normal corridor coaches was a mystery, but perhaps there were too many without extra coaches.

Junior clerks on the LMS had to pass a Pitman's shorthand exam to qualify for an increase in salary at the age of 18. You were allowed three attempts and if you failed to pass you had to leave. I managed to pass the exam although it seemed at the time to be of no assistance to me; it came in useful in later years.

I was at Blandford with the well-known Joe Penny. He was a real character. He was the porter who will go down in S&D folklore as the man who was heard to say "Stop that dog he's a parcel", when a dog which was in transit escaped with Joe running after him. Another story about Joe was when he was seen rushing to work pushing his bike. On asking why he didn't get on his bike he replied, "I haven't got time to do that because I'll be late". He was also heard to say: "The steepest ladder I went up was down a well". There were many more stories about Joe and I certainly missed him when I was transferred to the booking office at Sturminster Newton. Mr Coombes was the stationmaster and another clerk was Bert Hill. In those days (1939) the late-turn clerk had to check if any passengers on the last up train were travelling towards Exeter; if so, and the local train was late, the Waterloo to Exeter would be held at Templecombe. On one occasion the porter gave the guard the right away and before I could get off, I was taken to Stalbridge and had to return to Sturminster on the last down train.

I recall an outbreak of Foot and Mouth in the cattle market at Sturminster. This of course caused havoc and lots of problems for everybody concerned. No movement of livestock was allowed and hundreds of cattle were burnt in the market itself, the smell was terrible.

I then moved from the booking office to the goods office located in the station yard. Even in those days problems with road transport started to appear; gradually cattle food from Avonmouth by rail began to decrease and lorries were coming into the station yard delivering direct to Blandford and Webb's grain store, much to Mr Coombes' concern and annoyance. He made representation to Blandford and Webb but all to no avail. He wanted to stop the lorries coming into the station yard but of course he could not.

Market day was Monday, I think every fortnight, but again cattle traffic gradually decreased by train. Cattle trucks had partitions, small, medium and large depending on the number of cattle. One trader always had enough cattle to warrant a large truck and was charged accordingly. Without fail he only paid for a small truck and the

difference was placed as outstanding, no doubt in the hope that someone would collect it one day? As far as I know it was never collected, due to the fact that what business the railway had it didn't want to lose.

Charlie Darke worked with me in the goods office, Bert Witt was the lorry driver and Bert Newman had the horse and cart, which was used for local deliveries. Charlie and I used to play cricket (when the stationmaster was at lunch) against the shed doors if we could close them; we only used a tennis ball.

Walter Fudge was the goods porter and Bob Marsh the checker. I am afraid we used to play tricks on Walt some days. He would push the trucks into the goods shed for unloading and whilst he was walking round to get into the shed we were inside, and would push the trucks back out. I don't think he ever found out the reason for this.

The office coal ration always seemed to be used up by the middle of February. However with Charlie Darke's connection with the Templecombe loco men we always had coal dropped off for our office fire and if it was really cold this would happen on a daily basis.

Conscription was introduced in 1939 for the first time in peacetime and unfortunately I was in the first age group to be called up. I left Sturminster in July 1939 to join HM Forces and didn't come back to the railway until I was demobbed in 1946. The staff office at Derby must have thought my service with the S&D and the army service warranted a clerical position in the LMS headquarters office, then located at Watford. I therefore did not return to the S&D. At the office the chief officer for labour and establishment, a Mr. Scragg, used to call me Sturminster Newton.

My cousin Hilda House worked in the office at Sturminster Newton station when the war started and perhaps she felt she was keeping my place for me. Staff on the S&D at that time were LMS, but all the accounts were done in accordance with Southern region practice. Card tickets were issued on the S&D and the LMS, but special paper tickets were used for journeys to stations on the other railway companies. In the end the railway clearance house located in Eversholt Street, Euston sorted out the financial position of each railway company to ensure each received what was due to it.

At the steps of Sturminster Newton signalbox in 1930 are S&D men Walt Fudge, unknown, and Harry Leach. (*Author's collection*)

(*above*) Sturminster Newton station looking north; the station where staff Elsie Clarke, Frank and Gerald Trowbridge, Bill Dyer and Sid Cox used to work, looks immaculate. It was a busy station for goods traffic, with the nearby milk factory and cattle market, and was the life blood of the community. It is now just a distant memory. (*Keith Barrett collection*)

BR class 5 No.73049 is awaiting the down train before moving off from Shillingstone station with the 15.40 Bournemouth to Bath train.
(*Keith Barrett collection*)

(*above*) The signalman is about to climb Shillingstone signalbox as an unidentified Standard class 4 is about to pull away northbound with a short passenger train in 1965. The North Dorset Railway Trust is working very hard to take control of the station with the aim of bringing it back to its former glory. (*E.T.Gill/R.K.Blencowe collection*)

In need of a clean, BR Standard class 4 No. 76005 is ready to leave Shillingstone with a southbound passenger train heading for Bournemouth two months before closure in 1966. (*C.L.Caddy*)

(*left*) Porter Bob Downes on the up platform at Shillingstone station in the 1960s. (*Bob Downes collection*)

(*below*) Shillingstone signalman George Ainsworth with his wife Cicely on his retirement in 1965. His colleagues in this photo are Bert Scammell, Don May, Reg Eaton, Wilf Savory, Len Farley, stationmaster Ken Forrester, Bill Dyer, Jack Bell, Alan Cox, Ivor Ridout, Bob Downes, Donald Ridout, Roy Yates, Ron Jackson and Jim Maidment. (*Bob Downes collection*)

(*above*) S&D Scottie goods No.38 is being loaded up with coal in Blandford yard in the 1890s. The driver looks very smart; two heads can be seen peering over the engine at the back of the photograph. (*Jack Hobbs collection*)

On the down platform at Blandford Forum is the very tall 27-lever signal-box. The previous box was destroyed by fire in 1906. Signalmen that worked this box over the years were Arthur Bowen, Ken Everleigh, Eric Miles, Harry Scammell and Charlie Whiting. (*C.L.Caddy*)

Roy White

Every Saturday while I was still at school during the winter months, I would be waiting at the down water column at Blandford Forum at 09.30 ready for the arrival of the goods from Templecombe which shunted the yard until about 12.45. It would go back after the arrival of the 12.23 passenger ex-Templecombe at 13.15 and I usually managed to spend the morning on the footplate. For a long time the engine always seemed to be 3F No.43194, then the Ivatt tanks arrived, either 41248 or 41249. As soon as the foreman Henry Hall had removed one label from each wagon, shunting could begin. The first job was to push the three road vans, one each from Bristol, Salisbury and Nine Elms, through the up platform into the dead end above the goods shed. Harold (Nobby) Whiting would then run them down into the shed for unloading. Everything for the town was delivered that morning, any outlying parcels probably within 2 days, as the three parcel delivery vans always did a country run in the afternoon. The fourth vehicle at that time was a Scammell mechanical horse usually delivering full loads, driven by Dennis Andrews.

There were three coal merchants based in the yard and I used to wonder why even though there was room in the sidings, wagons of coal were left out of position. Later on I learnt about demurrage, obviously more wagons had arrived than the coal merchant could handle, so he would have spoken to shunter Ivor (Ginger) Ridout. These wagons were marked 'NIP' on the daily sheet.

I also remember when playing cricket in the recreation ground in 1954, hearing a chime whistle from the station, running across to the fence and seeing Standard class 5 engine No.73051 for the first time. Perhaps these childhood memories show my destiny in joining the railway at my home station as a junior goods clerk in May 1956, and what an adventure it was. Some of my colleagues I can recall were junior porters David Brine and Pat Holmes, signalmen Arthur Bowen and Les Garlick, porters Walt Warren and Bob Short and goods porter Fred Dominey.

The up Pines Express was always busy for both passengers and parcels. Alan Cobham's firm, Flight Refuelling, used to bring a lot of parcels in for various aircraft firms in the Midlands and the North of England. They would get there the same day, with the Pines having connections to so many places. On occasions we would get a ram from Tory's farm that bred Dorset Downs but I never understood why a ram had to be weighed for charging as they travelled on the hoof and were tied up in the brakevan.

I will always remember Henry Hall, the station foreman. The only time you saw him on the platform was Monday to Saturday when the Pines was due, also on summer Saturdays when there was no goods service. The rest of the time he was kept busy in the goods yard. As the train pulled in he would call out "Sheffield in the front, Liverpool next, Manchester in the rear", then it was all systems go as the train only stopped for two minutes. Summer Saturdays always seemed like you were on the main line somewhere, with the succession of up expresses, most of which stopped at Blandford. When one pulled out there would always be passengers waiting for the next one. Whereas on a weekday when the Pines had gone, the next passenger train did not arrive for two hours. When the down Pines was due at 16.53, we would lock up the booking office and go over to the down platform, which only held six coaches. The Pines had to pull up to let the passengers out of the rear half of the train, plus any parcels from Liverpool and Sheffield. As the platform was on the outside of a curve this involved at least two people plus the guard.

As well as going to rules and regulations classes conducted by Albert Powis, the Blandford stationmaster, I also went to commercial classes at Bournemouth Central. This involved catching the Pines to Poole where I got a Southern train round to Bournemouth. As the last train from Bournemouth was at 18.50 I was issued with a brakevan pass, which allowed me to travel back on the 20.10 freight from Poole. It was quite an experience, as I had to find the train in Poole yard; at least the engine was the last leg of the Pines working, so I knew the number.

Work on a railway like the S&D provided many characters and stories. Blandford porter Joe Penny and another porter were once loading bales of straw in an open wagon. It was eventually loaded up to the maximum height allowed, ready to be sheeted and roped. Joe called up to his mate and said "Don't come down that ladder, I've just taken it away".

Stationmaster Sid Cox was in the booking office at Sturminster Newton one Saturday afternoon. All was quiet; the booking clerk was doing the pay bills when there was a scratching noise at the booking office hatch. Sid knew

that the station cat was fond of coming in that way so he whipped up the hatch with the words: "Where the bloody hell do you think you're going", only to be confronted by a lady wishing to make an enquiry.

I recall working on the late shift at Blandford when the platelayer's gang came in for their pay led by Jack Parsons. He always came in with the remark: "What about we poor laddies down on the bank then, we don't get no cooked Sunday dinner?" He knew to the penny how much they were due and would soon put you right if he found a mistake.

When I had finished my late turn at 20.00 I would join signalman Arthur Bowen for a cup of tea and play a game of cribbage with him until 22.00; I used to enjoy those evenings. Arthur organised the Blandford station First Aid team which I was part of. Other members were stationmaster Sid Cox, signalman Bert Scammell and junior porter Pat Holmes. We used to go to Yeovil for competitions and Exeter for area finals. We held our classes at the Labour club in Damory Street.

At Blandford we had special names for two stations on the Somerset end of the line. Wincanton was called Winnie Can't Come and Shepton Mallet was called Shat and Smell It – a bit rude, but it always raised a smile when parcels arrived from these two places.

I do remember a funny story concerning Pat. He lived at Sturminster Newton and would cycle to the station and then catch a train to Blandford. The late shift came in early on a Saturday, so the early shift could go to Bournemouth if they wanted to. Anyway this particular Saturday Pat brings a suitcase with his smart clothes in it. He changes out of his uniform and goes to Bournemouth. We on the late shift took his uniform out of the case and tied it up in a bundle. Then we dismantled his bike putting the pedals, handle bar, saddle and other items into the case. The case was then covered in various parcel labels, stuck on with the horrible thick railway glue of those days. When Pat arrives back at about 22.45 he doesn't say a word, he picks up the case, puts it on the guard's van and carries on home. Apparently, so he told us the following

Blandford Forum station's ambulance team in action in the 1950s. From left to right are the examining doctor, stationmaster Sid Cox, signalman Bert Scammell, junior porter Pat Holmes and clerk Roy White. (*Roy White collection*)

Monday, his dad burst out laughing when he got home, but Pat's retort was "I don't know what you're laughing about, it's your case".

The army camp at Blandford brought in a lot of business for goods and passenger traffic; National Service was still in operation. There were two main units, 1 REME and 15 RASC. The latter amongst other things taught the squaddies to drive a 3-ton truck. Quite a lot of these succumbed to accident damage, so Lomacs were high on the list of wagons required to be sent to a maintenance unit at Bulwell, Nottinghamshire. In the booking office you always seemed to be dealing with tickets for the army, either for long lists that had been sent down in advance or else for individuals at the window. When they went home on weekend leave, there was no Sunday service so you would be issuing singles. When they came back to Salisbury, which was twenty miles away, lorries would pick them up. On Saturdays, the late shift always came on at 12.00 noon instead of 13.00, so that you could go to Bournemouth on the 12.23 ex Templecombe, as the next train to Bournemouth was the down Pines. I remember once I was in a compartment with two soldiers; we had got as far as Parkstone, when one said: "Where are we?" Looking out of the window his mate replied: "Gentlemen".

The large number of public schools in the area also provided regular business for both passenger and luggage in advance. There were five that used Blandford, the largest of which was Bryanston. When they went away two clerks and two porters spent all day at the school booking in the luggage. I think it took about six lorry loads to move it to the station where it was loaded straight onto parcel vans. We were provided with lunch, which always seemed to be mince, boiled carrots and potatoes. It was worse when they came back as the luggage was all mixed up for various schools, although it was probably spread over a week, the down waiting room being used as storage. Most of it came from the Templecombe direction. In my opinion school luggage was the cause of more aching backs than anything else.

One day a Stilton cheese arrived cracked so it was refused. When this had happened previously we had been told to send it to the railway manager's restaurant at Waterloo. On this occasion we were told to sell to best advantage. The parcels/booking office smelt of cheese for sometime afterwards; I was glad it was only the one.

Virtually everything relied on the railways; although people complained, most things arrived when they should.

For instance there were two fishmongers in the town who were on the platform every morning to meet the first down train at 08.21 to collect their fish sent from Grimsby and Hull. There were boxes and boxes of Lyons cakes, which always arrived on the same train on the same day from Kensington for all the surrounding village shops. Also there were cigarettes from Wills at Bristol and Players at Nottingham. At that time Mail Order was getting into full swing, with parcels from Gratton's of Bradford, Kay's of Worcester and Empire Stores at Manchester. All this, plus much more, used to keep the four road vehicles busy all the time; in fact we used to deliver for the first of the road competition, Carter-Patterson, who later became BRS Parcels.

I met my wife Gillian on the S&D; she used to travel from Shillingstone to Poole daily to work. She never missed the train even if she was late, as the line crossed over the road from Child Okeford where she lived. Even if the train went over the bridge in front of her, with still about 400 yards to go on her bike, it would be waiting for her. We actually got married earlier than planned as I had applied for the cottage at Green Lane Crossing, north of Bailey Gate. The cottage became available earlier than I expected. We never actually bought any coal all the time we lived there, as footplate staff like Percy Hobbs, Mike Baker, Gerald Trowbridge, Tony Axford, Reg Darke, John Holt, Len Hardee, David Walker, Stan Morey, Dick Isaacs, Eddie and George Skinner, Leo Elkins and Bert Short always dropped off lots of coal for us. One of us always had to be outside to see the first up train as our daily paper was delivered to Bailey Gate; the guard did the rest depending on how good a shot he was. It could finish up on the roof, in the water butt or in numerous other places.

One Sunday morning we were both sitting up in bed with the curtains drawn when we heard the tinkle, tinkle of a 4F coasting. We didn't take any notice. It was a ballast train with PW men standing up in all of the wagons. They all gave a cheer as they went slowly past. Of course I heard about it before I had taken my coat off the next day. I left the S&D in 1961; it was a wonderful education in life and it is something I have never forgotten. There were many people I worked with that I will always remember like booking clerks Don Newman, Don Ridout and David Highman, van drivers Dennis Andrews, Norman Weldon, Roy Caines and Reg Macey, relief stationmaster Sid Everett and Bailey Gate porter Charlie Stroud. Happy days.

(*above left*) Footplate crew Rodney Scovell (left) and Roy Hix on Standard class 5 No.73028. (*Rodney Scovell collection*)

(*above right*) Shunter Ivor Ridout on Blandford Forum station on the last day of passenger service in March 1966. To the left of Ivor is Catholic priest Father Pedrick who, with his dog Leo, was well known to S&D staff. (*Ivor Ridout collection*)

Hats off to the Blandford Forum permanent way gang for winning the best kept length award in the Exeter district in 1952. The length went from Blandford to Bailey Gate. From left to right are Sid Howe, Bill Chilcott, Reg Giles, Bert Kenison, unknown, George Passion, George Christopher, Fred Parsons and Ern Matthews. (*Dan Matthews collection*)

(*above*) Standard class 3 No.82001 waits at Blandford Forum with the 15.35 Templecombe to Bailey Gate train. (*R.K.Blencowe collection*)

(*right*) Ivatt class 2 No.41243 has just taken on water at Blandford Forum ready to go northwards with the 17.30 Bournemouth West to Templecombe train. (*Graham O'Donnell collection*)

(*below*) Class 9F No.92245 leaves Blandford Forum with a down express. Fireman Peter Smith is seen leaning out of the cab. (*R.K.Blencowe collection*)

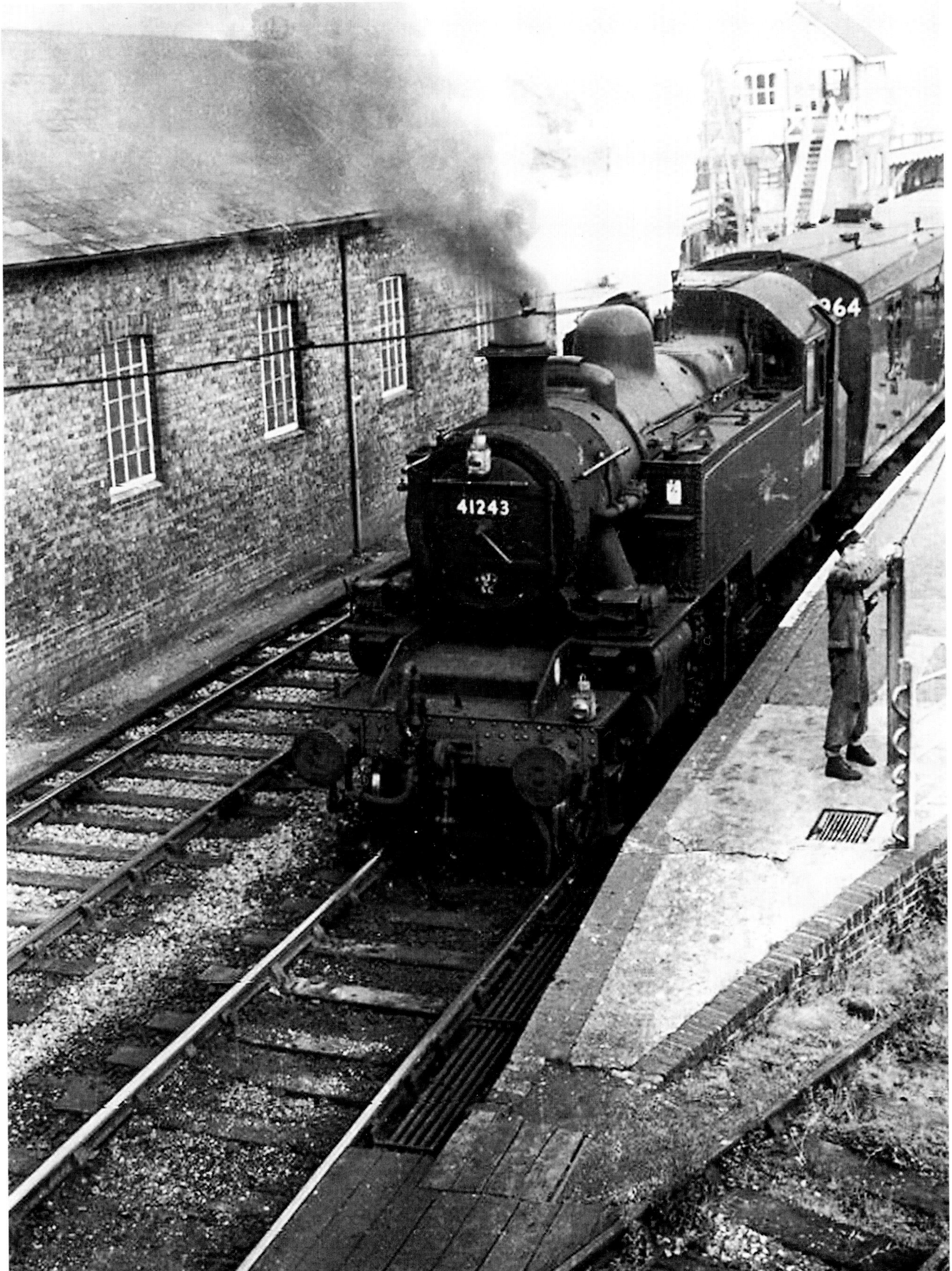
41243

Class 2 No.41242 is about to leave Blandford Forum from the down platform bound for Templecombe. (*Graham O'Donnell collection*)

Viewed from the lineside, BR class 5 No.73052 with an up local is passing Charlton Marshall Halt and about to go under bridge No.203. (*Graham O'Donnell collection*)

Swinging through near Spetisbury on a lovely summer's day in 1957 is Standard class 5 No.73049. Driver Ray Stokes is seen looking out of the cab. (*C.L.Caddy*)

In the heart of the Dorset countryside, class 2P No.40697 is captured at Spetisbury Halt in 1950. How tidy the station looks. (*S.C.Townroe/R.K.Blencowe collection*)

BR class 4 Tank No.80013 enters Bailey Gate with a short passenger train in 1965. It appears the white lines have been freshly painted on the platform. (*E.T.Gill/R.K.Blencowe collection*)

BR class 4 No.80043 pulls away from Bailey Gate with a three-coach set going southbound. (*C.L.Caddy*)

Bailey Gate station staff taken in the station yard in 1919, from left to right, are Percy Carter, George Biles, George Dennis and Harry Scovell.
(*Bill Coomer collection*)

(*below right*) The well-respected stationmaster George Pitman, seen here on the right, at Bailey Gate. George was also stationmaster at Blandford and Glastonbury.
(*SDRT collection*)

(*below left*) Joan Miles with pet dog Sue at Bailey Gate station. Joan, who worked on the S&D in the restaurant room at Bath Green Park and Templecombe, is awaiting the return of husband Roy who was a guard on the Bailey Gate milky, c.1959. (*Lesley Miles collection*)

BR Standard class 4 No.75073 has just passed Corfe Mullen signalbox with a mixed train in 1964. (*C.L.Caddy*)

2P No.40563 under the covered footbridge to the four platforms is about to leave Broadstone with a southbound train. (*R.K.Blencowe collection*)

Standard class 5 No.73049 with driver Bert Rendle (left) and fireman Ray Coates at Broadstone. It seems that the engine is off the road. (*Jim Milton collection*)

(*below*) A spruce looking BR class 5 No.73051 enters Broadstone in 1962. On the right, tucked in the corner, is a Standard Vanguard and what appear to be four trainspotters on the platform. (*C.L.Caddy*)

Looking resplendent is 4-4-0 No.15, on a down Bournemouth train on Parkstone Bank. This photograph is pre-1928 as the loco was withdrawn in August of that year. (*Jack Hobbs collection*)

Poole station with its sharp curve. All S&D trains stopped here including the Pines Express. Fortunately for residents and holidaymakers Poole still has its station. (*C.L. Caddy*)

Bill Harford

I joined the S&D at Branksome in 1952 as a cleaner; colleagues there at that time were fellow cleaners George Skinner and John Curtis; firemen Jack Thorne, Bert Short, Eddie Skinner, Steve Penny; and drivers Bert Freakley, Arthur Clist, Alec Bolwell and Donald Beale. I found the Branksome depot very friendly and everybody was most helpful to me. Within a couple of weeks I was made a passed cleaner. My first trip was with passed fireman Bill Bailey; we had to take a West Country class engine to Bath Green Park, which had failed at Branksome, for repair. The trip was quite memorable as the Mendips were covered in fog and as the junior hand I had to carry out rule 55 – the protection of a train at Midford; not a pleasant job walking over the viaduct in thick fog to the signalbox.

I fired a lot to Bert Brewer and what a turn he was. Bert had many interests, one of which was to take a couple of hours to select a horse from the morning papers and then place a bet of 6d each way. When working the Pines northbound Bert would disappear at Bath Green Park to collect the rent money from houses he owned in Bath. On the return journey to Bournemouth you fired to a very rich driver. I used to go fishing with Bert at Longham on the River Stour; his rod consisted of a makeshift billiard cue. Whilst sitting on the bank with Bert one day he related a story about one time he was fishing there. On this particular day a rabbit was feeding quietly on the bank when suddenly there was a large splash and a huge pike jumped out of the water and grabbed the rabbit. Bert immediately put more bait on his line; about half an hour later he was into something big, he had landed a huge pike. Lo and behold when he took it home and opened it up he discovered a rabbit inside. That night Bert and his wife had rabbit pie for tea and the next day roast pike.

One day Bert decided to help his fireman when they were on a goods train climbing the bank from Corfe Mullen to Broadstone. He climbed into the tender to get some coal down and hit his head on a bridge. The next thing the fireman knew was Bert sliding down through the shovelling plate; fortunately he was not badly hurt. Another time when going over Blandford River Bridge, he leant out of the cab and his false teeth fell out and hit the sleepers.

One summer Saturday evening I was firing to Arthur Clist and we were on the last train down from Templecombe to Bournemouth. The train ran in with six coaches headed by 2P No.40700. At Templecombe another four coaches were added to the train to compensate Bournemouth for the coaches on the 22.00 (SO) Bournemouth to Templecombe train. On arrival at Poole Arthur was informed that there was no banker for Parkstone Bank. Arthur being a very religious man put his finger in the collar of his shirt, muttering "shocking, shocking what are we going to do?" Suddenly there was a whistle from the guard, Arthur opened up and away we went. On this last passenger train of the day we had to stop at Parkstone and Branksome. Anyone who knows Parkstone Bank will know that ten coaches for a 2P was too many to manage without a banker. We stopped at Parkstone; then got the right away from the guard. Arthur said to me (bearing in mind I was only a young hand at the time): "Put your shoulder under the regulator and put it right across when I put her in full forward gear", which I did. The 2P shuddered and strained, but she started with the ten coaches and as we pulled away from Parkstone you could hear the crisp bark from the exhaust of the engine in the night air. We made Bournemouth West without losing time, what a loco; after this she was one of my favourite engines.

Bournemouth West signalman Fred Brown made me laugh one day. He had accepted a light engine off the last down passenger from the S&D and was looking out to see if it was coming. He could see a light moving slowly from the West station. Minutes went by and as it arrived at the box Fred could see it was Arthur Clist driving. With a grin on his face he said to me: "I believe Arthur gets out and pushes the engine to save coal".

One Christmas I was on the Bailey Gate goods. We were ready to depart when Charlie the shunter came up with a sack and asked us to burn the contents; it was full of chicken feathers. I put it in the firebox and when the driver opened the regulator the air was full of burning feathers; the smell wasn't that good either. I also recall buying a raffle ticket from Bath loco ambulance class and winning a chicken, which was dispatched on the 20.00 down passenger to Branksome, just in time for Christmas.

Whilst shunting on the Bailey Gate goods my driver forgot his sandwiches as he had left them on the messroom table at Branksome. We then got a call from Jock Ferguson, the steamraiser, to say that the driver of the up Pines was going to drop them off for him. Unfortunately as he was doing 70mph at the time, the Oxo tin, which was about six inches square, ended up as a mangled heap of tin; needless to say my driver wasn't very happy.

I remember a story about driver Donald Beale who had arrived at Blandford station with the up Pines. A steam pipe to the steam chest had broken so he got a spanner, took the pipe and fitting off and walked down the road to a garage and got them to weld the pipe back together. He returned to the engine, fitted it back on and continued the journey to Bath.

There was a Catholic priest, Father Pedrick, who would always be standing with his dog Leo at Milldown looking at all the engines going by and often he would come for a ride on the footplate to Bath. Whenever he rode with Bill Bailey and they arrived at Bath they would go off and enjoy a pint together.

When I qualified as a driver in 1959 I drove many different engines. I would say that the West Country class were very good locos; they were built for the Southern region, where most of the track was straight and flat. Of course the Somerset & Dorset was exactly the opposite with bends and plenty of hills where nearly every station had a climb out of it. When the West Countrys arrived on the S&D they were nicknamed Spam Cans. They were the worst as they were very hot, and with the casing the look out was very poor, as the smoke and steam would bellow down the side of the loco and cover the cab. The rebuilds were a lot better as you had a superior look out and they were not as hot; there seemed to be more air in the cabs. I drove both types and preferred the rebuilds as you also had more control over your driving. The originals had steam reversers, which kept going wrong. These were done away with when they were rebuilt.

On the S&D we had Nos.34040, 41 and 42, which were shedded at Bath Green Park. On Saturdays in the summer we used to have No.34043 *Combe Martin* allocated to Bournemouth Central. It was believed by Branksome crews that Bournemouth used to keep 34043 for the S&D, as she was one of the worst steaming engines in the class and no one knew why. Maybe it was because of the modifications they used on the loco. No.34040 *Crewkerne* was my favourite; I don't know why, but every time I was working on her I had a good trip. I remember one morning No.34041 *Wilton* caught fire at Blandford Forum on the Pines. The fire brigade was called and took nearly an hour to put out the fire. All the paint was burnt off the front of the cab. After about a week it looked a sorry sight, she was as rusty as a horseshoe. Someone at Bath loco took pity and painted her on the one side with a light green paint, which was completely different from the rest of the loco and tender. What with the colour and some smokebox ash, which got on to the paint before it was dry, she looked a mess. The engine remained like that until she went to Eastleigh for her refit.

I have just recently retired from the railway and my days on the S&D were the best. I still remember my work-mates at Branksome, the likes of Donald Beale, Jack Thorne, Eric Elford, Ron Hyde, Aubrey Punter, Jock Ferguson, Charlie Merryfield, Frank Cook, Bert Short and Peter Smith.

Derby-built 4-4-0 No.78 waits on Branksome shed ready for its return working. This engine was withdrawn in 1938. (*Jack Hobbs collection*)

Bournemouth West station in the early 1900s. It had six platforms and was the terminus for S&D trains. (*Author's collection*)

Two very different shots of S&D passenger guards:
(*left*) An exquisite background setting in the 1920s, as Bournemouth guard Alf Metcalfe poses for his photo at the start of his long and distinguished career on the railway. (*Ray Metcalfe collection*)
(*right*) Stan Poole (left) and Roy Miles relaxing between excursion duties at Bournemouth in 1958. (*Roy Miles collection*)

With pen at the ready, a trainspotter looks on as 7F No.53807 and class 4F No.44558 are about to leave Bournemouth West in 1960. (*R.K.Blencowe collection*)

Class 2 No.41248 viewed from the platform at Bournemouth West in 1957. This engine was withdrawn in 1964 and scrapped by D.Woodham of Barry in 1965. (*Keith Barrett collection*)

On the footplate we have fireman John Dimmock (left) with driver Johnny Walker, who was a legend on the S&D. (*Angela Holttum collection*)

(*below*) 4F No.44417 is seen here reversing stock to the carriage sidings at Bournemouth West. Lord Nelson class No.30853 *Sir Richard Grenville* is seen on the right of this 1949 picture. (*Keith Barrett collection*)

WINDSOR
RICHMOND
EVERY SATURDAY & MONDAY
EVERY
LONDON
MONDAYS,
BURNHAM
CHEAP EXCURSIONS
BATH
MONDAY,
MIDLAND
TEA
COCOA
TOWER
TEA

A picture of Pylle station one hundred years ago. On the platform are stationmaster W. Grossey and his wife with signalman Frank Hamblin and porter/signalman Alf Packer. There are a number of churns on the platform and posters for such destinations as Windsor, Richmond, London and Bath. (*Peter Bridges collection*)

Collett No.3218 climbing Pylle bank with a freight train from Highbridge to Evercreech Junction. (*John Dray collection*)

Pylle Halt nearing closure as class 2 No.41307 brings in the 09.55 Evercreech Junction to Highbridge train in September 1965. The station is already looking very neglected. (*C.L.Caddy*)

(*above*) BR class 3 No.82001 enters West Pennard while 2P No.40563 with a Highbridge to Evercreech Junction train is travelling in the opposite direction. (*E.T.Gill/R.K.Blencowe collection*)

(*below left*) Three-year-old Glen Church gives a big smile in the station yard at West Pennard. His grandfather, signalman Tom Salisbury, lived in the station house. The signalbox can be seen in the background. Behind Glen is his favourite pedal car held up by a professional-looking jack, quite ironic as he is now a mechanic. (*Joy Church collection*)

(*below right*) Signalman Tom Salisbury stands proudly on the veranda of West Pennard signalbox where he worked for many years. (*Joy Church collection*)

A fine view of West Pennard station looking towards Evercreech. The only movement is a young lad gazing out of the signalbox. *(R.K.Blencowe collection)*

In bright sunshine Collett class No.2219 trundles through West Pennard in 1962. Note the stationmaster's house on the left-hand side which is still there today. *(E.T.Gill/R.K.Blencowe collection)*

A busy scene with the loading and unloading of parcels at Glastonbury station. 2251 class No.3200 is in charge of this 08.15 Templecombe to Highbridge train. (*John Dray collection*)

0-6-0 No.2247 leaving Glastonbury with the 13.20 Evercreech Junction to Highbridge train on 13 April 1963. The Tor can be clearly seen on the skyline. (*R.E.Toop*)

(*above*) Ivatt class 2MT No.41307 runs past Dyehouse Lane Crossing with a train for Highbridge. (*Stan Blacker collection*)

Taken with the backdrop of Glastonbury goods shed in the 1930s are S&D railwaymen, from left to right, Bert Rodd, Owen Hatherall, not known, Bill Milton, Walter Giles, Arthur Lester, not known and Aubrey Barnstable. (*Fred Lester collection*)

On a bright spring day 2251 class No.2219 is about to leave Glastonbury with the 14.20 Highbridge to Templecombe train. *(E.T.Gill/R.K.Blencowe collection)*

A close up of fireman Robin Gould looking out of his cab as he is about to pass Glastonbury signal-box. A Collett 0-6-0 can be seen in the background. (*Robin Gould collection*)

Collett 2251 class No.2204 passing the ten-lever ground frame at Ashcott in 1962. Note the signs on the left-hand side. (*E.T.Gill/R.K.Blencowe collection*)

(*above left*) S&D lady Edna Atwell and family friend, driver George Wheadon, have their photo taken in front of the station house at Ashcott where Edna lived with her husband Archie, who also worked at the station. (*Janet & Tony Rossiter collection*)

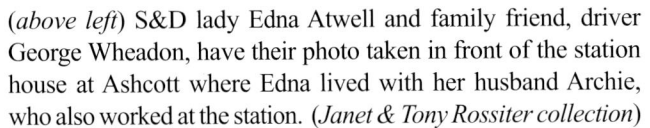

(*above right*) Ashcott porter Guy Parsons who spent many years on the S&D. He was renowned for breeding budgerigars. (*SDRT collection*)

On a sunny August day in 1964, 2251 class No.3210 is nearing Ashcott and Meare station with a short parcels train. On the right is a Commer EDV, Bedford CA and a Ford 100E. (*C.L.Caddy*)

Under a lowering sky on the Somerset levels, Shapwick station is still and quiet. It is a year since closure and nothing has moved. There will be no more mayflies annoying signalmen Reg Biffin, Walter Cook, Eric Miles, Bill Vowles and Ernie Brown in the 17-lever signalbox, nor creaking from the crossing gates. The signals are on danger as if protecting this now redundant station. What would former staff Ray George, Ron Keirle, Aubrey Simmons, and Elton King think of the demise of their station? (*C.L.Caddy*)

Class 2 No.41206 passes the signalbox at Shapwick where peat was the mainstay for traffic. (*E.T.Gill/R.K.Blencowe collection*)

Fireman Robin Gould exchanging tablets with Shapwick signalman Bill Vowles. (*Robin Gould collection*)

(*below*) The view from Shapwick signalbox of Collett No.2247 with a short passenger train. On the left can be seen a Vespa scooter; memories of the sixties roll back. (*E.T.Gill/R.K.Blencowe collection*)

Johnson Tank No.58072 with a passenger train passes the station house at Edington with the 13.40 from Bridgwater in 1952. (*H.C.Casserley*)

An unidentified 2251 class 0-6-0, shorn of her number plate on the smokebox door, is seen at Edington with the 14.20 Highbridge to Templecombe mixed train. (*John Dray collection*)

Edington Junction looking towards Shapwick in 1952 – an impressive layout for modellers. The 39-lever signalbox, station buildings with canopy, wooden shelter with stationmaster's house beyond and a magnificent array of signals. (*S.C.Townroe/ R.K.Blencowe collection*)

LMS class 2MT No.41307 with a down freight leaving Edington. (*Maurice Cook collection*)

Porter Eric Powell looks on as No.3206 enters Bason Bridge with a two-coach set for Highbridge in 1962. *(E.T.Gill/R.K.Blencowe collection)*

An unusual sight as two passengers awaiting the Burnham train tend the station's garden at Bason Bridge in the 1950s. (*Mrs Zoe Stowe collection*)

Class 2 No.41296 engulfed in smoke and steam with a number of milk tanks at Bason Bridge. (*Tony Haggett*)

Change of motive power at Bason Bridge Dairy, as two Dennis Pax lorries are unloading milk churns. (*Tony Haggett*)

2251 class 0-6-0 No.3206 comes into platform five at Highbridge station. Three members of staff are ready to unload the freight. Four churns on a trolley are probably for the outward journey, to be dropped off at crossing keepers' cottages. (*E.T.Gill/R.K.Blencowe collection*)

LMS 0-6-0 No.2889 is in store alongside the carriage cleaning and testing shed at Highbridge. (*Jack Hobbs collection*)

3F No.43682 setting off from Highbridge with the 16.00 departure for Evercreech and Templecombe. The fireman is receiving the single-line token from the signalman at Highbridge East box in 1961. Firemen at Highbridge who would have carried this procedure out in the fifties and sixties were Roger Parker, John Baker, Tony Rossiter, George Stent, Terry Fry, John Rice and Mike Lewis. (*R.E.Toop*)

Bernard Andrews

Many words have been said about my father Ronald (Chummy) Andrews and his life as an S&D driver. He was quite a character and had many hobbies besides driving trains. In his younger days he was a very good swimmer. He belonged to Highbridge Swimming club which used to practice and hold competitions in the River Brue at Highbridge near the loco sheds. He won a gold medal for being first in the Steart Island swim from the beach at Burnham.

Another of his hobbies was first aid with the St.John Ambulance. Harry Miller, who worked as a carriage cleaner, and my father were founder members of the Highbridge division. He was also captain of the Highbridge Railway team and travelled all over the West of England to enter in competitions; they usually came home with a prize.

I can remember when the staff of the S&D took part in their yearly exams in first aid. If they passed the test they gained an extra free travel pass, so it was well worth passing the exam. My brother Cecil and I were of school age and were used as casualties each year. We went down to the loco shed with our father and were laid out on the floor with a notice around our necks. These were placed by the doctors carrying out the judging, indicating that we had some form of broken bones or other injuries. The staff would treat us and hopefully be passed out.

Other hobbies were beekeeping and gardening. He also had an allotment, as did nearly all the S&D staff, on a piece of land known as Daisy Farm, which ran alongside Highbridge Recreation Field opposite Grange Avenue. This is where my father kept his seven beehives behind some blackberry bushes. Two plots away was my father's fireman, George Brooks's plot. He had a fairly large apple tree in the middle of it; my father was sure it was George's apple blossom that produced the best honey. Every summer, at the right time, he would go down to the allotment with a pair of trucks and come back with it full of honeycombs. My mother Violet and he spent many hours filtering it and filling up loads of honey jars. I also remember my father taking early retirement to save a younger driver being made redundant. Bruce Barnes the official from the Western Region came to our home to explain the terms of his early retirement. After he had finished talking, my father said to him: "You have given me a golden handshake, now I will give you one" and he gave him a pot of honey. Mr. Barnes thought that was a nice gesture.

One memory I have of the S&D is when my brother, sister Ruth and myself were very young and my father was a fireman to George Hurley. When they used to work the early turn to Burnham-on-Sea we would always have a treat. While the engine was at Burnham my father would nip across to Marchent's bakery next to the S&D hotel and buy what was called a twister loaf of bread; it was like today's stick loaf. He would put it in a bag my mother had made and take it back to the engine for the journey back to Highbridge. We lived in Newtown at this time and the train would run alongside Bland's Timber Yard. Opposite the yard there was a field where we would wait for the train and my father would throw the twister to us. There was nothing nicer than a piece of hot twister with butter, courtesy of the S&D.

When I was 16 in 1943 my father got me a job as a cleaner and callboy at Highbridge loco. My mother had shortened a pair of father's overalls for my first day. I had to report to the loco shed foreman Bill Bready; he greeted me by saying 'Hello, young Chummy' and that nickname stuck with me. He took me down to the running shed to introduce me to the staff; we stopped by a man and Mr. Bready said: "This is Frank Parsons, I want you to look after young Chummy Andrews and show him the ropes". Frank Parsons was a real nice man, his first words to me were. "Well, young Chummy, the first thing to learn is how to make a good cup of tea". He made the tea in his billycan, I had a cup and it was really good. He said: "I hope you were watching because you are making the next one". The reason I was on my own was because all the other passed cleaners were out acting as firemen. As it was during the war a lot of special trains were being run and the use of footplate staff was being stretched.

Frank introduced me to the rest of the staff in the shed. I first met Jack Swain and Ralph Barry, they were engine fitters and then Charlie Samson, a fitter's mate, Joe Ryan, steamraiser, Stan Washer, boilerman and George Cross, firebox maintenance man. We went outside to the coaling stage where I met the two coalmen, George James and Bill Barrett. Those two worked hard keeping all the engines coaled up ready for use. George was always joking and one thing I can remember about him was that he liked kippers. Every morning when he went to the messroom for breakfast he would take a whole kipper

out of his bag and stick it on the end of a huge toasting fork and grill it in front of the fire that was always burning there. He used to say it was the best way to cook a kipper and by the smell of it he was right.

About 12.00 that first day Bill Bready came out to Frank and asked him if he would drive some locos over to the coal stage for coaling. Frank could turn his hand to anything including driving an engine. I found out afterwards he was a very useful handyman. His main job seemed to be soldering and repairing hand and engine lamps, he was a wizard with a soldering iron. I followed Frank and we climbed on to a Bulldog No.3216, and took her for coaling. He showed me how to fire and put coal in the firebox, so there I was on my first day riding on an engine. He then showed me how to couple two engines together; I learnt a lot from Frank Parsons. Another task I did later was to help build new brick arches in the front of the fireboxes of different locos with George Cross.

Soon I was put on the nightshift to perform the duties of cleaning the boiler tubes. Also I had to do the calling up which meant getting on my bike at about 04.00 to go to the drivers' houses to wake them up for the early shift.

17-year-old passed cleaner Bernard Andrews at Highbridge in 1944. (*Bernard Andrews collection*)

There was always something different going on, especially when the American troops moved into Burnham-on-Sea. They were stationed in Nissan huts off Oxford Street and would go to work to Highbridge in a fleet of army trucks and jeeps. They used the fields, which is now Walrow Industrial Estate, to store thousands of five-gallon cans of petrol, covering them with camouflage nets. They had their own steam engine, which would shunt wagons of petrol around the area. Trains would come in from the GWR bringing the fuel wagons and be brought over to the S&D where the army would take over. The troops were all young lads in their twenties, who were very friendly and generous. For instance cigarettes were hard to come by in the local shops and the Americans could get as many as they wanted in their PX canteen. They used to buy them for the railway staff at ten shillings for two hundred. I still remember the names of the packets, Camel, Lucky Strike, Chesterfield, Fifth Avenue, and Phillip Morris. For the pipe smoker it was Sir Walter Raleigh tobacco. The Yanks wore lovely soft rubber boots and it was noticed one day that one of our drivers was sporting a pair of these new boots so it wasn't long before we all had a pair.

One day I went on my bike to call up Harry Pearce at Huntspill. I set off as usual and I was just about to cycle over Walrow Bridge, where the GWR railway line ran under, when a German plane flying low came over the bridge. A freight train was travelling along the up line towards Bristol. The plane machine-gunned it from Walrow Bridge to Bristol Bridge. It made one hell of a noise and the bullets were hitting the bridge before hitting the train. Had I been a few seconds earlier I would have been on top of the bridge and Harry Pearce might not have been called that morning. I learnt later there was no serious damage to the train. I always cycled quickly over that bridge after that. When I got back to the loco shed the steamraiser Ewart Hayes was most concerned and made me a cup of tea. When I told my mother about the incident she looked at me very concerned and said: "I've always told you to be careful going over Walrow Bridge" as though it was all my fault. The American troops were running around with their rifles at the ready as they had heard the machine-gunning and thought they were under attack. With all the petrol that was about I can understand why they were a bit jumpy.

Another time when they got a bit alarmed was when the Germans dropped incendiary bombs around the fields near the petrol dump. Hundreds of them failed to go off

but the ones that did lit up the area. It was a good job for Highbridge loco and of course the residents that they didn't land on the dump.

Two weeks before D-Day and two weeks after, all the petrol was taken away. The soldiers had gone, too. No longer could they be seen walking around the loco shed; they were sadly missed. At least I had a pair of their boots. I often wonder how they got on in the D-Day landings.

After a while I went back on days again and my firing career began. I was still a passed cleaner but could go on fireman's duties as required. My first firing turn was with driver Charlie King on a milky to Templecombe. After that I fired to most of the other drivers including my father. I was always amazed at the different kinds of produce that was brought back on the footplate from along the line to Evercreech. Staff from the different stations would bring up boxes of apples, pears, plums, rabbits and wild ducks for the footplate crews, payment would be a few shillings. Everything seemed to be ordered and collected on certain days and shifts.

To supplement the coal during the war years someone had the idea of using briquettes on the engines; these were made at Cardiff and consisted of coal dust held together by cement and were made in large blocks. They were dirty to use and unless they were mixed with some coal the engines did not steam too well with them. One night I was on the last passenger train from Evercreech firing to Lou Moxey and the engine had no coal only these to burn. We set off from Evercreech and at Glastonbury we found the engine was steaming very badly but we struggled on and Lou kept saying: "We aren't going to make Highbridge" despite everything we did. We stopped for steam alongside Highbridge loco, some little way from the station. Lou was really annoyed and what he said about these briquettes is unprintable. They got an engine from the shed and pulled us into the station. We found out later that the tube face was all clinked up with cement dust, which prevented the engine from steaming. Lou wrote a stinking report about the use of briquettes without coal and the next night we had a different engine and no briquettes, only coal to burn.

One day I was with driver Bill May and we were called into Bill Bready's office. He said to me: "I want you to be at your best today. On your trip back from Evercreech, Mr. Arkwright the Bath Green Park inspector will be taking Alan Jones and Fred Meaker on their driving test and you will be firing to both of them." Alan and Fred travelled up on the cushions with us. The inspector took Bill May off the engine at Evercreech and Alan Jones took over for his test – he was to drive to Glastonbury. On the way Mr. Arkwright said to Alan: "Come on the train can go faster than this." Alan replied: "There is a speed restriction over this branch and I am sticking to it." Mr. Arkwright smiled and said: "Good job you said that or I would have failed you." At Glastonbury Fred took over to Highbridge and Mr. Arkwright asked the same question; Fred answered correctly. It was a question he tried to trick all of them with when they were on their test. Both Alan and Fred passed their test and became passed firemen. At the end of the journey Mr. Arkwright said to me: "Well done, fireman" so in some small way I had helped them pass.

I had one mishap when I was firing to my father going to Burnham-on-Sea. You had to catch the tablet from the signalman at the level crossing in Church Street. Of course without the tablet you couldn't proceed. I was ready to put my arm through the loop as we passed the signalbox, when the signalman Ernie Oram who was holding the tablet sneezed. His arm dropped and I knocked the tablet out of his hand. My father had to stop the train and I walked back to retrieve it. Ernie was walking towards me and said as he handed it to me: "Sorry about that, I couldn't help it, I had a sneezing fit." We proceeded to Burnham station where the porter Miss Pursey said: "You are late." I said: "Have a word with Ernie in the box, he will tell you all about it."

Some of the loco staff I worked with at Highbridge were drivers George Hurley, Lou Moxey, Ern Cook, George Wheadon, Horace Green, Sergeant Hansford, Bill Peck and Harry Pearce. Others included passed firemen and cleaners Monarch Baker, Jack Meaker, Alan Jones, Fred Meaker, Jim Bradner, Cecil Andrews, Les Haines, Maurice and Norman Cook, Dennis Young, Ray Gibbs, Horace Hardwich, Walt Parsons, Bill Parsons and Jack Davis. Guards I recall were Sam Talbot, Frank Salter, Ted Christopher and Walt Pople, and fitter's mate George Gulliver. I left the S&D in 1946 to join HM Forces, and with my railway knowledge I was drafted into the Royal Engineers to train as a military engine driver at Longmoor Military Railway Depot. I passed out and became a driver at last and was posted to 10th Railway Depot in Egypt. When I came out of the army I became a signalman in various signalboxes on the Western region. My days on the S&D bring back many happy memories to me, which I will always remember with fondness.

Class 2 No.41296 takes a rest at the bay platform at Highbridge, before going across the Somerset levels with a Templecombe bound train. (*C.L.Caddy*)

Bulldog class 3F No.43356 is seen at Highbridge Wharf carrying out some freight shunting in 1950. (*S.C.Townroe/ R.K.Blencowe collection*)

(*above*) Walt Jeans leans out of the cab of class 2 No.41283 at Highbridge. Walt was a top link driver and gave over 50 years service to the railway. (*Trevor Jeans collection*)

3F No.43419 is in the background as Highbridge railwaymen pose for this 1950s photograph. From left to right are Keith Conibeer, David Rutherford, John Lancastle and in the front Bill Conibeer. (*John Lancastle collection*)

(*above*) In the cab of 3F No.3218 are fireman Les Haines (left) and driver Horace Green taken at Highbridge in 1949.
(*Mrs B.Reading collection*)

Footplate team at Highbridge in 1965 are fireman Mike Lewis (left) and guard Walter (Paddy) Smyth, with driver George Wheadon in the cab of class 2 No.41307.
(*Walter Smyth collection*)

Fitter Cyril (Captain) Burrows is seen here at Highbridge. Cyril started on the railway in 1952 and helped maintain turntables and plant on the S&D. (*Cyril Burrows collection*)

Fireman Maurice Cook (left) and driver Bill Peck are dressed up for the Centenary Special of the Somerset Central Railway on 28 August 1954. (*Maurice Cook collection*)

Guard Ted Christopher, in the garden with his pet dog, is about to set off for work on the branch in the 1950s. Note his SJC cap badge. (*Mrs M.Brown collection*)

Workmates at Highbridge, firemen John Lancastle (left) and Keith Conibeer. (*John Lancastle collection*)

From left to right are the loco foreman, Maurice Cook and Charlie King in front of Ivatt 2MT No.41241. In the background is the old Highbridge breakdown van. (*Maurice Cook collection*)

Highbridge West signalbox in the 1940s. This box controlled the S&D crossing over the Great Western. Third from the left is Albert Martin who also worked on the S&D as a foreman at Highbridge and as a porter at Bason Bridge. *(Bernard Martin collection)*

Burnham-on-Sea station looking towards the sea. The 4-lever signalbox is now on the S&D Railway Trust's site at Washford. To the left is the excursion platform, which was mostly used for summer specials. (*Author's collection*)

Class 4F No.44557 edges out of Burnham's station overall roof. The hut on the right is still there; the rest of the site is home to Somerfield's. (*Norman Ashman collection*)

Driver Stan Bedford gives a ride to his grand-daughter Martina Bunnett before he goes off to work. Stan worked on the railway for 49 years, many being on the S&D. (*Barbara Burdge collection*)

(*left*) Fireman Maurice Cook wearing a beard looks out from the cab of 3F No.43201 at Burnham-on-Sea on 28 August 1954. This special train from Glastonbury marked the Centenary of the Somerset Central Railway. Over 500 passengers were on board, many from Clarks Shoe Company.
(*John Mansfield collection*)

A rare photograph of Wells S&D signalbox taken in 1948. The gentlemen on the veranda are ganger Clifford Mock (left) and signalman Bert Baker who used to catch flies in his cap and take them back to his signalbox for a huge spider he kept in the locking frame under the box. (*Trevor Sprague collection*)

(*below*) 0-6-0 Pannier Tank No.8714 on shunting duties at Wells Priory Road. At Wells there was a shunter called Stan Ford who liked his cider. He had a habit of relieving himself on the buffer stops between two wagons in the goods shed. Stan was often warned that not only was he in grave danger of the wagons being moved, but also of the possibility of being coupled up to the vacuum pipe of one of the wagons. (*Jack Hobbs collection*)

(*left*) S&D 0-4-4T No.53, built by Vulcan Foundry in 1885, seen here at Wells. The footplate crew are possibly driver Walt Fowler and fireman Frank Banwell. (*R.K.Blencowe collection*)

(*right*) Porter Vaughan Wills, with his mother Harriet, about to set off for work at Polsham station in the 1930s. The dog in the photo is Dash, which was a very appropriate name. He must be the only dog banned from going to Wells. Water from the springs at Wells would at times travel down the gutters of the pavement. Dash delighted in running up and down the gutters scattering water everywhere, much to the annoyance of people on the pavement. (*Gordon Lee collection*)

(*left*) Polsham Halt after closure. For such a small station it boasted a stationmaster's house at the end of the 200-foot platform. The station closed in 1951. (*Author's collection*)

(*above*) What were six men with regulation hats and coats doing on Cossington station on 18 March 1952? Was it anything to do with the station closing nine months later? (*S.C.Townroe/R.K.Blencowe collection*)

(*left*) The grey stone buildings of Cossington station which are still there today as private dwellings. The station was situated between Bridgwater and Edington. (*Will Locke collection*)

London and South Western Ry.
787
FROM WATERLOO TO
COSSINGTON

A very rare picture of Bawdrip Halt, with an unidentified Vulcan 0-4-4T hauling a two-coach train to Bridgwater, c.1920s. Note the period dress of the passengers. (*David Milton collection*)

A presentation of long-service awards to five railwaymen in the goods department at Bridgwater, their total service between them being 240 years. The men with the awards in their hands are, from left to right, Gilbert Ashill (with clock), Jessie Manning, Albert Rawles, Reg Walford and William Heal. Some others in the group are Charlie Fuller, David Fisher, S. Alford, Bill Hill, D. Crocker, A. Baker, Sam Farthing and Jack Warren. (*Dennis Ashill collection*)

LMS 0-6-0 No.3248 (22c) Bath shedcode on 11.00 ex-Edington Junction seen here at Bridgwater North in 1947. The platform staff and footplate crew are clearly enjoying having their photograph taken. (*Richard Dagger collection*)

Bridgwater North station was home to such well-known railwaymen and women as Joyce Fear, Gilbert and Dennis Ashill, Les Green, Will Locke, Fred Lester, Reg Brewer and Fred Allen. The station was demolished in the 1980s and is now a Sainsbury's supermarket. (*Keith Barrett collection*)

Index

Achilles, Bert 52
Adams, Ray 11
Ainsworth, Cicely 98
Ainsworth, George 98
Ainsworth, Joyce 17
Alford, S. 156
Allan, John 66
Allen, Fred 157
Amos, Bill 25
Andrews, Bernard (Chummy) 140-142
Andrews, Cecil 142
Andrews, Dennis 100, 102
Andrews, Ronald (Chummy) 140, 142
Appleby, Bill 11
Arkwright, Mr. 142
Arlett, Mike 22-23
Ashfield, Norman 75, 79
Ashill, Dennis 157
Ashill, Gilbert 156, 157
Atkins, Ken 62
Attwood, Albert 68
Atwell, Archie 131
Atwell, Edna 131
Axford, Tony 102

Bailey, Bill 114, 115
Baker, A. 156
Baker, Bert 152
Baker, George 46-47, 52-53
Baker, John 139
Baker, Mike 102
Baker, Monarch 142
Ball, Vic 34
Ballantyne, Hugh 66
Banwell, Frank 153
Barnard, Doug 86-87
Barnes, Bruce 140
Barnes, Mr. 52
Barnes, Oliver 25
Barnstable, Aubrey 127
Barrett, Bill 140
Barry, Ralph 140
Beale, Donald 114, 115
Bean, Ron (Runner) 65
Bedford, Stan 151
Beeho, Vic 55
Bell, Jack 98
Bell, Joyce 54
Berryman, Hugh 88
Berryman, Joan 88
Berryman, Mabel 88
Biffin, Reg 132
Biles, George 109
Bird, Dickie 74

Blacker, Kate (*née* Russ) 54
Blacker, Stan 52-54
Blacker, Ted 49, 52, 55
Boase, Mr. 66
Bolwell, Alec 114
Bonfield, Stan 11
Boston, Dave 18
Bowen, Arthur 99, 100, 101
Box, Fred 54, 68
Box, Freda 54, 68
Boyce, Hubert 52
Bradner, Jim 142
Bready, Bill 140, 141, 142
Brewer, Bert 114
Brewer, Reg 74, 157
Brine, David 100
Brooks, George 140
Brooks, Len 49
Brooks, Rose 53
Brown, Ernie 132
Brown, Fred 114
Bryant, Fred 46-47
Bunnett, Ian 19
Burford, Harold 7
Burrows, Cyril (Captain) 146
Burt, D. 66
Bushrod, Fred 75

Cable, Kath 53
Caines, Roy 102
Candy, Ted 85
Carter, Albert 46-47, 53
Carter, Percy 109
Carter, Reg 56
Chilcott, Bill 103
Chinock, Reg 52
Christopher, George 103
Christopher, Ted 142, 147
Church, Glen 123
Clark, Horace 34
Clarke, Elsie 96
Clist, Arthur 114
Coates, Ray 111
Cockrell, Graham 45
Coles, Derek 19
Coles, George 56, 94
Colwell, Doug 75
Conibeer, Bill 144
Conibeer, Keith 144, 147
Cook, Charlie 78
Cook, Ern 142
Cook, Frank 115
Cook, Maurice 142, 146, 147, 151
Cook, Norah 54
Cook, Norman 142
Cook, Walter 132
Coombes, Bill 42
Coombes, H. 35
Coombes, Mr. 94

Corbin, Tom 48
Cornell, Bill 74
Counsell, Len 85
Cox, Alan 98
Cox, Sid 96, 100, 101
Crocker, D. 156
Croft, Dick 66
Cross, George 140, 141
Crossey, Harold 16
Crouchen, Joe 35, 37
Crouchen, Phil 32
Cull, Jim 82
Cummings, Bill 55
Cummings, Harold 49, 55
Curtis, John 114

Darke, Charlie 95
Darke, Reg 86-87, 102
Davies, May 53
Davis, Ernie 75, 78
Davis, Jack 142
Day, Bert 82
Dennis, George 109
Dimmock, John 119
Dominey, Fred 100
Doulting, F. 55
Downes, Bob 98
Dray, John 63, 82, 84
Durnford, Fred 46-47
Dyer, Bill 96, 98

Eames, Roger 19
Eaton, Reg 98
Elford, Eric 115
Elkins, Leo 102
Elliott, Alf 69, 74, 75
Elliott, Arthur 10, 18
Evans, Ken 32
Everett, Sidney 102
Everleigh, Ken 99
Eyre, Charlie 22
Farley, Len 94, 98
Farthing, Sam 156
Fear, Harry 52
Fear, Joyce 157
Fell, Chris 19
Ferguson, Jock 115
Filer, Fred 81
Fisher, David 156
Fisher, Fred 83, 91
Fishleigh, Bill 75
Flay, Bill 46-47
Foot, Bob 75, 78
Foot, Den 82
Ford, Stan 152
Forrester, Ken 98
Fowler, Walt 153
Franks, Bill 52
Franks, Frank 35

Fraser, Mary 53
Freak, Vic 68
Freakley, Bert 114
Fry, Bob 67
Fry, Terry 139
Fudge, Leonard 88
Fudge, Vera 88
Fudge, Walt 95
Fuller, Charlie 156

Gane, Jack 52
Garlick, Les 100
George, Ray 132
Gibbs, Ray 142
Giles, Reg 103
Giles, Walter 127
Gilham, Bob 56
Gilson, Charlie 52
Good, James 69
Good, William & Mrs. 69
Goodland, Dill 54
Goodland, Harry 54
Gould, Bob 74
Gould, Charlie 83
Gould, Jim 59, 75
Gould, Norman 79
Gould, Robin 12, 129, 133
Gray, Edgar 10
Gray, Ron 10
Green, Horace 142, 145
Green, Les 157
Green, Oliver 52
Gregory, Fred 52
Griggs, Mr. 54
Grossey, W. & Mrs. 120-121
Gulliver, George 142
Gunning, Archie 10, 56-57
Gunning, Bill 10, 56-57
Gunning, Tom 10
Gunning, Walter 52, 53
Guppy, Ted 55

Haines, Bert 32
Haines, Les 142, 145
Hall, Eddie 55
Hall, Henry 100
Hamblin, Eric 79
Hamblin, Frank 120-121
Hamblin, Percy 82
Hamer, Lew 68
Hannam, Alwyn 82
Hannam, Percy 78
Hansford, Harry 85
Hansford, Sergeant 142
Hardee, Len 102
Harding, George 78
Hardwick, Horace 142
Harford, Bill 114-115
Harris, Bill 52

Hartnell, Charlie 74
Hatcher, Art 85
Hatherall, Owen 127
Hawkins, Kathleen 53
Hayes, Bob 74
Hayes, Ewart 141
Heal, William 156
Hemmings, Ernie 10
Hemmings, Fred 10, 43
Hicks, Fred 62
Hicks, Tony 83
Higgins, Harry 55
Higgins, Ted 46-47, 55
Highman, David 102
Hill, Bert 94
Hill, Bill 156
Hill, Percy 52
Hix, Roy 103
Hobbs, Percy 102
Hodges, Frank 67
Holden, Doug 7, 10
Holden, Ralph 10
Holder, Chris 19
Holmes, Pat 100, 101-102
Holt, John 102
House, Hilda 95
Howe, Sid 103
Hughes, Joan 53
Hughes, Maurice 75,78
Hurford, Chris 66
Hurle, Frank 55
Hurley, George 140, 142
Hurst, Ron 66
Hyde, Ron 115

Isaacs, Dick 102

Jackson, Ron 98
James, Fred 75
James, George (Highbridge 140-141
James, George (Wincanton) 75
Jeans Reg 67
Jeans, Walt 144
Jones, Alan (Tankard) 54, 142
Jones, Davy 66
Judd, George 74-75

Keirle, Ron 132
Kelson, Richard 19
Kenison, Bert 103
Kiddle, Mary 72-73
Kiddle, Norris 79
Kilmister, Bernard 11
King, Arthur (senior) 10,11
King, Arthur (junior) 10-11
King, Charlie 142, 148
King, Elton 132
King, Gordon 10,14

Lamb, C. 35
Lambert, Mark 52
Lambert, Ted 59
Lancastle, John 144, 147
Lawrence, Fritz 62
Lay, Basil 59
Leach, Harry 95
Lee, Mr. 66
Lemon, Harry 52
Lester, Arthur 127
Lester, Fred 157
Lewis, Mike 139, 145
Light, Harry 75
Lintern, Bill 52, 94
Locke, Will 157
Lockwood, Mary 54
Lockwood, Norman 54
Lodder, Mike 29
Long, Lou 91

Macey, Reg 102
Machin, Jimmy 29
McKenzie, Robert (Jock) 92
Maidment, Jim 98
Maidment, Thomas 23
Manning, Jessie 156
Marsh, Bob 95
Martin, Albert 149
Martin, Jeff 75
Mason, Alan 54
Massey, David 16
Matthews, Ern 103
May, Bill 142
May, Don 98
Mayo, Wayne 19
Meader, Ivor 46-47, 66
Meaker, Fred 142
Meaker, Jack 142
Merchant, Ron 11
Merryfield, Charlie 115
Metcalfe, Alf 17, 117
Miles, Eric 99, 132
Miles, Joan 109
Miles, Roy 4, 74, 75, 109, 117
Miller, Harry 140
Milton, Bill 127
Mock, Clifford 152
Moody, Harold
Moore, Graham 94-95
Morey, Stan 102
Morris, Charlie 10
Morris, Harold 66
Moulton, Tom 55
Moxey, Lou 142

Nash, Harry 75
Nettley, Trevor 86-87
Newman, Bert 95
Newman, Don 102

Newman, Phil 94
Newsome, Harry 52
Nicol, Jock 75, 78
Norman, David 19
Norris, Ambrose 49
Norris, Dennis 12

Oram, Ernie 142

Packer, Alf 120-121
Packer, Frank 35
Padfield, Ern 54
Padfield, Frank 54
Padfield, Ken 46-47, 66
Padfield, Reg 54
Padfield, Win 54
Parfitt, Stan 94
Parker, Roger 139
Parsons, Albert 25, 34
Parsons, Bill 142
Parsons, Frank 140, 141
Parsons, Fred 103
Parsons, Guy 131
Parsons, Jack 101
Parsons, Walt 142
Pass, Nigel 16
Passion, George 103
Paul, Tom 46-47
Paulley, Ted 7
Pearce, Fred 35
Pearce, Harry 141, 142
Peck, Bill 142, 146
Pedrick, Father 103, 155
Penny, Joe 94, 100
Penny, Steve 114
Peters, Ivo 66
Phillips, Ern 68
Pike, Jack 67
Pitman, George 109
Pitt, Oscar 10
Pitt, Sid 59, 74
Pitt, Tony 10
Poole, Emily 54, 56
Poole, Stan 117
Pople, Walt 142
Powell, Eric 136
Powis, Albert 100
Powis, Colin 19
Pullen, Oliver 66
Punter, Aubrey 115
Pursey, Miss 142

Rallison, Norman 75
Rawles, Albert 156
Rawles, Bill 65
Rawles, Clarence 54, 62
Ray, Frank 85
Reakes, Dai 46-47, 55
Reakes, Dorothy 54

Reakes, Joyce 54
Reed, Bert 11
Rendle, Bert 83,111
Rendle, Dave 85
Rendle, Richard 81
Reynolds, Bev 16
Reynolds, Howard 14, 16
Rice, John 139
Ricketts, Lou 10, 11
Ridout, Don 94, 98, 102
Ridout, Ivor (Ginger) 98, 100, 103
Riggs, Eddie 62
Rodd, Bert 127
Robbins, B. 66
Rossiter, Len 74
Rossiter, Tony 139
Routley, Stan 42
Russ, Bob 79
Russ, Tom 52, 54
Russell, Alf 68
Rutherford, David 144
Ryall, Mike 19
Ryan, Joe 140

Salisbury, Tom 123
Salter, Frank 142
Samson, Charlie 140
Savage, Percy 22
Savory, Wilf 98
Sawyer, John 19
Scammell, Bert 98, 101
Scammell, Harry 99
Scovell, Harry 109
Scovell, Rodney 83,103
Shellard, Stan 15
Shore, Max 48
Short, Bert 102, 114, 115
Short, Bob 100
Simmons, Aubrey 132
Simms, Betty 54
Simms, Edna 54
Simms, Jack 74
Simms, Ted 59, 68
Skinner, Eddie 102, 114
Skinner, George 102, 114
Skinner, Mr. 66
Smith, Alfie
Smith, Cliff 15
Smith, Peter 104, 115
Smyth, Walter (Paddy) 75, 145
Spiller, Betty 54
Staddon, Frank 10
Staddon, Reg 10
Stamp, John 11, 14
Starkey, Harry 11
Steele, Harry 75
Stent, George 139
Stock, Fred 52
Stokes, Ray 107

Stowe, Alec 66
Stroud, Charlie 102
Swain, Jack 140

Talbot, Sam 142
Taylor, Albert 68
Thick, Fred 74
Thorne, Jack 114, 115
Toghill, Graham 7
Toose, Mary 53
Tooze, John 19
Tosio, K. 66
Trott, Frank 56
Trowbridge, Frank 96
Trowbridge, Gerald 96, 102
Tucker, George 11
Turner, Arthur 11

Vaughan, Charlie 66, 68
Vowles, Bill 132, 133

Walford, Reg 156
Walker, David 102
Walker, Johnny 119
Ware, Bernard 11, 18
Warren, Jack 156
Warren, Walt 100
Washer, Stan 140
Webb, Bill 63
Webb, Walt 80
Webber, Eric 16
Welch, George 81
Weldon, Norman 102
West, Cliff 11
Wheadon, George 131, 142
White, Roy 100-102
White, S. 66
White, Sid 11
Whiting, Charlie 99
Whiting, Harold (Nobby) 100
Whittle, Irving 75, 78
Willimas, Phil 66
Wills, Vaughan 153
Willsher, Les 10, 32
Willshire, Ivor 11
Wilson, Eric 34
Wiltshire, Harry 22,23
Withers, Clive 74
Witt, Bert 95
Wollard, Roy 52, 56
Woods, Walt 32
Woolley, Harry 75

Yates, Roy 98
Yeoman, Bryn 67
Young, Dennis 142

Principles Of Mechanics

Synge, John. L, Griffith, Byron. A

This work has been selected by scholars as being culturally important, and is part of the knowledge base of civilization as we know it. This work was reproduced from the original artifact, and remains as true to the original work as possible. Therefore, you will see the original copyright references, library stamps (as most of these works have been housed in our most important libraries around the world), and other notations in the work.

This work is in the public domain in the United States of America, and possibly other nations. Within the United States, you may freely copy and distribute this work, as no entity (individual or corporate) has a copyright on the body of the work.

As a reproduction of a historical artifact, this work may contain missing or blurred pages, poor pictures, errant marks, etc. Scholars believe, and we concur, that this work is important enough to be preserved, reproduced, and made generally available to the public. We appreciate your support of the preservation process, and thank you for being an important part of keeping this knowledge alive and relevant.

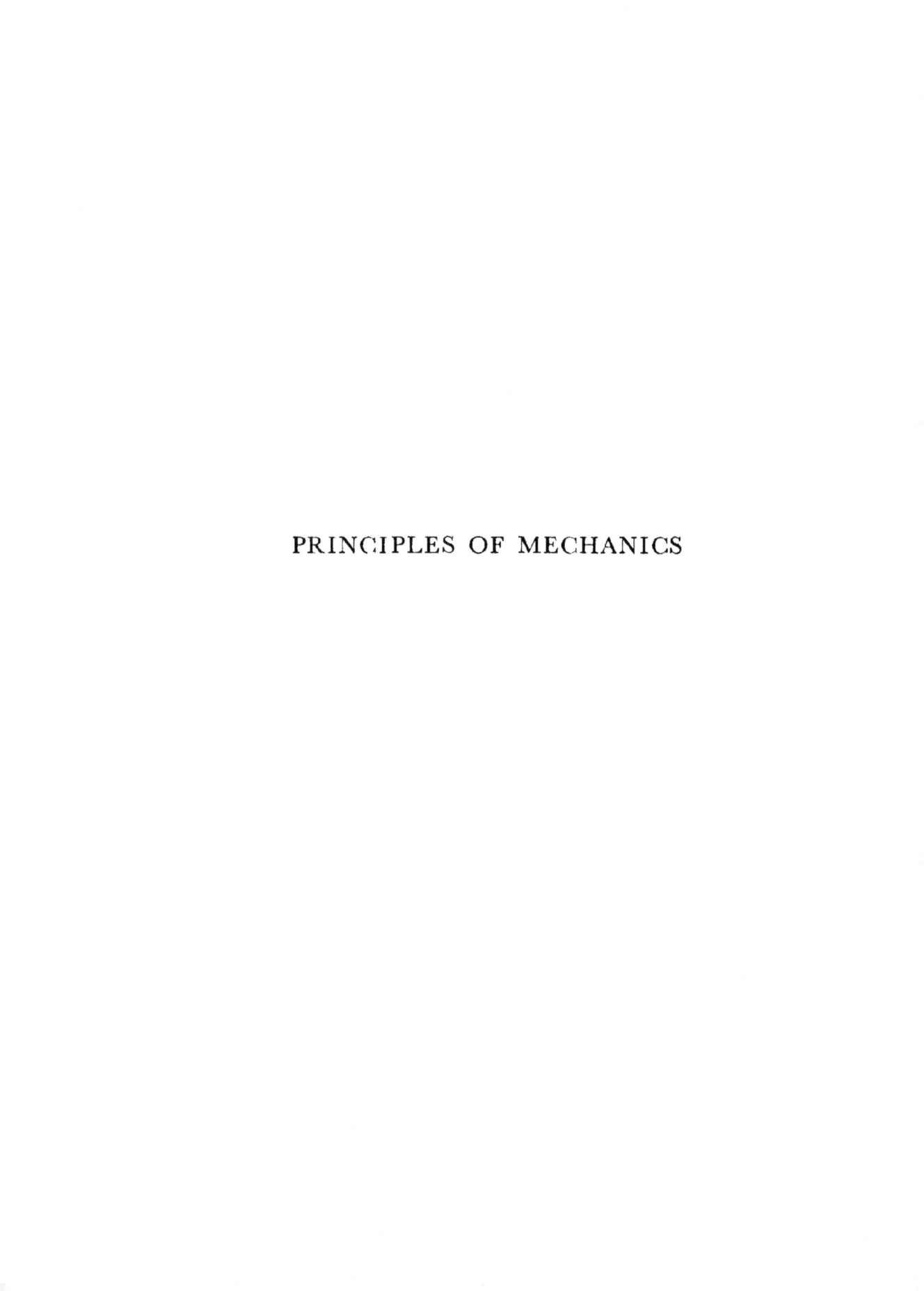

PRINCIPLES OF MECHANICS

PRINCIPLES
of
MECHANICS

BY

JOHN L. SYNGE
Professor of Mathematics
Carnegie Institute of Technology

AND

BYRON A. GRIFFITH
Assistant Professor of Mathematics
University of Toronto

SECOND EDITION

NEW YORK　　　TORONTO　　　LONDON
McGRAW-HILL BOOK COMPANY, INC.
1949

PRINCIPLES OF MECHANICS

Copyright, 1942, 1949, by the McGraw-Hill Book Company, Inc. Printed in the United States of America. All rights reserved. This book, or parts thereof, may not be reproduced in any form without permission of the publishers

PRINTED BY THE MAPLE PRESS COMPANY, YORK, PA.

Le savant doit ordonner; on fait la science avec des faits comme une maison avec des pierres, mais une accumulation de faits n'est pas plus une science qu'un tas de pierres n'est une maison.

Henri Poincaré

PREFACE TO THE SECOND EDITION

This edition differs in no essential way from the first. The principal revision occurs in Chap XIII, where the account of the motion of a particle in an electromagnetic field has been completely rewritten. The treatment of principal axes of inertia in Chap XI has been amplified, and some revisions have been made in the treatments of Foucault's pendulum, the spinning projectile, and the gyrocompass. The emphasis on units and dimensions has been increased by the inclusion in the earlier part of the book of a few short paragraphs, with references to the Appendix, where these matters are discussed in detail. A few additional exercises have been inserted, and numerous minor corrections have been made. We wish to thank all those readers who have contributed to the improvement of this second edition by their suggestions, and, in particular, Professors L. Infeld, A E. Schild, and A. Weinstein.

JOHN L. SYNGE
BYRON A. GRIFFITH

PITTSBURGH, PA.
TORONTO, ONT.
July, 1948

PREFACE TO THE FIRST EDITION

In a sense this is a book for the beginner in mechanics, but in another sense it is not. From the time we make our first movements, crude ideas on force, mass, and motion take shape in our minds. This body of ideas might be reduced to some order at high school (as crude ideas of geometry are reduced to order), but that is not the educational practice in North America. There is rather an accumulation of miscellaneous facts bearing on mechanics, some mathematical and some experimental, until a state is reached where the student is in danger of being repelled by the subject, as a chaotic jumble which is neither mathematics nor physics.

This book is intended primarily for students at this stage. The authors' ambition is to reveal mechanics as an orderly self-contained subject. It may not be quite so logically clear as pure mathematics, but it stands out as a model of clarity among all the theories of deductive science.

The art of teaching consists largely in isolating difficulties and overcoming them one by one, without losing sight of the main problem while attending to the details. In mechanics, the main problem is the problem of equilibrium or motion under given forces—the details are such things as the vector notation, the kinematics of a rigid body, or the theory of moments of inertia. If we rush straight at the main problem, we become entangled in the details and have to retrace our steps in order to deal with them. If, on the other hand, we decide to settle all details first, we are apt to find them uninteresting because we do not see their connection with the main problem. A compromise is necessary, and in this book the compromise consists of the division into Plane Mechanics (Part I) and Mechanics in Space (Part II). These titles must, however, be regarded only as rough indications of the contents. Part I includes some of the easier portions of three-dimensional theory, while Part II contains an introduction to the special theory of relativity, with mechanics in only one spatial dimension.

There is, of course, nothing novel in regarding plane mechanics as the preliminary field; but it is rather unusual to divide the subject in this way in a single volume, or even in a sequence of volumes. It has made the task of writing more difficult, but the authors have felt it worth while. Many of the most interesting results in statics and dynamics belong to the plane theory, and it is unfair to deny the reader access to them until he has mastered the more elaborate technique required for three dimensions.

Part 1 is complete in itself and might be used as a textbook in plane statics and dynamics, with some excursions into three-dimensional theory. Vector notation is introduced, but used sparingly. The reader should have a fair knowledge of calculus, elementary differential equations, and some analytical geometry. Practical experience in physics is not essential but very desirable; mechanics is at root a physical subject and should not be treated merely as an excuse for the exercise of mathematical techniques.

In Part II the language of vectors is used extensively. A knowledge of three-dimensional analytical geometry is required and greater power in the use of mathematical processes. This part is complete in itself, except for occasional references to Part I. The selection of particular applications follows conventional lines, except for one novel feature—a section on electron optics. Chapters on Lagrange's equations and on the special theory of relativity are included.

The book has developed from lectures delivered by both authors to Honor Students in their second and third years at the University of Toronto. These lectures cover about 110 periods of 50 minutes, and it has been found that the work can be done fairly adequately in that time. But this does not allow sufficiently for the working of problems with the classes; it is felt that 150 periods might well be spent on the contents of the book, were it not for other demands on the students' time.

Each chapter is followed by a summary. The summaries to the chapters dealing with methods are naturally the more fundamental—there is little hope of being able to attack problems unless one is thoroughly familiar with the general principles outlined there. On the other hand, the summaries to the chapters dealing with applications are intended to provide only a synopsis of what has been done.

Many of the exercises are taken with permission from examination papers set in the University of Toronto and printed by the University Press. In each set of exercises, the first few problems are so simple that failure to solve them will reveal a lack of understanding of basic methods, rather than a deficiency in skill and ingenuity.

The equations are numbered in such a way that, when read as decimals, they stand in their proper order. The integer represents the chapter, the first decimal place represents the section, and the last two decimal places the position of the equation in the section.

Debts to other textbooks are too numerous to acknowledge But we would like to pay tribute to two books and recommend them to the reader who wishes to pursue the subject further. They are E. T. Whittaker's Analytical Dynamics (Cambridge University Press) and P. Appell's Mécanique rationnelle (Gauthier-Villars). These books have suggested the possibility of reconciling in a textbook on mechanics two opposing goals—the reduction of the subject to a compact and classified form and its exposition with sufficient fullness to make the arguments easy to follow.

We gratefully acknowledge assistance and advice received from our colleagues, Professor H. S. M Coxeter, Professor A. F. Stevenson, Dr. A Weinstein, and Mr. A. W. Walker. We are under a particular debt to Professor L. Infeld, who read most of the manuscript and has been unsparing in frank criticism and suggestions; if we have succeeded in avoiding dullness and obscurity, it is due in no small measure to him.

J. L. SYNGE
B. A GRIFFITH

TORONTO, ONTARIO
MEDICINE HAT, ALBERTA
December, 1941

PART I
PLANE MECHANICS

CHAPTER I

FOUNDATIONS OF MECHANICS

1.1. SOME PHILOSOPHICAL IDEAS

Why do we study mechanics? There are at least three reasons. First, we live in an age of machinery, which cannot be designed without a knowledge of mechanics; in fact, it is the most fundamental subject in engineering. Secondly, mechanics plays a basic part in physics and astronomy, contributing to our knowledge of the working of nature. Thirdly, the mathematician is interested in mechanics, both in the logic of its foundations and in the methods employed; a considerable portion of mathematics was developed for the express purpose of solving mechanical problems.

The subject of mechanics is not a mere collection of facts. From certain simple hypotheses an elaborate theory is built up. Anyone who has studied the subject should be able to answer questions of interest to engineers and physicists; that is to say, he should be able to *apply* his knowledge. But he should also have a fair idea of the logical structure. A successful textbook has to steer a middle course between undue concentration on the mere working out of problems on the one hand, and an over-elaborate development of logical structure on the other.

The two ways of thinking.

What the student of mechanics requires more than anything else is the development of a certain point of view which is difficult to describe in a few words. Since the reader is expected to have a fair knowledge of geometry, it will be helpful to consider the ways in which we think about that subject.

Every student of geometry learns to think in two ways. First, there is the *physical* way, in which a point is a small dot on a sheet of paper, a straight line a mark made by drawing a sharp pencil along a straight edge, a circle a mark made by a pair of compasses, and so on. Secondly, there is the ideal or

mathematical way, in which a point is no longer a dot on paper, but an ideal thing which the dot serves only to suggest. Anyone who uses geometry has both these ways of thinking at his disposal, switching from one to the other without confusion. The engineer and the physicist generally think in the physical way, but when there is a theorem to be proved they subconsciously switch to the mathematical way. On the other hand the mathematician will think primarily in the mathematical way, but he will change to the physical way when he wants to aid his thought with a diagram.

This duality in point of view is confusing to the beginner in geometry. But it is fortunate that he has to face this difficulty at an early stage in his career, because it prepares him for a similar duality in mechanics, about which he has also to learn to think in two different ways.

First, there is the physical way. We think of actual physical things, natural or man-made. We seek to understand the laws governing their behavior and to predict how they will behave under given circumstances—to be able to trace the paths of comets in advance, or design machinery and bridges with confidence as to their behavior when constructed.

On the other hand, there is the mathematical way. Often without realizing it consciously, the physicist, astronomer, or engineer slips over from the physical way of thinking to the mathematical. Thus the astronomer may treat the earth as a perfect sphere—an abstract mathematical concept which does not exist in nature—or the engineer may discuss a wheel as if it were a perfect circle.

The transition from the physical to the mathematical and back again is a source of more confusion than may be suspected, but it is unavoidable. There is no doubt that the physical way of thought is the more natural; but as long as it is the only way, progress is slow. Physical things are very complicated and hard to think about. Slowly we come to distinguish between properties which are essential and properties which are incidental. We learn to simplify problems by forgetting the incidental properties and concentrating on those which are essential.

To illustrate, suppose we are interested in the periodic time of a bar suspended from one end, oscillating as a pendulum. Which properties of the bar is it essential for us to bear in mind,

and which may we neglect as incidental? Can we predict the periodic time of oscillation without knowing the material of which the bar is constructed? Does the form of the cross section of the bar matter? Does it make any difference whether the bar is supported on a knife-edge or by bearings? The cautious well-informed physicist would say that all these things mattered and many others. One material yields more than another, the form of cross section influences the distribution of material, and a change in the mode of suspension may alter the axis about which the pendulum oscillates. But if we were as cautious as this we should have no science of mechanics. To start on the problem, at any rate, we must simplify it ruthlessly. So we think of the bar as a rigid mathematical straight line and the support as a fixed mathematical point. Now we have a problem which is reasonably simple to handle mathematically. Strictly speaking, no properties are incidental. Even the color of the bar affects the pressure of light on it; a subway train stopping five hundred miles away may cause a vibration in the support and affect the motion of the bar. Common sense, which is the accumulated experience of centuries, gives us some guide as to the factors which we may neglect.

Mathematical models.

Gradually stripping physical things of attributes which are unimportant for the question in hand, we arrive at a mathematical way of thinking about nature. The particular mathematical model* to be used on a given occasion depends on that occasion. Consider the earth, for example. The simplest model of the earth is a particle, a mathematical point with mass. This model suffices to obtain the earth's orbit round the sun, but obviously will not do for the discussion of tides or lunar eclipses. For these phenomena we may think of the earth as a rigid sphere, but this model will not serve for the discussion of the precession of the equinoxes (for which we require an ellipsoidal rigid body) or for the discussion of earthquakes (for which we require an elastic sphere). Thus there are many mathe-

---

* The reader will of course understand that when we speak of a "model" we do not mean an actual physical reproduction on a small scale. We use the word—for want of a better—to describe our simplified mental picture of a physical object.

matical models for the earth, and the one which we choose depends on the question we are discussing at the moment.

In fact, mechanics—and indeed all theoretical science—is a game of mathematical make-believe. We say: *If* the earth *were* a homogeneous rigid ellipsoid acted on by such and such forces, how would it behave? Working out the answer to this mathematical question, we compare our results with observation. If there is agreement, we say that we have chosen a good model; if disagreement, then the model or the laws assumed are bad

Let us now sum up the general procedure in theoretical mechanics in the following five steps.

(1) A physical system is an object of curiosity; we wish to predict its behavior under various circumstances. (The system in question might be a pendulum, or a pair of stars attracting one another.)

(2) An ideal or mathematical model of the physical system is constructed mentally. (The pendulum is regarded as a rigid straight line, and the stars are regarded as two particles.)

(3) Mathematical reasoning is applied to the mathematical model. (This means that differential or finite equations are set up and solved. Formulas are developed to give answers to interesting questions, such as those concerning the periodic time of the pendulum or the orbit of one star relative to the other.)

(4) The mathematical results are interpreted physically in terms of the physical problem.

(5) The results are compared with the results of observation, if possible.

Certain remarks should be made about these five steps. First, (1) implies a physical curiosity. In spite of the fact that theoretical mechanics is a part of mathematics, we should not forget that its roots lie in physics and the actual world around us.

Secondly, as has been remarked above, the construction of a mathematical model (2) at once simple and adequate is by no means easy in all cases. However, mechanics is an old subject, and there is much accumulated experience to fall back on. The concepts of particles, rigid bodies, forces, etc. (all mathematical idealizations), have been designed for this purpose. These will be discussed in

Step (3) belongs largely to pure mathematics, requiring no particular knowledge of, or interest in, the physical problem. Nevertheless, it is often of the greatest assistance to the mathematician to bear the physical problem continually in mind; in this way, methods of attack may be suggested to him.

The fourth step in general presents no difficulty, provided that we are clear as to the things in nature which correspond to the things in our mathematical model.

The technical details of the fifth step belong to experimental physics or observational astronomy, and with them we shall not be concerned. But we are interested in the fact that the conclusions drawn from a mathematical theory are, or are not, physically true, within the limits of accuracy of observation.

It is necessary to distinguish between *mathematical* truth and *physical* truth. In developing the theory of mechanics, we shall try to make the mathematical arguments fairly complete, so that we can have confidence that the conclusions follow logically from the hypotheses, i.e., that they are mathematically true. We should not undertake this work, however, if we had not confidence that our conclusions are also physically true, in the sense that they agree with observation. A vast accumulation of physical results confirms our confidence. Nevertheless, it would be too much to claim that *all* our conclusions are physically valid.

Attempts to construct a successful model of an atom on the basis of Newtonian mechanics have failed. This failure led to the invention of quantum mechanics. We may say in general that Newtonian models of small-scale phenomena have not been successful, whereas at the other end of the scale we find difficulty also in the large-scale phenomena of astronomy. In spite of the many triumphs of Newtonian mechanics in dynamical astronomy, there remain a few phenomena which are in apparent disagreement with it; the best-known concerns the orbit of the planet Mercury. This difficulty was overcome when Einstein created the general theory of relativity.

To explore with any degree of completeness the theories referred to above would demand a course of study far wider than that covered in this book. The reader may feel disappointed that at this stage he cannot reach the forefront of our mechanical knowledge. To encourage him, however, it may be pointed out that as long as the physical problems concern only apparatus

of an intermediate scale, i.e., neither atomic on the one hand nor astronomical on the other, one may have complete confidence that no experimental technique can reveal any discrepancy between observation and the conclusions drawn from Newtonian mechanics. This confidence may even be extended to astronomy, because there the relativistic effects are extremely minute; the vast body of calculations of dynamical astronomy are still safely based on Newtonian mechanics.

Relativity and quantum mechanics not only enable us to obtain results which are physically true—they also throw light on such basic philosophical ideas as simultaneity and causality. Chapter XVI contains an introduction to the special theory of relativity. The general theory of relativity and quantum mechanics both lie outside the scope of this book.

1.2. THE INGREDIENTS OF MECHANICS

In any subject there are words which occur again and again, like the words "point," "line," and "circle" in elementary geometry. As well as these technical words, there occur ordinary words with the meanings of which we are supposed to be familiar When we start a new subject, we are not expected to know what the technical words mean They are introduced with some formality, being in fact given definitions A definition is itself only a set of words and may not mean much; the general idea is to explain a new thing in terms of things already familiar

We are now to try to create mathematical models of physical things. We start with a fair general unprecise knowledge of the world around us; the places in our minds reserved for the mathematical models are supposed to be absolutely blank. If we opened these places for the actual world to rush in, we should be overwhelmed with confusion. We guard the door and admit only a few ingredients of simple mathematical character.

Particles.

The first thing we admit is a *particle*. We have seen tiny scraps of matter and it is not difficult for us, with our training in geometry, to think of a scrap of matter with no size at all, but with a definite position; that is a particle. When we have to deal with a physical problem in which a body is very small in comparison with distances or lengths involved (for example,

the earth in comparison with its distance from the sun, or the bob of a pendulum in comparison with the string), we may represent that body in our mathematical model by a particle.

Mass.

Primitive trade was a matter of barter; later, money was introduced as a standard scale for comparison of values, and equivalence in value is now expressed by equality of price. This exemplifies a process of deep importance in science, namely, a concentration on some characteristic (value) of a thing and its expression by means of a number (price). A barrel of apples is very different from a pair of shoes, but they may be equivalent if value is the only characteristic in which we are interested. That the price is the same expresses complete equivalence as far as our purse is concerned.

Consider now a great variety of bodies—pieces of stone, iron, gold, wood, etc.—and mechanical experiments performed on them. As examples, we mention two experiments:

(i) The body is placed in the pan of a spring balance and the reading noted.

(ii) The body is fired from a gun by means of a definite explosive charge and passes into a block of wood, the resulting displacement of which is noted.

If A and B are two pieces of iron, as nearly identical in shape and size as it is possible to make them, they will of course give the same results when used in any experiment, performed first using A and then repeated using B instead. But it is a remarkable fact, resting on long experience, that two bodies A and B may differ in material, size, shape, etc., and yet give the same result in a great variety of mechanical experiments. We then say that they are *mechanically equivalent*. A piece of wood and a piece of gold may be mechanically equivalent, just as a barrel of apples and a pair of shoes may be equivalent in value.

As we assign a price to each article of trade, so we may assign a number to each piece of matter, equality of these numbers implying mechanical equivalence. This number is called *mass* and is usually denoted by m. Following the analogy of money, based on a standard substance (gold), it is easy to see how a scale of mass is to be constructed. We start with a number of identical pieces of some standard material such as platinum,

and we assign to the mass of each the value unity ($m = 1$). When n of these pieces are lumped together, we assign to the mass of the lump the value $n(m = n)$. By cutting the pieces, we can construct bodies with fractional masses and so obtain a set of standard bodies of all possible masses. Then, to assign a mass to a body A (not of the standard material), we subject it to experiments and find that standard body B to which it is mechanically equivalent. We then say that the mass of A is the same as the mass of B.

The comparison of masses is usually made by weighing as in the experiment (i) mentioned above, except that for reasons of accuracy the spring balance is replaced by a laboratory balance. Thus, in practice, two bodies are said to have the same mass when they have the same weight

The above considerations deal with physical bodies. In the mathematical model in which these bodies are represented by particles, we are to regard each particle as having attached to it a positive number m, its mass, which does not change during the history of the particle.

In dealing with a system of particles, we define the mass of the system to be the sum of the masses of the particles which compose it.

Rigid bodies.

We have now admitted as a mathematical model the particle with mass. The next thing to consider is the *rigid body*.

It is a matter of common experience that bodies may be soft like rubber or hard like steel. Even the hardest body, however, changes its size and shape by measurable amounts under the action of sufficiently great forces. But just as we idealized the small body of our experience into the particle with position but no size, so we idealize the hard body of our experience into the rigid body, which never undergoes any change of size or shape. The rigid body is now admitted as a mathematical model.

We pause for a moment to examine critically something written just above. We spoke of a body changing its size and shape. What does this really mean? Suppose, for example, we have a bar of steel with two marks on it. Alongside the bar we lay a graduated measuring scale and note the readings on the scale opposite the two marks on the bar. Then we pull the ends of the bar and note the readings again. The difference between

them is greater than it was before; hence we say that the bar has increased in length.

However, an argumentative person might assert that this was an incorrect statement; he might hold that the length of the bar was the same as before but that the measuring scale had shrunk. We cannot say that he is wrong in taking this point of view until we clarify our ideas as to the meaning of the word "length."

The idea of length is one that involves the comparison of two bodies. We decide once for all on a unit of length by making two marks on a piece of metal and stating conditions with regard to temperature and pressure under which measurements are to be made with this piece of metal. We were perhaps a little hasty in admitting a rigid body as a mathematical model, because there is no sense in talking about a single rigid body; we must have some means of measuring it and testing that it is rigid. So when we admit the rigid body, we shall at the same time admit a *measuring scale*. When we say that a body is rigid, we mean that measurements of distances between marks on it always have the same values, the measurements being made with the measuring scale

Events.

The word *event* is familiar in ordinary speech. It usually denotes something a little out of the ordinary, something that occurs in a fairly limited region of space and is of fairly short duration. Thus a football game or the arrival of a train might be described as an event. The word has now acquired an idealized scientific meaning, the idealization involved being rather similar to that by which we created the concept of particle. Instead of occupying a fairly limited region in space, an event (in our mathematical model) occurs at a mathematical point; and instead of being of fairly short duration, it occurs instantaneously. We do not carry over into our mathematical model the slightly dramatic meaning attached to the word in ordinary life. Anything that happens may be called an event. Even the continued existence of a particle forms a series of events.

Frames of reference.

In describing an event in ordinary life, it is usual to specify the place and time. Thus it is recorded of the sinking of a ship that it occurred at a certain latitude and longitude, and

at a certain Greenwich mean time. Latitude and longitude define position on the earth's surface; we are here using the earth as a *frame of reference*. This is the most familiar frame of reference, but others may be used. Astronomers prefer a frame of reference in which the sun is fixed and which does not share in the earth's motion of rotation. Also, the interior of a train, streetcar, elevator, or airplane may be used. The essential thing about a frame of reference is that it should be fairly rigid

In our mathematical model, we employ a rigid body as frame of reference. As we may introduce any number of rigid bodies moving relative to one another, we have thus at our disposal any number of frames of reference Selecting one of these and taking rectangular axes of coordinates in it, we assign to any event a set of three numbers x, y, z, the coordinates in the frame of reference of the point where the event occurs.

Time.

An event has not only position; it also has a time of occurrence This we have now to consider.

The possibility of repeating an experiment forms the basis of experimental science. It is assumed that, if an experiment is repeated under the same conditions, the same results will be obtained. Consider, for example, a tank of water drained through a hole in the bottom, and then refilled and drained again. Strictly speaking, it is impossible to reproduce conditions exactly, and we have to use judgment to decide whether the new conditions are sufficiently near the old. But in an ideal sense we may think of an experiment repeated over and over again under exactly the same conditions.

To define *time*, we think of some experiment which can be repeated over and over again, a new experiment starting just when the preceding one ends Denoting time by t, we assign the value $t = 0$ to the beginning of the first experiment, $t = 1$ to the beginning of the second experiment, $t = 2$ to the beginning of the third experiment, and so on. The repeated experiment thus forms a *clock* for the measurement of time; we shall call the unit of time given by some such ideal experiment a *Newtonian unit*. This is the procedure actually adopted in practice. In a watch, the experiment is an oscillation of the balance wheel; in a pendulum clock, it is an oscillation of the pendulum. In

As has been pointed out already, we are not to expect a mathematical model to have all the complexity of nature. The model which we shall use resembles in some ways the modern physicist's concept of a solid body, but it is greatly simplified. It was invented long before the development of modern atomic physics, and was originally supposed to be a more complete representation of nature than we now know it to be. Nevertheless, it enables us to predict to a high degree of accuracy an immense number of phenomena; it is in fact the basis of a great deal of Newtonian mechanics.

This mathematical model of a solid body is discontinuous—a collection of a vast number of particles. In a rigid body the distances between the particles remain invariable, but in an elastic body these distances may change. Since this model involves a very large number of things, statistical methods may be used; instead of following individual particles, we may direct our attention to their average behavior. In fact, we mentally replace the discontinuous body, consisting of a great number of particles, by a continuous distribution of matter. This simplifies the determination of mass centers and moments of inertia, because the methods of integral calculus can then be used.

To avoid lengthy and perhaps uninteresting arguments, we shall leave certain gaps in the logical development of our subject. We shall not give arguments of a statistical nature in order to pass from a result established for a discontinuous system to the corresponding result for a continuous one It is usually easier to establish general theorems for discontinuous systems and to solve special problems for continuous systems

Force.

Let us now introduce into our mathematical model the concept of *force*, idealizing as usual from our somewhat vague physical concepts. Our primitive concept of force arises out of our sensation of muscular exertion. We push and pull objects, sometimes with small exertion, sometimes with great effort. But the same effects as those produced by muscular effort may be produced in other ways. In this machine age, direct muscular effort is used to a great extent only to control much greater forces due to the pressure of steam, the weight of water, the explosive pressure of gasoline, or forces of electromagnetic type. One also admits the

existence of huge forces beyond human control, such as the gravitational attraction exerted by the sun on the earth.

On the basis of our experience with simple muscular forces, we think of the idealized force of our mathematical model as something which has

(i) a point of application,
(ii) a direction,
(iii) a magnitude.

For the development of general results in theoretical mechanics, it would be sufficient to represent the magnitude of a force by a letter, standing for some unspecified numerical value. But when we wish to make predictions regarding a physical system subject to forces, we require a definite procedure by means of which we may assign numerical values to their magnitudes. We must, in fact, define a *unit of force*.

There has been some controversy about this question. Though all are agreed as to the form of theory which we should ultimately obtain, there has been disagreement regarding the proper order of introduction of the various parts of the theory. Thus we might assume a statement A as an axiom and deduce a statement B from it, or alternately we might assume B and deduce A. The order of presentation chosen in this book seems to the authors the most natural; but it is hoped that the reader will explore for himself the possibility of a different approach.*

We define the unit of force in terms of a stretched spring; it is that force which produces some standard extension in some standard spring. Later we shall link up the unit of force with the units of mass, length, and time; but for the present the unit is to be regarded as arbitrary.

To measure a force, we examine the extension which it produces in a battery of standard springs side by side, all identical with one another. If the standard extension is produced in n springs, then the force is of magnitude n. If the magnitude of the force in question is not an integer, we reproduce it m times so as to get

---

* See treatments in E. T. Whittaker, Analytical Dynamics (Cambridge University Press, 1927), p 29; H. Lamb, Statics (Cambridge University Press, 1928), p 12, and Dynamics (Cambridge University Press, 1929), p 17; J. S. Ames and F. D. Murnaghan, Theoretical Mechanics (Ginn and Company, Boston, 1929), p. 104. For a critical and historical account of the development of mechanics, see E Mach, The Science of Mechanics (Open Court Publishing Company, Chicago, 1919).

the standard extension in some number n of standard springs; then the magnitude of the force is n/m.

Having thus given a means of measuring force, we may construct a simplified apparatus. Taking any spring, fixed at one end, we mark its extensions under the action of measured forces. In this way, we *calibrate* the spring; the calibrated spring may be used directly for the measurement of a force.

We have preferred to use the tension in a spring rather than the weight of a body as the foundation of our definition of force It is customary for many practical purposes to speak of a force of so many pounds weight (lb wt.); by a force of 10 lb wt., we mean a force equal to the weight of a mass of 10 lb. Although this practice is convenient and adequate for many purposes, it is open to objection on the following ground: If the weight of a body is measured by means of a calibrated spring at two different latitudes, the results are not the same (see Sec. 5.3). A definition of force based on the extension of a spring gives a consistent theory without contradictions, whereas a definition based on weight would involve us in explanations as to why a spring, showing the same definite extension in Toronto and in Panama, should exert different forces in the two places.

In describing particles, rigid bodies, and forces we have introduced the basic ingredients of mechanics. As we proceed, other ingredients will appear, but it is remarkable how much of the subject turns on the simple concepts just mentioned.

1.3. INTRODUCTION TO VECTORS. VELOCITY AND ACCELERATION

Definition of a vector.

In order to reproduce a game of chess, we must be able to describe the moves There is, of course, an accepted way of doing this, but we shall describe another. Let letters A, B, C, $\cdots$ (supplemented with other symbols to make up 64) be assigned to the squares of the board, one letter to each square. Then symbols such as $\vec{AB}$, $\vec{CF}$, $\vec{UB}$ will represent definite moves, the symbol $\vec{AB}$, for example, meaning that a piece is moved from the square A to the square B.

More generally, if we carry a particle from a position A to a position B in space, the operation which we perform may be

represented symbolically by $\vec{AB}$. The directed segment drawn from A to B, or the carrying operation—or indeed any physical quantity which can be represented by the directed segment—is called a *vector*,* and the symbol $\vec{AB}$ is used for any of them.

A vector $\vec{AB}$ has the following characteristics:
(i) an origin or point of application (A);
(ii) a direction (defined analytically by the three direction cosines of $\vec{AB}$ with respect to rectangular axes);
(iii) a magnitude (the length AB).

A number of fundamental physical quantities have these characteristics—for example, a force or the velocity of a particle; each of these quantities may be represented by a directed segment and is therefore a vector. They are to be distinguished from quantities such as mass or kinetic energy, which do not involve the idea of direction and are described each by a single number. Quantities of this latter type are called *scalars*.

It is convenient to employ the word "vector" in a slightly wider sense than that given above and to define the following:
(i) free vector;
(ii) sliding vector;
(iii) bound vector.

A *free vector* is any one of a system of directed segments having a common direction and magnitude but different origins. A physical quantity equally well represented by any one of such directed segments is also called a free vector. Such, for example, is the displacement, without rotation, of a rigid body, which is equally well represented by any one of the directed segments giving the displacements of its various points.

A *sliding vector* is any one of a system of directed segments obtained by sliding a directed segment along its line. A physical quantity equally well represented by any one of such directed segments is also called a sliding vector. Such, for example, is a force acting on a rigid body, which (by the principle of the transmissibility of force proved on page 64) may equally well be applied at any point on its line of action.

A *bound vector* is a unique directed segment, or a physical quantity so represented. Such, for example, is a force acting on

---

* The word "vector" is derived from the Latin *veho*, I carry.

an elastic body; we cannot in general alter this force, by any displacement of the directed segment representing it, without changing its effect.

By the word "vector," without an adjective, we shall generally understand "free vector"; but where we have to speak of bound or sliding vectors, it will be unnecessary to use the qualifying adjective when it may be understood from the context. Throughout the rest of this section, the vectors are to be regarded as free.

Notation.

A vector is indicated in print by a boldface letter (**P**): in manuscript work the symbol may be underlined ($\underline{P}$) or an arrow may be written on top ($\vec{P}$). Its magnitude is denoted by the same letter in ordinary type, or by an unmarked symbol in manuscript work (P). A vector of unit magnitude is called a *unit vector*. To refer to a bound or sliding vector, we may write "**P** acting at the point A" or "**P** acting on the line L," if there is any doubt as to the origin or line.

Two vectors are equal to one another when they may be represented by equal parallel directed segments with the same sense. We use the usual sign of equality and write

$$\mathbf{P} = \mathbf{Q}$$

The sign of equality carries the usual algebraic property: vectors equal to the same vector are equal to one another.

Multiplication of a vector by a scalar.

Let **P** be a vector and m a scalar. We define the product of m and **P** (written $m\mathbf{P}$ or $\mathbf{P}m$) as follows: If m is positive, then $m\mathbf{P}$ has the same direction as **P** and a magnitude mP; if m is negative, then $m\mathbf{P}$ has a direction opposite to that of **P** and a magnitude $-mP$.

We write $(-1)\mathbf{P} = -\mathbf{P}$; thus $-\mathbf{P}$ is the vector **P** reversed.

Addition of vectors.

The sum of two vectors **P** and **Q** is written $\mathbf{P} + \mathbf{Q}$; it is defined as the vector represented by the diagonal $\vec{AD}$ of a parallelogram of which two adjacent sides $\vec{AB}$, $\vec{AC}$ represent **P** and **Q**, respec-

tively (Fig. 1). Obviously, an alternative way of constructing
P + Q is the following (Fig. 2): Draw a segment $\vec{AB}$ to represent
P, and from its extremity draw $\vec{BD}$ to represent **Q**; then $\vec{AD}$
represents **P + Q**.

This is a mathematical definition of **P + Q**. It does not
contain the implication that **P + Q** is the physical resultant of
P and **Q**, although in almost all cases we shall find that **P + Q**
is actually the physical resultant. Finite rotations are the outstanding exceptions; a finite rotation is a vector, but the resultant
of two finite rotations is not the sum of the vectors (cf. Sec. 10.5).

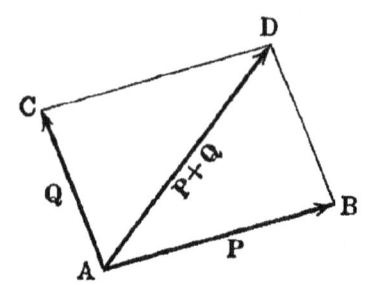

Fig. 1 —Addition of vectors by parallelogram.

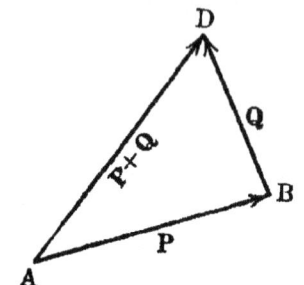

Fig. 2 —Addition of vectors by triangle.

When two vectors **P** and **Q** have the same direction or opposite
directions, the parallelogram constructed to give their sum
collapses into a straight line. But that does not prevent us
from applying the above definition, regarded as a limiting process.
It is easily seen that, if **P** and **Q** have the same direction, then
P + Q has also that direction and a magnitude $P + Q$; if they
have opposite directions and **P** is the greater, then **P + Q** has
the direction of **P** and a magnitude $P - Q$. Comparing this
with the definition of the product of a vector by a scalar, we
find in particular that

$$\mathbf{P} + \mathbf{P} = 2\mathbf{P},$$

and we verify generally that the multiplication of a vector by a
scalar is *distributive* both with respect to the scalar and to the
vector; this means that we have

(1.301) $\qquad (m + n)\mathbf{P} = m\mathbf{P} + n\mathbf{P},$
(1.302) $\qquad m(\mathbf{P} + \mathbf{Q}) = m\mathbf{P} + m\mathbf{Q}.$

It is an immediate consequence of the definition that the addition of vectors is *commutative*, that is,

$$P + Q = Q + P.$$

The subtraction of vectors is immediately effected by writing

$$P - Q = P + (-Q)$$

and applying the rule for addition. The difference between **P** and **Q** is easily constructed as follows: Draw $\vec{AB}$, $\vec{AC}$ to represent **P**, **Q**, respectively (Fig. 3); then $\vec{CB}$ represents **P** − **Q**.

Applying the rule for subtraction to the case **P** − **P**, we obtain a vector of zero magnitude, which we denote by **0**, so that

Fig. 3—Subtraction of vectors.

$$P - P = 0.$$

We call **0** the *zero vector*, all vectors of zero magnitude are regarded as equal to one another.

Any unfamiliar symbol containing vectors must be approached with caution. It may mean nothing at all (for example, we never attempt to define the sum of a scalar and a vector, $m + P$); on the other hand, it may be given a meaning. On the basis of previous definitions, $P + Q + R$ has no meaning, because we have defined the sum of *two* vectors, not *three*. But

$$(P + Q) + R$$

has a meaning, if we regard the parentheses as carrying the instruction to add **P** and **Q**, and then add **R** to that sum;

$$P + (Q + R)$$

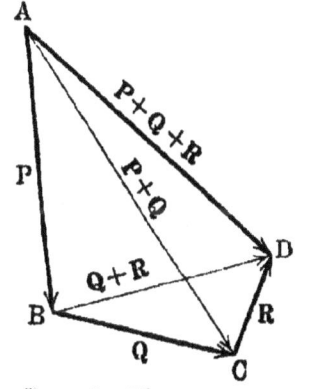

Fig. 4—The associative property of vector addition

has a meaning, also. It is then easy to see that

$$(P + Q) + R = P + (Q + R),$$

by means of the construction shown in Fig. 4, where $\vec{AB}$, $\vec{BC}$, $\vec{CD}$ represent **P**, **Q**, **R**, respectively, and $\vec{AD}$ either of the above sums.

22   PLANE MECHANICS   [SEC. 1.3

Thus a unique meaning can be attached to $\mathbf{P} + \mathbf{Q} + \mathbf{R}$. We say that vector addition is *associative*

Exercise. If
$$\mathbf{P} + 2\mathbf{Q} = \mathbf{R},$$
$$\mathbf{P} - 3\mathbf{Q} = 2\mathbf{R},$$

show that $\mathbf{P}$ has the same direction as $\mathbf{R}$, and $\mathbf{Q}$ the opposite direction.

Components of a vector.

Let L be a straight line and $\mathbf{P}$ a vector represented in Fig. 5 by $\overrightarrow{AB}$. If we draw through A and B planes perpendicular to L, these planes cut off on L a directed segment $\overrightarrow{CD}$, the orthogonal projection of $\overrightarrow{AB}$; $\overrightarrow{CD}$ is a common perpendicular to the pair of planes. If we take a different directed segment $\overrightarrow{A'B'}$ to represent $\mathbf{P}$, we get a projection $\overrightarrow{C'D'}$ on L. Now if we give $\overrightarrow{AB}$ and the

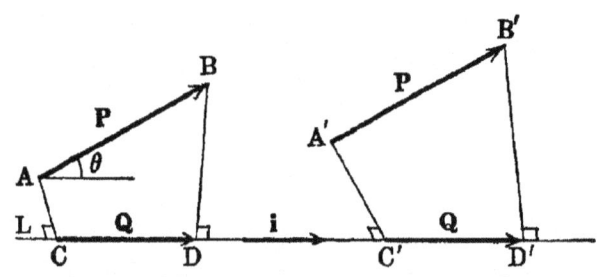

FIG. 5.—The component of a vector on a line.

pair of planes associated with it a displacement (without rotation) which carries A to A', then B will go to B' and the pair of planes associated with $\overrightarrow{AB}$ will coincide with the pair of planes associated with $\overrightarrow{A'B'}$. $\overrightarrow{CD}$ will become a common perpendicular to the latter pair of planes, and so $\overrightarrow{CD}$ and $\overrightarrow{C'D'}$ are equal in magnitude and direction. Thus the vector obtained by projecting on L a directed segment representing $\mathbf{P}$ is independent of the particular segment chosen. Writing $\mathbf{Q}$ for the vector represented by $\overrightarrow{CD}$ or $\overrightarrow{C'D'}$, we say that $\mathbf{Q}$ is the *vector component* of $\mathbf{P}$ on L.

Of the two senses on the line L, let us pick out one and call it the *positive* sense, the other being *negative;* the line L is then said to be *directed*. Let **i** be a vector of unit magnitude, lying on L and pointing in the positive sense. Then it is possible to

express the projection **Q** in the form

$$\mathbf{Q} = c\mathbf{i},$$

where c is a scalar, positive if **Q** has the same sense as **i** and negative if **Q** has the opposite sense to **i**. The scalar c is called the *scalar component* of **P** on the directed line L.

Since **Q** is represented by any common perpendicular (in the proper sense) to the projecting planes, it is easy to see that the scalar component of **P** on L is $P\cos\theta$, where θ is the angle between **P** and the positive sense of L.

In speaking of a component (without qualification), it will be clear from the context whether the vector or scalar component is to be understood.

Unit coordinate vectors.

In a frame of reference S, let $Oxyz$ be rectangular Cartesian axes. Let **i**, **j**, **k** be unit vectors lying on Ox, Oy, Oz, respectively, each in the positive sense. The set **i**, **j**, **k** is called a *unit orthogonal triad*. Let **P** be any vector, and P_1, P_2, P_3 its components on Ox, Oy, Oz, respectively. These components, obtained by projection, are independent of the particular directed segment chosen to represent **P**; we may therefore take the representative segment with its origin at O (Fig. 6). From the rule of vector addition, it is clear that

(1.303) $\quad \mathbf{P} = P_1\mathbf{i} + P_2\mathbf{j} + P_3\mathbf{k}.$

This reduction of a vector to the sum of three vector components along a unit orthogonal triad is of great service in mechanics, for it

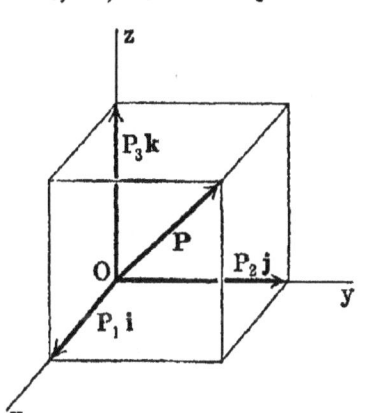

Fig. 6.—Resolution along unit coordinate vectors.

represents the link between the vector methods and the more usual methods of analysis. Vector notation is only a shorthand for the expression of fairly general statements. In the end, we must work in ordinary numbers, and the above formula is the bridge by which we pass from vectors to ordinary numbers.

We note that the magnitude of a vector **P** is expressed in terms of its scalar components by

$$(1.304) \qquad P = \sqrt{P_1^2 + P_2^2 + P_3^2}.$$

The components are given in terms of P and λ, μ, ν, the direction cosines of **P**, by

$$(1.305) \qquad P_1 = \lambda P, \qquad P_2 = \mu P, \qquad P_3 = \nu P.$$

The following facts are important but may be left to the reader to verify, using Fig. 2 in the case of the second:

(i) The components of $m\mathbf{P}$ are mP_1, mP_2, mP_3.

(ii) The components of $\mathbf{P} + \mathbf{Q}$ are $P_1 + Q_1, P_2 + Q_2, P_3 + Q_3$.

If P_1, P_2, P_3 are the components of a vector **P** on the coordinate axes and L is a directed line with direction cosines λ, μ, ν, then the angle θ between **P** and L is given by

$$\cos \theta = \lambda \frac{P_1}{P} + \mu \frac{P_2}{P} + \nu \frac{P_3}{P}.$$

Hence the scalar component of **P** on L is

$$(1.306) \qquad P \cos \theta = \lambda P_1 + \mu P_2 + \nu P_3.$$

Exercise. The components of a vector on axes Oxy in a plane are X, Y. What are the components X', Y' on axes $Ox'y'$, obtained by rotating Oxy through an angle θ?

Position vector.

Let A be a particle, moving relative to a frame of reference S in which $Oxyz$ are rectangular Cartesian axes. The vector $\overrightarrow{OA}$ is called the *position vector* of A relative to O. If we denote it by **r** and the coordinates of A by x, y, z, we have

$$(1.307) \qquad \mathbf{r} = x\mathbf{i} + y\mathbf{j} + z\mathbf{k},$$

where **i**, **j**, **k** is the unit orthogonal triad along the axes.

As the particle moves, the vector **r** changes. In fact, **r** may be regarded as a *vector function* of the time t; we may express this by writing

$$\mathbf{r} = \mathbf{r}(t).$$

Differentiation of a vector.

The above considerations lead naturally to a more general concept, namely, a vector **P** which is a function of a scalar u, a relation expressed by writing

$$\mathbf{P} = \mathbf{P}(u).$$

We need no longer think of **P** as a position vector or of u as the time.

We are familiar with the idea of differentiating a scalar function of a scalar: can we enlarge the familiar method to obtain a process for differentiating a vector function of a scalar?

We may follow the familiar plan almost word for word. We consider two values of the parameter, u and $u + \Delta u$, and the corresponding increment in **P**,

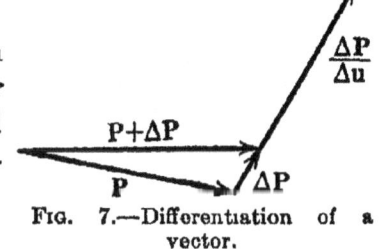

$$\Delta \mathbf{P} = \mathbf{P}(u + \Delta u) - \mathbf{P}(u).$$

Fig. 7.—Differentiation of a vector.

We multiply by $1/\Delta u$, to form the quotient $\Delta \mathbf{P}/\Delta u$ (Fig. 7) and let Δu tend to zero. Thus we get a limiting vector

(1.308) $$\frac{d\mathbf{P}}{du} = \lim_{\Delta u \to 0} \frac{\Delta \mathbf{P}}{\Delta u},$$

which we call the *derivative* of **P** with respect to u.

To find the components of the derivative we introduce unit coordinate vectors, so that

(1.309) $$\mathbf{P} = P_1 \mathbf{i} + P_2 \mathbf{j} + P_3 \mathbf{k};$$

P_1, P_2, P_3 are scalar functions of u. Increasing u to $u + \Delta u$, we have

$$\mathbf{P} + \Delta \mathbf{P} = (P_1 + \Delta P_1)\mathbf{i} + (P_2 + \Delta P_2)\mathbf{j} + (P_3 + \Delta P_3)\mathbf{k}.$$

Subtraction gives

$$\Delta \mathbf{P} = \Delta P_1 \mathbf{i} + \Delta P_2 \mathbf{j} + \Delta P_3 \mathbf{k}$$

Dividing by Δu, we get

$$\frac{\Delta \mathbf{P}}{\Delta u} = \frac{\Delta P_1}{\Delta u}\mathbf{i} + \frac{\Delta P_2}{\Delta u}\mathbf{j} + \frac{\Delta P_3}{\Delta u}\mathbf{k},$$

and so, letting Δu tend to zero,

(1.310) $$\frac{d\mathbf{P}}{du} = \frac{dP_1}{du}\mathbf{i} + \frac{dP_2}{du}\mathbf{j} + \frac{dP_3}{du}\mathbf{k},$$

the derivatives on the right being of course derivatives of scalars —the usual derivatives of the differential calculus. Thus the

components of $d\mathbf{P}/du$ are
$$\frac{dP_1}{du}, \quad \frac{dP_2}{du}, \quad \frac{dP_3}{du}.$$

In words, the components of the derivative are equal to the derivatives of the components.

The following results are easy to prove, either directly from the definition of the derivative or from (1.310):

(1.311)
$$\begin{cases} \dfrac{d}{du}(\mathbf{P}+\mathbf{Q}) = \dfrac{d\mathbf{P}}{du} + \dfrac{d\mathbf{Q}}{du}, \\ \dfrac{d}{du}(p\mathbf{P}) = \dfrac{dp}{du}\mathbf{P} + p\dfrac{d\mathbf{P}}{du}, \end{cases}$$

where $\mathbf{P}$, $\mathbf{Q}$ are vector functions of u, and p is a scalar function of u.

It will be observed that (1.310) can be obtained directly from (1.309) by differentiation, using the rules (1.311); in this process the vectors $\mathbf{i}$, $\mathbf{j}$, $\mathbf{k}$ are treated as constants.

To avoid possible confusion, let us ask the question: What do we mean by saying that a vector $\mathbf{Q}$ is constant? This is meaningless without a statement (explicit or understood) regarding the frame of reference employed. In a frame of reference S, a vector $\mathbf{Q}$ is constant if it may be represented permanently by a directed segment joining two points fixed in S. But viewed from another frame of reference this same vector $\mathbf{Q}$ may not be constant. Thus, in (1.309), $\mathbf{i}$, $\mathbf{j}$, $\mathbf{k}$ are constants in S because they are unit vectors along the axes; they may not be constants in another frame of reference moving relative to S.

If the vector $\mathbf{P}(u)$ is of constant magnitude, then the triangle shown in Fig 7 is isosceles. As Δu tends to zero, the vector $\Delta \mathbf{P}/\Delta u$ tends to perpendicularity with $\mathbf{P}$, or, in other words, *for a vector $\mathbf{P}(u)$ of constant magnitude, $d\mathbf{P}/du$ is perpendicular to $\mathbf{P}(u)$.*

Velocity and acceleration.

Let S be a frame of reference and O a point fixed in S. Let A be a moving particle, its position vector relative to O being $\mathbf{r}$. We define the *velocity* of A relative to S to be the vector

(1.312)
$$\mathbf{q} = \frac{d\mathbf{r}}{dt}.$$

Using dots to indicate differentiation with respect to time, we have

(1.313)
$$\mathbf{q} = \dot{\mathbf{r}} = \dot{x}\mathbf{i} + \dot{y}\mathbf{j} + \dot{z}\mathbf{k},$$

where x, y, z are the coordinates of A relative to rectangular axes $Oxyz$ coincident with the unit orthogonal triad $\mathbf{i}, \mathbf{j}, \mathbf{k}$. Thus the components of velocity are $(\dot{x}, \dot{y}, \dot{z})$. The magnitude q of the velocity is called *speed*.*

We define the *acceleration* of A relative to S to be the vector

(1.314) $$\mathbf{f} = \frac{d\mathbf{q}}{dt},$$

or

(1.315) $$\mathbf{f} = \dot{\mathbf{q}} = \ddot{x}\mathbf{i} + \ddot{y}\mathbf{j} + \ddot{z}\mathbf{k}.$$

The components of acceleration are $(\ddot{x}, \ddot{y}, \ddot{z})$.

If the velocity is resolved into components,

$$\mathbf{q} = u\mathbf{i} + v\mathbf{j} + w\mathbf{k},$$

then

(1.316) $$\mathbf{f} = \dot{u}\mathbf{i} + \dot{v}\mathbf{j} + \dot{w}\mathbf{k}.$$

We could, of course, continue this process, defining a super-acceleration $d\mathbf{f}/dt$. However, acceleration is the important vector in Newtonian mechanics, and so we stop our definitions here.

As a simple illustration of these ideas, consider a car traveling along a straight road. It follows from (1.312) and the definition of the derivative of a vector that the velocity $\mathbf{q}$ lies along the road and points in the direction in which the car is going. Similarly, it follows from (1.314) that the acceleration $\mathbf{f}$ lies along the road, but now there is an important difference. The vector of acceleration does not necessarily point in the direction of motion; this is the case only if the speed is increasing. If the speed is decreasing under application of the brakes, the vector $\mathbf{f}$ points backward. It is not hard to show that when the car rounds a curve the velocity continues to point along the road, but the acceleration points off the road toward the inside of the curve.

The formulas (1.313) and (1.315) are particularly useful for direct calculation when the motion is described by giving x, y, z as functions of t. Suppose, for example, that

---

* Thus velocity is a vector and speed is a scalar. However, when no confusion is likely to arise, the word "velocity" is often used in the scalar sense to denote the magnitude of the velocity vector; for example, the expression "velocity of light" is used instead of the correct expression "speed of light."

$$x = a \cos \omega t, \qquad y = a \sin \omega t, \qquad z = 0,$$

where a and ω are constants Then

$$\mathbf{r} = a \cos \omega t \; \mathbf{i} + a \sin \omega t \cdot \mathbf{j},$$
$$\mathbf{q} = -a\omega \sin \omega t \cdot \mathbf{i} + a\omega \cos \omega t \cdot \mathbf{j},$$
$$\mathbf{f} = -a\omega^2 \cos \omega t \cdot \mathbf{i} - a\omega^2 \sin \omega t \cdot \mathbf{j}.$$

It is easy to see that this is motion in a circle, the velocity pointing along the tangent and the acceleration in along the radius.

Units of velocity and acceleration.

In the c.g s. system of units, the components of $\mathbf{r}$ are measured in centimeters. Any component of the velocity $\mathbf{q}$ is obtained by dividing a number of centimeters by a number of seconds, and the result is expressed as so many centimeters per second or, briefly, cm. sec.$^{-1}$ *The unit of velocity is one centimeter per second.*

Any component of the acceleration $\mathbf{f}$ is obtained by dividing a velocity component by time or, more precisely, a number of centimeters per second by a number of seconds, and the result is expressed as so many centimeters per second per second or, briefly, cm. sec.$^{-2}$ *The unit of acceleration is one centimeter per second per second.*

If f p.s. units are used, the above italicized statements are modified by changing the word "centimeter" to "foot."

Although the c.g s. and f p.s. units are commonly used in scientific work, there is no necessity to limit ourselves to them. The units of length and time may be chosen arbitrarily. Indeed, velocities are frequently expressed in miles per hour (m p.h.).

Since velocity is obtained by dividing length by time, we say it has the "dimensions" $[LT^{-1}]$; similarly, acceleration has the dimensions $[LT^{-2}]$. This notation is discussed in the Appendix.

Gradient vector.

When to each point of space, or to each point of a plane, a scalar is assigned, we say that we are dealing with a *scalar field*. Thus the distribution of pressure (or temperature) in the atmosphere at a certain time gives a scalar field. Or consider a map on which heights are marked; the height gives a scalar field over the map.

When to each point of space or to each point of a plane a vector is assigned, we have a *vector field*. The wind velocity in the atmosphere gives a vector field.

We shall now show that a scalar field defines an associated

vector field in a very simple way. For generality, we shall make the argument three-dimensional, but the reader will find it interesting to consider by way of illustration the map marked with heights.

Let $Oxyz$ be rectangular Cartesian axes and $V(x, y, z)$ a scalar field. (For the map, we suppress z; $V(x, y)$ is the height of the land at the point x, y.) The surfaces $V = $ constant are called *level surfaces*. (On the map the level surfaces become the contour lines.) Let A be any point and S the level surface passing through A (Fig 8). Let us draw the normal to S on the side on which V increases, and proceed an arbitrary distance n along this normal. Then V is a function of n, and

$$\frac{dV}{dn} > 0$$

at A, since V is increasing.

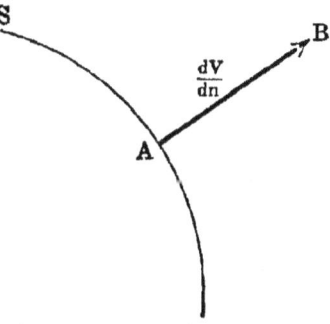

FIG. 8--The gradient vector

We now introduce a vector $\vec{AB}$, called the *gradient* of V at A, or briefly grad V. (It is also denoted by ∇V.) The defining properties of grad V are as follows·

(i) Its direction is along the normal to S at A, in the sense of V increasing

(ii) Its magnitude is dV/dn, calculated at A.

In the case of the map, grad V is perpendicular to the contour line and points in the uphill sense; its magnitude is the rate of increase of height.

We now proceed to find the components of grad V on the axes of coordinates. Let α, β, γ be the direction cosines of the normal to S in the sense of V increasing. Then any infinitesimal displacement lying in S, i.e., making

$$dV = \frac{\partial V}{\partial x} dx + \frac{\partial V}{\partial y} dy + \frac{\partial V}{\partial z} dz = 0,$$

also makes $\alpha\, dx + \beta\, dy + \gamma\, dz = 0$. Hence,

(1.317) $\qquad \dfrac{\partial V}{\partial x} = \phi\alpha, \qquad \dfrac{\partial V}{\partial y} = \phi\beta, \qquad \dfrac{\partial V}{\partial z} = \phi\gamma,$

where ϕ is some factor of proportionality. As we proceed along

the normal to S at A, we have, since V is a function of x, y, z, which in turn are functions of n,

$$\frac{dV}{dn} = \frac{\partial V}{\partial x}\frac{dx}{dn} + \frac{\partial V}{\partial y}\frac{dy}{dn} + \frac{\partial V}{\partial z}\frac{dz}{dn}$$
$$= \frac{\partial V}{\partial x}\alpha + \frac{\partial V}{\partial y}\beta + \frac{\partial V}{\partial z}\gamma.$$

Substitution from (1.317) gives

(1.318) $$\frac{dV}{dn} = \phi(\alpha^2 + \beta^2 + \gamma^2) = \phi.$$

When we substitute this value of ϕ in (1.317), we get

(1.319) $$\frac{\partial V}{\partial x} = \alpha\frac{dV}{dn}, \quad \frac{\partial V}{\partial y} = \beta\frac{dV}{dn}, \quad \frac{\partial V}{\partial z} = \gamma\frac{dV}{dn},$$

and so by (1.305) *the components of grad V on the axes are*

$$\frac{\partial V}{\partial x}, \quad \frac{\partial V}{\partial y}, \quad \frac{\partial V}{\partial z}.$$

If $\mathbf{i}$, $\mathbf{j}$, $\mathbf{k}$ is the unit orthogonal triad along the axes, then

(1.320) $$\operatorname{grad} V = \frac{\partial V}{\partial x}\mathbf{i} + \frac{\partial V}{\partial y}\mathbf{j} + \frac{\partial V}{\partial z}\mathbf{k}$$

By (1.306) the component of grad V on a directed line L is

(1.321) $$\lambda\frac{\partial V}{\partial x} + \mu\frac{\partial V}{\partial y} + \nu\frac{\partial V}{\partial z},$$

where λ, μ, ν are the direction cosines of L. Since

$$\lambda = \frac{dx}{ds}, \quad \mu = \frac{dy}{ds}, \quad \nu = \frac{dz}{ds},$$

where ds is an element of L, this component is

$$\frac{\partial V}{\partial x}\frac{dx}{ds} + \frac{\partial V}{\partial y}\frac{dy}{ds} + \frac{\partial V}{\partial z}\frac{dz}{ds} = \frac{dV}{ds}.$$

The component of grad V in any direction is the rate of change of V in that direction.

We have seen how to obtain a vector field (grad V) from a scalar field (V). It is not in general possible to express an *arbitrary* vector field as the gradient of a scalar field, but we find in mathematical physics many vector fields that can be so expressed. In Sec. 2.4 we shall discuss fields of force; in most cases of physical interest a field of force is the gradient of a scalar

field of potential energy (with a change of sign). Since the description of a vector field requires three functions and a scalar field only one function, a considerable simplification results from the use of the scalar field.

Exercise. If in a plane $V = x^2 + y^2$, find the component of grad V at the point $(1, 0)$ in a direction making an angle of $45°$ with the x-axis.

1.4 FUNDAMENTAL LAWS OF NEWTONIAN MECHANICS

Let us suppose that we are conducting experiments in which small bodies of measured masses are acted on by measured forces. We choose some frame of reference and observe the motions of the bodies relative to it. We shall use the following notation:

$$\mathbf{P} = \text{force},$$
$$m = \text{mass},$$
$$\mathbf{f} = \text{acceleration}.$$

The units of force, mass, length, and time are chosen arbitrarily.

We ask this question: As a physical fact, is there any simple relation connecting $\mathbf{P}$, m, and $\mathbf{f}$ for the motion of a body? The answer to this question is, in general: There is no simple relation.

We have thought of the experiments as conducted in any frame of reference—it might be the cabin of an airplane looping the loop, or it might be an ordinary laboratory. We ask a second question: Is it possible to *choose* a frame of reference so that there is a simple relation connecting $\mathbf{P}$, m, and $\mathbf{f}$? The answer is: Yes.

One frame of reference yielding a simple relation among $\mathbf{P}$, m, and $\mathbf{f}$ is the *astronomical frame of reference*, in which the sun[*] is fixed and which is without rotation relative to the fixed stars as a whole. The simple relation is

$$\mathbf{P} = km\mathbf{f},$$

where k is a universal positive constant, the value of which depends only on the units employed.[†]

[*] More accurately, the mass center of the solar system (see Sec. 3.1); actually this point is not far from the center of the sun.

[†] This relation is in excellent agreement with astronomical observations, but there are exceptions; the orbit of the planet Mercury reveals a minute discrepancy. Although few modern astronomers accept this relation as absolute physical truth, its validity is so high that it is taken as the basis of celestial mechanics. To take a deeper point of view, we must recast our whole mode of thought and follow the general theory of relativity.

The three laws.

We shall now state the fundamental laws on which Newtonian mechanics is based. These are the laws according to which our mathematical model of nature works. The laws as stated here are equivalent to those used by Newton, but they are expressed in a different form.*

LAW OF MOTION. *Relative to a basic frame of reference a particle of mass m, subject to a force* **P**, *moves in accordance with the equation*

$$(1.401) \qquad \mathbf{P} = km\mathbf{f},$$

where **f** *is the acceleration of the particle and k a universal positive constant, the value of which depends only on the choice of units of force, mass, length, and time.*

Any frame of reference relative to which (1.401) holds is called *Newtonian*.

If $\mathbf{P} = 0$, then $\mathbf{f} = 0$ by (1.401). Since $\mathbf{f} = d\mathbf{q}/dt$ as in (1.314), it follows that **q** is a constant vector. In words, *a particle under the influence of no force travels with constant velocity;* i.e., it travels in a straight line with constant speed. This important special case was stated separately by Newton as his first law of motion, his second law dealing with the case where **P** is not zero. Thus, his first two laws are included in our law of motion as stated above.

LAW OF ACTION AND REACTION. *When two particles exert forces on one another, these forces are equal in magnitude and opposite in sense and act along the line joining the particles.*

This is often summed up by saying: Action and reaction are equal and opposite.

LAW OF THE PARALLELOGRAM OF FORCES. *When two forces* **P** *and* **Q** *act on a particle, they are together equivalent to a single force* **P** + **Q**, *the vector sum being defined by the parallelogram construction as in Sec. 1.3.*

It is usual to call **P** + **Q** the *resultant* of **P** and **Q**; **P** and **Q** are called the *vector components* of **P** + **Q**.†

In setting up a system of laws or axioms, it is generally con-

---

* For the original form of Newton's laws, see Sir Isaac Newton's Mathematical Principles, translation revised by F. Cajori (Cambridge University Press, 1934), pp. 13, 644.

† In Sec. 1.3 we used the expression *vector component* only in the case where the components were perpendicular to one another. It is convenient to use it also in the present more general sense.

sidered desirable to make them independent, in the sense that no one of them can be deduced from the others. Many attempts have been made to deduce the parallelogram of forces, but all these deductions require the statement of other laws, which are individually simpler than the parallelogram law but rather long to state; so, for brevity, we accept the parallelogram law directly.*

The three laws stated above form the logical basis of mechanics Their full meaning can be understood only by applying them, and we shall not delay the development of the subject by further general discussion. We should, however, point out their significance for the prediction of the results of ordinary laboratory experiments.

Let us suppose that we are discussing the motion of a billiard ball which rolls down an inclined plane in a laboratory Our problem is to predict the behavior of the ball by mathematical reasoning. On the one hand, we have the actual physical apparatus, on the other our mathematical model, in which the ball, the plane, and the forces acting are replaced by their mathematical idealizations. There is a precise *correspondence* between the physical things and the ingredients of our mathematical model.

But here there enters an important question: What physical frame of reference corresponds to the basic Newtonian frame mentioned in the law of motion—the frame relative to which (1 401) holds? We have already indicated the answer: The physical frame in question is the astronomical frame of reference.

But we do not want to know the behavior of the billiard ball relative to the astronomical frame of reference; we want to know its behavior relative to the walls and floor of the laboratory, i e., relative to the earth's surface. Is it legitimate to regard the earth's surface as a physical frame corresponding to the Newtonian frame of (1.401)? Strictly speaking, it is not. Very refined experiments would enable us to detect differences between the physical behavior of the billiard ball and the theoretical predictions based on that correspondence. These differences are due to the rotation of the earth † But they are very minute

* For an interesting "proof" of the parallelogram of forces, see W. R. Hamilton, Mathematical Papers (Cambridge University Press, 1940), Vol. II, p. 284.

† In Sec. 13 5 we shall discuss some of the dynamical consequences of the earth's rotation.

in the vast majority of experiments made in a laboratory and in all problems connected with engineering structures; excellent predictions may be made from our three laws by taking the earth's surface to be the physical frame of reference corresponding to the Newtonian frame.

Units and dimensions.

In the equation (1.401), a constant k appears, and if the equation is left in this form, this constant k will occur throughout our dynamical equations. To avoid this, we make $k = 1$ by a special choice of the unit of force; the unit so chosen is called the *dynamical unit.* When it is used, (1.401) reads

$$(1.402) \qquad \mathbf{P} = m\mathbf{f}.$$

Clearly the dynamical unit of force produces unit acceleration in unit mass, since if $P = 1$ and $m = 1$, then $f = 1$. In the c.g.s. and f.p.s. systems, the dynamical units of force are called the *dyne* and the *poundal,* respectively. A force of one dyne produces an acceleration of one centimeter per second per second in a mass of one gram, and a force of one poundal produces an acceleration of one foot per second per second in a mass of one pound.

Since, in (1.402), force is the product of a mass by an acceleration, the dyne may be described as one gram centimeter per second per second, or briefly,

$$1 \text{ dyne} = 1 \text{ gm. cm. sec.}^{-2}$$

Similarly,

$$1 \text{ poundal} = 1 \text{ lb. ft. sec.}^{-2}$$

Force measured in dynamical units has the dimensions $[MLT^{-2}]$.

In dynamical problems, we shall always assume that the dynamical unit of force is used, so that the law of motion is (1.402). In statical problems, on the other hand, we shall leave the unit of force arbitrary, since there is no additional simplicity to be gained by restricting it.

At this point the reader is advised to study the Appendix at the end of the book in order that he may understand the references in the text to units and dimensions. In particular, attention is directed to the use of the theory of dimensions as an easy and rapid check against slips in calculation—a check which is of great value both in elementary and advanced work. *In any equation in mechanics, all terms must have the same dimensions.*

For example, if we had carelessly derived the formula (cf. page 28)

$$\mathbf{f} = -a\omega \cos \omega t \cdot \mathbf{i} - a\omega^3 \sin \omega t \cdot \mathbf{j},$$

a glance would show that something is wrong with this formula. The acceleration $\mathbf{f}$ has dimensions $[LT^{-2}]$, $a\omega$ has dimensions $[LT^{-1}]$, $a\omega^3$ has dimensions $[LT^{-3}]$, while the trigonometrical functions and the vectors $\mathbf{i}$, $\mathbf{j}$ are dimensionless.

1.5. SUMMARY OF THE FOUNDATIONS OF MECHANICS

The purposes of this first chapter have been (i) to dig down to the fundamental physical ideas and (ii) to lay the foundations of a logical structure. Before proceeding to the next chapter, we now extract and emphasize those concepts and laws which will be required later. ∴

I. The ingredients of mechanics.

(a) A *particle* has position and mass (m).

(b) A *rigid body* is a system of particles, the distances between which remain unchanged. It may also be regarded as a continuous distribution of matter.

(c) A *frame of reference* is a rigid body in which axes of coordinates are taken.

(d) A *force* has point of application, direction, and magnitude.

(e) The *units* of mass, length, and time are arbitrary. So also is the unit of force, but it is convenient in dynamics to connect the unit of force with the units of mass, length, and time.

II. Vectors.

(a) Addition of vectors is carried out by means of a parallelogram.

(b) The usual simple algebraic rules apply to vectors, but we do not yet define the multiplication of vectors by one another.

(c) A vector function of a scalar may be differentiated; the derivative is another vector function.

(d) If

$$\mathbf{P} = P_1\mathbf{i} + P_2\mathbf{j} + P_3\mathbf{k},$$

then P_1, P_2, P_3 are the scalar *components* of the vector on the unit orthogonal triad ($\mathbf{i}, \mathbf{j}, \mathbf{k}$).

(e) The components of grad V are

$$\frac{\partial V}{\partial x}, \quad \frac{\partial V}{\partial y}, \quad \frac{\partial V}{\partial z}.$$

(f) The component of grad V in any direction is dV/ds.

III. Velocity and acceleration of a particle.

(a) Position vector: $\mathbf{r} = x\mathbf{i} + y\mathbf{j} + z\mathbf{k}$
(b) Velocity vector: $\mathbf{q} = \dot{\mathbf{r}} = \dot{x}\mathbf{i} + \dot{y}\mathbf{j} + \dot{z}\mathbf{k}$.
(c) Acceleration vector: $\mathbf{f} = \dot{\mathbf{q}} = \ddot{x}\mathbf{i} + \ddot{y}\mathbf{j} + \ddot{z}\mathbf{k}$.

IV. Basic laws of mechanics.

(a) Law of motion: $\mathbf{P} = m\mathbf{f}$,   ($\mathbf{P}$ = force).
(b) Law of action and reaction: Action and reaction are equal and opposite.
(c) Law of the parallelogram of forces: $\mathbf{P} + \mathbf{Q}$ is the resultant of $\mathbf{P}$ and $\mathbf{Q}$.

EXERCISES I

1. If two forces of magnitude P and Q act at an inclination θ to one another, prove that the magnitude of the resultant R is given by
$$R^2 = P^2 + Q^2 + 2PQ\cos\theta.$$

2. A particle is acted on by forces of magnitudes P and Q, their lines of action making an angle θ with one another. They are to be balanced by two equal forces, acting at right angles to one another. Find the common magnitude of these forces

3. Show that if the magnitudes of a number of coplanar vectors are multiplied by a common factor, the directions of the vectors being unchanged, the magnitude of the sum is multiplied by the same factor and its direction is unchanged. Show also that if all the vectors are rotated through a common angle in their plane, without change of magnitude, their sum is rotated through the same angle without change of magnitude.

4. Forces of magnitudes 3, 4, and 5 lb wt. act at a point in directions parallel to the sides of an equilateral triangle taken in order. Find their resultant.

5. Two forces acting in opposite directions on a particle have a resultant of 34 lb wt ; if they acted at right angles to one another, their resultant would have a magnitude of 50 lb. wt. Find the magnitudes of the forces

6. An airplane dives at 400 miles per hour, losing height at the rate of 220 ft per sec. What is the horizontal component of its velocity in miles per hour?

7. Coplanar forces of magnitudes P, $2P$, $4P$ act on a particle How should they be directed to make the resultant (i) a maximum, (ii) a minimum?

8. If any number of coplanar vectors all of the same magnitude are drawn from a point, arranged symmetrically so that the angles between adjacent vectors are all equal, prove that their sum is zero

9. If $V = x^2 + y^2 + z^2 + xy + x$, at what points in space is the vector grad V parallel to the z-axis?

10. A scalar field is given over a plane by
$$V = \frac{x^2 + y^2}{2x}.$$

What are the level curves? Show that, at the point with polar coordinates (r, θ), grad V is inclined to the x-axis at an angle 2θ and its magnitude is $\frac{1}{2} \sec^2 \theta$.

11. A train, starting at time $t = 0$, has moved in time t a distance

$$x = at(1 - e^{-bt}),$$

where a and b are positive constants. Find its velocity and acceleration; what do these become after a long time has elapsed?

12. A particle travels along a straight line with constant acceleration f. Prove

$$s = ut + \tfrac{1}{2}ft^2, \qquad v = u + ft, \qquad v^2 = u^2 + 2fs,$$

where s is the distance covered from the instant $t = 0$, u the initial velocity, and v the final velocity.

13. A uniformly accelerated automobile passes two telephone poles with velocities 10 m.p.h. and 20 m.p.h., respectively. Calculate its velocity when it is halfway between the poles.

14. What curve is described by a particle moving in accordance with the equation

$$\mathbf{r} = a \cos ct \cdot \mathbf{i} + b \sin ct \cdot \mathbf{j},$$

where a, b, c are constants and $\mathbf{i}$, $\mathbf{j}$ fixed unit vectors perpendicular to one another? Show that the acceleration is directed toward the origin.

15. An elevator weighing one ton starts upward with constant acceleration and attains a velocity of 15 ft. sec.$^{-1}$ in a distance of 10 ft. Find in tons weight the tension in the supporting cable during the accelerated motion.

16. A car weighing 2 tons comes to rest with uniform deceleration from a speed of 30 m.p.h. in 100 ft. Find the force exerted by the car on the road, showing its direction in a diagram.

17. A particle of mass m moves on the axis Ox according to the equation

$$x = a \sin pt,$$

where a and p are constants. Express the force acting on it as a function of x.

18. A tug tows a barge A, which in turn tows another barge B. They start to move with an acceleration f. Find the tensions in the towing cables, in terms of f and m, m' (the masses of the barges).

19. Indicate the fallacy in the following argument: A locomotive pulls a train. But to every action there is an equal and opposite reaction. Therefore the train pulls the locomotive backward with a force equal to the pull of the locomotive, and so there can be no motion.

20. If the fundamental law of mechanics for a particle moving on a straight line were

$$m \frac{d}{dt} \left(\frac{\dot{x}}{\sqrt{1 - (\dot{x}^2/c^2)}} \right) = P,$$

instead of (1.402), m and c being constants, find the distance traveled from rest in time t under the action of a constant force P. (This is the relativistic equation of motion; see Chap. XVI.)

CHAPTER II

METHODS OF PLANE STATICS

2.1. INTRODUCTORY NOTE

In order to deal systematically with the subject of mechanics, we have to break it up into parts. The first division is into *statics* and *dynamics:* statics deals with the equilibrium of systems at rest, and dynamics with the motion of systems. As we have already seen, rest and motion are terms which have meanings only when a frame of reference has been specified. Thus the question at once arises: When we say that statics deals with systems at rest, what physical frame of reference have we in mind? The mathematical theory of statics is based on the fundamental laws of Sec. 1.4. Thus we should be confident of a close agreement between theory and observation if we were to develop statics relative to the astronomical frame. But that would not be physically interesting, because there are actually no systems at rest in that frame; the earth's surface is the physically interesting frame of reference for statics. Although (1.401) is not satisfied with great precision relative to the earth's surface, it is possible by a modification of the forces (i.e., by inclusion of centrifugal force) to obtain extremely satisfactory results in statics relative to the earth's surface. Thus in the mathematical theory of statics the frame of reference will be such that the fundamental laws hold, and in the physical interpretation of the results the frame of reference will be the earth's surface.

But there is another division of the subject of mechanics, namely, a division into *plane mechanics* and *mechanics in space.* This division is artificial from a physical point of view but is convenient in learning the subject, because the mathematics of the plane theory is simpler than the mathematics of the space theory. This is due to the fact that certain quantities (moments of forces, angular velocity, and angular momentum) appear as scalars in the plane theory but as vectors in the space theory.

Accordingly, to avoid undue mathematical complications in the development, we shall deal first with plane mechanics, but where the space theory presents no difficulty we shall develop it simultaneously.

To be precise, the subject of plane mechanics deals with

(i) The statics and dynamics of a system of particles lying in a fixed plane.

(ii) The statics and dynamics of rigid bodies which can move only parallel to a fixed plane, the displacement or velocity of every particle being parallel to the fixed plane.

As an example of (i), we may mention the problem of the motion of the earth relative to the sun, both being treated as particles, and as an example of (ii) the motion of a cylinder rolling down an inclined plane.

The plane in which the system lies, or to which the motion is parallel, will be called the *fundamental plane*.

We shall find in both statics and dynamics that the basic laws lead to certain general principles or methods. When any specific problem presents itself, we do not attack it directly from first principles as a rule; we can avoid waste of energy by applying to the problem one of the general methods. The present chapter is devoted to general methods in plane statics, with inclusion of the space theory where it presents no difficulty.

2.2. EQUILIBRIUM OF A PARTICLE

According to (1.401) a particle will have an acceleration unless the force acting on it vanishes. Thus if $\mathbf{P}$ is the force acting on a particle, the necessary and sufficient condition for equilibrium is

(2.201) $$\mathbf{P} = 0.$$

If several forces $\mathbf{P}, \mathbf{Q}, \mathbf{R} \cdots$ act on a particle, the necessary and sufficient condition for equilibrium is the vanishing of the resultant force, i.e.,

(2.202) $$\mathbf{P} + \mathbf{Q} + \mathbf{R} + \cdots = 0.$$

This vector condition may also be expressed in scalar form by means of components. Let a particle be acted on by forces whose components on an orthogonal triad are indicated as follows:

$$\mathbf{P}(P_1, P_2, P_3),$$
$$\mathbf{Q}(Q_1, Q_2, Q_3),$$
$$\mathbf{R}(R_1, R_2, R_3),$$
$$\ldots\ldots\ldots\ldots\ldots.$$

Then the conditions for equilibrium are

(2.203)
$$\begin{cases} P_1 + Q_1 + R_1 + \cdot & = 0, \\ P_2 + Q_2 + R_2 + \cdot & = 0, \\ P_3 + Q_3 + R_3 + \cdot & = 0. \end{cases}$$

All the above remarks hold whether the forces acting on the particle lie in a plane or not. The particular feature of the plane case is that only two components are to be considered instead of three.

No difficulty will be found in using (2.202) to prove the following theorems which are often useful:

(i) THE TRIANGLE OF FORCES. If a particle is in equilibrium under the action of three forces, these forces may be represented in magnitude and direction by the three sides of a triangle, taken in order (Fig. 9).

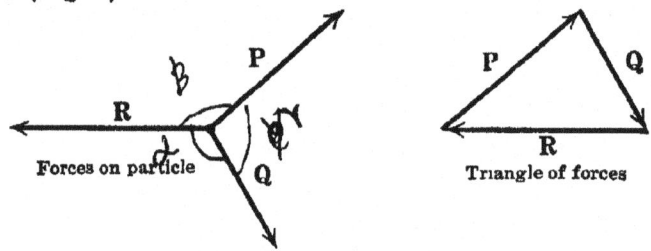

FIG. 9.—The triangle of forces

(ii) THE POLYGON OF FORCES. If a particle is in equilibrium under the action of several forces, these forces may be represented by the sides of a closed polygon, taken in order.

(iii) LAMY'S THEOREM. If a particle is in equilibrium under the action of three forces $\mathbf{P}, \mathbf{Q}, \mathbf{R}$, then

(2.204)
$$\frac{P}{\sin \alpha} = \frac{Q}{\sin \beta} = \frac{R}{\sin \gamma},$$

where α is the angle between $\mathbf{Q}$ and $\mathbf{R}$, β the angle between $\mathbf{R}$ and $\mathbf{P}$, and γ the angle between $\mathbf{P}$ and $\mathbf{Q}$.

Exercise. A particle is in equilibrium under three forces. Two of the forces act at right angles to one another, one being double the other. The

third force has a magnitude 10 lb. wt. Find the magnitudes of the other two.

2.3. EQUILIBRIUM OF A SYSTEM OF PARTICLES
Systems of particles.

Let us now consider a system of particles. We must in all cases come to a clear understanding as to what is included in the system under consideration. Let us suppose that we are dealing with a book which rests on a table, the table standing on the floor. The book and the table are regarded (in our mathematical model) as composed of a very great number of particles. In talking about this arrangement of matter, we are not compelled to think of the "system" under consideration as composed of the book and the table. If we like, we may think of the table alone as a system, or the book alone as a system, or the hundredth page of the book as a system

It is important to realize that the system under consideration is something we pick out from the given arrangement in an arbitrary manner. It is necessary to understand this in order to appreciate the distinction between *external* and *internal* forces.

External and internal forces.

The book presses down on the table and the table presses up on the book with an equal and opposite force (law of action and reaction) If the system is book + table, these forces are both exerted by particles of the system. But if the system consists of the book only, this is no longer the case; the force exerted by the table on the book is due, not to particles of the system, but to particles lying outside the system.

We make the following general definition:

A force acting on a particle of a given system is an *internal* force when it is exerted by another particle of that system; otherwise it is an *external* force.

In accordance with the law of action and reaction, internal forces occur in equal and opposite pairs, each pair representing the mutual interactions of a pair of particles of the system.

Figure 10 shows three particles A, B, C, the broken line indicating the boundary of the system. The forces are classified as follows:

at B about a line L is equal to the moment about L of the projection of the vector on the line through B perpendicular to the plane containing B and L.

Since the projection on any line of the sum of any number of vectors is equal to the sum of their projections on that line, the theorem of Varignon follows immediately:

The sum of the moments about a line L of vectors $\mathbf{P}, \mathbf{Q}, \mathbf{R}, \cdots$, with common origin B, is equal to the moment about L of the single vector $\mathbf{P} + \mathbf{Q} + \mathbf{R} + \cdots$ with origin B.

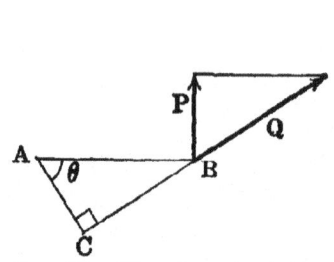

Fig. 15.—The plane containing P and Q.

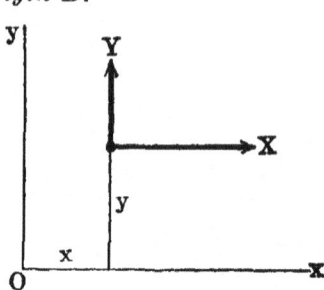

Fig 16.—Analytical method of finding the moment of a vector.

In statics the only vectors whose moments we have occasion to consider are forces. But it should be noted that the above definitions and theorems hold for any vectors. We shall have occasion to use them in Chap. V in discussing angular momentum.

The following analytical result is important; it is obvious from Fig 16, which shows the projection on the plane Oxy. *If a vector with components (X, Y, Z) acts at the point (x, y, z), then its moment about the perpendicular to the plane Oxy at O is*

$$(2.303) \qquad M = xY - yX.$$

The moment about the perpendicular to the plane Oxy at the point (a, b) is

$$(2.304) \qquad M = (x - a)Y - (y - b)X.$$

These formulas take care of the sign of M automatically.

Exercise A force, of fixed magnitude R and variable inclination θ to the x-axis, acts in the plane Oxy at the fixed point (a, b). Find its moment about the origin as a function of θ, and obtain the values of θ for which this moment (i) is a maximum, (ii) is a minimum, (iii) vanishes.

Necessary conditions for equilibrium (moments).

Let us now return to the consideration of a system of particles in equilibrium. Let L be any line. Consider any particle. Since it is in equilibrium, the resultant of all the forces acting on

moment about L of the projection of **P** on a plane perpendicular to L, the latter moment having already been defined above.

The following facts are now obvious:

(i) The moment of **P** about L is unaltered if **P** is made to slide along its line of action without change of magnitude or sense. (It is seen at once that this only slides the projection along its line of action, without change of magnitude or sense.)

(ii) The sum of the moments about any line L of two vectors **P**, $-$**P** situated on the same line is zero. (Their moments are equal in magnitude but opposite in sign.)

(iii) The moment about L of a vector **P** is unaltered if **P** is moved without change of magnitude or direction in a direction parallel to L. (This does not change its projection on a plane perpendicular to L.)

When we deal with the moments of coplanar vectors about a line perpendicular to their plane, we often refer to these moments as moments about a point, namely, the point where the line cuts the plane.

The theorem of Varignon.

Consider a line L and a bound vector **R** at a point B (Fig. 14). Let A be the foot of the perpendicular dropped from B on L. Let **Q** be the projection of **R** on the plane through B perpendicular to L. Let N be the line through B perpendicular to AB and to L, and let **P** be the projection of **Q** on N. It is clear that **P** is also the projection of **R** on N. We wish to prove that the moment of **R** about L is equal to the moment of **P** about L.

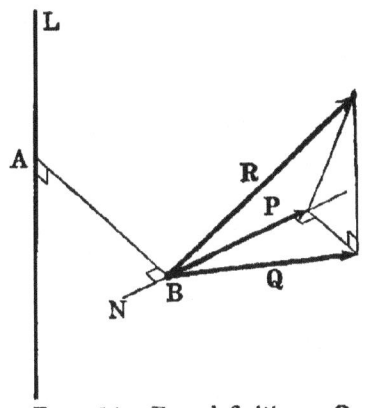

Fig. 14.—By definition, **Q** and **R** have the same moment about L; it is to be proved that **P** also has the same moment.

Figure 15 shows the plane containing **P**, **Q**, and AB. Let AC be drawn perpendicular to the line of action of **Q**, and let the angle CAB be denoted by θ. Then the moment M of **R** about L equals the moment of **Q** about L (by definition), so that*

$$M = Q \cdot AC = Q \cdot AB \cos \theta = AB \cdot Q \cos \theta = AB \cdot P,$$

which is the moment of **P** about L. Hence, *the moment of a vector*

* For simplicity, we have taken the case where M is positive; the other case is dealt with similarly.

The vector sum of all external forces and all internal forces is zero.
From the equality of action and reaction,
The vector sum of all internal forces is zero.
Comparing this with the preceding statement, we have

(2.301)   *The vector sum of all external forces is zero.*

Here we have the first of the necessary conditions for the equilibrium of a system of particles

Exercise. Consider a glass of water standing on a table, taking as the system (i) the water only, (ii) the water and the glass. What are the external forces in each case, and what does (2.301) tell us about them?

The moment of a vector about a line.

Consider a line L and a bound vector **P**, perpendicular to L but not intersecting it. Let a be the length of the common

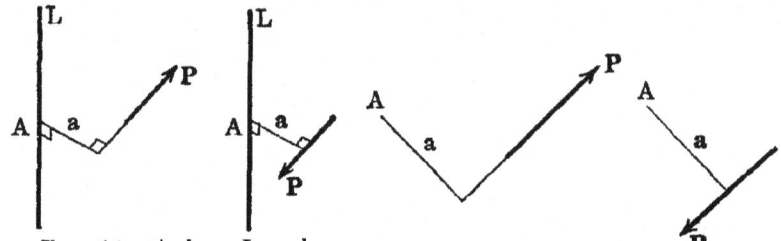

Fig. 12.—A line L and a vector **P** perpendicular to it. The moments in the two cases have opposite signs.

Fig. 13.—(a) $M = aP$. (b) $M = -aP$.

perpendicular to L and the line of action of **P**. The *moment* of **P** about L is defined to be

(2.302) $$M = \pm aP.$$

The ambiguous sign is introduced in order that we may distinguish between the two cases shown in Fig. 12, in which the vector **P** indicates rotations in opposite senses about L. Having decided to use the $+$ sign for vectors indicating rotations in one sense, we use the $-$ sign for vectors indicating rotations in the opposite sense. The significance of the signs will be better understood when Sec. 9.3 has been read, but for the present the following description of the convention will serve.

Let us suppose the line L drawn perpendicular to the plane of the paper, intersecting it at the point A (Figs. 13a and b); the moment is $+aP$ when **P** indicates a counterclockwise rotation around A in the plane, and $-aP$ when a clockwise rotation is indicated.

Consider now a line L and a bound vector **P** which is not perpendicular to L. The moment of **P** about L is defined to be the

External: **P** at A, **Q** at B, **R** at C.
Internal: **U** at B, $-$**U** at C, **V** at C, $-$**V** at A,
W at A, $-$**W** at B

Figure 11 shows these particles situated precisely as in Fig. 10 and subject to the same forces. The only difference between the two diagrams lies in the position of the broken line, indicating the boundary of the system under consideration. In Fig. 11 the system contains only the particles A and B. Now **P** at A, $-$**V** at A, **Q** at B, **U** at B are external; and **W** at A, $-$**W** at B are internal. If we reduce the system under consideration to one particle only, there are no longer any internal forces.

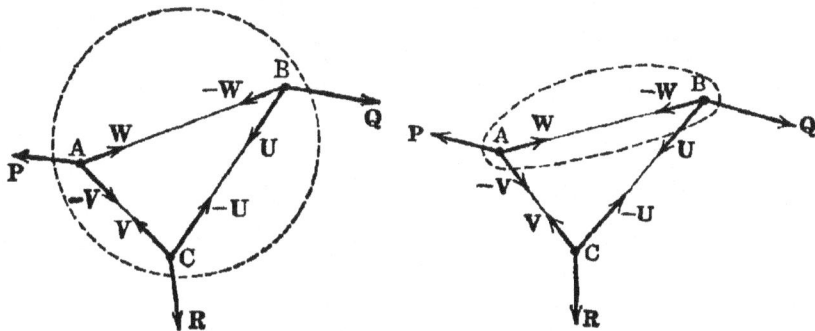

FIG. 10.—External and internal forces. The "system" is enclosed by the broken line.

FIG. 11.—The same particles and forces as in Fig. 10, but a different "system."

The only essential difference between the treatment of this question of internal and external forces in a plane and its treatment in space is that in the former case we may delimit the system by a closed curve, whereas in the latter case we require a closed surface.

Necessary conditions for equilibrium (forces).

We shall now obtain necessary conditions for the equilibrium of any system of particles. The meaning of the word "necessary" should be emphasized: these conditions must be satisfied if the system is in equilibrium, but the satisfaction of the conditions does not imply that there is equilibrium.

Consider any particle of the system, assumed in equilibrium. That particle is itself in equilibrium, and hence the vector sum of all forces acting on it is zero. Similarly for all particles. Hence,

The vector sum of all forces acting on all particles is zero.

But the forces are some external, some internal. We may state

it is zero; hence, by Varignon's theorem the sum of the moments about L of all forces acting on the particle is zero. Similarly for all particles. Hence,

The sum of the moments about L of all external forces and all internal forces is zero.

But the sum of the moments of a pair of equal and opposite internal forces is zero. Hence,

The sum of the moments about L of all internal forces is zero.

Comparing this with the preceding statement, we have

(2.305) *The sum of the moments about L of all external forces is zero.*

From (2.301) and (2.305) we may now state necessary conditions for the equilibrium of any system of particles.

If a system of particles is in equilibrium, then

(i) *The vector sum of all EXTERNAL forces is zero.*

(ii) *The sum of the moments of all EXTERNAL forces about any line is zero.*

This result is the key to the solution of statical problems, and it should be remembered.

The particular form of the above statement applicable to plane statics is as follows:

If a system of particles is in equilibrium, then

(2.306) $$\mathbf{F} = \mathbf{0}, \qquad N = 0,$$

where $\mathbf{F}$ is the vector sum of the projections of all EXTERNAL forces on the fundamental plane, and N the sum of the moments of all EXTERNAL forces about any line perpendicular to the fundamental plane.

It is convenient to have an explicit form of (2.306). Let axes be chosen so that the fundamental plane is $z = 0$. We shall take moments about the z-axis. Suppose now that the system is acted on by external forces with components (X_1, Y_1, Z_1), $(X_2, Y_2, Z_2), \cdots (X_n, Y_n, Z_n)$ at points (x_1, y_1, z_1), (x_2, y_2, z_2), $\cdots (x_n, y_n, z_n)$. By projection on the fundamental plane, it follows that $\mathbf{F}$ and N are unaltered if we replace this system by forces in the fundamental plane with components (X_1, Y_1), $(X_2, Y_2), \cdots (X_n, Y_n)$ at points $(x_1, y_1), (x_2, y_2), \cdots (x_n, y_n)$. Hence, by (2.303) we see that if (X, Y) are the components of $\mathbf{F}$, then

(2.307) $$X = \sum_{i=1}^{n} X_i, \qquad Y = \sum_{i=1}^{n} Y_i, \qquad N = \sum_{i=1}^{n} (x_i Y_i - y_i X_i),$$

and so necessary conditions for equilibrium are

(2.308) $\qquad \sum_{i=1}^{n} X_i = 0, \qquad \sum_{i=1}^{n} Y_i = 0, \qquad \sum_{i=1}^{n} (x_i Y_i - y_i X_i) = 0$

It might be thought that, by taking moments about other lines perpendicular to the fundamental plane, new conditions might be obtained; but this is not so. For, by (2.304), if moments are taken about a perpendicular to the plane at (a, b), then the total moment is

$$\sum_{i=1}^{n} [(x_i - a)Y_i - (y_i - b)X_i] = \sum_{i=1}^{n} (x_i Y_i - y_i X_i) - a \sum_{i=1}^{n} Y_i + b \sum_{i=1}^{n} X_i,$$

and this vanishes automatically if (2.308) are satisfied. Thus conditions of the type (2.306) or (2.308) are actually three in number, and no more.

The following important results are easy to establish from the principles laid down above:

(i) If a system is in equilibrium under the action of only two external forces, then these forces have a common line of action, equal magnitudes, and opposite senses.

(ii) If a system is in equilibrium under the action of only three external forces, these forces lie in a plane and their lines of action are either concurrent or parallel.

If a force is measured in dynamical units, its moment has dimensions $[ML^2T^{-2}]$ (see Appendix). In the c.g.s. system, the unit moment is 1 dyne cm. or 1 gm. cm.^{2} sec^{-2}; in the f.p.s. system, it is 1 ft. poundal or 1 lb. ft.^{2} sec^{-2}. In statics we frequently use a unit of force which is not a dynamical unit, such as the lb. wt. or the ton wt. (contracted to read lb. and ton). The corresponding moments are measured in ft. lb. or ft. ton.

Equipollent systems of forces.

Two systems of forces are said to be *equipollent** when the following conditions are satisfied:

---

* The word *equivalent* is often used. But there is a danger of confusion in using a common word in a technical sense. We might think that the effects of two such force systems were the same; this is not always the case. If we pull a string with equal and opposite forces at its ends, we produce a very different effect from that caused by pushing it with these forces reversed in direction; yet the two force systems are equipollent.

(i) The vector sum of all the forces of one system is equal to the vector sum of all the forces of the other system.

(ii) The sum of the moments of all the forces of one system about an arbitrary line is equal to the sum of the moments of all the forces of the other system about that line.

For the discussion of plane mechanics, we require only a restricted type of equipollence, which we shall call *plane equipollence*. Two systems of forces are said to be *plane-equipollent* for the fundamental plane if

(i) The vector sum of the projections on the fundamental plane of all the forces of one system is equal to the vector sum of the projections on that plane of all the forces of the other system.

(ii) The sum of the moments of all the forces of one system about an arbitrary line perpendicular to the fundamental plane is equal to the sum of the moments of all the forces of the other system about the same line.

It is evident that if $\mathbf{F}, \mathbf{F}'$ are the vector sums of the projections of the forces of the two systems, and N, N' the moments about some line, then the conditions for plane equipollence are

(2.309) $$\mathbf{F} = \mathbf{F}', \qquad N = N'.$$

If $\mathbf{F} = \mathbf{0}, N = 0$, we say that the system is *plane-equipollent to zero*. Thus, if a system of particles is in equilibrium, the forces acting on it are plane-equipollent to zero.

The idea of equipollence is extremely useful in statics. The solutions of problems in plane statics turn on the conditions (2.306), and difficulties may arise in the calculation of $\mathbf{F}$ and N. These difficulties are reduced by splitting up the calculation into parts, each of which is simple. This reduction depends on the following fact (obvious from the definition of equipollence): *For the calculation of the vector sum of the projections of the forces of a system on the fundamental plane and the sum of their moments about a line perpendicular to that plane, any system of forces may be replaced by a system plane-equipollent to it.*

In what follows below, we shall speak only of forces in the fundamental plane. This makes for simplicity of expression without any real loss of generality, because in problems of plane mechanics we are actually interested in projections on the fundamental plane and moments about lines perpendicular to it,

for the calculation of these, we may replace a given force system by a plane-equipollent system in the fundamental plane.

Exercise Find a system of two forces equipollent to a system of three forces represented by the sides of an equilateral triangle taken in order.

Couples.

A couple is defined as a pair of forces acting on parallel lines, equal in magnitude and opposite in sense. In fact, a couple consists of a pair of forces **P**, −**P**. A line drawn perpendicular to the two lines of action and terminated by them is called the *arm* of the couple.

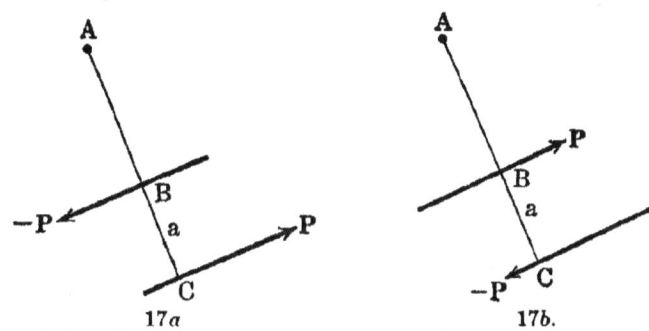

FIG. 17.—(a) Couple with positive moment. (b) Couple with negative moment

Thus the vector sum of the forces constituting a couple is zero. Consider now the sum of the moments of the forces forming a couple about any line L, perpendicular to the plane of the couple and cutting it at A (Figs. 17a and 17b). If AB, AC are the perpendiculars dropped from A on the lines of action, the sum of the moments is

$$M = P \cdot AC - P \cdot AB = P \cdot BC = Pa \qquad \text{(Fig. 17a)},$$
$$M = P \cdot AB - P \cdot AC = -P \cdot BC = -Pa \qquad \text{(Fig. 17b)},$$

where a is the arm of the couple. The rule for sign is easily seen to be as follows:

(2 310) $$M = \pm Pa,$$

where the + or − sign is to be taken according as the forces indicate a positive (counterclockwise) rotation or a negative (clockwise) rotation in the plane of the couple about any point taken between their lines of action.

We observe that the sum of the moments of the forces forming a couple about a line perpendicular to its plane is the same for all

such lines. Hence, we may speak in an absolute sense of the *moment of a couple*. Since the vector sum of forces in a couple is zero, it follows that *two couples in the fundamental plane are plane-equipollent if they have the same moment.*

It is evident that two couples of moments M, M' in the fundamental plane are together plane-equipollent to a single couple of moment $M + M'$ in that plane.

Reduction of a general plane force system.

Consider a system of forces in the fundamental plane. Let F be their vector sum and N the sum of their moments about some point O in the plane.* Consider on the other hand a single force $\mathbf{F}$ at O and a couple of moment N in the fundamental plane. Obviously, this simple system is plane-equipollent to the given system. Hence, we may state the following general result:

A system of forces in the fundamental plane is plane-equipollent to a single force applied at an arbitrary point in the plane, together with a couple

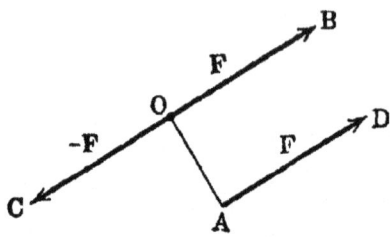

Fig. 18.—Reduction of a force and a couple to a single force.

It is customary also to express this by saying that a system of forces in the fundamental plane may be *reduced* to a force and a couple.

Expressed analytically, a system of forces (X_1, Y_1), (X_2, Y_2), $\cdots (X_n, Y_n)$ at points (x_1, y_1), (x_2, y_2), $\cdots (x_n, y_n)$ may be reduced to a single force at the origin with components X, Y, together with a couple N, where

$$(2.311) \quad X = \sum_{i=1}^{n} X_i, \qquad Y = \sum_{i=1}^{n} Y_i, \qquad N = \sum_{i=1}^{n} (x_i Y_i - y_i X_i)$$

We shall now show that a still greater reduction is possible.

Let O be an arbitrary point. The force system, as we already know, may be reduced to a force $\mathbf{F}$ at O, together with a couple of moment N. In Fig. 18, the force $\mathbf{F}$ at O is shown as $\overrightarrow{OB}$. We now consider the following two cases:

---

* That is, the moments about a line perpendicular to the fundamental plane, cutting it at O (see p. 44).

Sec. 2.3] METHODS OF PLANE STATICS 51

CASE (i): $\mathbf{F} \neq \mathbf{0}$. Let us suppose N positive for simplicity, the case where N is negative being similarly dealt with. We draw OA perpendicular to OB as in Fig. 18 and measure off OA equal to N/F. Then the couple is equipollent to the pair of forces

$$\overrightarrow{OC} \text{ (or } -\mathbf{F} \text{ at } O); \quad \overrightarrow{AD} \text{ (or } \mathbf{F} \text{ at } A).$$

Thus the given system is reduced to the three forces

$$\mathbf{F} \text{ at } O, \quad -\mathbf{F} \text{ at } O, \quad \mathbf{F} \text{ at } A$$

These are equipollent to a single force $\mathbf{F}$ at A.

CASE (ii): $\mathbf{F} = \mathbf{0}$. Here the system is reduced to a couple.

Hence we may state the following general result:

Any force system in the fundamental plane may be reduced either to a single force or to a couple.

It may be noted that reduction to a single force will occur much more frequently than reduction to a couple, because reduction to a couple occurs only when a special condition is satisfied, viz., $\mathbf{F} = \mathbf{0}$, or, in other words, when the vector sum of the forces in the system is zero.

Let us now carry out this reduction to a single force or to a couple analytically, the given plane force system being specified as consisting of forces with components (X_1, Y_1), (X_2, Y_2), $\cdots$ (X_n, Y_n) at points with coordinates (x_1, y_1), (x_2, y_2), $\cdots$ (x_n, y_n). Let us suppose that this system may be reduced to a force with components (X, Y) at (x, y). The conditions of plane equipollence are

$$(2.312) \quad X = \sum_{i=1}^{n} X_i, \quad Y = \sum_{i=1}^{n} Y_i,$$

$$xY - yX = \sum_{i=1}^{n} (x_i Y_i - y_i X_i).$$

The first two equations determine the components of the single force. The last equation gives one relation between the coordinates of the point of application; this relation, being linear, defines a straight line. It is seen at once that this line points in the direction of the force with components (X, Y); it is, in fact, the line of action of that force. The last equation of (2.312) leaves the point of application indeterminate to a certain extent—it may take any position on a certain line. One particu-

lar point on this line is given by the symmetrical formulas

$$(2.313) \qquad x = \frac{\sum_{i=1}^{n} x_i Y_i}{\sum_{i=1}^{n} Y_i}, \qquad y = \frac{\sum_{i=1}^{n} y_i X_i}{\sum_{i=1}^{n} X_i}.$$

If it should happen that

$$(2.314) \qquad \sum_{i=1}^{n} X_i = 0, \qquad \sum_{i=1}^{n} Y_i = 0, \qquad \sum_{i=1}^{n} (x_i Y_i - y_i X_i) \neq 0,$$

it is evident that we cannot find X, Y, x, y to satisfy (2.312). Then the system cannot be reduced to a single force. To find the couple to which it can be reduced, we compare it with the couple consisting of forces $(0, -Y)$, $(0, Y)$ at the points $(0, 0)$, $(0, x)$, respectively. The conditions of equipollence are

$$0 + 0 = 0, \qquad -Y + Y = 0, \qquad xY = \sum_{i=1}^{n} (x_i Y_i - y_i X_i).$$

These equations are satisfied provided that the moment of the couple is

$$(2.315) \qquad M = \sum_{i=1}^{n} (x_i Y_i - y_i X_i).$$

To sum up: *In general a plane system of forces is plane-equipollent to a single force whose components and line of action are given by* (2.312). *If*

$$(2.316) \qquad \sum_{i=1}^{n} X_i = 0, \qquad \sum_{i=1}^{n} Y_i = 0,$$

the system is plane-equipollent to a couple with moment given by (2.315). *If* (2.316) *are satisfied and also*

$$(2.317) \qquad \sum_{i=1}^{n} (x_i Y_i - y_i X_i) = 0,$$

then the given system is plane-equipollent to zero.

Exercise. Forces of magnitudes 2 and 3 act parallel to the x-axis at points $(1, 3)$ and $(2, 4)$, respectively. Reduce them (i) to a force at the origin and a couple, (ii) to a single force.

2.4. WORK AND POTENTIAL ENERGY

Definition of work.

Consider a particle A on which a force $\mathbf{P}$ acts. Let the particle be given an infinitesimal displacement of magnitude δs, represented by $\overrightarrow{AB}$ (Fig. 19). The *work* done by $\mathbf{P}$ in this displacement is defined to be the product of δs and the component of $\mathbf{P}$ in the direction of the displacement; in fact, the work δW is

$$(2.401) \qquad \delta W = P \cos \theta \cdot \delta s,$$

where θ is the angle between $\mathbf{P}$ and the displacement.* It will be positive or negative according as θ is acute or obtuse.

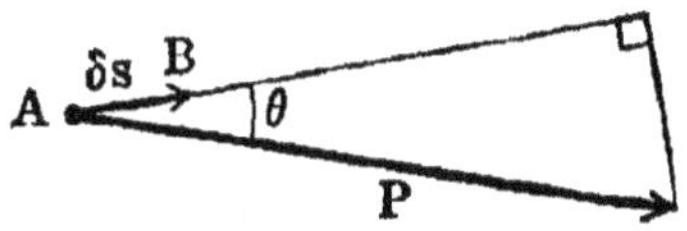

Since the sum of components in any direction is equal to the component of the sum in that direction, it follows that the total work done by any number of forces $\mathbf{P}, \mathbf{Q}, \mathbf{R}, \cdots$, acting on a particle, is equal to the work done by their resultant $\mathbf{P} + \mathbf{Q} + \mathbf{R} + \cdots$.

Fig. 19.—The force $\mathbf{P}$ does work when the particle on which it acts receives the displacement AB.

It is evident that δW is also equal to the product of P and the component of the displacement in the direction of $\mathbf{P}$. Hence the work done by $\mathbf{P}$ in a succession of small displacements is equal to the work done by $\mathbf{P}$ in the resultant displacement.

Let X, Y, Z be the components of $\mathbf{P}$ in the directions of the axes of coordinates, and let the coordinates of A, B be (x, y, z), $(x + \delta x, y + \delta y, z + \delta z)$, respectively. Then, since the direction cosines of $\mathbf{P}$ are $X/P, Y/P, Z/P$ and those of the displacement $\overrightarrow{AB}$ are $\delta x/\delta s, \delta y/\delta s, \delta z/\delta s$, we have

$$(2.402) \qquad \cos \theta = \frac{X}{P}\frac{\delta x}{\delta s} + \frac{Y}{P}\frac{\delta y}{\delta s} + \frac{Z}{P}\frac{\delta z}{\delta s},$$

and so the work done by $\mathbf{P}$ in the displacement $\overrightarrow{AB}$ is

$$(2.403) \qquad \delta W = X\,\delta x + Y\,\delta y + Z\,\delta z.$$

---

* The use of the symbol δ instead of the more usual d (for differential) is traditional, and not of much importance as far as statics is concerned. But in dynamics it is necessary to distinguish between a purely hypothetical (or virtual) displacement δx and the displacement dx actually occurring in time dt (i.e., $dx = \dot{x}\,dt$).

We note that no work is done when the displacement is perpendicular to the force.

If force is measured in dynamical units, work has dimensions $[ML^2T^{-2}]$ (see Appendix). In the c.g.s. system, the unit of work is the erg, which is 1 dyne cm. or 1 gm cm.^{2} sec.$^{-2}$; in the f.p.s. system, it is 1 ft. poundal or 1 lb. ft.^{2} sec.$^{-2}$ In statics, the ft. lb. and ft. ton are used.

Rate of working is called *power*. In dynamical units, power has dimensions $[ML^2T^{-3}]$. A unit commonly employed is the horsepower (550 ft. lb. wt. sec.$^{-1}$ = 1 hp.).

Forces which do no work.

Consider a particle in contact with the surface of a fixed rigid body, and suppose that a force acts on the particle tending to drive it into the body. If no other force acted, the particle would have to penetrate the body, in accordance with (1.401). Since, however, we regard such penetration as impossible we must assume the existence of another force, the *reaction* of the surface, which prevents the penetration from taking place. The particle in question may be an isolated particle, or it may be one of the particles of a rigid body.

In a mechanical problem the reactions between particles and surfaces, or between pairs of surfaces, are not in general to be regarded as known forces. They are called into play solely to prevent violation of the condition of non-penetration.

The words "smooth" and "rough" are familiar in ordinary life; we speak of polished steel, glass, ice, etc., as smooth, and sandpaper, cloth, etc., as rough. We make such a classification primarily on the basis of our sense of touch. A more scientific classification is obtained by examining the directions of the reactions between bodies. It is found that with smooth bodies the reactions always lie very close to the common normal of the surfaces in contact. As an idealization of such bodies, we admit into our mathematical model the concept of a *smooth surface* with the following property:

The reaction at a smooth surface is normal to the surface, and is of such a magnitude as just to prevent penetration or overlapping in space from taking place.

The reaction at a rough surface has more complicated properties which will be discussed in Sec. 3.2.

Since the reaction at a smooth surface is normal to the surface, the following result is evident from (2.401):

Sec. 2.4] METHODS OF PLANE STATICS 55

No work is done by the reaction at a smooth fixed surface in an infinitesimal displacement which preserves the contact.

In any contact there are actually two equal and opposite forces involved, one acting on each body. In what has been said above, one body was supposed fixed, so that the force acting on it did no work. Suppose now that both bodies, having smooth contact, are displaced infinitesimally. The displacements of the particles of the two bodies in contact with one another may now have components along the common normal, and so work is done by each of the two forces of reaction. But it is not difficult to see that *the sum of these two works is zero.*

Let us now consider a rolling contact, confining our attention here, for simplicity, to the rolling of a rigid circle on a fixed line in the fundamental plane (Fig. 20).

We say that the circle C rolls on the line L if it passes continuously through a sequence of positions such that (i) L is always tangential to C; (ii) if any two points A, B of C make contact with points A', B' of L, then arc $AB = A'B'$. (Consider a motor tire and the pattern it leaves on the road.)

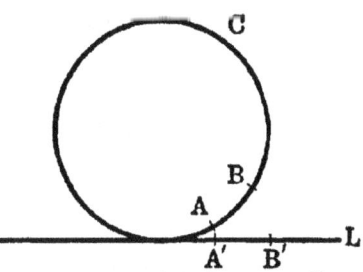

Fig. 20.—A circle rolling on a line.

If C advances a distance Δx while it turns through an angle $\Delta \theta$, it is clear that

(2.404) $$\Delta x = a\, \Delta \theta,$$

where a is the radius of C. During this advance the point of C initially in contact with L receives the following displacements:

Horizontal: $\Delta x - a \sin \Delta \theta$,
Vertical: $a - a \cos \Delta \theta$.

If the displacement Δx is infinitesimal, then these displacements are infinitesimals of the orders $(\Delta x)^3$, $(\Delta x)^2$, respectively. This is easily seen on using the well-known series for sine and cosine.

Suppose now that there is a reaction **R** exerted by L on C. We shall not assume that **R** is perpendicular to L. The work W done by **R** in a succession of infinitesimal rolling operations

will be a function of x, the final displacement. It may be written

$$W = \int \frac{dW}{dx} dx.$$

But since the displacement of the point of contact is an infinitesimal of higher order than the increment in x, we have $dW/dx = 0$ and hence $W = 0$. Thus, *no work is done by the reaction at a rolling contact*. It is true that our proof deals only with the case of a circle rolling on a line; the general case of a moving curve rolling on a fixed curve may be discussed by a slightly more complicated argument leading to the same result. The condition of rolling is the equality of arcs on the two curves between points of contact; the essential point in the proof is the fact that the displacement of the point of the moving curve instantaneously in contact is an infinitesimal of higher order than the infinitesimal angle through which the moving curve turns.

When rolling takes place between two moving surfaces, the sum of the works done by the equal and opposite reactions is zero. This follows from the fact that the displacements of the two particles in contact (one belonging to each body) are equal, to the first order of small quantities.

The fact that no work is done at a rolling contact is of enormous importance in modern transport, which moves on wheels in contrast to the dragged vehicles of primitive civilizations. It explains why boats are launched or hauled out of the water with much greater ease when placed on rollers, and why machinery operates more easily on ball or roller bearings than on plain bearings.

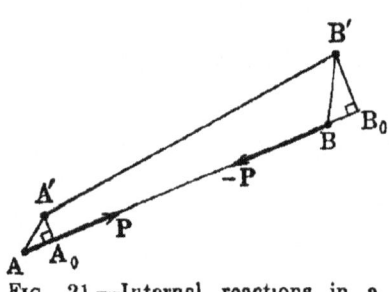

Fig. 21.—Internal reactions in a rigid body.

Let us now consider the work done by a pair of equal and opposite reactions, exerted on one another by two particles of a rigid body, when the body receives an infinitesimal displacement. Let A, B be the positions of the two particles before displacement, and A', B' their positions after displacement (Fig. 21). The lines AB, $A'B'$ make an infinitesimal angle with one another, and

(2.405) $$AB = A'B',$$

since the body is rigid. If A_0, B_0 are the projections of A', B' respectively on the line AB, we have obviously

$$(2.406) \qquad AA_0 + A_0B_0 = AB + BB_0$$

Since the inclination of $A'B'$ to AB is infinitesimal, $A_0B_0 = A'B'$ to the first order of infinitesimals; hence, $A_0B_0 = AB$ by (2.405) and so (2.406) gives

$$(2.407) \qquad AA_0 = BB_0.$$

If the forces on A, B are respectively $\mathbf{P}$, $-\mathbf{P}$, the amounts of work done by them are

$$P \cdot AA_0, \qquad -P \cdot BB_0,$$

and the sum of these is zero. Hence, *no work is done by a pair of equal and opposite reactions, exerted on one another by two particles of a rigid body.*

To sum up, we have seen that no work is done by

(i) the reaction on a movable body in smooth contact with a fixed body;

(ii) the pair of reactions at a smooth contact;

(iii) the reaction on a body rolling on a fixed body;

(iv) the pair of reactions at a rolling contact;

(v) the pair of reactions between two particles of a rigid body.

In the cases considered above, the particles forming the systems are not wholly free. The systems are, in fact, subject to *constraints*, and the reactions are brought into play to prevent the violation of these constraints. Since these *reactions of constraint* do no work in permissible displacements, we speak of these constraints as *workless*.

The principle of virtual work.

Let us start by considering the simple system shown in Fig. 22. AB is a rigid bar; a small hole is drilled in it at C, and a smooth pin passes through the hole, attaching the bar to some fixed support (not shown). Thus the bar can turn about C in the plane of the paper. Forces $\mathbf{P}$ and $\mathbf{Q}$ are applied at A and B, respectively, in directions perpendicular to AB.

There are two ways of regarding this system:

(i) It is just a rigid body, which can turn round C and which is subjected to the forces $\mathbf{P}$ and $\mathbf{Q}$.

(ii) It is a collection of a vast number of particles, subjected not only to the forces **P** and **Q**, but also to a vast number of reactions between the particles and a reaction at C, all adjusted so that the distances between the particles remain constant and the particles near C do not move away from the pin.

For present purposes we regard (ii) as the more useful view

In developing the principle of virtual work, we have to deal with *displacements, forces,* and *work*.

The only displacement consistent with the constraints is a rotation around C. But if we take the point of view (ii) above, we may think of other displacements in which the constraints are violated—for example, only one particle of the bar might be moved from its position. Such a displacement is merely a mathematical device. In either case (whether the constraints are satisfied or not) the displacement is called "virtual," this word implying that the displacement is a hypothetical one and not a displacement actually experienced. We note then that virtual displacements are of two types:

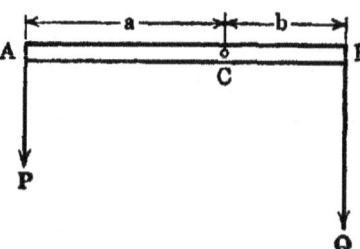

FIG. 22.—A rigid bar pinned at C.

(a) virtual displacements satisfying the constraints,
(b) virtual displacements violating the constraints.

As for forces, we have **P** and **Q** and the reactions of constraint We need a word to distinguish **P** and **Q** from the latter; we cannot use the word "external" because the reaction exerted by the pin at C is external. So we shall call **P** and **Q** *applied* forces, with this general definition for any system with workless constraints: *Forces other than reactions of constraint are called applied forces.* Thus the forces acting on the system are of two types.

(a) applied forces,
(b) reactions of constraint.

As for the work done in a virtual displacement (called *virtual work*), we are to observe that no work is done by the reactions of constraint provided that the constraints are of the workless type and are satisfied by the virtual displacement.

We shall now proceed to state and prove the principle of virtual work. The argument will be quite general, covering

the case of any system in which the constraints are of the workless type.

PRINCIPLE OF VIRTUAL WORK. *A system with workless constraints is in equilibrium under applied forces if, and only if, zero virtual work is done by the applied forces in an arbitrary infinitesimal displacement satisfying the constraints.*

It will be noticed that this statement contains both a sufficient (if) condition for equilibrium and a necessary (only if) condition. There are two theorems here, requiring separate proofs.

Let us first prove the *necessity* of the condition; that is, we are given that the system is in equilibrium, and we have to prove that zero virtual work is done by the applied forces in any infinitesimal displacement satisfying the constraints. Consider any particle of the system; it is in equilibrium, and so the resultant of all forces acting on it is zero. Thus, zero virtual work is done by the forces acting on that particle in any displacement of it. This holds for all particles; and so, in any displacement of the system, zero virtual work is done by *all* forces acting. But the reactions of constraint do no work in any displacement which satisfies the constraints. Hence the applied forces do no work in such a displacement, and so the necessity of the condition is proved.

Let us now prove its *sufficiency;* that is, we are given that zero virtual work is done by the applied forces in any infinitesimal displacement satisfying the constraints, and we have to prove that the system is in equilibrium. *Suppose it is not in equilibrium;* then it starts to move. It is clear from (1.401) that each particle starts to move in the direction of the resultant force acting on it. Referring to (2.401), we see that a *positive* amount of work is done in the initial displacement, since $\theta = 0$ and $\cos \theta = 1$. This is true for every particle; and so, in the initial displacement of the system, positive (not zero) virtual work is done by all the forces. But such an initial displacement must of course satisfy the constraints, and so the reactions of constraint do no work. Thus, on the basis of our assumption that the system is not in equilibrium, we see that it must undergo a displacement which satisfies the constraints and in which the applied forces do positive work. But this contradicts the given information, according to which zero work is done.

Since our assumption leads to a contradiction, it must be false, and so the system does remain in equilibrium. The sufficiency of the condition is proved.

Returning to the system shown in Fig. 22, let us give the bar a rotation about C in a counterclockwise sense through an infinitesimal angle $\delta\theta$. The work done by **P** is $Pa\,\delta\theta$ and the work done by **Q** is $-Qb\,\delta\theta$, and so the total work is

$$\delta W = (Pa - Qb)\,\delta\theta$$

If the system is in equilibrium, then $\delta W = 0$ and hence

$$\frac{P}{Q} = \frac{b}{a}.$$

On the other hand, if $P/Q = b/a$, then $\delta W = 0$ for this displacement. But this is the most general displacement satisfying the constraints; hence the bar must be in equilibrium if the condition $P/Q = b/a$ is satisfied.

Although the chief merit of the principle of virtual work lies in the fact that it does not involve the reactions of constraint, nevertheless it can be used to find these reactions should they be required. Suppose, for example, we wish to know the reaction at C in the system considered. If this reaction is **R**, it is obvious that the equilibrium will not be disturbed if we remove the pin at C and apply at C a force **R**. Since there is now no constraint at C, other virtual displacements are permissible. We may slide the bar along its length. In this displacement, **P** and **Q** do no work; hence **R** does no work, and consequently **R** acts at right angles to AB. If we now push the bar through a small distance δx, perpendicular to AB in the upward direction, the work done by **P** and **Q** is $-(P+Q)\,\delta x$. Hence the work done by **R** is $(P+Q)\,\delta x$; therefore, **R** has a magnitude $P+Q$ and acts in the direction opposite to the common direction of **P** and **Q**.

We have developed the principle of virtual work for the simplest and most interesting systems, namely, those for which the constraints are workless. But it is easily extended to cover more general cases by means of the device employed above, namely, the replacement of a constraint by an unknown "applied" force.

Exercise. A lever, in the form of the letter L, is pivoted at the angle. It is in equilibrium under forces applied at the ends of the arms, and per-

Sec. 2.4] METHODS OF PLANE STATICS 61

pendicular to them. Use the method of virtual work to find the force at the end of one arm and the reaction at the pivot, the other force and the lengths of the arms being given

Infinitesimal displacements of a rigid body parallel to a fixed plane.

Let us consider a rigid body which is permitted to move only parallel to a fixed fundamental plane. The section of the body by this plane is itself a two-dimensional rigid body; we call it the *representative lamina*. A description of the motion of this lamina specifies the motion of the body, and vice versa. We may therefore discuss infinitesimal displacements of the lamina

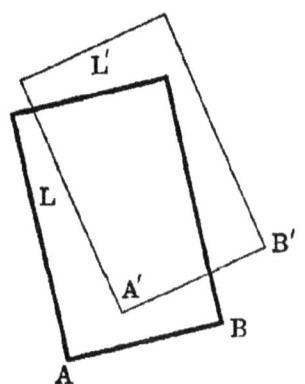

Fig. 23.—General displacement of a lamina in its plane

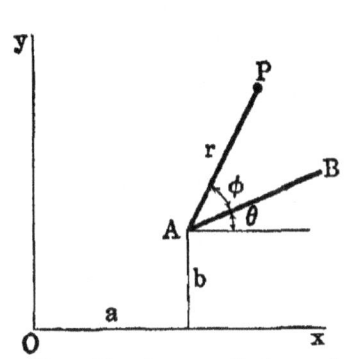

Fig. 24.—In an infinitesimal displacement the quantities a, b, and θ receive infinitesimal increments, while r and ϕ remain constant.

in the fundamental plane instead of displacements of the rigid body parallel to that plane; they come to the same thing.

In Fig. 23, L is the lamina before and L' the lamina after an arbitrary displacement. Let A, B be any two points of the lamina before displacement and A', B' their positions after displacement. Obviously the displacement from L to L' may be achieved in two steps:

(i) a *translation*, in which each point of L receives a displacement equal and parallel to $\overrightarrow{AA'}$;

(ii) a *rotation* about A' through an angle equal to the angle between AB and $A'B'$.

The point A, used in describing the displacement, is called a *base point*.

Let us now consider an *infinitesimal displacement*. For fixed axes Oxy in the fundamental plane (Fig. 24), let (a, b) be the coordinates of A, and θ the inclination of AB to Ox. Then the increments δa, δb describe the translational displacement, and the increment $\delta\theta$ describes the rotation. Let P be any particle of the lamina; let us put $r = AP$, $\phi = B\hat{A}P$. Since the lamina is rigid, r and ϕ remain constant as the lamina moves.

Now if (x, y) are the coordinates of P, we have

(2.408) $\quad x = a + r \cos (\theta + \phi), \quad y = b + r \sin (\theta + \phi).$

Hence the displacement of P in the infinitesimal displacement δa, δb, $\delta\theta$ of the lamina is

$$\delta x = \delta a - r \sin (\theta + \phi) \delta\theta, \quad \delta y = \delta b + r \cos (\theta + \phi) \delta\theta.$$

Substituting for $r \sin (\theta + \phi)$, $r \cos (\theta + \phi)$ from (2.408), we obtain

(2.409) $\quad \delta x = \delta a - (y - b) \delta\theta, \quad \delta y = \delta b + (x - a) \delta\theta.$

This gives the infinitesimal displacement of any point in the lamina (or in the rigid body of which the lamina is a section) in terms of the translation $(\delta a, \delta b)$ of the base point (a, b), and the rotation $\delta\theta$. By giving arbitrary infinitesimal values to δa, δb, $\delta\theta$, we get the most general infinitesimal displacement of a lamina in a plane or of a rigid body parallel to a plane.

Exercise Find the displacement of the particle at the highest point of a rolling wheel, when the wheel advances a small distance δs.

Sufficient conditions for the equilibrium of a rigid body movable parallel to a fixed plane.

We now consider the equilibrium of a rigid body which can move only parallel to a fixed fundamental plane. There are no constraints limiting the motion of the body parallel to the plane, but there are constraints preventing other motions. These are supposed to be of the workless type. In addition to the reactions of these constraints, there act applied forces, not necessarily parallel to the fundamental plane. Let (x_1, y_1), $(x_2, y_2), \cdots (x_n, y_n)$ be the projections on the fundamental plane $(z = 0)$ of the points at which these forces are applied, and let $(X_1, Y_1), (X_2, Y_2), \cdots (X_n, Y_n)$ be the components of these forces in the directions of the axes Oxy.

In an infinitesimal virtual displacement δa, δb, $\delta\theta$, as described above, the work done is

[Sec. 2.4] METHODS OF PLANE STATICS

$$(2.410) \quad \delta W = \sum_{i=1}^{n} X_i[\delta a - (y_i - b)\delta\theta]$$
$$+ \sum_{i=1}^{n} Y_i[\delta b + (x_i - a)\delta\theta]$$
$$= \left(\sum_{i=1}^{n} X_i\right) \delta a + \left(\sum_{i=1}^{n} Y_i\right) \delta b$$
$$+ \sum_{i=1}^{n} [(x_i - a)Y_i - (y_i - b)X_i] \delta\theta$$
$$= X \delta a + Y \delta b + N \delta\theta,$$

where X, Y are the components of the vector sum of the applied forces and N is their moment about the point (a, b).

Thus, if

$$(2.411) \quad X = 0, \quad Y = 0, \quad N = 0,$$

we have $\delta W = 0$ for the most general infinitesimal displacement consistent with the constraints. Thus, by the principle of virtual work, the body is in equilibrium if (2.411) are satisfied. These are therefore sufficient conditions for the equilibrium of the body. Let us restate this important result, as follows:

If a rigid body is constrained to move parallel to a fixed fundamental plane, then the body is in equilibrium under the action of any system of external forces plane-equipollent to zero; i.e., there is equilibrium provided that the vector sum of the projections of these forces on the fundamental plane vanishes, and the moment of these forces about some one line perpendicular to the fundamental plane vanishes also.

We note that (2.411) are the same as (2.306) or (2.308), written in a slightly different form. In Sec. 2.3 these conditions were shown to be *necessary* for the equilibrium of any system; now we find them to be *sufficient* for the equilibrium of a rigid body movable parallel to the plane $z = 0$.

Let S and S' be two plane-equipollent force-systems acting on a rigid body; then X, Y, N have the same values for S and S'. It follows from (2.410) that, if δW is the virtual work done by S and $\delta W'$ that done by S' in the *same displacement* of the body parallel to the fundamental plane, then

$$\delta W = \delta W'.$$

It is evident that two plane-equipollent force systems are equivalent in all statical problems concerning the equilibrium

of a rigid body movable parallel to the fundamental plane, in the sense that one system may be replaced by a plane-equipollent system without disturbing equilibrium. In particular, two forces are equivalent if they are equal in magnitude, with the same sense and with a common line of action. Thus, we may slide a force along its line of action without changing its effect. This is known as the principle of *transmissibility of force* for a rigid body, and it enables us to regard a force acting on a rigid body as a sliding vector.

In the same way, two couples in the same plane are equivalent if they have the same moment N. Since $X = Y = 0$ for a couple, it follows from (2.410) that *the work done by a couple of moment N in an infinitesimal rotation $\delta\theta$ is $N\,\delta\theta$.*

There is no unique way in which the principles of mechanics must be developed. Two rival methods exist, the method of forces as used in Sec. 2.3 and the method of virtual work as used here. In developing the theory up to this stage, we have used one method to establish some points and the other method to establish other points. The reader may prefer to work out some other logical development of the subject, and indeed is most likely to appreciate the critical points in the chain of reasoning by so doing.

Exercise. A card lies on a table. Along the edges, there are applied forces represented in magnitude and direction by the edges, taken in order. The card is given any small displacement. Show that the work done is represented by twice the area of the card, multiplied by the angle of rotation.

Potential energy.

Consider any system of particles. We shall refer to a set of positions of all the particles as a *configuration* of the system. Let A_0 be some configuration selected as a *standard configuration*, and let A be any other configuration. Let us take the system from A to A_0, and denote by W the work done by all forces acting on the system during this process.

If the system consists of a single particle in the plane Oxy, we might take the origin O as standard configuration A_0. Then if X, Y are the components of force acting on it, the work done in bringing it from the position A is

$$(2.412) \qquad W = \int_A^O (X\,dx + Y\,dy),$$

the integral being taken along the curve by which the particle is brought to the origin. For example, if the force depends on the

position of the particle according to the equations $X = 2x$, $Y = 6y$ and if the coordinates of A are a, b, then

$$(2.413a) \quad W = \int_{a,b}^{0,0} (2x\,dx + 6y\,dy) = \Big[x^2 + 3y^2\Big]_{a,b}^{0,0}$$
$$= -a^2 - 3b^2.$$

This value is independent of the particular path along which the particle is brought to O.

To take another example, if $X = 6y$, $Y = 2x$, we have

$$(2.413b) \quad W = \int_{a,b}^{0,0} (6y\,dx + 2x\,dy).$$

The value of this integral is not independent of the path of integration, as is easily seen by taking the two paths along the sides of the rectangle $x = 0$, $y = 0$, $x = a$, $y = b$. Thus it is only in some cases that W is independent of the path.

Passing from the case of a single particle to a general system, we make the following definition.

When the forces acting on a system are such that the work done by them, in the passage of the system from a configuration A to the standard configuration A_0, is independent of the way in which this passage is carried out, then the system is said to be *conservative*. The work done by the forces in the passage from A to A_0 is called the *potential energy*[*] of the system at the configuration A.

Since the standard configuration may be chosen arbitrarily, the potential energy of a conservative system is indeterminate to within an additive constant, the value of which depends on the standard configuration chosen.

Potential energy will be denoted by V. Thus, in the case of (2.413a), the system (a single particle) is conservative and the potential energy V at the position x, y is

$$(2.414) \quad V = -x^2 - 3y^2.$$

Generally speaking, most of the systems considered in mechanics are conservative. The outstanding exceptions are systems in which frictional resistances are involved. Cases like that of (2.413b) occur rarely.

Let there be a conservative system, A_0 being the standard configuration. We shall use the following notation:

[*] Since potential energy is defined as work done, it has the same dimensions $[ML^2T^{-2}]$ and is measured in the same units as work (cf. p. 54).

$V(A)$ = potential energy at configuration A,
$W(A, B)$ = work done by forces in passage from A to B.

By the definition of V, we have

(2.415) $$V(A) = W(A, A_0).$$

Now give the system an infinitesimal displacement from A to B; let δV be the increment in potential energy and δW the work done. We have

$$\delta V = V(B) - V(A)$$
$$= W(B, A_0) - W(A, A_0).$$

But since work done is independent of path and additive, we have

$$W(B, A_0) = W(B, A) + W(A, A_0),$$

and

$$W(B, A) = -W(A, B) = -\delta W.$$

Hence we have

(2.416) $$\delta V = -\delta W.$$

In words, *the increment in potential energy equals the work done, with its sign changed.*

Consider a particle which can move in a plane subject to the action of a force which depends only on the position of the particle. If X, Y are the components of force and x, y the coordinates of the particle, then X, Y are functions of x, y. This is called a *field of force*. It is said to be a *conservative field* if the particle under its influence is a conservative system. In that case, denoting the potential energy by V, we have by (2.403) and (2.416) the equation

(2.417) $$X\,\delta x + Y\,\delta y = -\delta V,$$

where δx, δy are the components of an arbitrary infinitesimal displacement given to the particle. It follows that

(2.418) $$X = -\frac{\partial V}{\partial x}, \quad Y = -\frac{\partial V}{\partial y}.$$

The preceding result may be extended without any difficulty to a conservative field in space; we have then

(2.419) $$X = -\frac{\partial V}{\partial x}, \quad Y = -\frac{\partial V}{\partial y}, \quad Z = -\frac{\partial V}{\partial z}.$$

In the language of Sec. 1.3: *In a conservative field, the force is the gradient of potential energy, with sign reversed.*

A *uniform* field of force is one in which X, Y, Z are constants. Such a field is conservative, with potential energy

(2.420) $$V = -(Xx + Yy + Zz).$$

Returning to a general conservative system, let us note a useful consequence of (2.416) in connection with the principle of virtual work. *If a conservative system is in equilibrium, the change in potential energy in any infinitesimal displacement is zero.* This is also expressed by saying that the potential energy has a *stationary value.*

Example. As an illustrative example of the principle of virtual work, consider the system shown in Fig 25. Two heavy particles of weights w, w' are connected by a light inextensible string and hang over a fixed smooth circular cylinder of radius a, the axis of which is horizontal. We wish to find the position of equilibrium.

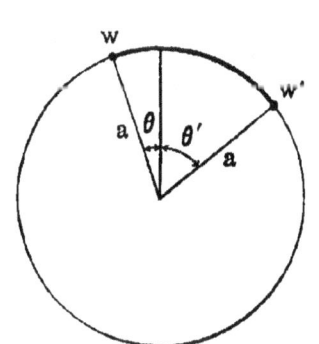

Fig. 25.—Two heavy particles balanced on a smooth cylinder.

Here we have a system of two particles. The forces acting on them are
(i) gravity,
(ii) forces due to the tension in the string,
(iii) reactions exerted by the cylinder.

If we give a virtual displacement satisfying the constraints, only gravity does work. The system is conservative, and the potential energy is, by (2.420), with suitable choice of the standard configuration,

$$V = wa \cos \theta + w'a \cos \theta',$$

where θ, θ' are the inclinations to the vertical of the radii drawn to the particles. In an infinitesimal displacement,

$$\delta V = -wa \sin \theta \, \delta\theta - w'a \sin \theta' \, \delta\theta'.$$

But $\theta + \theta'$ is constant, since the string is inextensible. Thus $\delta\theta' = -\delta\theta$, and

$$\delta V = a \, \delta\theta (w' \sin \theta' - w \sin \theta).$$

Hence, when the system is in equilibrium, the following condition must be satisfied:

$$\frac{\sin \theta}{\sin \theta'} = \frac{w'}{w}.$$

2.5. STATICALLY INDETERMINATE PROBLEMS

Consider a rigid body which can move parallel to a fixed fundamental plane, in equilibrium under external forces in that plane. Let X and Y be the total components of the external forces on axes of coordinates in the fundamental plane and N their total moment about the origin. Then, as in (2.411), we have the scalar equations of equilibrium

(2.501) $\qquad X = 0, \qquad Y = 0, \qquad N = 0$

It is important to note that these equations are *three* in number. This means that, in any problem concerning the plane statics of a rigid body, we can find *three* unknowns and no more. If there are more than three unknowns, the problem is *statically*

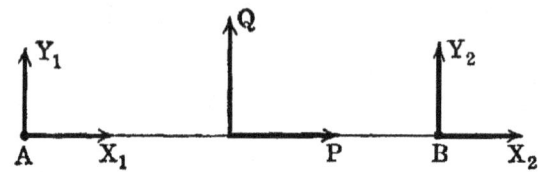

FIG. 26.—A statically indeterminate problem

indeterminate, which means that it cannot be solved by means of the conditions of equilibrium alone. We shall illustrate with a simple example.

A rigid bar AB (Fig. 26) is fixed at its ends; at its middle point there is applied a force with components P, Q along and perpendicular to the bar. Find the reactions on the bar at A and B.

Let the components of the reactions be X_1, Y_1 at A and X_2, Y_2 at B, and let $AB = 2a$. Taking components along and perpendicular to the bar and moments about A, by (2.501) we have

(2.502) $\qquad \begin{cases} X = X_1 + P + X_2 = 0, \\ Y = Y_1 + Q + Y_2 = 0, \\ N = aQ + 2aY_2 = 0. \end{cases}$

Hence,

(2.503) $\quad Y_2 = -\tfrac{1}{2}Q, \qquad Y_1 = -\tfrac{1}{2}Q, \qquad X_1 + X_2 = -P.$

We have only *three* equations for *four* unknowns; the problem is statically indeterminate, and nothing more can be found out about the reactions from the conditions of equilibrium alone.

If such a problem were to occur in physical reality, the four unknown quantities would have values which might be measured. Apparently our mathematical methods have failed us; they have not provided us with the answer to a question of physical interest. The fault actually lies in the selection of a mathematical model. Rigid bodies do not exist in nature, and this problem is one where the use of a rigid body as a mathematical model is not justified. We should take an elastic bar as a model instead (cf. Sec. 3.3).

A simple modification in the constraints may render an indeterminate problem determinate. Consider the same problem, altered by the condition that the end B, instead of being

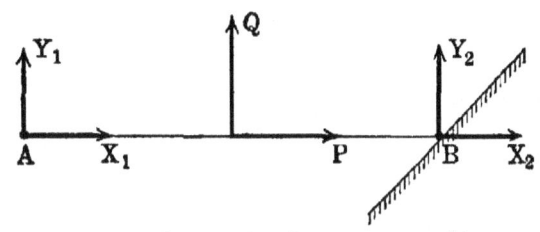

FIG. 27.—A statically determinate problem.

fixed, slides on a smooth plane inclined at an angle of 45° to AB (Fig. 27). Again, we have (2.503), but also an additional equation

(2.504) $$X_2 + Y_2 = 0,$$

arising from the condition that the reaction at B is perpendicular to the plane. Now the problem is statically determinate, and we have

(2.505) $$\begin{cases} X_1 = -P - \tfrac{1}{2}Q, & Y_1 = -\tfrac{1}{2}Q, \\ X_2 = \tfrac{1}{2}Q, & Y_2 = -\tfrac{1}{2}Q. \end{cases}$$

Had we taken one of the axes parallel to the plane of constraint at B, we should have obtained a slightly simpler treatment, because only three unknowns would have appeared.

2.6. SUMMARY OF METHODS OF PLANE STATICS

I. Conditions of equilibrium.

(a) For single particle (necessary and sufficient):

(2.601)   Vector sum of all forces vanishes,

or

(2.602) Total components in two perpendicular directions vanish.

(b) For any system (necessary) or for rigid body (necessary and sufficient):

(2.603) $\mathbf{F} = \mathbf{0}$, $N = 0$; or $X = 0$, $Y = 0$, $N = 0$.

(c) For any system with workless constraints (necessary and sufficient):

(2.604) $\delta W = 0$ (work done by applied forces).

II. Moment of a vector in a plane about a point in that plane.

(2.605) $\quad M = \pm aP \quad$ (+ for counterclockwise),
(2.606) $\quad M = xY - yX \quad$ (about origin).

III. Plane equipollence.

(a) Conditions for plane equipollence:

(2.607) $\quad \mathbf{F} = \mathbf{F}', \quad N = N'$.

(b) General system of forces can be reduced to a single force at an assigned point, together with a couple.

(c) General system of forces can be reduced to a single force or to a single couple (latter case exceptional).

IV. Work and potential energy.

(a) Definition of work:

(2.608) $\quad \delta W = P \cos \theta \cdot \delta s = X \delta x + Y \delta y$.

(b) Reactions do no work at smooth contacts, rolling contacts, and inside rigid body.

(c) For the infinitesimal displacement of a rigid body,

(2.609) $\quad \delta W = X \delta a + Y \delta b + N \delta \theta$.

(d) Potential energy:

(2.610) $\quad \delta V = -\delta W$,
(2.611) $\quad X = -\dfrac{\partial V}{\partial x}, \quad Y = -\dfrac{\partial V}{\partial y}$.

(Force is gradient of potential energy with sign reversed.)

EXERCISES II

The method of virtual work may be used in any of these problems; it will be found particularly useful in the case of those marked with an asterisk.

1. A particle is in equilibrium under the action of six forces. Three of these forces are reversed, and the particle remains in equilibrium. Prove that it will still remain in equilibrium if these three forces are removed altogether.

2. A ladder of weight W rests at an angle α to the horizontal, with its ends resting on a smooth floor and against a smooth vertical wall. The lower end is joined by a rope to the junction of the wall and the floor. Find, in terms of W and α, the tension of the rope and the reactions at the wall and the ground. (Assume that the weight of the ladder acts at its middle point.)

3. The corner A of a square plate $ABCD$ is held fixed by means of a smooth hinge which permits the plate to turn freely in its own plane. Four forces, each of magnitude P, act along the four sides in order. Find the single additional force which, applied at the center of the plate parallel to the side AB, will keep the plate in equilibrium. What is the corresponding reaction at the hinge?

4. A door of weight W, height $2a$, and width $2b$ is hinged at the top and bottom. If the reaction at the upper hinge has no vertical component, find the components of reaction at both hinges. (Assume that the weight of the door acts at its center.)

5. A particle of weight W is suspended from a fixed point by a light string. A horizontal force H is applied to it, and the particle takes up a position of equilibrium with the string inclined to the vertical. If the string breaks when the tension in it reaches a value T_0, find the smallest value of H necessary to break the string.

6. A heavy beam AB, 8 ft long, rests horizontally on two supports, one at A and the other 3 ft from B. If the greatest weight that can be hung from B without upsetting the beam is 20 lb., find the weight of the beam. (Assume that the weight of the beam acts at its middle point.)

7. Show that if a light cable passes round a pulley mounted on smooth bearings, the tensions in the portions on either side of the pulley are equal. Hence find the tension T in the cable for the pulley system shown, supporting a weight W, the pulleys and cable being supposed light and the distance between the upper and lower pulleys so great that the cables may be regarded as vertical.

8. A force of magnitude P, acting up and along a smooth inclined plane, can support a weight W; when acting horizontally, it can support a weight w. Find a relation among P, W, and w, not involving the inclination of the plane.

9. Four lamps each weighing 4 lb. are suspended across a road between posts 40 ft. apart by light cords attached at points B, C, D, E of a cord

$ABCDEF$, whose ends A and F are fixed at the same level to the posts The cords supporting the lamps divide the horizontal distance between the posts into equal parts. C and D are 12 ft below AF Find the tension in CD.

***10.** A light rigid rod of length $2b$, terminated by heavy particles of weights w, W, is placed inside a smooth hemispherical bowl of radius a, which is fixed with its rim horizontal If the particle of weight w rests just below the rim of the bowl, prove that

$$wa^2 = W(2b^2 - a^2).$$

11. A system of forces acting on a rigid body consists of n forces acting along the n sides of a closed polygon taken in order. If the magnitudes of the forces are proportional to the lengths of the sides along which they act, show that the system reduces to a couple whose moment is proportional to the area enclosed by the polygon, a proper convention as regards the sign of this area being made. Give a simple example of such a system of forces which would keep a rigid body in equilibrium

12. Explain why in a motion picture the spokes of a rotating wheel sometimes appear to be moving the wrong way

13. A force P of constant magnitude and fixed direction is applied to one end of an arm of length a, which can turn about the other end in a plane containing the direction of P Find the total work done by the force as it pulls the arm into its own direction from a position perpendicular to it.

14. Show that a field of force with components (X, Y) is conservative if, and only if,

$$\frac{\partial X}{\partial y} = \frac{\partial Y}{\partial x}$$

15. Find the potential energy of a particle attracted toward a fixed point by a force of magnitude k^2/r^n, r being the distance from the fixed point and k, n any constants.

*16. A light lever, in the form of a letter L with arms a and b, is pivoted at the angle so that it can turn freely in a vertical plane. Weights W, w are suspended from the ends. Show that there are just two positions of equilibrium.

*17. To a number of fixed points $A_1, A_2, \cdots, A_n$, situated at equal intervals a on a straight line inclined at an angle θ to the horizontal, there are attached rods all of the same length a and weight w. The other ends of these rods, $B_1, B_2, \quad , B_n$, are connected by rods of the same length a and weight w The system hangs in a vertical plane, forming a set of squares, A_1 and B_2 being connected by a light rigid rod Find the reaction in this rod, assuming that all the joints are smooth and that the weight of each rod acts as its middle point.

*18. A framework $ABCD$ consists of four equal, light rods smoothly jointed together to form a square; it is suspended from a peg at A, and a weight W is attached to C, the framework being kept in shape by a light rod connecting B and D. Determine the thrust in this rod

19. A number of coplanar forces act on a rigid body All the forces are turned in their plane through the same angle θ about their points of application, without change of magnitude. Show that their resultant turns through the angle θ about a fixed point in the body. (This point is called the *astatic center*)

20. Four forces of magnitudes 1, 3, 4, 6 act in order along the sides of a square $ABCD$ of side a, the force of magnitude 1 acting along AB. Choosing as axes in the plane the lines AB and AD, find the equation of the line of action of the resultant force Find also the position of the astatic center (see Exercise 19), if one force only is considered as acting through each corner of the square and the force of magnitude 1 acts at A.

CHAPTER III

APPLICATIONS IN PLANE STATICS

In this chapter we shall be concerned chiefly with systems lying in a plane. However, mass centers and centers of gravity are here discussed for systems in space; the presence of a third coordinate causes no real complication.

3.1. MASS CENTERS AND CENTERS OF GRAVITY

Definition of mass center.

Consider a system of n particles of masses $m_1, m_2, \cdots m_n$, situated at points $P_1, P_2, \cdots P_n$. If the position vectors of these points relative to some assigned point are $\mathbf{r}_1, \mathbf{r}_2, \cdots \mathbf{r}_n$, we define the *linear moment* of the system with respect to that point to be the vector

$$\sum_{i=1}^{n} m_i \mathbf{r}_i.$$

The *mass center* of the system is defined to be that point with respect to which the linear moment vanishes. To show that this definition is significant, we have to prove two things: (i) a mass center exists; (ii) there is only one mass center.

To establish the existence of a mass center, we take any point O; let the position vectors of $P_1, P_2, \cdots P_n$ relative to O be $\mathbf{r}_1, \mathbf{r}_2, \cdots \mathbf{r}_n$. Let C be the point such that

(3.101) $$\overrightarrow{OC} = \frac{\sum_{i=1}^{n} m_i \mathbf{r}_i}{\sum_{i=1}^{n} m_i}.$$

Then the position vector of the point P_i relative to C is

$$\mathbf{r}_i - \overrightarrow{OC},$$

and so the linear moment of the system with respect to C is

$$\sum_{i=1}^{n} m_i(\mathbf{r}_i - \overrightarrow{OC}) = \sum_{i=1}^{n} m_i \mathbf{r}_i - \overrightarrow{OC} \sum_{i=1}^{n} m_i.$$

But this vanishes by (3 101), and therefore C is a mass center.

To establish the uniqueness of the mass center, we assume that there are two mass centers C, C', relative to which the position vectors of the particles are $\mathbf{r}_1, \mathbf{r}_2, \cdots \mathbf{r}_n$ and $\mathbf{r}'_1, \mathbf{r}'_2, \cdots \mathbf{r}'_n$, respectively. Then,

(3.102) $$\sum_{i=1}^{n} m_i \mathbf{r}_i = 0, \qquad \sum_{i=1}^{n} m_i \mathbf{r}'_i = 0.$$

But

$$\mathbf{r}_i = \mathbf{r}'_i + \overrightarrow{CC'};$$

combined with (3 102), this leads to $\overrightarrow{CC'} = 0$, so that C and C' coincide

Equation (3.101) gives the position vector of the mass center relative to an arbitrary origin O; *this position vector is the quotient of the linear moment by the total mass.* It follows that the linear moment of a system is the same as that of a particle, having a mass equal to the total mass of the system, situated at its mass center.

If the system consists of only two particles, with masses m_1, m_2, the definition shows that the mass center lies on the line joining them and divides it in the ratio $m_2:m_1$.

For the calculation of mass centers, it is convenient to have (3.101) in scalar form; referred to any axes, the coordinates of the mass center are

(3.103) $$\bar{x} = \frac{\sum_{i=1}^{n} m_i x_i}{\sum_{i=1}^{n} m_i}, \qquad \bar{y} = \frac{\sum_{i=1}^{n} m_i y_i}{\sum_{i=1}^{n} m_i}, \qquad \bar{z} = \frac{\sum_{i=1}^{n} m_i z_i}{\sum_{i=1}^{n} m_i}.$$

The numerators are, of course, the components of the linear moment with respect to the origin.

It is important to note that when we move a system of particles rigidly (i.e., without changing mutual distances), the mass center is carried along as if rigidly attached to the system.

This follows from (3.103). For let $Oxyz$ be any set of axes and $O'x'y'z'$ a new set of axes, such that the new position of the system relative to $O'x'y'z'$ is the same as the old position relative to $Oxyz$; this means that $x_i' = x_i$, $y_i' = y_i$, $z_i' = z_i$. Then the coordinates of the new mass center relative to $O'x'y'z'$ will be the same three numbers as the coordinates of the old mass center relative to $Oxyz$, and hence the new mass center occupies the same position relative to the system as the old one did.

Let us now consider a continuous distribution of matter instead of a system of particles. Viewing the continuous distribution as the limit of the discontinuous system, we are led to associate a definite mass with any volume in the continuous distribution. *Density* is defined as mass per unit volume; by this we mean that the density ρ is

$$(3.104) \qquad \rho = \lim \frac{\Delta m}{\Delta v},$$

where Δm is the mass in the volume Δv and the sign "lim" means "limit as Δv contracts to a point." In an infinitesimal volume dv the mass is

$$(3.105) \qquad dm = \rho\, dv.$$

In *homogeneous* bodies (with which we shall be chiefly concerned), ρ is a constant. If ρ varies from point to point in a body, the body is said to be *heterogeneous*.

The definition given above for the linear moment of a discontinuous system suggests that the linear moment of a continuous system should be defined as

$$\iiint \mathbf{r}\rho\, dx\, dy\, dz,$$

where $\mathbf{r}$ is the position vector of a general point of the system and ρ the density at that point. This vector has components

$$\iiint x\rho\, dx\, dy\, dz, \qquad \iiint y\rho\, dx\, dy\, dz, \qquad \iiint z\rho\, dx\, dy\, dz$$

The previous definition of mass center leads us to the statement that the mass center is that point for which, taken as origin, we have

$$(3.106) \quad \iiint x\rho\, dx\, dy\, dz = 0, \quad \iiint y\rho\, dx\, dy\, dz = 0,$$
$$\iiint z\rho\, dx\, dy\, dz = 0.$$

SEC. 3.1]   APPLICATIONS IN PLANE STATICS   77

To find the mass center we may use (3.103), changed into continuous form. Thus, for any axes, the mass center has coordinates

(3.107) $\quad \bar{x} = \dfrac{\iiint x\rho\, dx\, dy\, dz}{\iiint \rho\, dx\, dy\, dz}, \qquad \bar{y} = \dfrac{\iiint y\rho\, dx\, dy\, dz}{\iiint \rho\, dx\, dy\, dz},$
$$\bar{z} = \dfrac{\iiint z\rho\, dx\, dy\, dz}{\iiint \rho\, dx\, dy\, dz}.$$

Consideration of a system of particles lying in or very close to a plane or surface leads to the idealized concept of a continuous distribution of matter on a plane or surface; we introduce a quantity σ called *surface density*, such that the mass of an infinitesimal area dS of the surface is $\sigma\, dS$. The mass center of a surface distribution has coordinates

(3.108) $\quad \bar{x} = \dfrac{\iint x\sigma\, dS}{\iint \sigma\, dS}, \qquad \bar{y} = \dfrac{\iint y\sigma\, dS}{\iint \sigma\, dS}, \qquad \bar{z} = \dfrac{\iint z\sigma\, dS}{\iint \sigma\, dS}$

Similarly, we consider a continuous distribution of matter along a line or curve; we introduce a quantity λ called the *line density*, such that the mass of an element ds is $\lambda\, ds$. The mass center of a curvilinear distribution has coordinates

(3.109) $\quad \bar{x} = \dfrac{\int x\lambda\, ds}{\int \lambda\, ds}, \qquad \bar{y} = \dfrac{\int y\lambda\, ds}{\int \lambda\, ds}, \qquad \bar{z} = \dfrac{\int z\lambda\, ds}{\int \lambda\, ds}.$

In (3.107), (3.108), and (3.109) the denominator in each case represents the total mass of the system.

In the case of uniform distributions of mass (i.e., distributions of constant volume density, surface density, or line density, as the case may be), the density factor comes outside the signs of integration and so disappears by cancellation from (3.107), (3.108), and (3.109).

Methods of symmetry and decomposition.

In cases of symmetry, it is possible to locate the mass center (or, at any rate, limit its position) without any calculation.

A system is said to have *central symmetry* with respect to a point O if the system is left unchanged by reflection in the point O. (By reflection we mean that a particle or element of mass m at A is replaced by a particle or element of mass m at B, where $\overrightarrow{OB} = -\overrightarrow{OA}$.) For such a system, it is immediately seen that the mass center coincides with the center of sym-

78   *PLANE MECHANICS*   [Sec. 3.1

metry, because the linear moment about that point consists of contributions which cancel in pairs.

A system has a *plane of symmetry* if the system is left unchanged by reflection in a plane. It is easily seen that in such cases the mass center lies in the plane of symmetry.

A system has an *axis of symmetry* if the system is left unchanged by a rotation of arbitrary magnitude about the axis. It is not difficult to show that the mass center lies on the axis of symmetry.

Thus, for example, it is evident that

(i) The mass center of a solid sphere lies at its geometrical center, when the sphere is homogeneous or when the density depends only on the distance from the center.

(ii) The mass center of a solid homogeneous hemisphere lies on the radius which is perpendicular to its plane face.

(iii) The mass center of a plate in the form of an equilateral triangle (of uniform density and thickness) lies at the centroid.

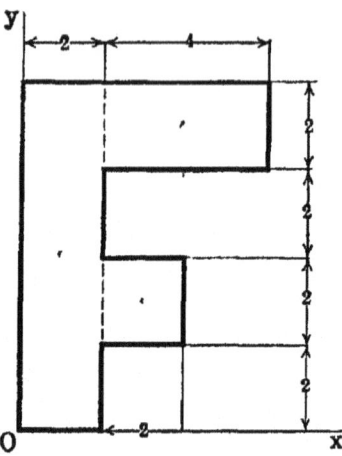

Fig. 28.—A letter F is cut out of metal sheeting. The position of the mass center is required.

Sometimes we meet distributions of matter which may be decomposed into simple parts, the mass centers of which can be found. Such a system is shown in Fig. 28, the lines of decomposition being dotted. We shall now establish the following *principle of decomposition:* If a system is decomposed into parts with masses $M_1, M_2, \cdots M_n$ and mass centers at the points $P_1, P_2, \cdots P_n$, then the mass center of the complete system is at the mass center of the system of n particles of masses $M_1, M_2, \cdots M_n$, situated at the points $P_1, P_2, \cdots P_n$.

We shall prove this principle for a system of particles, the proof for a continuous system being similar. Further, for simplicity we shall suppose that the system is decomposed into three parts, since the proof for n parts is similar. The proof rests on the fact that linear moments are additive; this is obvious from the definition of linear moment. Thus the linear moment

of the complete system is the sum of the linear moments of the three parts. But by (3.101) the linear moment of each part is the same as the linear moment of a particle situated at its mass center, having a mass equal to the mass of the part in question. Hence the linear moment of the complete system is equal to the sum of the linear moments of the three particles, and both vanish when they are calculated relative to the mass center of the complete system. This point is therefore the mass center of the three particles.

In the case of the plate shown in Fig. 28, the reader should verify by this method that the mass center lies at $x = \frac{15}{7}$, $y = \frac{33}{7}$.

The principle of decomposition may also be expressed as follows: For the calculation of mass centers, any part of a system may be replaced by a representative particle, situated at the mass center of the part and having a mass equal to the mass of the part.

In applying the method of decomposition, it is often convenient to decompose the system into infinitesimal portions. Generally the use of such a decomposition will require a process of integration, but sometimes this can be avoided. Thus, if a triangular plate is decomposed into thin strips, the representative particles lie on the median of the triangle which bisects these strips. Hence the mass center lies on each of the medians; the mass center of a triangle is therefore at the centroid.

By an extension of the same method, it is easily seen that the mass center of a solid tetrahedron lies at the point of intersection of the lines joining the vertices to the centroids of the opposite faces.

If we wish to find the mass center of a body with a hole in it, we can regard the body as a superposition of the complete body with no hole and a fictitious body of negative density (equal in absolute value to the density of the body) occupying the position of the hole. Thus, if a circular hole of radius 1 in. is punched from a circular disk of radius 4 in., the edge of the hole passing through the center of the disk, the mass center is that of a pair of particles with masses in the ratio $16 : -1$ situated at the centers of the circles. Hence the mass center lies at a distance of $\frac{1}{15}$ in. from the center of the larger circle.

Theorems of Pappus.

Our knowledge of certain surface areas and volumes enables us to calculate some mass centers quickly by means of the theorems of Pappus, which state

I. Let there be a uniform distribution of mass along a plane curve C, which does not cross a straight line L in the same plane. Let p be the distance of the mass center from L, l the length of C, and S the surface area generated by rotating C about L, to form a surface of revolution. Then

$$(3.110) \qquad 2\pi p l = S$$

II. Let there be a uniform distribution of mass on a region R of a plane. Let L be a line in the plane, not crossing R. Let p be the distance of the mass center from L, A the area of R, and V the volume generated by rotating R about L, to form a solid of revolution. Then

$$(3.111) \qquad 2\pi p A = V.$$

To prove these theorems, we take axes Oxy, Ox lying along L in each case. Then, in the case of I, by (3.109) we have

$$p = \int y \, ds / l$$

the integral being taken along C. But

$$S = \int 2\pi y \, ds,$$

and hence (3.110) follows. In the case of II, by (3.108) we have

$$p = \int y \, dx \, dy / A,$$

the integral being taken over R. But

$$V = \int 2\pi y \, dx \, dy,$$

and hence (3.111) follows. Thus the theorems of Pappus are established.

As an example of the use of the first theorem, consider a wire bent into the form of a semicircle of radius a. We take for L the diameter joining the ends. Then

$$(3.112) \qquad l = \pi a, \qquad S = 4\pi a^2, \qquad p = \frac{S}{2\pi l} = \frac{2a}{\pi}.$$

As an example of the use of the second theorem, consider a flat semicircular plate. We take for L the terminating diameter. Then

$$(3.113) \qquad A = \tfrac{1}{2}\pi a^2, \qquad V = \tfrac{4}{3}\pi a^3, \qquad p = \frac{V}{2\pi A} = \frac{4a}{3\pi}.$$

SEC. 3 1]   APPLICATIONS IN PLANE STATICS   81

Mass centers found by integration.

Though much labor may be saved by using the methods of symmetry and decomposition or the theorems of Pappus, it is evident from (3.107), (3 108), and (3 109) that when these methods fail we can fall back on direct integration. Usually a judicious mixture of the several methods will yield the result most rapidly. As illustrations, we shall calculate the mass centers of a wire bent to form a quadrant of a circle, a solid hemisphere, and a thin hemispherical shell.

In terms of polar coordinates r, θ in its plane, the equation of a quadrant of a circle may be written $r = a$, with θ running from 0 to $\frac{1}{2}\pi$. The length of an element is $r\, d\theta$; and with $x = r \cos \theta$, $y = r \sin \theta$, the Cartesian coordinates of the mass center are, by (3 109),

$$(3.114) \quad \begin{cases} \bar{x} = \int_0^{\frac{1}{2}\pi} a \cos \theta \cdot a\, d\theta \Big/ \int_0^{\frac{1}{2}\pi} a\, d\theta = \frac{2a}{\pi}, \\ \bar{y} = \int_0^{\frac{1}{2}\pi} a \sin \theta \cdot a\, d\theta \Big/ \int_0^{\frac{1}{2}\pi} a\, d\theta = \frac{2a}{\pi}. \end{cases}$$

The mass center lies on the radius bisecting the arc at a distance $2\sqrt{2} \cdot a/\pi$ from the center. The reader may compare (3.114) with (3.112) and consider how (3 114) might have been deduced from (3.112) without calculation

We may decompose a solid hemisphere into thin circular plates parallel to the plane face. The distance of the mass center from the plane face is thus

$$\bar{z} = \int_{z=0}^{a} z \cdot \pi r^2\, dz \Big/ \int_{z=0}^{a} \pi r^2\, dz,$$

where r is the radius of the circular section at a distance z from the plane face. But $r^2 = a^2 - z^2$, where a is the radius of the spherical surface. Hence,

$$(3.115) \quad \bar{z} = \tfrac{3}{8}a.$$

We may decompose a thin hemispherical shell into thin circular bands by means of planes drawn parallel to the open face. If θ is the angle between any radius and the radius perpendicular to the open face, the area of the band between θ and $\theta + d\theta$ is $2\pi a^2 \sin \theta\, d\theta$, where a is the radius of the shell. Hence the height of the mass center above the open face is

$$\text{(3.116)} \qquad \bar{z} = \frac{\int_0^{\frac{1}{2}\pi} a \cos\theta \cdot 2\pi a^2 \sin\theta\, d\theta}{\int_0^{\frac{1}{2}\pi} 2\pi a^2 \sin\theta\, d\theta} = \tfrac{1}{2}a.$$

Historically, this result is famous; it was obtained by Archimedes through comparison of the shell with a cylinder of the same radius, and length equal to the radius, containing the hemisphere and touching it along the edge of its open face. It is easy to show that two adjacent planes parallel to the open face intercept the same areas on the hemisphere and the cylinder. These two areas contribute the same linear moment, and so the mass centers of the hemisphere and the cylinder coincide; from this fact the result follows.

Gravitation.

A body falls to the ground unless it is held up by suitable forces. This is due to gravitational attraction between the body and the earth. Every body attracts every other body, and we accept as one of our hypotheses the following law:

NEWTON'S LAW OF GRAVITATION. *If two particles of masses m_1, m_2 are at a distance r apart, each attracts the other with a gravitational force of magnitude*

$$\frac{Gm_1m_2}{r^2},$$

where G is a universal constant, called the constant of gravitation. The forces act along the line joining the particles, in accordance with the law of action and reaction stated in Sec. 1.4.

If we think of the particle of mass m_1 as fixed and that of mass m_2 as free to take up various positions, we recognize that the mass m_1 produces a field of force. It is usual to take $m_2 = 1$ for simplicity in discussing this field; then the magnitude of the force of attraction is Gm_1/r^2.

If we take coordinates with origin O at m_1, the direction cosines of the line drawn from O to any point A with coordinates x, y, z are $x/r, y/r, z/r$. Hence the components of force on unit mass at A are

$$\text{(3.117)} \quad X = -\frac{Gm_1 x}{r^3}, \qquad Y = -\frac{Gm_1 y}{r^3}, \qquad Z = -\frac{Gm_1 z}{r^3},$$

the minus sign occurring since the force is directed from A toward O. Now

$$r^2 = x^2 + y^2 + z^2, \quad r\frac{\partial r}{\partial x} = x, \quad \frac{\partial r}{\partial x} = \frac{x}{r}, \quad \frac{\partial}{\partial x}\left(\frac{1}{r}\right) = -\frac{x}{r^3};$$

therefore (3.117) may be written

(3.118) $\quad X = -\dfrac{\partial V}{\partial x}, \quad Y = -\dfrac{\partial V}{\partial y}, \quad Z = -\dfrac{\partial V}{\partial z},$

where

(3.119) $\quad\quad\quad\quad V = -\dfrac{Gm_1}{r}.$

This is the potential energy (cf. 2.419) of a particle of unit mass in the gravitational field of a particle of mass m_1, or, briefly, the *potential* of the field. Thus *the force of attraction is the gradient of the potential, with sign reversed.* When a number of attracting particles are present, the resultant force of attraction is the vector sum of the individual forces of attraction. This resultant force is equal to the negative of the gradient of the total potential, i.e., the sum of the potentials due to the several particles. In calculating the force of attraction due to a system of particles (or a continuous distribution of matter), it is often convenient to find the potential first.

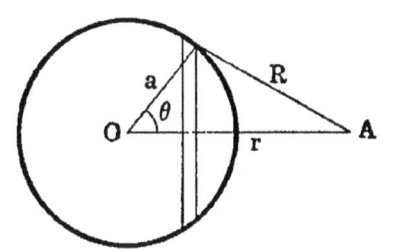

FIG. 29.—A spherical shell divided into thin rings for the calculation of the potential at A.

Let us consider a thin spherical shell of matter of radius a (Fig. 29). We wish to find the potential at an external point A, at a distance r from the center O.

Let us draw cones with O for vertex, OA for axis, and semivertical angles θ, $\theta + d\theta$. These cut off from the shell a ring of area $2\pi a^2 \sin\theta\, d\theta$. The elements of this ring are all at the same distance (R) from A, and so the potential due to the ring is

$$-2\pi G\sigma a^2 \sin\theta\, d\theta/R,$$

where σ is the mass per unit area of the shell. Expressing R in terms of a, r, θ and integrating over the shell, we find for the potential

$$(3.120) \quad V = -\int_0^\pi \frac{2\pi G\sigma a^2 \sin\theta\, d\theta}{\sqrt{r^2 + a^2 - 2ra\cos\theta}}$$
$$= -\frac{2\pi G\sigma a}{r}[\sqrt{(r+a)^2} - \sqrt{(r-a)^2}],$$

the positive values of the square roots being understood. Since $r > a$, the last square root is $r - a$, and so

$$(3.121) \qquad V = -\frac{4\pi G\sigma a^2}{r} = -\frac{GM}{r},$$

where M is the total mass of the shell.

Thus we have the following result. *The potential (and hence the force of attraction) of a thin spherical shell at any external point is the same as if the whole mass of the shell were concentrated at its center.*

If the point A lies inside the shell instead of outside, we proceed as before down to (3.120). But now $a > r$, and so the last square root is $a - r$. Hence

$$V = -4\pi G\sigma a,$$

a constant. Thus, inside a thin spherical shell the potential is constant, and the force of attraction is zero.

We can now discuss the gravitational field of the earth, supposing it to be composed of thin spherical shells, each of constant density. Each shell attracts as if its mass were concentrated at the center of the earth. Hence we have the following result: *At a point A, outside the earth, the force of attraction is directed toward the center of the earth and is of magnitude*

$$(3.122) \qquad \frac{GM}{r^2},$$

where M is the mass of the earth and r the distance of A from the center of the earth.

In particular, if r is the radius of the earth, (3.122) gives the force of attraction at the earth's surface. The constant G is very small (6.67×10^{-8} c.g.s. unit), and so gravitational forces are insignificant unless the masses involved are great. For this reason we usually neglect the mutual attractions of bodies on the earth's surface in comparison with the earth's attraction.

Centers of gravity.

We consider now a body near the earth's surface, the body being small in comparison with the earth's radius (We have in mind a piece of laboratory apparatus or even a large engineering structure, but not anything which would be of appreciable size on a map of the world.) Throughout this body the direction and

SEC. 3.1]   APPLICATIONS IN PLANE STATICS   85

magnitude of the earth's attraction are nearly constant. This leads us to the construction of the following model for the discussion of gravity near the earth's surface: *The earth's surface (or the ground) is represented by a plane (the horizontal plane). The earth's attraction on a particle of mass m is of magnitude mg, where g is a constant; it is directed vertically downward (i e., perpendicular to and toward the ground).* The value of g is approximately 32 ft. sec.$^{-2}$, or 980 cm. sec.$^{-2}$

We shall now show that there is just one point C, the *center of gravity* of a body, which satisfies the following conditions:

(i) *The potential energy of the body is equal to that of a single particle with mass equal to the total mass of the body, situated at C.*

(ii) *The whole system of forces due to gravity is plane-equipollent (with respect to any vertical plane) to a single vertical force through C.*

Let us take axes $Oxyz$, Ox and Oz being horizontal and Oy vertical. Let us choose O as standard position for each of the particles forming the body. Then a particle of mass m_i at the point (x_i, y_i, z_i) has by (2.120) potential energy $m_i g y_i$, and so the whole potential energy is (for n particles)

$$(3.123) \qquad V = g \sum_{i=1}^{n} m_i y_i.$$

Let the coordinates of C be x, y, z; condition (i) is equivalent to

$$(3.124) \qquad V = Mgy,$$

where M is the total mass of the body. Hence, comparing the two expressions for V, we have

$$y = \frac{\sum_{i=1}^{n} m_i y_i}{M}$$

The condition of plane equipollence with respect to the plane $z = 0$ demands that

$$Mgx = \sum_{i=1}^{n} m_i g x_i,$$

these being moments about Oz. Hence

$$x = \frac{\sum_{i=1}^{n} m_i x_i}{M}.$$

Similarly,
$$z = \frac{\sum_{i=1}^{n} m_i z_i}{M}.$$

Thus the center of gravity C exists, with coordinates

(3.125) $\quad x = \dfrac{\sum_{i=1}^{n} m_i x_i}{M}, \quad y = \dfrac{\sum_{i=1}^{n} m_i y_i}{M}, \quad z = \dfrac{\sum_{i=1}^{n} m_i z_i}{M}.$

We note, on referring to (3.103), that the center of gravity is in fact the same point as the mass center.

The force Mg, directed downward through the center of gravity, is called the *weight* of the body.

An accurate treatment of statics on the earth's surface is complicated by the earth's rotation about its axis and its motion round the sun. However, the effects due to these causes are very small, and we may neglect them without making serious physical errors. In fact, we get satisfactory results by treating the earth as a Newtonian frame of reference. Likewise, another simplification introduced above (the assumption that the earth is flat, with a uniform gravitational field) does not cause serious physical errors. So, if we do not wish to obtain results of extremely high physical accuracy, we may use the model described above; this is, in fact, the procedure throughout the rest of the chapter

The effects of the rotation of the earth are considered in Sec. 5.3 and also in Sec. 13.5. It will be shown that, as far as statics is concerned, this introduces no real complication; it merely modifies the value of g.

3.2. FRICTION

In Sec. 2.4 we introduced the concept of a smooth surface; the essential property is that, at a smooth contact, the reaction is normal to the surface. We shall now discuss the reaction at a rough contact and state the laws of friction.

Laws of static and kinetic friction.

Let A and B (Fig. 30) be two bodies in contact. Let **R** be the reaction exerted by B on A. **R** can be resolved in a unique manner into the forces **N** and **F**, **N** lying along the normal at the point of contact and **F** lying in the plane of contact. **N** is called the *normal reaction* and **F** the *force of friction*. (At a smooth contact, **F** = 0.)

On the basis of experiment, certain *laws of friction* are accepted. These are mathematical idealizations from the experimental results, and a high degree of accuracy in predictions based on these laws is not to be expected.

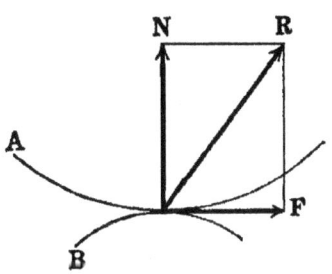

FIG. 30.—The reaction **R** at a rough contact resolved into the normal reaction (**N**) and the force of friction (**F**).

LAW OF STATIC FRICTION. *When two surfaces are in contact and no slipping takes place, the ratio F/N cannot exceed a number μ, the coefficient of static friction, which depends only on the nature of the surfaces.*

In statical problems the two bodies will be at rest, but the above statement is sufficiently general to cover the case where one body rolls on another.

The acute angle λ defined by

$$(3.201) \qquad \tan \lambda = \mu$$

is called the *angle of friction*. It is seen at once that the law of static friction

$$(3.202) \qquad \frac{F}{N} \leq \mu$$

implies

$$(3.203) \qquad \theta \leq \lambda,$$

where θ is the inclination of the reaction **R** to the normal. Thus the direction of **R** must lie inside the *cone of static friction*, formed by drawing all lines inclined to the normal at an angle λ.

When one body slides on another, the behavior of the reaction is controlled by the law of kinetic friction. We shall state this law for the case where one body is at rest.

LAW OF KINETIC FRICTION. *When one surface slides on another which is at rest, the force of friction **F** on the former acts*

in the direction opposed to the direction of motion of the particle at the point of contact, and

$$(3.204) \qquad \frac{F}{N} = \mu',$$

where μ' is the *coefficient of kinetic friction*, which depends only on the nature of the surfaces.*

If both surfaces are moving, the law has the same form except that the direction of the force of friction is opposed to the direction of relative motion.

The *angle of kinetic friction* λ' is defined by

$$(3.205) \qquad \tan \lambda' = \mu'.$$

As an experimental result, μ' is less than μ; μ is always less than unity.†

Problems in static friction often present considerable difficulty because the fundamental relation (3.202) is an inequality and, in mathematics, inequalities are usually more difficult to handle than equations. This difficulty may, however, be overcome by treating cases of *limiting friction*, for which

$$(3.206) \qquad \frac{F}{N} = \mu.$$

When this relation holds, the system is on the point of slipping

Some problems on friction.

Example 1. A light ladder is supported on a rough floor and leans against a smooth wall. How far up the ladder can a man climb without slipping taking place?

In Fig. 31, AB is the ladder and C is the man (replaced by a particle) Only three forces act on the ladder: (i) the weight of the man (W); (ii) the reaction at the wall, this reaction being horizontal on account of the smoothness of the wall; (iii) the reaction of the ground. The lines of action of the first two meet at D. Hence the line of action of (iii) must pass through D, and hence the angle DBE, where BE is vertical, must not exceed the angle of friction λ. Thus the highest position that the man can reach may be found as follows: Draw a line through B, making an angle λ with BE; let it cut the horizontal through A at D; through D, draw a vertical; the point C

---

* This quantity will be denoted by μ when there can be no confusion with the coefficient of static friction

† For further details regarding friction, see P P. Ewald, Th Pöschl, and L. Prandtl, The Physics of Solids and Fluids (Blackie & Son, Ltd., Glasgow, 1930), p. 67.

where this line cuts the ladder is the required highest position. This method is called *descriptive* or *graphical*, because the result may be obtained by drawing to scale.

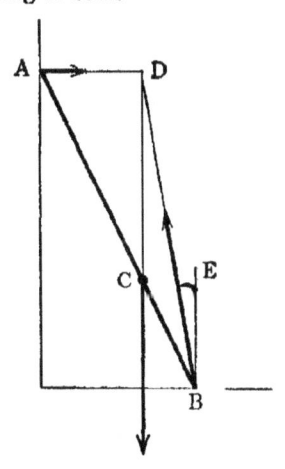

Fig. 31.—The ladder problem for a smooth wall (descriptive method).

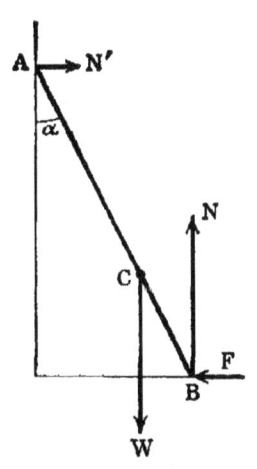

Fig. 32.—The ladder problem for a smooth wall (analytical method).

Let us now discuss the same problem analytically. Figure 32 shows the forces acting on the ladder. Let α be the inclination of the ladder to the vertical. The total vertical component must vanish, thus

$$N - W = 0.$$

The total horizontal component must vanish; thus

$$N' - F = 0$$

The total moment about B must vanish; thus

$$W \cdot BC \sin \alpha - N' \cdot AB \cos \alpha = 0$$

Hence

$$F = N' = W \frac{BC}{AB} \tan \alpha,$$
$$N = W,$$
$$\frac{F}{N} = \frac{BC}{AB} \tan \alpha.$$

Thus, by (3.202),

$$\frac{BC}{AB} \tan \alpha \leq \mu.$$

The highest point C attainable is given by

(3.207) $$BC = AB\mu \cot \alpha$$

The analytical method appears more complicated than the descriptive, but it has the advantage of being more systematic. Moreover, since the

three conditions of equilibrium give all possible information, the solution of the problem is reduced to algebra as soon as they are written down.

It might be thought that in drawing the arrow for the force of friction to the left in Fig. 32, we were anticipating the result. This is not actually the case. When we draw an arrow in connection with a component of a force, we are simply indicating the sense in which this component is considered positive. Had we drawn the arrow to the right in Fig. 32, we should have obtained equations as above, but with the sign of F reversed. The final physical result would have been the same.

However, since positive quantities are easier to think of than negative quantities, it is advisable whenever possible to draw the arrows in the senses in which the forces really act. Thus, in the case of N, we draw the arrow upward. As for friction, it is generally found that the force of friction acts in the direction opposed to the motion which would take place in its absence. That is why the arrow for F in Fig. 32 was drawn to the left.

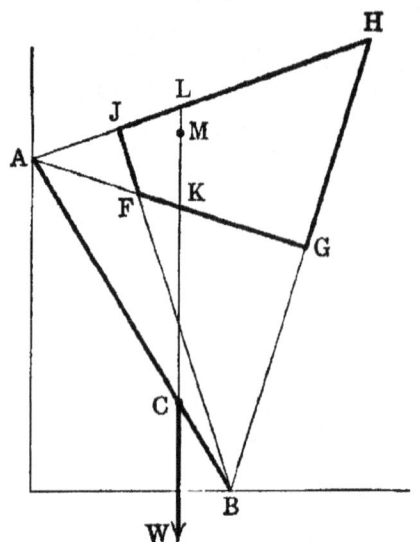

FIG. 33.—The ladder problem for a rough wall (descriptive method)

FIG. 34.—The ladder problem for a rough wall (analytical method)

Example 2. The preceding problem modified by supposing both wall and floor to be rough, with the same coefficient of friction μ.

Consider the cones of friction at A and B. They will cut the plane of the paper in four lines as shown in Fig. 33, these four lines giving the quadrilateral $FGHJ$. Draw the vertical through C, the position of the man, and let this vertical cut the sides of the quadrilateral at K, L. Let M be any point on the segment KL. Now the weight W may be resolved into forces along MA, MB, and hence W can be balanced by forces along AM, BM. Since these lines lie inside the cones of friction, the law of friction is satisfied. We have here a case of statical indeterminacy (cf. Sec. 2.5): provided that the vertical through C cuts the quadrilateral $FGHJ$, the ladder will be in equilibrium, but we cannot tell precisely what the reactions of the wall and floor will be.

Sec. 3.2]   APPLICATIONS IN PLANE STATICS   91

Now let us ask: How far can the man go up the ladder before slipping takes place? Obviously, he can climb until the vertical through his position passes through the point J. When he passes that position, it will no longer be possible to find reactions satisfying the conditions of equilibrium and the law of friction

The question may also be treated analytically. Consider the man slowly climbing the ladder. If the ladder slips at all, just at the point of slipping the reactions at *both* contacts must correspond to limiting friction. Thus, at the point of slipping, the force system is as shown in Fig. 34, with $F = \mu N$. $F' = \mu N'$. Taking vertical and horizontal components and moments about B, we have the three equations

$$\mu N' + N - W = 0,$$
$$N' - \mu N = 0,$$
$$W\ BC \sin \alpha - \mu N'\ AB \sin \alpha - N'\ AB \cos \alpha = 0.$$

These three equations determine N, N', BC: we find

(3 208) $N = \dfrac{W}{1 + \mu^2}, \qquad N' = \dfrac{\mu W}{1 + \mu^2}, \qquad \dfrac{BC}{AB} = \dfrac{\mu}{1 + \mu^2}(\mu + \cot \alpha).$

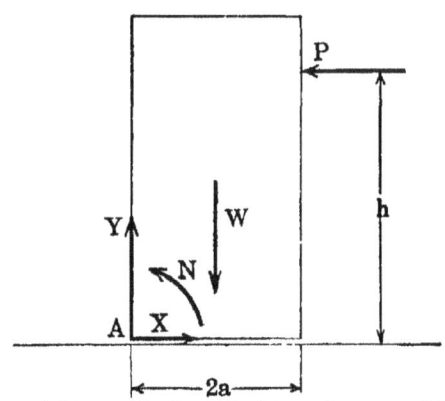

Fig. 35.—A heavy block pushed by a horizontal force **P**.

Example 3. *A block rests on a rough horizontal floor and is pushed by a gradually increasing horizontal force. Will the block slide, or will it topple over an edge?*

Let the thickness of the block be $2a$, its weight W, and the coefficient of static friction μ. Let the horizontal force P be applied at a height h above the floor. The first question is: Given W and P as shown in Fig 35, can there be a system of reactions exerted by the ground, satisfying simultaneously the law of friction and the conditions of equilibrium for the block? Any such system of reactions will be plane-equipollent to forces X, Y at A as shown, together with a couple N. If equilibrium exists, it is clear that the following conditions are demanded by the law of friction and the fact that the floor cannot pull the block downward:

(3.209) $X \leq \mu Y, \qquad Y \geq 0, \qquad N \geq 0$

Taking horizontal and vertical components and moments about A, we have
$$X = P, \quad Y = W, \quad N = aW - hP,$$
and so (3.209) give
$$(3.210) \qquad P \leq \mu W, \qquad P \leq \frac{aW}{h}.$$

Starting with a small value of P, these inequalities are both satisfied; but as P is increased, one or other will be violated, and then equilibrium will cease. If
$$(3.211) \qquad \mu < \frac{a}{h},$$
the first inequality of (3.210) will be broken first. At the instant when $P = \mu W$, we have
$$X = \mu Y, \quad N > 0.$$
This is a state of limiting friction; and so, if (3.211) holds, equilibrium of the block will be broken by sliding along the plane. On the other hand, if
$$(3.212) \qquad \mu > \frac{a}{h},$$
then the second inequality of (3.210) will be violated first. At the instant when $P = aW/h$, we have
$$X < \mu Y, \quad Y > 0, \quad N = 0.$$
The friction is not limiting, and so slipping cannot take place. But any further increase in P will cause violation of the last inequality of (3.209). Hence we conclude that, if (3.212) holds, equilibrium will be broken by the block turning over the edge A.

The result is in agreement with common experience: the smaller we make h, the more likely is sliding to occur.

3.3. THIN BEAMS

Tension, shearing force, and bending moment.

Let us consider a straight beam of uniform section (Fig. 36) and a plane P parallel to its length. P may be regarded as the

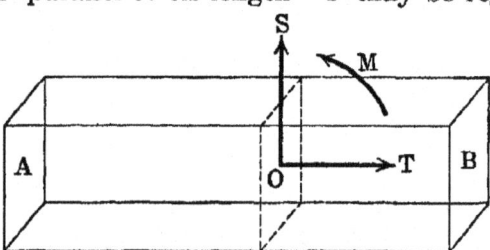

FIG. 36.—Reactions across a section of a beam

plane of the paper. External forces, parallel to P, act on the beam. (These forces are not shown. They may consist of the weight of the beam or loads placed on it.) Let a cross section

be drawn through a point O, perpendicular to the length of the beam. Let us take as our "system" the portion of the beam extending from the end A up to this section. The external forces acting on this system will consist of

(i) the external forces already mentioned, acting on this portion of the beam,

(ii) the reactions exerted across the section by the particles in the portion of the beam extending from the section to the end

FIG. 37.—A thin beam

R. These reactions are *internal* forces as far as the whole beam is concerned, but they are *external* forces for the system at present under consideration.

Let us take P as the fundamental plane. The reactions across the section are plane-equipollent to a force acting at O, together with a couple M. The force may be resolved into components T, S along the beam and perpendicular to its length, respectively. We define the following terms:

T = tension,
S = shearing force,
M = bending moment.

We shall confine our attention to *thin beams*. The thin beam is a mathematical idealization, in which the cross section is reduced to a point and the beam to a straight line.

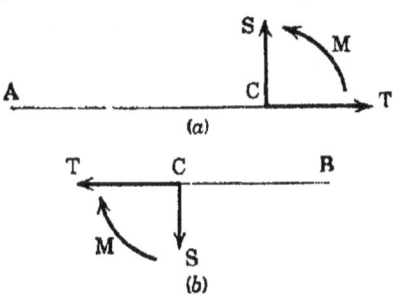

FIG. 38.—(a) Reactions exerted on AC by CB (b) Reactions exerted on CB by AC.

Figure 37 shows a thin beam AB; C is any point of it. To draw the reactions on AC across the section at C without confusion, we delete the line CB as in Fig. 38a. Figure 38b shows the reactions on CB; these have the same magnitudes as, but opposite senses to, those shown in Fig. 38a, on account of the law of action and reaction.

Let us take an origin on the beam, the x-axis along the beam and the y-axis perpendicular to it. Consider a small length of the beam extending from x to $x + dx$ (Fig. 39). Let T, S, M be the values of tension, shearing force, and bending moment at x, and $T + dT$, $S + dS$, $M + dM$ the values at $x + dx$. To allow for gravity or other continuous external loading, we shall

add a force with components $X\,dx$, $Y\,dx$ (not shown in Fig. 39) acting at the middle point of the portion x, $x + dx$. By taking components and moments about the point x and neglecting

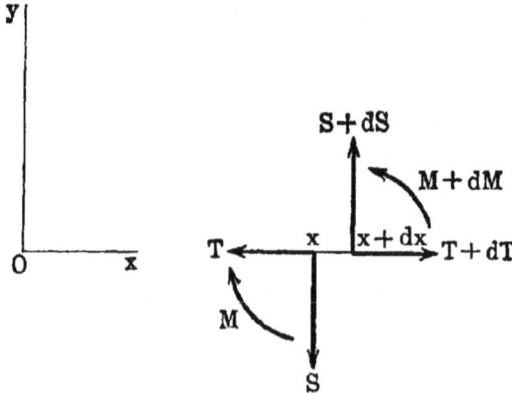

Fig. 39.—Reactions on the ends of a small element of a beam.

infinitesimals of the second order, we have, as conditions of equilibrium for the small length of the beam,

$$dT + X\,dx = 0, \qquad dS + Y\,dx = 0, \qquad dM + S\,dx = 0.$$

Thus

$$(3.301) \qquad \frac{dT}{dx} = -X, \qquad \frac{dS}{dx} = -Y, \qquad \frac{dM}{dx} = -S.$$

These are the general differential equations for the equilibrium of thin beams. But in statically determinate cases we can obtain all required information regarding internal reactions without using these equations, or rather by using them in integrated form.

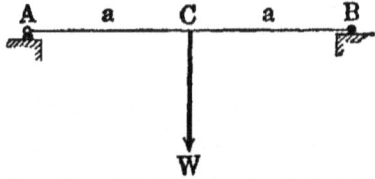

Fig. 40.—A light beam loaded at its middle point.

Statically determinate problems.

We shall illustrate the method by the solution of a problem A light beam AB of length $2a$ is hinged at A and supported on a smooth horizontal plane at B (Fig. 40). A load W is placed at the middle point C. Find the bending moment and shearing force along the beam.

First, by application of the conditions of equilibrium (2.306) to the whole beam, we find the reactions on the beam at A and B.

Sec. 3.3]   APPLICATIONS IN PLANE STATICS   95

These are each of magnitude $\tfrac{1}{2}W$, directed upward. Let us take our origin at A and the x-axis along the beam. Consider the

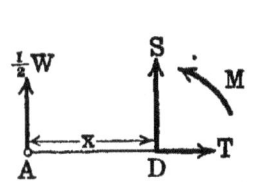

Fig. 41.—External forces on a portion of the beam shown in Fig. 40 $(AD < AC)$.

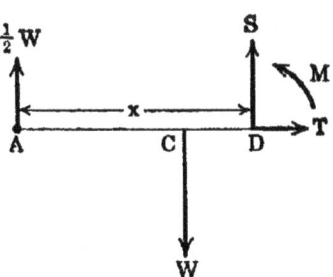

Fig. 42.—External forces on a portion of the beam shown in Fig. 40 $(AD > AC)$.

portion of the beam AD, where D lies in AC; let $AD = x$ (Fig 41). From the equilibrium of AD, we have

(3.302) $\quad \begin{cases} T = 0, \quad S = -\tfrac{1}{2}W, \\ M = -xS = \tfrac{1}{2}xW, \quad (x < a). \end{cases}$

These give the shearing force and bending moment for any point in AC; there is no tension. Since S is negative, the shearing force actually acts in the *downward* direction.

Now take D in CB (Fig. 42). Instead of (3.302), we have

(3.303) $\quad \begin{cases} T = 0, \quad S = W - \tfrac{1}{2}W = \tfrac{1}{2}W, \\ M = aW - xS = (a - \tfrac{1}{2}x)W, \quad (x > a). \end{cases}$

The shearing force is now positive. We note that the last of (3.301) is satisfied by (3.302) and (3.303).

The graphs of S and M along the beam are shown in Fig. 43.

The Euler-Bernoulli theory of thin elastic beams.

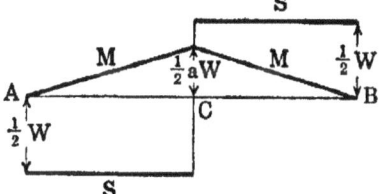

Fig. 43.—Graphs of shearing force (S) and bending moment (M) along the beam shown in Fig. 40.

If a straight beam rests on three supports, the problem of finding the reactions due to the supports is statically indeterminate (cf. Sec. 2.5), and we cannot find the shearing force and bending moment by elementary statical principles. But this indeterminacy disappears when we take into consideration the elasticity of the beam. Although straight initially, an elastic beam will stretch and bend under the influence of forces. We

suppose the stretching and bending to be very small and accept the law of Hooke for stretching and the law of Euler and Bernoulli for bending *

HOOKE'S LAW. When a beam is slightly stretched,

$$(3.304) \qquad T = k'e,$$

where e is the extension (increase in length per unit length) and k' a constant for the beam. (Actually $k' = EA$, where E is Young's modulus for the material and A the area of the cross section.)

THE EULER-BERNOULLI LAW. When a beam is slightly bent, the bending moment is connected with the curvature by the relation

$$(3.305) \qquad M = \frac{k}{\rho},$$

where ρ is the radius of curvature and k a constant for the beam. (Actually $k = EI$, where E is Young's modulus and I the "moment of inertia" of the cross section about an axis through its mean center perpendicular to the plane of the couple M.)

When the beam is approximately straight and the axes as in Fig. 39,

$$\frac{1}{\rho} = \frac{d^2y}{dx^2} \qquad \text{approximately,}$$

and (3.305) may be written

$$(3.306) \qquad M = k\frac{d^2y}{dx^2}.$$

Let us refer to Fig. 39 and to the equations (3.301). We shall suppose that the beam is subject to a force w per unit length in the negative sense of the y-axis, due either to its own weight or to a load placed on it. Then $X = 0$, $Y = -w$, and (3.301) read

$$(3.307) \qquad \frac{dT}{dx} = 0, \qquad \frac{dS}{dx} = w, \qquad \frac{dM}{dx} = -S.$$

We see that the tension T is constant. Elimination of M and S from (3.306) and (3.307) gives

$$(3.308) \qquad k\frac{d^4y}{dx^4} = -w.$$

* The law of Euler and Bernoulli follows from that of Hooke; the proof belongs to the theory of elasticity.

Sec. 3.3]   APPLICATIONS IN PLANE STATICS   97

This is the fundamental differential equation in the theory of thin elastic beams. If it is solved, the bending moment and shearing force are given by

(3.309) $$M = k \frac{d^2y}{dx^2}, \qquad S = -\frac{dM}{dx}$$

It must be realized that the differential equation (3.308) holds only between isolated loads or supports. To deal with these a special treatment is necessary. Figure 44 shows an element Δx of a thin beam with an isolated load W suspended from its middle point P. (The case of a support is covered by making W negative.)

The element is in equilibrium under four forces and two couples: the continuous load on Δx (not shown), the isolated load W, the shearing force $S + \Delta S$, and the bending moment $M + \Delta M$ on the right, and the shearing force S and the bending moment M on the left, positive senses being as indicated.

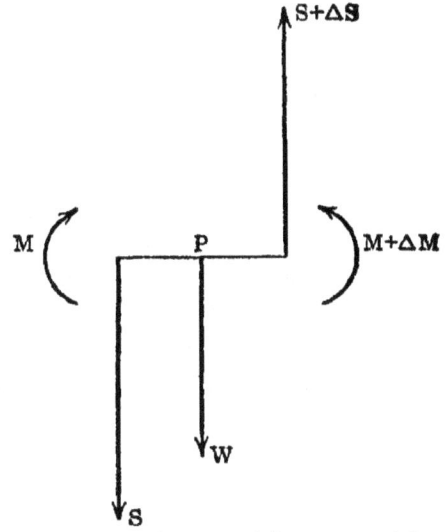

Fig. 44.—Element of beam containing isolated load.

If Δx tends to zero, the continuous load tends to zero and so does the moment of this load about P. Hence the conditions of equilibrium give, in the limit, $\Delta S = W$, and (taking moments about P) $\Delta M = 0$.

This means that the bending moment M is continuous across an isolated load or support, but the shearing force S changes abruptly. In terms of y and its derivatives (since the beam is not broken at the isolated load or support) we have continuity in y, dy/dx, d^2y/dx^2, but discontinuity in d^3y/dx^3.

Example. A uniform heavy beam OP of length $2a$ and weight W is hinged at O and rests on two smooth supports, one at P and the other at its middle point Q. Find the reactions on the supports, if O, P, Q are all at the same height.

We shall take the origin of coordinates at O, the x-axis horizontal, and the y-axis directed vertically upward. Integration of (3.308) along OQ gives

(3.310) $$ky = -\tfrac{1}{24}wx^4 + Ax^3 + Bx, \qquad (OQ)$$

where A, B are constants of integration; two other constants of integration have been put equal to zero on account of the vanishing of y and d^2y/dx^2 at O (There can be no bending moment at a hinge or free end) Similarly, we have along QP

(3.311) $\quad ky = -\tfrac{1}{24}w(x - 2a)^4 + A'(x - 2a)^3 + B'(x - 2a),\quad (QP)$

where A', B' are constants of integration. In these two equations, we have four unknown constants, they are to be found from the conditions that $y = 0$ at Q, while dy/dx and d^2y/dx^2 are continuous there. Thus, we have the four equations

$$Aa^3 + Ba - \tfrac{1}{24}wa^4 = 0,$$
$$A'a^3 + B'a + \tfrac{1}{24}wa^4 = 0,$$
$$3Aa^2 + B - \tfrac{1}{6}wa^3 = 3A'a^2 + B' + \tfrac{1}{6}wa^3,$$
$$6Aa - \tfrac{1}{2}wa^2 = -6A'a - \tfrac{1}{2}wa^2$$

We find
$$A = -A' = \tfrac{1}{16}wa, \qquad B = -B' = -\tfrac{1}{48}wa^3,$$

and substitution in (3.310) and (3 311) gives the equations of the two portions of the beam

(3 312) $\quad \begin{cases} ky = -\tfrac{1}{24}wx^4 + \tfrac{1}{16}wax^3 - \tfrac{1}{48}wa^3x, & (OQ), \\ ky = -\tfrac{1}{24}w(2a - x)^4 + \tfrac{1}{16}wa(2a - x)^3 - \tfrac{1}{48}wa^3(2a - x), & (QP) \end{cases}$

In OQ the bending moment is
$$M = k\frac{d^2y}{dx^2} = -\tfrac{1}{2}wx^2 + \tfrac{3}{8}wax.$$

Its maximum value occurs at $x = \tfrac{3}{8}a$ The portion OQ is a system in equilibrium, hence, taking moments about Q, we have for the reaction R_O at O

$$R_O a = M_Q + \tfrac{1}{2}wa^2 = \tfrac{3}{8}wa^2 = \tfrac{3}{16}Wa.$$

When one reaction has been found, the others follow from the usual statical methods. Hence

(3.313) $\quad R_O = \tfrac{3}{16}W, \qquad R_Q = \tfrac{10}{16}W, \qquad R_P = \tfrac{3}{16}W$

3.4. FLEXIBLE CABLES

A flexible cable differs from a stiff rod in the ease with which it can be bent into a curve. The bending moment per unit curvature is much less for the cable. In mechanics, we idealize this property and understand by a flexible cable a material curve such that there can be no bending moment across any section. By considering the equilibrium of a small portion of the cable, it is easily seen that the shearing force must also vanish. Hence the only surviving component of the reaction across a section of a flexible cable is a tension T, which acts along the tangent to the curve in which the cable lies.

We use the word "cable" exclusively, but it is to be understood that the practical applications cover chains, ropes, strings, and threads. The theoretical predictions will agree well with the

APPLICATIONS IN PLANE STATICS

results of experiments conducted on cables in which the bending moments are small.

General formulas for all flexible cables hanging freely.

Let us consider a flexible cable hanging under the influence of its own weight, and perhaps additional continuous vertical loads attached to it. For the present, we shall not make any special assumptions regarding the nature of the cable or the load.

We pass over the trivial case in which the cable hangs from one end in a vertical line. When suspended from two points, it hangs in a vertical plane. Let Oxy be axes in this plane, Ox being horizontal and Oy directed vertically upward (Fig 45). Let A be a point on the cable with coordinates (x, y), and B an adjacent point with coordinates $(x + dx, y + dy)$. Let ds be the infinitesimal length of AB, and let $w\,ds$ be the total load on AB, including the weight of the cable. The portion AB is a system in equilibrium under the action of the tensions at its ends and the load. Let θ be the inclination of the tangent at A to the horizontal. Then $dx/ds = \cos\theta$, $dy/ds = \sin\theta$; and so, taking horizontal and vertical components, we have

$$\left(T\frac{dx}{ds}\right)_B - \left(T\frac{dx}{ds}\right)_A = 0,$$

$$\left(T\frac{dy}{ds}\right)_B - \left(T\frac{dy}{ds}\right)_A - w\,ds = 0$$

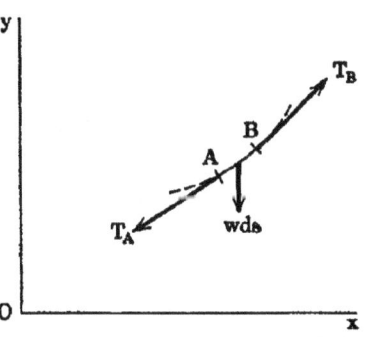

FIG 45 —Forces acting on an element of a hanging cable.

By the first of these equations, *the horizontal component of the tension is constant*. The second equation may be written

(3.401) $$\frac{d}{ds}\left(T\frac{dy}{ds}\right) = w.$$

If H is the constant horizontal component of tension, we have

(3.402) $$T\frac{dx}{ds} = H;$$

substitution in (3.401) gives

(3.403) $$\frac{d}{ds}\left(\frac{dy}{dx}\right) = \frac{w}{H}.$$

This is a differential equation satisfied by the curve in which the cable hangs When this equation has been solved, the tension may be found from (3.402).

The suspension bridge.

Let us now suppose that a weightless cable supports a load uniformly distributed on a horizontal line; for the load on a horizontal length dx, we write $w_0\, dx$ This approximates to the condition of a cable of a suspension bridge (Fig. 46), the load consisting of the roadway AB, of weight w_0 per unit length.

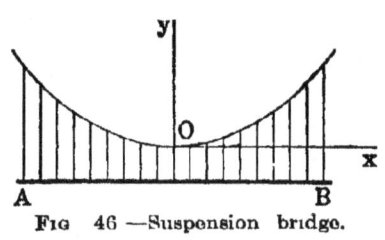

Fig 46 —Suspension bridge.

With the notation used above, we have $w\, ds = w_0\, dx$, and so

$$w = w_0 \frac{dx}{ds};$$

thus (3.403) reads

$$\frac{d}{ds}\left(\frac{dy}{dx}\right) = \frac{w_0}{H}\frac{dx}{ds},$$

or

$$\frac{d^2y}{dx^2} = \frac{w_0}{H}.$$

If the origin is chosen at the lowest point of the cable, so that $y = dy/dx = 0$ when $x = 0$, we obtain as the equation of the cable

(3 404)
$$y = \tfrac{1}{2}\frac{w_0 x^2}{H}.$$

This is a *parabola*. The tension in the cable is given by (3.402). Since

(3.405)
$$ds^2 = dx^2 + dy^2, \qquad \frac{ds}{dx} = \sqrt{1 + \left(\frac{dy}{dx}\right)^2},$$

we have

(3.406)
$$T = H\sqrt{1 + \left(\frac{dy}{dx}\right)^2} = \sqrt{H^2 + w_0^2 x^2}.$$

The common catenary.

We shall now consider a uniform cable hanging freely under its own weight, w per unit length. The fundamental equation is

(3.403), in which w is now a constant. We write it in the form

$$\frac{d^2y}{dx^2} = \frac{w}{H}\frac{ds}{dx},$$

or, by (3.405),

(3.407) $$\frac{d^2y}{dx^2} = \frac{w}{H}\sqrt{1 + \left(\frac{dy}{dx}\right)^2}$$

Introducing a variable z defined by

(3.408) $$\sinh z = \frac{dy}{dx},$$

we reduce (3.407) to

$$\frac{dz}{dx} = \frac{w}{H},$$

and so

$$z = \frac{wx}{H} + A,$$

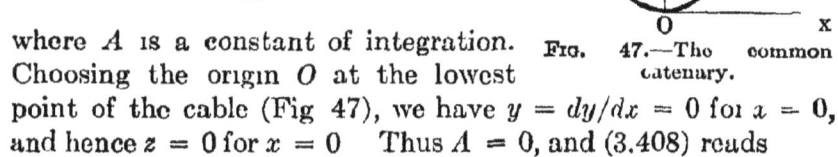

where A is a constant of integration. Choosing the origin O at the lowest point of the cable (Fig 47), we have $y = dy/dx = 0$ for $x = 0$, and hence $z = 0$ for $x = 0$. Thus $A = 0$, and (3.408) reads

Fig. 47.—The common catenary.

(3.409) $$\frac{dy}{dx} = \sinh \frac{wx}{H}$$

Hence

(3.410) $$y = \frac{H}{w}\left(\cosh \frac{wx}{H} - 1\right),$$

when account is taken of the conditions at O. This curve is called the *common catenary*, the lowest point O is called its *vertex*.

It is customary to define the *parameter* c of the catenary by

(3.411) $$c = \frac{H}{w};$$

then (3.410) reads

(3.412) $$y = c\left(\cosh \frac{x}{c} - 1\right)$$

To find the tension from (3.402), we note that from (3.405) and (3.409)

(3.413) $$\frac{ds}{dx} = \sqrt{1 + \sinh^2 \frac{x}{c}} = \cosh \frac{x}{c},$$

and so

$$(3.414) \qquad T = H\frac{ds}{dx} = H \cosh \frac{x}{c} = H + wy.$$

So far we have concentrated our attention on two things, the curve in which the cable hangs and the tension at any point in it. These have been found in (3.412) and (3.414) But other problems suggest themselves, and we need other formulas to solve them. Such problems may involve the length of the cable and the inclination of its tangent to the horizontal Let us denote the length by s (measured from the vertex to a general point) and the inclination by θ; there are then five variables involved in the theory of the cable,

$$x, y, T, s, \theta.$$

Any one of these variables is expressible in terms of any other, and it is an interesting exercise to prepare a table of five rows and columns showing all the twenty expressions. We shall note here only the expressions giving s in terms of x, y, and θ, as follows:

$$(3.415) \qquad s = c \sinh \frac{x}{c}, \qquad s^2 = y^2 + 2yc,$$

$$(3.416) \qquad s = c \tan \theta.$$

These equations are easy to obtain from (3.413), combined with (3.412); to get (3.416), we use the fact that $dy/dx = \tan \theta$. The equation (3.416) is the *intrinsic equation* of the catenary.

Examples. Problems connected with freely hanging cables usually involve the solution of a transcendental equation As illustrations, two problems will be considered These problems may be stated briefly as follows:

(i) *Given the span and length, to find the maximum tension.*

(ii) *Given the length and sag, to find the span*

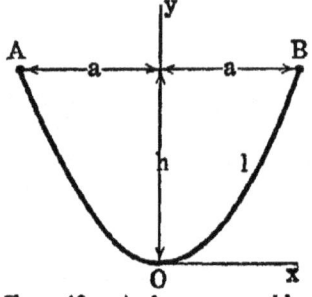

Fig. 48.—A hanging cable.

A cable, of weight w per unit length and length $2l$, hangs from two points A and B, at the same height and at a distance $2a$ apart (Fig. 48). We wish to find the maximum tension in the cable.

It is clear from (3.414) that the maximum tension occurs at A and B, and the value is

$$(3.417) \qquad T_{max} = H \cosh \frac{a}{c} = wc \cosh \frac{a}{c}.$$

Here, as in most problems on the catenary, the solution depends on finding the parameter c. Applying the first of (3.415) at the point B, we have

$$(3.418) \qquad l = c \sinh \frac{a}{c}$$

This is an equation to determine c in terms of a and l; it may be written

$$(3.419) \qquad \frac{\sinh (a/c)}{a/c} = \frac{l}{a}.$$

If tables of $(\sinh X)/X$ are available, the numerical value of a/c may be obtained at once.* The solution of the problem is given by (3.417) on inserting the value for c, found from (3.419).

If the ratio l/a is nearly unity, i.e., if the cable is only a little longer than the span, the solution of (3.419) for a/c is small, because

$$\lim_{X \to 0} \frac{\sinh X}{X} = 1.$$

In fact, the parameter c is large. Then we can obtain an approximate solution of (3.419) without recourse to numerical tables. Retaining only the first two terms of the expansion for $\sinh a/c$, we have

$$(3.420) \qquad 1 + \tfrac{1}{6}\left(\frac{a}{c}\right)^2 = \frac{l}{a}, \qquad \frac{a}{c} = \sqrt{\frac{6(l-a)}{a}},$$

$$c = \sqrt{\frac{a^3}{6(l-a)}}.$$

Since c is large, $T_{\max}$ as given by (3.417) is large; it is approximately equal to H, where

$$(3.421) \qquad H = wc = wa\sqrt{\frac{a}{6(l-a)}}.$$

The second problem arises when the distance between two points A and B at the same height is measured by a measuring tape which sags under its own weight. With the notation of Fig. 48, we are given h, l; we wish to find a.

Applying the second of (3.415) at the point B, we have

$$(3.422) \qquad c = \frac{l^2 - h^2}{2h}.$$

The answer to the problem is given by (3.418). This is a quadratic equation for $e^{a/c}$, and the positive root gives†

$$(3.423) \qquad a = c \log\left(\frac{l}{c} + \sqrt{1 + \frac{l^2}{c^2}}\right) = \frac{l^2 - h^2}{2h} \log \frac{l+h}{l-h}$$

* J. W. Campbell, Numerical Tables of Hyperbolic and Other Functions (Houghton Mifflin Company, Boston, 1929), p. 30. These tables were prepared with the solution of catenary problems in mind.
† Throughout this book "log" means the natural logarithm, that is, log$_e$.

If the ratio h/l is small, we have approximately

(3.424) $$\log \frac{l+h}{l-h} = 2\left(\frac{h}{l} + \frac{1}{3}\frac{h^3}{l^3}\right),$$

and hence

(3.425) $$a = l\left(1 - \frac{2}{3}\frac{h^2}{l^2}\right),$$

with an error of the order of $(h/l)^4$.

Cables in contact with smooth curves.

So far the cables considered have been unconstrained. Let us now consider the case of a cable lying against a smooth surface, or, as we may say in two-dimensional language, against a smooth curve. Gravity will be neglected.

Figure 49 shows a small portion AB of a cable lying in equilibrium in contact with a smooth curve. Let O be any assigned point on the cable and s the length of the cable between O and A. Let the length AB be ds, and let the inclinations to some fixed direction of the tangents to the cable at A and B be θ and $\theta + d\theta$. The element AB is in equilibrium under three forces, namely, the tension T at A, the tension $T + dT$ at B, and a normal reaction due to the curve. This last may be written $N\,ds$ and may be supposed to act along the normal at A. Resolving forces along the tangent and normal at A, we obtain from the conditions of equilibrium

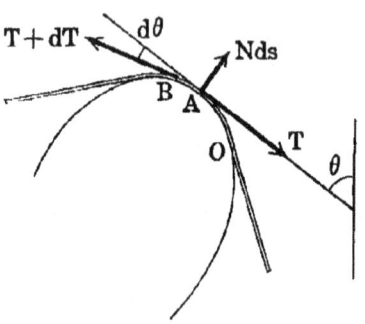

FIG. 49.—Forces on an element of light cable in contact with a smooth curve.

(3.426) $$dT = 0, \qquad N\,ds = T\,d\theta.$$

Hence, *the tension is constant along a light cable in contact with a smooth curve.* Also, since $ds/d\theta = \rho$, the radius of curvature, we have

(3.427) $$N = \frac{T}{\rho}.$$

An example of the significance of this last formula occurs in tying up a parcel: the sharper the edge of the parcel, the smaller ρ and hence the greater the tendency of the string to bite into the parcel.

Cables in contact with rough curves.

Let us now suppose that the curve shown in Fig. 49 is rough and that the cable is just on the point of slipping in the direction AB. In addition to the forces already considered, there is now a force of friction $F\,ds$ on the element, acting along the tangent at A and opposing motion. The conditions of equilibrium are now

(3.428) $\qquad dT = F\,ds, \qquad N\,ds = T\,d\theta.$

But $F = \mu N$, where μ is the coefficient of friction. Hence

(3.429) $\qquad \dfrac{dT}{ds} = \mu N, \qquad N = T\dfrac{d\theta}{ds},$

and so

(3.430) $\qquad \dfrac{dT}{d\theta} = \mu T.$

Integration gives

(3.431) $\qquad T = T_0 e^{\mu\theta},$

where T_0 is a constant of integration.

The rapid increase of the exponential with increasing θ is of great practical importance. As a numerical example, consider a rope wrapped twice around a post, for which the coefficient of friction is $\frac{1}{2}$. Then

$$T = T_0 e^{4\mu\pi} = T_0 e^{2\pi},$$

where T_0, T are the tensions in the rope where it meets and leaves the post, slipping being about to occur in the direction of T. We have

$$\frac{T_0}{T} = e^{-2\pi} = 0.0019.$$

If $T = 2000$ lb., $T_0 = 3.8$ lb. Thus, a load of one ton can be sustained by application of a force of less than 4 lb.; and, of course, a much greater load might be sustained if the rope were wrapped more often round the post. This principle is used in holding ships by ropes passed round mooring posts and in hoists in which a rope is passed round a revolving drum, the end being held in the hand.

3.5. FRAMES

Just-rigid frames.

Figure 50 shows a simple frame or truss, as used in bridges. It consists of steel girders riveted together at the joints. For mathematical discussion we simplify the system as follows: (i) the girders are treated as light rigid bars, (ii) the joints are

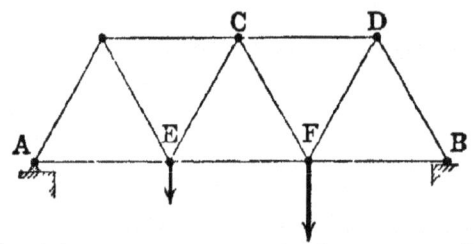

Fig 50.—A just-rigid frame with loads applied at E and F.

supposed to be smoothly working hinges, each bar being capable of rotation about the joints on it without any resisting couple. We shall discuss only frames with joints lying in a plane, and we shall not consider displacements out of that plane.

In Fig 50, we suppose the joint A fixed and the joint B constrained to slide on a horizontal line. Inspection shows that the whole frame is fixed by these conditions. In fact, the frame is a rigid body and is fixed when one of its points is fixed and another of its points constrained to move on a line. If one bar, for example CD, were removed, the frame would cease to be a rigid body. Hence it is called *just-rigid*. The following is the general definition: *A frame is just-rigid when the removal of any one of its bars destroys its rigidity.*

If an additional bar is inserted in a just-rigid frame, it becomes *over-rigid*. We shall deal only with just-rigid frames.

We shall now show that *a just-rigid frame with j joints has $2j - 3$ bars*. Taking any axes in the plane of the frame, we denote the coordinates of the joints by (x_1, y_1), (x_2, y_2), $\cdots$ (x_j, y_j); there are $2j$ coordinates altogether. If the first two joints are connected by a bar of length l, their coordinates must satisfy

$$(x_1 - x_2)^2 + (y_1 - y_2)^2 = l^2.$$

Thus if there are b bars, the $2j$ coordinates are subjected to b relations of this type. If we fix one joint and constrain another

Sec. 3.5]   APPLICATIONS IN PLANE STATICS   107

joint to move on a line, we impose 3 more conditions. If the frame is just-rigid, these $b + 3$ conditions suffice to fix the whole frame, i.e., to determine the $2j$ coordinates of the joints. Hence $b + 3 = 2j$, which gives the stated result:

(3.501) $\qquad b = 2j - 3.$

If $b < 2j - 3$, the frame is not rigid.

Fig. 51.—Frame with three joints and three bars.

The smallest number of joints possible in a just-rigid frame is $j = 3$. Then the number of bars is $2j - 3 = 3$. In this case, we have a triangular frame (Fig. 51).

Now take $j = 4$; then the number of bars is $2j - 3 = 5$. Examples are shown in Fig. 52. (When two bars cross in a

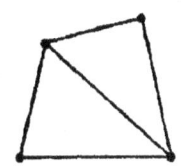

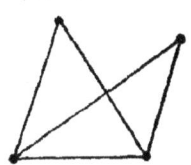

Fig. 52.—Frames with four joints and five bars

diagram, without indication of a joint, they are supposed capable of free motion past one another.)

If $j = 5$, the number of bars is $2j - 3 = 7$. Examples are shown in Fig. 53

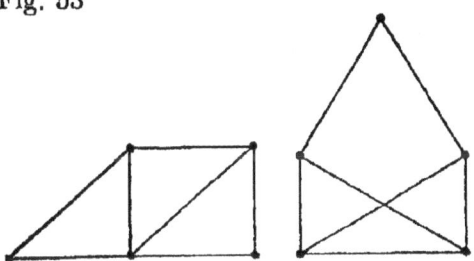

Fig 53.—Frames with five joints and seven bars

A simple way to build up a just-rigid frame is to start with a triangle and add two bars at a time. Since, in each operation, we add one joint and two bars, after p operations we have $3 + p$ joints and $3 + 2p$ bars; the identity

$$3 + 2p = 2(3 + p) - 3$$

shows that the condition for a just-rigid frame is satisfied. However, all just-rigid frames cannot be constructed in this way.

Stresses in bars.

Suppose that a just-rigid frame is fixed by external constraints so that it cannot move. (The normal plan is to fix one joint and constrain another joint to move on a line, as in Fig. 50.) Now let external forces, or loads, be applied to some or all of the joints. Each bar is in equilibrium under two forces, the reactions at its ends. These two forces must be equal in magnitude and act in opposite senses along the bar. If the forces act away from one another (so that the bar tends to be torn in two), the bar is said to be in *tension*; if the forces act toward one another (so that the bar tends to buckle), the bar is said to be in *thrust*. The word *stress*

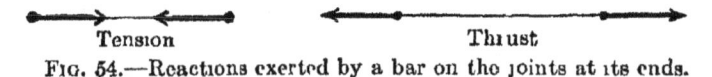

FIG. 54.—Reactions exerted by a bar on the joints at its ends.

is used to cover both cases. A plus sign is associated with tension and a minus sign with thrust. Thus, if we say that the stress in a bar is $+3$ tons, we mean that there is a tension of 3 tons in it; if the stress is -5 tons, we mean that there is a thrust of 5 tons. In Fig. 54 the arrows indicate forces exerted *on* the joints *by* the bars. The forces exerted on the bars by the joints act in the reverse directions.

For a frame in equilibrium, two problems arise:
(i) to determine the external reactions at the supported joints;
(ii) to determine the stresses in the bars.

The first problem is elementary. It is a question of the equilibrium of a system, as discussed in Secs. 2.3 and 2.4 and summarized in Sec. 2.6. It is with the second problem that we are concerned.

Method of joints.

The following argument is general, but the reader may consider the frame shown in Fig. 50 as an example, the loads being indicated by arrows at the joints E and F. The loads are given, and the stresses are to be found. Each joint may be considered as a particle in equilibrium, under the action of a load (if any) and the reactions of the bars meeting there. (Since the joint is the system considered, this method is called the *method of joints*.) As the forces lie in a plane, there are two equations of equilibrium for each joint, and thus $2j$ equations in all if the number of joints is j. These equations involve 3 unknown components of external

SEC. 3 5]   *APPLICATIONS IN PLANE STATICS*   109

reactions at the supports and a number of unknown stresses equal to the number of bars, i.e., $2j - 3$. Thus the total number of unknowns is $2j$, and we have $2j$ linear equations to find them. *Thus, in a just-rigid frame the problem of finding the external reactions at the supports and the stresses in the bars is a determinate problem, involving the solution of a number of simultaneous linear equations equal to twice the number of joints.*

If the frame were over-rigid, the number of unknowns would exceed the number of equations, and the problem would be indeterminate. We should have to consider the elastic properties of the bars.

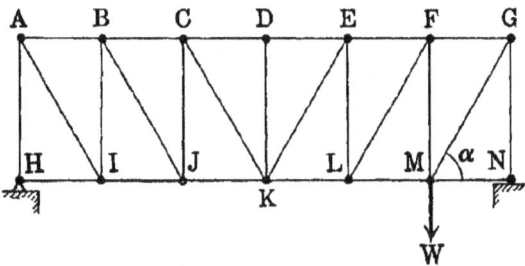

FIG 55a.—A frame with 14 joints, supporting a load at M

The problem of the just-rigid frame having been thus reduced to the solution of simultaneous linear equations, it might be thought that nothing remained to be said. However, the system of equations obtained in the manner described above may be very involved, and much labor may be avoided by modifying the method. This is particularly true if we only require the stresses in certain bars. But the reader should realize that these are only laborsaving devices. If he cannot discover the particular device suited to a certain problem, he can always fall back on the direct laborious method.

Before turning to the special devices, let us see how the method of joints may be applied without undue complication to the frame shown in Fig. 55a. This frame has 14 joints, and hence a direct attack involves 28 simultaneous equations.

The load at M is W. We find at once (by taking components and moments) that the reactions at H and N are both vertical and of magnitudes $R_H = \tfrac{1}{6}W$, $R_N = \tfrac{5}{6}W$. Let $S_{AB}, S_{BC} \cdots$ be the stresses in the bars. From the equilibrium of the joint N, we have

$$S_{GN} = -R_N = -\tfrac{5}{6}W, \qquad S_{MN} = 0.$$

Passing to G, we have

$$S_{GM} \sin \alpha = -S_{GN} = \tfrac{5}{6}W,$$
$$S_{FG} = -S_{GM} \cos \alpha = -\tfrac{5}{6}W \cot \alpha,$$

where α is the inclination of the oblique bars to the horizontal. Proceeding in this way, step by step, we can find all the stresses. Incidentally, we shall get a check on our work when we reach the last joint. It will be noted that, to start the method, we must begin with a joint where only two bars meet.

Method of sections.

When we require the stresses in only some of the bars, the method of joints may prove unnecessarily laborious. Let us recall the fact, emphasized in Sec. 2 3, that we may choose any part of the given system as the system to which the conditions of

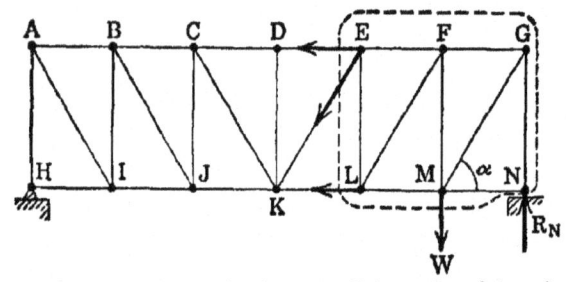

Fig. 55b.—Method of sections. the "system" is enclosed by the broken line.

equilibrium are applied. Up till now we have been thinking of a single bar, the whole frame, or a single joint as the system. But here we take a different approach, following the *method of sections*.

Figure 55b shows the same frame as that of Fig. 55a, with the same load. We wish to find the stresses in KL, KE, DE. We consider as a system the part of the frame enclosed within a curved line cutting the bars KL, KE, DE, but no others. This system is acted on by the following external forces:

the load W at M;
the reaction R_N at N;
the stresses in KL, KE, DE.

Taking moments about E, we have

$$S_{KL} \cdot EL + W \; EF = R_N \cdot EG.$$

But R_N may be found by consideration of the equilibrium of the whole frame; hence
$$S_{KL} = \tfrac{2}{3}W \cot \alpha.$$
From consideration of the total vertical component of force, we have
$$S_{KE} = -\tfrac{1}{6}W \csc \alpha;$$
and, from the total horizontal component,
$$S_{DE} = -S_{KL} - S_{KE} \cos \alpha = -\tfrac{1}{2}W \cot \alpha.$$

We note that the method would not have worked had the three bars cut by the section met in a point.

Method of virtual work.

The method of virtual work may be applied to the problem just treated. To find S_{KL}, we suppose the bar KL removed and forces applied to the joints K and L equal to the (unknown) stress in KL. The frame is no longer rigid, but it is in equilibrium. Hence the virtual work done in an infinitesimal displacement is zero. For infinitesimal displacement, let us take a rotation about E of the right-hand portion of the frame. The only forces to do work are the load W, the reaction R_N, and the force at L replacing the stress S_{KL}. Equating the work done by them to zero, we obtain the expression for S_{KL} given above.

To get the stress in EK, we replace the bar KL and remove EK, at the same time applying to the joints E and K forces equal to the (unknown) stress in EK. Now we give a virtual displacement, holding the left-hand portion fixed. The right-hand side rises slightly with parallel displacement of its bars, the bar DE hinging at D and KL hinging at K. The only working forces are the load W, the reaction R_N, and the force at E replacing the stress S_{KE}. Equating to zero the work done, we find for S_{KE} the value given above. S_{DE} is found similarly without difficulty.

Complex frames.

Frames constructed by adding successive pairs of bars to a basic triangular frame are called *simple* frames. Those so far discussed have been of this type. But there are also just-rigid frames which cannot be built up in this way; such frames are called *complex*. An example is shown in Fig. 56, in which

the bars are supposed to cross without touching. The stresses may be found by solving the 12 equations of equilibrium of the joints, but that method is complicated. We cannot use the step-by-step method of joints, because there is no joint at which only two bars meet. We modify the method by assigning an unknown value to one of the stresses; we find the other stresses in terms of this one unknown by the conditions of equilibrium of the joints and finally, on closing the calculation, determine the unknown stress and hence all the stresses

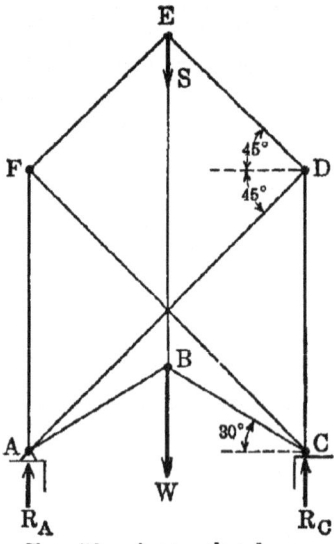

Fig. 56.—A complex frame.

Let us work this out in the case shown in Fig. 56, in which the bars FE, ED, AD, FC are inclined to the horizontal at 45°, and AB, BC inclined to the horizontal at 30°. Write $S_{EB} = S$. Then

at E, $S_{ED} = S_{EF} = -S/\sqrt{2}$,

at D, $S_{AD} = -S_{ED} = S/\sqrt{2}$,   ($= S_{FC}$, by symmetry),

at D, $S_{CD} = (S_{ED} - S_{AD})/\sqrt{2} = -S$,

at C, $S_{CD} + S_{FC}/\sqrt{2} + S_{BC}/2 + R_C = 0$,

at C, $S_{FC}/\sqrt{2} + S_{BC}\sqrt{3}/2 = 0$.

Elimination of S_{BC} from the last two equations gives

$$S_{CD}\sqrt{3} + S_{FC}(\sqrt{3} - 1)/\sqrt{2} + R_C\sqrt{3} = 0$$

Since $R_C = W/2$, $S_{CD} = -S$, $S_{FC} = S/\sqrt{2}$, we obtain

$$S = \tfrac{1}{2}W(3 - \sqrt{3});$$

all the stresses are now easily written down.

Concluding remarks.

The methods described above are adequate in simple cases, and the reduction of the problem of determining the stresses to the solution of a set of $2j$ simultaneous linear equations is complete and satisfactory mathematically, although often complicated. When we have written down the equations, we know that we have given complete mathematical expression to all the

conditions of equilibrium and that the stresses can be found from the equations *provided they are consistent.*

It may happen that the equations of equilibrium are inconsistent; this occurs in the case of *critical forms*, of which an example is shown in Fig. 57. This frame is just-rigid; but since the bars AB, BC lie in a straight line, no stresses in them can give equilibrium of the joint B, when a load W is applied there. Such a frame would be an unsound engineering structure. Actually the joint B would be slightly depressed (owing to stretching of the bars), and there would be very great tensions in the bars AB, BC.

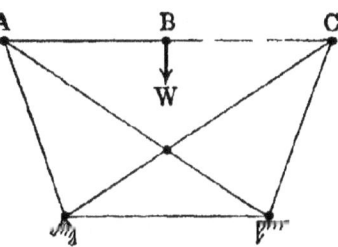

Fig. 57.—A critical form.

On account of its importance in engineering, the theory of frames has been elaborately developed. For a more complete account, with special reference to engineering problems, the reader is referred to S. Timoshenko and D. H. Young, Engineering Mechanics (McGraw-Hill Book Company, Inc., New York, 1940).

Most statical problems admit two methods of attack. On the one hand, we may reduce the problem to the solution of equations; this is the *analytical method.* On the other hand, we may represent forces by segments, and compound and resolve them by actual drawing; this is the *graphical method.* Each method has its advantages, but throughout this book we have preferred to use the analytical method, because it is easier to explain and has a wider range of application. For the graphical method in statics and its application to frames, the reader may consult for example H. Lamb, Statics (Cambridge University Press, 1928).

3.6. SUMMARY OF APPLICATIONS IN PLANE STATICS

I. Mass centers and centers of gravity.

(a) Formulas for the mass center:

$$(3.601) \qquad \bar{\mathbf{r}} = \frac{\sum_{i=1}^{n} m_i \mathbf{r}_i}{\sum_{i=1}^{n} m_i} \qquad \text{(system of particles);}$$

$$\tag{3.602} \bar{\mathbf{r}} = \frac{\iiint \mathbf{r}\rho \, dx \, dy \, dz}{\iiint \rho \, dx \, dy \, dz} \quad \text{(continuous system)}.$$

(b) Devices for finding mass centers:

(i) symmetry, (ii) decomposition, (iii) theorems of Pappus.

(c) Center of gravity coincides with mass center   Potential energy $= Mg\bar{y}$. With respect to any vertical plane, the weights of all the particles of a system are plane-equipollent to a single force (total weight) acting through the center of gravity.

II. Friction.

Static friction: $F/N \le \mu$ or $\theta \le \lambda$; $(\tan \lambda = \mu)$.
Kinetic friction: $F/N = \mu'$ or $\theta = \lambda'$; $(\tan \lambda' = \mu')$.

III. Thin beams.

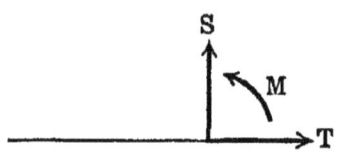

(a)

T = tension, S = shearing force, M = bending moment.

(b) Basic assumptions:

  (i) Hooke's law: $T = k'e$,   (e = extension, $k' = EA$).
  (ii) Euler-Bernoulli law: $M = k/\rho$,
                       (ρ = radius of curvature, $k = EI$).

(c) Differential equation of a thin heavy beam:

$$\tag{3.603} k \frac{d^4 y}{dx^4} = -w.$$

$$\tag{3.604} M = k \frac{d^2 y}{dx^2}, \quad S = -\frac{dM}{dx}.$$

(d) Continuity conditions: y, dy/dx, d^2y/dx^2 are continuous

IV. Flexible cables.

(a) General formulas:

$$\tag{3.605} T \frac{dx}{ds} = H \quad \text{(a constant)}; \quad \frac{d}{ds}\left(\frac{dy}{dx}\right) = \frac{w}{H}.$$

(b) Cable of suspension bridge hangs in a parabola.

(c) Common catenary:

$$(3.606) \qquad y = c\left(\cosh\frac{x}{c} - 1\right), \qquad c = \frac{H}{w},$$

$$(3.607) \qquad s = c \sinh\frac{x}{c},$$

$$(3.608) \qquad s^2 + c^2 = (y + c)^2,$$

$$(3.609) \qquad T = H + wy.$$

(d) Light cable in contact with a smooth curve:

$$(3.610) \qquad T = \text{constant}, \qquad N = \frac{T}{\rho}.$$

(e) Light cable in contact with a rough curve:

$$(3.611) \qquad T = T_0\, e^{\mu\theta} \qquad \text{(for cable on point of slipping)}.$$

V. Frames.

(a) Just-rigid frame:

$$(3.612) \qquad b = 2j - 3$$

(b) Method of joints. Begin with a joint where only two bars meet.

(c) Method of sections. Section must not cut more than three bars, and these three bars must not meet at a point.

(d) Method of virtual work. Remove a bar.

(e) Complex frames: (b) and (c) not applicable directly. Assume one stress S, and use (b).

EXERCISES III

1. Find the mass center of a cubical box with no lid, the sides and bottom being made of the same thin material.

2. A ladder leans against a smooth wall, the lower end resting on a rough floor for which the coefficient of friction is $\frac{1}{4}$. Find the inclination of the ladder to the vertical, if it is just on the point of slipping.

3. A square frame is braced by two diagonal bars. One of these contains a turnbuckle, which is tightened until there is a tension T in the bar. Find the stresses in the other bars.

4. A man of weight W walks slowly along a light plank of length a, supported at its ends. Find the bending moment in the plank directly beneath his feet as a function of his distance from one end of the plank. Find also the shearing forces just in front of him and just behind him. Draw diagrams to show the senses of the bending moment and shearing forces.

5. Find the mass center of a wire bent into the form of an isosceles right-angled triangle.

6. A rod 4 ft. long rests on a rough floor against the smooth edge of a table of height 3 ft. If the rod is on the point of slipping when inclined at an angle of 60° to the horizontal, find the coefficient of friction.

7. A body of weight w rests on a rough inclined plane of inclination i, the coefficient of friction (μ) being greater than $\tan i$. Find the work done in slowly dragging the body a distance a up the plane and then dragging it back to the starting point, the applied force being in each case parallel to the plane.

8. A heavy cable rests in contact with a smooth curve in a vertical plane Show that the difference in the tension at two points of the cable is proportional to the difference in level at these points.

9. Two light rings can slide on a rough horizontal rod. The rings are connected by a light inextensible string of length a, to the mid-point of which is attached a weight W. Show that the greatest distance between the rings, consistent with the equilibrium of the system, is

$$\mu a/\sqrt{1+\mu^2},$$

where μ is the coefficient of friction between either ring and the rod.

10. A heavy beam $ABCD$, of weight 2 lb. per ft., is supported horizontally by knife-edges at B and D. The beam is subjected to an additional vertical load of 20 lb. at C. If $AB = BC = CD = 4$ ft., determine the shearing force and bending moment for all points of the beam.

11. A portion of a circular disk of radius r is cut off by a straight cut of length $2c$. Find the position of the mass center of the larger portion

If $r = 1$ ft., $c = 6$ in., calculate the distance of the mass center from the center of the circle.

12. A light cable connects two weights W, w ($W > w$) and passes over a rough circular cylinder whose axis is horizontal. W rests on the ground, and w is suspended in the air. Find the least value of the coefficient of friction between the cylinder and the cable in order that W may be raised from the ground by slowly rotating the cylinder, and find expressions for the work done in turning the cylinder through one revolution (i) if W is raised, (ii) if W is not raised.

Find also the work done in turning the cylinder through one revolution in the opposite sense.

13. For the frame shown in Fig. 55a, take $\alpha = 45°$, and find the stresses in all the bars. Make a sketch of the frame, marking with a double line each bar in which there is a thrust.

14. A uniform semicircular wire hangs on a rough peg, the line joining its extremities making an angle of 45° with the horizontal If it is just on the point of slipping, find the coefficient of friction between the wire and the peg.

15. An elastic beam rests on three props, two being situated at the ends of the beam and at the same height, and the third at the middle point of the beam. Find the height of this central prop if the pressures on all three props are equal.

16. A cable 200 ft. long hangs between two points at the same height. The sag is 20 ft., and the tension at either point of suspension is 120 lb. wt Find the total weight of the cable.

17. A uniform cable hangs across two smooth pegs at the same height, the ends hanging down vertically. If the free ends are each 12 ft. long

and the tangent to the catenary at each peg makes an angle of 60° with the horizontal, find the total length of the cable.

18. Consider a frame as in Fig. 50, the triangles being equilateral. It is to carry a load $2W$, either as a single load at E or equally divided between E and F. In which case is there greater danger of collapse, it being assumed that collapse is due to a thrust in a bar exceeding some definite value, the same for all bars?

19. Four rods each of length a and weight w are smoothly jointed together to form a rhombus $ABCD$, which is kept in shape by a light rod BD. The angle BAD is 60°, and the rhombus is suspended in a vertical plane from A. Find the tension or thrust in BD and the magnitude and direction of the force exerted by the joint C on the rod CD.

20. Two equal spheres, each of weight W, rest on a horizontal plane in contact with one another. All three contacts are equally rough, with coefficient of friction μ. The spheres are pressed together by forces of magnitudes P, Q $(P > Q)$ acting inward along the line of centers. Show that there will be equilibrium if, and only if,

$$P - Q \leq \mu(P + Q), \qquad P - Q \leq \mu[2W - (P - Q)].$$

If P and Q are increased, their ratio remaining fixed, how will equilibrium be broken?

21. Find the stresses in the frame shown in Fig. 56 if the joint F is fixed, instead of A.

22. A hanging cable consists of two portions for which the weights per unit length are w_1 and w_2. Show that there is a discontinuity of curvature where the two portions are connected, the radii of curvature (ρ_1, ρ_2) on the two sides of the join satisfying the equation $\rho_1 w_1 = \rho_2 w_2$.

23. A beam AB, of length l and weight W, rests in a horizontal position with A clamped and a load W' is suspended from B. If the weight per unit length of the beam varies as the square of the distance from B, show that at distance x from A the shearing force S and the bending moment M are given by

$$S = W' + \frac{W}{l^3}(l - x)^3,$$

$$M = W'(l - x) + \frac{W}{4l^3}(l - x)^4.$$

24. Prove that at a point inside a uniform solid sphere the force of attraction varies directly as the distance from the center.

25. Find the potential of a circular disk at a point on its axis. Use the result to calculate the potential of a solid sphere at an external point

CHAPTER IV

PLANE KINEMATICS

4.1. KINEMATICS OF A PARTICLE

Having completed our study of plane statics, we now prepare for the study of dynamics by developing some results in *kinematics;* this subject deals with the motions of particles and rigid bodies without any consideration of the forces required to produce these motions. In the present chapter we discuss kinematics in a plane.

Tangential and normal components of velocity and acceleration.

Consider a particle P moving in a plane, in which Oxy are fixed axes. The position vector of the particle (cf. Sec. 1.3) is $r = \overrightarrow{OP}$, and the velocity is $q = dr/dt$. If the path of the particle is the curve C, then dr is an infinitesimal displacement along C, so that

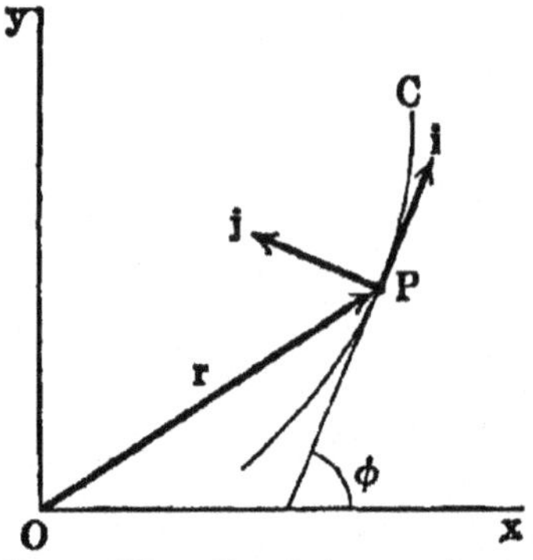

$$dr = i\, ds,$$

where ds is an element of length on C and i is the unit vector tangent to C. Thus

(4.101) $\quad q = i\dfrac{ds}{dt}, \quad q = \dfrac{ds}{dt};$

or, in words, *the velocity of a moving particle has a direction tangent to the path and a magnitude ds/dt*.

Fig. 58a.—Resolution along tangent and normal.

Let j be the unit normal vector to C (Fig. 58a), and let ϕ be the inclination of i to the x-axis. As we move along C, i and j are functions of ϕ. Figure 58b shows the vectors i and $i + \Delta i$ (corresponding to ϕ and $\phi + \Delta\phi$, respectively) transferred to a common origin. Since these are both unit vectors, the triangle formed by the three vectors i, $i + \Delta i$, Δi is isosceles. The magni-

tude of $\Delta\mathbf{i}$ is $2\sin\frac{1}{2}\Delta\phi$, and so the limit of the magnitude of $\Delta\mathbf{i}/\Delta\phi$ is unity. Thus $d\mathbf{i}/d\phi$ is a unit vector, pointing in the limiting direction defined by $\Delta\mathbf{i}$ as $\Delta\phi$ tends to zero. This direction is clearly that of $\mathbf{j}$, and so $d\mathbf{i}/d\phi = \mathbf{j}$. When a similar argument is used to evaluate $d\mathbf{j}/d\phi$, we readily see that $d\mathbf{j}/d\phi$ is perpendicular to $\mathbf{j}$, but since the limiting direction of $\Delta\mathbf{j}$ is that

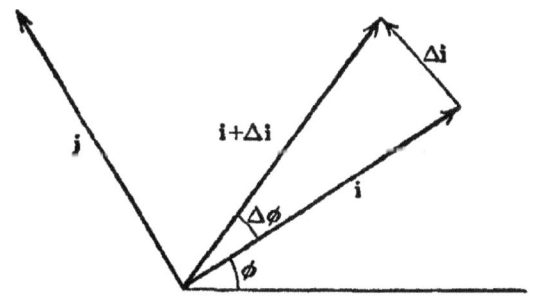

Fig. 58b —Change in unit tangent vector.

of $-\mathbf{i}$, we get $d\mathbf{j}/d\phi = -\mathbf{i}$. Combining these results we have

(4.102) $$\frac{d\mathbf{i}}{d\phi} = \mathbf{j}, \qquad \frac{d\mathbf{j}}{d\phi} = -\mathbf{i}.$$

To find the acceleration $\mathbf{f}$, we differentiate (4.101); this gives

(4.103) $$\mathbf{f} = \frac{d\mathbf{q}}{dt} = \mathbf{i}\frac{d^2s}{dt^2} + \frac{d\mathbf{i}}{d\phi}\frac{d\phi}{ds}\left(\frac{ds}{dt}\right)^2.$$

Hence, by (4.102) and the fact that the radius of curvature of C is $\rho = ds/d\phi$, we have

(4.104) $$\mathbf{f} = \mathbf{i}\frac{dq}{dt} + \mathbf{j}\frac{q^2}{\rho};$$

or, in words, *the acceleration of a moving particle has a component dq/dt along the tangent and a component q^2/ρ along the normal to the path.* The tangential component may also be expressed in the form $q\,dq/ds$.

It is easily seen that the normal component of acceleration always points to the concave side of the path.

As an example, consider a particle traveling in a circle of radius r with a speed q which is (a) constant, (b) proportional to t. In case (a), the acceleration vector is directed inward along the radius and has a magnitude q^2/r; in case (b), the acceleration vector has a constant component along the tangent and a component along the radius which varies as t^2.

Radial and transverse components.

Consider a particle P moving in a plane, its position being described by polar coordinates r, θ (Fig. 59). Let $\mathbf{i}$ be the unit vector along OP and $\mathbf{j}$ the unit vector perpendicular to $\mathbf{i}$, drawn in the sense shown. We note that

$$(4.105) \quad \frac{d\mathbf{i}}{d\theta} = \mathbf{j}, \quad \frac{d\mathbf{j}}{d\theta} = -\mathbf{i}.$$

We have then $\mathbf{r} = r\mathbf{i}$, and the velocity is

$$(4.106) \quad \mathbf{q} = \dot{\mathbf{r}} = \dot{r}\mathbf{i} + r\dot{\theta}\mathbf{j},$$

the dot indicating d/dt. Thus $(\dot{r}, r\dot{\theta})$ *are the components of velocity along and perpendicular to the radius vector.* For the acceleration we find, on differentiating (4.106) and using (4.105),

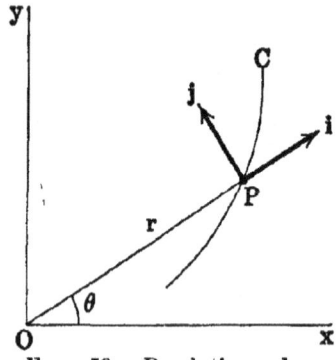

Fig 59.—Resolution along and perpendicular to radius vector

$$(4.107) \quad \mathbf{f} = \dot{\mathbf{q}} = (\ddot{r} - r\dot{\theta}^2)\mathbf{i} + \frac{1}{r}\frac{d}{dt}(r^2\dot{\theta})\mathbf{j}.$$

Thus

$$\ddot{r} - r\dot{\theta}^2, \quad \frac{1}{r}\frac{d}{dt}(r^2\dot{\theta})$$

are the components of acceleration along and perpendicular to the radius vector.

It is usual to call the components in the directions $\mathbf{i}$ and $\mathbf{j}$ the *radial* and *transverse* components, respectively.

The hodograph.

It is easy to form an intuitive picture of the velocity of a particle; we have merely to visualize the small displacement it receives in a small time and then imagine that small displacement greatly magnified without change of direction. But it is much more difficult to form an intuitive picture of the acceleration. The *hodograph* is a device to facilitate this. Figure 60a shows the path C of a particle, with its velocity $\mathbf{q}$ and acceleration $\mathbf{f}$ at the position P. Imagine now a fictitious particle P' moving in the plane (Fig. 60b) with a motion correlated to the motion

of P by the following rule: *the position vector of P', relative to some chosen origin O', is equal to the velocity of P.* The path described by P' is called the *hodograph* of the motion of P.

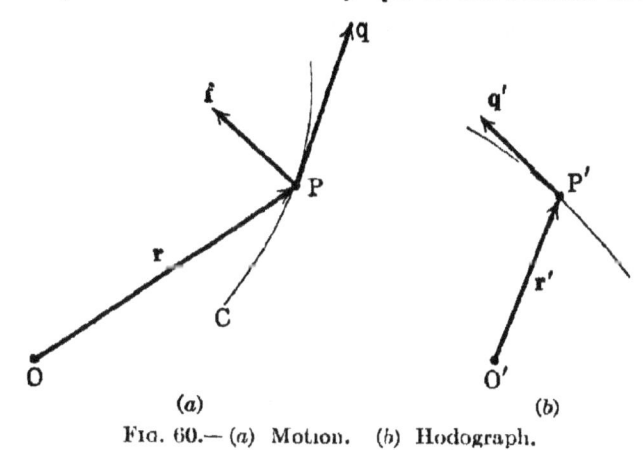

Fig. 60.—(a) Motion. (b) Hodograph.

Denoting by $\mathbf{r'}$, $\mathbf{q'}$ the position vector and velocity of P', we have

$$(4.108) \qquad \mathbf{r'} = \mathbf{q}$$

Hence, on differentiation,

$$(4.109) \qquad \mathbf{q'} = \mathbf{f};$$

in words, *the velocity in the hodograph is equal to the acceleration in the actual motion.*

Exercise. Verify the following statements:
(i) If a particle has an acceleration which is constant in magnitude and direction, the hodograph is a straight line described with constant speed.
(ii) If a particle moves in a circle with constant speed, the hodograph is a circle described with constant speed.

4.2. MOTION OF A RIGID BODY PARALLEL TO A FIXED PLANE

Description of the motion.

As already remarked in Sec. 2.4, the motion of a rigid body parallel to a fixed plane is completely described by the motion of the representative lamina, i.e., the section of the body by the plane. We may therefore confine our attention to the representative lamina. We also discussed in Sec. 2.4 the general infinitesimal displacement of a lamina in its plane. This displacement was described by selecting a base point A in the lamina

and giving (i) the infinitesimal displacement of A and (ii) the infinitesimal angle through which the lamina is turned.

A continuous motion of a lamina may be considered as a sequence of infinitesimal displacements received in infinitesimal intervals of time. We select some particle A of the lamina as base point. At any time t, A has a velocity, say $\mathbf{q}_A$. At time t the angle between a line fixed in the lamina and a line fixed in the plane is increasing at some rate which we shall denote by ω: ω is called the *angular velocity* of the lamina.* In a small time interval dt the particle A receives a small displacement $\mathbf{q}_A\, dt$, and in the same interval the lamina is turned through a small angle $\omega\, dt$. Hence the specification of $\mathbf{q}_A$ and ω as functions of t describes the succession of infinitesimal displacements which the body undergoes. To sum up: *The motion of a lamina in a plane is described by* (i) *selecting a base point A in the lamina,* (ii) *specifying the velocity $\mathbf{q}_A$ of A as a function of the time t, and* (iii) *specifying the angular velocity ω of the lamina as a function of t.*

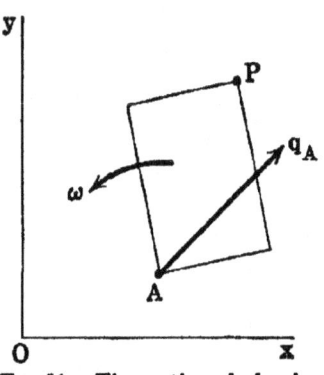

Fig. 61.—The motion of a lamina described by $\mathbf{q}_A$ and ω.

This description, for the instant t, is shown diagrammatically in Fig. 61, the curved arrow being used to indicate angular velocity.

The instantaneous velocity of any point P of the lamina can be found from (2.409), which gives the infinitesimal displacement of a point. Let (a, b) be the coordinates of A and (x, y) those of P, both measured on fixed axes Oxy. Then the infinitesimal displacement of P in the time interval dt has components

$$(4.201) \quad \begin{cases} dx = u_A\, dt - (y - b)\omega\, dt, \\ dy = v_A\, dt + (x - a)\omega\, dt, \end{cases}$$

where u_A, v_A are the components of $\mathbf{q}_A$. Thus the velocity of P has components

$$(4.202) \quad \begin{cases} u = u_A - (y - b)\omega, \\ v = v_A + (x - a)\omega. \end{cases}$$

---

* Since the angle between two lines fixed in a rigid body is constant, it is easily seen that the value of ω is the same no matter what lines are chosen in the lamina and in the plane.

Instantaneous center.

At any instant, there is just one point of a moving lamina which has no velocity. Its coordinates are found from (4.202), on putting $u = v = 0$; they are

(4 203) $\qquad x = a - v_A/\omega, \qquad y = b + u_A/\omega.$

This point is called the *instantaneous center* Under one exceptional condition no instantaneous center exists, namely, when $\omega = 0$. We may then say that the instantaneous center is at infinity.

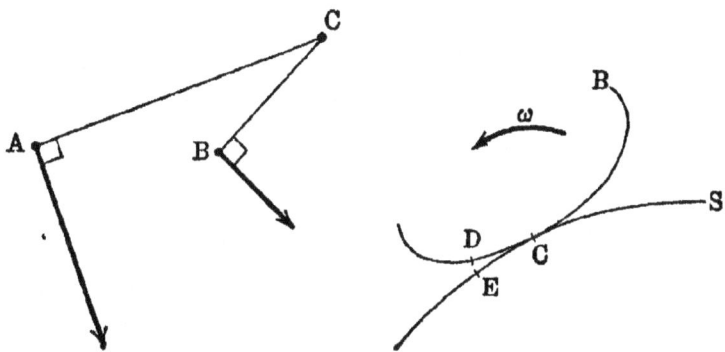

Fig. 62.—Determination of the instantaneous center from the velocities of two points.

Fig. 63 —The body centrode B rolls on the space centrode S.

Once the instantaneous center C is known, it is very easy to visualize what happens to the lamina in a small interval of time dt: the lamina rotates about C through a small angle $\omega\, dt$. This fact enables us to find C when the directions of the velocities of two points A and B of the lamina are known. For, since the lamina is turning about C at the instant, the velocity of any point P is perpendicular to CP. Hence, C is located at the intersection of the lines drawn through A and B perpendicular to the velocities of those points (Fig. 62).

From the definition of the rolling of one curve on another, given in Sec. 2.4, it is now clear that *a moving curve rolls on a fixed curve when the curves touch and the instantaneous center of the moving curve is at the point of contact*. In fact, this statement may be taken as a definition of rolling, instead of that given in Sec. 2 4. If both curves are in motion, we define rolling by the conditions that the curves touch and that the instantaneous

velocities of the two particles at the point of contact (one on each curve) are equal to one another.

As a lamina moves, the instantaneous center C moves in the fixed plane; the curve described by it is called the *space centrode* (S). But C also moves in the lamina; the curve described by C in the lamina is called the *body centrode* (B). At any instant, S and B have the point C in common, and B is turning about C, since B is carried along with the lamina. The situation at time t is shown in Fig. 63. A little later, at time $t + dt$, a point D of B has moved into coincidence with a point E of S to form the new instantaneous center, and this is done by turning B about C through the small angle $\omega\, dt$. Hence, it is evident that B cannot cut S at a finite angle; therefore B touches S at C, and since C is the instantaneous center of B, we have the following result: *The body centrode rolls on the space centrode.*

Exercise. Verify the following statements:
(i) When a wheel rolls on a track, the space centrode is the track itself and the body centrode the circumference of the wheel.
(ii) When a rod of length $2a$ slides with its extremities on two lines which intersect at right angles, the body centrode is a circle of radius a and the space centrode a circle of radius $2a$.

Example. As an example of our analysis of the motion of a rigid body, let us consider two wheels W_1 and W_2 of radii a_1 and a_2, respectively, lying in a plane. Their centers are connected by a rod R of length $a_1 + a_2$, and the wheels engage without slipping. If we fix the center of W_1, then W_1 and R can turn independently about this center, and W_2 will roll on W_1. Each of the three bodies W_1, W_2, R has an angular velocity, say ω_1, ω_2, Ω. These three angular velocities are not independent; let us find the relation connecting them.

The particles of W_1 and W_2 at their point of contact have the same velocity. We can find two different expressions for this common velocity, equating them, we obtain the required relation. Since W_1 turns about its center with angular velocity ω_1, the velocity of its particle at the point of contact is tangential and of magnitude $a_1\omega_1$. The wheel W_2 has a motion which may be described by means of a base point taken at its center. The velocity of this base point is perpendicular to R and of magnitude $(a_1 + a_2)\Omega$. Hence the velocity of the particle of W_2 at the point of contact with W_1 is tangential and of magnitude

$$(a_1 + a_2)\Omega - a_2\omega_2.$$

Therefore we have, as the required relation in symmetric form,

$$a_1\omega_1 + a_2\omega_2 = (a_1 + a_2)\Omega.$$

As an alternative method of finding ω_2 when ω_1 and Ω are given, the following general method of finding angular velocity may be used. Take two particles of the body, say A and B. Resolve their velocities perpendicular to AB. The difference of these component velocities, divided by AB, is the required angular velocity. The proof of this is left as an exercise.

4.3. SUMMARY OF PLANE KINEMATICS

I. Kinematics of a particle.

(a) Components of velocity and acceleration:

	Velocity	Acceleration
Tangential	$q = \dot{s}$	$\ddot{s}$ or $q \dfrac{dq}{ds}$
Normal	0	$\dfrac{q^2}{\rho}$
Radial	$\dot{r}$	$\ddot{r} - r\dot{\theta}^2$
Transverse .	$r\dot{\theta}$	$\dfrac{1}{r}\dfrac{d}{dt}(r^2\dot{\theta})$

(b) Position in hodograph is velocity in motion; velocity in hodograph is acceleration in motion.

II. Kinematics of a rigid body.

(a) The angular velocity ω of a lamina is the rate of change of the angle between a line fixed in the lamina and a line fixed in the plane of reference.

(b) For base point A (a, b) the velocity at (x, y) has components

$$(4.301) \quad u = u_A - (y - b)\omega, \quad v = v_A + (x - a)\omega$$

(c) The space centrode (S) is the locus of the instantaneous center in the plane of reference. The body centrode (B) is the locus of the instantaneous center in the body. B rolls on S.

EXERCISES IV

1. A particle moves in a plane with constant speed. Prove that its acceleration is perpendicular to its velocity.

2. A particle moves in an elliptical path with constant speed. At what points is the magnitude of the acceleration (i) a maximum, (ii) a minimum?

3. A particle moves along a curve $y = a \sin px$, where a and p are constants. The component of velocity in the x-direction is a constant (u). Find the acceleration, and describe the hodograph.

4. AB, BC are two rods, each 2 ft. long, hinged at B. A and C are made to slide in a straight groove in opposite directions, each with a speed of 8 ft

per sec. Find the velocity and acceleration of B at the instant when the rods are perpendicular to one another.

5. Starting from

$$x = r \cos \theta, \qquad y = r \sin \theta,$$

calculate $\ddot{x}$ and $\ddot{y}$. Hence, by resolving the acceleration vector along and perpendicular to the radius vector, establish the formula (4.107).

6. A wheel of radius a rolls without slipping along a straight road. If the center of the wheel has a uniform velocity v, find at any instant the velocity and acceleration of the two points of the rim which are at a height h above the road. Examine in particular the cases $h = 0$, $h = 2a$.

7. Is it possible for a particle to move in a circle and have a hodograph which is a straight line? Give reasons for your answer.

8. A wheel of radius a rolls along a straight track, the center having a constant acceleration f. Show that there is, at any instant, just one point of the wheel with no acceleration; find its position relative to the center of the wheel.

9. A rectangular plate $ABCD$ moves in its plane with constant angular velocity ω. At a given instant the point A has a velocity of magnitude V along the diagonal AC. Find the velocity of B at this instant in terms of V, ω, and the dimensions of the rectangle.

10. A uniform circular hoop of radius a rolls on the outer rim of a fixed wheel of radius b, the hoop and the wheel being coplanar. If the angular velocity ω of the hoop is constant, find

(i) the velocity and acceleration of the center of the hoop;
(ii) the acceleration of that point of the hoop which is at the greatest distance from the center of the wheel.

11. A motorboat experiences a resistance proportional to the square of the speed. The engine is switched off when the speed is 50 ft. per sec. When the boat has moved through a distance of 60 ft., its speed has been reduced to 20 ft. per sec. Find (to the nearest foot) the total distance traversed when the speed has been reduced to 10 ft. per sec.

12. A point A has a uniform circular motion about a fixed point O with angular velocity m. A point B has a uniform circular motion about A with angular velocity n. What relation connects m and n if the acceleration of B is always directed toward O?

13. A circular ring of radius b turns in its plane about its center with constant angular velocity Ω. A second circular ring of radius a ($<b$) rolls in the same plane on the inner side of the first ring. The angular velocity of the center of the smaller ring about the center of the larger ring is ω, a constant with the same sign as Ω. Find the space and body centrodes for the smaller ring.

14. A particle P moving in a plane has an acceleration directed toward a fixed point O in the plane and varying as $1/OP^2$. Show that the curvature of the hodograph is constant and hence that the hodograph is a circle.

CHAPTER V

METHODS OF PLANE DYNAMICS

5.1. MOTION OF A PARTICLE

Equations of motion.

In accordance with (1.402) a particle, under the influence of a force **P**, moves so as to satisfy the equation

(5.101) $$m\mathbf{f} = \mathbf{P},$$

where m is the mass of the particle and $\mathbf{f}$ its acceleration relative to a Newtonian frame of reference. If $Oxyz$ are rectangular axes in this frame, then (5.101) gives, on resolution into components,

(5.102) $$m\ddot{x} = X, \quad m\ddot{y} = Y, \quad m\ddot{z} = Z,$$

where X, Y, Z are the components of **P** along the axes.

The above statements hold for a particle moving in space; let us now confine our attention to a particle moving in a plane, the force **P** being supposed to act in the plane of motion.

We may resolve **P** into components along the tangent and normal to the path of the particle (Fig. 64). If these components are P_t, P_n, respectively, the vector equation of motion (5.101) gives, on resolution along the tangent and normal [cf. (4.104)],

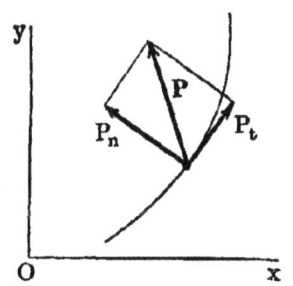

Fig. 64.—Resolution of force along the tangent and normal to the path.

(5.103) $$m\frac{dq}{dt} = P_t, \quad \frac{mq^2}{\rho} = P_n.$$

An interesting deduction may be noted. If the force acting on a particle is always perpendicular to its velocity (so that $P_t = 0$), then the speed of the particle is constant. If, further, the force is of constant magnitude, then P_n is constant; then

ρ is constant, so that the particle describes a circle. This occurs when an electrically charged particle moves in a uniform magnetic field with lines of force perpendicular to the plane of motion.

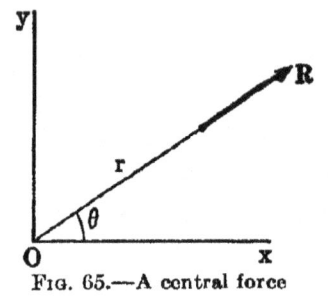

Let us now consider a particle moving in a plane under the influence of a force always directed away from, or toward, the origin (Fig. 65). Such a force is called a *central* force. Let R be the component of force in the direction away from the origin, so that R is positive when the force is repulsive and negative when it is attractive. Then, by (5 101), on resolution along and perpendicular to the radius vector [cf. (4.107)],

FIG. 65.—A central force

$$(5\ 104) \qquad m(\ddot{r} - r\dot{\theta}^2) = R, \qquad \frac{d}{dt}(r^2\dot{\theta}) = 0.$$

Equations (5.102), (5.103), and (5 104) are all very useful forms of the equations of motion of a particle.

Exercise. Referring to (3 122), write down the equations of motion of a particle in the earth's gravitational field, using (i) polar coordinates and (ii) rectangular Cartesians

Principle of angular momentum.

The *momentum* of a particle of mass m, moving with velocity **q**, is defined as the vector $m\mathbf{q}$. (This is sometimes called *linear* momentum, to distinguish it from angular momentum, defined below.) The components of momentum for motion in a plane are

$$m\dot{x}, \qquad m\dot{y},$$

where Oxy are rectangular axes in the plane. Since momentum is a vector, it has a moment about any point A in the plane; this moment is called *moment of momentum* or *angular momentum* about A. In Chap. II, we discussed moments of vectors; we saw that the moment of a vector is the sum of the moments of its components, and so by (2.303) the angular momentum of a moving particle about the origin is

$$(5.105) \qquad h = m(x\dot{y} - y\dot{x}).$$

If, instead of resolving the momentum vector along the axes, we

Sec. 5.1]   *METHODS OF PLANE DYNAMICS*   129

resolve it along and perpendicular to the radius vector drawn from the origin, we obtain components [cf. (4.106)]

$$m\ddot{r}, \quad mr\ddot{\theta}.$$

The former component has no moment about the origin; hence

(5.106) $$h = mr^2\dot{\theta}.$$

Consider now a particle moving in a plane under the action of a force with components X, Y. The rate of change of angular momentum about the origin is

$$\dot{h} = m(x\ddot{y} - y\ddot{x}) = xY - yX = N,$$

where N is the moment of the force about the origin. Hence we have the *principle of angular momentum: For a particle moving in a plane the rate of change of angular momentum about any fixed point in the plane is equal to the moment of the force about that point.*

We note that, in the case of a central force, the second equation of (5.104) is equivalent to the statement that the angular momentum about the origin is constant.

Linear momentum, being the product of mass and velocity, has the dimensions $[MLT^{-1}]$. In the c.g.s. system, it is measured in gm. cm. sec.$^{-1}$; in the f.p.s. system in lb. ft. sec.$^{-1}$. On account of the equivalence of dimensions (see Appendix), these units may also be called dyne sec. and poundal sec., respectively. Angular momentum has the dimensions $[ML^2T^{-1}]$ and is measured in gm. cm.^{2} sec.$^{-1}$ or lb. ft.^{2} sec.$^{-1}$

Principle of energy.

The *kinetic energy** of a particle of mass m moving with velocity q is defined to be $\tfrac{1}{2}mq^2$. It will be denoted by T. Thus, for a particle moving in space,

(5.107) $$T = \tfrac{1}{2}mq^2 = \tfrac{1}{2}m(\dot{x}^2 + \dot{y}^2 + \dot{z}^2).$$

The rate of change of kinetic energy is

$$\dot{T} = m(\dot{x}\ddot{x} + \dot{y}\ddot{y} + \dot{z}\ddot{z}) = X\dot{x} + Y\dot{y} + Z\dot{z},$$

where X, Y, Z are the components of the force acting on the particle. The increase in kinetic energy in the interval (t_0, t_1)

---

* Dimensions $[ML^2T^{-2}]$, as for work or potential energy and measured in the same units (cf. p. 54).

is therefore
$$T_1 - T_0 = \int_{t_0}^{t_1} (X\dot{x} + Y\dot{y} + Z\dot{z})\, dt.$$

Let W denote the work done by the force during this time interval. By (2.403) the work done in an infinitesimal displacement is
$$dW = X\, dx + Y\, dy + Z\, dz = (X\dot{x} + Y\dot{y} + Z\dot{z})\, dt,$$
and so
$$W = \int_{t_0}^{t_1} (X\dot{x} + Y\dot{y} + Z\dot{z})\, dt.$$
Hence

(5.108) $$T_1 - T_0 = W.$$

This establishes the *principle of energy*: *The increase in kinetic energy is equal to the work done by the force.*

Differentiating (5.108) with respect to t_1 and then dropping the subscript 1, we have

(5.109) $$\dot{T} = \dot{W};$$

in words, *the rate of increase of kinetic energy equals the rate of working of the force.*

If the particle moves in a conservative field of force with potential energy V, then, as in (2.419),
$$X = -\frac{\partial V}{\partial x}, \qquad Y = -\frac{\partial V}{\partial y}, \qquad Z = -\frac{\partial V}{\partial z}.$$
Then
$$W = \int_{t_0}^{t_1} (X\dot{x} + Y\dot{y} + Z\dot{z})\, dt = -\int_{t_0}^{t_1} \dot{V}\, dt = -V_1 + V_0,$$

where V_1, V_0 are the potential energies at times t_1, t_0, respectively. Comparison with (5.108) gives
$$T_1 - T_0 = -V_1 + V_0, \qquad T_1 + V_1 = T_0 + V_0.$$
Hence, in general,

(5.110) $$T + V = E,$$

where E is a constant, called the *total energy*. Thus *the sum of the kinetic and potential energies is constant*. This is called *the principle of the conservation of energy.*

The principle expressed mathematically by (5.110) is one of

the fundamental formulas of mechanics, and it is of great use in the solution of problems. It represents one relation among the three coordinates and the three components of velocity, V being supposedly known as a function of the coordinates. In the absence of a conservative field, we no longer have (5.110), only (5.108). This is much less useful because W is *not* a function of the coordinates. It is an integral the value of which depends on the path of the particle and thus is unknown, since the path of the particle is precisely what we have to find in the majority of problems on the dynamics of a particle.

Exercise. A particle slides down a smooth inclined plane. Use (5.110) to find its speed in terms of the distance traveled from rest.

5.2. MOTION OF A SYSTEM

Anyone familiar with the usual type of problems posed as exercises in mechanics must have been struck by their artificial character. The mechanical systems considered are often too simple to be of much practical interest. Attention is concentrated on such simple systems as rigid bodies swinging about fixed axes or wheels rolling along lines, instead of on complicated realities like trains, automobiles, or airplanes. This is because it has become traditional in the study of mechanics to direct attention to problems which are soluble, in the sense that the behavior of the system can be described by simple formulas. This is an unfortunate practice, because it fails to emphasize one of the greatest achievements of the applied mathematician, namely, his capacity to make general statements about complicated systems without paying much attention to the details of the systems.

To extract the fullest interest from the present section, the reader should bear in mind the striking generality of the statements. Since, however, it is tiring and confusing to think too much in terms of generalities, he should bear in mind a few concrete examples and think of them in connection with the various principles about to be discussed. The following systems are suggested as suitable examples:

(i) a stick sliding on a frozen pond;
(ii) a complete automobile;
(iii) a wheel of an automobile;

(iv) an airplane;
(v) a man on a trapeze;
(vi) the solar system.

As attention is at present directed toward plane dynamics, it is advisable to think primarily of two-dimensional motions of the above systems; e.g., the automobile and the airplane are traveling straight ahead. For the first five systems, we may accept the earth's surface as a Newtonian frame. As for the solar system, we may merely assume that there is *some* Newtonian frame and try to identify it by examining the consequences of the laws of motion.

The system under consideration is regarded as composed of particles. The forces acting on the particles are in part internal and in part external, the internal forces satisfying the law of action and reaction (Sec. 1.4) A rigid body is a particular type of system, in which the internal forces are such as to prevent the alteration of the distances between the particles The internal forces in a system are, as a rule, complicated; the purpose of the general principles which we are about to establish is to make important statements about the motion of the system which involve, not these complicated forces, but only the external forces which as a rule are comparatively simple For example, in the case of the automobile, the only external forces are (i) gravity, (ii) reactions at the contacts of the tires with the ground, and (iii) resistance of the air.

Principle of linear momentum; motion of the mass center.

The *linear momentum* of a system is defined as the sum of the linear momenta of the several particles of the system. Thus, if the masses of the particles are $m_1, m_2, \cdots m_n$, and their velocities $q_1, q_2, \cdots q_n$, the linear momentum of the system is the vector

$$(5.201) \qquad \mathbf{M} = \sum_{i=1}^{n} m_i \mathbf{q}_i.$$

We shall now prove the *principle of linear momentum: The rate of change of linear momentum of a system is equal to the vector sum of the external forces*

From (5 201), we have

$$(5.202) \qquad \dot{\mathbf{M}} = \sum_{i=1}^{n} m_i \mathbf{f}_i,$$

where $\mathbf{f}_i$ is the acceleration of the ith particle. Thus,

$$(5.203) \qquad \dot{\mathbf{M}} = \sum_{i=1}^{n} (\mathbf{P}_i + \mathbf{P}'_i),$$

where $\mathbf{P}_i$ is the external force on the ith particle and $\mathbf{P}'_i$ the internal force on it. But, from the equality of action and reaction, we see that

$$(5.204) \qquad \sum_{i=1}^{n} \mathbf{P}'_i = 0,$$

because this summation consists of vectors which are formed from pairs of forces that are equal and opposite. Hence, (5.203) gives

$$(5.205) \qquad \dot{\mathbf{M}} = \sum_{i=1}^{n} \mathbf{P}_i,$$

which proves the principle of linear momentum.

The last equation may be written

$$(5.206) \qquad \dot{\mathbf{M}} = \mathbf{F},$$

where $\mathbf{F}$ is the vector sum of the external forces.

We shall now prove the *law of motion of the mass center: The mass center of a system moves like a particle, having a mass equal to the total mass of the system, acted on by a force equal to the vector sum of the external forces acting on the system.*

From (3.101) it follows that the velocity of the mass center of a system of particles is

$$(5.207) \qquad \bar{\mathbf{q}} = \sum_{i=1}^{n} m_i \mathbf{q}_i / m,$$

where m is the total mass of the system. Thus if $\bar{\mathbf{f}}$ is the acceleration of the mass center, we have

$$(5.208) \qquad m\bar{\mathbf{f}} = m\dot{\bar{\mathbf{q}}} = \sum_{i=1}^{n} m_i \mathbf{f}_i = \dot{\mathbf{M}},$$

and so, by (5.206),

$$(5.209) \qquad m\bar{\mathbf{f}} = \mathbf{F}.$$

This is the equation of motion of a particle of mass m acted on by a force $\mathbf{F}$, and so the law is established.

We note that, by (5.207),

$$(5.210) \qquad m\bar{q} = \sum_{i=1}^{n} m_i q_i,$$

so that the linear momentum of the fictitious particle moving with the mass center is equal to the linear momentum of the system.

The conclusions to be drawn from the preceding principles are simple and interesting when the vector sum of the external forces is zero. Then the linear momentum of the system remains constant, and its mass center travels in a straight line with constant speed. This is true in particular for a stick sliding on a frozen pond. As for the solar system, we see that any Newtonian frame of reference must be such that the mass center of the solar system has a constant velocity relative to it.

Principle of angular momentum; motion relative to mass center.

The *angular momentum* of a system about a line (or about a point in its plane if the system is confined to a plane) is defined as the sum of the angular momenta of the particles composing it. Thus if the particle of mass m_i has coordinates x_i, y_i, z_i and velocity components $\dot{x}_i$, $\dot{y}_i$, $\dot{z}_i$, the angular momentum of the system about Oz is

$$(5.211) \qquad h = \sum_{i=1}^{n} m_i (x_i \dot{y}_i - y_i \dot{x}_i).$$

The rate of change of angular momentum about Oz is then

$$(5.212) \qquad \dot{h} = \sum_{i=1}^{n} m_i (x_i \ddot{y}_i - y_i \ddot{x}_i).$$

But

$$m_i \ddot{x}_i = X_i + X'_i, \qquad m_i \ddot{y}_i = Y_i + Y'_i,$$

where X_i, Y_i are the components of external force acting on the particle and X'_i, Y'_i the components of internal force. Thus,

$$(5.213) \qquad \dot{h} = \sum_{i=1}^{n} (x_i Y_i - y_i X_i) + \sum_{i=1}^{n} (x_i Y'_i - y_i X'_i)$$
$$= N + N',$$

where N is the total moment about Oz of all the external forces acting on the system and N' the total moment of all the internal

forces. But since the internal forces occur in balanced pairs, their total moment is zero; hence

(5.214) $$h = N.$$

This equation expresses the *principle of angular momentum: The rate of change of the angular momentum of a system about a fixed line is equal to the total moment of the external forces about that line.*

If we think, for example, of a man on a trapeze, the only external forces are (i) gravity and (ii) a reaction at the point of suspension. But the latter has no moment about the point of suspension. Hence the rate of change of angular momentum about the point of suspension is equal to the moment of the gravitational forces about that point.

Let $\bar{x}$, $\bar{y}$, $\bar{z}$ be the coordinates of the mass center of a system and let x'_i, y'_i, z'_i be the coordinates of the ith particle relative to the mass center, so that

(5.215) $$x_i = \bar{x} + x'_i, \qquad y_i = \bar{y} + y'_i.$$

The components of velocity of the particle relative to the mass center are $\dot{x}'_i$, $\dot{y}'_i$, $\dot{z}'_i$, and so the angular momentum relative to a line through the mass center parallel to Oz is

(5.216) $$h = \sum_{i=1}^{n} m_i(x'_i \dot{y}'_i - y'_i \dot{x}'_i),$$

where we use, in computing angular momentum, the velocities relative to the mass center. We shall refer to this briefly as the *angular momentum relative to the mass center.*

From (5.216), we obtain

(5.217) $$\dot{h} = \sum_{i=1}^{n} m_i(x'_i \ddot{y}'_i - y'_i \ddot{x}'_i),$$

and hence by (5.215), differentiated twice,

(5.218) $$\dot{h} = \sum_{i=1}^{n} m_i[x'_i(\ddot{y}_i - \ddot{\bar{y}}) - y'_i(\ddot{x}_i - \ddot{\bar{x}})]$$
$$= -\left(\sum_{i=1}^{n} m_i x'_i\right)\ddot{\bar{y}} + \left(\sum_{i=1}^{n} m_i y'_i\right)\ddot{\bar{x}}$$
$$+ \sum_{i=1}^{n}(x'_i Y_i - y'_i X_i) + \sum_{i=1}^{n}(x'_i Y'_i - y'_i X'_i);$$

as before, X_i, Y_i are components of external force and X_i', Y_i' components of internal force. But, from the defining property of the mass center, we have

$$\sum_{i=1}^{n} m_i x_i' = \sum_{i=1}^{n} m_i y_i' = 0,$$

so that the first two terms on the right-hand side of our last equation vanish. The fourth term vanishes through the balancing of the internal forces in pairs, and so we have

(5.219) $$\dot{h} = N,$$

where N is the total moment of the external forces about the mass center. This is the *principle of angular momentum relative to the mass center: The rate of change of angular momentum relative to the mass center is equal to the moment of the external forces about the mass center.*

Exercise Check to see that the two sides of (5 219) have the same dimensions.

It will be noticed that we have a principle of angular momentum relative to a fixed axis and a principle of angular momentum relative to the mass center. The principle does not hold for an arbitrarily moving axis with fixed direction.

As an illustration of the principle of angular momentum relative to the mass center, consider the front wheel of an automobile. The external forces on it are (i) gravity, (ii) the reaction of the axle, and (iii) the reaction of the ground. The force of gravity and the reaction of the axle have no moment about the central line of the axle, which passes through the mass center. Hence the rate of change of angular momentum relative to the center of the wheel equals the moment of the reaction of the ground about the center. In particular, if the car is traveling at constant speed, the angular momentum is constant, and so the reaction of the ground must act vertically up through the center of the wheel, no force of friction is called into play. Further, if the wheel bumps off the ground, its angular momentum will remain constant as long as it is in the air. These statements are made on the assumption that the bearings are smooth; the reader can supply the qualitative description of the modifications which arise when there is friction in the bearings.

The principle of energy.

The *kinetic energy* of a system is defined as the sum of the kinetic energies of its constituent particles; the formal expression

is

(5.220) $$T = \tfrac{1}{2} \sum_{i=1}^{n} m_i(\dot{x}_i^2 + \dot{y}_i^2 + \dot{z}_i^2).$$

Then,

(5.221) $$\dot{T} = \sum_{i=1}^{n} m_i(\dot{x}_i \ddot{x}_i + \dot{y}_i \ddot{y}_i + \dot{z}_i \ddot{z}_i)$$
$$= \sum_{i=1}^{n} (X_i \dot{x}_i + Y_i \dot{y}_i + Z_i \dot{z}_i),$$

where X_i, Y_i, Z_i are the components of the total force, external and internal, acting on the ith particle. Thus, if W is the work done by the forces from time t_0 to time t, we have

(5.222) $$\dot{T} = \dot{W}.$$

This is formally the same as (5.109), but here we are considering a system instead of a single particle. For a system, the *principle of energy* takes the following form: *The rate of change of kinetic energy of a system is equal to the rate of working of all the forces, external and internal.*

There is a sharp difference between the principles of linear and angular momentum on the one hand and the principle of energy on the other. In the principles of momentum the internal forces are eliminated; in the principle of energy they are not eliminated, except in the special case where they do no work and so contribute nothing to $\dot{W}$. In our idealized mathematical models, consisting of rigid bodies with smooth contacts, no work is done by the internal forces, and so they disappear from the principle of energy. In cases of collision, however, work may be done by the internal forces (see Chap. VIII); that is because, in such cases, it is impossible to regard the bodies as absolutely rigid.

When the system is conservative, with potential energy V, we have $\dot{W} = -\dot{V}$ by (2.416); then (5.222) leads to the *principle of the conservation of energy*

(5.223) $$T + V = E,$$

where E is the constant total energy.

D'Alembert's principle.

The principle about to be discussed adds nothing essential to the principles already given, but it is interesting as an alternative expression.

We have regarded "force" as a primitive concept in mechanics, and we shall not abandon that point of view. One must guard against logical confusion in accepting the following definitions, in which we use the conventional terms. Consider a particle of mass m, having at a certain instant an acceleration $\mathbf{f}$. The vector $m\mathbf{f}$ is called the "effective force" acting on the particle, and that vector reversed, i.e., $-m\mathbf{f}$, the "reversed effective force." Now consider a system (S) of n particles in motion, the reversed effective force on the ith particle being $-m_i\mathbf{f}_i$. Alongside the mental picture of this system, think of another (S') in which the particles are at rest at the same positions as they have instantaneously in S and are acted on by the same forces, external and internal, as in S; in addition let there act in the statical system S' a set of real forces identical with the reversed effective forces of S. Now, by the equations of motion of the particles in S, we have

$$\mathbf{P}_i - m_i\mathbf{f}_i = 0, \qquad (i = 1, 2, \cdots n),$$

where $\mathbf{P}_i$ is the real force on the ith particle in S; hence it follows that S' is in statical equilibrium since the total force on each particle is zero. Thus we have *D'Alembert's principle: The reversed effective forces and the real forces together give statical equilibrium.*

To deal with problems in plane dynamics, we introduce a fundamental plane to which the motion is parallel. Since the internal forces are plane-equipollent to zero, it follows that *the external forces, together with the reversed effective forces, form a system plane-equipollent to zero.* We recall that this means that the vector sum and the moment vanish.

The statement of D'Alembert's principle may give the impression that it reduces dynamics to statics. This is partly true in the sense that the statement involves only the conditions of statical equilibrium. However, it must be remembered that the reversed effective forces involve derivatives of coordinates and that therefore conditions of statical equilibrium involving these forces are actually differential equations of motion. To determine

motion under given forces, these differential equations must be solved—a dynamical, rather than a statical, problem On the other hand, if the motion is known, D'Alembert's principle enables us to use the methods of statics to determine the forces acting on the system.

Exercise Three equal particles are joined by light rods to form an equilateral triangle. If the triangle rotates in its plane about its centroid with constant angular velocity, find the tensions in the rods

5.3. MOVING FRAMES OF REFERENCE

In developing dynamics up to this point, we have assumed the existence of a frame of reference relative to which bodies move in accordance with the Newtonian laws. To get accurate agreement between theoretical prediction and observation, we take for frame of reference one in which the mass center of the solar system is fixed and which has no rotation relative to the stars as a whole. For a slightly less accurate agreement in the case of experiments on the earth, we may take the earth itself as frame of reference.

We now raise the question: Knowing that a body behaves relative to a Newtonian frame of reference in accordance with the laws and principles discussed earlier, how does a body appear to behave when viewed from a frame of reference moving relative to the Newtonian frame?

Frames of reference with uniform translational velocity.

Let S be a Newtonian frame of reference and S' a frame of reference which has, relative to S, a uniform (i.e., unaccelerated) translational motion. (If S is the earth's surface, S' might be a train running smoothly on straight tracks at constant speed.)

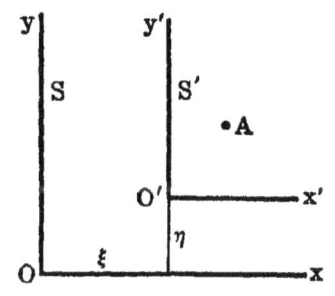

Fig. 66.—Frames of reference in relative motion without rotation.

We shall consider only two dimensions, but the argument can be extended to space immediately.

In S we take axes Oxy and in S' we take parallel axes $O'x'y'$ (Fig. 66). Let ξ, η be the coordinates of O' relative to O. Then

(5.301) $$\dot{\xi} = u_0, \quad \dot{\eta} = v_0,$$

where u_0, v_0 are the constant components of the velocity of S' relative to S. Let A be the position of any moving particle; it has coordinates (x, y) relative to Oxy and coordinates (x', y') relative to $O'x'y'$. These coordinates are connected by the relations

$$x = x' + \xi, \qquad y = y' + \eta,$$

and, on differentiation,

(5.302) $$\dot{x} = \dot{x}' + \dot{\xi}, \qquad \dot{y} = \dot{y}' + \dot{\eta}.$$

If we denote by **q** the velocity of A relative to S, by **q'** the velocity of A relative to S', and by **q**$_0$ the velocity of S' relative to S, (5.302) may be expressed in the form

(5.303) $$\mathbf{q} = \mathbf{q}' + \mathbf{q}_0.$$

This is called the *law of composition of velocities* and is exhibited graphically in Fig. 67.

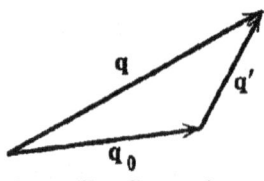

Fig. 67.—Composition of velocities

Exercise. A man stands on the deck of a steamer, traveling east at 15 miles per hour. To him the wind appears to blow from the south with a speed of 10 miles per hour. What is the true speed and direction of the wind?

Since ξ, η are constants, differentiation of (5.302) gives

(5.304) $$\ddot{x} = \ddot{x}', \qquad \ddot{y} = \ddot{y}';$$

thus the acceleration relative to S' is equal to the acceleration relative to S, and this may be expressed in vector form as $\mathbf{f}' = \mathbf{f}$. Thus the law of motion

(5.305) $$m\mathbf{f} = \mathbf{P}$$

may also be written

(5.306) $$m\mathbf{f}' = \mathbf{P},$$

and so *Newton's law of motion holds in S' as well as in S.*

From this we draw an important conclusion. Given one Newtonian frame of reference S, we can find an infinity of other Newtonian frames of reference, namely, all those frames of reference which have a uniform motion of translation relative to S.

In Sec. 5.2 we saw that if a Newtonian frame exists—and of

course we suppose that it does, since otherwise there would be no Newtonian mechanics—then the mass center of the solar system must have a constant velocity relative to it. From what has been shown above, it follows that we may change to another Newtonian frame in which the mass center of the solar system is at rest. This is, in fact, the astronomical frame, to which we have referred before.

If the earth is regarded as a satisfactory Newtonian frame of reference, then we must regard as equally satisfactory the interior of any vehicle which moves over the earth with constant velocity. This is in accordance with common experience. we are not conscious of the smooth uniform motion of a train when we are traveling in it; we become conscious of the motion only when the train lurches or brakes or rounds a corner.

Frames of reference with translational acceleration.

Let us now suppose that S is a Newtonian frame and that S' has relative to it a translational motion with constant acceleration. Then (cf Fig 66), we have

$$(5.307) \qquad \xi = \alpha_0, \qquad \eta = \beta_0,$$

where α_0, β_0 are constants. The relations (5 302) hold in this case also, and differentiation gives

$$(5.308) \qquad x = x' + \alpha_0, \qquad y = y' + \beta_0$$

Let $\mathbf{f}$, $\mathbf{f}'$ denote, respectively, the accelerations of A relative to S and S', and let $\mathbf{f}_0$ denote the acceleration of S' relative to S; then (5.308) may be written

$$(5.309) \qquad \mathbf{f} = \mathbf{f}' + \mathbf{f}_0.$$

This is called the *law of composition of accelerations*

The equation of motion (5.305) now leads to

$$(5.310) \qquad m\mathbf{f}' = \mathbf{P} - m\mathbf{f}_0.$$

Thus the Newtonian law of motion does *not* hold relative to S'. But we can say that the Newtonian law holds provided that we add to the *true* force $\mathbf{P}$ a *fictitious* force $-m\mathbf{f}_0$.

As an illustration, consider an elevator descending with constant acceleration f_0. Relative to the elevator, everything takes place as if the elevator

were at rest and every particle experienced an upward force mf_0, where m is the mass of the particle, in addition to the downward force mg. These fictitious forces alter the reactions among the particles constituting the human body, and so we are conscious of an acceleration, even though we cannot look outside our frame of reference.

Frames of reference rotating with constant angular velocity.

Let us now suppose that S is a Newtonian frame of reference and S' a frame of reference rotating about a point O of S with constant angular velocity ω. Let $\mathbf{i}, \mathbf{j}$ be perpendicular unit vectors, fixed in S' (Fig. 68). Let A be a moving particle. (We may think of A as a fly walking on a rotating sheet of cardboard.)

Taking axes Oxy in S', in the directions of $\mathbf{i}$ and $\mathbf{j}$, the position vector of A is

$$(5.311) \quad \mathbf{r} = x\mathbf{i} + y\mathbf{j}.$$

Now

$$(5.312) \quad \frac{d\mathbf{i}}{dt} = \omega \mathbf{j}, \quad \frac{d\mathbf{j}}{dt} = -\omega \mathbf{i};$$

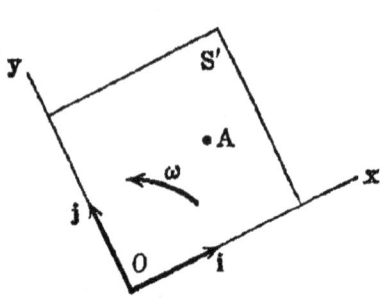

Fig. 68.—Rotating frame of reference.

and so differentiation of (5.311) gives, for the velocity of A (relative to S),

$$(5.313) \quad \mathbf{q} = \dot{\mathbf{r}} = (\dot{x} - \omega y)\mathbf{i} + (\dot{y} + \omega x)\mathbf{j}.$$

Another differentiation gives, for the acceleration of A (relative to S),

$$(5.314) \quad \mathbf{f} = \dot{\mathbf{q}} = (\ddot{x} - 2\omega \dot{y} - \omega^2 x)\mathbf{i} + (\ddot{y} + 2\omega \dot{x} - \omega^2 y)\mathbf{j}.$$

Thus, if X, Y are the components of true force in the directions of $\mathbf{i}, \mathbf{j}$, respectively, we have the equations of motion

$$(5.315) \quad m(\ddot{x} - 2\omega \dot{y} - \omega^2 x) = X, \quad m(\ddot{y} + 2\omega \dot{x} - \omega^2 y) = Y.$$

These may also be written

$$(5.316) \quad m\ddot{x} = X + X' + X'', \quad m\ddot{y} = Y + Y' + Y'',$$

where

$$(5.317) \quad \begin{cases} X' = 2m\omega \dot{y}, & Y' = -2m\omega \dot{x}, \\ X'' = m\omega^2 x, & Y'' = m\omega^2 y. \end{cases}$$

Thus we may say that *the particle moves relative to the rotating frame of reference in accordance with Newton's law of motion, provided that we add to the true force the two fictitious forces* (X', Y') *and* (X'', Y'').

The fictitious force (X', Y') is called the *Coriolis force*. Its magnitude is proportional to the angular velocity of S' and to the speed q' of the particle relative to S'; its direction is perpendicular to the velocity q' relative to S', and is obtained from the direction of q' by rotation through a right angle in a sense opposite to the sense of the angular velocity (Fig. 69). The fictitious force (X'', Y'') is called the *centrifugal force*. Its magnitude is proportional to the square of the angular velocity

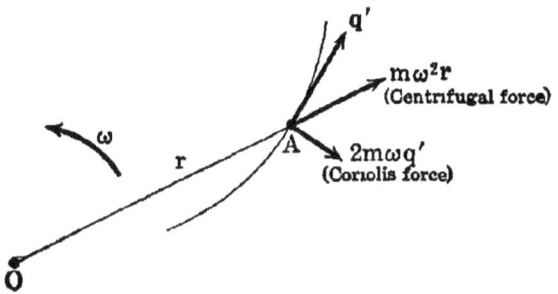

Fig. 69—Centrifugal force and Coriolis force in a rotating frame of reference

of S' and to the distance of the particle from the center of rotation; it is directed radially outward from the center of rotation.

The frame of reference which we employ in ordinary life is the earth. It rotates relative to the astronomical frame with an angular velocity of 2π radians per sidereal day; since one sidereal day contains 86,164.09 seconds (cf. page 14), the angular velocity of the earth is 7.29×10^{-5} radians per second. This is a very small angular velocity, and hence the Coriolis force and the centrifugal force arising from the earth's rotation are not noticeable in our daily lives. They are important geographically, however; the centrifugal force is responsible for the equatorial bulge on the earth, and the Coriolis force is responsible for the trade winds.

When frames of reference turning rapidly relative to the earth are employed, these fictitious forces may assume serious proportions. Thus, in an airplane turning in aerial combat or coming out of a dive, centrifugal force may be much greater than the force of gravity.

Statical effects of the earth's rotation.

In Sec. 3.1 we gave an introductory discussion of the force of gravity and the weight of a body near the earth's surface, leaving the earth's rotation out of account, i.e., treating the earth as a Newtonian frame. We now see that it may indeed be so treated provided that the proper fictitious forces are added. If we deal only with statical problems, i.e., those in which the system is at rest relative to the earth, there is no Coriolis force, and so the only fictitious force is centrifugal. The "weight" of a particle is the resultant of the force of gravity and the

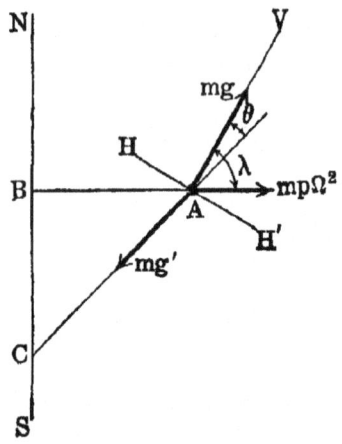

Fig. 70—Plumb line on the rotating earth.

centrifugal force, instead of being merely the force of gravity alone. Thus the weight of a particle is proportional to its mass, and the theory of Sec. 3.1 is valid provided that we understand by mg the weight as just defined.

We shall now bring our theory still closer to reality by taking a more accurate model of the earth. As a first crude approximation, the earth may be regarded as a sphere of radius R, where $R = 3960$ miles. More accurately, it is an oblate spheroid with an equatorial radius of 3963 miles and a polar radius of 3950 miles. This is the model which we shall accept for the present discussion, and we shall assume that the model rotates about its polar axis with constant angular velocity Ω.

In Fig. 70, SN is the earth's axis, A any point on its surface, and AB the perpendicular dropped on SN. The gravitational attraction of the earth on a particle at A acts along some line

AC which intersects SN; its magnitude is proportional to the mass m of the particle, and we shall denote it by mg'. The centrifugal force is directed along BA, and its magnitude is $mp\Omega^2$, where $p = BA$.

In order that the particle may remain in equilibrium relative to the earth, a third force must be applied to balance the gravitational force and the centrifugal force. This force must lie in the plane ABC, and its magnitude must be proportional to m. We denote it by mg; it may be supplied by the tension in a string or plumb line, or by the reaction of a smooth plane. We define the *vertical* AV at A as the direction of this force and the *horizontal plane* HAH' as the plane perpendicular to it.

We now ask: As we range over the earth's surface, what is the relation between g and g', and what is the inclination of the vertical to the direction of the gravitational force?

The *astronomical latitude* λ is defined as the elevation of the astronomical pole above the horizontal plane, i.e., the angle between SN and $H'AH$, or (equivalently) the angle between BA and AV. Let us denote by θ the angle between CA and AV. Resolution of forces along and perpendicular to AC gives as conditions of equilibrium

$$(5.318) \quad \begin{cases} g' = g \cos \theta + p\Omega^2 \cos(\lambda - \theta), \\ g \sin \theta = p\Omega^2 \sin(\lambda - \theta). \end{cases}$$

Now the ratio $p\Omega^2/g$ is small; hence θ is small, and $\cos \theta$ differs from unity by a small quantity of the second order. To the first order of small quantities, we have

$$(5.319) \quad g' = g + p\Omega^2 \cos \lambda, \qquad \theta = \frac{p\Omega^2}{g} \sin \lambda.$$

The terms involving Ω are small, and to our order of approximation we are entitled to replace p and λ by approximate values. Now λ is approximately equal to the angle BAC, and so

$$p = CA \cos \lambda,$$

approximately. According to a well-known law of hydrostatics, the surface of the ocean must be tangent to the horizontal plane; in fact, AV is normal to the surface of our model of the earth. Thus, since θ is small, CA is very nearly normal to this surface, and so $CA = R$ approximately, where R is the radius of the

earth in the first crude model. Hence (5.319) may be written

$$(5.320) \qquad g' = g + R\Omega^2 \cos^2 \lambda,$$

$$(5.321) \qquad \theta = \frac{R\Omega^2}{g} \sin \lambda \cos \lambda.$$

Thus we can find the gravitational intensity g' in terms of measurable quantities, g being measured by means of a pendulum (cf. Sec. 6.3). Theoretically, g is given by a measurement of the tension in a plumb line, but this is not a practical method. At the North and South Poles, $g = 983$ cm. sec^{-2}; at the Equator, $g = 978$ cm. sec.$^{-2}$ Equation (5.321) gives the deviation of the plumb line from the direction of the gravitational force; it is a maximum at a latitude of 45°.

Other effects of the earth's rotation will be treated in Sec. 13.5.

5.4. SUMMARY OF METHODS OF PLANE DYNAMICS

I. Equations of motion of a particle.

$$(5.401) \qquad m\mathbf{f} = \mathbf{P} \qquad \text{(vector form)};$$
$$(5.402) \qquad m\ddot{x} = X, \quad m\ddot{y} = Y \quad \text{(Cartesian coordinates)};$$
$$(5.403) \qquad m\dot{q} = P_t, \quad \frac{mq^2}{\rho} = P_n \quad \text{(resolution along tangent and normal)};$$
$$(5.404) \qquad m(\ddot{r} - r\dot{\theta}^2) = R, \quad r^2\dot{\theta} = \text{const.} \quad \text{(central force)}.$$

II. Principle of angular momentum for a particle.

$$(5.405) \qquad \dot{h} = N,$$

where

$$h = m(x\dot{y} - y\dot{x}) = mr^2\dot{\theta}.$$

III. Principle of energy for a particle.

$$(5.406) \qquad \dot{T} = \dot{W},$$

where

$$T = \tfrac{1}{2}mq^2 = \tfrac{1}{2}m(\dot{x}^2 + \dot{y}^2), \quad W = \text{work done};$$

$$(5.407) \qquad T + V = E \qquad \text{(conservation of energy)}.$$

IV. Principle of linear momentum for a system.

$$(5.408) \qquad \dot{\mathbf{M}} = \mathbf{F},$$

where

$$M = \sum_{i=1}^{n} m_i q_i;$$

(5.409) $\qquad m\bar{f} = F \qquad$ (motion of mass center).

V. Principle of angular momentum for a system.

(5.410) $\qquad \dot{h} = N,$

where

$$h = \sum_{i=1}^{n} m_i(x_i\dot{y}_i - y_i\dot{x}_i), \qquad N = \text{moment of external forces}.$$

(This holds with respect to a fixed point and with respect to the mass center.)

VI. Principle of energy for a system.

(5.411) $\qquad \dot{T} = \dot{W},$

where

$$T = \tfrac{1}{2} \sum_{i=1}^{n} m_i q_i^2, \qquad W = \text{work done};$$

(5.412) $\qquad T + V = E \qquad$ (conservation of energy).

VII. D'Alembert's principle.

The reversed effective forces $(-m_i f_i)$ and the real forces together give statical equilibrium.

VIII. Moving frames of reference.

(i) A frame of reference having a translation with constant velocity relative to a Newtonian frame is also Newtonian.

(ii) A frame of reference having a translation with constant acceleration f relative to a Newtonian frame may be treated as Newtonian if a fictitious force $-mf$ is applied to each particle.

(iii) A frame of reference rotating with constant angular velocity ω relative to a Newtonian frame may be treated as a Newtonian frame if to each particle there are applied two fictitious forces:

Coriolis force with components $(2m\omega\dot{y}, -2m\omega\dot{x})$,
Centrifugal force with components $(m\omega^2 x, m\omega^2 y)$.

EXERCISES V

1. At a certain instant, a particle of mass m, moving freely in a vertical plane under gravity, is at a height h above the ground and has a speed q. Use the principle of energy to find its speed when it strikes the ground.

2. What is the least number of revolutions per minute of a rotating drum, 2 feet in internal diameter, in order that a stone placed inside the drum may be carried right round? Assume that the contact between the stone and the drum is rough enough to prevent sliding. (The reaction of the drum on the stone must be directed inward.)

3. A skier, starting from rest, descends a slope 117 yards long and inclined at an angle of $\sin^{-1} \frac{5}{13}$ to the horizontal. If the coefficient of friction between the skis and the snow is $\frac{1}{5}$, find his speed at the bottom of the slope. If the skier with his equipment weighs 200 lb., how much energy is dissipated in overcoming friction?

4. A bead of mass m slides on a smooth wire in the form of a parabola with axis vertical and vertex downward. If the bead starts from rest at an end of the latus rectum (of length $4a$), find the speed with which it passes through the vertex. Find also the reaction of the wire on the bead at this point.

5. A heavy particle rests on top of a smooth fixed sphere. If it is slightly displaced, find the angular distance from the top at which it leaves the surface.

6. Two barges of masses m_1, m_2 at a distance d from each other are connected by a cable of negligible weight. One barge is drawn up to the other by winding in the cable. If neither barge is anchored, find the distance through which each barge moves. (Neglect any frictional effects due to the water.)

7. An airplane with an air speed of 120 miles per hour starts from A to go to B which is northeast of A. If there is a wind blowing from the north at 20 miles per hour, in what direction must the pilot point the airplane if he wishes to go in a straight line from A to B?

8. A heavy particle is suspended from a fixed point by a light string of length a. If the string would break under a tension equal to twice the weight of the particle, find the greatest angular velocity at which the string and particle can rotate as a conical pendulum without the string breaking.

9. A steamer sailing east at 24 knots is 1000 feet to the north of a launch which is proceeding north at 7 knots. Find the shortest subsequent distance between them if these courses are maintained. Draw rough diagrams, showing
  (i) the tracks relative to the water,
  (ii) the track of the steamer relative to the launch,
  (iii) the track of the launch relative to the steamer.

10. An automobile travels round a curve of radius r. If h is the height of the center of gravity above the ground and $2a$ the width between the wheels, show that it will overturn if the speed exceeds $\sqrt{gra/h}$, assuming no side-slipping takes place.

11. Every second n gas molecules, each of mass m, strike the side of a box. Use the principle of linear momentum to find the force required to hold the side of the box in place, assuming that each molecule has the same speed q before and after hitting the side and that the molecules move at right angles to the side. Explain precisely what dynamical "system" you use.

12. Explain how a man standing on a swing can increase the amplitude of the oscillations by crouching and standing up at suitable times.

13. A light string is attached to a fixed point O and carries at its free end a particle of mass m. The particle is describing complete revolutions about O under gravity, and the string is just taut when the particle is vertically above O. Find the tension in the string when in a horizontal position.

14. Show that, if an airplane of mass M in horizontal flight drops a bomb of mass m, the airplane experiences an upward acceleration mg/M.

15. A chain of any number of links hangs suspended from one end. The suspension and the connections between the links are smooth. The chain is displaced in a vertical plane and released from rest. Show that in the resulting oscillations the center of gravity of the chain never rises higher than its initial position, and that if it does ever rise to that same height, the whole chain is at rest at that instant.

16. A wheel spins in a horizontal plane about a vertical axis through its center, the bearings are supposed frictionless, and there is a mass clipped on one spoke. During the motion the mass slips along the spoke out to the rim. Does this cause an increase or decrease in the angular velocity of the wheel?

17. Assuming that a skier keeps his legs and body straight and neglecting friction and air resistance, show that he must keep his body perpendicular to the slope of a hill in order that he may preserve his balance without support from the forward or rear ends of his skis. Give a general discussion of the proper direction for his body when friction and air resistance are taken into account.

18. An ice floe with mass 500,000 tons is near the North Pole, moving west at the rate of 5 miles a day. Neglecting the curvature of the earth, find the magnitude and direction of the Coriolis force. Express the magnitude in tons wt.

19. A particle moves in a smooth straight horizontal tube which is made to rotate with constant angular velocity ω about a vertical axis which intersects the tube. Prove that the distance of the particle from the axis is given by

$$r = Ae^{\omega t} + Be^{-\omega t},$$

where A and B are constants depending on the initial position and velocity of the particle.

If when $t = 0$ the particle is at a distance $r = a$ from the axis, what velocity must it have along the tube in order that after a very long interval of time it may be very close to the axis?

20. A loop of string is spinning in the form of a circle about a diameter of the loop with constant angular velocity. Neglecting gravity, prove that the mass per unit length of the string must be proportional to $\operatorname{cosec}^3 \theta$, θ being measured from the diameter.

21. A particle moves with constant relative speed q round the rim of a wheel of radius a; the wheel rolls along a fixed straight line with uniform velocity V. Taking the wheel as frame of reference, find the Coriolis force and the centrifugal force. Indicate them in a diagram.

22. A system of particles moves in a plane. Prove that, provided the mass center is not at rest, there exists at time t a straight line L such that the angular momentum about any point on L is zero. Further, show that, if no external forces act on the system, the line L is fixed for all values of t.

CHAPTER VI

APPLICATIONS IN PLANE DYNAMICS—MOTION OF A PARTICLE

6.1. PROJECTILES WITHOUT RESISTANCE

The science of *ballistics* is concerned with the motion of projectiles. The theory of the explosion of the charge and the motion of the projectile in the barrel of the gun belong to *interior* ballistics, with which we shall not be concerned. After the projectile leaves the barrel of the gun, it moves under the influence of gravity and the resistance of the air; the purpose of *exterior* ballistics is to predict, from given muzzle velocity and angle of elevation of the gun, the path or *trajectory* of the projectile.

On account of the complicated nature of the resistance of the air, an accurate mathematical prediction is not possible. The greatest difficulties arise from the fact that the projectile is of finite size. To avoid these, we regard the projectile as a particle.

In the present section, we shall make a further and much more drastic simplification; we shall assume that no resistance is offered by the air. We cannot claim that the theory based on this hypothesis gives results of much practical value in ballistics, except in the case of projectiles thrown with small velocities.[*]

The parabolic trajectory.

Let Oxy be rectangular axes, Ox being horizontal and Oy vertical, directed upward. The equations of motion of a particle under the influence of gravity are

(6.101) $$m\ddot{x} = 0, \quad m\ddot{y} = -mg.$$

Integration gives

(6.102) $$\dot{x} = u_0, \quad \dot{y} = v_0 - gt,$$
(6.103) $$x = x_0 + u_0 t, \quad y = y_0 + v_0 t - \tfrac{1}{2}gt^2,$$

where x_0, y_0, u_0, v_0 are constants of integration. It is evident

---

[*] Cf. C. Cranz and K Becker, Handbook of Ballistics (H M Stationery Office, London, 1921), Vol. I, p. 17

that (x_0, y_0) is the position and (u_0, v_0) the velocity, both at time $t = 0$. The equations (6.103) give the path, or trajectory, of the particle.

Obviously, at a certain instant $(t = v_0/g)$, we have $\dot{y} = 0$, so that at that instant the velocity is horizontal. Now the origin O and the instant from which t is measured may be chosen as we please. Let us choose O at the point where the velocity is horizontal and measure t from that instant. Then we have

(6.104) $\qquad$ for $t = 0, \quad x = y = 0, \quad y = 0,$

Substituting in (6.102) and (6.103), we obtain

$$x_0 = y_0 = 0, \quad v_0 = 0,$$

and so the equations of the trajectory become

(6.105) $\qquad x = u_0 t, \quad y = -\tfrac{1}{2} g t^2.$

Elimination of t gives the equation of the trajectory in the form

(6.106) $$y = -\frac{gx^2}{2u_0^2},$$

a *parabola* with its vertex at the origin (Fig. 71).

The focus F of the parabola is situated at a distance $a = \tfrac{1}{2} u_0^2/g$ below the vertex, and the directrix L is at the same height above the vertex. At any point on the trajectory the speed q is given by

(6.107) $\quad q^2 = \dot{x}^2 + \dot{y}^2 = u_0^2 + g^2 t^2$
$\qquad\qquad = u_0^2 - 2gy = 2g(a - y);$

thus *the speed at any point P on the trajectory is equal to the speed acquired in free fall to P from rest at the directrix L.*

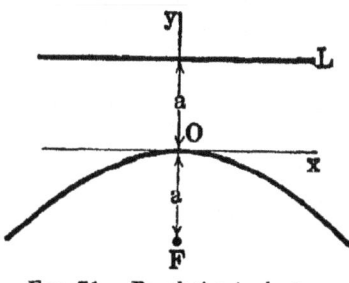

Fig. 71 —Parabolic trajectory, with focus F, vertex O, and directrix L.

From this it follows that, when a projectile is fired from a point P with speed q_0, the directrix of its parabolic trajectory is at the greatest height reached by a second projectile, fired straight up from P with the same speed q_0. In particular, we note that all trajectories obtained by firing projectiles at various inclinations in one vertical plane, but with a common initial speed q_0, have a geometrical property in common, namely, a common directrix.

The axes shown in Fig. 71 are the simplest for the discussion of general properties of the trajectory. But in ballistic problems it is preferable to take the origin at the point of projection and measure the time from the instant of firing (Fig. 72).

If α is the inclination of the initial velocity to the horizontal, we have, as in (6.102) and (6.103),

(6.108) $\quad\begin{cases} x = (q_0 \cos \alpha)t, \\ y = (q_0 \sin \alpha)t - \tfrac{1}{2}gt^2. \end{cases}$

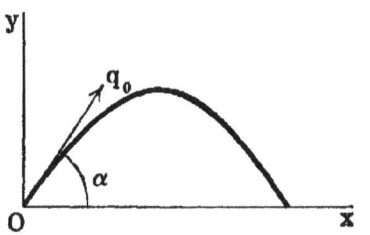

Fig. 72.—Parabolic trajectory referred to the point of projection

The projectile strikes the ground when $y = 0$, that is, when

(6.109) $$t = \frac{2q_0}{g} \sin \alpha;$$

then

(6.110) $$x = \frac{q_0^2}{g} \sin 2\alpha.$$

This is the *range* of the projectile. We note that it is a maximum (for given q_0) when $\alpha = 45°$.

The greatest height attained by the projectile is obtained by putting $\dot{y} = 0$. Then, by (6.108),

(6.111)

$$t = \frac{q_0}{g} \sin \alpha, \qquad y = \frac{q_0^2}{2g} \sin^2 \alpha$$

Limits of range.

Let us suppose that a gun gives to a projectile a muzzle velocity q_0. The gun can be pointed in any direction. What region in space can be reached by the projectile?

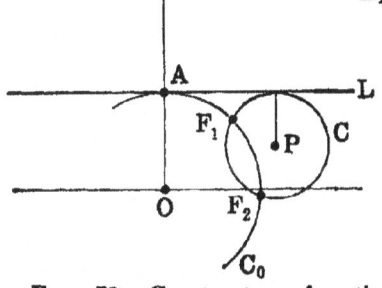

Fig. 73.—Construction for the foci of the two parabolic trajectories passing through P.

The question may be answered analytically, but the most elegant solution is geometrical.

We may confine our attention to one vertical plane through the gun, which is at O in Fig. 73. First we ask: Where is the focus of the trajectory passing through an assigned point P? The answer is given by the following construction:

Draw the directrix L, at a height $\frac{1}{2}q_0^2/g$ above O. Draw the circle C_0 with center O, touching L at A. Since O is a point on the parabolic trajectory, the focus must lie at a distance OA from O, and so it must lie on C_0. Similarly, if the circle C is drawn with center P to touch L, the focus must lie on C also. Hence the focus must lie at an intersection of the circles C_0 and C. In general, there will be either two points of intersection, F_1 and F_2, or none. In the former case, P is within range and F_1, F_2 are the foci of the *two* trajectories through it. In the latter case, P is out of range.

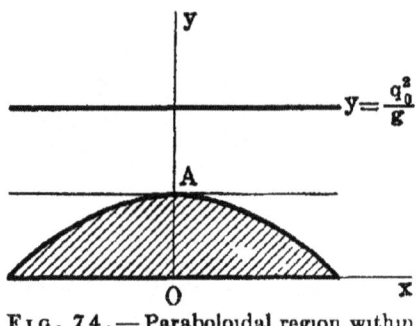

Fig. 74.—Paraboloidal region within range

If P is at the limit of range, the circles C_0 and C touch. Then P is equidistant from O and a horizontal line L_1, drawn at a height twice that of L, i.e., at a height q_0^2/g. Thus the locus of P in space is a paraboloid of revolution, having O for focus and A for vertex (Fig. 74). All points inside this paraboloid are within range, and all points outside it are out of range.

6.2. PROJECTILES WITH RESISTANCE

General equations.

We turn now to the more practical problem in which the air exerts on the projectile (still regarded as a particle) a force R acting in a direction opposite to the velocity (Fig. 75).

In resolving forces and acceleration in order to obtain equations of motion in scalar form, we have a choice of two procedures: (i) resolution along horizontal and vertical directions, and (ii) resolution along the tangent and normal to the trajectory as in (5.103).

Fig. 75.—The forces acting on a projectile.

Denoting by θ the inclination to the horizontal of the tangent to the trajectory, we obtain by (i) the equations

Sec. 6.2] MOTION OF A PARTICLE 155

(6.201) $\quad m\ddot{x} = -R\cos\theta, \quad m\ddot{y} = -R\sin\theta - mg.$

Denoting by ρ the radius of curvature of the trajectory, we obtain by (ii) the equations

(6.202) $\quad mq\dfrac{dq}{ds} = -R - mg\sin\theta, \quad \dfrac{mq^2}{\rho} = mg\cos\theta,$

where q is the speed and ds an element of arc of the trajectory. The equations (6.202) are, of course, only a different mathematical expression of (6.201).

The resistance experienced by a given projectile depends on its speed and on the density of the air. Regarding the air as stratified into horizontal layers each of constant density, so that the density is a function of y only, we may express R in the form

(6.203) $\quad\quad\quad\quad R = R(y, q),$

to show that it is a function of y and q only.

Since

(6.204) $\quad\quad\quad \cos\theta = \dfrac{\dot{x}}{q}, \quad \sin\theta = \dfrac{\dot{y}}{q},$

we may write (6.201) in the form

(6.205) $\quad\quad\quad \ddot{x} = -\Phi\dot{x}, \quad \ddot{y} = -\Phi\dot{y} - g,$

where Φ is a function of y, q, namely,

(6.206) $\quad\quad\quad \Phi(y, q) = \dfrac{R(y, q)}{mq}.$

The mathematical problem of the determination of the trajectory is made much more difficult by the fact that there is no physically valid formula expressing R as a function of q. For small values of q, R varies as q; but this simple law breaks down before we reach those velocities which are of interest in ballistics. For low ballistic velocities, R varies as q^2; but this law again breaks down when the velocity of the projectile approaches the velocity of sound. The law of dependence is then complicated and can be represented only graphically or by tables of values obtained experimentally. Hence, we must not expect to find any simple formulas for trajectories. In general, (6.205) must be integrated by a tedious process of step-by-step numerical integration. The differential equations are integrated approximately over small intervals of time; the errors due to approximation become insignificant when the intervals are very small.

The difficulties involved in the above method lead us to do what we so often do in applied mathematics—replace the complicated physical problem by one that is simpler mathematically. Thus, we shall confine our attention below to the case where R is independent of y and devote particular attention to the cases where R varies as q^2 or as q.

Resistance independent of height.

If the resistance depends on the speed only, so that $R = R(q)$, the problem is most easily attacked by means of (6.202). Let us write

(6.207) $$R = mg\phi(q)$$

for convenience. Noting that θ decreases as the arc length s increases, we have $\rho = -ds/d\theta$, and elimination of ds from (6.202) gives

(6.208) $$\frac{1}{q}\frac{dq}{d\theta} = \frac{\phi(q) + \sin\theta}{\cos\theta}.$$

This is called the *equation of the hodograph*, since q, θ are the polar coordinates of a point on the hodograph.

If we can solve (6.208), all desired information about the trajectory may be obtained by quadratures. By (6.202), we have

(6.209)
$$\begin{cases} \dfrac{dx}{d\theta} = \dfrac{dx}{ds}\dfrac{ds}{d\theta} = -\rho\cos\theta = -\dfrac{q^2}{g}, \\ \dfrac{dy}{d\theta} = \dfrac{dy}{ds}\dfrac{ds}{d\theta} = -\rho\sin\theta = -\dfrac{q^2\tan\theta}{g}, \\ \dfrac{dt}{d\theta} = \dfrac{dt}{ds}\dfrac{ds}{d\theta} = -\dfrac{\rho}{q} = -\dfrac{q\sec\theta}{g}. \end{cases}$$

Let us suppose that the projectile is fired from the origin at time $t = 0$ with speed q_0 at an angle of elevation θ_0. Let

(6.210) $$q = f(\theta)$$

be the solution of (6.208), supposed known. Then integration of (6.209) gives

(6.211)
$$\begin{cases} x = -\dfrac{1}{g}\int_{\theta_0}^{\theta} [f(\theta)]^2\, d\theta, \\ y = -\dfrac{1}{g}\int_{\theta_0}^{\theta} \tan\theta\, [f(\theta)]^2\, d\theta, \\ t = -\dfrac{1}{g}\int_{\theta_0}^{\theta} \sec\theta\, f(\theta)\, d\theta. \end{cases}$$

These equations express x, y, t as functions of one parameter θ and so determine the trajectory.

But we cannot use (6.211) until the function $f(\theta)$ is known, i.e., until the differential equation (6.208) is integrated. If the function $\phi(q)$ is general, the integration of (6.208) cannot even be reduced to quadratures. For some special forms of $\phi(q)$ the integration can be reduced to quadratures, and in some cases the solution $f(\theta)$ can be expressed in terms of elementary functions. We shall consider below the case $\phi(q) = Cq^2$, but before making this special choice of ϕ we shall transform (6.208) by changing to a new independent variable ψ, defined by

$$\tanh \psi = \sin \theta.$$

It is easily seen that (6.208) transforms into

(6.212) $$\frac{1}{q}\frac{dq}{d\psi} = \tanh \psi + \phi(q).$$

Resistance varying as the square of the velocity.

Let us take the law of resistance to be

(6.213) $$R = mg\phi(q), \qquad \phi(q) = Cq^2,$$

where C is a constant. Division of (6.212) by $-\tfrac{1}{2}q^2$ gives

(6.214) $$\frac{d}{d\psi}\left(\frac{1}{q^2}\right) = -\frac{2}{q^2}\tanh \psi - 2C;$$

this is a standard type of equation, with solution

(6.215) $$\frac{1}{q^2} = \operatorname{sech}^2 \psi \left(A - 2C \int \cosh^2 \psi \, d\psi\right)$$
$$= \cos^2 \theta \left[A - C \tanh^{-1}(\sin \theta)\right] - C \sin \theta,$$

where A is a constant of integration, to be fixed by the initial conditions.

Theoretically at least, the equations (6.211) now determine the trajectory, $f(\theta)$ being the reciprocal of the square root of the right-hand side of (6.215). But it is evident that the calculations involved are very complicated.

When the projectile moves in a vertical line, the problem is much simpler. If $\mathbf{i}$ is a unit vector directed vertically upward and the position vector of the projectile is $y\mathbf{i}$, the acceleration is $\ddot{y}\mathbf{i}$. The force of gravity is $-mg\mathbf{i}$. The resistance is $-mgC\dot{y}^2\mathbf{i}$ for motion upward ($\dot{y} > 0$) and $mgC\dot{y}^2\mathbf{i}$ for motion downward

$(\dot{y} < 0)$. Hence the equation of motion is

(6.216a) $$\ddot{y} = -gC\dot{y}^2 - g \quad \text{for motion upward;}$$
(6.216b) $$\ddot{y} = gC\dot{y}^2 - g \quad \text{for motion downward}$$

Since
$$\ddot{y} = \dot{y}\frac{d\dot{y}}{dy},$$

we have

(6.217a) $$\frac{\dot{y}\,d\dot{y}}{1 + C\dot{y}^2} = -g\,dy \quad \text{for motion upward;}$$

(6.217b) $$\frac{\dot{y}\,d\dot{y}}{1 - C\dot{y}^2} = -g\,dy \quad \text{for motion downward.}$$

Thus, on integration,

(6.218a) $$y = -\frac{1}{2gC}\log(1 + C\dot{y}^2) + A \quad \text{for motion upward,}$$

(6.218b) $$y = \frac{1}{2gC}\log(1 - C\dot{y}^2) + A' \quad \text{for motion downward,}$$

where A, A' are constants of integration.

Let us consider two special cases, corresponding to (a) a shell fired vertically upward, and (b) a bomb dropped vertically downward

(a) Let q_0 be the initial velocity of the shell, fired from $y = 0$. Then, by (6.218a), we have

(6.219) $$y = \frac{1}{2gC}\log\frac{1 + Cq_0^2}{1 + C\dot{y}^2}$$

The height h to which the shell rises is found by putting $\dot{y} = 0$; thus,

(6.220) $$h = \frac{1}{2gC}\log(1 + Cq_0^2).$$

If the resistance is small, this gives, approximately,

(6.221) $$h = \tfrac{1}{2}\frac{q_0^2}{g} - \tfrac{1}{4}\frac{Cq_0^4}{g},$$

in which the first term is the well-known expression for height attained under no resistance.

(b) Let the bomb be dropped from $y = 0$ with no velocity. Then (6.218b) gives

(6.222) $$y = \frac{1}{2gC}\log(1 - C\dot{y}^2),$$

y being, of course, negative When the bomb has dropped a distance h, we have

$$\log(1 - C\dot{y}^2) = -2gCh,$$

and hence its speed is

$$(6.223) \qquad q = \sqrt{\frac{1 - e^{-2gCh}}{C}}.$$

As h tends to infinity, q tends to $C^{-\frac{1}{2}}$. This is the *limiting velocity*; its value is

$$(6.224) \qquad C^{-\frac{1}{2}} = q \sqrt{mg/R},$$

where R is the resistance at any speed q.

Relations connecting y and t may be obtained from (6.216) by integration. Thus, (6.216a) may be written

$$\frac{d\dot{y}}{1 + C\dot{y}^2} = -g\, dt.$$

One integration gives $\dot{y}$ in terms of t, and a second integration gives y.

Resistance varying directly as the velocity.

Although the law of resistance

$$(6.225) \qquad R = mgCq$$

is not accurate physically, it is so simple to treat mathematically that it is a useful approximation—at least an improvement over the assumption of no resistance at all.

Turning back to (6.206), we note that Φ is now a constant ($\Phi = gC$), and the equations (6.205) are easy to handle, because the variables x and y are separated. We obtain, on integration,

$$(6.226) \qquad \begin{cases} x = x_0 + \dfrac{u_0}{\Phi}(1 - e^{-\Phi t}), \\ y = y_0 - \dfrac{gt}{\Phi} + \left(\dfrac{v_0}{\Phi} + \dfrac{g}{\Phi^2}\right)(1 - e^{-\Phi t}), \end{cases}$$

where x_0, y_0 are the coordinates and u_0, v_0 the components of velocity for $t = 0$.

When Φ is small, these equations yield approximately

$$(6.227) \qquad \begin{cases} x = x_0 + u_0 t - \tfrac{1}{2}\Phi u_0 t^2, \\ y = y_0 + v_0 t - \tfrac{1}{2}gt^2 - \tfrac{1}{2}\Phi v_0 t^2 \left(1 - \tfrac{1}{3}\dfrac{gt}{v_0}\right), \end{cases}$$

in which the terms independent of Φ correspond to the parabolic trajectory.

6.3. HARMONIC OSCILLATORS

The simple pendulum.

A simple pendulum consists of a heavy particle attached to one end of a light rod or inextensible string, the other end of the rod or string being attached to a fixed point. We con-

sider only motions of the pendulum in which the string remains in a definite vertical plane. In Fig. 76, B is the point of attachment and A is the particle (of mass m), drawn aside from its position of equilibrium O. Oxy are rectangular axes in the plane of motion, Ox being horizontal.

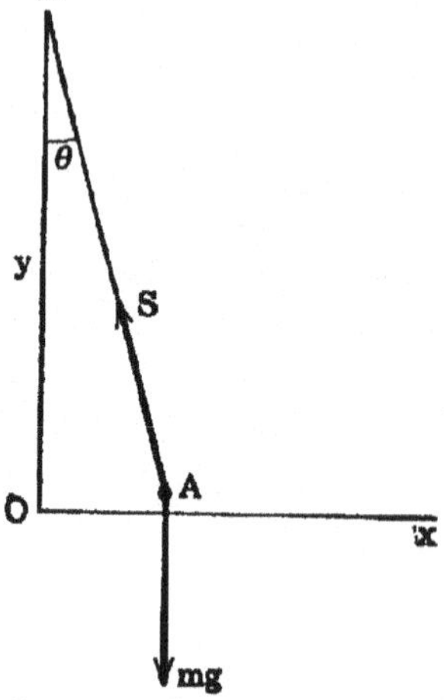

The particle moves under the influence of two forces: (i) its weight mg, and (ii) the tension S in the string. Since S acts along the normal to the circular path of the particle, it is clear that the dynamical problem presented by the simple pendulum is precisely the same as that of the motion of a particle on a smooth circular supporting curve, fixed in a vertical plane.

Fig. 76.—The simple pendulum.

Let $AB = l$, $O\widehat{B}A = \theta$; then

(6.301) $\quad \cos \theta = \dfrac{l - y}{l}, \quad \sin \theta = \dfrac{x}{l},$

where x, y are the coordinates of A. The equations of motion are

(6.302) $\quad m\ddot{x} = -S \sin \theta, \quad m\ddot{y} = S \cos \theta - mg.$

Let us investigate small oscillations about the position of equilibrium, assuming x and its derivatives to be small. Then y and its derivatives are small, of the second order, and $\cos \theta$ differs from unity by a small quantity of the second order. Thus, to the first order inclusive, the second of (6.302) gives

(6.303) $\quad\quad\quad\quad\quad S = mg,$

and substitution from this and from (6.301) in (6.302) gives

(6.304) $\quad\quad\quad \ddot{x} + p^2 x = 0, \quad p = \sqrt{\dfrac{g}{l}}.$

The general solution of this differential equation is

(6.305) $\quad\quad\quad x = A \cos pt + B \sin pt,$

where A, B are constants, to be determined by the initial conditions. A motion given by an equation of this form is called *simple harmonic*.

Differentiation of (6.305) gives

(6.306) $\quad\quad\quad \dot{x} = -Ap \sin pt + Bp \cos pt.$

We note that x and $\dot{x}$ have the same pair of values at times

$$t_1, \quad t_1 + \tau, \quad t_1 + 2\tau, \quad t_1 + 3\tau, \cdots$$

where t_1 is arbitrary, and

(6.307) $$\tau = \frac{2\pi}{p} = 2\pi\sqrt{\frac{l}{g}}.$$

When the position and velocity of a particle are repeated over and over again at equal intervals of time, we say that the motion is *periodic;* the interval is called its *periodic time.* Hence the above motion of a simple pendulum is periodic, with periodic time given by (6.307).

In Sec. 13.2 the finite oscillations of a pendulum will be discussed, and it will be found that the finite oscillations are periodic but not simple harmonic; the formula for the periodic time is different.

The harmonic oscillator.

The simple pendulum, executing small oscillations, is only one physical example of a type of dynamical system of frequent occurrence. Many problems of oscillation can be discussed in a single mathematical form; so we create a single mathematical model for them all. This model is called the *harmonic oscillator* (Fig. 77).

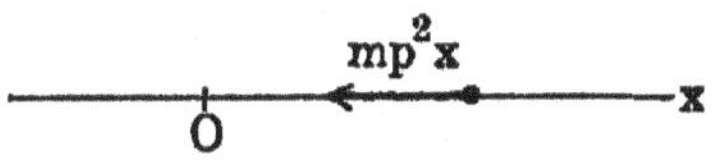

Fig. 77.—The harmonic oscillator.

The harmonic oscillator consists of a particle which can move on a straight line, which we shall take for x-axis. It is attracted toward the origin by a controlling force varying as the distance. If **i** is a unit vector in the positive direction of the x-axis, the controlling force may be written $-mp^2 x\mathbf{i}$, where m is the mass of the particle and p is a constant. The acceleration is $\ddot{x}\mathbf{i}$, and hence the equation of motion is

(6.308) $$m\ddot{x}\mathbf{i} = -mp^2 x\mathbf{i},$$

or, in scalar form,

(6.309) $$\ddot{x} + p^2 x = 0.$$

The general solution of this equation may be written in the form (6.305), that is,

(6.310) $$x = A \cos pt + B \sin pt,$$

so that the motion is simple harmonic.

Let us now define constants a, ϵ by the equations

(6.311) $$a = \sqrt{A^2 + B^2},$$
$$\cos \epsilon = \frac{A}{\sqrt{A^2 + B^2}}, \quad \sin \epsilon = - \frac{B}{\sqrt{A^2 + B^2}}.$$

Then (6.310) may be written

(6.312) $$x = a \cos (pt + \epsilon)$$

We observe that x covers the range $(-a, a)$ and that the motion is periodic with periodic time $2\pi/p$. The following terminology is used in connection with the harmonic oscillator:

amplitude $= a$,
period or periodic time $= \tau = 2\pi/p$,
frequency $=$ number of oscillations per unit time
$= 1/\tau = p/2\pi$,
phase $= pt + \epsilon$.

Effect of a disturbing force.

Let us now suppose that, in addition to the controlling force, there acts on the harmonic oscillator a force whose component in the positive direction of the x-axis is mX. The equation of motion (6.308) is now modified to the form

(6.313) $$m\ddot{x}\mathbf{i} = - mp^2 x\mathbf{i} + mX\mathbf{i},$$

or, in scalar form,

(6.314) $$\ddot{x} + p^2 x = X.$$

First let us suppose that X is constant. The general solution of (6.314) is then

(6.315) $$x = \frac{X}{p^2} + a \cos (pt + \epsilon)$$

This motion is simple harmonic, but the center of the oscillations is displaced to the position $x = X/p^2$, as is seen by writing (6.315) in the form

(6.316) $$x - \frac{X}{p^2} = a \cos (pt + \epsilon).$$

When the oscillation or vibration has a high frequency, so that p is large, the displacement of the center is small.

Let us now suppose that X is itself simple harmonic, varying according to the formula

(6.317) $$X = k \cos ct,$$

where k, c are constants Then the equation of motion (6.314) reads

(6.318) $$\ddot{x} + p^2 x = k \cos ct.$$

In the general case where $c \neq p$, the solution is

(6.319) $$x = a \cos (pt + \epsilon) + \frac{k}{p^2 - c^2} \cos ct,$$

where a, ϵ are constants, to be determined by the initial conditions. Thus the motion is a superposition of an undisturbed simple harmonic motion and a second motion; the latter has the same period as the force, and an amplitude which becomes large when the difference between the periods of the free oscillator and the disturbing force becomes small. The great increase in the amplitude of the oscillations under this last condition is called *resonance*. We shall discuss it again below, taking resistance into consideration

Damped oscillations.

Let us now suppose that, in addition to the controlling force, there acts on the particle of a harmonic oscillator a force of resistance proportional to the velocity, called the *damping force*. The component of this force in the positive direction of the x-axis may be written $-2m\mu \dot{x}$, where μ is a positive constant. The equation of motion (6.308) is modified to

(6.320) $$m\ddot{x}\mathbf{i} = -mp^2 x\mathbf{i} - 2m\mu\dot{x}\mathbf{i},$$

or, in scalar form,

(6.321) $$\ddot{x} + 2\mu\dot{x} + p^2 x = 0.$$

Now,

(6.322) $$x = Ce^{nt}$$

will satisfy this equation provided that n satisfies the *characteristic equation*

(6.323) $$n^2 + 2\mu n + p^2 = 0.$$

This equation has two roots, which may be real or complex; they are

(6.324) $$n_1, n_2 = -\mu \pm \sqrt{\mu^2 - p^2}.$$

Let us define a real positive number l by

(6.325) $$l = \sqrt{|\mu^2 - p^2|},$$

the sign $||$ indicating absolute value. We have then two cases to discuss: (i) light damping, $\mu < p$; (ii) heavy damping, $\mu > p$.

CASE (i) *Light damping* ($\mu < p$).

In this case,

(6.326) $$n_1, n_2 = -\mu \pm il,$$

and the general solution of (6.321) is

(6.327) $$x = C_1 e^{(-\mu+il)t} + C_2 e^{(-\mu-il)t}.$$

This may be written

(6.328) $$x = e^{-\mu t}(A \cos lt + B \sin lt),$$

where

(6.329) $$A = C_1 + C_2, \quad B = i(C_1 - C_2).$$

Since, for physical reasons, we are interested only in real values of x, it is evident that, although the differential equation is satisfied by (6.327) with C_1, C_2 complex constants, we should adopt as our final solution (6.328) with *real* constants A, B. These may be chosen to satisfy the initial conditions, i.e., to give assigned values to x and $\dot{x}$ for $t = 0$.

The motion given by (6.328) may also be written

(6.330) $$x = ae^{-\mu t} \cos(lt + \epsilon),$$

where a, ϵ are constants chosen to fit the initial conditions. This is not a simple harmonic motion, not being of the form (6.312). The factor $e^{-\mu t}$ indicates a general decay of the oscillations, x tending to zero as t tends to infinity.

By changing the instant from which t is measured, we can get rid of ϵ in (6.330), obtaining the simpler expression

(6.331) $$x = ae^{-\mu t} \cos lt.$$

On plotting x as a function of t, we obtain the graph shown in Fig. 78. (The graph of the simple harmonic motion

$$x = a \cos lt$$

is a cosine curve, resembling the above curve, except for the latter's tendency to die away) The curve of (6.331) should be compared with the curves

(6.332a) $$x = ae^{-\mu t},$$
(6.332b) $$x = -ae^{-\mu t},$$

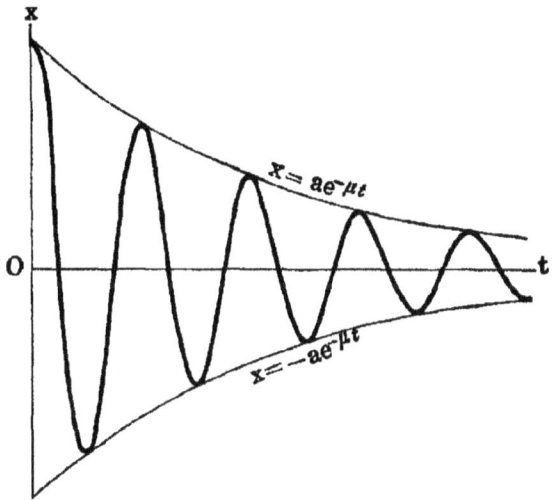

Fig. 78.—Position-time graph for a lightly damped harmonic oscillator.

also shown in Fig 78 It is easily seen that (6.331) touches (6.332a) and (6.332b) at

(6.333a) $$t = \frac{2n\pi}{l},$$

(6.333b) $$t = \frac{(2n+1)\pi}{l},$$

respectively, n being any integer.

We may regard (6.331) as a harmonic motion with decaying amplitude, given by $ae^{-\mu t}$. But the following is a more accurate description.

The maxima and minima of (6.331) occur at instants $t = t_n$, where

(6.334) $$lt_n = n\pi - \alpha, \quad \tan \alpha = \frac{\mu}{l},$$

n being any integer. The common interval is

(6.335)
$$\tau = \frac{\pi}{l};$$

thus $2\pi/l$ may be referred to as the *period* of the oscillations. The values of x corresponding to (6.334) are

(6.336) $\qquad x_n = (-1)^n a e^{-\mu t_n} \cos \alpha.$

Thus successive values are connected by

(6.337) $\qquad \dfrac{x_{n+1}}{x_n} = -e^{-\mu(t_{n+1}-t_n)} = -e^{-\pi\mu/l}.$

The ratio of successive swings to opposite sides is, in absolute value,

(6.338) $\qquad \left|\dfrac{x_{n+1}}{x_n}\right| = e^{-\pi\mu/l}$

It is usual to define the *logarithmic decrement* of the damped oscillation as the logarithm of the reciprocal of this ratio to base 10; its value is $(\pi\mu/l)\log_{10} e$.

Case (ii) *Heavy damping* ($\mu > p$).

In the case of heavy damping, we have, by (6.324),

(6.339) $\qquad n_1, n_2 = -\mu \pm l,$

and so the general solution of (6.321) is

(6.340) $\qquad x = e^{-\mu t}(A e^{lt} + B e^{-lt}).$

Then,

(6.341) $\qquad \dot{x} = e^{-\mu t}[A(l-\mu)e^{lt} - B(l+\mu)e^{-lt}].$

This vanishes only if

(6.342) $\qquad e^{2lt} = \dfrac{B(l+\mu)}{A(l-\mu)}.$

Since e^{2lt} is a steadily increasing function of t, there can be at most one solution. Hence the velocity of the oscillator vanishes at one instant at most. The motion is non-oscillatory, or *deadbeat*, x tending to zero as t tends to infinity, since $\mu > l$.

Forced oscillations.

Finally, let us suppose that a harmonic oscillator is subject to
(i) a controlling force ($-mp^2 x$),
(ii) a damping force ($-2m\mu \dot{x}$),
(iii) a disturbing force ($mk \cos ct$).

Sec. 6.3]   MOTION OF A PARTICLE   167

The equation of motion is now

(6.343) $$\ddot{x} + 2\mu\dot{x} + p^2 x = k \cos ct.$$

The general solution is

(6.344) $$x = x_1 + x_2,$$

where x_1 satisfies

(6.345) $$\ddot{x}_1 + 2\mu\dot{x}_1 + p^2 x_1 = 0,$$

and contains two constants of integration, while x_2 is any particular solution of

(6.346) $$\ddot{x}_2 + 2\mu\dot{x}_2 + p^2 x_2 = k \cos ct.$$

Then x_1 corresponds to the motion of the damped oscillator without disturbing force; it is given by (6.330) or (6.340), according as the damping is light or heavy.

As for x_2, (6.346) is satisfied by the expression

(6.347) $$x_2 = E \cos ct + F \sin ct,$$

where

(6.348) $$E = \frac{k(p^2 - c^2)}{(p^2 - c^2)^2 + (2\mu c)^2}, \qquad F = \frac{2\mu ck}{(p^2 - c^2)^2 + (2\mu c)^2}.$$

This solution is most easily found by replacing $\cos ct$ by e^{ict} in (6.346) and finding a complex constant G so that Ge^{ict} is a solution; x_2 will then be the real part of this solution. Alternatively, we may substitute (6.347) directly in (6.346) to find the constants.

If we define

(6.349) $$b = \frac{k}{\sqrt{(p^2 - c^2)^2 + (2\mu c)^2}},$$

$$\cos \eta = \frac{p^2 - c^2}{\sqrt{(p^2 - c^2)^2 + (2\mu c)^2}}, \qquad \sin \eta = \frac{-2\mu c}{\sqrt{(p^2 - c^2)^2 + (2\mu c)^2}},$$

we may write (6.347) in the form

(6.350) $$x_2 = b \cos (ct + \eta).$$

Thus the general motion of the damped oscillator under the influence of the disturbing force is

(6.351) $$x = x_1 + b \cos (ct + \eta).$$

As $t \to \infty$, $x_1 \to 0$; thus after a long time the motion tends to the *forced oscillation*

(6.352) $$x = b \cos (ct + \eta).$$

This is a simple harmonic motion of amplitude b and period equal to that of the disturbing force, but there is a difference in phase.

If the period of the disturbing force is equal to the free period of the oscillator, we have the case of *resonance*. Then $c = p$, $\eta = -\tfrac{1}{2}\pi$, and so

(6.353) $$x = \frac{k}{2\mu p} \cos (pt - \tfrac{1}{2}\pi) = \frac{k}{2\mu p} \sin pt,$$

the disturbing force being $mk \cos pt$. The difference of $\tfrac{1}{2}\pi$ in phase is interesting.

6.4. GENERAL MOTION UNDER A CENTRAL FORCE

Cartesian equations and the law of direct distance.

Consider a particle of mass m attracted toward a fixed point O by a force mP. (We may include the case of repulsion by taking P negative.) For rectangular Cartesian coordinates Oxy, the equations of motion are

(6.401) $$m\ddot{x} = -\frac{mPx}{r}, \quad m\ddot{y} = -\frac{mPy}{r},$$

where $r^2 = x^2 + y^2$. We refer to this as motion under a *central force*, because the line of action of the force passes through a fixed center O.

As an application of (6.401), let us consider the *law of direct distance*, meaning thereby that P is proportional to r. Let us confine our attention to an attractive force, putting

(6.402) $$P = k^2 r,$$

where k is a constant.

Then (6.401) read

(6.403) $$\ddot{x} + k^2 x = 0, \quad \ddot{y} + k^2 y = 0;$$

these equations have the general solutions

(6.404) $$\begin{cases} x = A \cos kt + B \sin kt, \\ y = C \cos kt + D \sin kt, \end{cases}$$

where the coefficients are constants, to be fixed by the initial conditions.

If we solve (6.404) for $\cos kt$ and $\sin kt$, and eliminate t by the identity

$$\cos^2 kt + \sin^2 kt = 1,$$

we get

(6.405) $\quad (Cx - Ay)^2 + (Dx - By)^2 = (BC - AD)^2.$

This is a central conic and necessarily an ellipse since x, y remain finite, as we see from (6.404). Thus *the orbit described under a central attractive force varying directly as the distance is an ellipse having its center at the center of force.* This motion is called *elliptic harmonic*.

To illustrate the significance of the constants in (6.404), let us suppose that at time $t = 0$ the particle is at $x = a, y = 0$, moving with velocity v_0 in the direction of the y-axis, so that $\dot{x} = 0, \dot{y} = v_0$. Putting this information into the equations (6.404), first as they stand and then in the form obtained by differentiation, we get

$$a = A, \quad 0 = C,$$
$$0 = B, \quad v_0 = Dk,$$

and so the motion is given by

(6.406) $\quad x = a \cos kt, \quad y = \dfrac{v_0}{k} \sin kt.$

Polar coordinates.

Returning to the general problem of motion under a central force, we shall now obtain equations easier to handle than (6.401). It is only in the case of the law of direct distance that (6.401) are convenient.

Since the force on the particle passes through O, it has no moment about O. Hence, by the principle of angular momentum (5.214), the angular momentum about O is constant. We shall change slightly the notation of Chap. V, now letting h denote angular momentum per unit mass; then, by (5.106),

(6.407) $\quad h = r^2 \dot\theta = \text{constant},$

where r, θ are the polar coordinates of the particle. An alter-

native expression for h is pq, where p is the perpendicular from O on the velocity vector q.

If we follow the radius vector, drawn from O to the particle, we observe that when it turns through an infinitesimal angle $d\theta$ it sweeps out an area $\frac{1}{2}r^2 d\theta$. Thus the *areal velocity* $\dot{A}$ may be defined as

(6.408) $$\dot{A} = \frac{1}{2}r^2\dot{\theta},$$

A being, in fact, the total area swept out from some initial instant. We observe that h is twice the areal velocity, and by (6.407) we have the following important result: *In motion under a central force, the areal velocity is constant.*

This fact is used to simplify the problem of determining the orbit. We define

(6.409) $$u = \frac{1}{r},$$

the reciprocal of the radius vector. Then, since (6.407) may be written

(6.410) $$\dot{\theta} = hu^2,$$

we have

(6.411) $$\begin{cases} \dot{r} = -\frac{1}{u^2}\frac{du}{d\theta}\dot{\theta} = -h\frac{du}{d\theta}, \\ \ddot{r} = -h\frac{d^2u}{d\theta^2}\dot{\theta} = -h^2u^2\frac{d^2u}{d\theta^2}, \\ \ddot{r} - r\dot{\theta}^2 = -h^2u^2\left(\frac{d^2u}{d\theta^2} + u\right), \\ \dot{r}^2 + r^2\dot{\theta}^2 = h^2\left[\left(\frac{du}{d\theta}\right)^2 + u^2\right]. \end{cases}$$

The vector equation of motion is

(6.412) $$m\mathbf{f} = m\mathbf{P},$$

where $\mathbf{P}$ is the attractive force per unit mass. Resolution along the radius vector gives, by (4.107),

(6.413) $$\ddot{r} - r\dot{\theta}^2 = -P,$$

where P is the inward component of $\mathbf{P}$. By (6.411), we obtain

(6.414) $$\frac{d^2u}{d\theta^2} + u = \frac{P}{h^2u^2}.$$

This is the *differential equation of the orbit of a particle moving under an attractive central force P per unit mass.* If we can solve this equation, obtaining u as a function of θ, we have the equation of the orbit in polar coordinates.

Henceforth, let us suppose that P is a function of r only. It is easy to see that the work done in passing from one position to another is then independent of the path described. Thus the system is conservative, and we may use the principle of energy. Let T, V, E be respectively the kinetic energy, potential energy, and constant total energy, all per unit mass. Then

(6.415) $$T + V = E.$$

Now, by (6.411),

(6.416) $$T = \tfrac{1}{2}(\dot r^2 + r^2\dot\theta^2) = \tfrac{1}{2}h^2\left[\left(\frac{du}{d\theta}\right)^2 + u^2\right].$$

The potential energy per unit mass is such that

$$\mathbf{P} = -\operatorname{grad} V,$$

so that, since P is the *inward* component of $\mathbf{P}$,

(6.417) $$P = \frac{dV}{dr}, \qquad V = \int_{r_0}^r P\,dr,$$

where r_0 is some constant. Hence, (6.415) gives

(6.418) $$\left(\frac{du}{d\theta}\right)^2 + u^2 = \frac{2(E - V)}{h^2}.$$

This equation is really equivalent to (6.414), as may be seen on differentiation. We are, of course, to remember that V, being a function of r, is also a function of u.

Apsides and apsidal angles.

An *apse* is a point on an orbit at a maximum or minimum distance from the center of force. The condition for an apse is $\dot r = 0$, or, equivalently,

(6.419) $$\frac{du}{d\theta} = 0.$$

From (6.418) it follows that, at an apse,

(6.420) $$u^2 = \frac{2(E - V)}{h^2}.$$

Since V is a function of u, this is an equation to determine the values of u at the apsides, supposing the constants E and h known.

As an illustration, let us return to the case $P = k^2 r$. Then

(6.421) $$V = \tfrac{1}{2} k^2 r^2 = \tfrac{1}{2} \frac{k^2}{u^2},$$

and so (6.420) may be written

(6.422) $$u^4 - \frac{2}{h^2}(Eu^2 - \tfrac{1}{2}k^2) = 0.$$

This quadratic equation in u^2 yields roots u_1^2, u_2^2, which will be the squares of the reciprocals of the semiaxes of the elliptical orbit.

By a study of apsides, we may obtain a general description of an orbit without actually solving the differential equation (6.414) To establish an important feature, let us temporarily forget the dynamical problem and think of a differential equation

(6.423) $$\frac{d^2 y}{dx^2} = f(y),$$

to be solved under the initial conditions $y = y_0$, $dy/dx = 0$ for $x = 0$. These initial conditions determine a unique solution. Since the transformation $x = -x'$ leaves the form of the differential equation and the initial conditions unaltered, it is evident that the curve $y = F(x)$, which satisfies (6.423) and the initial conditions, is symmetric with respect to the y-axis

Since P is a function of u, it is clear that (6.414) and (6.423) are equations of the same form, with the correspondence $u \to y$, $\theta \to x$. If we measure θ from an apse, the initial conditions for (6.414) are the same as those for (6.423). Hence, *a central orbit is symmetric with respect to the line drawn from the force center to an apse.*

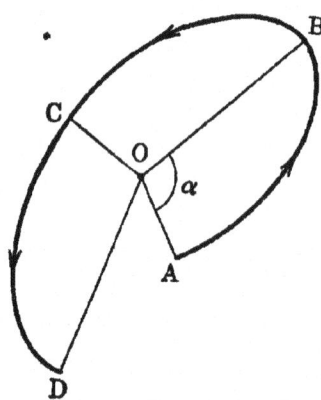

Fig. 79.—Symmetry of a central orbit with respect to an apse line.

This result throws much light on the general structure of a central orbit. Let A and B (Fig. 79) be consecutive apsides, and

let us suppose that the portion AB of the orbit is known. The orbit is symmetrical about OB; hence, we may obtain some more of the orbit by folding the portion AB over the line OB, obtaining BC, with an apse at C by symmetry. The apsidal distance OC is equal to the apsidal distance OA. Again, folding BC over OC, we get CD with an apse at D, and $OD = OB$

The following facts are now clear:

(i) Any central orbit has only two apsidal distances. The orbit is a curve touching two concentric circles, the radii of which are the two apsidal distances.

(ii) Once the orbit between two consecutive apsides is known, the whole of the orbit may be constructed by operations of folding over apsidal radii.

(iii) The angle subtended at the center by the arc joining consecutive apsides is a constant. It is called the *apsidal angle*.

In some cases, (i) may be violated. The radius of the inner circle may be zero, or that of the outer circle may be infinite. But these are to be regarded as exceptional cases.

Let us now consider how the apsidal angle is to be found. When u is increasing, (6.418) gives

$$(6.424) \qquad \frac{du}{d\theta} = \sqrt{F(u)},$$

where

$$(6.425) \qquad F(u) = \frac{2(E - V)}{h^2} - u^2.$$

Thus

$$d\theta = \frac{du}{\sqrt{F(u)}};$$

and so, if u_1, u_2 are the reciprocals of the apsidal distances (with $u_1 < u_2$), the apsidal angle α is

$$(6.426) \qquad \alpha = \int_{u=u_1}^{u=u_2} d\theta = \int_{u_1}^{u_2} \frac{du}{\sqrt{F(u)}}.$$

As an illustration, let us consider the law of direct distance, where V is given by (6.421). Here $F(u)$ is of the form

$$F(u) = \frac{1}{u^2}(A + Bu^2 - u^4),$$

where A and B are constants. But $F(u) = 0$ at an apse; hence $u = u_1$, $u = u_2$ are roots of $F(u) = 0$, and so

$$F(u) = \frac{(u_2^2 - u^2)(u^2 - u_1^2)}{u^2}.$$

Thus, by (6.426),

(6.427) $$\alpha = \int_{u_1}^{u_2} \frac{u\, du}{\sqrt{(u_2^2 - u^2)(u^2 - u_1^2)}} = \tfrac{1}{2}\pi,$$

as we already know from the fact that the orbit is a central ellipse

Stability of circular orbits.

In a circular orbit u is constant. Hence by (6.414) the possible radii of circular orbits are determined by

(6.428) $$u = \frac{P(u)}{h^2 u^2}.$$

With an attractive force ($P > 0$), we can obtain a circular orbit of any radius, by projecting the particle at right angles to the radius vector with that velocity which makes

(6.429) $$h^2 = \frac{P(u)}{u^3}.$$

But the question arises: Are these circular orbits *stable* or *unstable?* In other words, if slightly disturbed, will the resulting orbit lie close to the original circular orbit, or will it deviate far from it? This question is important physically, because in nature small disturbances are always present, and they will destroy an unstable circular orbit. The only circular orbits we can hope to observe are those that are stable.

It should be clearly understood that we shall not consider the effects of disturbing forces which *continue* to act on the particle; we assume that the position and velocity of the particle have been disturbed and investigate the resulting motion under the original central force.

Let $u = u_0$ and $h = h_0$ in the circular orbit. Then, by (6.429),

(6.430) $$h_0^2 = \frac{P(u_0)}{u_0^3}.$$

To study the disturbance, we put

(6.431) $$u = u_0 + \xi,$$

SEC. 6.4]   MOTION OF A PARTICLE   175

where ξ and its derivatives are assumed to be small. We also assume that $h - h_0$ is small. Substitution in (6.414) gives

(6.432) $$\frac{d^2\xi}{d\theta^2} + u_0 + \xi = \frac{P(u_0 + \xi)}{h^2(u_0 + \xi)^2}.$$

Now, on expansion in powers of ξ,

(6.433) $$\frac{P(u_0 + \xi)}{h^2(u_0 + \xi)^2} = \frac{1}{h^2 u_0^2}\left(1 + \frac{\xi}{u_0}\right)^{-2}(P_0 + \xi P_0' + \cdots)$$
$$= \frac{P_0}{h^2 u_0^2}\left[1 + \xi\left(\frac{P_0'}{P_0} - \frac{2}{u_0}\right) + \cdots\right],$$

where $P' = dP/du$, and the subscript 0 indicates evaluation for $u = u_0$.

Then, to the first order in small quantities, (6.432) becomes

(6.434) $$\frac{d^2\xi}{d\theta^2} + A\xi = B,$$

where

(6.435) $$A = 1 - \frac{P_0}{h_0^2 u_0^3}\left(\frac{P_0'}{P_0} - \frac{2}{u_0}\right) = 3 - \frac{u_0 P_0'}{P_0},$$

by (6.430); B is another constant whose value does not interest us. The solution of (6.434) is

(6.436a) $\quad \xi = \frac{B}{A} + C_1 \cos(\sqrt{A} \cdot \theta) + C_2 \sin(\sqrt{A} \cdot \theta),$

(6.436b) $\quad \xi = \frac{B}{A} + C_1 \cosh(\sqrt{-A} \cdot \theta) + C_2 \sinh(\sqrt{-A} \cdot \theta),$

(6.436c) $\quad \xi = \frac{1}{2}B\theta^2 + C_1\theta + C_2,$

according as $A > 0$, $A < 0$, or $A = 0$.

Of these solutions, only (6.436a) remains permanently small; the others increase indefinitely with θ. Hence *the circular orbit of radius $1/u_0$ is stable if, and only if,*

(6.437) $$\frac{u_0 P_0'}{P_0} < 3.$$

In particular, let us consider the case of a force varying inversely as the nth power of the distance so that

(6.438) $$P = \frac{k}{r^n} = ku^n.$$

Then

$$\frac{uP'}{P} = n,$$

and so *circular orbits under the attractive force* (6.438) *are stable if, and only if,*

(6.439) $$n < 3.$$

Thus the law of direct distance ($n = -1$) and the law of the inverse square ($n = 2$) give stable circular orbits; the law of the inverse cube ($n = 3$) gives unstable circular orbits.

6.5. PLANETARY ORBITS

The law of the inverse square.

As already remarked in Sec. 3.1, Newton's law of gravitational attraction states that two particles of masses m, m', at a distance r apart, attract one another with equal and opposite forces of magnitude

(6.501) $$\frac{Gmm'}{r^2},$$

where G is the gravitational constant.

Coulomb's law of electrostatic attraction states that two particles carrying electric charges e, e' (in electrostatic units), at a distance r apart, repel one another with equal and opposite forces of magnitude

(6.502) $$\frac{ee'}{r^2}.$$

If e and e' have opposite signs, this force is a force of attraction.

Here we have two examples of *the law of the inverse square.* The law (6.501) governs astronomical phenomena—in particular, the motion of a planet round the sun. The law (6.502) governs atomic phenomena—in particular, the motion of an electron in an atom about the central nucleus. In this case, of course, the charges e, e' have opposite signs, so that the force is one of attraction, as in the gravitational case. It is remarkable that the same form for the law of attraction should hold on such different scales.

The expressions (6.501) and (6.502), combined with Newton's law of motion, constitute two hypotheses regarding phenomena in gravitational and electrostatic fields. For a long time, they were accepted as completely valid from a physical point of view, but that is no longer the case. The modern astronomer knows

that gravitational attraction should be discussed in terms of the general theory of relativity, and the physicist insists that problems on the atomic scale belong to quantum mechanics. It would, however, create a completely false impression if we were to say that the law of the inverse square has disappeared from modern science. Nearly all the calculations of astronomers are still based on (6.501) and give results in excellent agreement with observation. Moreover, the physicist often falls back on the simple atomic picture based on (6.502) and Newton's law of motion.

In what follows, we shall discuss the motion of a planet attracted by the sun. Obviously, by a mere change of constant, the same reasoning will apply to the motion of an electron in an atom

Determination of the orbit.

The sun and a planet are regarded as particles, of masses M and m, respectively. The attraction of the sun on the planet, given by (6.501), produces an acceleration GM/r^2; and the attraction of the planet on the sun produces an acceleration Gm/r^2. These accelerations are in the ratio M/m, which is actually a very large number. Hence, without any serious departure from reality, we may neglect the acceleration of the sun and treat it as if it were at rest. Later we shall see how to treat the problem exactly.

We consider then the case of a particle attracted toward a fixed center by a force P per unit mass, where

(6.503) $$P = \frac{\mu}{r^2},$$

μ being some positive constant. The differential equation (6.414) for the orbit now reads

(6.504) $$\frac{d^2 u}{d\theta^2} + u = \frac{\mu}{h^2}.$$

The general solution is

(6.505) $$u = \frac{\mu}{h^2} + C \cos(\theta - \theta_0),$$

where C and θ_0 are constants of integration. *This is, in polar coordinates, the equation of the most general orbit described under a central force varying as the inverse square of the distance.*

The potential energy per unit mass is

(6.506) $$V = \int P\, dr = -\frac{\mu}{r} = -\mu u,$$

the constant of integration being chosen to make V vanish at infinity.

Let us now substitute from (6.505) in (6.418), the equation of energy, in order to express the constant C in terms of E and h (the total energy and angular momentum per unit mass). We get

$$C^2 + \frac{\mu^2}{h^4} + 2C\frac{\mu}{h^2}\cos(\theta - \theta_0) = \frac{2}{h^2}\left[E + \frac{\mu^2}{h^2} + \mu C \cos(\theta - \theta_0)\right],$$

so that

(6.507) $$C^2 = \frac{\mu^2}{h^4} + \frac{2E}{h^2}.$$

By rotating the base line $\theta = 0$, we can make $\theta_0 = 0$ and $C > 0$ in (6.505); this we shall suppose done. Then the equation (6.505) for the orbit reads

(6.508) $$u = \frac{\mu}{h^2}\left(1 + \sqrt{1 + \frac{2Eh^2}{\mu^2}}\cos\theta\right).$$

From the focus-directrix property of a conic, we know that its equation in polar coordinates may be written

(6.509) $$u = \frac{1}{l}(1 + e \cos\theta),$$

where l is the semi-latus-rectum (i.e., half the focal chord parallel to the directrix) and e the eccentricity; θ is measured from the perpendicular dropped from the focus on the directrix. The conic may be of any of the following types:

$$\begin{array}{ll}\text{ellipse} & (e < 1), \\ \text{parabola} & (e = 1), \\ \text{hyperbola} & (e > 1).\end{array}$$

In the case of the hyperbola, (6.509) gives only the branch adjacent to the focus.

Comparing (6.508) and (6.509), we note that it is always possible to bring the equations into complete agreement by choosing for l and e the values

(6.510) $$l = \frac{h^2}{\mu}, \quad e = \sqrt{1 + \frac{2Eh^2}{\mu^2}}.$$

Accordingly, we may say: *The orbit described by a particle, attracted to a fixed center by a force varying as the inverse square of the distance, is a conic having the center of force for focus. The semi-latus-rectum and the eccentricity are given by (6.510) in terms of the angular momentum and energy per unit mass. The orbit may be of the following types:*

$$\begin{aligned}&\textit{ellipse} \quad (E < 0),\\ &\textit{parabola} \ (E = 0),\\ &\textit{hyperbola} \ (E > 0).\end{aligned}$$

The fact that orbits may be classified thus in terms of the total energy is remarkable.

The most important orbits in astronomy (those of the planets) are ellipses. Recurring comets describe orbits which are elongated ellipses, approximating to parabolas. A body with a parabolic or hyperbolic orbit would pass out from the solar system, never to return.

Constants of the elliptical orbit.

Let us now confine our attention to the elliptical orbit. Since the orbits of the planets are of this type, a great wealth of technical detail has been developed about the elliptical orbit. We shall here give only a brief treatment.

It is evident from (6.509) that the shape and size of an orbit (but not its orientation in space) are determined by the two constants l, e. These are related to the constants E, h by (6.510). Thus, of the various constants which appear in our equations, we are to regard μ (the intensity of the force center) as given once for all, whereas the constants l, e, E, h take different values for different orbits. On account of (6.510), only two of these constants are independent. We may use as an independent pair any two which prove convenient.

Instead of using (l, e) as fundamental constants, it is better to use (a, e), where a is the semiaxis major of the orbit. Now,

(6.511) $$l = \frac{b^2}{a} = a(1 - e^2),$$

b being the semiaxis minor. We shall refer to (a, e) as the *geometrical* constants of an orbit and (E, h) as its *dynamical*

constants. The formulas of transformation from one set to the other are as follows:

$$(6.512) \quad \begin{cases} a = -\dfrac{\mu}{2E}, & e = \sqrt{1 + \dfrac{2Eh^2}{\mu^2}}; \\ E = -\dfrac{\mu}{2a}, & h = \sqrt{\mu a(1 - e^2)}. \end{cases}$$

There is a simple formula giving the speed q at any point of the orbit in terms of the radius vector. By the equation of energy, we have

$$\tfrac{1}{2}q^2 - \frac{\mu}{r} = E.$$

Substituting for E from (6.512), we obtain

$$(6.513) \quad q^2 = \mu\left(\frac{2}{r} - \frac{1}{a}\right).$$

The periodic time.

We now ask: How long does the particle take to describe the elliptical orbit? This time is called the *periodic time* (τ). We seek an expression for τ in terms of the fundamental constants.

The periodic time cannot be obtained from (6.414), because the time has been eliminated from this equation. We refer instead to (6.408), which gives for the areal velocity

$$\dot{A} = \tfrac{1}{2}h.$$

If F is the focus at which the center of force is situated, it follows at once that the particle describes an arc VP, starting from the vertex* V nearer to F, in a time $2A/h$, where A is the area of the sector subtended at F by this arc (Fig. 80). Following the point P right round the orbit, we get for the periodic time

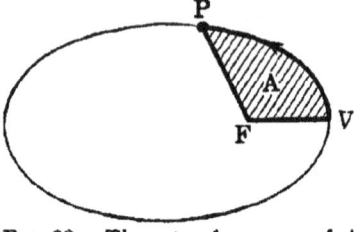

Fig. 80.—The rate of increase of A is constant.

$$(6.514) \quad \tau = \frac{2A}{h},$$

* The vertex V is called *perihelion*—the point closest to the sun—the other vertex being called *aphelion*—the point away from the sun.

where A is now the total area of the ellipse. We might substitute $A = \pi ab$; but, to be systematic, we should express τ in terms of either the geometrical constants or the dynamical constants. Since
$$b = a \sqrt{1 - e^2},$$
we obtain, by some easy calculations,

(6.515) $$\tau = 2\pi \sqrt{\frac{a^3}{\mu}} = \frac{2\pi\mu}{\sqrt{(-2E)^3}}.$$

(We remember that $E < 0$ for the elliptical orbit.)

It is remarkable that the formula involves only one geometrical constant or one dynamical constant. All orbits with the same semiaxis major have the same periodic time; so also have all orbits with the same total energy.

Kepler's laws.

Before the mathematical theory given above had been developed by Newton, Kepler deduced the following laws of planetary motion from a careful study of the results of astronomical observations:

I. Each planet describes an ellipse with the sun in one focus

II. The radius vector drawn from the sun to a planet sweeps out equal areas in equal times.

III. The squares of the periodic times of the planets are proportional to the cubes of the semiaxes major of their orbits.

Starting from Newton's law of gravitation, we have shown that all these statements are true. But it is interesting to adopt the historical point of view and face the problem as it presented itself to Newton: *Given Kepler's laws as a statement of fact, what is the law of gravitational attraction?*

Law II tells us that h—the angular momentum per unit mass—is constant, and hence that the force must be directed toward the sun From Law I, we know that the equation of an orbit may be written
$$u = \frac{1}{l}(1 + e \cos \theta).$$

Then by (6.414) the force per unit mass is

(6.516) $$P = h^2 u^2 \left(\frac{d^2 u}{d\theta^2} + u\right) = \frac{h^2 u^2}{l}.$$

Thus for each planet the force varies inversely as the square of the distance. But it remains to prove that the force is of the form

$$mP = \frac{m\mu}{r^2}, \tag{6.517}$$

where m is the mass of the planet and μ a constant, the same for all the planets. To show this, we appeal to Law III. We know that for an elliptical orbit, described under a central force directed to a focus,

$$\tau = \frac{2\pi ab}{h},$$

and so

$$\frac{\tau^2}{a^3} = \frac{4\pi^2 b^2}{h^2 a} = \frac{4\pi^2 l}{h^2}.$$

But, by Law III, this is a constant, the same for all planets. Thus h^2/l is the same for all planets; and so, by (6.516), $P = \mu u^2$, where μ is the same for all planets. Hence (6.517) is true, and Newton's law of gravitation is thus deduced as a consequence of Kepler's laws.

If Kepler's laws were accurately true, we should have to regard the sun as fixed and the planets as attracted *only* by the sun. More precise measurements show that Kepler's laws are only an approximation and that the inverse-square law of attraction holds for every pair of bodies. It is fortunate that the observations of Kepler's time were crude, because otherwise the simplicity of the law of gravitation would have been obscured.

The two-body problem.

An accurate dynamical treatment of the solar system involves complexities far greater than those encountered in the above discussion. First, the sun is accelerated by the attractions of the planets; secondly, the mutual attractions of the planets influence their motions. A full treatment of the problem belongs to the subject of celestial mechanics, and we make no attempt to discuss it here.

We may however ask: *What is the behavior of two bodies which attract one another according to the law of the inverse square?* This

Sec. 6.5]   MOTION OF A PARTICLE   183

problem presents itself in nature in the case of a double star and in the problem of the moon's motion relative to the earth, the attraction of the sun being neglected

We showed in Sec. 5.2 that, if there are no external forces, the mass center of a system moves in a straight line with constant velocity, relative to a Newtonian frame of reference. We can then take another Newtonian frame in which the mass center C is at rest. We suppose this done for the two-body problem in Fig. 81.

Let m, m' be the masses of the particles, $\mathbf{r}$, $\mathbf{r}'$ their position vectors relative to C, and $\mathbf{i}$ a unit vector drawn parallel to the line joining m' to m. Then the equations of motion are, in vector form,

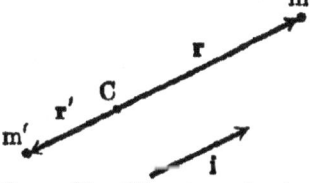

Fig. 81.—The two-body problem.

(6.518) $$\begin{cases} m\ddot{\mathbf{r}} = -\dfrac{Gmm'}{(r+r')^2}\mathbf{i}, \\ m'\ddot{\mathbf{r}}' = \dfrac{Gmm'}{(r+r')^2}\mathbf{i}. \end{cases}$$

Now, from the definition of mass center,

(6.519) $$\frac{m}{r'} = \frac{m'}{r} = \frac{m+m'}{r+r'};$$

hence (6.518) may be written

(6.520) $$\begin{cases} m\ddot{\mathbf{r}} = -\dfrac{GmM'}{r^2}\mathbf{i}, & M' = \dfrac{m'^3}{(m+m')^2}, \\ m'\ddot{\mathbf{r}}' = \dfrac{Gm'M}{r'^2}\mathbf{i}, & M = \dfrac{m^3}{(m+m')^2}. \end{cases}$$

But these equations have the form of equations of motion under central forces varying as the inverse square of the distance. Therefore, *each body moves about the fixed mass center as if attracted to it by the gravitational force due to a mass M' in the first case and a mass M in the second case.*

To find the motion of m relative to m', we note that the relative position vector is

(6.521) $$\mathbf{R} = \mathbf{r} - \mathbf{r}'.$$

Thus, by (6.518),

(6.522) $$m\ddot{\mathbf{R}} = m\ddot{\mathbf{r}} - \frac{m}{m'} m'\ddot{\mathbf{r}}' = -\frac{Gm(m+m')}{R^2}\mathbf{i},$$

since $R = r + r'$.

This result may be expressed as follows: *The motion of one of the bodies (m) relative to the other (m') takes place precisely as if the latter were fixed and its mass increased from m' to m + m'.*

It is evident from symmetry that, when a particle is attracted by a fixed center O, its orbit lies in a plane, i.e., the plane containing O and the initial velocity vector. In the case of the two-body problem, the orbits both lie in one plane when viewed in a frame of reference in which the mass center C is fixed. But in any other Newtonian frame the motion appears very complicated.

6.6. SUMMARY OF APPLICATIONS IN PLANE DYNAMICS—MOTION OF A PARTICLE

I. Ballistics.

(a) No resistance; the trajectory is a parabola.

(b) Resistance independent of height [$R = mg\phi(q)$]; the trajectory may be found by quadratures when the following differential equation of the hodograph has been integrated:

(6.601) $$\frac{1}{q}\frac{dq}{d\theta} = \frac{\phi(q) + \sin\theta}{\cos\theta} \quad \text{or} \quad \frac{1}{q}\frac{dq}{d\psi} = \tanh\psi + \phi(q).$$

(c) Resistance proportional to q^2; (6.601) may be integrated in terms of elementary functions, but the complete determination of the trajectory is very complicated. Motion in a vertical line is easily determined.

(d) Resistance proportional to q; the trajectory is easily found.

II. Harmonic oscillators.

(a) Simple harmonic oscillations:

(6.602) $$\ddot{x} + p^2 x = 0,$$

(6.603) $\quad x = A \cos pt + B \sin pt, \quad \text{or} \quad x = a \cos(pt + \epsilon);$

$$\left(\tau = \frac{2\pi}{p} = 2\pi\sqrt{\frac{l}{g}} \text{ for simple pendulum}\right).$$

(b) Oscillations with disturbing force mX:

(6.604) $\quad X = \text{constant}; \quad$ center of oscillation displaced.

(6.605) $X = k \cos ct;$ $x = a \cos (pt + \epsilon) + \dfrac{k}{p^2 - c^2} \cos ct.$

(c) Oscillations with damping $(-2m\mu\dot{x})$:
  (i) Light damping $(\mu < p)$ or oscillatory:

(6.606) $x = ae^{-\mu t} \cos (lt + \epsilon),$ $l = \sqrt{p^2 - \mu^2}.$

(Ratio of successive swings to opposite sides $= e^{-\pi\mu/l}.$)
  (ii) Heavy damping $(\mu > p)$ or deadbeat.

(6.607) $x = Ae^{-(\mu-l)t} + Be^{-(\mu+l)t},$ $l = \sqrt{\mu^2 - p^2}.$

(d) Forced oscillations (periodic disturbing force $mk \cos ct$): after a long time the motion approximates to

(6.608) $x = b \cos (ct + \eta),$

where b and η are independent of the initial conditions.

III. General motion under a central force (mP toward center).

(a) Equations of motion:

(6.609) $\ddot{x} = -\dfrac{Px}{r},$ $\ddot{y} = -\dfrac{Py}{r};$

(6.610) $\begin{cases} \dfrac{d^2u}{d\theta^2} + u = \dfrac{P}{h^2 u^2}, \quad u = \dfrac{1}{r}; \\ h = r^2\dot{\theta} = pq = \text{twice the areal velocity;} \end{cases}$

(6.611) $\left(\dfrac{du}{d\theta}\right)^2 + u^2 = \dfrac{2(E - V)}{h^2},$ ($E =$ constant total energy).

(b) Orbit symmetric with respect to apse line.
(c) If $P = k^2 r$, the orbit is a central ellipse.

IV. Planetary orbits.

(a) The orbit under an attraction $m\mu/r^2$ is a conic section with one focus at the center of force: ellipse for $E < 0$, parabola for $E = 0$, hyperbola for $E > 0$.

(b) For elliptical orbit

(6.612) $\dfrac{l}{r} = 1 + e \cos \theta,$ $l = a(1 - e^2);$ $q^2 = \mu\left(\dfrac{2}{r} - \dfrac{1}{a}\right);$

(6.613) $\begin{cases} E = -\dfrac{\mu}{2a}, \quad h = \sqrt{\mu a(1 - e^2)}, \\ \text{periodic time} = \tau = 2\pi \sqrt{\dfrac{a^3}{\mu}}. \end{cases}$

V. Two-body problem.

Relative motion is the same as if one body were held fixed and its mass increased to the sum of the two masses.

EXERCISES VI

1. A particle is projected upward in a direction inclined at 60° to the horizontal. Show that its velocity when at its greatest height is half its initial velocity. (Neglect the resistance of the air.)

2. A particle of mass m moves on a straight line under the influence of a force directed toward the origin O on the line and proportional to the distance from O; the force at unit distance is of magnitude mk^2. The particle passes O with a velocity u. If x is its coordinate at time t and v its velocity at that instant, show that $v^2 + k^2x^2 = u^2$.

3. Prove by a general argument, not involving any particular law of resistance, that a body thrown vertically upward in a resisting medium will return to the point of projection with a velocity less than that with which it was projected.

4. A gun is mounted on a hill of height h above a level plain. Show that, if the resistance of the air is neglected, the greatest horizontal range for given muzzle velocity V is obtained by firing at an angle of elevation θ such that
$$\operatorname{cosec}^2 \theta = 2(1 + gh/V^2).$$

5. Find the greatest distance that a stone can be thrown inside a horizontal tunnel 10 feet high with a velocity of projection of 80 feet per second. Find also the corresponding time of flight.

6. In a resisting medium two identical bodies are let fall from the same position at instants separated by an interval t. Show that the distance between them tends to the limit vt, where v is the limiting velocity.

7. Calculate the rate of loss of energy (kinetic + potential) for a damped harmonic oscillator vibrating as in (6.330).

8. A spring with compression modulus λ supports a mass m. Show that the period of vertical oscillations under gravity is $2\pi \sqrt{ml/\lambda}$, where l is the natural length of the spring. (The *compression modulus* is the ratio of the force producing compression to the compression per unit length.)

9. A particle moves in a plane, attracted to a fixed center by a force varying as the inverse cube of the distance. Find the equation of the orbit, distinguishing the three different cases which may arise.

10. A particle is attracted toward a fixed center by a force μ/r^2 per unit mass, μ being a constant and r the distance from the center. It is projected from a position P with a velocity of magnitude q_0, making an angle α with OP. Assuming that $OP < 2\mu/q_0^2$, show that the orbit is an ellipse; determine (in terms of μ, q_0, α and the distance OP) the eccentricity of the orbit and the inclination of the major axis to OP.

11. A particle moves under the influence of a center which attracts with a force $[(b/r^2) + (c/r^4)]$, b and c being positive constants and r the distance from the center. The particle moves in a circular orbit of radius a. Prove that the motion is stable if, and only if, $a^2b > c$.

12. A particle of mass m moves in a central field of attractive force of which the intensity is

$$mkr^{-2}e^{-r^2},$$

where k is a constant. Prove that a circular orbit of radius r is stable if, and only if, $r^2 < \tfrac{1}{2}$.

13. Deduce the following relations for an elliptical orbit under the Newtonian law of attraction,

$$r = a(1 - e \cos E),$$
$$M = E - e \sin E,$$

where r is the radius vector drawn from the center of attraction, a the semiaxis major of the orbit, E the eccentric anomaly, and M the mean anomaly (These *anomalies* are angles, defined as follows. Let O be the geometrical center of the orbit, V its perihelion, and P the position of the particle at time t. Then E is the eccentric angle of P—vanishing when P is at V. To define M, we consider a point moving on the orbit with constant angular velocity about O, starting from V with P and completing the circuit in the actual periodic time If Q is the position of this point at time t, then the value of M corresponding to P is the angle QOV.)

14. A simple pendulum of mass m and length a is hanging in equilibrium. At time $t = 0$ a small horizontal disturbing force X comes into operation and continues to act, varying with time according to the formula

$$X = mb \sin 2pt,$$

where $p^2 = g/a$ Find a formula giving the position of the pendulum at any time.

15. A body of mass m is projected vertically upward in a medium for which the resistance is mk^2v^2 If the initial velocity is v_0, show that the body returns to the point of projection with a velocity v_1 such that

$$v_1^2 = \frac{gv_0^2}{g + k^2v_0^2}.$$

16. Mud is thrown off from the tire of a wheel (radius a) of a car traveling at a speed V, where $V^2 > ga$. Neglecting the resistance of the air, show that no mud can rise higher than a height

$$a + \frac{V^2}{2g} + \frac{ga^2}{2V^2}$$

above the ground.

17. A shell is fired vertically upward with speed q_0. The resistance is $mgCq^2$. Show that it attains its greatest height at time t, given by

$$\tan (gt \sqrt{C}) = q_0 \sqrt{C}.$$

Deduce that, no matter how large q_0 may be, t cannot exceed $\tfrac{1}{2}\pi g^{-1}C^{-\frac{1}{2}}$.

18. A particle of mass m describes an elliptical orbit of semiaxis major a under a force $m\mu/r^2$ directed to a focus. Prove that the time average of

reciprocal distance is

$$\frac{1}{\tau}\int \frac{dt}{r} = \frac{1}{a}$$

and deduce that the time average of the square of the speed is

$$\frac{1}{\tau}\int q^2\, dt = \frac{\mu}{a}$$

The integrals are evaluated for a complete revolution.

19. A bomb is dropped from an airplane flying horizontally at a height h with speed U. Assuming the linear law of resistance $R = mgCq$ as in (6.225), and further assuming that this resistance is small, show that the time of fall is approximately

$$\sqrt{\frac{2h}{g}}\left(1 + \tfrac{1}{6}gC\sqrt{\frac{2h}{g}}\right).$$

Show also that the horizontal distance through which the bomb falls is approximately

$$U\sqrt{\frac{2h}{g}}\left(1 - \tfrac{1}{3}gC\sqrt{\frac{2h}{g}}\right).$$

20. In the problem of two bodies attracting according to the inverse square law, there are four orbits: the orbits of either body relative to the other and the orbits of either body relative to the mass center. Show that all four orbits have simultaneous apsides and the same eccentricity.

21. Two particles of masses m, m' distant a apart are projected with velocities q, q', respectively, the directions of projection and the line joining the particles are mutually perpendicular. Find the condition that the relative orbits under their mutual attraction may be ellipses; assuming the condition to be satisfied, find the periodic time.

22. The motion of an oscillator may be represented graphically in a plane, x being shown as abscissa and $\dot{x}$ as ordinate. The history of the oscillator is then a curve. Show that for an undamped harmonic oscillator this curve is an ellipse, and for a lightly damped oscillator it is a curve spiraling in to the origin. Investigate the curve for a heavily damped oscillator, and show that it will be a straight line through the origin for special initial conditions.

CHAPTER VII

APPLICATIONS IN PLANE DYNAMICS—MOTION OF A RIGID BODY AND OF A SYSTEM

7.1. MOMENTS OF INERTIA. KINETIC ENERGY AND ANGULAR MOMENTUM

Definition of moment of inertia and some direct calculations.

The moment of inertia of a particle about a line is defined as $I = mr^2$, where m is the mass of the particle and r its perpendicular distance from the line. The moment of inertia of a system of particles is defined as the sum of the moments of inertia of the separate particles. Thus,

$$(7.101) \qquad I = \sum_{i=1}^{n} m_i r_i^2,$$

if the system consists of n particles of masses $m_1, m_2, \cdots m_n$, situated at distances $r_1, r_2, \cdots r_n$ from the line about which the moment of inertia is taken

It is evident that the method of decomposition is applicable to moments of inertia. Thus, if a system is split into two parts with moments of inertia I_1 and I_2, the moment of inertia of the complete system is

$$(7.102) \qquad I = I_1 + I_2.$$

It is convenient to define a length k called the *radius of gyration*. If a system of total mass m has a moment of inertia I, the radius of gyration k is defined by the equation

$$(7.103) \qquad mk^2 = I.$$

When the system consists of a single particle, it is evident that the radius of gyration about any line is simply the distance from the line.

In the case of a continuous distribution of matter, the definition (7.101) passes over into

$$(7.104) \qquad I = \int r^2 \, dm,$$

where the integration sign indicates the limit of a process in which the system is divided into a great number of very small parts, and the sum taken; dm is the mass of an infinitesimal

element, and r is its distance from the line about which the moment of inertia is to be found.

Moment of inertia has the dimensions $[ML^2]$ and is measured in gm cm^2 in the c g s system and in lb. ft.^{2} in the f p s. system. The square of the radius of gyration has the dimensions [moment of inertia]/[mass], or $[ML^2]/[M]$, i e, $[L^2]$. Thus radius of gyration has dimensions $[L]$ and so is a length.

Let us now calculate some simple moments of inertia.

Hoop It is evident that the moment of inertia of a thin hoop of mass m and radius a about a line through its center perpendicular to its plane is ma^2.

Rod. Let us calculate the moment of inertia of a uniform rod of mass m and length $2a$ about a line through its center perpendicular to its length. Taking the rod for x-axis, with the origin at the center of the rod, the mass of an element dx is

$$dm = \frac{m\,dx}{2a}.$$

Hence, by (7.104), we have

$$(7.105) \qquad I = \int_{-a}^{a} x^2 \frac{m\,dx}{2a} = \tfrac{1}{3}ma^2.$$

Rectangular plate Consider now a uniform rectangular plate of mass m and edges of lengths $2a$, $2b$. We wish to calculate the moment of inertia about the line in its plane passing through the center and parallel to the edge $2b$. We imagine the plate split into thin strips parallel to the edge $2a$ Let dm be the mass of a strip. Then the moment of inertia of the strip is $\tfrac{1}{3}a^2\,dm$, by (7.105), and hence the moment of inertia of the whole plate is $\tfrac{1}{3}ma^2$.

Circular disk. We wish to find the moment of inertia of a uniform circular disk of mass m and radius a about a line through its center perpendicular to its plane. We imagine the disk split up into thin rings by a great number of circles concentric with the boundary. If r, $r + dr$ are the inner and outer radii of a ring, the area of the ring is $2\pi r\,dr$, and its mass is

$$dm = m \cdot \frac{2\pi r\,dr}{\pi a^2}.$$

The moment of inertia is

$$(7.106) \qquad I = \int r^2\,dm = \int_0^a \frac{2m}{a^2} r^3\,dr = \tfrac{1}{2}ma^2.$$

Sec. 7.1] *MOTION OF A RIGID BODY AND OF A SYSTEM* 191

Circular cylinder. The moment of inertia of a solid circular cylinder about its axis follows immediately from (7.106). For we may imagine the cylinder split up by planes perpendicular to its axis into a great number of thin disks. When we add together their moments of inertia, we get $I = \frac{1}{2}ma^2$, where m is the mass of the cylinder and a its radius. The length of the cylinder does not appear explicitly in the formula.

Sphere. To find the moment of inertia of a solid sphere of mass m and radius a about a diameter, we imagine it split into thin circular disks by planes perpendicular to the diameter in question. Figure 82 shows the section of the sphere by a plane through the diameter (Ox) about which the moment is to be calculated. If ρ is the density of the material, the mass of the disk between planes at distances x, $x + dx$ from the center is

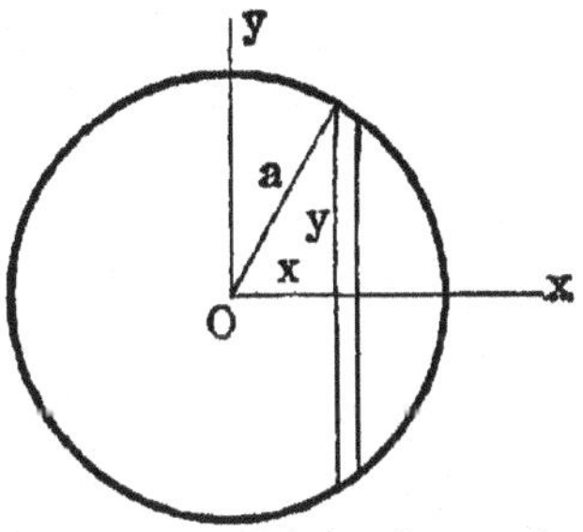

$$\rho \cdot \pi y^2 \, dx,$$

Fig. 82.—Solid sphere split into thin circular disks for the calculation of moment of inertia.

where y is the radius of the disk. By (7.106), the moment of inertia of the disk is

$$dI = \tfrac{1}{2}\pi\rho y^4 \, dx.$$

But $y^2 = a^2 - x^2$, and so

$$I = \tfrac{1}{2}\pi\rho \int_{-a}^{a} (a^2 - x^2)^2 \, dx = \tfrac{8}{15}\pi\rho a^5.$$

But

$$m = \tfrac{4}{3}\pi\rho a^3,$$

and so the moment of inertia of the sphere is

(7.107) $$I = \tfrac{2}{5}ma^2.$$

Exercise. Show by the theory of dimensions, without calculations, that the above moments of inertia of the hoop, the rod, the circular disk, the circular cylinder, and the sphere are all necessarily of the form Cma^2, where C is a pure number.

Theorem of parallel axes.

The theorem of parallel axes gives us an easy method of calculating the moment of inertia of a system about any line, when the moment of inertia about a parallel line through the mass center is known. Figure 83 shows a projection onto a

plane perpendicular to the two lines, O' being the projection of the line through the mass center and O the projection of the other line. Introducing parallel coordinate axes as shown, let (a, b) be the coordinates of O' relative to O. If x, y are the coordinates of any point relative to the axes Oxy, and x', y' the coordinates of the same point relative to $O'x'y'$, then

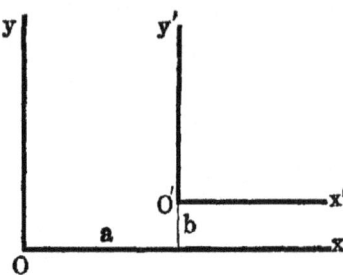

FIG. 83.—Coordinates for the proof of the theorem of parallel axes

$$(7.108) \quad \begin{cases} x = x' + a, \\ y = y' + b. \end{cases}$$

With the notation used at the beginning of this section, the moments of inertia about the lines through O and O' are, respectively,

$$(7.109) \quad I = \sum_{i=1}^{n} m_i(x_i^2 + y_i^2), \quad I' = \sum_{i=1}^{n} m_i(x_i'^2 + y_i'^2).$$

Then, by (7.108),

$$(7.110) \quad I = \sum_{i=1}^{n} m_i[(x_i' + a)^2 + (y_i' + b)^2]$$
$$= I' + m(a^2 + b^2),$$

where m is the total mass of the system, since

$$\sum_{i=1}^{n} m_i x_i' = \sum_{i=1}^{n} m_i y_i' = 0$$

from the definition of mass center. We may state (7.110) in words as follows: *The moment of inertia of a system about an axis L is equal to the moment of inertia of the same system about an axis through the mass center parallel to L, together with the moment of inertia about L of a particle with a mass equal to the total mass of the system, placed at its mass center.*

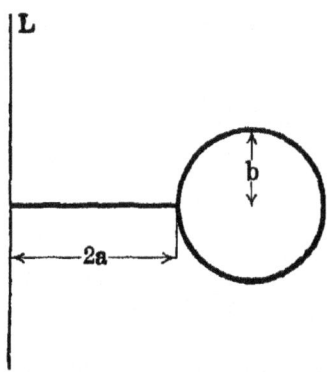

FIG. 84.—Rod and sphere: the moment of inertia about L is required.

As an application of this theorem of parallel axes, we note that by (7.105) the moment of inertia of a rod of length $2a$ about a line through one end, perpendicular to the rod, is $\frac{4}{3}ma^2$.

As another application, suppose we wish to find the moment of inertia about the line L of the apparatus shown in Fig. 84, consisting of a rod of mass m and length $2a$, with a sphere of mass M and radius b attached to the end of the rod. From (7.105) and (7.107), combined with the theorem of parallel axes, we obtain at once

(7.111) $\quad I = \frac{4}{3}ma^2 + M[\frac{2}{5}b^2 + (2a + b)^2].$

Theorem of perpendicular axes.

The theorem of perpendicular axes is useful for the calculation of moments of inertia of plane distributions of matter. Let $Oxyz$ be rectangular axes, and let there be a distribution of matter in the plane $z = 0$. Denoting by A, B, C the moments of inertia about the three axes, we have

(7.112) $\quad A = \sum_{i=1}^{n} m_i y_i^2, \quad B = \sum_{i=1}^{n} m_i x_i^2, \quad C = \sum_{i=1}^{n} m_i(x_i^2 + y_i^2).$

Obviously,

(7.113) $\quad\quad\quad C = A + B;$

this result constitutes the theorem of perpendicular axes.

As an application, suppose we wish to find the moment of inertia of a rectangular plate of edges $2a$, $2b$, about a line through its center perpendicular to its plane. Taking the origin at the center, the axes Oxy parallel to the edges, and the axis Oz perpendicular to the plate, we have, as already established,

(7.114) $\quad\quad\quad A = \frac{1}{3}mb^2, \quad B = \frac{1}{3}ma^2.$

Hence the required moment of inertia is

(7.115) $\quad\quad\quad C = A + B = \frac{1}{3}m(a^2 + b^2).$

More information about moments of inertia will be found in Sec. 11.3.

Exercise. The moment of inertia of a hoop of mass m and radius a about a diameter is $\frac{1}{2}ma^2$ and that of a circular disk of the same mass and radius about a diameter is $\frac{1}{4}ma^2$. Verify these statements.

Kinetic energy and angular momentum.

As we have seen in Sec. 5.2, kinetic energy and angular momentum play an important part in the dynamics of systems. We

shall now show how these quantities are to be calculated when the system is a rigid body moving parallel to a plane.

Let us first suppose that the rigid body is *rotating about a fixed axis*. Let ω be the instantaneous value of the angular velocity. Then the kinetic energy of a particle of mass m_i situated at a distance r_i from the axis is $\frac{1}{2}m_i r_i^2 \omega^2$, and so the kinetic energy of the rigid body (supposed to consist of n particles) is

$$(7.116) \qquad T = \tfrac{1}{2}\omega^2 \sum_{i=1}^{n} m_i r_i^2 = \tfrac{1}{2} I \omega^2,$$

where I is the moment of inertia about the axis. The angular momentum of a particle about the axis of rotation is $m_i r_i^2 \omega$, and so the angular momentum of the rigid body is

$$(7.117) \qquad h = \omega \sum_{i=1}^{n} m_i r_i^2 = I\omega.$$

Let us now suppose that the rigid body no longer rotates about a fixed axis but moves in a general manner parallel to a fixed fundamental plane (cf. Sec. 4.2). Let us imagine an observer traveling with one of the particles (A) of the rigid body and observing the motion of the particles relative to him. He can compute a *relative* kinetic energy and a *relative* angular momentum about a line through A perpendicular to the fundamental plane, using in these computations the velocities of the particles relative to him. Since relative to him the body rotates with angular velocity ω about a fixed axis through A, the formal calculations are precisely as above and lead to formulas (7.116) and (7.117) for the relative kinetic energy and angular momentum.

Although this is true for any particle A of the body, the results are most useful when A is the mass center. Let us restate them: *The kinetic energy and angular momentum, both relative to the mass center, of a rigid body moving parallel to a plane are*

$$(7.118) \qquad T = \tfrac{1}{2}I\omega^2, \qquad h = I\omega,$$

where ω is the angular velocity of the body and I its moment of inertia about an axis through the mass center perpendicular to the plane of motion.

The following theorem of Konig enables us to complete the calculation of the kinetic energy of a rigid body moving parallel to a plane. We shall prove it in general three-dimensional form.

Sec. 7.1] MOTION OF A RIGID BODY AND OF A SYSTEM 195

THEOREM OF KÖNIG. *The kinetic energy of a moving system is equal to the sum of* (i) *the kinetic energy of a fictitious particle moving with the mass center and having a mass equal to the total mass of the system and* (ii) *the kinetic energy of the motion relative to the mass center.*

Let $Oxyz$ be fixed axes and $O'x'y'z'$ parallel axes through the mass center. Let $\bar{x}$, $\bar{y}$, $\bar{z}$ be the coordinates of the mass center referred to $Oxyz$. Then, for any particle, we have

$$(7.119) \quad x_i = \bar{x} + x'_i, \quad y_i = \bar{y} + y'_i, \quad z_i = \bar{z} + z'_i.$$

The kinetic energy of the system is

$$(7.120) \quad T = \tfrac{1}{2}\sum_{i=1}^{n} m_i(\dot{x}_i^2 + \dot{y}_i^2 + \dot{z}_i^2)$$

Let us differentiate (7.119) and substitute for $\dot{x}_i$, $\dot{y}_i$, $\dot{z}_i$ in (7.120). Certain terms vanish on account of the relations

$$(7.121) \quad \sum_{i=1}^{n} m_i x'_i = \sum_{i=1}^{n} m_i y'_i = \sum_{i=1}^{n} m_i z'_i = 0,$$

which are consequences of the definition of mass center given in Sec. 3.1. We obtain

$$(7.122) \quad T = \tfrac{1}{2}m(\dot{\bar{x}}^2 + \dot{\bar{y}}^2 + \dot{\bar{z}}^2) + \tfrac{1}{2}\sum_{i=1}^{n} m_i(\dot{x}'^2_i + \dot{y}'^2_i + \dot{z}'^2_i),$$

where $m = \sum_{i=1}^{n} m_i$, the total mass of the system. Thus the theorem is proved.

It is convenient to refer to the kinetic energy of the fictitious particle as the "kinetic energy of the mass center," so that our result reads

$$(7.123) \quad T = T_0 + T',$$

where T_0 is the kinetic energy of the mass center and T' the kinetic energy relative to the mass center. This general result holds even though the system is not a rigid body.

In the case of a rigid body, we have the important formula

$$(7.124) \quad T = \tfrac{1}{2}mq^2 + \tfrac{1}{2}I\omega^2,$$

where m = mass of body,
q = speed of mass center,
I = moment of inertia about mass center,*
ω = angular velocity.

Exercise. Find the kinetic energy of a disk of mass m and radius a, rolling along the ground with speed q.

7.2. RIGID BODY ROTATING ABOUT A FIXED AXIS

General methods.

In Sec 5.2 we developed the principle of angular momentum (5.214) and the principle of energy (5.223). Let us insert in these equations the values of h and T given in (7.117) and (7.116); then we have

(7.201) $\qquad I\dot{\omega} = N \qquad$ (principle of angular momentum),
(7.202) $\qquad \tfrac{1}{2}I\omega^2 + V = E \qquad$ (principle of energy).

These equations represent the two fundamental methods of finding the motion of a rigid body which turns about a fixed axis. Let us recall the meanings of the terms:

I = moment of inertia about the fixed axis,
ω = angular velocity,
N = moment of external forces about the fixed axis, or *torque*.
V = potential energy,
E = total energy (a constant).

It must be remembered that (7.201) is always valid; (7.202), on the other hand, holds only when the system is conservative. It would not hold, for example, if there were a frictional torque.

Flywheels.

Let us consider a flywheel rotating about a fixed axis which passes through its mass center. Gravity contributes nothing to the moment about the axis and so does not influence the motion. We suppose the torque N supplied by a motor or brakes. Since the forces involved here will not, in general, be conservative, we use (7.201) as the equation of motion; so we write

(7.203) $\qquad\qquad I\dot{\omega} = N.$

We may note the resemblance between this equation and the

---
* More precisely, the moment of inertia about the line through the mass center perpendicular to the plane of motion.

equation of motion of a particle moving on a straight line,
$$m\dot{u} = X;$$
mass corresponds to moment of inertia, linear velocity to angular velocity, force to torque. This mathematical similarity may be used to solve a problem in the dynamics of a rotating flywheel, when the solution of the analogous problem for a particle moving on a straight line is already known.

If the torque N is constant, (7.203) gives

(7.204) $$\omega = \frac{N}{I} t + A,$$

where A is a constant of integration; hence, if θ is the angle turned through, we have $\dot{\theta} = \omega$ and

(7.205) $$\theta = \frac{N}{2I} t^2 + At + B,$$

where B is another constant of integration. This motion is analogous to the motion of a particle under a constant force.

The importance of the flywheel in machinery lies in its capacity to smooth out motion. In a steam or gasoline engine the torque is not uniform, and without a flywheel (or something equivalent) the motion would be jerky. As an illustration, let us work out the case where a flywheel of moment of inertia I is under the action of a torque with a fluctuating part,
$$N = N_0 + N_1 \cos ct, \quad (N_0, N_1 \text{ constants}),$$
and a load proportional to angular velocity. The equation of motion is

(7.206) $$I\dot{\omega} = N_0 + N_1 \cos ct - L\omega,$$

the last term corresponding to the load; thus

(7.207) $$\dot{\omega} + \frac{L}{I} \omega = \frac{1}{I} (N_0 + N_1 \cos ct)$$

This is a standard type of differential equation, which has the integrating factor $e^{Lt/I}$; the solution is

(7.208) $$\omega = e^{-Lt/I} \left[A + \frac{1}{I} \int e^{Lt/I}(N_0 + N_1 \cos ct) \, dt \right],$$

where A is a constant of integration. Using R to denote "real part of," we have

$$(7.209) \quad \int e^{Lt/I} \cos ct \, dt = R \int e^{(L/I+ic)t} \, dt$$
$$= R \frac{1}{(L/I)+ic} e^{(L/I+ic)t}$$
$$= e^{Lt/I} R \frac{(L/I)-ic}{(L/I)^2+c^2} (\cos ct + i \sin ct)$$
$$= e^{Lt/I} \frac{\cos(ct+\epsilon)}{[(L/I)^2+c^2]^{\frac{1}{2}}},$$

where ϵ is a constant; its value is of no present interest. Hence,

$$(7.210) \quad \omega = Ae^{-Lt/I} + \frac{N_0}{L} + \frac{N_1}{I[(L/I)^2+c^2]^{\frac{1}{2}}} \cos(ct+\epsilon).$$

The first term dies away as t increases. The ratio of the amplitude of the third term to the second term is

$$(7.211) \quad \frac{N_1}{N_0} \cdot \frac{L}{I[(L/I)^2+c^2]^{\frac{1}{2}}}.$$

By increasing the moment of inertia of the flywheel, we can make this ratio as small as we please and so approximate to the steady motion $\omega = N_0/L$, even though the fluctuating part $N_1 \cos ct$ may be greater in magnitude than the steady torque N_0.

The compound pendulum.

In Sec. 6.3, we discussed the small oscillations of a simple pendulum, consisting of a heavy particle attached to a fixed point by a light string. We shall now discuss the *compound pendulum*, which is a rigid body free to oscillate under the influence of gravity about a fixed horizontal axis. We shall use the equation of energy (7.202), but the results may be obtained with equal ease from (7.201).

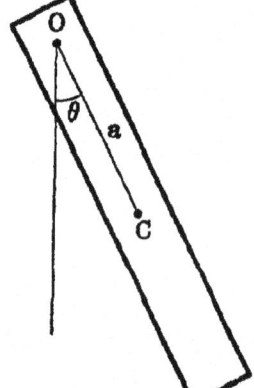

FIG. 85.—A compound pendulum.

In Fig. 85 the plane of the paper is the plane through the mass center C perpendicular to the axis of suspension. The axis cuts it at O, which is called the *point of suspension*. We shall use the following notation:

$a = OC$,
$m = $ mass of pendulum,
$k_c = $ radius of gyration about C,
$k_0 = $ radius of gyration about O.

If θ denotes the inclination of OC to the vertical, the potential energy is
$$V = -mga \cos \theta,$$
and (7.202) gives

(7.212) $\qquad \frac{1}{2}mk_0^2\dot\theta^2 - mga \cos \theta = E,$

where E is a constant.

This equation gives the angular velocity at any position, when E has been found from the initial conditions.

For example, if the pendulum starts with C directly below O and with angular velocity ω_0, we have
$$E = \tfrac{1}{2}mk_0^2\omega_0^2 - mga;$$
equation (7.212) gives

(7.213) $\qquad \dot\theta^2 = \omega_0^2 - \dfrac{4ga}{k_0^2} \sin^2 \tfrac{1}{2}\theta.$

This will vanish when θ takes the values $\pm \alpha$, where
$$\sin^2 \tfrac{1}{2}\alpha = \frac{k_0^2 \omega_0^2}{4ga},$$
and so the pendulum oscillates through the range $(-\alpha, \alpha)$.

Since $\sin^2 \tfrac{1}{2}\theta$ cannot exceed unity, it is evident from (7.213) that $\dot\theta$ never vanishes if
$$\omega_0^2 > \frac{4ga}{k_0^2};$$
if started with such an angular velocity, the pendulum travels right around.

Differentiation of (7.212) gives

(7.214) $\qquad k_0^2 \ddot\theta + ga \sin \theta = 0,$

as an alternative form for the equation of motion of a compound pendulum. Had we used (7.201), we should have obtained this equation directly without differentiation.

For small oscillations, we replace $\sin \theta$ by θ and obtain the solution

(7.215) $\qquad \theta = \alpha \cos (pt + \epsilon),$

where α, ϵ are constants of integration and $p^2 = ga/k_0^2$. This

is a simple harmonic motion with periodic time

$$\tag{7.216} \tau = \frac{2\pi}{p} = \frac{2\pi k_0}{\sqrt{ga}}.$$

The simple pendulum is a special case of the compound pendulum; for a simple pendulum of length l, we have $k_0 = l$, $a = l$, and so (7.214) gives

$$\tag{7.217} l\ddot{\theta} + g \sin \theta = 0,$$

as the general equation of motion of a simple pendulum. The equation (6.304) was valid only for small oscillations.

If we compare the motion of a compound pendulum, given by (7.214), with the motion of a simple pendulum, given by (7.217), we note that the two equations are mathematically identical provided that

$$\tag{7.218} l = \frac{k_0^2}{a}.$$

Thus, corresponding to any compound pendulum, we can construct a simple pendulum of length given by this formula, which will oscillate in unison with the compound pendulum; it is called the *equivalent simple pendulum*.

Exercise. Show that a square plate of side $2b$ suspended from one corner oscillates in unison with a simple pendulum of length $(4\sqrt{2}/3)b = 1.89b$.

Let us now suppose that a rigid body is given, with a number of thin parallel holes drilled through it. We can form a compound pendulum by passing an axis of suspension through any one of the holes. How does the periodic time of small oscillations depend on the position of the hole chosen?

To answer this question, we note that, by the theorem of parallel axes (7.110),

$$\tag{7.219} k_0^2 = a^2 + k_c^2.$$

Hence the formula (7.216) for the periodic time may be written

$$\tag{7.220} \tau^2 = \frac{4\pi^2}{g}\left(a + \frac{k_c^2}{a}\right).$$

If we change the position of the point of suspension in the body, a changes but k_c does not change. We see that τ tends to

infinity if a tends to zero or if a tends to infinity. Thus, we can obtain very slow oscillations by moving the point of suspension close to the mass center or far from it.

On differentiating (7.220) with respect to a, we get

$$\frac{d}{da}(\tau^2) = \frac{4\pi^2}{g}\left(1 - \frac{k_c^2}{a^2}\right).$$

Thus *the periodic time is a minimum when the point of suspension is at a distance from the mass center equal to the radius of gyration about the mass center.*

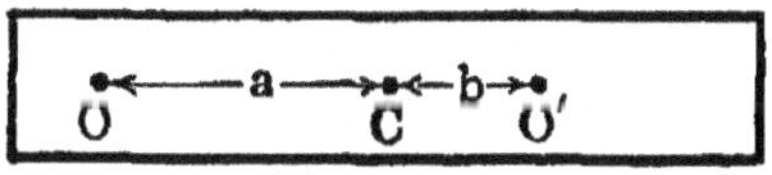

We now ask whether it is possible to shift the point of suspension from a position O to a new position O' (Fig. 86) on the line OC without changing the periodic time. With $OC = a$, $CO' = b$, the condition for equality of periodic times is, by (7.220),

$$a + \frac{k_c^2}{a} = b + \frac{k_c^2}{b},$$

which is satisfied if

(7.221) $$ab = k_c^2.$$

Fig. 86.—The periodic time is the same whether O or O' is used as point of suspension.

The point O', related in this way to the point of suspension O, is called the *center of oscillation*.

7.3. GENERAL MOTION OF A RIGID BODY PARALLEL TO A FIXED PLANE

General methods.

Probably the most useful principle available for the solution of problems in mechanics is the principle of energy in the form (5.223), namely

(7.301) $$T + V = E.$$

One must of course make sure, before attempting to apply this principle, that the system is conservative, i.e., that it has a potential energy V.

When the system consists of a single rigid body moving parallel to a fixed plane, we may write (7.301) in the form

(7.302) $$\tfrac{1}{2}mq^2 + \tfrac{1}{2}I\omega^2 + V = E,$$

where m = mass of body,
q = speed of mass center,
I = moment of inertia about mass center,
ω = angular velocity of body.

However, (7.302) is only *one* equation. Sometimes we require more equations, and then we may employ the principles of linear and angular momentum in the forms (5.209) and (5.219). If Oxy are fixed axes in the fundamental plane, we have

(7.303) $\qquad m\ddot{x} = X, \qquad m\ddot{y} = Y, \qquad I\dot{\omega} = N,$

where x, y are the coordinates of the mass center, X, Y are the total components of external forces in the directions of the axes, and N is the total moment of external forces about the mass center. Of the four equations (7.302) and (7.303), at most *three* are independent.

Cylinder rolling down an inclined plane.

Consider a cylinder of mass m and radius a, rolling down a plane inclined at an angle α to the horizontal (Fig. 87). We wish to determine the motion, and as an illustration we shall do so by two methods, first using the principle of energy and then the principles of linear and angular momentum. We assume the mass center to be situated on the geometrical axis of the cylinder.

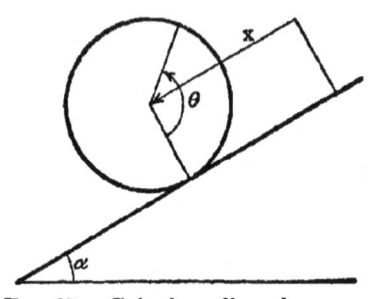

FIG. 87.—Cylinder rolling down an inclined plane

Let x be the displacement at time t of the center of the cylinder from its initial position at rest at $t = 0$, and θ the angle through which it has turned. Then, by the condition of rolling,

(7.304) $\qquad x = a\theta.$

If k is the radius of gyration of the cylinder about its axis, its kinetic energy is

(7.305) $\qquad T = \tfrac{1}{2}m\dot{x}^2 + \tfrac{1}{2}mk^2\dot{\theta}^2,$

or, by (7.304),

(7.306) $\qquad T = \tfrac{1}{2}m\left(1 + \dfrac{k^2}{a^2}\right)\dot{x}^2.$

Sec. 7.3] MOTION OF A RIGID BODY AND OF A SYSTEM 203

The potential energy is

(7.307) $$V = -mgx \sin \alpha.$$

Hence, by (7.301),

(7.308) $$\tfrac{1}{2}m\left(1 + \frac{k^2}{a^2}\right)\dot{x}^2 - mgx \sin \alpha = E,$$

where E is the constant total energy. Actually $E = 0$, since $x = \dot{x} = 0$ for $t = 0$. Differentiating (7.308) with respect to t, we obtain

(7.309) $$\ddot{x} = \frac{g \sin \alpha}{1 + (k^2/a^2)}.$$

Thus the cylinder rolls down the inclined plane with a constant acceleration.

A particle would slide down a smooth plane of inclination α with an acceleration $g \sin \alpha$. The value given by (7.309) is always less than $g \sin \alpha$, except in the limiting case $k = 0$, which corresponds to a concentration of all the mass of the cylinder on its axis. If the cylinder is a thin shell, we have $k = a$, and hence

(7.310) $$\ddot{x} = \tfrac{1}{2}g \sin \alpha$$

If the cylinder is solid and uniform, we have $k^2 = \tfrac{1}{2}a^2$, and hence

(7.311) $$\ddot{x} = \tfrac{2}{3}g \sin \alpha.$$

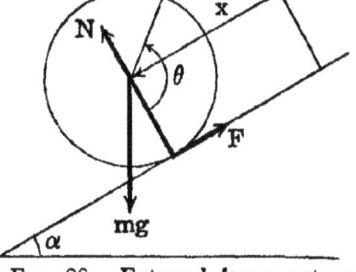

Fig. 88.—External forces acting on cylinder.

The method of energy does not tell us the reaction between the cylinder and the plane, or how rough the plane must be in order that slipping may be avoided. To find out these things, we turn to the principles of linear and angular momentum, using (7.303).

The reaction of the plane on the cylinder may be resolved into a normal component N and a component F in the plane (Fig. 88). These forces, with the weight mg, form the complete system of external forces. Thus, we have

(7.312) $$\begin{cases} m\ddot{x} = mg \sin \alpha - F, \\ 0 = mg \cos \alpha - N, \\ mk^2\ddot{\theta} = Fa, \end{cases}$$

the second equation coming from resolution perpendicular to the plane. Using (7.304) and eliminating F, we get

$$(7.313) \qquad \ddot{x} = \frac{g \sin \alpha}{1 + (k^2/a^2)},$$

as in (7.309). Hence the components of the reaction are

$$(7.314) \quad F = m\frac{k^2}{a^2} \ddot{x} = \frac{mgk^2 \sin \alpha}{a^2 + k^2}, \qquad N = mg \cos \alpha.$$

In order that rolling may occur without slipping, we must have $F/N \le \mu$, or

$$(7.315) \qquad \mu \ge \frac{k^2 \tan \alpha}{a^2 + k^2},$$

where μ is the coefficient of static friction as in (3.202).

Self-propelled vehicle.

Consider an automobile (Fig 89). The external forces acting on it are
  (i) gravity,
  (ii) the reactions of the ground on the wheels,
  (iii) resistance of the air.
Without knowing any further details, we can apply the principle of linear momentum in the form (5 209) to the complete auto-

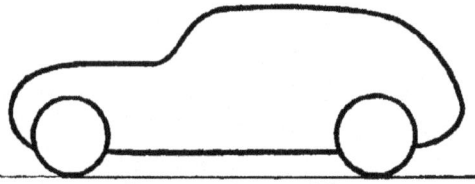

Fig. 89.—Automobile.

mobile. If its mass is m and it is traveling on a horizontal road with acceleration f, then mf equals the total horizontal component of ground reactions and air resistance. The total vertical component of gravity, ground reactions, and air resistance is zero.

Application of the principle of angular momentum in the form (5.219) requires a little care. For simplicity, we shall suppose that the wheels have no mass and hence no angular momentum. The angular momentum of the automobile about

Sec 7 3]   *MOTION OF A RIGID BODY AND OF A SYSTEM*   205

its mass center is then zero. Hence the total moment about the mass center of ground reactions and air resistance is zero.

We can use the above results to find the greatest possible acceleration of an automobile on a street for which the coefficient of friction between ground and tire is μ. Since, by hypothesis, the mass of each wheel is zero, the rate of change of angular momentum of a wheel about its center is zero; hence the total moment of external forces on a wheel is zero. These forces consist of a force exerted by the axle, a couple due to engine or brakes, and a ground reaction. If the couple is absent, the ground reaction can have no moment about the center of the wheel. In fact, *in the case of a wheel without mass, undriven and unbraked, the ground reaction has no frictional component.*

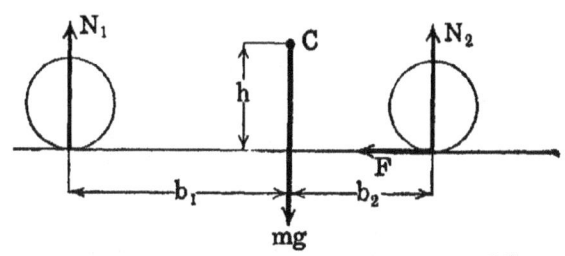

Fig. 90.—External forces acting on automobile.

Figure 90 shows the external forces acting on an automobile, driven through the rear wheels on the right, air resistance being neglected.

Let h = height of mass center above ground,
b_1 = distance of front axle in front of mass center,
b_2 = distance of rear axle behind mass center,
N_1 = resultant of vertical reactions at two front wheels,
N_2 = resultant of vertical reactions at two rear wheels,
F = resultant of frictional forces at two rear wheels

Then,

(7 316) $$\begin{cases} mf = F, \\ 0 = N_1 + N_2 - mg, \\ 0 = b_2 N_2 - b_1 N_1 - hF. \end{cases}$$

Solving for N_1, N_2, F, we obtain

(7.317) $N_1 = m \dfrac{gb_2 - fh}{b_1 + b_2},$ $N_2 = m \dfrac{gb_1 + fh}{b_1 + b_2},$ $F = mf.$

By the law of static friction (3.202) $F/N_2 \leq \mu$, and so

$$\text{(7.318)} \qquad \frac{f(b_1 + b_2)}{gb_1 + fh} \leq \mu,$$

or

$$\text{(7.319)} \qquad f \leq \frac{\mu g b_1}{b_1 + b_2 - \mu h}.$$

This fraction represents the greatest acceleration possible without slipping.

The maximum negative acceleration obtainable by the application of brakes, without slipping between the tires and the ground, may be found in a similar way

Internal reactions.

The principles of linear and angular momentum do not involve the internal reactions between the particles of a rigid body. Nevertheless these reactions exist, and when they become excessive the body may break. As we shall now see, the principles of linear and angular momentum may be used to find the reactions. D'Alembert's principle (cf. Sec. 5.2) may also be used.

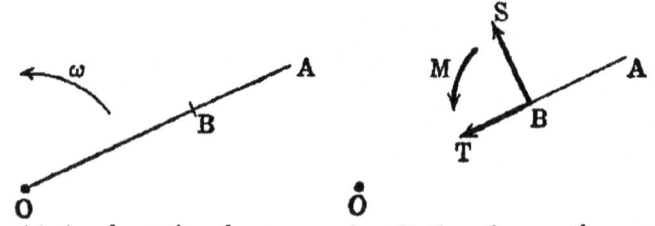

FIG. 91.—(a) A rod rotating about one end. (b) Reactions on the portion BA.

The essential point to note is that, when internal reactions are sought, the dynamical system considered is only *part* of the rigid body. We shall illustrate the method with an example.

Figure 91a shows a uniform rod OA rotating about O with angular velocity ω, which we shall first suppose to be constant B is any point in the rod. We seek the reaction across the section of the rod at B. As in Sec. 3.3, the reaction exerted by OB on BA consists of a tension T, a shearing force S, and a bending moment M (Fig. 91b). Let us regard gravity as non-existent. Then T, S, M constitute the whole system of external forces acting on BA.

Let $OA = l$, $OB = r$. The acceleration of the mass center of BA is of magnitude $\frac{1}{2}(l + r)\omega^2$, directed along AB. If m

is the mass of the rod, the mass of BA is $m(l - r)/l$. Hence the principle of linear momentum, applied to BA as a dynamical system, gives

(7.320) $$T = \tfrac{1}{2}\frac{m\omega^2}{l}(l^2 - r^2), \qquad S = 0.$$

The angular momentum of BA about its mass center is constant. Hence, by the principle of angular momentum, $M = 0$. Thus, when ω is constant, the reaction in the rod at B is a tension, as given by (7.320). As a check, we note that $T = 0$ for $r = l$, and $T = \tfrac{1}{2}m\omega^2 l$ for $r = 0$.

Let us now consider the more general case where ω is a variable function of t. By (4.107) the acceleration of the mass center of BA has components

(7.321) $\qquad \tfrac{1}{2}(l + r)\omega^2$ along AB, $\qquad \tfrac{1}{2}(l + r)\dot{\omega}$ perpendicular to AB

Hence,

(7.322) $$T = \tfrac{1}{2}\frac{m\omega^2}{l}(l^2 - r^2), \qquad S = \tfrac{1}{2}\frac{m\dot{\omega}}{l}(l^2 - r^2).$$

If k is the radius of gyration of BA about its mass center, the angular momentum of BA about its mass center is $mk^2\omega(l - r)/l$. Hence, by the principle of angular momentum,

(7.323) $$M - \tfrac{1}{2}S(l - r) = \frac{mk^2\dot{\omega}}{l}(l - r).$$

Thus,

(7.324) $$M = \frac{m\dot{\omega}(l - r)}{l}[k^2 + \tfrac{1}{4}(l^2 - r^2)].$$

But

$$k^2 = \tfrac{1}{12}(l - r)^2,$$

and so

(7.325) $$M = \tfrac{1}{6}\frac{m\dot{\omega}}{l}(l - r)^2(2l + r).$$

Exercise. Find where the rod is most likely to break, assuming that this occurs where the bending moment is greatest.

7.4. NORMAL MODES OF VIBRATION

Degrees of freedom.

The position of a simple pendulum is determined by the value of one variable, namely, its inclination to the vertical, or the horizontal component of the displacement of the bob. A system

whose position may be specified by one variable or coordinate is said to be a system with *one degree of freedom.*

A rod which can move in a plane, with one end constrained to move on a fixed line, can be described as to position by two variables, namely, the distance of the constrained end from a fixed point on the constraining line and the inclination of the rod to the line. Each of these variables can take arbitrary values. A system whose position may be specified by two arbitrary and independent variables or coordinates is said to be a system with *two degrees of freedom.*

Similarly, there are systems with n degrees of freedom, where $n = 3, 4, \cdots$.

In Sec. 6.3 we discussed the oscillations or vibrations of a simple pendulum and in Sec. 7.2 those of a compound pendulum. Each of these is a system with one degree of freedom. We now proceed to discuss systems with two degrees of freedom.

Particles on a stretched string.

Let there be a light elastic string of length $3a$, stretched between points A, B. Let two particles, each of mass m, be

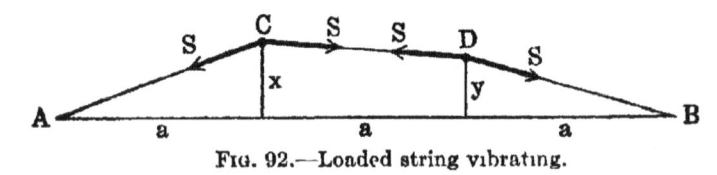

Fig. 92.—Loaded string vibrating.

attached to the string at the points of trisection. For simplicity, we shall neglect gravity; or, equivalently, we may suppose the particles supported on a smooth horizontal plane.

Initially the particles are at rest and the tension in the string is a constant (S) throughout. The particles are given small displacements perpendicular to the string and then released. We wish to investigate the resulting oscillations.

Figure 92 shows the situation at time t. The particles are at C and D, their displacements from the positions of equilibrium being denoted by x and y, which are small quantities. The inclinations of the portions of the string to AB are small, of the same order as x and y. Hence, since the cosine of a small angle differs from unity by a small quantity of the second order, it is seen that the lengths AC, CD, DB are each equal to a, to

[Sec. 7.4] MOTION OF A RIGID BODY AND OF A SYSTEM 209

the first order of small quantities inclusive. Hence the tensions in these portions are equal to S to this order.

Resolving forces in the direction perpendicular to AB, we obtain the following equations of motion.

(7.401) $\quad m\ddot{x} = -S\dfrac{x}{a} - S\dfrac{x-y}{a}, \qquad m\ddot{y} = S\dfrac{x-y}{a} - S\dfrac{y}{a}.$

Writing

(7.402) $\qquad k^2 = \dfrac{S}{ma},$

we simplify these equations to

(7.403) $\quad \ddot{x} + 2k^2 x - k^2 y = 0, \qquad -k^2 x + \ddot{y} + 2k^2 y = 0.$

We try solutions of the form

(7.404) $\quad x = A \cos(nt + \epsilon), \qquad y = B \cos(nt + \epsilon),$

where A, B, n, ϵ are constants. The equations (7.403) are satisfied provided A, B, n satisfy the equations

(7.405) $\qquad \begin{cases} A(-n^2 + 2k^2) - Bk^2 = 0, \\ -Ak^2 + B(-n^2 + 2k^2) = 0. \end{cases}$

Elimination of A and B gives the determinantal equation

(7.406) $\qquad \begin{vmatrix} n^2 - 2k^2 & k^2 \\ k^2 & n^2 - 2k^2 \end{vmatrix} = 0,$

or

(7.407) $\qquad n^4 - 4k^2 n^2 + 3k^4 = 0;$

the solutions are n_1, n_2, where

(7.408) $\qquad n_1^2 = k^2, \qquad n_2^2 = 3k^2$

When n is known, either of the equations (7.405) gives, for the ratio B/A,

(7.409) $\qquad \dfrac{B}{A} = 2 - \dfrac{n^2}{k^2}.$

Thus for $n = n_1$, $B/A = 1$; and for $n = n_2$, $B/A = -1$.

Hence if A_1, ϵ_1 are arbitrary constants, the following is a solution of (7.403):

(7.410) $\quad x = A_1 \cos(kt + \epsilon_1), \qquad y = A_1 \cos(kt + \epsilon_1).$

Also, if A_2, ϵ_2 are arbitrary constants, the following is a solution of (7.403):

(7.411) $\quad x = A_2 \cos (kt \sqrt{3} + \epsilon_2), \qquad y = -A_2 \cos (kt \sqrt{3} + \epsilon_2).$

Thus, (7.410) and (7.411) represent possible vibrations of the particles. The most general vibration is given by adding these expressions, thus:

(7.412) $\quad \begin{cases} x = A_1 \cos (kt + \epsilon_1) + A_2 \cos (kt \sqrt{3} + \epsilon_2), \\ y = A_1 \cos (kt + \epsilon_1) - A_2 \cos (kt \sqrt{3} + \epsilon_2). \end{cases}$

We know that this is the general solution, because it contains four constants of integration which may be chosen to satisfy initial conditions corresponding to given positions and velocities of the particles at $t = 0$.

Let us suppose, for example, that when $t = 0$ we have

$$x = y = \dot{x} = 0, \qquad \dot{y} = v.$$

This corresponds to the case where the motion is started by giving a blow to D. Putting $t = 0$ in (7.412) and the equations obtained by differentiating (7.412), we obtain

(7.413) $\quad \begin{cases} A_1 \cos \epsilon_1 + A_2 \cos \epsilon_2 = 0, \\ A_1 \cos \epsilon_1 - A_2 \cos \epsilon_2 = 0, \\ -A_1 \sin \epsilon_1 - A_2 \sqrt{3} \sin \epsilon_2 = 0, \\ -A_1 \sin \epsilon_1 + A_2 \sqrt{3} \sin \epsilon_2 = \dfrac{v}{k}, \end{cases}$

which are four equations for A_1, A_2, ϵ_1, ϵ_2. The solution is

(7.414) $\quad \epsilon_1 = \epsilon_2 = \tfrac{1}{2}\pi, \qquad A_1 = -\dfrac{v}{2k}, \qquad A_2 = \dfrac{v}{2k \sqrt{3}},$

so that the motion of the particles is given by

(7.415) $\quad \begin{cases} x = \dfrac{v}{2k} \left[\sin kt - \dfrac{1}{\sqrt{3}} \sin (kt \sqrt{3}) \right], \\ y = \dfrac{v}{2k} \left[\sin kt + \dfrac{1}{\sqrt{3}} \sin (kt \sqrt{3}) \right]. \end{cases}$

This motion is complicated, but the simple harmonic motions of which it is composed are easy to describe. These simple harmonic vibrations are called *normal modes of vibrations*. They

Sec. 7.4] MOTION OF A RIGID BODY AND OF A SYSTEM 211

are executed by a vibrating system when the initial conditions are properly chosen.

The vibration given in (7.415) is not a normal mode of vibration, nor in general is that given by (7.412). But if the initial conditions are chosen so that $A_2 = 0$, we have the normal mode of vibration (7.410), whereas, if the initial conditions are chosen so that $A_1 = 0$, we have the normal mode of vibration (7.411). The periodic times and frequencies of normal modes are called *normal periods* and *normal frequencies*. In the above problem the normal periods are

$$\frac{2\pi}{k}, \quad \frac{2\pi}{k\sqrt{3}}.$$

When a system is executing a normal vibration, its configurations are usually simple to describe. Thus, in the mode (7.410) we have $x = y$, and in (7.411) we have $x = -y$. Typical configurations for the normal modes are shown in Figs 93a and b.

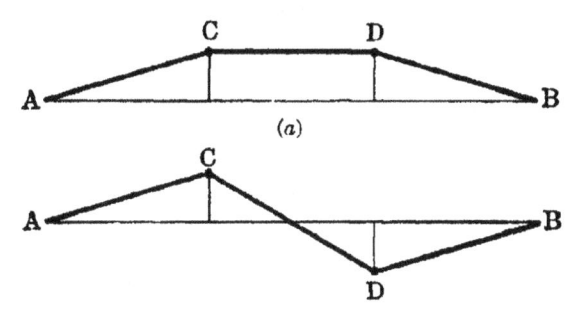

Fig. 93.—(a) Loaded string vibrating in first normal mode. (b) Loaded string vibrating in second normal mode

We have been discussing the vibrations of a particular system—two particles on a taut string. All problems of vibration have certain features in common; and although we shall not attempt here to prove these facts, it will be useful to sum them up:

(i) A vibration may be regarded as a superposition, or addition, of simple harmonic vibrations.

(ii) Each simple harmonic vibration is called a normal mode of vibration. It is possible to make a system vibrate in a normal mode by starting with suitable initial conditions.

(iii) The periods and frequencies of the normal modes are called the normal periods and frequencies.

(iv) The number of normal modes is equal to the number of degrees of freedom of the system.

(v) The normal periods are found by solving a determinantal equation, e.g., (7.406).

Vibrations of a particle in a plane.

As another example of a vibrating system with two degrees of freedom, let us consider a particle which moves in a plane in a field of force such that the potential energy per unit mass is

$$(7.416) \qquad V = \tfrac{1}{2}(ax^2 + 2hxy + by^2),$$

where a, h, b are constants. The force components per unit mass are then

$$(7.417) \qquad X = -(ax + hy), \qquad Y = -(hx + by).$$

These vanish at the origin, which is therefore a position of equilibrium.

The equations of motion are

$$(7.418) \qquad \ddot{x} = -ax - hy, \qquad \ddot{y} = -hx - by.$$

Trying a solution

$$(7.419) \qquad x = A \cos(nt + \epsilon), \qquad y = B \cos(nt + \epsilon),$$

we see that (7.418) are satisfied provided A, B, n satisfy

$$(7.420) \qquad \begin{cases} A(n^2 - a) - Bh = 0, \\ -Ah + B(n^2 - b) = 0. \end{cases}$$

Hence, n must satisfy the determinantal equation

$$(7.421) \qquad \begin{vmatrix} n^2 - a & -h \\ -h & n^2 - b \end{vmatrix} = 0,$$

or

$$(7.422) \qquad n^4 - n^2(a + b) + ab - h^2 = 0;$$

the solutions are n_1, n_2, where

$$(7.423) \qquad \begin{cases} n_1^2 = \tfrac{1}{2}[(a + b) + \sqrt{(a - b)^2 + 4h^2}], \\ n_2^2 = \tfrac{1}{2}[(a + b) - \sqrt{(a - b)^2 + 4h^2}]. \end{cases}$$

If one of these values should be negative, the corresponding n would be imaginary, and the solution (7.419) would contain hyperbolic instead of trigonometrical functions. This case will

be discussed in Sec. 7.5; for the present, we assume that n_1, n_2 are real.

Then the normal periods are $2\pi/n_1$, $2\pi/n_2$, and the normal modes of vibration are

$$(7.424) \quad x = A_1 \cos(n_1 t + \epsilon_1), \quad y = \frac{n_1^2 - a}{h} A_1 \cos(n_1 t + \epsilon_1),$$

and

$$(7.425) \quad x = A_2 \cos(n_2 t + \epsilon_2), \quad y = \frac{n_2^2 - a}{h} A_2 \cos(n_2 t + \epsilon_2),$$

where A_1, A_2, ϵ_1, ϵ_2 are arbitrary constants. The general motion is found by adding the solutions (7.424) and (7.425), just as we added (7.410) and (7.411).

The preceding discussion is actually more general than might appear. Let us again suppose that a particle moves in a plane under a conservative force system, with potential energy V per unit mass; but instead of assuming the simple expression (7.416) for V, we shall merely assume that it is a function which can be expanded in a Taylor series.

Let x_0, y_0 be a position of equilibrium. Since the components of force must vanish there, we have

$$(7.426) \quad \left(\frac{\partial V}{\partial x}\right)_0 = 0, \quad \left(\frac{\partial V}{\partial y}\right)_0 = 0,$$

the suffix zero indicating evaluation at $x = x_0$, $y = y_0$. If we expand V in a Taylor series about x_0, y_0, two terms in the expansion vanish on account of these equations, and so

$$(7.427) \quad V = V_0 + \tfrac{1}{2}\left[(x - x_0)^2 \left(\frac{\partial^2 V}{\partial x^2}\right)_0 \right.$$
$$\left. + 2(x - x_0)(y - y_0)\left(\frac{\partial^2 V}{\partial x \partial y}\right)_0 + (y - y_0)^2 \left(\frac{\partial^2 V}{\partial y^2}\right)_0 \right] + \cdots,$$

the terms not written being of a higher order of smallness if $x - x_0$, $y - y_0$ are small.

Now V is always undetermined to within an additive constant; there is therefore no loss of generality in putting $V_0 = 0$. If we shift the origin to the position of equilibrium (x_0, y_0) and define a, h, b by

$$(7.428) \quad a = \left(\frac{\partial^2 V}{\partial x^2}\right)_0, \quad h = \left(\frac{\partial^2 V}{\partial x\, \partial y}\right)_0, \quad b = \left(\frac{\partial^2 V}{\partial y^2}\right)_0,$$

the principal part of V for small values of x and y is

$$(7.429) \quad V = \tfrac{1}{2}(ax^2 + 2hxy + by^2),$$

which is formally the same as (7.416) The deductions based on (7.416) were exact; the same formal deductions hold approximately for small vibrations about any position of equilibrium. The normal modes of vibration are given by (7.424) and (7.425), where n_1, n_2 are given by (7.423), a, h, b having the values (7.428).

7.5. STABILITY OF EQUILIBRIUM

A position of equilibrium for any system is said to be *stable* when an arbitrary small disturbance does not cause the system to depart far from the position of equilibrium. Otherwise, it is *unstable*. By "small disturbance" we mean that, at the initial instant, the particles of the system are displaced from their positions of equilibrium through small distances and their velocities are small The system is stable if in the resulting motion the particles remain at small distances from their positions of equilibrium.

Thus a compound pendulum hanging from its axis of support is in stable equilibrium. If it is balanced with its mass center above the axis of support, the equilibrium is unstable, because a small disturbance will cause the pendulum to move right away from the position of equilibrium.

Condition of minimum potential energy.

Let a system have a potential energy V. We know by the principle of virtual work (cf. Sec. 2.4) that, for a system in equilibrium, no work is done in a small displacement. Thus $\delta V = 0$ for any small displacement from a position of equilibrium, and so V has a stationary value there.

Stationary values are of various kinds; the question of stability turns on the character of the stationary value of V. We make the following statement: *If, in a position of equilibrium, the potential energy is a minimum, then the equilibrium is stable.*

To prove this, let us recall the principle of energy,

$$(7.501) \quad T + V = E,$$

where E is a constant. Since potential energy is always undetermined to within an additive constant, there is no loss of generality in assuming $V = 0$ at the position of equilibrium. Then, since V is a minimum there, we have $V > 0$ for all positions near that of equilibrium. The constant E is found from the small initial disturbance. Let T_0, V_0 be the initial kinetic and potential energies. Then $E = T_0 + V_0$, which is small and positive. In the subsequent motion,

$$(7.502) \qquad V = E - T \leq E,$$

since T cannot be negative. Thus V always remains less than the small positive constant E, and so the equilibrium is stable, since to escape to a finite distance from the position of equilibrium the potential energy would have to become finite.

As an illustration, consider a simple pendulum of mass m and length a. At an inclination θ to the downward vertical, the potential energy is

$$V = mga(1 - \cos \theta),$$

if we choose $V = 0$ at the position in which the pendulum hangs vertically. Then V is a minimum for $\theta = 0$. Suppose that the pendulum is disturbed to an angle θ_0 and is given a kinetic energy T_0. In the subsequent motion, as in (7.502),

$$mga(1 - \cos \theta) \leq T_0 + mga(1 - \cos \theta_0),$$

where the right-hand side is small. Thus $\cos \theta$ must remain nearly equal to unity, or, in other words, θ must remain small.

If, on the other hand, we consider that position of equilibrium in which the pendulum is balanced directly above the point of support (the string being replaced by a light rod) and measure θ from this position, we have

$$V = mga(\cos \theta - 1)$$

Then V is a maximum for $\theta = 0$. Our inequality (7.502) is still valid; it reads

$$mga(\cos \theta - 1) \leq T_0 + mga(\cos \theta_0 - 1),$$

where θ_0, T_0 refer to the initial disturbance. But this inequality is not violated as θ increases from θ_0 to π, and so it does not

restrict the motion. The position of equilibrium is actually unstable, but this inequality shows only that it may be so

The following statement is true for a system with any number of degrees of freedom, but we shall prove it here only for systems with one degree of freedom: *If the potential energy at a position of equilibrium is not a minimum, then the equilibrium is unstable.**

Let x be the variable which fixes the position of the system Consider the graph of the potential energy V against x (Fig. 94)

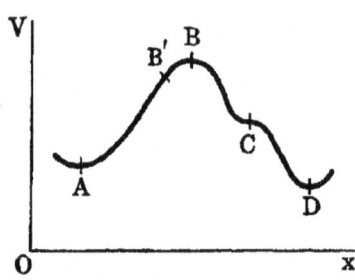

Fig 94—Graph of potential energy against position; stable equilibrium at A and D, unstable equilibrium at B and C.

By the principle of virtual work, we have $\delta V = 0$ for an infinitesimal displacement δx from a position of equilibrium. In fact, at a position of equilibrium

(7.503) $$\frac{dV}{dx} = 0,$$

so that the positions of equilibrium correspond to those points on the graph where the tangent is parallel to the x-axis, i.e., the points A, B, C, D. At A and D, V is a minimum, and hence we know that equilibrium at A or D is stable.

Let us now consider the position corresponding to B. Suppose the system is displaced to a neighboring position B' and is then released from rest. Since the tangent at B' is not parallel to the x-axis, the system cannot remain in equilibrium at B'. It must start to move; and since its kinetic energy (being positive) must increase in comparison with its initial zero value, V must decrease, and so the system must move still farther away from B. It can come to rest only when V takes the same value as at B'. Thus it cannot stop moving until it has passed the position corresponding to A. Clearly, this is a case of instability

At C the potential energy has a stationary value, but it is neither a maximum nor a minimum. By considering an initial displacement in the direction of D, it is seen that the equilibrium

---

*In the particular case where V is constant (as for a sphere resting on a horizontal table), the equilibrium is often called *neutral*. Actually, it is unstable in the sense of our definition.

is unstable. This completes the proof of the italicized statement on the preceding page.

To sum up: *A position of equilibrium is stable if, and only if, the potential energy is a minimum.*

Hence, in the case of a system with one degree of freedom, a sufficient condition for stability is

(7.504) $$\frac{d^2V}{dx^2} > 0,$$

at the position of equilibrium. This condition is also necessary, unless $d^2V/dx^2 = 0$ at the position of equilibrium; in that exceptional case, we have to examine the higher derivatives.

It is clear from Fig 94 that between any two positions of stable equilibrium there must be at least one position of unstable equilibrium. Points such as C, where a point of inflection on the graph coincides with a tangent parallel to the x-axis, are exceptional. In general, positions of stability and instability alternate.

Stability of equilibrium of a particle in a plane.

It was shown in (7 429) that, near a position of equilibrium, the potential energy per unit mass of a particle in a plane may be written

(7.505) $$V = \tfrac{1}{2}(ax^2 + 2hxy + by^2),$$

where a, h, b are constants. It is known, from the analytical geometry of conics, that we may choose new rectangular axes $Ox'y'$ such that

(7.506) $$ax^2 + 2hxy + by^2 = a'x'^2 + b'y'^2,$$

where a', b' are new constants.

Let us recall how a', b' are found. For any constant value of λ,

(7.507) $$ax^2 + 2hxy + by^2 - \lambda(x^2 + y^2)$$
$$= a'x'^2 + b'y'^2 - \lambda(x'^2 + y'^2).$$

If $\lambda = a'$ or $\lambda = b'$, the right-hand side is a perfect square. For either of these values of λ, the left-hand side must also be a perfect square. Thus, if $\lambda = a'$ or $\lambda = b'$,

(7.508) $$(a - \lambda)(b - \lambda) - h^2 = 0,$$

or, in determinantal form,

(7 509) $$\begin{vmatrix} a - \lambda & h \\ h & b - \lambda \end{vmatrix} = 0.$$

In fact, a' and b' are the roots of this quadratic equation.

Suppose the transformation carried out, so that, near the position of equilibrium,

(7.510) $$V = \tfrac{1}{2}(a'x'^2 + b'y'^2).$$

The equations of motion are

(7.511) $$\begin{cases} x'' = -\dfrac{\partial V}{\partial x'} = -a'x', \\ y'' = -\dfrac{\partial V}{\partial y'} = -b'y', \end{cases}$$

or

(7.512) $$x'' + a'x' = 0, \qquad y'' + b'y' = 0.$$

Various cases have now to be distinguished:

(i) $a' > 0$, $x' = A \cos(\sqrt{a'} \cdot t) + B \sin(\sqrt{a'} \cdot t)$,
(ii) $a' = 0$, $x' = At + B$,
(iii) $a' < 0$, $x' = Ae^{\sqrt{-a'}\, t} + Be^{-\sqrt{-a'}\, t}$.

These are the solutions of the first of (7.512), according to the sign of a'. The solutions of the second equation for y' may be similarly classified according to the sign of b'.

The solution for case (i) indicates that x' remains permanently small, so that there is stability as far as x' is concerned. The solutions for cases (ii) and (iii) indicate instability. Thus, there is stability if, and only if, both a' and b' are positive; since a', b' are the roots of (7.509), we may state our result as follows:

When the origin is a position of equilibrium, the potential energy for adjacent positions is given by (7.505). The equilibrium is stable if, and only if, the two roots of the determinantal equation (7.509) are positive.

It is clear from (7.510) that V is a minimum at the origin if, and only if, the roots of (7.509) are positive. Hence, we have a direct proof in this case that minimum potential energy is the condition for stability, both necessary and sufficient.

In the case of stability, oscillations along the axes of x' and y' are normal modes and the normal periods are

$$\frac{2\pi}{\sqrt{\lambda_1}}, \qquad \frac{2\pi}{\sqrt{\lambda_2}},$$

where λ_1, λ_2 are the roots of (7.509).

SEC. 7.5] *MOTION OF A RIGID BODY AND OF A SYSTEM* 219

Problems of balancing.

Theoretically it is possible to balance a needle on its point, but in practice it is extremely difficult to do so. There is a position of equilibrium with the needle vertical, but it is unstable. The instability is obvious in view of the general test given above, because the height of the center of gravity is decreased as the needle is displaced from the vertical position, and so the potential energy is a maximum for the vertical position.

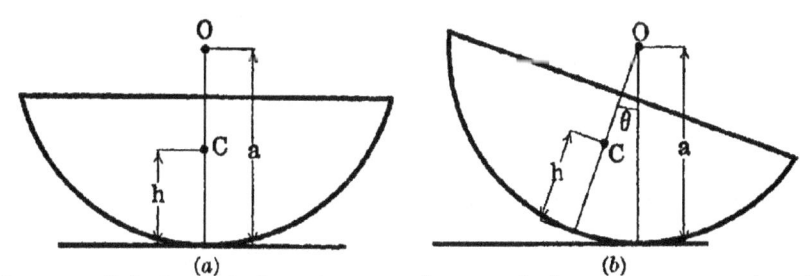

Fig. 95.—Cylindrical body rolling on a horizontal plane (a) position of equilibrium, (b) displaced position

If, instead of a needle, we try to balance a body with a rounded base, it is not immediately evident whether the equilibrium in the position of balancing is stable or not. But the condition of minimum energy gives us an easy test. We shall confine our attention to cases where the possible motion of the body is two-dimensional.

Figures 95a and b show end views of a cylindrical body in contact with a rough horizontal plane; the lower part of the section is a circular arc of radius a. In equilibrium (Fig. 95a) the center of gravity C must lie vertically above the point of contact, since the body is in equilibrium under two forces (the weight and the reaction) and their lines of action must coincide. Let h be the height of the center of gravity above the point of contact.

Figure 95b shows a displaced position, in which the body has been turned through an angle θ. If W is the weight of the body, the potential energy is

(7.513) $$V = W[a - (a - h)\cos\theta].$$

Hence,

(7.514) $$\left(\frac{d^2V}{d\theta^2}\right)_{\theta=0} = W(a - h).$$

Thus the equilibrium is stable if, and only if, $a > h$, i.e., if the center of gravity lies below the center of the circle.

Let us now consider a more general problem, which includes the preceding as a special case. Let A be a cylinder of any section, balanced on a fixed cylinder A', the contact being rough and the common tangent horizontal (Fig 96a). C is the center of gravity of A. D, D' are the centers of curvature of the sections of the cylinders at the point of contact, and ρ, ρ' are the radii of curvature; the height of C above the point of contact is h.

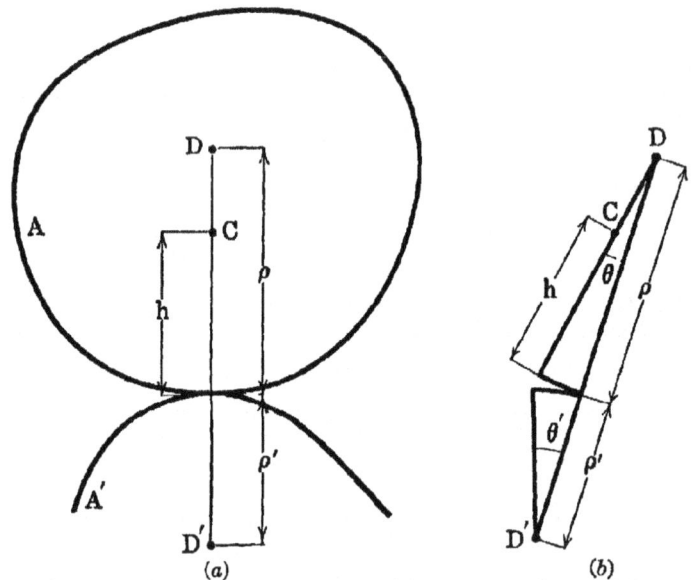

FIG. 96 —One cylinder rolling on another. (a) position of equilibrium, (b) displaced position.

Figure 96b shows a displaced position, in which the point of contact has moved through a small angle θ' about D', and the line DC now makes a small angle θ with DD'. Since we are concerned only with small values of θ and θ', it is legitimate to regard the sections in the neighborhood of the point of contact as circular arcs of radii ρ and ρ'. Then, by the condition of rolling,

(7.515) $$\rho\theta = \rho'\theta'.$$

If W is the weight of A, the potential energy is

(7.516) $\quad V = W[(\rho' + \rho)\cos\theta' - (\rho - h)\cos(\theta + \theta')],$

or, since θ, θ' are small,

(7.517) $\quad V = \frac{1}{2}W[(\rho - h)(\theta + \theta')^2 - (\rho' + \rho)\theta'^2] + C$,

approximately, where C is a constant. By (7.515), this may be written

(7.518) $\quad V = \frac{1}{2}W\theta'^2\left[(\rho - h)\left(1 + \frac{\rho'}{\rho}\right)^2 - (\rho' + \rho)\right] + C$.

The condition that this shall be a minimum for $\theta' = 0$ is

(7.519) $\quad (\rho - h)\left(1 + \frac{\rho'}{\rho}\right)^2 - (\rho' + \rho) > 0$,

or, equivalently,

(7.520) $\quad h < \frac{\rho\rho'}{\rho + \rho'}$.

This is the condition of stability. On letting $\rho' \to \infty$, it reads $h < \rho$, agreeing with the result established earlier. If on the other hand we let $\rho \to \infty$, we get $h < \rho'$ as the condition for the stability of a body with a flat base balanced on a cylinder with radius of curvature ρ'.

By means of the principle of energy, it is easy to find the period of small oscillations of a stable balanced system when disturbed. For example, the body shown in Fig. 95 has the potential energy given by (7.513). To convert to dynamical units, we put $W = mg$, where m is the mass of the cylinder. Thus, when θ is small, the potential energy is approximately

(7.521) $\quad V = mgh + \frac{1}{2}mg(a - h)\theta^2$.

Since, at any instant, the cylinder is turning about the line of contact, the velocity of the mass center is approximately $h\dot\theta$; the angular velocity of the cylinder is $\dot\theta$. Hence (7.302) gives

(7.522) $\quad \frac{1}{2}mh^2\dot\theta^2 + \frac{1}{2}I\dot\theta^2 + mgh + \frac{1}{2}mg(a - h)\theta^2 = E$,

where I is the moment of inertia about a line through C parallel to the generators. If we write

(7.523) $\quad k^2 = h^2 + \frac{I}{m}$,

and differentiate (7.522), we get

(7.524) $\quad k^2\ddot\theta + g(a - h)\theta = 0$;

this gives a simple harmonic motion with period

(7.525) $\qquad \tau = 2\pi k/\sqrt{g(a - h)}.$

7.6. SUMMARY OF APPLICATIONS IN PLANE DYNAMICS—MOTION OF A RIGID BODY AND OF A SYSTEM

I. Moments of inertia.

(a) Definitions:

(7.601) $\quad I = \sum_{i=1}^{n} m_i r_i^2 \quad \text{or} \quad I = \int r^2\, dm = \iiint \rho(x^2 + y^2)\, dx\, dy\, dz;$

$$mk^2 = I.$$

(b) Devices for calculation:
  (i) Theorem of parallel axes (all moments of inertia follow immediately when those for axes through mass center are known).
  (ii) Theorem of perpendicular axes (for a plane distribution, the moments of inertia about axes perpendicular to the plane follow immediately when those for axes in the plane are known).

(c) Standard results:

Body	Axis	k^2
Hoop of radius a	Perpendicular to plane at center	a^2
Circular disk of radius a	Perpendicular to plane at center	$\tfrac{1}{2}a^2$
Circular cylinder of radius a	Geometrical axis	$\tfrac{1}{2}a^2$
Rod of length $2a$	Perpendicular to rod at center	$\tfrac{1}{3}a^2$
Rectangular plate of edges $2a$, $2b$	Through center parallel to edge $2b$	$\tfrac{1}{3}a^2$
	Perpendicular to plate at center	$\tfrac{1}{3}(a^2 + b^2)$
Sphere of radius a	Diameter	$\tfrac{2}{5}a^2$

II. Kinetic energy (T) and angular momentum (h).

(a) Rigid body turning about fixed axis:

(7.602) $\qquad T = \tfrac{1}{2}I\omega^2, \qquad h = I\omega.$

(b) Rigid body in general plane motion:

(7.603) $T = \tfrac{1}{2}mq^2 + \tfrac{1}{2}I\omega^2$, $h = I\omega$ (h, I about mass center).

III. Motion of a rigid body.

(a) Rotation about fixed axis:

(7.604) $I\dot\omega = N$ (angular momentum),
(7.605) $\tfrac{1}{2}I\omega^2 + V = E$ (energy).

(b) Compound pendulum:
  (i) Exact equation of motion:

(7.606) $k^2\ddot\theta + ga \sin\theta = 0$,   ($k$ relative to axis).

  (ii) Periodic time for small oscillations:

(7.607) $$\tau = \frac{2\pi k}{\sqrt{ga}}.$$

  (iii) Equivalent simple pendulum:

(7.608) $$l = \frac{k^2}{a}.$$

(c) General motion parallel to plane:

(7.609) $m\ddot x = X$, $m\ddot y = Y$, $I\dot\omega = N$ (momentum);
(7.610) $\tfrac{1}{2}mq^2 + \tfrac{1}{2}I\omega^2 + V = E$ (energy).

IV. Normal modes of vibration.

(a) A vibration is in general not periodic; it is composed of simple harmonic vibrations with different frequencies. These are the normal modes. A system vibrates in a normal mode if started under special initial conditions.

(b) The normal frequencies are found by assuming a simple harmonic solution of the equations of motion and solving a determinantal equation obtained on this assumption.

V. Stability of equilibrium.

Necessary and sufficient condition for stability: the potential energy is a minimum.

EXERCISES VII

1. A uniform rod of length l and mass M is free to rotate in a vertical plane about an axis at a distance a from its center. If it is released from a

horizontal position, find its angular velocity when passing through the vertical position.

2. A bucket of mass M is fastened to one end of a light rope, the rope is coiled round a windlass in the form of a circular cylinder (radius a) which is left free to rotate about its axis. Prove that the bucket descends with acceleration
$$\frac{g}{1 + (I/Ma^2)},$$
where I is the moment of inertia of the cylinder about its axis.

3. Three uniform rods, each of mass m, form an equilateral triangle of side $2a$. The triangle is suspended from one corner. Find the lengths of the equivalent simple pendulums for oscillations under gravity

(i) when the triangle oscillates in its own plane;
(ii) when the plane of oscillation is perpendicular to the plane of the triangle.

4. A wheel consists of a thin rim of mass M and n spokes each of mass m, which may be considered as thin rods terminating at the center of the wheel. If the wheel is rolling with linear velocity v, express its kinetic energy in terms of M, m, n, v.

With what acceleration will it roll down a rough inclined plane of inclination α?

5. A buoy is formed by joining the edge of a thin metal conical shell to the edge of a hemispherical shell of the same material and thickness. The radii of the hemisphere and of the mouth of the cone are each equal to 5 ft., and the slant height of the cone is 10 ft. The buoy is placed with the hemisphere in contact with the rough horizontal surface of a dock so that the axis is vertical. If slightly disturbed, determine whether or not it will return to the vertical position.

6. One end of a heavy chain is attached to a drum and the chain is wrapped around the drum, making n complete turns, with a small piece of chain hanging free. The drum is mounted on a smooth horizontal axle, and the chain is allowed to unwrap itself. Apply the principle of energy to find the angular velocity of the drum at the instant when the chain is completely unwrapped, in terms of the mass of the chain (m), the radius of the drum (r), and the moment of inertia of the drum (I).

7. A rectangular plate swings in a vertical plane about one of its corners. If its period is 1 sec., find the length of the diagonal.

8. A particle of mass m moves in a plane under the action of a force with components
$$X = -k^2(2x + y), \qquad Y = -k^2(x + 2y),$$
where k is a constant. What is the potential energy? Find the normal periods of oscillation about the position of equilibrium.

9. A uniform circular plate of radius a and mass M is dragged along a smooth sheet of ice by means of a long string attached to a point A on the

rim of the plate. The tension T in the string is kept constant throughout. If initially the plate is at rest and the diameter through A makes a small angle with the string, show that this diameter oscillates about the direction of the string with a period equal to

$$2\pi \sqrt{\frac{Ma}{2T}}$$

10. A particle A hangs from a fixed point by a light string, and another particle B of the same mass hangs from A by a second light string of the same length. Find the normal periods of oscillation, and sketch the normal modes.

11. A homogeneous solid cylinder, whose section is a semicircle of radius a, rests with its flat face horizontal and in contact with a fixed rough circular cylinder of radius b, the generators of the two cylinders being parallel. Find the greatest value of a/b for which there is stability.

12. Find the radius of gyration of a uniform semicircular plate about a line through the mass center perpendicular to the plate.

13. A ladder (length $2a$) rests against a smooth vertical wall and a smooth horizontal floor, the inclination to the floor being initially α. Find the inclination of the ladder to the floor at the instant when the upper end leaves the wall as it slides down under the action of gravity.

14. A pendulum consists of a bob of mass m at the end of a light rod of length $3a$. It is suspended from the point of the rod distant $2a$ from the bob. A horizontal force $mb \cos nt$ (where b and n are constants and b is small) is applied to the rod at its upper end. Find the angular amplitude of the forced oscillations of period $2\pi/n$.

15. A uniform solid ellipsoid of revolution of semiaxes a, b (the axis of revolution being $2a$) is cut in two by a plane through the center perpendicular to the axis of revolution. If either half will balance in stable equilibrium with its vertex on a horizontal plane, prove that

$$\frac{b^2}{a^2} > \tfrac{1}{5}.$$

16. When a ship rolls through a small angle, the upward thrust of the water intersects the central plane of the ship at a point called the *metacenter*. Find a formula for the periodic time of rolling of a ship in terms of h, the height of the metacenter above the mass center of the ship, and k, the radius of gyration of the ship about a fore-and-aft axis through the mass center.

Is the periodic time increased or decreased by shifting cargo horizontally from the center of the ship to the sides, this shift being done symmetrically with respect to the central plane of the ship?

17. A square frame, consisting of four equal uniform rods of length $2a$ rigidly joined together, hangs at rest in a vertical plane on two smooth pegs P, Q at the same level. If $PQ = c$ and the pegs are not both in contact with the same rod, show that there are three positions of equilibrium, provided $a < c\sqrt{2}$.

Of these positions, show that the only unstable one is the symmetrical position. If, however, $a > c\sqrt{2}$, show that the only possible position of equilibrium is stable

18. A particle is suspended by a light string of length a from the lower end of a rod of the same mass and length $2a$, which is free to turn about its upper end For vibrations about equilibrium in a vertical plane, show that the two normal frequencies are given by

$$\frac{1}{2\pi}\sqrt{\frac{gp}{a}},$$

where p satisfies

$$4p^2 - 25p + 9 = 0.$$

19. A rod of length $2a$ hangs from a support which is given a small horizontal displacement ξ varying with time according to the equation $\xi = b \sin pt$, where b and p are constants Find the equation of motion for small oscillations. Integrate the equation, obtaining a result with two arbitrary constants Find these constants on the assumption that when $t = 0$ the rod is hanging vertically and has no angular velocity, hence show that the inclination θ of the rod to the vertical is given by

$$\theta = \frac{bp^2 n}{g(n^2 - p^2)}(n \sin pt - p \sin nt), \qquad \left(n^2 = \frac{3g}{4a}\right).$$

20. Two simple pendulums, each of mass m and length a, hang from a trolley of mass M which can run without friction along horizontal rails A small impulse, parallel to the rails, is applied to one of the pendulums and imparts to it an angular velocity ω, the other pendulum and the trolley having no velocity at that instant Investigate the resulting motion, and express the displacement of the trolley and the inclinations of the pendulums to the vertical as functions of the time.

Show that, if the ratio m/M is small, the motions of the pendulums relative to the trolley may be regarded as simple harmonic motions with slowly varying amplitudes, the amplitudes being given by the absolute values of

$$\frac{\omega}{p} \cos \frac{mpt}{2M}, \qquad \frac{\omega}{p} \sin \frac{mpt}{2M},$$

where

$$p^2 = \frac{g}{a}$$

CHAPTER VIII

PLANE IMPULSIVE MOTION

8.1. GENERAL THEORY OF PLANE IMPULSIVE MOTION

The concept of an impulsive force.

For a particle moving in a plane under the action of a force with components X, Y, the equations of motion are

(8.101) $\qquad m\ddot{x} = X, \qquad m\ddot{y} = Y.$

Multiplying by dt and integrating from t_0 to t_1, we obtain

(8.102) $\qquad \Delta(m\dot{x}) = \int_{t_0}^{t_1} X\,dt, \qquad \Delta(m\dot{y}) = \int_{t_0}^{t_1} Y\,dt,$

where Δ denotes an increment during the time interval (t_0, t_1).

The vector with components

(8.103) $\qquad \int_{t_0}^{t_1} X\,dt, \qquad \int_{t_0}^{t_1} Y\,dt$

is called the *impulse* on the particle during the time interval (t_0, t_1). We may state (8.102) in words as follows: *The increment in momentum is equal to the impulse.*

Let us now suppose that a particle of mass m can move along the x-axis. At time $t = 0$, it is at rest at $x = 0$. At this instant a force

(8.104) $\qquad X = A \sin \dfrac{\pi t}{\tau}$

commences to act and acts until $t = \tau$ (A and τ are constants.) During this time the equation of motion of the particle is

(8.105) $\qquad m\ddot{x} = A \sin \dfrac{\pi t}{\tau},$

and so

$$u = \dot{x} = \frac{A\tau}{\pi m}\left(1 - \cos\frac{\pi t}{\tau}\right),$$

$$x = \frac{A\tau t}{\pi m} - \frac{A\tau^2}{\pi^2 m}\sin\frac{\pi t}{\tau},$$

the constants of integration having been chosen to fit the initial conditions. Thus in the time interval $(0, \tau)$ the particle receives increments in velocity and position given by

$$(8.106) \quad \Delta u = \frac{2A\tau}{\pi m}, \quad \Delta x = \frac{A\tau^2}{\pi m}.$$

The mean value of the force is

$$(8.107) \quad \bar{X} = \frac{1}{\tau} \int_0^\tau A \sin \frac{\pi t}{\tau} dt = \frac{2A}{\pi},$$

and so (8.106) may be written

$$(8.108) \quad \Delta u = \frac{\bar{X}\tau}{m}, \quad \Delta x = \tfrac{1}{2} \frac{\bar{X}\tau^2}{m}.$$

The experiment may be repeated using different values of A and τ. We note that as long as the product $\bar{X}\tau$ remains unchanged the value of Δu remains the same. If we let A (and therefore $\bar{X}$) tend to infinity and let τ tend to zero in such a way that $\bar{X}\tau$ maintains a fixed value C, we have

$$(8.109) \quad \Delta u \to \frac{C}{m}, \quad \Delta x \to 0.$$

We note that, in this limiting case of "an infinite force acting for an infinitesimal time," there is an instantaneous change in velocity but no change in position.

Returning to the general equations (8.102), we may let the force components (X, Y) tend to infinity and the time interval $t_1 - t_0$ to zero in such a way that the integrals remain constant or approach finite limits. Under these circumstances a particle moving in a plane experiences (in the limit) an instantaneous change of velocity. Since the velocity remains finite during this change, the displacement is zero in the limit. The instantaneous change in momentum is given by

$$(8.110) \quad \Delta(m\dot{x}) = \lim_{t_1 \to t_0} \int_{t_0}^{t_1} X \, dt, \quad \Delta(m\dot{y}) = \lim_{t_1 \to t_0} \int_{t_0}^{t_1} Y \, dt.$$

Have we here introduced a new ingredient or concept into mechanics? It must be admitted that we have, because no force, however large, can produce an *instantaneous* change in momentum. To place our new ideas on a secure foundation, we admit the concept of an *impulsive force*, with components denoted

Sec 8.1]   IMPULSIVE MOTION   229

by $\hat{X}, \hat{Y}$: it is such that, when applied to a particle, the impulsive force causes an instantaneous change in momentum given by

(8.111) $\quad \Delta(m\dot{x}) = \hat{X}, \quad \Delta(m\dot{y}) = \hat{Y}.$

We must, however, regard the impulsive force, not as something absolutely new, but as connected with the ordinary force (X, Y) by the relations

(8.112) $\quad \hat{X} = \lim_{t_1 \to t_0} \int_{t_0}^{t_1} X \, dt, \quad \hat{Y} = \lim_{t_1 \to t_0} \int_{t_0}^{t_1} Y \, dt,$

obtained by comparison of (8.110) and (8.111).

On account of this connection, it is unnecessary to repeat for impulsive forces results already obtained for ordinary forces. We draw attention to the fact that impulsive reactions between the particles in a rigid body obey the law of action and reaction. The theory of moments applies to impulsive forces, and we may speak of an impulsive couple. The idea of equipollence may also be used.

It is clear from (8.112) that forces which remain finite as $t_1 \to t_0$ (e.g., gravity) contribute nothing to the impulsive force.

An impulsive force is the product of an ordinary force and a time and is equal to a change in momentum. Hence, impulsive force has the dimensions $[MLT^{-1}]$; its magnitude is expressed in dyne sec. or gm cm sec $^{-1}$ in the c.g.s. system and in poundal sec. or lb. ft. sec.$^{-1}$ in the f.p.s. system.

Principles of linear and angular momentum.

We expressed in (5.206) the law that, for any system, the rate of change of linear momentum is equal to the sum of the external forces. If M_x, M_y are the components of linear momentum in the directions of axes Ox, Oy, and X, Y the total components of external force in those directions, then

(8.113) $\quad \dot{M}_x = X, \quad \dot{M}_y = Y.$

Let us multiply by dt, integrate from $t = t_0$ to $t = t_1$, and then proceed to the limit $t_1 \to t_0$, supposing the forces to tend to infinity. Then

(8.114) $\quad \Delta M_x = \hat{X}, \quad \Delta M_y = \hat{Y},$

where $\hat{X}, \hat{Y}$ are the sums of the components of the external impulsive forces. In words, *the sudden change in the linear momentum of a system is equal to the total external impulsive force.*

These equations may also be written in vector form:

(8.115) $$\Delta \mathbf{M} = \hat{\mathbf{F}},$$

where $\hat{\mathbf{F}}$ is the vector sum of the external impulsive forces. Similarly, we obtain from (5.209) the vector equation

(8.116) $$m\Delta \bar{\mathbf{q}} = \hat{\mathbf{F}},$$

where m is the mass of the system and $\Delta \bar{\mathbf{q}}$ the sudden change in the velocity of the mass center.

If there are no external impulsive forces, we have $\hat{\mathbf{F}} = \mathbf{0}$, and hence $\Delta \bar{\mathbf{q}} = \mathbf{0}$. Thus, when the impulsive forces are purely internal, there is no sudden change in the velocity of the mass center.

This result is of interest in connection with collisions and explosions. Here, in physical reality, we find large forces acting for short intervals of time, and we may treat the phenomena mathematically by means of impulsive forces. Thus, if a shunting locomotive strikes a car, the mass center of the system "locomotive + car" has the same velocity just before and just after the collision. The bursting of a shell in the air produces a set of fragments, the mass center of which has the same velocity as the mass center of the shell before bursting.

Consider now the change in angular momentum about a fixed line due to the action of impulsive forces. Equation (5.214) applies. Multiplying by dt, integrating over the range (t_0, t_1) and proceeding to the limit as usual, we find

(8.117) $$\Delta h = \lim_{t_1 \to t_0} \int_{t_0}^{t_1} N \, dt = \hat{N}.$$

In words, *the sudden change in angular momentum about the fixed axis is equal to the moment of the external impulsive forces about the axis.**

We may treat similarly the equation (5.219) which concerns motion relative to the mass center. We find that *the sudden change in angular momentum relative to the mass center is equal to the moment of the external impulsive forces about the mass center.*

If the system is a rigid body with a fixed axis, (8.117) may be written

(8.118) $$I \Delta \omega = \hat{N},$$

---

* It is easily proved that $\hat{N}$, defined as the limit of the time integral of the moment, is equal to the moment of the impulsive forces.

where I is the moment of inertia about the fixed axis, $\Delta\omega$ the change in angular velocity, and $\hat{N}$ the moment of the impulsive forces about the axis.

For a rigid body which can move parallel to a plane, (8.118) holds, provided we understand I to be the moment of inertia about the mass center and $\hat{N}$ the moment of impulsive forces about the mass center.

We have now converted the principles of linear and angular momentum into forms valid in the case where impulsive forces act. Since the application of impulsive forces leads to sudden changes in velocity, we may call the theory of impulsive motion a *discontinuous* theory, reserving the word *continuous* for those cases in which no sudden changes in velocity occur.

In the continuous theory the principle of energy is useful for determining motions, either completely or in part. But it must be used with great caution in the discontinuous theory, because we find in general that when impulsive forces act the law of conservation of mechanical energy does not hold. Actually, the energy is not lost; it is converted into heat or employed to deform the bodies on which the impulses act. But *mechanical energy disappears*, and it is with mechanical energy alone that we are concerned in this book.

Exercise. An impulsive force $\hat{P}$ is applied at one end of a bar of mass m and length $2a$, in a direction perpendicular to the bar. Find the velocity imparted to the other end of the bar, assuming (i) that the center of the bar is fixed, (ii) that the bar is free.

8.2. COLLISIONS

As remarked above, a collision between two bodies gives rise (in physical reality) to large reactions acting for a short time, and so we treat the problem of collision mathematically by means of impulsive forces.

The collision of spheres and the coefficient of restitution.

As an illustrative example, we shall discuss the problem of the collision of two spheres which are moving along the line joining their centers (Fig. 97).

Taking the axis Ox along the line of centers, let us use the following notation:

m_1, m_2 = masses of the spheres,
u_1, u_2 = velocities of centers before collision,
u_1', u_2' = velocities of centers after collision,
$\widehat{P}$ = magnitude of impulsive reaction.

We have then

(8.201) $\quad m_1(u_1' - u_1) = -\widehat{P}, \quad m_2(u_2' - u_2) = \widehat{P},$

and so

(8.202) $\quad m_1 u_1' + m_2 u_2' = m_1 u_1 + m_2 u_2,$

as indeed we might have deduced directly from the fact that there is no external impulsive force.

Our problem is to find the result of the collision, i.e., to find u_1', u_2' when u_1, u_2 are given. But for this we have only one equation (8.202), and that is not enough to give two unknowns. We can proceed no further without an additional hypothesis, and here we introduce the idea of the *coefficient of restitution*.

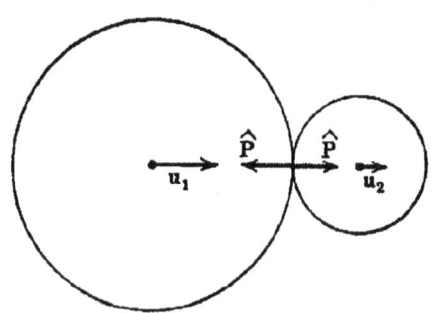

Fig. 97.—Collision of two spheres

Consider the problem of collision as it might occur in reality, say between two tennis balls. Actually the balls would become distorted during the collision and then would bound away from one another, regaining their spherical shapes. This is a complicated process which we cannot follow through mathematically, and we are obliged to substitute some simple hypothesis based on experimental results.

We introduce the expressions *speed of approach* q_a and *speed of separation* q_s. For a general collision, these speeds are calculated for the particles of the two bodies at the point of contact, components of velocity along the common normal at that point being used. In our problem of colliding spheres, we have

(8.203) $\quad q_a = u_1 - u_2, \quad q_s = u_2' - u_1'.$

The following general hypothesis is adopted: *The speeds of separation and approach are connected by the relation*

(8.204) $$q_s = eq_a,$$

where *e is a positive number, called the coefficient of restitution.* The value of e depends on the materials of which the bodies are composed and also on their shapes and sizes; it never exceeds unity in value. When $e = 1$ the bodies are said to be *perfectly elastic*, and when $e = 0$ they are said to be *perfectly inelastic*.

In the problem of the spheres, we now have

(8.205) $$\begin{cases} m_1 u_1' + m_2 u_2' = m_1 u_1 + m_2 u_2, \\ u_2' - u_1' = e(u_1 - u_2). \end{cases}$$

Hence,

(8.206) $$\begin{cases} u_1' = \dfrac{m_1 - em_2}{m_1 + m_2} u_1 + (1 + e) \dfrac{m_2}{m_1 + m_2} u_2, \\ u_2' = (1 + e) \dfrac{m_1}{m_1 + m_2} u_1 + \dfrac{m_2 - em_1}{m_1 + m_2} u_2, \end{cases}$$

and so the problem is solved.

In the case of perfectly inelastic spheres ($e = 0$), we have $u_1' = u_2'$; there is no rebound.

If the spheres are of the same mass ($m_1 = m_2$) and there is perfect elasticity ($e = 1$), we have

(8.207) $$u_1' = u_2, \qquad u_2' = u_1;$$

this means that the spheres exchange velocities. This case is particularly interesting because, in the kinetic theory of gases, the mathematical model represents the molecules by perfectly elastic spheres.

Compression and restitution.

The hypothesis (8.204) appears artificial; we generally prefer to adopt hypotheses which have some plausibility. The hypothesis may however be put in another form, which suggests rather better its connection with physical reality. To do this, we return to the physical picture of the collision of two tennis balls. At first the centers of the balls are approaching one another, and the balls are being distorted. Then they start to regain their spherical shapes, pressing against one another until they separate. Thus the whole period of collision is divided

into a period of *compression* and a period of *restitution*. We may adopt, instead of (8.204), the following hypothesis: The impulse during restitution bears to the impulse during compression a definite ratio e. Or, passing to the limit of infinite forces and vanishing time, we may make the following formal statement of our hypothesis: *If $\widehat{P}_1$ is the magnitude of the impulsive reaction of compression required to reduce the speed of approach to zero, then the magnitude $\widehat{P}_2$ of the impulsive reaction of restitution is*

$$(8.208) \qquad \widehat{P}_2 = e\widehat{P}_1$$

where e is the coefficient of restitution. These two impulsive reactions act in the same direction.

It is by no means obvious that (8.208) is equivalent to (8.204), but it can be proved without much difficulty. We shall here merely establish the equivalence for the problem of the spheres. We have, for compression,

$$(8.209) \qquad m_1 u - m_1 u_1 = -\widehat{P}_1, \qquad m_2 u - m_2 u_2 = \widehat{P}_1,$$

where u is the common velocity when the speed of approach is zero. For restitution, we have by (8.208)

$$(8.210) \qquad m_1 u_1' - m_1 u = -e\widehat{P}_1, \qquad m_2 u_2' - m_2 u = e\widehat{P}_1.$$

We have here four equations, which can be solved for $u_1', u_2', u, \widehat{P}_1$. To prove that we get the same result as that given by (8.204), we eliminate u from (8.209) and also from (8.210); we obtain

$$(8.211) \qquad \begin{cases} m_1 m_2 (u_1 - u_2) = (m_1 + m_2)\widehat{P}_1, \\ m_1 m_2 (u_2' - u_1') = e(m_1 + m_2)\widehat{P}_1, \end{cases}$$

from which (8.204) follows at once.

Motion relative to the mass center.

The mathematics of discontinuous motions is much simpler than that of continuous motions, because the equations to be solved are algebraic, not differential. But the algebra may become complicated, and it is sometimes advisable to use a special Newtonian frame of reference. Thus, in the case of the two spheres considered above, we may use a frame of reference in which the mass center is at rest before collision. It is, of course, at rest in this frame after collision also. We have then

(8.212) $$\begin{cases} m_1 u_1 + m_2 u_2 = 0, \quad m_1 u_1' + m_2 u_2' = 0, \\ u_2' - u_1' = e(u_1 - u_2); \end{cases}$$

hence,

(8.213) $$u_1' = -e u_1, \quad u_2' = -e u_2.$$

As a result of the collision, the components of velocity are reversed in sign and multiplied by the coefficient of restitution.

If the kinetic energy is T before collision and T' after collision, we have

$$T = \tfrac{1}{2}(m_1 u_1^2 + m_2 u_2^2), \quad T' = \tfrac{1}{2}(m_1 u_1'^2 + m_2 u_2'^2) = e^2 T,$$

and so the loss of kinetic energy is

(8.214) $$T - T' = (1 - e^2)T.$$

Since $e \leq 1$, kinetic energy is lost in every case except that of perfect elasticity ($e = 1$)

We have discussed the collision of spheres in the case where their centers move along the line joining the centers. Provided the spheres are smooth, the extension to the case where the spheres have general motions is immediate; the components of momentum (and hence velocity) in directions parallel to the common tangent plane of the spheres undergo no changes, and the components of velocity along the common normal change as described above.

8.3. APPLICATIONS

We shall now illustrate the application of the principles of linear and angular momentum by two examples.

The ballistic pendulum.

Consider a rigid body, hanging in equilibrium from a horizontal axis O (Fig. 98). A bullet, traveling horizontally, strikes the body at A and becomes embedded in it. As a result of the impact, the body swings as a compound pendulum, rising through an angular displacement α before coming to rest. On account of its importance in ballistics, the apparatus is called a *ballistic pendulum*. From the angle α and the constants of the system, we can compute the velocity of the bullet, as we shall now show.

Fig. 98.—Ballistic pendulum.

Let us take as dynamical system the body and the bullet. Then the forces between the body and the bullet are internal. During the brief interval of impact the only external forces acting are (i) gravity and (ii) the reaction at O. The force of gravity is a finite force and so contributes no impulsive force. Since the reaction at O has no moment about O, it is evident that the principle of angular momentum enables us to state that

angular momentum of system about O before impact
= angular momentum of system about O after impact.

Let ON be the vertical through O, AN being horizontal Let m be the mass of the bullet, q its speed, I the moment of inertia of the body about O, and ω the angular velocity immediately after impact. Then the angular momentum of the system about O is

before impact: $mq \cdot ON$,
after impact: $(m \cdot AO^2 + I)\omega$.

If the mass of the bullet is very small in comparison with that of the body, we may neglect $m \cdot AO^2$ in comparison with I; thus we have

(8.301) $$mql = I\omega,$$

where $l = ON$.

Although we cannot apply the principle of energy during impact, we can apply it in the subsequent motion. Thus, again neglecting the mass of the bullet in comparison with that of the body, we have

(8.302) $$\tfrac{1}{2}I\omega^2 = Mgh(1 - \cos \alpha),$$

where M is the mass of the body and h the distance of its mass center from O. Hence, from (8.301),

(8.303) $$q = \frac{\sqrt{2IMgh(1 - \cos \alpha)}}{ml},$$

which gives the speed of the bullet in terms of α and constants of the system.

Linked rods.

Two uniform rods AB, BC, each of mass m and length $2a$, are connected by a smooth joint at B and lie in one straight line

on a smooth horizontal table (Fig. 99a). A horizontal blow $\hat{P}$ is struck at C, in a direction perpendicular to BC. We wish to find the motion generated.

Let us draw a schematic diagram (Fig. 99b), separating the rods in order to represent the reactions without confusion.

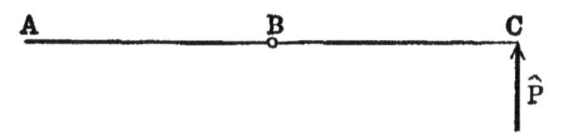

Fig. 99a.—A pair of rods, linked at B, receive a blow at C.

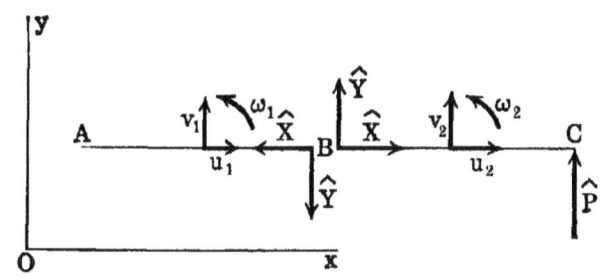

Fig. 99b.—Diagram of velocities and impulsive forces.

Taking rectangular axes Oxy, with Ox parallel to ABC and Oy in the sense of $\hat{P}$, we shall use the following notation:

u_1, v_1 = components of velocity of center of AB,
u_2, v_2 = components of velocity of center of BC,
ω_1 = angular velocity of AB,
ω_2 = angular velocity of BC,
$\hat{X}, \hat{Y}$ = components of reaction on BC at B,
$-\hat{X}, -\hat{Y}$ = components of reaction on AB at B.

Since the rods are joined at B, this point must have the same velocity whether considered as a point of AB or of BC. Thus,

(8.304) $\qquad u_1 = u_2, \qquad v_1 + a\omega_1 = v_2 - a\omega_2.$

The principle of linear momentum applied to each rod gives

(8.305) $\qquad \begin{cases} mu_1 = -\hat{X}, & mu_2 = \hat{X}, \\ mv_1 = -\hat{Y}, & mv_2 = \hat{Y} + \hat{P}; \end{cases}$

the principle of angular momentum gives

(8.306) $\qquad mk^2\omega_1 = -a\hat{Y}, \qquad mk^2\omega_2 = -a\hat{Y} + a\hat{P},$

where k is the radius of gyration of each rod about its center, so that $k^2 = \tfrac{1}{3}a^2$.

From the first equation of (8.304) and the first two of (8.305), we see that

(8.307) $\quad u_1 = u_2 = 0, \quad \hat{X} = 0.$

There now remain in (8.304), (8.305), and (8.306) five equations for the following five unknowns:

$$v_1, v_2, \omega_1, \omega_2, \hat{Y}.$$

It is most symmetrical to find $\hat{Y}$ first by substitution in (8.304) from the other equations; we find

(8.308) $\quad \hat{Y} = \tfrac{1}{4}\hat{P},$

and hence

(8.309) $\quad \begin{cases} v_1 = -\tfrac{1}{4}\dfrac{\hat{P}}{m}, & v_2 = \tfrac{5}{4}\dfrac{\hat{P}}{m}, \\ \omega_1 = -\tfrac{3}{4}\dfrac{\hat{P}}{ma}, & \omega_2 = \tfrac{9}{4}\dfrac{\hat{P}}{ma}. \end{cases}$

The velocity of B is $\hat{P}/m$, downward in the diagram.

8.4. SUMMARY OF PLANE IMPULSIVE MOTION

I. Components of impulsive force.

(8.401) $\quad \hat{X} = \lim\limits_{t_1 \to t_0} \int_{t_0}^{t_1} X\, dt, \quad \hat{Y} = \lim\limits_{t_1 \to t_0} \int_{t_0}^{t_1} Y\, dt.$

II. Instantaneous change in motion.

(a) Particle:

(8.402) $\quad \Delta(m\dot{x}) = \hat{X}, \quad \Delta(m\dot{y}) = \hat{Y}.$

(b) Any system:

(8.403) $\quad \Delta M_x = \hat{X}, \quad \Delta M_y = \hat{Y}, \quad \Delta h = \hat{N}.$

($\hat{X}, \hat{Y}, \hat{N}$ = total components and moment of external impulsive forces.)

(c) Rigid body with fixed axis:

(8.404) $\quad I\, \Delta\omega = \hat{N}.$

(d) Rigid body moving parallel to a fixed plane:

(8.405) $\quad m\, \Delta u = \hat{X}, \quad m\, \Delta v = \hat{Y}, \quad I\, \Delta\omega = \hat{N}.$

(u, v = components of velocity of mass center; $\hat{N}$ = impulsive moment about mass center.)

III. Collisions.

Either

(8.406) $$q_\bullet = e q_a$$

or

(8.407) $$\hat{P}_2 = e\hat{P}_1.$$

(e = coefficient of restitution; $e \leq 1$.)

EXERCISES VIII

1. A bar 2 ft long, of mass 10 lb., lies on a smooth horizontal table. It is struck horizontally at a distance of 6 in from one end, the blow being perpendicular to the bar, the magnitude of the blow is such that it would impart a velocity of 3 ft. per sec. to a mass of 2 lb. Find the velocities of the ends of the bar just after it is struck.

2. A uniform rod of mass m and length $3a$ hangs from a pin passing through it at a distance a from the upper end. Find in terms of m, a, g the magnitude of the smallest blow, struck at the lower end of the rod, which will make the rod describe a complete revolution.

3. A ball is dropped on the floor from a height h. If the coefficient of restitution is e, find the height of the ball at the top of the nth rebound.

4. A bar, 6 ft. long, is swinging about a horizontal axle passing through it at a distance of 1 foot from one end. At what point must a blow be struck to bring it to rest without causing any impulsive reaction on the axle? (This point is called the *center of percussion*.)

5. A particle moving with a speed of 30 feet per second in a direction making an angle of 60° with the horizontal strikes a smooth horizontal plane and rebounds, the coefficient of restitution being $\frac{1}{2}$. Find the speed and the direction of motion of the particle immediately after impact.

6. A uniform square plate of mass M and side $2a$ rests on a smooth horizontal table. A horizontal impulsive force of magnitude $\hat{P}$ is applied at a corner in a direction perpendicular to the diagonal at that corner. Show that the angular velocity generated by this impulsive force is

$$\frac{3\sqrt{2}\,\hat{P}}{2Ma}.$$

7. A tug of mass m tons is attached to a barge of mass M tons by a cable the mass of which may be neglected. The cable is slack. The tug moves and has acquired a speed of v ft. per sec when the cable becomes taut and the barge is jerked into motion. Assuming that the cable has a coefficient of restitution $\frac{1}{2}$ and neglecting the impulsive resistance of the water, find

(i) the speed imparted to the barge;

(ii) the mean tension (in tons wt.) in the cable during the jerk, supposing this to take t sec.

8. A billiard ball of radius a and mass M rests on a horizontal table. In a vertical plane through the center of the ball there is applied a horizontal

impulsive force of magnitude $\hat{P}$. If the line of action of the impulse is at a height h above the table, find the initial velocity of that point of the ball which is in contact with the table.

9. Two gear wheels of radii a_1, a_2 and axial moments of inertia I_1, I_2, respectively, can rotate freely about fixed parallel axles. Initially the wheel of radius a_1 is rotating with angular velocity ω, while the other wheel is at rest. If the gear wheels are suddenly engaged, find the angular velocity of each wheel afterward

10. A beam of mass 100 lb. and length 6 ft. hangs from an axle passing through it at a distance of 1 ft from one end. It is drawn aside through an angle of 30° and then released. It is stopped dead at the lowest point of its swing by a horizontal blow which strikes it at a height of 2 ft. above its lower end. What is the impulsive reaction on the axle, expressed in lb. ft sec.$^{-1}$?

11. Two uniform rods AB, BC, each of mass M and length $2a$, are smoothly jointed together and rest on a smooth horizontal plane, the angle between the rods being 45°. A horizontal impulsive force $\hat{P}$ is applied at A in a direction at right angles to AB and away from the rod BC. Find the initial angular velocity of BC.

12. A smooth rod of length $2a$ and mass M rests on a horizontal plane A small body of mass m moves in this plane with velocity v in a direction inclined to the rod at an angle of 45°, it strikes the rod at a point distant c from the center If the coefficient of restitution between the rod and the body is e, find the angular velocity of the rod and the velocity of the body after collision.

13. A flywheel whose axial moment of inertia is 200 lb. ft.^{2} rotates with an angular velocity of 300 revolutions per minute Find in ft. lb. wt. sec the angular impulse which would be required to bring the flywheel to rest Hence find the frictional torque at the bearings if the flywheel comes to rest in 10 minutes under friction alone.

14. One end of each of four equal uniform rods is smoothly jointed to the circumference of a uniform disk of radius a and mass M. The length of a rod is $2a$ and its mass is m. The points of attachment are at equal angular intervals. Initially the system is at rest on a smooth horizontal plane with each rod lying along a radius of the disk produced A horizontal impulsive force of magnitude $\hat{P}$ is applied to the outer end of one rod in a direction perpendicular to it Show that the initial angular velocity of the disk is

$$\frac{\hat{P}}{a(M + 2m)},$$

in a sense opposed to the direction of the impulse

15. A uniform rod of mass m and length $2a$ is moving on a smooth horizontal plane. At a certain instant, its center has velocity components u along the rod and v perpendicular to it, and the rod has an angular velocity ω What impulsive force must be applied to a point of the rod at a distance b from the center in order to bring that point to rest instantaneously?

16. Two uniform circular plates A and B, each of radius a and mass m, are connected by a rod of length $2a$ and mass m, each end of which is linked

smoothly to a point on the circumference of one of the plates. The system is at rest on a smooth horizontal plane with the centers of the plates in the line of the rod produced. An impulsive couple $\hat{N}$ acts on the plate A. Determine the initial motion of the plate B.

17. AB, BC, CD are three equal rods, smoothly hinged to one another at B and C. They lie on a smooth horizontal plane, forming three sides of a square. AB can turn freely about A, which is fixed. An impulsive force applied to D sets D in motion with a velocity v directed away from A. Prove that the initial velocity of B is opposite in direction to that of D and equal in magnitude to $\tfrac{1}{10}v$.

18. For the collision of two smooth laminas moving in a plane, prove that the assumption that the impulsive reaction of restitution is equal to e times the impulsive reaction of compression leads to the result that the ratio of the speeds of separation and approach is e.

19. On a straight line L, there are situated n particles all of the same mass. Initially the particles are at the points A_1, A_2, $\cdots A_n$ where $OA_1 < OA_2 < \cdot < OA_n$, O being a fixed point of L, and the velocity of the rth particle is in the direction OA_r and of magnitude u_r.

If $u_1 > u_2 > \cdots > u_n$ and the particles are all perfectly elastic, find the final velocity of each particle. What would be the result if all the particles were perfectly inelastic?

20. A number of equal uniform rods are smoothly jointed together to form a chain which hangs at rest under gravity. The upper end A of the chain is free to slide on a smooth horizontal axis. If an impulsive force is applied to A along the axis, show that the initial angular velocities of the last three rods are in the ratios $11 . -3 . 1$.

PART II
MECHANICS IN SPACE

CHAPTER IX

PRODUCTS OF VECTORS

Up to the present, our development of mechanics has been restricted, for the most part, to two dimensions. We now come to the systematic treatment of mechanics in space. Here we must make a decision as to notation. On the one hand, we have the ordinary notation of coordinates; on the other hand, the vector symbolism. Each has its advantages, but on the whole the vector notation has proved more useful on account of its compactness. We shall therefore use it extensively (but not exclusively) throughout the rest of the book. The present chapter, together with Sec. 1.3, explains the mathematical language to be employed later.

9.1. THE SCALAR AND VECTOR PRODUCTS

In developing the theory of vectors, we try to extend to vectors the operations of ordinary (scalar) algebra, as far as possible. In Sec. 1.3, this was done successfully for the addition and subtraction of vectors and for the multiplication of a vector by a scalar. We now consider the multiplication of vectors by one another, and here the methods of ordinary algebra are not so easy to generalize. Actually, we define two types of product— the *scalar product* and the *vector product*.

As in Sec. 1.3, we use P_1, P_2, P_3 to denote the components of a vector **P** on rectangular axes Ox, Oy, Oz, and P to denote its magnitude.

Scalar product.

The scalar product of two vectors **P** and **Q**, written **P · Q**, is defined by

$$(9.101) \qquad \mathbf{P} \cdot \mathbf{Q} = PQ \cos \theta,$$

where θ is the angle between **P** and **Q**. Since $Q \cos \theta$ is the component of **Q** in the direction of **P** (cf. Sec 1.3), it is clear that **P · Q** is equal to the magnitude of **P** multiplied by the component of **Q** in the direction of **P**.

In particular, $\boldsymbol{\lambda} \cdot \mathbf{P}$ is the component of a vector $\mathbf{P}$ in the direction of a unit vector $\boldsymbol{\lambda}$. Thus the work done by a force $\mathbf{P}$ in an infinitesimal displacement $\boldsymbol{\lambda}\, \delta s$ is, by (2.401),

$$\delta W = \mathbf{P} \cdot \boldsymbol{\lambda}\, \delta s.$$

Since the direction cosines of $\mathbf{P}$ are P_1/P, P_2/P, P_3/P and those of $\mathbf{Q}$ are Q_1/Q, Q_2/Q, Q_3/Q, we have

$$\cos \theta = \frac{P_1 Q_1 + P_2 Q_2 + P_3 Q_3}{PQ}.$$

Hence, using (9.101), we have the following expression for the scalar product of two vectors in terms of their components:

(9.102) $\quad\quad \mathbf{P} \cdot \mathbf{Q} = P_1 Q_1 + P_2 Q_2 + P_3 Q_3.$

From the definition, it is clear that *the scalar product of two perpendicular vectors vanishes.*

Either from the definition (9.101) or from (9.102), it follows that the order of the factors in a scalar product is immaterial. Thus,

$$\mathbf{P} \cdot \mathbf{Q} = \mathbf{Q} \cdot \mathbf{P};$$

in fact, scalar multiplication is *commutative*. It is also *distributive*; that is,

$$\mathbf{P} \cdot (\mathbf{Q} + \mathbf{R}) = \mathbf{P} \cdot \mathbf{Q} + \mathbf{P} \cdot \mathbf{R}.$$

To show this, we recall that the components of $\mathbf{Q} + \mathbf{R}$ are $Q_1 + R_1$, $Q_2 + R_2$, $Q_3 + R_3$; and therefore, by (9.102),

$$\begin{aligned}\mathbf{P} \cdot (\mathbf{Q} + \mathbf{R}) &= P_1(Q_1 + R_1) + P_2(Q_2 + R_2) + P_3(Q_3 + R_3) \\ &= (P_1 Q_1 + P_2 Q_2 + P_3 Q_3) + (P_1 R_1 + P_2 R_2 + P_3 R_3) \\ &= \mathbf{P} \cdot \mathbf{Q} + \mathbf{P} \cdot \mathbf{R}\end{aligned}$$

A third law governing the operation of multiplication in ordinary algebra, namely, the *associative law*, does not concern us here since we attach no meaning to $\mathbf{P} \cdot \mathbf{Q} \cdot \mathbf{R}$. However, we have defined such quantities as $(\mathbf{P} \cdot \mathbf{Q})\mathbf{R}$ and $\mathbf{P}(\mathbf{Q} \cdot \mathbf{R})$, each being the product of a vector by a scalar. These quantities are, of course, quite different, one being a vector with the direction of $\mathbf{R}$ and the other a vector with the direction of $\mathbf{P}$.

Exercise A vector has components $(1, 3, -2)$ in the directions of rectangular axes $Oxyz$. What is its component along the line $x = y = z$, the positive sense being that in which x increases?

Positive rotations.

Before defining the vector product, we shall introduce a convention concerning the sign of a rotation.

A rotation about a directed line L is said to be *positive* if it bears to the direction of L the same relation as the rotation of a right-handed screw bears to its direction of travel

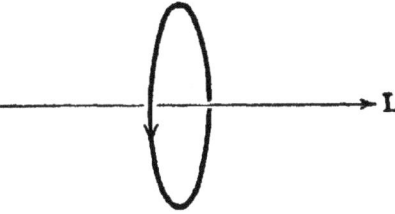

FIG. 100.—A positive rotation.

(Fig. 100). Thus a rotation from south to east is a positive rotation about the upward vertical; the earth's rotation about its axis drawn from south to north is also positive.

Right-handed triads.

Consider three non-coplanar vectors. These three vectors, taken in some order, form an *ordered triad*. Since all the triads of which we shall speak are ordered, the adjective will be understood in future, and a *triad* will mean an ordered triad. Let **P**, **Q**, **R** be an orthogonal triad, the order being as indicated. This triad is said to be *right-handed* if the rotation through a right angle from **P** to **Q** is a positive rotation about **R**. Any other triad is said to be right-handed if it can be deformed continuously into a right-handed orthogonal triad without its vectors becoming coplanar at any stage in the deformation.

If the triad **P**, **Q**, **R** is right-handed, then the triad **Q**, **P**, **R** is said to be *left-handed*.

If the triad of unit coordinate vectors **i**, **j**, **k**, introduced in Sec. 1.3, is a right-handed triad, the axes $Oxyz$ are said to be right-handed. We shall always use right-handed axes for the sake of consistency.

Vector product.

Given two vectors **P** and **Q**, we draw the unit vector **n** perpendicular to both **P** and **Q**, such that the triad **P**, **Q**, **n** is a right-handed triad. We define the vector product of **P** and **Q**, written **P** × **Q**, by

$$(9.103) \qquad \mathbf{P} \times \mathbf{Q} = PQ \sin \theta \, \mathbf{n},$$

where θ is the angle between **P** and **Q** (Fig. 101).

It is clear from the definition that a rotation from **P** to **Q**, through an angle less than two right angles, is a positive rotation about **P** × **Q**. We note that the magnitude of **P** × **Q** is $PQ \sin \theta$; this is equal to the area of the parallelogram whose adjacent sides are **P** and **Q**.

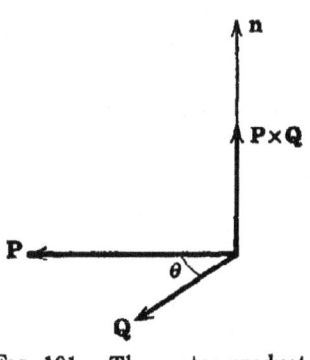

The vector product **P** × **Q** of two non-zero vectors vanishes if, and only if, **P** and **Q** are codirectional or opposite; in particular,

$$\mathbf{P} \times \mathbf{P} = 0.$$

Fig. 101.—The vector product

Let us now find the components of **P** × **Q**. If we denote this vector by **R**, then **R** is perpendicular to both **P** and **Q**, and we have

$$R_1 P_1 + R_2 P_2 + R_3 P_3 = 0,$$
$$R_1 Q_1 + R_2 Q_2 + R_3 Q_3 = 0.$$

Therefore,

(9.104) $$\begin{cases} R_1 = k(P_2 Q_3 - P_3 Q_2), \\ R_2 = k(P_3 Q_1 - P_1 Q_3), \\ R_3 = k(P_1 Q_2 - P_2 Q_1), \end{cases}$$

where k is an undetermined factor. Now,

$$\begin{aligned} R^2 &= R_1^2 + R_2^2 + R_3^2 \\ &= k^2[(P_2 Q_3 - P_3 Q_2)^2 + (P_3 Q_1 - P_1 Q_3)^2 + (P_1 Q_2 - P_2 Q_1)^2] \\ &= k^2[(P_1^2 + P_2^2 + P_3^2)(Q_1^2 + Q_2^2 + Q_3^2) \\ &\qquad\qquad - (P_1 Q_1 + P_2 Q_2 + P_3 Q_3)^2] \\ &= k^2 P^2 Q^2 \sin^2 \theta. \end{aligned}$$

But, by definition,

$$R = PQ \sin \theta,$$

and hence

$$k = \pm 1$$

From considerations of continuity, it is evident that k is to have the same sign in all cases. This sign may therefore be determined by considering the particular case where **P** and **Q** are unit vectors directed along the positive axes of x and y, respectively; then,

$$P_1 = 1, \quad P_2 = 0, \quad P_3 = 0,$$
$$Q_1 = 0, \quad Q_2 = 1, \quad Q_3 = 0,$$

and hence, by (9.104),

$$R_1 = 0, \quad R_2 = 0, \quad R_3 = k.$$

But $\mathbf{P} \times \mathbf{Q}$ is, in this case, a unit vector directed along the positive axis of z, so that $R_3 = 1$. Hence, $k = +1$ here, and so in all cases. Thus, quite generally, the components of $\mathbf{R} = \mathbf{P} \times \mathbf{Q}$ are

$$(9.105) \quad \begin{cases} R_1 = P_2Q_3 - P_3Q_2, \\ R_2 = P_3Q_1 - P_1Q_3, \\ R_3 = P_1Q_2 - P_2Q_1. \end{cases}$$

Note that the number describing the component and the subscripts in the leading term of the expression for that component are a cyclic permutation of the numbers 1, 2, 3.

From the definition (9.103), it is evident that

$$(9.106) \quad \mathbf{P} \times \mathbf{Q} = -\mathbf{Q} \times \mathbf{P}.$$

Again, using (9.105), it is easily shown that

$$(9.107) \quad \mathbf{P} \times (\mathbf{Q} + \mathbf{R}) = \mathbf{P} \times \mathbf{Q} + \mathbf{P} \times \mathbf{R}.$$

Thus, vector multiplication is *not commutative* but does obey the usual *distributive* law for multiplication.

For the unit coordinate vectors $\mathbf{i}, \mathbf{j}, \mathbf{k}$, it is easily seen that the following relations hold:

$$(9.108) \quad \begin{cases} \mathbf{i} \cdot \mathbf{i} = \mathbf{j} \cdot \mathbf{j} = \mathbf{k} \cdot \mathbf{k} = 1, \\ \mathbf{j} \cdot \mathbf{k} = \mathbf{k} \cdot \mathbf{i} = \mathbf{i} \cdot \mathbf{j} = 0, \\ \mathbf{j} \times \mathbf{k} = \mathbf{i}, \quad \mathbf{k} \times \mathbf{i} = \mathbf{j}, \quad \mathbf{i} \times \mathbf{j} = \mathbf{k}. \end{cases}$$

If we assume the distributive law for scalar and vector products and the formulas (9.108), we can establish (9.102) and (9.105) directly. Thus,

$$\begin{aligned} \mathbf{P} \cdot \mathbf{Q} &= (P_1\mathbf{i} + P_2\mathbf{j} + P_3\mathbf{k}) \cdot (Q_1\mathbf{i} + Q_2\mathbf{j} + Q_3\mathbf{k}) \\ &= P_1Q_1 + P_2Q_2 + P_3Q_3, \end{aligned}$$

and

$$\begin{aligned} \mathbf{P} \times \mathbf{Q} &= (P_1\mathbf{i} + P_2\mathbf{j} + P_3\mathbf{k}) \times (Q_1\mathbf{i} + Q_2\mathbf{j} + Q_3\mathbf{k}) \\ &= (P_2Q_3 - P_3Q_2)\mathbf{i} + (P_3Q_1 - P_1Q_3)\mathbf{j} + (P_1Q_2 - P_2Q_1)\mathbf{k} \end{aligned}$$

If we multiply a vector by a scalar m, we do not alter its line of action; we merely change its magnitude, and reverse its

direction if m is negative. From this fact and the definitions of the scalar and vector products, we see that

(i) $\qquad (m\mathbf{P}) \cdot \mathbf{Q} = \mathbf{P} \cdot (m\mathbf{Q}) = m(\mathbf{P} \cdot \mathbf{Q});$
(ii) $\qquad (m\mathbf{P}) \times \mathbf{Q} = \mathbf{P} \times (m\mathbf{Q}) = m(\mathbf{P} \times \mathbf{Q}).$

Hence, if a scalar factor appears in a product of vectors, its position is actually of no importance; it may be shifted to any position without altering the value of the product as a whole.

Exercise. If $\mathbf{P} \times \mathbf{Q} = \mathbf{R}$ and $\mathbf{P} \times \mathbf{R} = \mathbf{Q}$, then the vectors $\mathbf{Q}$ and $\mathbf{R}$ both vanish.

Differentiation of products of vectors.

The derivative of a vector with respect to a scalar has been defined in Sec. 1.3. We saw there that the derivative of the sum of two vectors is equal to the sum of their derivatives, as in ordinary calculus. The ordinary rule holds also for the derivatives of the scalar and vector products. This is shown as follows:

$$(9.109) \quad \frac{d}{du}(\mathbf{P} \cdot \mathbf{Q}) = \lim_{\Delta u \to 0} \frac{(\mathbf{P} + \Delta \mathbf{P}) \cdot (\mathbf{Q} + \Delta \mathbf{Q}) - \mathbf{P} \cdot \mathbf{Q}}{\Delta u}$$
$$= \lim_{\Delta u \to 0} \frac{\Delta \mathbf{P} \cdot \mathbf{Q} + \mathbf{P} \cdot \Delta \mathbf{Q} + \Delta \mathbf{P} \cdot \Delta \mathbf{Q}}{\Delta u}$$
$$= \frac{d\mathbf{P}}{du} \cdot \mathbf{Q} + \mathbf{P} \cdot \frac{d\mathbf{Q}}{du}.$$

Similarly, writing "cross" for "dot," we obtain

$$(9.110) \quad \frac{d}{du}(\mathbf{P} \times \mathbf{Q}) = \frac{d\mathbf{P}}{du} \times \mathbf{Q} + \mathbf{P} \times \frac{d\mathbf{Q}}{du}.$$

It is important to preserve the order of $\mathbf{P}$ and $\mathbf{Q}$ in (9.110), but not in (9.109)

9.2. TRIPLE PRODUCTS

Mixed triple product.

Let us consider three vectors $\mathbf{P}$, $\mathbf{Q}$, and $\mathbf{R}$. From them we can form the product $\mathbf{P} \cdot (\mathbf{Q} \times \mathbf{R})$, called their *mixed triple product*. This is the scalar product of $\mathbf{P}$ and the vector $\mathbf{V} = \mathbf{Q} \times \mathbf{R}$, and so is a scalar. We shall now express it in terms of the com-

ponents of the three vectors. From (9.102) and (9.105), we have

$$\mathbf{P} \cdot (\mathbf{Q} \times \mathbf{R}) = \mathbf{P} \cdot \mathbf{V}$$
$$= P_1 V_1 + P_2 V_2 + P_3 V_3$$
$$= P_1(Q_2 R_3 - Q_3 R_2) + P_2(Q_3 R_1 - Q_1 R_3)$$
$$+ P_3(Q_1 R_2 - Q_2 R_1),$$

or, in determinantal form,

$$(9.201) \qquad \mathbf{P} \cdot (\mathbf{Q} \times \mathbf{R}) = \begin{vmatrix} P_1 & Q_1 & R_1 \\ P_2 & Q_2 & R_2 \\ P_3 & Q_3 & R_3 \end{vmatrix}.$$

From the rule governing the interchange of columns in a determinant, it follows that

$$\mathbf{P} \cdot (\mathbf{Q} \times \mathbf{R}) = \mathbf{Q} \cdot (\mathbf{R} \times \mathbf{P}) = \mathbf{R} \cdot (\mathbf{P} \times \mathbf{Q}),$$

and

$$\mathbf{P} \cdot (\mathbf{Q} \times \mathbf{R}) = -\mathbf{P} \cdot (\mathbf{R} \times \mathbf{Q}) = -\mathbf{Q} \cdot (\mathbf{P} \times \mathbf{R}).$$

Thus a mixed triple product is not changed by a cyclic permutation of the vectors; its sign is reversed when two of the vectors are interchanged.

We may interpret the mixed triple product geometrically as follows: As we have seen, the magnitude of $\mathbf{Q} \times \mathbf{R}$ is equal to the area of the parallelogram whose adjacent sides represent $\mathbf{Q}$ and $\mathbf{R}$. Now $\mathbf{P} \cdot (\mathbf{Q} \times \mathbf{R})$ is the product of the magnitude of $\mathbf{Q} \times \mathbf{R}$ by the component of $\mathbf{P}$ in the direction of $\mathbf{Q} \times \mathbf{R}$ (that is, perpendicular to the plane of $\mathbf{Q}$ and $\mathbf{R}$). Hence the *magnitude* of $\mathbf{P} \cdot (\mathbf{Q} \times \mathbf{R})$ is equal to the volume of the parallelepiped whose adjacent edges represent $\mathbf{P}$, $\mathbf{Q}$, and $\mathbf{R}$ (Fig. 102). The *sign* of $\mathbf{P} \cdot (\mathbf{Q} \times \mathbf{R})$ is also significant; it is positive or negative according as the angle between $\mathbf{P}$ and $\mathbf{Q} \times \mathbf{R}$ is acute or obtuse, i.e., according as $\mathbf{P}$, $\mathbf{Q}$, $\mathbf{R}$ form a right- or left-handed triad.

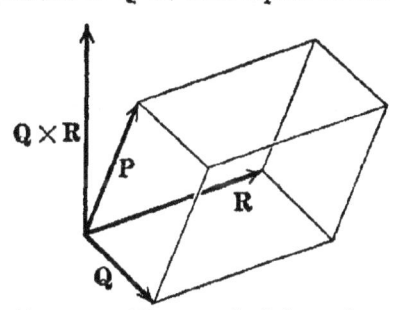

Fig. 102 —The mixed triple product

From the geometrical interpretation, it is obvious that

$$\mathbf{P} \cdot (\mathbf{Q} \times \mathbf{R}) = 0$$

if the vectors $\mathbf{P}$, $\mathbf{Q}$, $\mathbf{R}$ are coplanar.

Vector triple product.

From the vectors **P**, **Q**, **R**, we can form another product, namely, $\mathbf{P} \times (\mathbf{Q} \times \mathbf{R})$; this is evidently a vector and is called the *vector triple product*.

We shall now express this product as the difference of two vectors. Denoting it by **U** and writing $\mathbf{V} = \mathbf{Q} \times \mathbf{R}$, we have

$$\mathbf{U} = \mathbf{P} \times \mathbf{V};$$

hence, using (9.105),

$$\begin{aligned} U_1 &= P_2 V_3 - P_3 V_2 \\ &= P_2(Q_1 R_2 - Q_2 R_1) - P_3(Q_3 R_1 - Q_1 R_3) \\ &= (P_1 R_1 + P_2 R_2 + P_3 R_3) Q_1 - (P_1 Q_1 + P_2 Q_2 + P_3 Q_3) R_1 \\ &= (\mathbf{P} \cdot \mathbf{R}) Q_1 - (\mathbf{P} \cdot \mathbf{Q}) R_1 \end{aligned}$$

Similarly,

$$\begin{aligned} U_2 &= (\mathbf{P} \cdot \mathbf{R}) Q_2 - (\mathbf{P} \cdot \mathbf{Q}) R_2, \\ U_3 &= (\mathbf{P} \cdot \mathbf{R}) Q_3 - (\mathbf{P} \cdot \mathbf{Q}) R_3. \end{aligned}$$

These three expressions for U_1, U_2, U_3 can be combined into the vector equation

(9.202) $\quad \mathbf{U} = \mathbf{P} \times (\mathbf{Q} \times \mathbf{R}) = (\mathbf{P} \cdot \mathbf{R}) \mathbf{Q} - (\mathbf{P} \cdot \mathbf{Q}) \mathbf{R}.$

The following remark is an aid in remembering this expression: since $\mathbf{Q} \times \mathbf{R}$ is perpendicular to the plane of **Q** and **R**, the vector $\mathbf{P} \times (\mathbf{Q} \times \mathbf{R})$ must be in this plane; hence,

$$\mathbf{P} \times (\mathbf{Q} \times \mathbf{R}) = q\mathbf{Q} + r\mathbf{R},$$

where q and r are scalars.

Exercise. Evaluate all the vector triple products of the unit coordinate vectors **i**, **j**, **k**, including those in which one of the vectors is repeated.

9.3. MOMENTS OF VECTORS

The moment of a vector about a line was defined in Sec. 2.3 as a scalar. There we spoke also of "the moment of a vector about a point A," but only as an abbreviation for "the moment about a line through A perpendicular to the plane containing A and the vector." Now that we are in possession of the powerful vector notation, we shall make a fresh start. We shall define the vector moment of a vector about a point, and (in terms of it)

Sec. 9 3]   PRODUCTS OF VECTORS   253

the scalar moment of a vector about a line; this latter definition will be shown to agree with that given in Sec. 2.3.

Moment of a vector about a point.

Let **P** be a vector with origin at B, and A any point in space (Fig. 103). We define the *vector moment* of **P** about A (or briefly the *moment* of **P** about A) as a vector **M**, given by

(9 301) $$\mathbf{M} = \mathbf{r} \times \mathbf{P},$$

where $\mathbf{r} = \overrightarrow{AB}$, the position vector of B relative to A. Thus **M**

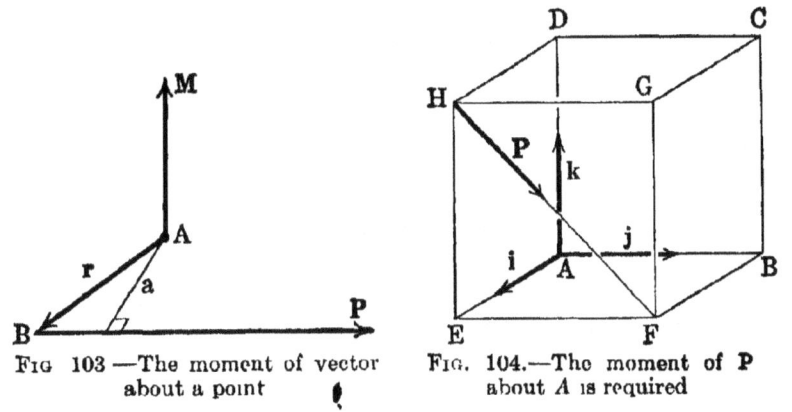

Fig 103.—The moment of vector about a point

Fig. 104.—The moment of **P** about A is required

is a vector perpendicular to the plane of **r** and **P**, with magnitude

(9.302) $$M = rP \sin \theta = aP,$$

where θ is the angle between **r** and **P**, and a the perpendicular from A on the line of action of **P**.

As an illustration, let us calculate the moment of a given force **P** about a point A In Fig 104, **P** is a force of known magnitude applied at H and acting along the diagonal HF of one face of the cube $ABC \cdots H$. If **i, j, k** is a triad of unit orthogonal vectors at A (as shown), we have

$$\overrightarrow{AH} = b(\mathbf{i} + \mathbf{k}),$$
$$\mathbf{P} = \frac{P}{\sqrt{2}}(\mathbf{j} - \mathbf{k}),$$

where b denotes an edge of the cube. The moment **M** of **P** about A is now easily calculated; it is

$$\mathbf{M} = b(\mathbf{i} + \mathbf{k}) \times \frac{P}{\sqrt{2}}(\mathbf{j} - \mathbf{k}).$$

Hence, by (9.108),

$$\mathbf{M} = \frac{bP}{\sqrt{2}}(-\mathbf{i} + \mathbf{j} + \mathbf{k}).$$

Thus the moment of P about A is a vector with components ($-bP/\sqrt{2}$, $bP/\sqrt{2}$, $bP/\sqrt{2}$) in the directions of the edges AE, AB, AD, respectively.

Returning to the situation shown in Fig. 103, let us investigate the effect of sliding P along its line of action. It becomes

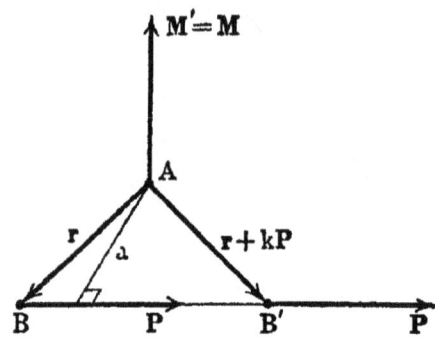

Fig. 105.—The moment of a vector is unchanged when we slide the vector along its line of action.

(Fig. 105) a vector **P** at B', where $\overrightarrow{AB'} = \mathbf{r} + k\mathbf{P}$ (k being some scalar). The moment about A is now

$$\mathbf{M}' = (\mathbf{r} + k\mathbf{P}) \times \mathbf{P}.$$

But $\mathbf{P} \times \mathbf{P} = 0$, and hence

$$\mathbf{M}' = \mathbf{r} \times \mathbf{P} = \mathbf{M}$$

Thus *the moment of a vector about a point is unaltered by sliding the vector along its line of action.*

We shall now make an important deduction from the above fact. Let **P** at B and $-\mathbf{P}$ at B' be two vectors with a common line of action L, and let A be any point. Sliding $-\mathbf{P}$ along L until its origin is at B, we do not alter its moment about A. Thus, if $\overrightarrow{AB} = \mathbf{r}$, the sum of the moments about A of **P** at B and $-\mathbf{P}$ at B' is

$$\mathbf{r} \times \mathbf{P} + \mathbf{r} \times (-\mathbf{P}) = \mathbf{r} \times (\mathbf{P} - \mathbf{P}) = 0.$$

In words, for two vectors in the same line, with equal magnitudes but opposite senses, the vector sum of moments about any point

is zero. In particular, by the fundamental law of action and reaction (cf. Sec. 1.4), we have

(9.303) *The vector sum of moments about an arbitrary point of the forces of interaction between two particles of any system is zero.*

By the distributive law for vector multiplication, we have, for any vectors,

(9.304) $\mathbf{r} \times \mathbf{P} + \mathbf{r} \times \mathbf{Q} + \mathbf{r} \times \mathbf{R} + \cdots$
$$= \mathbf{r} \times (\mathbf{P} + \mathbf{Q} + \mathbf{R} + \cdots).$$

Let $\mathbf{P}, \mathbf{Q}, \mathbf{R}, \cdots$ be vectors with common origin B, and let $\mathbf{r}$ be the position vector of B relative to a point A. Then, for vector moments about a point, we have the theorem of Varignon (cf. Sec. 2.3): *The sum of the vector moments about a point A of vectors $\mathbf{P}, \mathbf{Q}, \mathbf{R}, \cdots$ with common origin B, is equal to the vector moment about A of the single vector $\mathbf{P} + \mathbf{Q} + \mathbf{R} + \cdots$ with origin B.*

Moment of a vector about a line.

Let $\mathbf{M}$ be the moment of a vector $\mathbf{P}$ about a point A, and let L be any line through A. Of the two senses on L, we choose one as positive and distinguish it by a unit vector $\boldsymbol{\lambda}$ lying on L. We define *the scalar moment of $\mathbf{P}$ about L* as the component M_λ of $\mathbf{M}$ in the positive sense of L; expressed in symbols,

(9.305) $\qquad M_\lambda = \boldsymbol{\lambda} \cdot \mathbf{M}.$

We shall now show that the above definition is equivalent to that given in Sec. 2.3. We take special axes $Oxyz$ as shown in Fig. 106; the origin O coincides with A, and Oz lies along the line L in the positive sense.

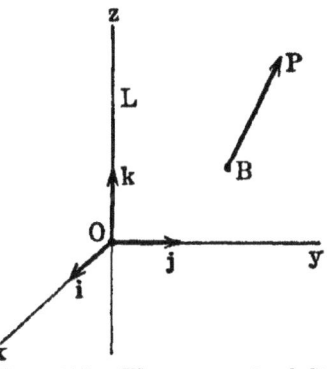

Fig. 106.—The moment of $\mathbf{P}$ about the line L is required.

Relative to these axes, $\mathbf{P}$ has components (X, Y, Z) and acts at a point B with coordinates (x, y, z). The moment $\mathbf{M}$ of $\mathbf{P}$ about A (or O) is

(9.306) $\mathbf{M} = (x\mathbf{i} + y\mathbf{j} + z\mathbf{k}) \times (X\mathbf{i} + Y\mathbf{j} + Z\mathbf{k})$
$= (yZ - zY)\mathbf{i} + (zX - xZ)\mathbf{j} + (xY - yX)\mathbf{k},$

where **i**, **j**, **k** are the unit coordinate vectors. Since $\pmb{\lambda} = \mathbf{k}$, we have

(9.307) $$M_\lambda = \mathbf{k} \cdot \mathbf{M} = xY - yX.$$

But this quantity is precisely the moment as given by (2.303); the two definitions of the moment of a vector about a line are now completely reconciled.

It might appear that the value of the moment M_λ of **P** about L, as given by (9.305), depends on the choice of a point A on this line. This is not actually the case. For let A' be any other point on L, so that $\overrightarrow{AA'} = k\pmb{\lambda}$, where k is some scalar. The moment about A' of **P** at B is

$$\mathbf{M}' = (-k\pmb{\lambda} + \mathbf{r}) \times \mathbf{P},$$

where $\mathbf{r} = \overrightarrow{AB}$. The component of $\mathbf{M}'$ in the positive sense of L is therefore

$$\begin{aligned} M'_\lambda &= \pmb{\lambda} \cdot [(-k\pmb{\lambda} + \mathbf{r}) \times \mathbf{P}] \\ &= -k\pmb{\lambda} \cdot (\pmb{\lambda} \times \mathbf{P}) + \pmb{\lambda} \cdot (\mathbf{r} \times \mathbf{P}) \\ &= \pmb{\lambda} \cdot \mathbf{M} = M_\lambda, \end{aligned}$$

since $\pmb{\lambda} \cdot (\pmb{\lambda} \times \mathbf{P}) = 0$.

The theorem of Varignon for scalar moments of vectors about a line follows directly from (9.304); we have merely to take the scalar product of each side with $\pmb{\lambda}$. This very simple proof by vector methods should be compared with that of Sec. 2.3, where only elementary methods were used.

There are occasions, however, where scalar methods are more direct than vector methods. On such occasions, we require formulas for the moments of a vector about the axes of coordinates. These are, by (9.306),

(9.308) $$yZ - zY, \qquad zX - xZ, \qquad xY - yX,$$

where (X, Y, Z) are the components of the vector applied at (x, y, z).

Exercise. A vector with components $(1, 2, 3)$ acts at the point $(3, 2, 1)$. What is its moment about the origin, and what are its moments about the coordinate axes?

9.4. SUMMARY OF PRODUCTS OF VECTORS

I. Scalar product.

(9.401) $\quad \mathbf{P} \cdot \mathbf{Q} = \mathbf{Q} \cdot \mathbf{P} = PQ \cos \theta = P_1Q_1 + P_2Q_2 + P_3Q_3.$

II. Vector product.

(9.402) $\quad \mathbf{P} \times \mathbf{Q} = -\mathbf{Q} \times \mathbf{P} = PQ \sin \theta \, \mathbf{n}.$

(n a unit vector perpendicular to **P** and **Q**; triad **P**, **Q**, **n** right-handed.)

III. Usual rules of algebra and calculus apply to products of vectors, if order in vector products is preserved.

IV. The mixed triple product.

(9.403) $\quad \mathbf{P} \cdot (\mathbf{Q} \times \mathbf{R}) = \begin{vmatrix} P_1 & Q_1 & R_1 \\ P_2 & Q_2 & R_2 \\ P_3 & Q_3 & R_3 \end{vmatrix}$

V. The vector triple product.

(9.404) $\quad \mathbf{P} \times (\mathbf{Q} \times \mathbf{R}) = (\mathbf{P} \cdot \mathbf{R})\mathbf{Q} - (\mathbf{P} \cdot \mathbf{Q})\mathbf{R}.$

VI. Moment of a vector about a point.

(9.405) $\quad \mathbf{M} = \mathbf{r} \times \mathbf{P}$
$\qquad = (yZ - zY)\mathbf{i} + (zX - xZ)\mathbf{j} + (xY - yX)\mathbf{k}.$

VII. Moment of a vector about a directed line (λ).

(9.406) $\quad M_\lambda = \lambda \cdot (\mathbf{r} \times \mathbf{P}).$

EXERCISES IX

1. Solve the equations

$$2\mathbf{A} + \mathbf{B} = \mathbf{M}, \quad \mathbf{A} + 2\mathbf{B} = \mathbf{N},$$

M and **N** being given vectors.

2. Three vectors are represented by the diagonals of three adjacent faces of a cube, all passing through the same corner and directed away from it. Find their sum.

3. What is the moment about the x-axis of a force of magnitude 3 applied at a point with coordinates (2, 3, 5), in a direction making angles of 60° with the axes of y and z and an acute angle with the axis of x?

4. A, B, C, D are any four vectors. Prove that there exist scalars a, b, c, d (not all zero), such that

$$a\mathbf{A} + b\mathbf{B} + c\mathbf{C} + d\mathbf{D} = 0.$$

5. If $\mathbf{A} \times \mathbf{B} = \mathbf{A} \times \mathbf{C}$, show that $\mathbf{B} = \mathbf{C} + k\mathbf{A}$, where k is some scalar.

6. If $\mathbf{A}$ and $\mathbf{B}$ are any two unit vectors, prove that the moment of $\mathbf{A}$ about $\mathbf{B}$ is equal to the moment of $\mathbf{B}$ about $\mathbf{A}$.

7. Find the moments, about a corner of a cube, of three unit vectors converging on the opposite corner along three edges. Show that the sum of the moments is zero. How could you obtain this result without calculation?

8. A force with components (X, Y, Z) acts at the point (a, b, c). What is its moment about a line through the origin with direction cosines (l, m, n)?

9. A force of magnitude P acts along the line joining opposite corners of a cube of edge $2a$. Find the moment of the force about a line which is a diagonal of a face of the cube and which does not cut the line of action of the force.

10. A directed line L passes through the point (a, b, c) with direction cosines (l, m, n). Prove that the moment about L of a unit vector pointing along the x-axis is $bn - cm$.

11. Prove that the moment of a vector about a line vanishes if, and only if, the vector cuts the line or is parallel to it.

12. Prove the identities

(i) $\qquad \mathbf{A} \times (\mathbf{B} \times \mathbf{C}) + \mathbf{B} \times (\mathbf{C} \times \mathbf{A}) + \mathbf{C} \times (\mathbf{A} \times \mathbf{B}) = 0,$

(ii) $\qquad \mathbf{A} \times [\mathbf{B} \times (\mathbf{C} \times \mathbf{D})] = (\mathbf{B} \cdot \mathbf{D})(\mathbf{A} \times \mathbf{C}) - (\mathbf{B} \cdot \mathbf{C})(\mathbf{A} \times \mathbf{D}),$

(iii) $\qquad (\mathbf{A} \times \mathbf{B}) \times (\mathbf{C} \times \mathbf{D}) = \mathbf{B}[\mathbf{A} \cdot (\mathbf{C} \times \mathbf{D})] - \mathbf{A}[\mathbf{B} \cdot (\mathbf{C} \times \mathbf{D})].$

13. $Oxyz, Ox'y'z'$ are two sets of rectangular Cartesian axes. $\mathbf{P}$ is a vector with components X, Y, Z on $Oxyz$ and components X', Y', Z' on $Ox'y'z'$. Show that

$$X' = a_{11}X + a_{12}Y + a_{13}Z,$$

where a_{11}, a_{12}, a_{13} are the direction cosines of Ox' with respect to $Oxyz$. Develop similar formulas for Y' and Z'.

14. Solve the differential equation

$$\frac{d^2\mathbf{r}}{dt^2} = \mathbf{a},$$

where $\mathbf{a}$ is a constant vector.

15. Show that the differential equation

$$\mathbf{a} \times \frac{d^2\mathbf{r}}{dt^2} = \mathbf{b},$$

where $\mathbf{a}$ and $\mathbf{b}$ are perpendicular constant vectors, has the general solution

$$\mathbf{r} = f(t)\mathbf{a} + t\mathbf{c} + \mathbf{e} - \frac{t^2}{2a^2}(\mathbf{a} \times \mathbf{b}),$$

here $f(t)$ is an arbitrary function and $\mathbf{c}, \mathbf{e}$ are arbitrary constant vectors.

CHAPTER X

STATICS IN SPACE

10.1. GENERAL FORCE SYSTEMS

Before proceeding to conditions of equilibrium, let us develop some results valid for any system of forces, whether they produce equilibrium or not.

The total force and the total moment.

Let there be a system of particles with position vectors r_1, $r_2, \cdots r_n$ relative to a point O, and let forces $\mathbf{P}_1, \mathbf{P}_2, \cdots \mathbf{P}_n$ act on them. We define the *total force* $\mathbf{F}$ of this system as the vector sum of the forces, i.e.,

$$(10.101) \qquad \mathbf{F} = \sum_{i=1}^{n} \mathbf{P}_i.$$

The moment of the force $\mathbf{P}_i$ about O is $\mathbf{r}_i \times \mathbf{P}_i$, by (9.301). We define the *total moment* $\mathbf{G}$ of the force system about the *base point* O as the sum of these moments, i.e.,

$$(10.102) \qquad \mathbf{G} = \sum_{i=1}^{n} \mathbf{r}_i \times \mathbf{P}_i.$$

The scalar components of the total force and the total moment on axes $Oxyz$ are easy to write down. Let x_i, y_i, z_i be the coordinates of the ith particle and X_i, Y_i, Z_i the components of $\mathbf{P}_i$. Then the components of $\mathbf{F}$ are

$$(10.103) \quad X = \sum_{i=1}^{n} X_i, \quad Y = \sum_{i=1}^{n} Y_i, \quad Z = \sum_{i=1}^{n} Z_i,$$

and the components of $\mathbf{G}$ are

$$(10.104) \quad L = \sum_{i=1}^{n} (y_i Z_i - z_i Y_i), \quad M = \sum_{i=1}^{n} (z_i X_i - x_i Z_i),$$

$$N = \sum_{i=1}^{n} (x_i Y_i - y_i X_i).$$

Since the scalar moment about Ox is the component along Ox of the vector moment about O, it is evident that L, M, N are the total scalar moments about the axes $Oxyz$; thus, for example, L is the sum of the scalar moments of all the forces about Ox.

Change of base point.

It is clear that $\mathbf{F}$ does not depend on the choice of base point O. On the other hand, $\mathbf{G}$ does depend on this choice. Let us see how $\mathbf{G}$ changes when we change the base point from O to O', where $\overrightarrow{OO'} = \mathbf{a}$.

If $\mathbf{r}'_1, \mathbf{r}'_2, \cdots \mathbf{r}'_n$ are the position vectors of the particles relative to O', we have

(10.105) $$\mathbf{r}_i = \mathbf{r}'_i + \mathbf{a}.$$

Then, if $\mathbf{G}'$ is the total moment about O', we have

$$\mathbf{G}' = \sum_{i=1}^{n} \mathbf{r}'_i \times \mathbf{P}_i$$
$$= \sum_{i=1}^{n} (\mathbf{r}_i - \mathbf{a}) \times \mathbf{P}_i;$$

and so, by (10.101) and (10.102),

(10.106) $$\mathbf{G}' = \mathbf{G} - \mathbf{a} \times \mathbf{F}.$$

This equation shows how the total moment changes with change of base point.

Equipollent force systems.

In Sec. 2.3, we gave the general definition of equipollence but used it only in the restricted sense of plane equipollence. We recall that two force systems are equipollent if (in the language used above) the total forces of the two systems are equal, and also their total scalar moments about an arbitrary line. We shall now establish the following fundamental theorem:

If two force systems are equipollent, they have the same total force and the same total moment about an arbitrary base point—the same for both systems. Conversely, if two force systems have the same total force and the same total moment about some one base point, then they are equipollent.

Let S_1 and S_2 be two force systems and O any base point. The total forces of the two systems will be denoted by $\mathbf{F}_1$, $\mathbf{F}_2$, and their total moments about O by $\mathbf{G}_1$, $\mathbf{G}_2$, respectively.

If S_1 and S_2 are equipollent, then $\mathbf{F}_1 = \mathbf{F}_2$ from the definition of equipollence. Further, the scalar moments of S_1 and S_2 about any line through O are equal, and so the vectors $\mathbf{G}_1$ and $\mathbf{G}_2$ have the same component along any line through O; hence $\mathbf{G}_1 = \mathbf{G}_2$. Thus, for an arbitrary base point O, we have

$$(10.107) \qquad \mathbf{F}_1 = \mathbf{F}_2, \qquad \mathbf{G}_1 = \mathbf{G}_2,$$

which establishes the first part of the theorem.

To prove the converse, we must show that S_1 and S_2 are equipollent if (10.107) hold for some one base point O. The first condition of equipollence, namely, the equality of total forces, is evidently satisfied; it remains to prove that the scalar moments of S_1 and S_2 about any line are equal. If the line passes through O, the equality of scalar moments follows at once by projecting the equal vectors $\mathbf{G}_1$, $\mathbf{G}_2$ on the line. If the line does not pass through O, let O' be any point on it. The total moment $\mathbf{G}'_1$ of S_1 about O' is expressed in terms of $\mathbf{F}_1$ and $\mathbf{G}_1$ as in (10.106); there is a similar expression for the total moment $\mathbf{G}'_2$ of S_2 about O'. These vectors are obviously equal by virtue of (10.107), and so the scalar moments in question are also equal. The proof of the theorem is now complete.

If the total force $\mathbf{F}$ of a system is zero, and also the total moment $\mathbf{G}$ about some one base point, it follows that $\mathbf{F}$ and $\mathbf{G}$ are zero for all base points. We say then that the system is *equipollent to zero*.

10.2. EQUILIBRIUM OF A SYSTEM OF PARTICLES

In Chaps. II and V, we developed the general principles of statics and dynamics in a plane. In establishing these principles, we sometimes gave the results in three-dimensional form, where there was no particular difficulty involved. Now we have to develop general principles in three dimensions, and it might be thought that the new work would have to be built on top of the old. That is not the case. Since we are now in possession of the powerful vector method, it is on the whole simpler to establish the general principles directly from the basic laws of Sec. 1.4. That is what we shall do, except

in those cases where the vector method offers no advantage. In the main, therefore, the rest of the book is logically independent of Part I, except for the laws of Sec. 1.4.

Necessary conditions of equilibrium.

For a single particle, the condition of equilibrium is

(10.201) $$\mathbf{P} = 0,$$

where $\mathbf{P}$ is the vector sum of the forces acting on the particle.

Let us now consider a system of n particles in equilibrium. Let $\mathbf{P}_i$ denote the resultant of the external forces acting on the ith particle. In addition to the external forces, there act on each particle a number of internal forces due to the other particles of the system. Let $\mathbf{P}_{ij}$ denote the force on the ith particle due to the jth particle; by the law of action and reaction, these internal forces satisfy

(10.202) $$\mathbf{P}_{ij} + \mathbf{P}_{ji} = 0$$

Since each particle is in equilibrium, it follows from (10.201) that the external and internal forces satisfy the equations

(10.203) $$\begin{cases} \mathbf{P}_1 + 0 + \mathbf{P}_{12} + \mathbf{P}_{13} + \cdots + \mathbf{P}_{1n} = 0, \\ \mathbf{P}_2 + \mathbf{P}_{21} + 0 + \mathbf{P}_{23} + \cdots + \mathbf{P}_{2n} = 0, \\ \cdots \cdots \cdots \cdots \cdots \cdots \cdots \cdots \cdots \cdots \\ \mathbf{P}_n + \mathbf{P}_{n1} + \mathbf{P}_{n2} + \cdots + \mathbf{P}_{n,n-1} + 0 = 0. \end{cases}$$

When we add these equations, the internal reactions cancel on account of (10.202), and so

(10.204) $$\mathbf{F} = 0,$$

where $\mathbf{F}$ is the total force of the external force system, viz., $\sum_{i=1}^{n} \mathbf{P}_i$.

Let $\mathbf{r}_i$ denote the position vector of the ith particle relative to a base point O. If we multiply the equations (10.203) vectorially by $\mathbf{r}_1, \mathbf{r}_2, \cdots \mathbf{r}_n$ in order, we obtain

(10.205) $$\begin{cases} \mathbf{r}_1 \times \mathbf{P}_1 + 0 + \mathbf{r}_1 \times \mathbf{P}_{12} + \mathbf{r}_1 \times \mathbf{P}_{13} + \cdots \\ \qquad\qquad\qquad\qquad + \mathbf{r}_1 \times \mathbf{P}_{1n} = 0, \\ \mathbf{r}_2 \times \mathbf{P}_2 + \mathbf{r}_2 \times \mathbf{P}_{21} + 0 + \mathbf{r}_2 \times \mathbf{P}_{23} + \cdots \\ \qquad\qquad\qquad\qquad + \mathbf{r}_2 \times \mathbf{P}_{2n} = 0, \\ \cdots \cdots \cdots \cdots \cdots \cdots \cdots \cdots \cdots \cdots \\ \mathbf{r}_n \times \mathbf{P}_n + \mathbf{r}_n \times \mathbf{P}_{n1} + \mathbf{r}_n \times \mathbf{P}_{n2} + \cdots \\ \qquad\qquad\qquad\qquad + \mathbf{r}_n \times \mathbf{P}_{n,n-1} + 0 = 0. \end{cases}$$

Now,

$$\mathbf{r}_1 \times \mathbf{P}_{12} + \mathbf{r}_2 \times \mathbf{P}_{21} = (\mathbf{r}_1 - \mathbf{r}_2) \times \mathbf{P}_{12} = 0,$$

since $\mathbf{r}_1 - \mathbf{r}_2$ and $\mathbf{P}_{12}$ lie in the same line [cf. (9.303)]. Hence, on addition of the equations (10.205), the terms symmetrically placed with respect to the line of zeros cancel in pairs, and we get

(10.206) $$\mathbf{G} = 0,$$

where $\mathbf{G}$ is the total moment about O of the external force system, viz., $\sum_{i=1}^{n} \mathbf{r}_i \times \mathbf{P}_i$.

Thus, for a system in equilibrium, $\mathbf{F}$ and $\mathbf{G}$ both vanish, and so (in the language of Sec. 10.1) we have the following general result:*
If a system of particles is in equilibrium, then the external force system is equipollent to zero.

In terms of the total force $\mathbf{F}$ and the total moment $\mathbf{G}$ about any base point O, the above statement is equivalent to the two vector equations

(10.207) $$\mathbf{F} = 0, \quad \mathbf{G} = 0.$$

Resolving vectors along rectangular axes $Oxyz$ and using the notation of (10.103) and (10.104), we get the following six scalar conditions of equilibrium:

(10.208) $\quad X = 0, \quad Y = 0, \quad Z = 0;$
(10.209) $\quad L = 0, \quad M = 0, \quad N = 0.$

In this form the conditions appear as generalizations of (2.308).

The whole theory of statics rests on the equations (10.207). Most frequently, these equations are applied to a rigid body, treated as a whole. But they are valid for *any* system, which may be a part of a rigid body or a piece of an elastic material, or even a volume of fluid. As an example, we shall presently discuss the equilibrium of a flexible cable in space (cf. Sec. 3.4 for the plane case). The equilibrium of a rigid body will be considered in more detail in Sec. 10.4.

---

* This condition is equivalent to the conditions obtained in Sec. 2.3.

Curves in space.

We require some elements of the geometry of curves in space; they are of importance apart from the present connection and will be used again later.

Let C be a curve in space and A any point on C. Let P be any other point on C, distant s from A (s being measured along the curve). The unit vector **i**, tangent to the curve at P, is clearly a vector function of s. Since $\mathbf{i} \cdot \mathbf{i}$ remains equal to unity along C, we have

$$(10.210) \qquad \mathbf{i} \cdot \frac{d\mathbf{i}}{ds} = 0.$$

It follows that the vector $d\mathbf{i}/ds$ is normal to C at each point P. Let $1/\rho$ (ρ is the *radius of curvature* of C at P) denote the magnitude of this vector. Then we may write

$$(10.211) \qquad \frac{d\mathbf{i}}{ds} = \frac{\mathbf{j}}{\rho},$$

where **j** is a unit vector normal to C; it is the unit *principal normal vector*. The plane of **i** and **j** is called the *osculating plane*.

The unit *binormal vector* **k** at P is defined as follows: It is normal to both **i** and **j** and is so directed that (**i**, **j**, **k**) is a right-handed triad.

The equation (10.211) is the first of the *Frenet-Serret formulas*. The complete set of formulas is

$$(10.212) \qquad \frac{d\mathbf{i}}{ds} = \frac{\mathbf{j}}{\rho}, \qquad \frac{d\mathbf{j}}{ds} = \frac{\mathbf{k}}{\tau} - \frac{\mathbf{i}}{\rho}, \qquad \frac{d\mathbf{k}}{ds} = -\frac{\mathbf{j}}{\tau},$$

where τ is a certain scalar, called the *radius of torsion*.* These formulas are easily proved. Since

$$\mathbf{j} \cdot \frac{d\mathbf{j}}{ds} = 0, \qquad \mathbf{k} \cdot \frac{d\mathbf{k}}{ds} = 0,$$

it follows that

$$(10.213) \qquad \frac{d\mathbf{j}}{ds} = a\mathbf{i} + b\mathbf{k}, \qquad \frac{d\mathbf{k}}{ds} = \alpha\mathbf{i} + \beta\mathbf{j},$$

---

* We note that ρ is necessarily positive, since it is defined as the reciprocal of the magnitude of $d\mathbf{i}/ds$; τ may be positive or negative.

where a, b, α, β are scalars. On differentiating the relations

(10.214) $\qquad \mathbf{i} \cdot \mathbf{j} = 0, \qquad \mathbf{j} \cdot \mathbf{k} = 0, \qquad \mathbf{k} \cdot \mathbf{i} = 0$

and using (10.211) and (10.213), we find

(10.215) $\qquad a = -\dfrac{1}{\rho}, \qquad \alpha = 0, \qquad b + \beta = 0.$

Hence, writing $b = 1/\tau$, we obtain (10.212).

For a curve C, drawn on a surface S, the vector $\mathbf{i}$ is necessarily a tangent to S. But the vector $\mathbf{j}$ is not necessarily normal to S; it may even be a tangent to S, as in the case where S is a plane. If $\mathbf{j}$ is normal to S at each point of C, the curve is called a *geodesic* on S.

Flexible cables.

Let us now consider a flexible cable in equilibrium under the action of known external forces and the tensions at its ends.

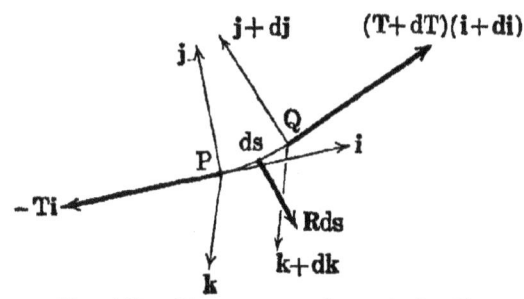

FIG. 107.—Forces on an element of cable.

Figure 107 shows an infinitesimal portion PQ, P being at a distance s from one end of the cable. Let $\mathbf{i}$, $\mathbf{j}$, $\mathbf{k}$ denote the unit tangent, principal normal, and binormal vectors at P. The forces acting on the element PQ (length ds) may now be described as follows:

(i) a force $-T\mathbf{i}$ at P, where T is the tension at P;

(ii) a force $(T + dT)(\mathbf{i} + d\mathbf{i}) = (T + dT)[\mathbf{i} + (\mathbf{j}/\rho)\,ds]$ at Q, where $T + dT$ is the tension at Q;

(iii) a force $\mathbf{R}\,ds = (R_1\mathbf{i} + R_2\mathbf{j} + R_3\mathbf{k})\,ds$, where $\mathbf{R}$ is the external force per unit length of the cable. (This force acts at some unspecified point of the element PQ.)

The element PQ is a system in equilibrium under these forces, and so we may apply the conditions (10.207) to it. From the first of these conditions, we have

$$(10.216) \quad -T\mathbf{i} + (T + dT)\left(\mathbf{i} + \frac{\mathbf{j}}{\rho} ds\right) + (R_1\mathbf{i} + R_2\mathbf{j} + R_3\mathbf{k}) ds = 0.$$

The second of the conditions (10.207) is satisfied identically to the first order in ds. From (10.216), we at once obtain the scalar equations

$$(10.217) \quad \begin{cases} \dfrac{dT}{ds} + R_1 = 0, \\ \dfrac{T}{\rho} + R_2 = 0, \\ \phantom{\dfrac{T}{\rho}} R_3 = 0. \end{cases}$$

These are the general equations of equilibrium. They enable us to find the form of the cable and also the variation in tension along it. In particular, the last of these equations tells us that the osculating plane at each point contains the external force vector.

Example. A light cable rests in contact with a smooth surface S, under no forces except the reaction of S and the tensions at its ends. It is required to find the curve C in which the cable rests, and also the tension at each point.

The external force vector $\mathbf{R}\, ds$ is the reaction of the surface S on the element. Since this reaction is normal to S, it is also normal to C, and so $R_1 = 0$. But $R_3 = 0$, by the last of (10.217), and so

$$\mathbf{R} = R_2 \mathbf{j}.$$

It follows that the principal normal vector $\mathbf{j}$ is normal to S at each point of C. Hence, C is a geodesic on S. Thus, to construct a geodesic joining two given points on a surface, we have merely to stretch a light thread between these points. If S is a sphere, C is an arc of a great circle; if S is a cylinder, C is a curve on the cylinder which maps into a straight line, when the cylinder is cut along a generator and unrolled on a plane.

Again, since $R_1 = 0$, the first equation in (10.217) gives

$$\frac{dT}{ds} = 0.$$

Thus the tension T is constant; in particular, the tensions at the ends are equal.

10.3. REDUCTION OF FORCE SYSTEMS

If we succeed in finding a simple force system S', equipollent to a given system S, we say that we have *reduced* the system S to the system S'. We shall presently consider, in some detail, the

reduction of force systems; but, before doing this, it is convenient to have a vector description of the particular force system known as a couple.

Moment of a couple.

As in Sec. 2.3, a couple is defined as a pair of parallel forces, equal in magnitude but opposite in sense. Figure 108 shows a couple consisting of the forces **P** and −**P** applied at the points A and B, respectively; O is any point in space. The vector

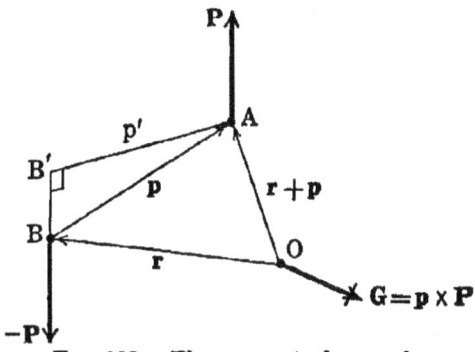

FIG. 108.—The moment of a couple.

moment **G** of this couple about O is easily found; denoting $\overrightarrow{OB}$ by r and $\overrightarrow{BA}$ by p, we obtain

$$(10.301) \quad \mathbf{G} = \mathbf{r} \times (-\mathbf{P}) + (\mathbf{r} + \mathbf{p}) \times \mathbf{P} = \mathbf{p} \times \mathbf{P}.$$

This value of **G** is independent of the position of the point O. In other words, *a couple has the same moment about all points in space.* Thus the vector **G** may be regarded as a free vector; it is perpendicular to the plane determined by the forces **P**, −**P** of the couple; its magnitude is $p'P$, where p' is the perpendicular distance between the lines of action of these forces (Fig. 108).

Since two couples which have the same moment are equipollent force systems, a couple is completely specified (as far as equipollence is concerned) by its free moment vector, or, briefly, its *moment*. Thus, when we speak of a couple **G**, we have in mind any one of an infinite number of couples, each of which has moment **G**.

To avoid confusion in diagrams, the arrowheads indicating couples may be marked with a crossbar, as in the figure.

Composition of couples.

Let there be a system of forces consisting of a number of couples $G_1, G_2, \cdots$. The total force of this system is zero, and the total moment about any point is clearly

$$(10.302) \qquad G = G_1 + G_2 + \cdots.$$

Thus, *a system consisting of couples is equipollent to a single couple; its moment is equal to the vector sum of the moments of the individual couples.* In other words, couples are compounded by the parallelogram law.

Exercise. Forces with components $(2, 0, 0)$, $(-1, 0, 0)$, $(-1, 0, 0)$ act at the points $(0, 0, 0)$, $(0, 1, 0)$, $(0, 0, 1)$, respectively. Show that they can be reduced to a couple, and find its magnitude and direction.

Reduction of a force system to a force and a couple.

Consider a general force system S, with total force F and total moment G with respect to a base point O. Consider also a second force system S', consisting only of a single force F applied at O and a single couple G. Obviously, S' is equipollent to S. Therefore *a general force system can always be reduced to a single force applied at an arbitrary base point, together with a couple.*

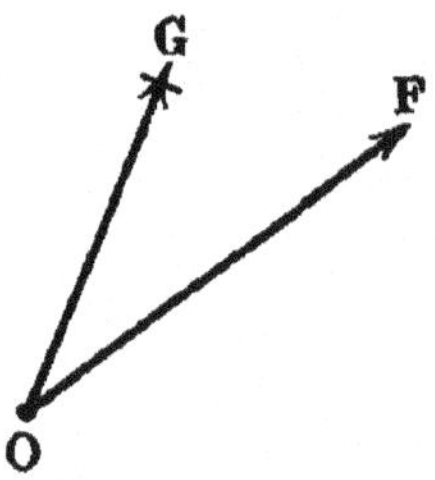

Fig. 109.—Representation of a general force system by a force F and a couple G.

Just as we represent a single force by an arrow, so we can represent a general force system by a diagram such as that in Fig 109, this shows a force F acting at a base point O and a couple G. Although the couple G is a free vector, it is convenient to draw it out from the base point O.

If we change the base point from O to O', where $\overrightarrow{OO'} = \mathbf{r}$, we do not alter F, but the moment about O' is not G; it is found by adding to G the moment of F about O'; this gives [cf. (10.106)]

$$G' = G - \mathbf{r} \times F.$$

Hence, under a change of base point from O to O', the force F and the couple G become F' and G', respectively, where

$$(10.303) \qquad F' = F, \qquad G' = G - \mathbf{r} \times F.$$

We note that $F' = F$ and $\mathbf{F}' \cdot \mathbf{G}' = \mathbf{F} \cdot \mathbf{G}$; in words, the scalars F and $\mathbf{F} \cdot \mathbf{G}$ are *invariant* under a change of base point. If either of these invariants vanishes for one choice of base point, then it vanishes for all choices of base point.

Reduction to a wrench.

A *wrench* consists of a force $\mathbf{F}$ and a couple $\mathbf{G}$ with parallel representative line segments. This relation between $\mathbf{F}$ and $\mathbf{G}$ is expressed by the vector equation

$$(10.304) \qquad \mathbf{G} = p\mathbf{F},$$

where p is some scalar having the dimensions of a length. The quantities p and F are called the *pitch* and *intensity* of the wrench, respectively. The line of action of the force $\mathbf{F}$ is called the *axis* of the wrench.

A general force system can always be reduced to a wrench. We shall now show how this is done. Let us first reduce the system in question to a force $\mathbf{F}$ at a base point O and a couple $\mathbf{G}$. Changing the base point to O', where $\overrightarrow{OO'} = \mathbf{r}$, we obtain a force $\mathbf{F}'$ and couple $\mathbf{G}'$. These constitute a wrench if

$$(10.305) \qquad \mathbf{G}' = p\mathbf{F}'.$$

Since, by (10.303),

$$\mathbf{F}' = \mathbf{F}, \qquad \mathbf{G}' = \mathbf{G} - \mathbf{r} \times \mathbf{F},$$

the equation (10.305) is satisfied if $\mathbf{r}$ and p satisfy

$$(10.306) \qquad \mathbf{G} - \mathbf{r} \times \mathbf{F} = p\mathbf{F}$$

This is, in fact, a vector equation for $\mathbf{r}$ (the position vector of O') and p (the pitch of the wrench).

Let us take O as origin of rectangular Cartesian coordinates, and let (F_1, F_2, F_3), (G_1, G_2, G_3) denote the components of $\mathbf{F}$, $\mathbf{G}$, respectively. The vector equation (10.306) is equivalent to the scalar equations

$$\frac{G_1 - yF_3 + zF_2}{F_1} = \frac{G_2 - zF_1 + xF_3}{F_2} = \frac{G_3 - xF_2 + yF_1}{F_3} = p,$$

where x, y, z are the coordinates of O'. These equations show that $\mathbf{F}'$, $\mathbf{G}'$ constitute a wrench provided O' lies on the straight

line with equations

$$(10.307)\quad \frac{G_1 - yF_3 + zF_2}{F_1} = \frac{G_2 - zF_1 + xF_3}{F_2} = \frac{G_3 - xF_2 + yF_1}{F_3}.$$

We note that, if (x, y, z) is any point on this line, then $(x + kF_1, y + kF_2, z + kF_3)$, where k is any scalar factor, is also on it. It follows that this line has the direction of $\mathbf{F}$; it is the axis of the wrench to which the system is reduced.

The pitch p is found by taking the scalar product of $\mathbf{F}$ and the vectors on the two sides of (10.306). We find

$$\mathbf{F} \cdot \mathbf{G} = pF^2;$$

therefore,

$$(10.308)\quad p = \frac{\mathbf{F} \cdot \mathbf{G}}{F^2}.$$

It is, of course, not accidental that the pitch of the resulting wrench is a function of the invariants F and $\mathbf{F} \cdot \mathbf{G}$.

If $p = 0$, the wrench degenerates into a single force; in this case $\mathbf{F} \cdot \mathbf{G} = 0$. If p is infinite, the wrench degenerates into a couple; in this case $F = 0$. In each of these special cases, we have a force system equipollent to a plane system of forces. Conversely, if the force system is equipollent to a plane system of forces, then one or other of these special cases must arise.

Exercise In the reduction of a given force system to a force and a couple, the couple G depends on the base point. For what base points is G least?

Reduction of a system of parallel forces.

A set of parallel forces is a system of particular importance in mechanics, e.g., the weights of a number of particles.

Any n parallel forces may be denoted by $k_1\mathbf{P}, k_2\mathbf{P}, \cdots k_n\mathbf{P}$, where $k_1, k_2, \cdots k_n$ are scalars. Selecting a base point O, we first reduce this system to a force $\mathbf{F}$ at O and a couple $\mathbf{G}$. Let $\mathbf{r}_s$ $(s = 1, 2, \cdots n)$ denote the position vectors, relative to O, of the points of application of the several forces. Then,

$$(10.309)\quad \begin{cases} \mathbf{F} = \sum_{s=1}^{n} (k_s\mathbf{P}) = k\mathbf{P}, \\ \mathbf{G} = \sum_{s=1}^{n} (\mathbf{r}_s \times k_s\mathbf{P}) = \left(\sum_{s=1}^{n} k_s\mathbf{r}_s\right) \times \mathbf{P} = \mathbf{r} \times \mathbf{F}, \end{cases}$$

where

(10.310) $$k = \sum_{s=1}^{n} k_s, \qquad \mathbf{r} = \Big(\sum_{s=1}^{n} k_s \mathbf{r}_s\Big)/k.$$

This reduced system is clearly equipollent to the single force **F**, applied at the point C with position vector **r**.

Thus a system of parallel forces can be reduced to a single force, unless $k = 0$. If $k = 0$, it can be reduced to a couple.

The point C, with position vector **r** given by (10.310), is called the *center of the system of parallel forces*. Its position is determined solely by the vectors $\mathbf{r}_s$ and the ratios of the numbers $k_1, k_2, \cdots k_n$. It is unaltered by turning the several forces about their points of application, provided they retain their magnitudes and remain parallel to one another.

If the forces in question are the weights of the particles of a system, the point C is the center of gravity of the system (cf. Sec. 3.1).

The reduction of some special force systems.

The force systems encountered in practical problems are often extremely complicated. However, the details of such a force system are relatively unimportant when it acts on a rigid body; if we know the *total force* and the *total moment*, we know all that is essential for the discussion of equilibrium. The total force and the total moment play an equally important part in dynamics (see Chap. XII).

1. Analysis of forces on an airplane.

Figure 110 shows an airplane in flight. C is the mass center. The orthogonal right-handed triad of unit vectors **i**, **j**, **k** is fixed in the airplane; **j** is perpendicular to the plane of symmetry and points to the right; **i** and **k** lie in the plane of symmetry. The direction of **i** is fixed in some conventional way (e.g., parallel to the airscrew axes), so as to be nearly horizontal and point forward when the plane is in normal flight, **k** will then be directed nearly vertically downward.

The forces acting on the airplane are as follows:

(i) The weights of the various parts. These constitute a system of parallel forces and can be reduced to a single force **W** acting vertically downward through C; W is the total weight of the airplane.

(ii) The thrust, or driving force, **P** due to the airscrews. This force is in the direction of the vector **i** or nearly so.

(iii) Forces arising from the action of the air. These forces are due mainly to variations in pressure over the wing surface and in a lesser degree

to friction; they form a very complicated system. Reducing this system to a force **F** at C and a couple **G**, we resolve as follows:

$$\mathbf{F} = X\mathbf{i} + Y\mathbf{j} + Z\mathbf{k}, \qquad \mathbf{G} = L\mathbf{i} + M\mathbf{j} + N\mathbf{k}$$

For normal flight, $-X$ is the *drag*, $-Z$ is the *lift*, and M is the *pitching moment*, Y, L, N are zero. The precise terminology of aerodynamic theory is not quite so simple as this. Under normal flight conditions, however, the differences are small.

The theoretical determination of the force system (**F**, **G**) is a very difficult problem in hydrodynamics; and, in practice, experimental methods are used. A model of the airplane (or the airplane itself) is mounted in a wind tunnel Direct measurements are then made of the force system required to keep the model at rest in a stream of air.

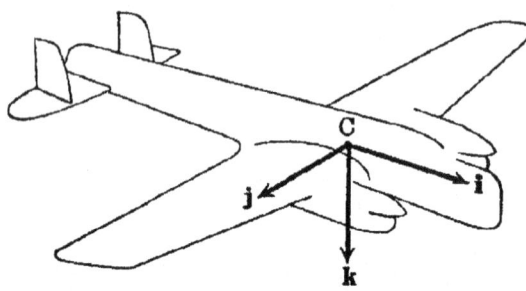

Fig 110—Reference vectors for an airplane

An analysis of the forces on a bullet or shell follows the same lines. In this case, however, the driving force **P** is absent.

2. Analysis of stresses in a beam.

Consider a beam in equilibrium and let Ox be a line in the direction of its length. We imagine the beam cut in two by a plane II perpendicular to Ox at A (Fig. 111). We shall denote by R the part of the beam to the right of II, and by L the part to the left.

The forces on L are as follows:

(i) Applied forces, such as gravity or external loads. These are equipollent to a single force **F** at A and a couple **G**.

(ii) Forces exerted across II by R on L. These are internal forces for the whole beam, but external forces for the system L. They are called the *stresses* across the plane section II and are equipollent to a force **S** at A and a couple **M**. Introducing the orthogonal triad of unit vectors **i**, **j**, **k**, as shown, we write

$$\mathbf{S} = S_1\mathbf{i} + S_2\mathbf{j} + S_3\mathbf{k}, \qquad \mathbf{M} = M_1\mathbf{i} + M_2\mathbf{j} + M_3\mathbf{k}.$$

The following terminology is used

$$S_1 = \text{tension},$$
$$S_2, S_3 = \text{shearing forces},$$
$$M_1 = \text{twisting couple},$$
$$M_2, M_3 = \text{bending moments}.$$

If the applied forces are known, then **F**, **G** are known and we can find **S**, **M**. We have merely to apply the conditions of equilibrium (10.207) to L, obtaining

$$\mathbf{S} = -\mathbf{F}, \qquad \mathbf{M} = -\mathbf{G}.$$

If we change the section II by varying the distance x of A from O, **F** and **G** are known functions of x; hence, **S** and **M** are known functions of x. In other words, there are two vector functions $\mathbf{S}(x)$, $\mathbf{M}(x)$ [or six scalar functions $S_1(x), S_2(x), \ldots M_3(x)$] which give, for each value of x, a force system equipollent to the stresses across the corresponding cross section of the beam

Failure in an engineering structure, such as a bridge, is due to excessive stress. The engineer must know in advance if any given beam or girder is likely to fail under the loads which it will be called on to support

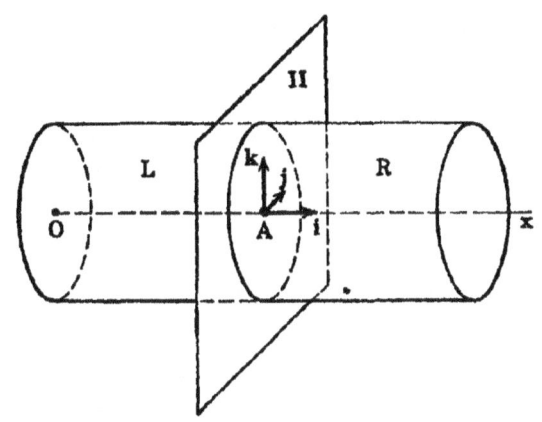

Fig. 111.—Reference vectors for reactions in a beam.

Although the values of **S** and **M** do not give a complete picture of the internal stresses, they are the quantities which the engineer calculates in order to see whether or not a structure is safe.

The above analysis also applies in naval architecture. Regarding the hull of a ship as a beam, subject to known applied forces, we can determine a force system (**S**, **M**) equipollent to the internal stresses across any section perpendicular to its length. A ship must be so constructed that it will withstand the action of stresses (**S**, **M**) arising from the applied forces of weight and buoyancy In a storm the ship may be supported by waves under bow and stern; then the forces of buoyancy are concentrated there, and the ship is in danger of "breaking its back"

10.4. EQUILIBRIUM OF A RIGID BODY

Necessary and sufficient conditions of equilibrium.

In our mathematical model, a rigid body is a set of particles whose mutual distances are invariable. Let us now consider a rigid body acted on by external forces. Reducing the force

system to a single force **F** at a base point O and a couple **G**, we know by (10.207) that the conditions

(10.401) $$\mathbf{F} = 0, \quad \mathbf{G} = 0$$

are *necessary* for equilibrium. We now make use of the rigidity of the body to prove that these conditions are also *sufficient*, so that the body must be in equilibrium if they are satisfied.

Let us suppose that a rigid body acted on by external forces, satisfying (10.401), is not in equilibrium; then the particles of the body will be on the point of moving. This motion will be prevented by introducing the following constraints (Fig. 112):

(i) The point O (taken in the body) is fixed; this leaves the body free to turn about O.

(ii) With origin O, we draw a unit vector **i**; the particle A at its extremity is constrained to slide in a smooth tube with axis in the direction of **i**. The two constraints now introduced fix all points of the body on the line OA, but still permit the body to turn about this line.

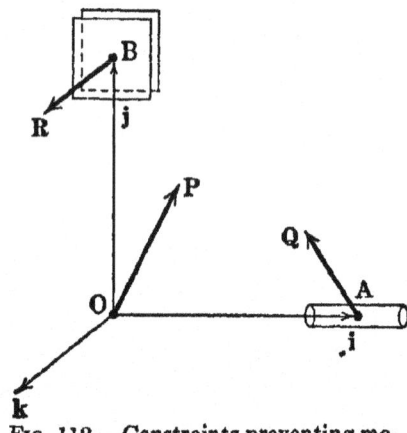

Fig. 112.—Constraints preventing motion of a rigid body

(iii) With origin O, we draw a unit vector **j**, perpendicular to **i**; the particle B at its extremity is constrained to move between two smooth planes parallel to the plane OAB. If these planes are close to each other, this constraint will prevent the motion of B.

These three constraints together prevent any motion of the body, and so it must remain at rest. It is therefore in equilibrium under the action of the given external force system and the reactions of these constraints.

Now the reactions of constraint are equipollent to a force **F'** at O and a couple **G'**. Since the body is in equilibrium,

$$\mathbf{F} + \mathbf{F'} = 0, \quad \mathbf{G} + \mathbf{G'} = 0;$$

and so, by (10.401),

(10.402) $$\mathbf{F'} = 0, \quad \mathbf{G'} = 0.$$

In view of the smoothness of the constraints at A and B, we see that the forces of constraint are

(i)   a force $\mathbf{P} = P_1\mathbf{i} + P_2\mathbf{j} + P_3\mathbf{k}$ applied at O;
(ii) a force $\mathbf{Q} = Q_2\mathbf{j} + Q_3\mathbf{k}$ applied at A (position vector $\mathbf{i}$ relative to O);
(iii) a force $\mathbf{R} = R_3\mathbf{k}$ applied at B (position vector $\mathbf{j}$ relative to O)

The vector $\mathbf{k}$ is a unit vector completing the orthogonal triad $\mathbf{i}, \mathbf{j}, \mathbf{k}$. On calculating $\mathbf{F}'$, $\mathbf{G}'$ in terms of $P_1, P_2, P_3, Q_2, Q_3, R_3$, we find that the six scalar equations contained in (10.402) imply

$$P_1 = P_2 = P_3 = Q_2 = Q_3 = R_3 = 0$$

Hence the constraints introduced actually exert no reactions, and so the body remains in equilibrium even if they are removed. The sufficiency of the conditions (10.401) is now established.

It is possible to state the conditions of equilibrium in forms other than (10.401). For example, it is easy to see that, if the external forces have no moment about each of three non-collinear points, then the conditions (10.401) are satisfied. Conversely, if the external forces satisfy (10.401) for some particular base point, they have no moment about any point. Thus, if $\mathbf{G}, \mathbf{G}', \mathbf{G}''$ denote the total moments of the external force system about each of three non-collinear points, the conditions

(10.403) $$\mathbf{G} = \mathbf{G}' = \mathbf{G}'' = 0$$

are both necessary and sufficient for equilibrium. Occasionally the conditions (10.403) are easier to apply than (10.401)

Applications.

The conditions (10.401) will now be applied to solve two problems.

Example 1. Figure 113 shows a pulley, with radius r and center A, rigidly attached to a horizontal shaft BCD. This shaft is free to turn in smooth bearings at B and C; the end D projects beyond the bearing at C, and to it is rigidly fastened a crank DE with handle EH. The angles BDE and DEH are right angles. A weight W is attached to the lower end of a cord passing round the pulley, the other end of the cord being fixed to the pulley. To raise W, a man applies a force $\mathbf{P}$ at H in a direction perpendicular to BCD and making an angle ϕ with the horizontal.

It is required to find the magnitude of $\mathbf{P}$ and also the directions and magnitudes of the reactions $\mathbf{R}$ and $\mathbf{R}'$ at B and C, respectively.

Let **i**, **j**, **k** be an orthogonal triad of unit vectors at A, **i** lying along AC and **k** pointing vertically upward. Lengths are denoted as follows: $BA = AC = a$, $CD = b$, $DE = c$, $EH = d$. Then, if DE makes an angle θ with the vertical, the forces acting on the whole system can be described as follows (position vectors being taken relative to A):

(10.404)
$$\begin{cases} \text{a force } \mathbf{P} = P \cos \phi\, \mathbf{j} - P \sin \phi\, \mathbf{k} \\ \qquad \text{at } (a + b + d)\mathbf{i} + c \sin \theta\, \mathbf{j} + c \cos \theta\, \mathbf{k}, \\ \text{a force } -W\mathbf{k} \text{ at } -r\mathbf{j}, \\ \text{a force } \mathbf{R} = R_2 \mathbf{j} + R_3 \mathbf{k} \text{ at } -a\mathbf{i}, \\ \text{a force } \mathbf{R}' = R_2' \mathbf{j} + R_3' \mathbf{k} \text{ at } a\mathbf{i} \end{cases}$$

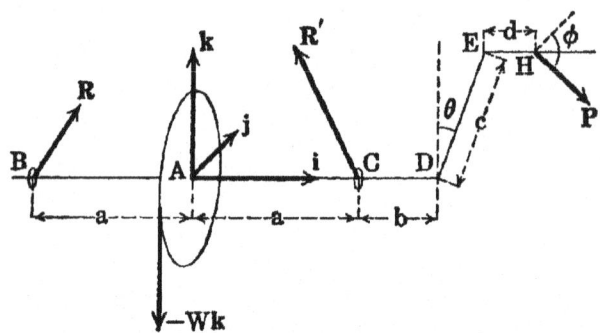

Fig. 113.—Pulley and shaft turned by a crank.

Reducing this force system to a force **F** at A and a couple **G**, we find

$$\mathbf{F} = (P \cos \phi + R_2 + R_2')\mathbf{j} + (-P \sin \phi - W + R_3 + R_3')\mathbf{k},$$
$$\mathbf{G} = [(a + b + d)\mathbf{i} + c \sin \theta\, \mathbf{j} + c \cos \theta\, \mathbf{k}] \times [P \cos \phi\, \mathbf{j} - P \sin \phi\, \mathbf{k}]$$
$$\qquad + r\mathbf{j} \times W\mathbf{k} - a\mathbf{i} \times (R_2 \mathbf{j} + R_3 \mathbf{k}) + a\mathbf{i} \times (R_2' \mathbf{j} + R_3' \mathbf{k})$$
$$= [Wr - Pc \cos (\theta - \phi)]\mathbf{i} + [P(a + b + d) \sin \phi + aR_3 - aR_3']\mathbf{j}$$
$$\qquad + [P(a + b + d) \cos \phi - aR_2 + aR_2']\mathbf{k}.$$

For equilibrium, these vectors must vanish. Equating them to zero and performing some simple calculations, we find

(10.405)
$$\begin{cases} P = \dfrac{Wr}{c} \sec (\theta - \phi), \\[4pt] R_2 = P \dfrac{(b + d)}{2a} \cos \phi, \qquad R_3 = \dfrac{W}{2} - P \dfrac{(b + d)}{2a} \sin \phi, \\[4pt] R_2' = -P \dfrac{(2a + b + d)}{2a} \cos \phi, \qquad R_3' = \dfrac{W}{2} + P \dfrac{(2a + b + d)}{2a} \sin \phi. \end{cases}$$

These equations constitute the solution of our problem.

The value of P given above is least when $\phi = \theta$, i.e., when the force at H is perpendicular to the crank DE; this may also be seen quite simply by taking moments about the line BD. Thus, to raise the weight with the least effort, the man should push at right angles to the crank. As far as the man is concerned, the actual position of the point H in the handle is of no importance; a change in d merely alters the reactions at B and C.

this is, therefore, the only position of equilibrium. As for stability, we observe that

$$V = (q_1 + \tfrac{3}{2}q_2)^2 + \tfrac{7}{4}q_2^2.$$

Since $V = 0$ for $q_1 = q_2 = 0$ and is positive for all other values, it follows that V is a minimum at the position of equilibrium, the equilibrium is stable.

Example 2. We shall now discuss a device known as Hooke's joint. This is used to transmit a torque or couple from one axis to another, inclined to the first

Figure 119 shows the essential features of the joint AB is a shaft or axis, branching into the fork BCD, $A'B'$ is another axis, with fork $B'C'D'$. These forks are connected by a rigid body composed of two bars CD, $C'D'$, joined perpendicularly at their common center O The lines AB, $A'B'$ meet at O when produced and are perpendicular to CD, $C'D'$, respectively. There are smooth bearings at C, D, C', D', and the axes AB, $A'B'$ are free to turn in smooth bearings at A and A'

Let $\mathbf{I}$ be a unit vector in the direction AB and $\mathbf{I'}$ a unit vector in the direction $B'A'$ When a couple $M\mathbf{I}$ is applied to $ABCD$, the system will move unless motion is prevented by other forces We propose to calculate the couple $M'\mathbf{I'}$ applied to $A'B'C'D'$, which (together with $M\mathbf{I}$ and the reactions at the bearings) gives equilibrium.

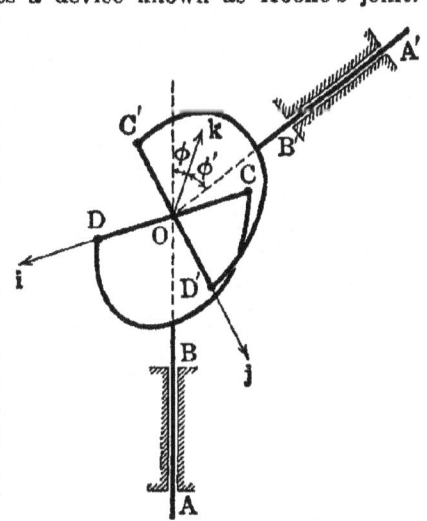

Fig. 119.—Hooke's joint.

To solve such a problem, the general plan is as follows: (i) select generalized coordinates q_1, q_2, $\cdots$ for the system, (ii) calculate an expression of the form (10.708) for the work done in a displacement; (iii) equate the generalized forces to zero, and solve.

We note that the fixed elements of the system are the lines AB, $A'B'$ and the point O. Since $ABCD$ can merely turn about AB, a single coordinate θ (the angle turned through) is sufficient to fix it. When $ABCD$ is fixed, the line CD is fixed Now the line $C'D'$ must be perpendicular to both CD and $A'B'$ (from the construction of the joint), hence $C'D'$ is fixed, and so the angle θ suffices to fix, not only $ABCD$, but $A'B'C'D'$ also The system has one degree of freedom, and θ is a generalized coordinate.

When θ increases to $\theta + \delta\theta$, $A'B'C'D'$ turns through some small angle $\delta\theta'$; the displacements of $ABCD$, $A'B'C'D'$, $CDC'D'$ are as follows:

$ABCD$: a rotation $\delta\theta\,\mathbf{I}$,
$A'B'C'D'$: a rotation $\delta\theta'\,\mathbf{I'}$,
$CDC'D'$: a rotation $\delta\mathbf{n} = \delta n_1\mathbf{i} + \delta n_2\mathbf{j} + \delta n_3\mathbf{k}$,

where **i**, **j**, **k** are unit vectors along CD, $C'D'$ and perpendicular to them. Since no work is done by the reactions at the bearings and the internal reactions at C, C', D, D', we have [cf. (10.704)]

(10.715)
$$\delta W = M\mathbf{I} \cdot \delta\theta\,\mathbf{I} + M'\mathbf{I}' \cdot \delta\theta'\,\mathbf{I}'$$
$$= M\,\delta\theta + M'\,\delta\theta'$$

We must now find $\delta\theta'$ in terms of $\delta\theta$. The point D belongs to two rigid bodies $ABCD$ and $CDC'D'$. Equating the two expressions for its displacement [cf. (10.501)], we have

(10.716)
$$\delta\theta\,\mathbf{I} \times a\mathbf{i} = \delta\mathbf{n} \times a\mathbf{i},$$

where $a = OD = OD'$. Similarly, by considering the displacement of D', we find

(10.717)
$$\delta\theta'\,\mathbf{I}' \times a\mathbf{j} = \delta\mathbf{n} \times a\mathbf{j}.$$

Now, resolving along **i**, **j**, **k**, we have

$$\mathbf{I} = -\sin\phi\,\mathbf{j} + \cos\phi\,\mathbf{k}, \qquad \mathbf{I}' = -\sin\phi'\,\mathbf{i} + \cos\phi'\,\mathbf{k},$$

where ϕ, ϕ' are the angles between **k** and AB, $B'A'$, respectively. Substituting these values for $\mathbf{I}$ and $\mathbf{I}'$ in (10.716) and (10.717), we obtain

(10.718)
$$\begin{cases} \cos\phi\,\delta\theta = \delta n_3, & -\sin\phi\,\delta\theta = \delta n_2, \\ \cos\phi'\,\delta\theta' = \delta n_3, & -\sin\phi'\,\delta\theta' = \delta n_1. \end{cases}$$

Equating the expressions for δn_3, we obtain

(10.719)
$$\delta\theta' = \cos\phi \sec\phi'\,\delta\theta.$$

Substituting this value in (10.715), we get

(10.720)
$$\delta W = (M + M'\cos\phi \sec\phi')\,\delta\theta,$$

and so the single generalized force Θ is

$$\Theta = M + M'\cos\phi \sec\phi'.$$

For equilibrium, this must vanish, and so the couple required to hold $A'B'C'D'$ is $M'\mathbf{I}'$, where

$$M' = -M\sec\phi \cos\phi'.$$

The fraction of the torque M transmitted through the joint is $\sec\phi\cos\phi'$.

Example 3. In Fig. 120, AB represents a shaft free to turn about a horizontal axis L, perpendicular to AB at A; DE represents a heavy bar threaded on the shaft AB and perpendicular to it. The pitch of the thread is p, so that, when DE turns through an angle ϕ about AB, E moves along AB through a distance $p\phi$. The points C, C' are the centers of gravity of AB, DE, respectively. We wish to find the possible positions of equilibrium of this system under gravity, all friction being neglected.

We start with a standard configuration in which AB is vertical and DE lies in the vertical plane Π perpendicular to L at A. Let x_0 denote the distance AE in this position. We pass to a general configuration by swing-

Sec. 10.7] STATICS IN SPACE 299

ing AB through an angle θ and turning DE to make an angle ϕ with Π. The angles θ and ϕ are generalized coordinates. In terms of them, the potential energy is

(10.721) $V = -wa \cos \theta - W[(x_0 + p\phi) \cos \theta + b \sin \theta \cos \phi]$,

where $a = AC$, $b = EC'$ and w, W denote the weights of AB, DE, respectively.

The conditions of equilibrium are

(10.722) $\begin{cases} \dfrac{\partial V}{\partial \theta} = wa \sin \theta + W(x_0 + p\phi) \sin \theta - Wb \cos \theta \cos \phi = 0, \\ \dfrac{\partial V}{\partial \phi} = -Wp \cos \theta + Wb \sin \theta \sin \phi = 0 \end{cases}$

Elimination of θ gives for ϕ the equation

(10.723) $\qquad Wb^2 \sin 2\phi = 2wpa + 2Wp(x_0 + p\phi)$

With numerical values for the constants, this equation can be solved graphically or otherwise. In terms of ϕ, θ is given by

(10.724) $\qquad \tan \theta = \dfrac{p}{b \sin \phi}.$

Some interesting results can be deduced without solving (10.723). If p is small, a position of equilibrium occurs for some small value of ϕ, i.e., with

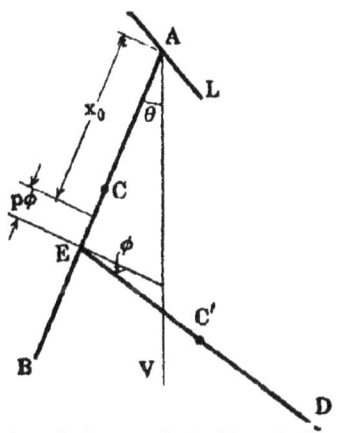

Fig 120.—A bar ED is threaded on a shaft AB, which can turn about a horizontal axis L.

DE close to Π. For this position, $\tan \theta$ is finite, since p and ϕ are small of the same order. Another position occurs near $\phi = \tfrac{1}{2}\pi$; for this, $\tan \theta$ is small, and so AB is nearly vertical. If p is large, the right-hand side of (10.723) may exceed Wb^2 for all ϕ; in this case, there is no position of equilibrium, and the bar DE simply runs down the shaft AB, turning as it goes.

Example 4. The last two examples considered above are three-dimensional in character. We conclude with an application of the methods of work and energy to a two-dimensional system with many degrees of freedom.

300   MECHANICS IN SPACE   [SEC. 10.7

Consider a chain of n equal uniform rods, smoothly jointed together and suspended from one end A_1. (Figure 121 shows the case $n = 5$.) A horizontal force **P** is applied to the other end A_{n+1} of this chain. It is required to find the equilibrium configuration.

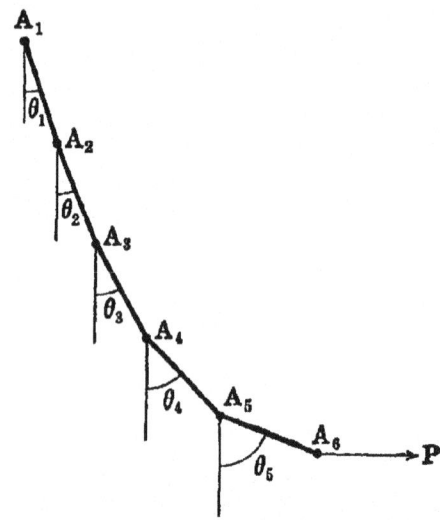

Fig. 121.—A chain of rods pulled by a horizontal force

As generalized coordinates, we take the inclinations (to the downward vertical) $\theta_1, \theta_2, \cdots \theta_n$ of the several rods in order. If each rod has length $2a$ and weight w, the potential energy in a general configuration is

$$V = -wa \cos \theta_1 - w(2a \cos \theta_1 + a \cos \theta_2) - \cdots$$
$$- w(2a \cos \theta_1 + 2a \cos \theta_2 + \cdots + 2a \cos \theta_{n-1} + a \cos \theta_n)$$
$$= -wa[(2n - 1) \cos \theta_1 + (2n - 3) \cos \theta_2 + \cdots + 3 \cos \theta_{n-1} + \cos \theta_n].$$

In a small virtual displacement the work done by gravity is

$$-\delta V = -wa[(2n - 1) \sin \theta_1 \, \delta\theta_1 + (2n - 3) \sin \theta_2 \, \delta\theta_2 \cdots + \sin \theta_n \, \delta\theta_n].$$

The work done by the force **P** is the product of P and the horizontal displacement of A_{n+1}, i.e.,

$$P\delta(2a \sin \theta_1 + 2a \sin \theta_2 + \cdots + 2a \sin \theta_n).$$

Adding these two expression, we find, for the total work done,

(10.725)
$$\begin{aligned}\delta W = \; & [2P \cos \theta_1 - (2n - 1)w \sin \theta_1]a \, \delta\theta_1 \\ & + [2P \cos \theta_2 - (2n - 3)w \sin \theta_2]a \, \delta\theta_2 \\ & + \cdots \\ & + [2P \cos \theta_n - w \sin \theta_n]a \, \delta\theta_n.\end{aligned}$$

This must vanish for arbitrary values of $\delta\theta_1, \delta\theta_2, \cdots \delta\theta_n$, if the displacement is from a position of equilibrium. Hence, equating to zero the brackets on the right of (10.725), we find

(10.726)
$$\begin{cases} \tan \theta_1 = \dfrac{2P}{w(2n-1)}, \\ \tan \theta_2 = \dfrac{2P}{w(2n-3)}, \\ \cdots \cdots \cdots \cdots \\ \tan \theta_n = \dfrac{2P}{w} \end{cases}$$

These equations give the inclinations of the rods to the downward vertical in the equilibrium configuration, the tangents form a harmonic progression.

10.8. SUMMARY OF STATICS IN SPACE

I. Conditions of equilibrium.

(a) For a single particle (necessary and sufficient):

(10.801) $$\mathbf{P} = 0,$$

or

(10.802) $$X = 0, \quad Y = 0, \quad Z = 0.$$

(b) For any system (necessary), or for a rigid body (necessary and sufficient):

(10.803) $$\mathbf{F} = 0, \quad \mathbf{G} = 0.$$

($\mathbf{F}$ = total force, $\mathbf{G}$ = total moment.)

(c) For any system with workless constraints (necessary and sufficient):

(10.804) $$\delta W = 0, \quad (\delta W = \text{work done by applied forces}).$$

II. Equipollence.

(a) Conditions of equipollence:

(10.805) $$\mathbf{F} = \mathbf{F}', \quad \mathbf{G} = \mathbf{G}'.$$

(b) Any system of forces can be reduced to a force $\mathbf{F}$ at an assigned point, together with a couple $\mathbf{G}$. If $\mathbf{G} = p\mathbf{F}$, the reduced system is a wrench.

III. Displacements of a rigid body.

(a) Finite displacements:
  (i) Any displacement of a rigid body with a fixed point is equivalent to a rotation $\mathbf{n}$ (Euler's theorem).

302   MECHANICS IN SPACE   [Ex. X

    (ii) A general displacement is equivalent to a translation **s**, followed by rotation **n**.

 (b) Infinitesimal displacements:

    (i) Infinitesimal rotations compound vectorially. The order of application is immaterial.

    (ii) For a rigid body with a fixed point, the displacement of a particle of the body is

(10.806) $$\delta \mathbf{n} \times \mathbf{r}.$$

    (iii) In general, the displacement of a particle of the body is

(10.807) $$\delta \mathbf{s} + \delta \mathbf{n} \times \mathbf{r}.$$

IV. Work and potential energy.

 (a) Work done on a particle:

(10.808) $$\delta W = \mathbf{P} \cdot \delta \mathbf{s} = X\,\delta x + Y\,\delta y + Z\,\delta z.$$

 (b) Work done on a rigid body:

(10.809) $$\delta W = \mathbf{F} \cdot \delta \mathbf{s} + \mathbf{G} \cdot \delta \mathbf{n}.$$

 (c) Work done on a general system:

(10.810) $$\delta W = Q_1\,\delta q_1 + Q_2\,\delta q_2 + \cdots + Q_n\,\delta q_n.$$

 (d) Work done on a conservative system:

(10.811) $$\delta W = -\delta V = -\sum_{r=1}^{n} \frac{\partial V}{\partial q_r}\,\delta q_r.$$

EXERCISES X

1. A force with components $(-7, 4, -5)$ acts at the point $(2, 4, -3)$. Find its moment about the origin. Find also its moment about the line

$$x = y = z,$$

the positive sense on the line being that in which x increases.

2. A rigid body is acted on by a force with components $(1, 2, 3)$ at a point $(3, 2, 1)$ and by a force with components $(-1, -2, -3)$ at a point $(-3, -2, -1)$. Give the components of the equipollent force and couple at the origin.

3. A particle of weight w is placed on a rough plane inclined to the horizontal at an angle α. If the coefficient of friction is $2 \tan \alpha$, find the least horizontal force across the plane which will cause the particle to move. Determine the direction in which the particle moves.

4. A tripod consisting of three uniform rigid legs, each of length $2a$ and weight w, supports a camera of weight W, the legs being smoothly jointed together at the top. The tripod stands on a rough horizontal plane (coefficient of friction μ), the feet forming an equilateral triangle. Find an expression for the greatest length of a side of this triangle consistent with equilibrium.

5. Prove, by the principle of virtual work, that for an inextensible cable (either free or in contact with a smooth surface) $T - V = $ constant, where T is the tension and Vds the potential of the external force acting on an element ds of the cable.

6. A force with components $(3, 5, 6)$ acts at a point with coordinates $(1, 2, 3)$, and a force with components $(-8, -2, Z)$ acts at a point with coordinates $(4, 6, -7)$. If the pair of forces has no resultant moment about the x-axis, find Z.

7. Determine the pitch of the wrench equipollent to two forces of magnitudes P, Q, inclined to one another at an angle α, the shortest distance between their lines of action being c.

8. A square gate $ABCD$, of weight W and edge a, has hinges at B and C, the line BC being vertical with B on top. The hinge at C can support a downward thrust, but that at B merely supplies a vertical axis of rotation. The wind blows on the gate, exerting a uniform pressure p. The gate is kept in position by a light rope attached to the outer upper corner A and to a point E on the ground, where $CE = a$ and CE is a perpendicular to the gate. Find in terms of W, p, a the tension in the rope and the magnitude of the reaction at each of the hinges.

9. Three identical spheres lie in contact with one another on a horizontal plane. A fourth identical sphere rests on them, touching all three. Show that the coefficient of friction between the spheres is at least $(\sqrt{3} - \sqrt{2})$ and that the coefficient of friction between each sphere and the plane is at least $(\sqrt{3} - \sqrt{2})/4$.

10. Denoting by θ, ϕ the usual polar angles, find the polar angles of the axis of an infinitesimal rotation equivalent to three infinitesimal rotations, all of the same magnitude, with axes whose polar angles are

$(\theta = 60°, \phi = 45°)$, $(\theta = 120°, \phi = 135°)$, $(\theta = 60°, \phi = 225°)$.

11. A rigid body receives in succession three rotations about three mutually perpendicular intersecting lines fixed in space, each rotation being through a right angle and the senses being cyclic. Find the axis and magnitude of the single equivalent rotation.

12. A rigid body receives a finite translation and a finite rotation (through an angle θ) about an axis D perpendicular to the translation. Show that the resultant displacement is equivalent to a rotation (through an angle θ) about an axis parallel to D, the position of this axis depending on the order in which the translation and rotation are applied.

13. Show that any finite displacement of a rigid body is equivalent to a screw, i.e., a translation and a rotation about an axis parallel to the translation (Chasles' theorem).

14. In coming to rest on a slippery road, the wheel of a car travels 10 feet forward and 2 feet sideways, at the same time turning through an angle of 180° about its axle. Locate the axis of the equivalent screw displacement.

15. Show that, in general, a force system may be reduced to a force acting along any given line together with another force. (The lines of action of the two forces are said to be *conjugate*.)

16. A rigid body is acted on by a force **F** at O and a couple **G**. P is an assigned point, with position vector **r** relative to O. Show that there is a single infinity of lines through P about which the force system has no moment; show that these lines lie in a plane and find, in Cartesian coordinates, the equation of this plane. (The lines are called *null lines*, and the plane a *null plane*.)

17. Show that, if a rigid body is in equilibrium under the action of four forces, the invariant ($\mathbf{F} \cdot \mathbf{G}$) of any two is equal to the invariant ($\mathbf{F} \cdot \mathbf{G}$) of the other two. Show also that the invariant ($\mathbf{F} \cdot \mathbf{G}$) of any three of the forces is zero.

18. A heavy uniform inextensible cable hangs in contact with a smooth right-circular cone of semivertical angle α, the axis of the cone being vertical. Prove that the cable hangs in a curve satisfying the equation

$$\left(\frac{dz}{d\phi}\right)^2 + z^2 \sin^2 \alpha = z^4(A + Bz)^2,$$

where z is the depth below the vertex of the cone, ϕ is the azimuthal angle, and A, B are constants.

19. In a Hooke's joint (Fig. 119) force systems (**F**, **G**) and (**F**′, **G**′) (including the reaction of the bearings at A, A') act on the parts $ABCD$, $A'B'C'D'$, respectively, O being taken for base point. For equilibrium, show that couples **G**, **G**′ must both be perpendicular to the plane $CDC'D'$.

20. There are two identical rough stones, each being an oblate spheroid of semiaxes a, b ($a > b$). One is laid on a horizontal floor and the other balanced on top of it, the axes of symmetry being vertical. Confining attention to displacements in a vertical plane through the axis of symmetry, show that the equilibrium is stable if $a^2 > 3b^2$.

21. Discuss the stability of any four successive positions of equilibrium for the system shown in Fig. 120. Consider only the case where p is small in comparison with a and b.

22. A force system is equipollent to a force **F** at O and a couple **G**, another force system is equipollent to a force **F**′ at O and a couple **G**′. Prove that, if the axes of the equivalent wrenches intersect, then

$$\mathbf{F} \cdot \mathbf{G}' + \mathbf{F}' \cdot \mathbf{G} = (p + p')\mathbf{F} \cdot \mathbf{F}',$$

where p, p' are the pitches of the wrenches.

23. In a Hooke's joint (Fig. 119) let the angle θ, through which $ABCD$ is turned about AB, be measured from zero when CD lies in the plane of AB and $A'B'$. Denoting by α the angle between AB and $B'A'$, find the angles ϕ and ϕ' in terms of θ and α. Check your answers by considering the special cases: (i) $\theta = 0$, (ii) $\theta = \frac{1}{2}\pi$.

CHAPTER XI

KINEMATICS. KINETIC ENERGY AND ANGULAR MOMENTUM

We now approach the study of dynamics in space. We shall require

(i) a simple way of describing the motions of particles and of rigid bodies;

(ii) methods of calculating kinetic energy and angular momentum

These items belong to kinematics (if we understand the word to include mass as well as motion) and form the subject matter of the present chapter.

11.1. KINEMATICS OF A PARTICLE

Let $Oxyz$ be rectangular axes fixed in a frame of reference and $\mathbf{I}, \mathbf{J}, \mathbf{K}$ unit vectors along them. For any particle, with coordinates x, y, z, we define the following vectors (cf. Sec. 1.3):

$$(11.101) \begin{cases} \text{Position vector: } \mathbf{r} = x\mathbf{I} + y\mathbf{J} + z\mathbf{K}, \\ \text{Velocity: } \mathbf{q} = \dfrac{d\mathbf{r}}{dt} = \dot{x}\mathbf{I} + \dot{y}\mathbf{J} + \dot{z}\mathbf{K}, \\ \text{Acceleration: } \mathbf{f} = \dfrac{d\mathbf{q}}{dt} = \ddot{x}\mathbf{I} + \ddot{y}\mathbf{J} + \ddot{z}\mathbf{K} \end{cases}$$

The simplest way of describing the motion of a particle is to give the vector function $\mathbf{r}(t)$ For, when $\mathbf{r}$ is known as a vector function of the time t (i.e, when x, y, z are known as scalar functions of t), we can trace the path of the particle and find its velocity and acceleration at any instant by differentiation.

We frequently require expressions for the components of velocity and acceleration in directions other than $\mathbf{I}, \mathbf{J}, \mathbf{K}$. Two particular resolutions of these vectors will now be considered.

Tangential and normal components of velocity and acceleration.

Figure 122 shows the path C of a moving particle A; A_0 is a fixed point on C. The arc length AA_0 is denoted by s. From

(11.101), we see that the vector $d\mathbf{r}/ds$ has components dx/ds, dy/ds, dz/ds along $\mathbf{I}$, $\mathbf{J}$, $\mathbf{K}$; it is the unit tangent vector to C at A and will be denoted by $\mathbf{i}$.

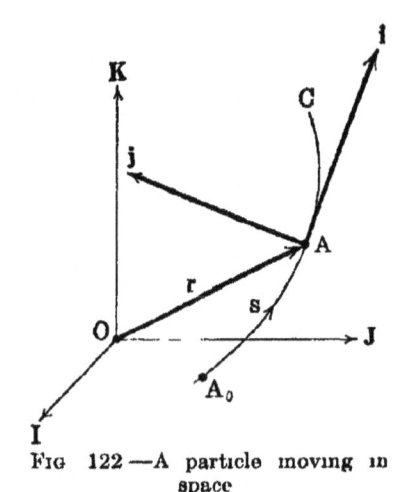

For the velocity of A we have

$$(11.102) \quad \mathbf{q} = \frac{d\mathbf{r}}{dt} = \frac{d\mathbf{r}}{ds}\frac{ds}{dt} = \dot{s}\mathbf{i}.$$

Hence, *the velocity of a particle is directed along the tangent to its path, and has magnitude $\dot{s}$.*

For the acceleration we have

$$\mathbf{f} = \frac{d\mathbf{q}}{dt} = \ddot{s}\mathbf{i} + \dot{s}\frac{d\mathbf{i}}{dt} = \ddot{s}\mathbf{i} + \dot{s}^2\frac{d\mathbf{i}}{ds}.$$

But, by (10.211),

$$\frac{d\mathbf{i}}{ds} = \frac{\mathbf{j}}{\rho},$$

Fig. 122.—A particle moving in space

where $\mathbf{j}$ is the unit principal normal vector and ρ the radius of curvature of C at A. Hence,

$$(11.103) \qquad \mathbf{f} = \ddot{s}\mathbf{i} + \frac{\dot{s}^2}{\rho}\mathbf{j},$$

and so we may state: *The acceleration of a particle lies in the osculating plane to its path; the components in the directions of the tangent and principal normal are $\ddot{s}$ and $\dot{s}^2/\rho$, respectively.* These results should be compared with those for the corresponding two-dimensional case (cf. Sec. 4.1).

Components of velocity and acceleration in cylindrical coordinates.

In Fig. 123, A is the position of a particle at time t and M the foot of the perpendicular from A on the plane Oxy. The polar coordinates (R, ϕ) of M, together with the z-coordinate of A, are the cylindrical coordinates (R, ϕ, z) of A. Let $\mathbf{i}, \mathbf{j}, \mathbf{k}$ be unit vectors at A in the directions of the parametric lines of these coordinates (i.e., those directions in each of which just one of the three coordinates R, ϕ, z increases, the other two remaining constant). We wish to find the components of the velocity and acceleration of A along $\mathbf{i}, \mathbf{j}, \mathbf{k}$.

Sec. 11.1] KINEMATICS 307

The vector **k** is constant in magnitude and direction. The directions of **i** and **j** do not depend on R and z; they are, however, dependent on ϕ. As in Sec. 4.1 (where r, θ correspond to R, ϕ), we have

(11.104) $$\frac{d\mathbf{i}}{d\phi} = \mathbf{j}, \qquad \frac{d\mathbf{j}}{d\phi} = -\mathbf{i}.$$

Since

$$\mathbf{r} = \overrightarrow{OA} = R\mathbf{i} + z\mathbf{k},$$

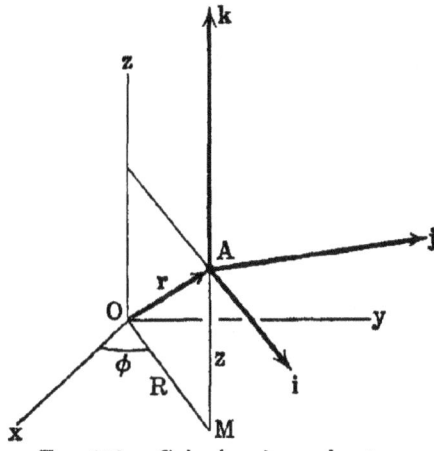

Fig 123.—Cylindrical coordinates

we obtain, on differentiating **r** with respect to t and using (11.104),

(11.105) $$\mathbf{q} = \frac{d\mathbf{r}}{dt} = \dot{R}\mathbf{i} + R\dot{\phi}\mathbf{j} + \dot{z}\mathbf{k}.$$

A second differentiation with respect to t gives

(11.106) $$\mathbf{f} = (\ddot{R} - R\dot{\phi}^2)\mathbf{i} + \frac{1}{R}\frac{d}{dt}(R^2\dot{\phi})\mathbf{j} + \ddot{z}\mathbf{k}.$$

From these equations, we can read off the components of the velocity (**q**) and the acceleration (**f**) in the directions of **i**, **j**, **k**, when required.

Composition of velocities and accelerations.

We often need to connect the velocities (or accelerations) of a particle relative to two different frames of reference, S and S'. We shall here think only of the case where there is no relative rotation of the frames. Let O be a point fixed in S and

O' a point fixed in S'. A particle A has position vectors $\mathbf{r} = \overrightarrow{OA}$ and $\mathbf{r}' = \overrightarrow{O'A}$; they are connected by

$$(11.107) \qquad \mathbf{r} = \mathbf{r}_0 + \mathbf{r}',$$

where $\mathbf{r}_0 = \overrightarrow{OO'}$. Differentiation gives

$$(11.108) \qquad \mathbf{q} = \mathbf{q}_0 + \mathbf{q}', \qquad \mathbf{f} = \mathbf{f}_0 + \mathbf{f}',$$

where $\mathbf{q}, \mathbf{f}$ = velocity and acceleration of A relative to S,
$\mathbf{q}', \mathbf{f}'$ = velocity and acceleration of A relative to S',
$\mathbf{q}_0, \mathbf{f}_0$ = velocity and acceleration of S' relative to S.

The equations (11.108) give the laws of composition of velocities and accelerations.

11.2. KINEMATICS OF A RIGID BODY

Motion of a rigid body with a fixed point.

Consider a rigid body constrained to rotate about a fixed point O. Let t_1, t_2 be two instants; in the time interval $t_2 - t_1$ the body receives a displacement which is equivalent (cf. Sec. 10.5) to a rotation $\mathbf{n}$ about O. If we keep t_1 fixed and let t_2 approach t_1, the direction of $\mathbf{n}$ will approach some limiting direction, which we denote by the unit vector $\mathbf{i}$. The ratio of the angle of rotation n to the time interval $t_2 - t_1$ will approach a limiting value ω. The vector $\boldsymbol{\omega} = \omega \mathbf{i}$ is called the *angular velocity* of the body at the instant t_1. At this instant the body is rotating about a line through O in the direction of $\boldsymbol{\omega}$; this line is called the *instantaneous axis of rotation*. The rate of turning is ω radians per unit time and is a rotation in the positive sense about the instantaneous axis.

In an infinitesimal time dt the body receives an infinitesimal rotation $\boldsymbol{\omega}\, dt$; and so the displacement of a particle of the body is, by (10.501),

$$d\mathbf{r} = \boldsymbol{\omega}\, dt \times \mathbf{r},$$

where $\mathbf{r}$ is the position vector relative to O. The velocity of this particle is

$$(11.201) \qquad \mathbf{q} = \frac{d\mathbf{r}}{dt} = \boldsymbol{\omega} \times \mathbf{r}.$$

This formula gives the velocity of any particle of the body in terms of the angular velocity vector $\boldsymbol{\omega}$. Thus, if $\boldsymbol{\omega}$ is known as

a vector function of the time, we can find the velocity of any particle at any time; in other words, the single vector function $\omega(t)$ suffices to describe the motion.

As the body turns about O, the instantaneous axis (determined by ω) will occupy different positions in the body. Since this axis always passes through O, its locus in the body is a cone with vertex O; it is called the *body cone* (or *polhode cone*). Similarly, the locus of the instantaneous axis in space is another cone with vertex O; it is called the *space cone* (or *herpolhode cone*).

A rigid body moving parallel to a fundamental plane may be regarded as a body turning about a point at infinity. In this case the body and space cones become cylinders; their intersections with the fundamental plane are the body and space centrodes of our earlier theory (cf. Sec. 4.2).

We saw in Sec. 4.2 that, in the motion of a rigid body parallel to a plane, the body centrode rolls on the space centrode. Similarly, in the motion of a rigid body with a fixed point, the body cone rolls on the space cone. To establish this result we must show that:

(i) the body cone touches the space cone;

(ii) the particles of the body on the line of contact of the cones are instantaneously at rest.

Let OA be the position of the instantaneous axis of rotation at some instant. It is a generator of the fixed space cone and also of the moving body cone. After an infinitesimal time dt, another generator OB of the body cone comes into coincidence with a generator OB' of the space cone. But the displacement in time dt is an infinitesimal rotation of magnitude $\omega\, dt$ about OA, and so the angle between the planes OAB, OAB' is an infinitesimal angle. Since these planes represent the tangent planes to the two cones along the generator OA, it follows that the tangent planes cannot cut at a finite angle; the cones must therefore touch. Since all particles of the body on the instantaneous axis OA are instantaneously at rest, the second of the above conditions is also satisfied, and the result is established.

The components of angular velocity in terms of the Eulerian angles.

In Sec. 10.6 we defined the Eulerian angles θ, ϕ, ψ; they describe (relative to a fixed triad $\mathbf{I}, \mathbf{J}, \mathbf{K}$) the position of a triad

of unit orthogonal vectors **i**, **j**, **k**, fixed in a rigid body turning about a point O (Fig. 118). The motion of the body is determined when θ, ϕ, ψ are known as functions of the time t; but this motion can also be described by the angular velocity $\omega(t)$. We write

$$\omega = \omega_1 \mathbf{i} + \omega_2 \mathbf{j} + \omega_3 \mathbf{k},$$

and seek expressions for ω_1, ω_2, ω_3 in terms of θ, ϕ, ψ, and their rates of change.

In an infinitesimal time dt the body receives the rotation $\omega \, dt$. But, by (10.607), this rotation is

$$(\sin \psi \, d\theta - \sin \theta \cos \psi \, d\phi)\mathbf{i} + (\cos \psi \, d\theta + \sin \theta \sin \psi \, d\phi)\mathbf{j} + (\cos \theta \, d\phi + d\psi)\mathbf{k},$$

where $d\theta$, $d\phi$, $d\psi$ are the infinitesimal increments in θ, ϕ, ψ in time dt. Equating this expression to $\omega \, dt$ and dividing by dt, we have

(11.202)
$$\begin{cases} \omega_1 = \sin \psi \, \dot\theta - \sin \theta \cos \psi \, \dot\phi, \\ \omega_2 = \cos \psi \, \dot\theta + \sin \theta \sin \psi \, \dot\phi, \\ \omega_3 = \cos \theta \, \dot\phi + \dot\psi. \end{cases}$$

These equations give the components of angular velocity when the motion is known, i.e., when θ, ϕ, ψ are known as functions of the time. Conversely, when the components of ω are known at any time t, we can solve the above equations for θ, ϕ, ψ as functions of t and so determine the motion.

Exercise. Find the components of ω on the fixed triad **I**, **J**, **K** (Fig. 118) in terms of θ, ϕ, ψ and their rates of change.

General motion of a rigid body.

Let us consider a rigid body moving in a general manner. We select a particle A of the body as a base point and denote its velocity by $\mathbf{q}_A$. In an infinitesimal time dt, the displacement of the body is equivalent to a translation $\mathbf{q}_A \, dt$, and a rotation $d\mathbf{n}$ about A (cf. Sec. 10.5). By (10.502), the displacement of any particle B of the body is

$$\mathbf{q}_A \, dt + d\mathbf{n} \times \mathbf{r},$$

where $\mathbf{r} = \overrightarrow{AB}$. Hence, for the velocity of B we have

(11.203)
$$\mathbf{q} = \mathbf{q}_A + \omega \times \mathbf{r},$$

where $\omega = d\mathbf{n}/dt$. We observe that this velocity consists of two parts: (i) the velocity $\mathbf{q}_A$ of the base point, and (ii) the velocity of B relative to A, viz., $\omega \times \mathbf{r}$. It is clear that the velocity of B relative to A is precisely the same as if the body were turning about A (as a fixed point) with angular velocity ω.

If we alter the base point A, the translation $\mathbf{q}_A\, dt$ is changed, but the rotation $d\mathbf{n}$ remains the same. It follows that the vector ω pertains to the motion of the body as a whole; it is the *angular velocity of the body* and is to be regarded as a free vector, since it does not depend on our choice of base point. The equation (11.203) gives the velocity of any point of the body when the angular velocity ω and the velocity $\mathbf{q}_A$ are known; thus, the two vectors ω and $\mathbf{q}_A$ completely describe the motion.

When ω and $\mathbf{q}_A$ are known as vector functions of the time, we have a picture of the motion at any instant. From the velocity $\mathbf{q}$ of any particle B, as given by (11.203), its acceleration $\mathbf{f}$ can be found by differentiation; thus,

$$\mathbf{f} = \frac{d\mathbf{q}_A}{dt} + \frac{d\omega}{dt} \times \mathbf{r} + \omega \times \frac{d\mathbf{r}}{dt}.$$

Here $d\mathbf{q}_A/dt$ is the acceleration $\mathbf{f}_A$ of the base point A; it depends solely on the motion of A and not on the angular velocity. As for the last term, $d\mathbf{r}/dt$ is the velocity of B relative to A; therefore, by (11.201), it equals $\omega \times \mathbf{r}$. We have then

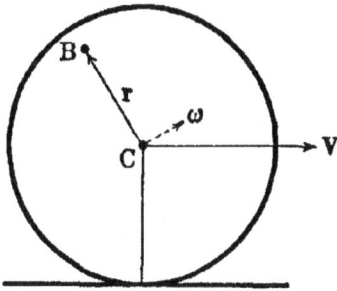

Fig. 124.—A wheel rolling on a straight track.

(11.204) $\qquad \mathbf{f} = \mathbf{f}_A + \dfrac{d\omega}{dt} \times \mathbf{r} + \omega \times (\omega \times \mathbf{r}).$

Example 1. As a simple illustration, let us consider a circular wheel rolling with constant speed along a straight level track (Fig. 124). We take as base point the center C of the wheel and denote its velocity by $\mathbf{V}$. This vector is constant, it lies in the plane of the wheel and is horizontal. The angular velocity ω of the wheel is a vector perpendicular to its plane; it also is a constant vector. By (11.203), a particle B of the wheel has velocity

$$\mathbf{V} + \omega \times \mathbf{r},$$

where $\mathbf{r} = \overrightarrow{CB}$. Since $\omega \times \mathbf{r}$ is a vector perpendicular to ω, this velocity lies in the plane of the wheel—a fact which is intuitively obvious. Since

312   MECHANICS IN SPACE   [Sec 11.2

ω and **V** are constant vectors, the acceleration of B is, by (11 204),

$$\mathbf{f} = \boldsymbol{\omega} \times (\boldsymbol{\omega} \times \mathbf{r}) = \boldsymbol{\omega}(\boldsymbol{\omega} \cdot \mathbf{r}) - \mathbf{r}\omega^2 = -\mathbf{r}\omega^2.$$

Thus, each particle of the wheel has an acceleration of magnitude $r\omega^2$, directed toward C.

Example 2 As a second illustration, let us consider the motion of the propeller of an airplane making a turn In particular, let us see how the velocity and acceleration of the tip of the propeller may be found

For simplicity, we shall suppose that the center O of the propeller describes a horizontal circle C with constant speed V, let b be the radius and A the center of C. Figure 125 shows the position of the propeller when the line from the center to the tip B makes an angle θ with the vertical.

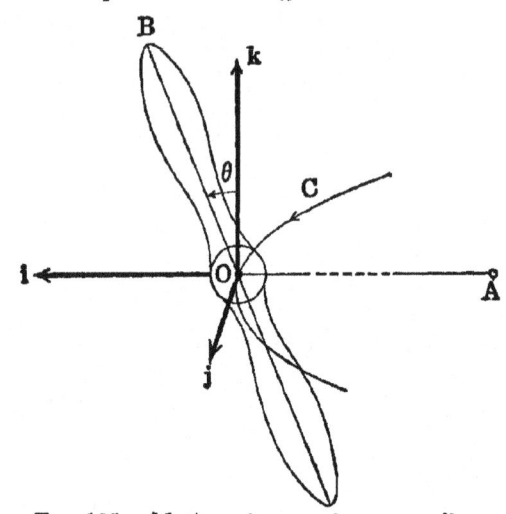

FIG. 125.—Motion of an airplane propeller

Let **i**, **j**, **k** be a triad of unit orthogonal vectors at O; **i** points along AO, **k** points vertically upward, and **j** completes the triad The vector **j** is clearly the unit tangent vector to C at O As a base point for the description of the motion, we take the point O; its velocity is $V\mathbf{j}$. The angular velocity ω of the propeller consists of two parts:

(i) an angular velocity or spin $s\mathbf{j}$ (where $s = \dot\theta$), imparted by the engine,

(ii) an angular velocity $(V/b)\mathbf{k}$, due to the turning of the airplane.

Hence,

$$\boldsymbol{\omega} = s\mathbf{j} + \frac{V}{b}\mathbf{k}.$$

The second part of ω arises from the fact that, in time $2\pi b/V$, the airplane (and the axis of the propeller) would turn through an angle 2π about the vertical

From (11.203), we have, for the velocity of any point of the propeller (position vector **r** relative to O),

$$\mathbf{q} = V\mathbf{j} + \boldsymbol{\omega} \times \mathbf{r}.$$

In particular, the velocity of B is

$$(11.205) \quad \mathbf{q}_B = V\mathbf{j} + \left(s\mathbf{j} + \frac{V}{b}\mathbf{k}\right) \times (a \sin\theta\, \mathbf{i} + a \cos\theta\, \mathbf{k})$$

$$= v \cos\theta\, \mathbf{i} + \left(1 + \frac{a}{b}\sin\theta\right) V\mathbf{j} - v \sin\theta\, \mathbf{k},$$

where $a = OB$ and $v = sa$, the speed of the tip relative to the airplane. Hence the absolute speed is given by

$$q_B^2 = v^2 + V^2 \left(1 + \frac{a}{b}\sin\theta\right)^2.$$

Actually, a/b will be small, and so $q_B^2 = v^2 + V^2$, approximately. If the trigonometrical term is retained, q_B takes maximum and minimum values when the propeller is horizontal.

The acceleration of B may be found by differentiating (11.205). We shall assume that s is constant, then the scalars v, V, b and the vector $\mathbf{k}$ are constant, whereas the scalar θ and the vectors $\mathbf{i}$ and $\mathbf{j}$ are variable. To find $d\mathbf{i}/dt$ and $d\mathbf{j}/dt$, we note that $\mathbf{i}$ and $\mathbf{j}$ may be regarded as the position vectors of points fixed in a body, turning about O with angular velocity $(V/b)\mathbf{k}$. Hence, by (11.201),

$$\frac{d\mathbf{i}}{dt} = \frac{V}{b}\mathbf{k} \times \mathbf{i} = \frac{V}{b}\mathbf{j}, \qquad \frac{d\mathbf{j}}{dt} = \frac{V}{b}\mathbf{k} \times \mathbf{j} = -\frac{V}{b}\mathbf{i}$$

It is left for the reader to verify that the acceleration of B is

$$(11.206) \quad \mathbf{f}_B = -\left(\frac{v^2}{a}\sin\theta + \frac{V^2}{b} + \frac{V^2 a}{b^2}\sin\theta\right)\mathbf{i} + \frac{2vV}{b}\cos\theta\, \mathbf{j} - \frac{v^2}{a}\cos\theta\, \mathbf{k}.$$

Under normal circumstances, the terms in v^2/a far exceed the other terms in magnitude, and so the acceleration is due almost entirely to the spin of the propeller.

11.3. MOMENTS AND PRODUCTS OF INERTIA

The *moment of inertia* of a system was defined in Sec. 7.1. For a particle of mass m distant p from a line L, the moment of inertia about L is mp^2. For a system of particles, the moment of inertia is the sum of the moments of inertia of the several particles.

We now define *products of inertia*. Let P, Q be two planes, and let p, q denote the perpendicular distances from them of a particle of mass m. The distance is counted positive or negative according as the particle lies on one side or the other of the corresponding plane. The product mpq is called the product of inertia of the particle with respect to the planes P, Q. For a system of particles, the product of inertia is the sum of the products of inertia of the several particles.

Let $Oxyz$ be rectangular axes; the moments of inertia of a system of particles about the axes Ox, Oy, Oz are, respectively,

(11.301) $\quad A = \Sigma m(y^2 + z^2), \quad B = \Sigma m(z^2 + x^2),$
$$C = \Sigma m(x^2 + y^2).$$

Here m is the mass of a typical particle, x, y, z are its coordinates, and the summation extends over all particles of the system. The products of inertia with respect to the coordinate planes, taken in pairs, are

(11.302) $\quad F = \Sigma myz, \quad G = \Sigma mzx, \quad H = \Sigma mxy.$

For a continuous distribution of matter the summations are replaced by integrations, the mass m being replaced by the mass $\rho d\tau$ (ρ = density) of a small volume element $d\tau$.

It is a remarkable fact that, when A, B, C, F, G, H are known, we can find the moment of inertia I of the system about *any* line through O. To see this, we recall that, by definition,

$$I = \Sigma mp^2,$$

where p is the perpendicular distance of a typical particle P (mass m) from the line L (Fig. 126). Now $p = OP \sin \theta$, where θ is the angle between OP and L; thus, p equals the magnitude of the vector product $\lambda \times \mathbf{r}$, where λ is a unit vector along L and $\mathbf{r} = \overrightarrow{OP}$. The components of λ are the direction cosines α, β, γ of L, and the components of $\mathbf{r}$ are the coordinates x, y, z of P. Hence, the components of $\lambda \times \mathbf{r}$ are

$$\beta z - \gamma y, \quad \gamma x - \alpha z, \quad \alpha y - \beta x.$$

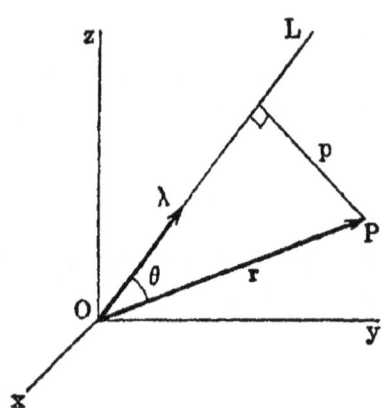

Fig. 126.—The moment of inertia about the line L is required.

Thus, since p is the magnitude of the vector with these components, we have

(11.303) $\quad I = \Sigma m[(\beta z - \gamma y)^2 + (\gamma x - \alpha z)^2 + (\alpha y - \beta x)^2]$
$\qquad = \alpha^2 \Sigma m(y^2 + z^2) + \beta^2 \Sigma m(z^2 + x^2) + \gamma^2 \Sigma m(x^2 + y^2)$
$\qquad \qquad - 2\beta\gamma \Sigma myz - 2\gamma\alpha \Sigma mzx - 2\alpha\beta \Sigma mxy$
$\qquad = A\alpha^2 + B\beta^2 + C\gamma^2 - 2F\beta\gamma - 2G\gamma\alpha - 2H\alpha\beta.$

This gives I in terms of A, B, C, F, G, H, and the direction cosines of L.

When A, B, C, F, G, H are known for any set of rectangular axes through the mass center, we can find the moment of inertia I of the system about any line L very easily. This is done in two steps:

(i) use (11.303) to find the moment of inertia I_0 about a line through the mass center parallel to L;

(ii) apply the theorem of parallel axes (cf. Sec. 7 1) to find I.

If A, B, C, F, G, H are known for a point other than the mass center, we can find I in a similar manner, but two applications of the theorem of parallel axes are required

The momental ellipsoid.

By varying α, β, γ in (11.303), we obtain the moments of inertia about all lines through O Let us measure off, along each line through O, a distance $OQ = 1/\sqrt{I}$, where I denotes the moment of inertia about the line in question. The locus of Q has the equation

(11.304) $\quad Ax^2 + By^2 + Cz^2 - 2Fyz - 2Gzx - 2Hxy = 1.$

This is the equation of a quadric surface with center O; in general, it is a closed surface, since I does not vanish for any line.* Hence, (11 304) is the equation of an ellipsoid; it is called the *momental ellipsoid* at O.

When the equation of the momental ellipsoid at a point is known, we find the moments and products of inertia with respect to the axes of coordinates by inspecting the coefficients in this equation. Under a rotation of axes from $Oxyz$ to $Ox'y'z'$, the equation of the momental ellipsoid changes from (11.304) to

$$A'x'^2 + B'y'^2 + C'z'^2 - 2F'y'z' - 2G'z'x' - 2H'x'y' = 1.$$

The coefficients A', B', C', F', G', H' give the moments and products of inertia for the new axes.

The quadric represented by the equation (11.304) sums up the inertial properties of the system with respect to axes through the origin. The form of the equation changes (in the sense that the values of the coefficients change) when we rotate the

---

* There is only one exceptional case. If all particles of the system lie on a line L, then $I = 0$ for L; the quadric is then a circular cylinder with axis L.

coordinate axes, but the quadric itself remains an invariant model of the inertial properties. The representation of physical properties by means of a quadric surface is of frequent occurrence—it is used in elasticity, hydrodynamics, and other branches of applied mathematics. Since the coefficients in the equation of the quadric change when we change the axes, they cannot be called scalars, in the sense that mass is a scalar. Nor are they components of a vector. The whole set of six coefficients, or more precisely the array

$$(11.305) \quad \begin{matrix} A & -H & -G \\ -H & B & -F \\ -G & -F & C \end{matrix}$$

is called a *tensor*. This is the simplest example of the concept which has played such an important part in the theory of relativity

An array is also called a *matrix*. Just as we use a single letter to denote a vector (which may be regarded as a matrix with three elements), so we may denote a matrix by a single letter. The operations of algebra may be applied to matrices, yielding a compact and powerful notation in mechanics.*

Existence of principal axes and moments of inertia.

Equation (11.303) gives us the moment of inertia about any line L through O in terms of the direction cosines of L and the six coefficients shown in the array (11.305). We shall now show that the number of coefficients may be reduced from six to three by making a suitable choice of the axes $Oxyz$.

Let $Oxyz$ be any axes. Then I, as given by (11.303), attains its maximum value for some line L_1. Let this maximum be I_1. Let us take axes $Ox'y'z'$ such that Ox' coincides with L_1; we leave the directions of the other two axes unspecified for the present, except for the conditions that they shall be perpendicular to Ox' and to one another. Then, for any line L, the moment of inertia is

$$I = A'\alpha'^2 + B'\beta'^2 + C'\gamma'^2 - 2F'\beta'\gamma' - 2G'\gamma'\alpha' - 2H'\alpha'\beta',$$

---

* See R. A. Frazer, W. J. Duncan, and A. R. Collar, Elementary Matrices (Cambridge University Press, London, 1938).

SEC. 113]   KINEMATICS   317

where A', B', C', F', G', H', are the moments and products of inertia for the axes $Ox'y'z'$, and α', β', γ' are the direction cosines of L relative to $Ox'y'z'$. If we put $\alpha' = 1$, $\beta' = \gamma' = 0$, then L coincides with L_1, and so $A' = I_1$, the maximum moment of inertia.

We shall now show that the vanishing of G' and H' is a necessary consequence of the fact that I is a maximum for $\alpha' = 1$, $\beta' = \gamma' = 0$. Since $\alpha'^2 + \beta'^2 + \gamma'^2 = 1$, we can write

$$I - I_1 = -2\alpha'(G'\gamma' + H'\beta') + (B' - I_1)\beta'^2 \\ + (C' - I_1)\gamma'^2 - 2F'\beta'\gamma'.$$

If we take a line L near L_1, α' will be nearly unity and β', γ' will be small. If at least one of G', H' is different from zero, we can choose β', γ' (reversing one or both signs if necessary) so that $(G'\gamma' + H'\beta')$ is negative. But, since β' and γ' are small, the sign of the right-hand side of the above equation is determined by the first term. Therefore, $I - I_1$ may be made positive. But this is impossible since I_1 is the maximum of I. Therefore the hypothesis we made about G' and H' is false, and we conclude that $G' = H' = 0$, so that for any line L,

$$I = I_1\alpha'^2 + B'\beta'^2 + C'\gamma'^2 - 2F'\beta'\gamma'.$$

This is true for all axes $Ox'y'z'$ such that Ox' coincides with L_1. Let us now subject Oy' to the condition that, of all lines perpendicular to Ox', Oy' has the maximum moment of inertia, say I_2. Then we have $B' = I_2$, and so for any line L,

$$I = I_1\alpha'^2 + I_2\beta'^2 + C'\gamma'^2 - 2F'\beta'\gamma'.$$

For lines L perpendicular to Ox' we have $\alpha' = 0$, $\beta'^2 + \gamma'^2 = 1$, and so

$$I - I_2 = -2F'\beta'\gamma' + (C' - I_2)\gamma'^2.$$

If we take a line near Oy', β' will be nearly unity and γ' will be small. It is evident that, if F' does not vanish, we can make I greater than I_2, which is impossible since I_2 is a maximum.

Therefore $F' = 0$, and we have for any line L,

$$I = I_1\alpha'^2 + I_2\beta'^2 + C'\gamma'^2.$$

Substituting $\gamma'^2 = 1 - \alpha'^2 - \beta'^2$, we get

$$I - C' = (I_1 - C')\alpha'^2 + (I_2 - C')\beta'^2 \geqq 0,$$

and so the third moment of inertia C' is the least of all moments of inertia for lines through O.

We may sum up as follows, simplifying the notation: *It is always possible to choose rectangular axes $Oxyz$ such that the moment of inertia I of a system about a line L through O is given by*

(11.306) $$I = A\alpha^2 + B\beta^2 + C\gamma^2,$$

where α, β, γ are the direction cosines of L relative to $Oxyz$. These axes are called *principal axes of inertia at O*, and the moments of inertia A, B, C about them are called *principal moments of inertia*. The planes defined by the principal axes are called *principal planes;* for any pair of principal planes, the product of inertia vanishes since F, G, and H are absent from (11.306). For principal axes, the equation of the momental ellipsoid is

(11.307) $$Ax^2 + By^2 + Cz^2 = 1.$$

Exercise. Find principal axes of inertia for a thin straight uniform rod at its middle point.

General method of finding principal axes and moments of inertia.

The principal axes and moments of inertia have been shown to exist. We shall now show how to find them, starting from general axes $Oxyz$ with moments and products of inertia A, B, C, F, G, H. Let $Ox'y'z'$ be the principal axes and A', B', C' the principal moments of inertia. Any point P has two sets of coordinates, (x, y, z) and (x', y', z'), according to the axes which are used. One set of coordinates are linear functions of the other, such that

$$x^2 + y^2 + z^2 = x'^2 + y'^2 + z'^2$$

for every point P. Also, for every point P, we have

$$Ax^2 + By^2 + Cz^2 - 2Fyz - 2Gzx - 2Hxy = A'x'^2 + B'y'^2 + C'z'^2,$$

since each side represents the moment of inertia about OP, multiplied by OP^2. Therefore, no matter how the constant K is chosen, we have the identity

$$Ax^2 + By^2 + Cz^2 - 2Fyz - 2Gzx - 2Hxy - K(x^2 + y^2 + z^2) = A'x'^2 + B'y'^2 + C'z'^2 - K(x'^2 + y'^2 + z'^2).$$

Let us denote each side of this identity by Φ. Consider the

equations

(11.308) $\quad \dfrac{\partial \Phi}{\partial x'} = 0, \quad \dfrac{\partial \Phi}{\partial y'} = 0, \quad \dfrac{\partial \Phi}{\partial z'} = 0.$

Explicitly, these equations read

$$(A' - K)x' = 0, \quad (B' - K)y' = 0, \quad (C' - K)z' = 0.$$

Rejecting the trivial solution $x' = y' = z' = 0$, we must choose K equal to A', B', or C'. We have then the following three solutions·

$$K = A', x' \text{ arbitrary}, y' = 0, z' = 0;$$
$$K = B', x' = 0, y' \text{ arbitrary}, z' = 0;$$
$$K = C', x' = 0, y' = 0, z' \text{ arbitrary}.$$

Thus (11.308) have nontrivial solutions provided K is equal to one of the principal moments of inertia; the corresponding values of x', y', z' give the principal axes

Now

$$\frac{\partial \Phi}{\partial x} = \frac{\partial \Phi}{\partial x'}\frac{\partial x'}{\partial x} + \frac{\partial \Phi}{\partial y'}\frac{\partial y'}{\partial x} + \frac{\partial \Phi}{\partial z'}\frac{\partial z'}{\partial x},$$

and similar equations could be written for $\partial \Phi / \partial y$ and $\partial \Phi / \partial z$. Therefore, (11.308) imply that

(11.309) $\quad \dfrac{\partial \Phi}{\partial x} = 0, \quad \dfrac{\partial \Phi}{\partial y} = 0, \quad \dfrac{\partial \Phi}{\partial z} = 0.$

If K, x', y', z' are chosen as above, (11.308) are satisfied, and therefore (11.309) are satisfied. Explicitly, (11.309) read

(11.310) $\quad \begin{cases} (A - K)x - Hy - Gz = 0, \\ -Hx + (B - K)y - Fz = 0, \\ -Gx - Fy + (C - K)z = 0. \end{cases}$

Since these equations have a solution other than $x = y = z = 0$, it follows that

(11.311) $\quad \begin{vmatrix} A - K & -H & -G \\ -H & B - K & -F \\ -G & -F & C - K \end{vmatrix} = 0.$

This is a cubic equation for K, and, as we have seen, its three roots are the three principal moments of inertia To sum up:

Starting with general axes Oxyz with moments and products of inertia A, B, C, F, G, H, the three principal moments of inertia at O are the values of K satisfying the cubic determinantal equation (11.311), and the directions of the three principal axes are given by the ratios $x:y:z$ determined by (11.310) when the above values of K are substituted.

The problem of finding principal axes and moments of inertia is essentially the same as the geometrical problem of finding the directions and magnitudes of the principal axes of an ellipsoid from its general equation.* The use of the equations (11.309) is most naturally suggested by the problem† of finding stationary values (including maximum and minimum values) of the expression

$$Ax^2 + By^2 + Cz^2 - 2Fyz - 2Gzx - 2Hxy,$$

subject to the condition $x^2 + y^2 + z^2 = 1$.

Method of symmetry.

For a body which exhibits symmetry, it is often possible to find principal axes of inertia very simply.

In Sec. 3.1 the idea of symmetry was used in connection with mass centers. A more thorough discussion requires the concept of a *covering operation*, which we now proceed to define.

If we rotate a body of revolution about its axis through any angle, we do not alter the distribution of matter—the whole body appears exactly as before. Similarly, if we turn a three-bladed propeller about its axis through an angle $2\pi/3$, the final distribution of matter is that with which we started. These rotations are examples of covering operations. In general, *a covering operation for a body is a transformation which does not alter the distribution of matter as a whole, although the individual particles are moved.* In the case of a curve or surface, where no distribution of matter is involved, a covering operation is a transformation which leaves the curve or surface unchanged as a whole. The covering operations which we shall consider are (i) a rotation about a line or axis, and (ii) a reflection in a plane.

---

* Cf. D. M. Y. Sommerville, Analytical Geometry of Three Dimensions (Cambridge University Press, 1934), Chap. VIII.

† Cf. R. Courant, Differential and Integral Calculus (Blackie & Sons, Ltd., Glasgow, 1936), Vol. II, pp. 188-191.

Whenever there exists a covering operation* for a body, the body is said to possess symmetry. If the covering operation is a rotation through an angle $2\pi/n$ about an axis (where n is a positive integer other than unity), this axis is called an *axis of n-gonal symmetry*; for $n = 2, 3, 4$ the symmetry is *digonal, trigonal, tetragonal*, respectively. Thus the axis of a three-bladed propeller is an axis of trigonal symmetry; for a two-bladed propeller the axis is of digonal symmetry. If the covering operation is a reflection in a plane, then that plane is a *plane of symmetry* for the body.

When we speak of an axis of symmetry, without qualification, we understand that a rotation through any arbitrary angle is a covering operation. A surface of revolution has this type of symmetry.

We now return to the problem of finding principal axes of inertia for a body possessing symmetry. In this connection we have the following theorem: *A covering operation for a body, which leaves a point O of the body unchanged, is a covering operation for the momental ellipsoid at O.* The proof of this theorem depends on the following facts, which hold for any distribution of matter whether symmetrical or not and are easily proved:

(i) when a body is rotated about a line, the momental ellipsoid at any point on the line turns with the body;

(ii) when a body is reflected in a plane, the momental ellipsoid at any point on the plane is also reflected in this plane.

When the rotation (or reflection) is a covering operation for the body, the distribution of matter is unaltered, and the momental ellipsoid at a point on the axis of rotation (or in the plane of reflection) is the same as before. The rotation (or reflection) is therefore a covering operation for the momental ellipsoid also, and so the theorem is proved.

Now we know from the geometry of the ellipsoid that, when the axes are unequal, there are only very special covering operations; these are (i) a rotation through an angle π about a principal axis and (ii) a reflection in a principal plane. If the ellipsoid has more general covering operations, it must necessarily be of revolution or, in particular, a sphere. Thus, for example, if a rotation through an angle $2\pi/3$ is a covering operation, the

---

* Other than a rotation through four right angles, this is a trivial operation, since it leaves every particle of the body back in its original position

ellipsoid must be of revolution. If a rotation through an angle π about a line L is a covering operation, then L must be a principal axis. If a reflection in a plane Π is a covering operation, then Π must be a principal plane.

We shall now apply these facts to the momental ellipsoid. The truth of the following statements will be obvious:

(i) An axis of n-gonal symmetry is a principal axis of inertia at any point of itself. (Example: a two-bladed propeller.)

(ii) At any point on an axis of trigonal or tetragonal symmetry, the momental ellipsoid has this axis for axis of revolution, and two of the principal moments of inertia are equal. (Example: a three- or four-bladed propeller.)

(iii) The normal to a plane of symmetry is a principal axis of inertia at the point where it cuts the plane of symmetry. (Example: the hull of a ship.)

Principal axes of inertia for a number of bodies are given in the table on page 324. In each case an argument, based on the ideas of symmetry, can be used to verify that the principal axes are given correctly.

The momental ellipse.

Let us now consider a distribution of matter in a plane Π, and let Ox, Oy be rectangular axes in this plane. Since Π is a plane of symmetry, its normal at O is a principal axis of inertia, and the section of the momental ellipsoid at O by the plane Π is a principal section; it is called the *momental ellipse* at O.

If A and B denote the moments of inertia about Ox, Oy, respectively, and H denotes the product of inertia with respect to planes through Ox, Oy, perpendicular to Π, the equation of this ellipse is

(11.312) $$Ax^2 - 2Hxy + By^2 = 1.$$

(We see this by introducing the third axis Oz and putting $z = 0$ in the equation of the momental ellipsoid.) It is clear that the principal axes of this ellipse are principal axes of inertia at O. To find them we proceed as follows.

Let Ox', Oy' be new axes at O, Ox' making an angle θ with Ox. If (x', y'), (x, y) denote the coordinates of a point referred to the axes $Ox'y'$, Oxy, respectively, then

$$x = x' \cos\theta - y' \sin\theta, \qquad y = x' \sin\theta + y' \cos\theta.$$

The equation of the ellipse (11.312) referred to the axes Ox', Oy' is

$$A(x' \cos \theta - y' \sin \theta)^2 \\ - 2H(x' \cos \theta - y' \sin \theta)(x' \sin \theta + y' \cos \theta) \\ + B(x' \sin \theta + y' \cos \theta)^2 = 1,$$

or, equivalently,

(11.313) $\qquad A'x'^2 - 2H'x'y' + B'y'^2 = 1,$

where

$$A' = A \cos^2 \theta - 2H \sin \theta \cos \theta + B \sin^2 \theta, \\ H' = (A - B) \sin \theta \cos \theta + H(\cos^2 \theta - \sin^2 \theta), \\ B' = A \sin^2 \theta + 2H \sin \theta \cos \theta + B \cos^2 \theta.$$

Now (11.313) represents the equation of an ellipse referred to principal axes at its center if $H' = 0$. Hence, Ox', Oy' are principal axes of inertia at O if

(11.314) $\qquad \tan 2\theta = \dfrac{2H}{B - A}.$

The two values of θ in the range $(0, \pi)$ satisfying this equation give the directions of the two principal axes. The complete set of principal axes at O are Ox', Oy', and a line perpendicular to them.

This method of finding principal axes of inertia at a point can be applied to any case where one principal axis at the point is known; it need not be restricted, as here, to the case of a plane distribution of matter. In particular, it applies to any body with a plane of symmetry or an axis of digonal symmetry.

Moments of inertia of some simple bodies.

The table on the following page gives the principal axes and moments of inertia at the mass center for some simple bodies. The moments of inertia about the axes Ox, Oy, Oz are denoted (as usual) by A, B, C, respectively. In all cases the bodies are homogeneous, i.e., of constant density.

Some of the moments of inertia given in the table have already been calculated in Sec. 7.1. We shall give the calculations for the ellipsoid and leave the reader to verify the others for himself.

The equation of an ellipsoid E with semiaxes a, b, c, referred to principal axes at its center, is

$$\frac{x^2}{a^2} + \frac{y^2}{b^2} + \frac{z^2}{c^2} = 1.$$

The moment of inertia about the x-axis is given by

$$\frac{A}{\rho} = \iiint\limits_{(E)} (y^2 + z^2)\, dx\, dy\, dz,$$

Body (mass = m)	Principal axes (at mass center O)	Principal moments of inertia
Rectangular plate (edges $2a$, $2b$).	Ox, Oy parallel to edges $2a$, $2b$, respectively, Oz perpendicular to plate.	$A = \frac{1}{3}mb^2$, $B = \frac{1}{3}ma^2$, $C = \frac{1}{3}m(a^2 + b^2)$
Solid rectangular cuboid (edges $2a$, $2b$, $2c$).	Ox, Oy, Oz parallel to edges $2a$, $2b$, $2c$, respectively	$A = \frac{1}{3}m(b^2 + c^2)$, $B = \frac{1}{3}m(c^2 + a^2)$, $C = \frac{1}{3}m(a^2 + b^2)$.
Circular plate (radius a)	Ox, Oy in plane of plate, Oz perpendicular to plate	$A = B = \frac{1}{4}ma^2$, $C = \frac{1}{2}ma^2$
Elliptical plate (semi-axes a, b).	Ox, Oy along semiaxes a, b, respectively, Oz perpendicular to plate.	$A = \frac{1}{4}mb^2$, $B = \frac{1}{4}ma^2$, $C = \frac{1}{4}m(a^2 + b^2)$.
Solid circular cylinder (radius a, length $2l$).	Ox, Oy perpendicular to axis; Oz along axis.	$A = B = \frac{1}{12}m(3a^2 + 4l^2)$, $C = \frac{1}{2}ma^2$
Solid elliptical cylinder (semiaxes a, b, length $2l$)	Ox, Oy along semiaxes a, b of section, respectively; Oz along axis of cylinder.	$A = \frac{1}{12}m(3b^2 + 4l^2)$, $B = \frac{1}{12}m(3a^2 + 4l^2)$, $C = \frac{1}{4}m(a^2 + b^2)$.
Sphere (radius a).	Ox, Oy, Oz any three perpendicular lines	$A = B = C = \frac{2}{5}ma^2$.
Solid ellipsoid (semiaxes a, b, c)	Ox, Oy, Oz along semiaxes a, b, c, respectively.	$A = \frac{1}{5}m(b^2 + c^2)$, $B = \frac{1}{5}m(c^2 + a^2)$, $C = \frac{1}{5}m(a^2 + b^2)$

where ρ is the density and the integration extends throughout the ellipsoid E. We put $x' = x/a$, $y' = y/b$, $z' = z/c$ and obtain

$$\frac{A}{\rho} = \iiint\limits_{(S)} (b^2 y'^2 + c^2 z'^2) abc\, dx'\, dy'\, dz',$$

where the range of integration is now the interior of a unit sphere S. From the symmetry of S,

$$\iiint\limits_{(S)} y'^2\, dx'\, dy'\, dz' = \iiint\limits_{(S)} z'^2\, dx'\, dy'\, dz'$$
$$= \tfrac{1}{2} \iiint\limits_{(S)} (y'^2 + z'^2)\, dx'\, dy'\, dz'.$$

But this last integral has already been calculated in Sec. 7.1; it is the moment of inertia of a sphere (of unit radius and density) about a diameter and has the value $8\pi/15$. Hence,

$$A = \frac{4\pi \rho abc}{15}(b^2 + c^2) = \tfrac{1}{5}m(b^2 + c^2),$$

as given in the table. The values for B and C follow in exactly the same way.

The following rule, known as *Routh's rule*, summarizes most of the results given in the table on page 324: *For solid bodies of the cuboid, elliptical cylindrical, and ellipsoidal types, the moment of inertia about a principal axis through the center (and parallel to the generators, in the case of the elliptical cylinder) is equal to*

$$\frac{m(a^2 + b^2)}{n},$$

where m is the mass of the body, a, b are the semiaxes perpendicular to the principal axis in question, and $n = 3$, 4, or 5 according as the body belongs to the cuboid, elliptical cylindrical, or ellipsoidal type.

The methods of decomposition and differentiation.

If we wish to calculate a moment of inertia, we can always do so by evaluating a multiple integral. But in many cases there are simpler methods. One method is to divide the body into a number of parts, for each of which the moment of inertia is known; by adding the moments of inertia of these parts, we obtain the required result. This is the *method of decomposition* and has been used already in Sec. 7.1.

Another method, known as the *method of differentiation*, can

be used to find the moment of inertia of a shell when the corresponding moment of inertia for a similar solid is known.

As an example, let us find the moment of inertia of a spherical shell about a diameter. We first consider a uniform solid sphere of density ρ and radius r. Its moment of inertia about a diameter is $(8\pi/15)\rho r^5$. If the radius of this sphere is increased to $r + dr$, the moment of inertia is increased by

$$dI = (8\pi/3)\rho r^4\, dr;$$

this is the moment of inertia of a spherical shell of radius r, thickness dr, and mass $4\pi\rho r^2\, dr$. Hence the moment of inertia of a spherical shell, of radius a and mass m, about a diameter is $\tfrac{2}{3}ma^2$.

Similarly, by considering the ellipsoid

$$\frac{x^2}{k^2 a^2} + \frac{y^2}{k^2 b^2} + \frac{z^2}{k^2 c^2} = 1$$

and increasing k to $k + dk$, we can find the principal moments of inertia at the center of a thin shell bounded by two such ellipsoids. The reader will have no difficulty in showing that, for $k = 1$, the results are

$$\tfrac{1}{3}m(b^2 + c^2),\ \tfrac{1}{3}m(c^2 + a^2),\ \tfrac{1}{3}m(a^2 + b^2),$$

where m is the mass of the shell.

Equimomental systems.

Two distributions of matter which have the same total mass and the same principal moments of inertia at the mass center are said to be *equimomental systems*. For example, a hoop of mass m and radius $a/\sqrt{2}$ is equimomental with a circular plate of mass m and radius a.

Such systems are interesting on account of the following fact: Two rigid bodies which are equimomental have the same dynamical behavior. By this we mean that two such bodies, when acted on by identical force systems, will behave in the same way; if the bodies were fixed inside two identical boxes, we should not be able to distinguish between them. This result will be evident when we have developed the general principles of dynamics in Chap. XII.

11.4. KINETIC ENERGY

The kinetic energy of a rigid body with a fixed point.

Consider a rigid body turning about a fixed point O with angular velocity ω. A particle P of this body, with velocity $\mathbf{q}$ and mass δm, has kinetic energy $\frac{1}{2}\delta m \cdot q^2$ (cf. Sec. 5.1); the kinetic energy of the body is

$$(11.401) \qquad T = \tfrac{1}{2}\Sigma\, \delta m \cdot q^2,$$

where the summation extends over all particles of the body. We seek an alternative expression for T, involving the angular velocity ω and the principal moments of inertia at O.

Let $Oxyz$ be any rectangular axes at O, and $\mathbf{i}, \mathbf{j}, \mathbf{k}$ unit vectors along them. Resolving vectors in the directions of these axes, we write

$$\mathbf{r} = x\mathbf{i} + y\mathbf{j} + z\mathbf{k}, \qquad \boldsymbol{\omega} = \omega_1\mathbf{i} + \omega_2\mathbf{j} + \omega_3\mathbf{k},$$

where $\mathbf{r} = \overrightarrow{OP}$. For the velocity $\mathbf{q}$ of P, we have, by (11.201),

$$(11.402)\quad \mathbf{q} = \boldsymbol{\omega} \times \mathbf{r}$$
$$= (\omega_2 z - \omega_3 y)\mathbf{i} + (\omega_3 x - \omega_1 z)\mathbf{j} + (\omega_1 y - \omega_2 x)\mathbf{k}.$$

Hence, by substitution from (11.402) in (11.401), we obtain

$$2T = \Sigma\, \delta m \cdot [(\omega_2 z - \omega_3 y)^2 + (\omega_3 x - \omega_1 z)^2 + (\omega_1 y - \omega_2 x)^2]$$
$$= \omega_1^2 \Sigma\, \delta m \cdot (y^2 + z^2) + \omega_2^2 \Sigma\, \delta m \cdot (z^2 + x^2) + \omega_3^2 \Sigma\, \delta m \cdot (x^2 + y^2)$$
$$- 2\omega_2\omega_3 \Sigma\, \delta m \cdot yz - 2\omega_3\omega_1 \Sigma \delta m\; zx - 2\omega_1\omega_2 \Sigma \delta m \cdot xy,$$

or

$$(11.403) \quad T = \tfrac{1}{2}(A\omega_1^2 + B\omega_2^2 + C\omega_3^2 - 2F\omega_2\omega_3 - 2G\omega_3\omega_1 - 2H\omega_1\omega_2),$$

where A, B, C, F, G, H are the moments and products of inertia for $Oxyz$. If the axes are principal axes of inertia, then

$$F = G = H = 0,$$

and we obtain, as the required expression for the kinetic energy,

$$(11.404) \qquad T = \tfrac{1}{2}(A\omega_1^2 + B\omega_2^2 + C\omega_3^2),$$

where A, B, C are now principal moments of inertia.

The expression (11.404) is valid only when the axes $Oxyz$ are principal axes of inertia at O; for other axes, it is evident

from (11.403) that T involves both products and moments of inertia. If we use axes with directions fixed in space, not only will T involve both products and moments of inertia—worse still, these will vary with the time. To avoid these complications, it is customary to use axes which are permanently principal axes of inertia at O, so that the simple formula (11.404) holds at any time and A, B, C are constants.

In general the principal axes at O are fixed in the body. But if the momental ellipsoid at O is of revolution, only one of them need be so fixed; the other two may be any perpendicular lines in the plane perpendicular to the axis of revolution. It might appear that the use of such axes, fixed neither in space nor in the body, would introduce a needless complication But actually it simplifies considerably the theory of tops and gyroscopes.

For a rigid body turning about a fixed line L through O, it is easily seen that the formula (11.403) simplifies to the formula (7.116), given in the two-dimensional theory. We have merely to take Oz along L; then $\omega_1 = \omega_2 = 0$. $\omega_3 = \omega$, and (11 403) gives

$$T = \tfrac{1}{2}C\omega^2,$$

where C is the moment of inertia about L.

The kinetic energy of a rigid body in general.

Let us now find the kinetic energy T of a rigid body moving quite generally in space. Applying the theorem of Konig (cf. Sec. 7.1), we have

(11.405) $$T = \tfrac{1}{2}mq_0^2 + T'',$$

where m = mass of body,
q_0 = speed of mass center,
T' = kinetic energy of motion relative to mass center.

But the mass center may be regarded as a base point in the body; and so, as explained in Sec. 11.2, the motion relative to the mass center is that of a rigid body turning about a fixed point. Thus, T' is given by (11.404) with a proper interpretation of the symbols. We therefore have

(11 406) $$T = \tfrac{1}{2}mq_0^2 + \tfrac{1}{2}(A\omega_1^2 + B\omega_2^2 + C\omega_3^2),$$

where A, B, C = principal moments of inertia at the mass center,
$\omega_1, \omega_2, \omega_3$ = components of the angular velocity ω in the directions of principal axes of inertia at the mass center.

In applying the principle of energy, proved in Sec. 5.2, to particular systems, we need expressions for kinetic energy. For a particle the kinetic energy is simply $\frac{1}{2}mq^2$; for a rigid body, we have the formulas (11.404) and (11.406). With the aid of these fundamental formulas, we find no difficulty in calculating the kinetic energy of any system.

11.5. ANGULAR MOMENTUM

The angular momentum of a particle about a line was defined in Sec. 5.1 as the moment of the linear momentum vector about the line in question. Now in dealing with moments of vectors in three dimensions, it is the *vector moment* about a point which is fundamental, rather than the *scalar moment* about a line. Accordingly, we define the angular momentum of a particle as a vector; the scalar angular momentum defined in Sec. 5.1 is, of course, merely one component of the vector defined here.

Angular momentum of a particle and of a system of particles.

Consider a particle of mass m, moving with velocity $\mathbf{q}$ relative to some frame of reference S. The linear momentum is $m\mathbf{q}$ (cf. Sec. 5.1). We define *the angular momentum* $\mathbf{h}$, *about any point* O, *as the moment of* $m\mathbf{q}$ *about* O, hence, by (9.301),

$$(11.501) \qquad \mathbf{h} = \mathbf{r} \times m\mathbf{q},$$

where $\mathbf{r}$ is the position vector of the particle relative to O. It is clear that $\mathbf{h}$ depends on the frame of reference used in the measurement of $\mathbf{q}$.

For a system of particles, the angular momentum is the vector sum of the angular momenta of the several particles. Let m_i, $\mathbf{r}_i$, $\mathbf{q}_i$ denote the mass, position vector (relative to a point O), and velocity of the ith particle, respectively. The angular momentum about O is

$$(11.502) \qquad \mathbf{h} = \sum_{i=1}^{n} (\mathbf{r}_i \times m_i \mathbf{q}_i),$$

where n is the number of particles in the system.

We note that, if O is fixed in the frame of reference, then $\mathbf{q}_i = \dot{\mathbf{r}}_i$. In that case the components of $\mathbf{h}$ along rectangular axes fixed in the frame are

$$(11.503) \quad \sum_{i=1}^n m_i(y_i\dot{z}_i - z_i\dot{y}_i), \quad \sum_{i=1}^n m_i(z_i\dot{x}_i - x_i\dot{z}_i),$$
$$\sum_{i=1}^n m_i(x_i\dot{y}_i - y_i\dot{x}_i).$$

Let us now consider the effect of changing the frame of reference. Let S' be a new frame, having a velocity $\mathbf{q}_0$ of translation relative to S. Then the velocities $\mathbf{q}_i$, $\mathbf{q}'_i$ of a particle relative to S, S', respectively, are connected by

$$(11.504) \quad \mathbf{q}_i = \mathbf{q}_0 + \mathbf{q}'_i,$$

according to (11.108). The angular momenta about O are then

$$\mathbf{h} = \sum_{i=1}^n (\mathbf{r}_i \times m_i\mathbf{q}_i) \text{ for } S; \quad \mathbf{h}' = \sum_{i=1}^n (\mathbf{r}_i \times m_i\mathbf{q}'_i) \text{ for } S'.$$

Substituting from (11.504) in the expression for $\mathbf{h}$, we find

$$(11.505) \quad \mathbf{h} = \left(\sum_{i=1}^n m_i\mathbf{r}_i\right) \times \mathbf{q}_0 + \mathbf{h}'.$$

If O is the mass center, $\sum_{i=1}^n m_i\mathbf{r}_i = \mathbf{0}$, and so the first term on the right vanishes. This gives the following remarkable result: *Angular momentum about the mass center is the same for all frames of reference in relative translational motion.* Generally it is most convenient to use a frame of reference in which the mass center is fixed.

In speaking of angular momentum about a point O, we shall in future always understand a frame of reference in which O is fixed.

Angular momentum of a rigid body.

The most interesting application of (11.502) is to the case of a rigid body turning about O. The formulas which we are about to develop are fundamental in gyroscopic theory.

In a slightly different notation, we have, for the angular momentum about O,

(11.506) $$\mathbf{h} = \Sigma(\mathbf{r} \times \delta m \cdot \mathbf{q}),$$

where δm is the mass of a typical particle, $\mathbf{r}$ its position vector, and $\mathbf{q}$ its velocity; the summation extends over all particles in the body. But, by (11.201),

$$\mathbf{q} = \boldsymbol{\omega} \times \mathbf{r},$$

where $\boldsymbol{\omega}$ is the angular velocity of the body. Hence,

(11.507) $$\mathbf{h} = \Sigma\, \delta m \cdot [\mathbf{r} \times (\boldsymbol{\omega} \times \mathbf{r})] = \Sigma\, \delta m \cdot [\boldsymbol{\omega} r^2 - \mathbf{r}(\boldsymbol{\omega} \cdot \mathbf{r})]$$

Let us resolve this vector along an orthogonal triad $\mathbf{i}, \mathbf{j}, \mathbf{k}$ at O. In the usual notation, we write

$$\mathbf{r} = x\mathbf{i} + y\mathbf{j} + z\mathbf{k}, \qquad \boldsymbol{\omega} = \omega_1 \mathbf{i} + \omega_2 \mathbf{j} + \omega_3 \mathbf{k}$$

and denote by A, B, C, F, G, H the moments and products of inertia with respect to the triad $\mathbf{i}, \mathbf{j}, \mathbf{k}$. The component of $\mathbf{h}$ in the direction of $\mathbf{i}$ is

$$\begin{aligned} h_1 &= \Sigma\, \delta m \cdot [\omega_1(x^2 + y^2 + z^2) - x(\omega_1 x + \omega_2 y + \omega_3 z)] \\ &= \omega_1 \Sigma\, \delta m\ (y^2 + z^2) - \omega_2 \Sigma\, \delta m \cdot xy - \omega_3 \Sigma\, \delta m\ zx \\ &= A\omega_1 - H\omega_2 - G\omega_3. \end{aligned}$$

Similar expressions for the components h_2 and h_3 are found in the same way; the complete set of components is

(11.508) $$\begin{cases} h_1 = A\omega_1 - H\omega_2 - G\omega_3, \\ h_2 = -H\omega_1 + B\omega_2 - F\omega_3, \\ h_3 = -G\omega_1 - F\omega_2 + C\omega_3 \end{cases}$$

The structure of these formulas should be compared with the array (11.305).

If $\mathbf{i}, \mathbf{j}, \mathbf{k}$ are principal axes of inertia at O, then $F = G = H = 0$, and these formulas are greatly simplified. They become

(11.509) $$h_1 = A\omega_1, \qquad h_2 = B\omega_2, \qquad h_3 = C\omega_3,$$

where A, B, C are now principal moments of inertia at O.

332   MECHANICS IN SPACE   [Sec 11.6

As in the case of kinetic energy, it is usual to choose the coordinate vectors **i**, **j**, **k** in directions which are permanently principal axes of inertia at O. With such a choice for these vectors, the simple formulas (11.509) hold at any time, and A, B, C are constants.

If the body is constrained to rotate about a fixed axis, we may take **k** along this axis. Then $\omega_1 = 0$, $\omega_2 = 0$, $\omega_3 = \omega$, and (11.508) gives

(11 510) $\qquad h_1 = -G\omega, \qquad h_2 = -F\omega, \qquad h_3 = C\omega.$

Thus the angular momentum vector does not lie along the axis of rotation, unless the latter is a principal axis of inertia. However, the component h_3 along the axis of rotation is equal to the product of the moment of inertia about that axis and the angular velocity. This is in agreement with (7 117).

11.6. SUMMARY OF KINEMATICS, KINETIC ENERGY, AND ANGULAR MOMENTUM

I. Kinematics of a particle.

Velocity:

(11.601) $\qquad \mathbf{q} = \dfrac{d\mathbf{r}}{dt} = s\mathbf{i}, \qquad (\mathbf{i} = \text{unit tangent vector}).$

Acceleration:

(11 602) $\qquad \mathbf{f} = \dfrac{d\mathbf{q}}{dt} = \ddot{s}\mathbf{i} + \dfrac{\dot{s}^2}{\rho}\mathbf{j}, \qquad (\mathbf{j} = \text{unit principal normal vector}).$

II. Kinematics of a rigid body.

(a) Rigid body with a fixed point:
Motion described by vector **ω**, velocity of any particle of the body is

(11.603) $\qquad \mathbf{q} = \boldsymbol{\omega} \times \mathbf{r}.$

(b) Rigid body in general motion:
Motion described by vectors $\mathbf{q}_A$, **ω**; velocity of any particle of the body is

(11.604) $\qquad \mathbf{q} = \mathbf{q}_A + \boldsymbol{\omega} \times \mathbf{r}.$

III. Moments and products of inertia.

(a) General formulas:

(11.605) $$\begin{cases} A = \Sigma m(y^2 + z^2), & B = \Sigma m(z^2 + x^2), \\ & C = \Sigma m(x^2 + y^2), \\ F = \Sigma myz, & G = \Sigma mzx, \quad H = \Sigma mxy; \end{cases}$$

(11.606) $I = A\alpha^2 + B\beta^2 + C\gamma^2 - 2F\beta\gamma - 2G\gamma\alpha - 2H\alpha\beta.$

(b) Momental ellipsoid ($r = 1/\sqrt{I}$):
General form:

(11.607) $Ax^2 + By^2 + Cz^2 - 2Fyz - 2Gzx - 2Hxy = 1.$

Form for principal axes:

(11.608) $$Ax^2 + By^2 + Cz^2 = 1$$

(A, B, C are principal moments of inertia, $F = G = H = 0$)

IV. Kinetic energy.

(a) Particle:

(11.609) $$T = \tfrac{1}{2} m q^2.$$

(b) Rigid body with a fixed point (principal axes):

(11.610) $$T = \tfrac{1}{2}(A\omega_1^2 + B\omega_2^2 + C\omega_3^2).$$

(c) Rigid body in general motion (principal axes at mass center):

(11.611) $$T = \tfrac{1}{2} m q_0^2 + \tfrac{1}{2}(A\omega_1^2 + B\omega_2^2 + C\omega_3^2).$$

V. Angular momentum.

(a) Particle:

(11.612) $$\mathbf{h} = \mathbf{r} \times m\mathbf{q}$$

(b) Rigid body turning about a point (principal axes):

(11.613) $$\mathbf{h} = A\omega_1 \mathbf{i} + B\omega_2 \mathbf{j} + C\omega_3 \mathbf{k}.$$

EXERCISES XI

1. What is the kinetic energy of a homogeneous circular cylinder, of mass m and radius a, rolling on a plane with linear velocity v?

2. For a certain orthogonal triad of axes at O the moments of inertia of a body are 3, 4, 5, and the products of inertia vanish. What is the greatest moment of inertia of the body about any line through O?

3. A rod, of length $2a$ and mass m, turns about one end O, describing a cone with semivertical angle α. It completes a revolution in time τ. Find the magnitude and direction of the angular momentum about O.

4. A rigid body is turning about a fixed point O, and $Oxyz$ are rectangular axes. If the components of velocity of the particle with coordinates $(1, 0, 0)$ are $(0, 2, 5)$, find the component in the direction of the x-axis of the velocity of the particle with coordinates $(0, 0, 1)$.

5. Find the length of a homogeneous solid circular cylinder of radius a, given that the momental ellipsoid at the mass center is a sphere.

6. A body turns about a fixed point. Prove that the angle between its angular velocity vector and its angular momentum vector (about the fixed point) is always acute. Show that, if the principal moments of inertia A, B, C are all different, then the angle vanishes only if the body is turning about a principal axis.

7. Find the moment of inertia of a solid homogeneous cube about an arbitrary line through its center.

What are the principal axes of inertia at a corner?

8. Find the moment of inertia of a rectangular plate 3 ft. by 4 ft., of mass 20 lb., about a diagonal.

9. Find the components of velocity and acceleration along the parametric lines of spherical polar coordinates r, θ, ϕ, for a particle moving in space.

Check your formulas by applying them to the following special cases.

(i) $\phi =$ constant;   (ii) $\theta = \tfrac{1}{2}\pi$

10. A car drives round a curve of constant curvature at constant speed. What is the magnitude and direction of the instantaneous acceleration of the highest point of a tire?

11. A uniform circular disk of radius a and mass m is rigidly mounted on one end of a thin light shaft CD, of length b. The shaft is normal to the disk at its center C. The disk rolls on a rough horizontal plane, D being fixed in this plane by a smooth universal joint. If the center of the disk rotates about the vertical through D with constant angular velocity n, find the angular velocity, the kinetic energy, and the angular momentum of the disk about D.

12. A car is turning a corner, the middle point of the back axle describing a circle of radius r. If the length of the axle is $2a$ and the wheels are regarded as uniform disks, each of radius b, prove that the ratio of the kinetic energies of the back wheels is

$$\frac{6(r+a)^2 + b^2}{6(r-a)^2 + b^2}.$$

13. An ellipsoid of revolution with fixed center rolls without slipping on a fixed plane. Describe the space and body cones.

14. A plane is fixed in space. Coordinate axes $Oxyz$ rotate about O. Their angular velocity has components $\omega_1, \omega_2, \omega_3$ along them. If the equation of the plane at any instant is

$$Ax + By + Cz = 1,$$

prove that

$$\frac{dA}{dt} = B\omega_3 - C\omega_2, \qquad \frac{dB}{dt} = C\omega_1 - A\omega_3, \qquad \frac{dC}{dt} = A\omega_2 - B\omega_1.$$

15. A governor consists of two equal spheres, of mass m and radius a. They are fixed to the ends of equal light rods, each of length $c - a$, which are hinged to a collar on a vertical axle. By means of a light linkage and sliding collar, the equality of the inclinations to the vertical of the two rods is ensured. If this angle of inclination is θ and the angular velocity of the governor about its vertical axle is ω, show that the kinetic energy is

$$A(\theta^2 + \omega^2 \sin^2 \theta) + C\omega^2 \cos^2 \theta,$$

where

$$A = m(\tfrac{2}{5}a^2 + c^2), \qquad C = \tfrac{2}{5}ma^2$$

16. Prove that the angular momentum of a moving system about a point O is the sum of the following parts:

(i) the angular momentum about O of a particle moving with the mass center and having a mass equal to the total mass of the system;
(ii) the angular momentum of the system about the mass center.

17. A steel ball is placed between two horizontal planes, which rotate with angular velocities ω, ω' about vertical axes L, L'. Assuming that no slipping takes place, show that the center of the ball describes a horizontal circle with center in the plane containing L and L'. Show that the distances of this center from L and L' are in the ratio $\omega' : \omega$.

18. For a rigid body in general motion, show that there is no point at rest. Show also that, in general, there is one point, and only one, with no acceleration.

19. For a system of particles, prove that the kinetic energy of motion relative to the mass center may be expressed in the form

$$T = \frac{1}{2m} \sum m_i m_j v_{i,j}^2,$$

where m = total mass of system,
$\quad m_i$ = mass of typical particle,
$\quad v_{i,j}$ = magnitude of velocity of m_i relative to m_j,
and the summation contains one term for each pair of particles.

20. *OA* is a light rod of length b which turns with angular velocity Ω about an axis *OB* perpendicular to it. *A* is the middle point of a rod *CD* of mass m and length $2a$, hinged to *OA* at *A* in such a way that *CD* is always coplanar with *OB*. If θ denotes the angle *OAC*, prove that the components of the angular momentum of *CD* about *O* in the directions *OA*, *OB* and a direction perpendicular to them are, respectively,

$$-\tfrac{1}{3}ma^2\Omega \sin\theta \cos\theta, \qquad m\Omega(b^2 + \tfrac{1}{3}a^2\cos^2\theta), \qquad \tfrac{1}{3}ma^2\dot\theta.$$

CHAPTER XII
METHODS OF DYNAMICS IN SPACE

The following three principles are fundamental in Newtonian mechanics:
  (i) the principle of linear momentum,
  (ii) the principle of angular momentum,
  (iii) the principle of energy.
General forms for the first and last of these principles have already been given in Chap. V; we shall merely recall them here, stressing their applications to dynamics in space. The treatment of the principle of angular momentum, given in this chapter, is independent of that given in Chap. V; there is reason for this, since in two dimensions angular momentum is a scalar, whereas in three dimensions it is a vector.

We begin our discussion of the above principles by considering the simplest of all systems—a single particle.

12.1. MOTION OF A PARTICLE

Equations of motion.

For a particle of mass m acted on by a force $\mathbf{P}$, we have, by the fundamental law (1 402),

$$(12.101) \qquad m\mathbf{f} = \mathbf{P},$$

where $\mathbf{f}$ is the acceleration relative to a Newtonian frame of reference. This vector equation can also be written in the form

$$(12.102) \qquad \frac{d}{dt}(m\mathbf{q}) = \mathbf{P},$$

where $\mathbf{q}$ is the velocity of the particle. In this form, it is often referred to as the *principle of linear momentum for a particle*: *The rate of change of linear momentum of a particle is equal to the applied force.*

By resolving the vectors $\mathbf{f}$ and $\mathbf{P}$ in the directions of rectangular axes $Oxyz$, fixed in the frame of reference, we obtain, as in Sec 5.1, the equations

$$(12.103) \qquad m\ddot{x} = X, \qquad m\ddot{y} = Y, \qquad m\ddot{z} = Z,$$

where X, Y, Z are the components of **P** along the axes. These are the equations of motion of a particle in rectangular Cartesians; other forms of the equations of motion are obtained below.

Let **i**, **j**, **k** be unit vectors along the tangent, principal normal and binormal to the path of the particle. By (11.103),

$$\mathbf{f} = \ddot{s}\mathbf{i} + \frac{\dot{s}^2}{\rho}\mathbf{j},$$

where s denotes arc length along the path and ρ is the radius of curvature Writing

$$\mathbf{P} = P_1\mathbf{i} + P_2\mathbf{j} + P_3\mathbf{k},$$

we obtain from (12 101) the following *intrinsic equations of motion*·

(12.104) $\qquad m\ddot{s} = P_1, \qquad \dfrac{m\dot{s}^2}{\rho} = P_2, \qquad 0 = P_3.$

Now let **i**, **j**, **k** be unit vectors in the directions of the parametric lines of cylindrical coordinates (R, ϕ, z). By (11.106), we have

$$\mathbf{f} = (\ddot{R} - R\dot{\phi}^2)\mathbf{i} + \frac{1}{R}\frac{d}{dt}(R^2\dot{\phi})\mathbf{j} + \ddot{z}\mathbf{k}.$$

Thus, if

$$\mathbf{P} = P_R\mathbf{i} + P_\phi\mathbf{j} + P_z\mathbf{k},$$

we obtain, as *equations of motion in cylindrical coordinates*,

(12.105) $\quad m(\ddot{R} - R\dot{\phi}^2) = P_R, \quad m\dfrac{1}{R}\dfrac{d}{dt}(R^2\dot{\phi}) = P_\phi, \quad m\ddot{z} = P_z.$

Equations (12.103), (12.104), and (12.105) are probably the most useful forms of the equations of motion of a particle. Other forms may be obtained by following the same general plan, namely, resolution of vectors along a suitably chosen orthogonal triad

When the path of a particle is to be found, it is better to use some form such as (12 103) or (12.105), rather than the intrinsic equations (12.104). However, if the path is known beforehand, the equations (12 104) are particularly convenient. For example, consider a particle sliding down a smooth curve under

gravity. In this case P_1 is simply the component of the particle's weight in the direction of the tangent and is therefore known. Integration of the first equation in (12.104) gives $\dot{s}$ (and s) in terms of the time. The other two equations then give the reaction of the curve on the particle without further integration.

There is a point of interest in connection with (12.104). From the last of these equations, it is clear that the path is such that the osculating plane contains the applied force. We recall that, for a flexible cable in equilibrium [cf. (10.217)], the osculating plane also contains the external force; there is a close analogy between the two problems.

Exercise A particle moves on a smooth surface under no forces except the reaction of the surface. Show that its path is a geodesic on the surface. Is this result true when the surface is rough?

Integration of the equations of motion.

To obtain the equations of motion of a particle is one question, but to solve them is another. The second task is much harder than the first. Indeed, we may say that only a very few of all possible problems in dynamics can be completely solved, if by *solution* we mean the expression of the coordinates as easily calculable functions of the time t. However, it is always possible to obtain solutions in the form of power series in t. Consideration of this process leads to the following important general theorem: *The motion of a particle is determined when its initial position and velocity are given.*

Let us sketch the proof of this theorem in the case of a free particle, moving in accordance with the equations (12.103). We shall suppose that X, Y, Z are given functions of x, y, z and perhaps of $\dot{x}$, $\dot{y}$, $\dot{z}$, t, also. (Consider, for example, a projectile under the action of gravity and air resistance, as in Sec. 6.2.) Then the equations (12.103) give $\ddot{x}_0$, $\ddot{y}_0$, $\ddot{z}_0$ in terms of

(12.106) $\qquad\qquad x_0,\ y_0,\ z_0,\ \dot{x}_0,\ \dot{y}_0,\ \dot{z}_0,$

the subscript indicating evaluation at $t = 0$. If we differentiate (12.103) and consider the resulting equations at $t = 0$, we see that they give the third derivatives of x, y, z with respect to t at $t = 0$ in terms of the quantities (12.106), since $\ddot{x}_0$, $\ddot{y}_0$, $\ddot{z}_0$ have already been found. Proceeding in this way, we can determine *all* derivatives of x, y, z at $t = 0$ in terms of the quan-

tities (12.106). Thus, we have all the coefficients in the following Taylor expansions for x, y, z:

$$x = x_0 + \dot{x}_0 t + \tfrac{1}{2}\ddot{x}_0 t^2 + \cdots,$$
$$y = y_0 + \dot{y}_0 t + \tfrac{1}{2}\ddot{y}_0 t^2 + \cdots,$$
$$z = z_0 + \dot{z}_0 t + \tfrac{1}{2}\ddot{z}_0 t^2 + \cdots.$$

The above series provide a formal solution of the equations of motion and, as we have seen, this solution depends only on $x_0, y_0, z_0, \dot{x}_0, \dot{y}_0, \dot{z}_0$. For the completion of the proof, it is necessary to discuss the convergence of the series; this belongs to the theory of differential equations, and we shall merely remark that the conditions of convergence (for some range of values for t) are satisfied in all the problems we shall consider.

In order that a solution for the motion of a free particle (not necessarily expressed in power series) may be made to fit the stated initial conditions, there must be available *six* constants of integration.

For a set of particles moving under forces depending on their positions and velocities, it may be shown by an argument similar to that given above that the motion is determined when the initial positions and velocities are given. (This is most easily seen by means of Lagrange's equations; cf. Chap XV.) The number of constants of integration is double the number of degrees of freedom.

If we regard the universe as composed of particles, this result leads to a rather surprising conclusion. If we knew at the present moment the position and velocity of every particle in the universe and could solve the differential equations of motion, we should be able to predict the whole future of the universe. Even more surprising, since the motions of all the particles could be followed backward in time as well as forward, we should be in a position to uncover the history of the universe from its beginning.

Is this practical science? It is not, for such a complete knowledge of present conditions is quite beyond our power. From a philosophical point of view, however, the question is of interest— the question as to whether the past and future are *determined* by the present. That they are so determined is implied in Newtonian mechanics, and it is here that quantum mechanics

introduces a new and revolutionary idea: Nothing is *certain*, only *probable*.

Principle of angular momentum.

By (11.501), the angular momentum of a particle about a fixed point O is

(12.107) $$\mathbf{h} = \mathbf{r} \times m\mathbf{q}$$

Let us calculate the rate of change of $\mathbf{h}$. Differentiating (12.107), we find

(12.108) $$\begin{aligned}\dot{\mathbf{h}} &= \dot{\mathbf{r}} \times m\mathbf{q} + \mathbf{r} \times m\dot{\mathbf{q}} \\ &= \mathbf{q} \times m\mathbf{q} + \mathbf{r} \times m\mathbf{f} \\ &= \mathbf{r} \times \mathbf{P},\end{aligned}$$

where $\mathbf{P}$ is the force acting on the particle. In words, *the rate of change of angular momentum of a particle about a fixed point is equal to the moment of the applied force about that point.*

If we take O as origin of rectangular axes $Oxyz$ and resolve vectors in the directions of these axes, we obtain

(12 109) $$\begin{cases} m(y\ddot{z} - z\ddot{y}) = yZ - zY, \\ m(z\ddot{x} - x\ddot{z}) = zX - xZ, \\ m(x\ddot{y} - y\ddot{x}) = xY - yX, \end{cases}$$

where X, Y, Z are the components of $\mathbf{P}$. The last of these equations is the same as that obtained in Sec. 5.1 for a particle moving in the plane Oxy, moments being taken about O (or Oz).

Principle of energy.

For a moving particle we have, as in Sec. 5.1,

(12.110) $$\dot{T} = \dot{W},$$

where $\dot{T}$ is the rate of increase of the kinetic energy and $\dot{W}$ is the rate at which the applied forces do work. This general form of the principle of energy is of little use, except in the case where the working forces are conservative. Then $\dot{W} = -\dot{V}$, where V is the potential energy of the particle and (12.110) gives, on integration,

(12 111) $$T + V = E,$$

where E is a constant, the *total energy.*

342   MECHANICS IN SPACE   [Sec.

The reader may ask: Seeing that the equations of mot (12.103) are three equations for three unknowns (and theref mathematically complete), why do we trouble to develop f more equations (12.109) and (12.111)? The answer is: latter equations often give directly pieces of information wh can be used in conjunction with (12.103) to simplify the worl

Example. Let us consider the motion of a particle on a smooth sph We use cylindrical coordinates (R, ϕ, z) with origin at the center of sphere, the axis of z being directed vertically upward. Then the equa of the sphere is

$$(12.112) \qquad R^2 = a^2 - z^2.$$

The forces acting on the particle are its weight mg and the normal reac $\mathbf{N}$ of the sphere. By resolving these forces along the parametric line R, ϕ, and z, we find P_R, P_ϕ, and P_z in (12.105); these equations, toget with (12.112), are four equations from which we can find N, R, ϕ, z as fu tions of the time. This plan of dealing with the motion, though straig forward, is not so simple as that given below.

We first note that, since $\mathbf{N}$ does no work, the principle of energy app Now the potential energy of the particle is mgz, and its kinetic energ $\tfrac{1}{2}mq^2$, where q is the velocity, with components given by (11.105). Her by (12.111),

$$(12.113) \qquad \tfrac{1}{2}m(\dot R^2 + R^2\dot\phi^2 + \dot z^2) + mgz = mE,$$

where E is here used to denote the constant energy per unit mass. Ag since $\mathbf{N}$ and the weight have no moment about Oz, the angular moment about Oz is constant. The components of linear momentum in the R- an directions have no moments about Oz, the ϕ-component is $mR\dot\phi$ and moment is $mR^2\dot\phi$. Hence,

$$(12.114) \qquad R^2\dot\phi = h,$$

where h is a constant. This result follows also from the second equa of (12.105), since $P_\phi = 0$ in this case. When the initial position and velo are known, the constants E and h can be found, and the equations (12.1 (12.113), and (12.114) provide three equations to determine R, ϕ, and z.

From (12.112), we have, by differentiation,

$$\dot R = -\frac{z\dot z}{\sqrt{a^2 - z^2}}.$$

When this value of $\dot R$ and the value of $\dot\phi$ from (12.114) are substituted (12.113), we get

$$(12.115) \qquad \dot z^2 = \frac{2g}{a^2}\left[(z^2 - a^2)\left(z - \frac{E}{g}\right) - \frac{h^2}{2g}\right].$$

This is a single equation for z as a function of t; when this equation has been solved, (12.112) gives R in terms of t directly, and ϕ can be found by a quadrature from (12.114). The solution of (12.115) is given in the next chapter.

12.2. MOTION OF A SYSTEM

Principle of linear momentum; motion of the mass center.

We now recall some results established in Sec. 5.2. If m_i and $\mathbf{q}_i$ denote the mass and velocity of the ith particle of a system, then the linear momentum is

$$(12.201) \qquad \mathbf{M} = \sum_{i=1}^{n} m_i \mathbf{q}_i,$$

where n is the number of particles. By (5.206), we have

$$(12.202) \qquad \dot{\mathbf{M}} = \mathbf{F},$$

where $\mathbf{F}$ is the vector sum of the external forces. This is the principle of linear momentum in its general form. It may be stated as follows: *The rate of increase of the linear momentum of a system is equal to the vector sum of the external forces.*

If $\mathbf{q}_0$ denotes the velocity of the mass center and m the total mass, the linear momentum $\mathbf{M}$ is $m\mathbf{q}_0$ and (12.202) gives

$$(12.203) \qquad m\dot{\mathbf{q}}_0 = \mathbf{F}.$$

This is the equation of motion for a single particle of mass m under a force $\mathbf{F}$, and so we have the following result, already stated in Sec. 5.2: *The mass center of a system moves like a particle, having a mass equal to the mass of the system, acted on by a force equal to the vector sum of the external forces acting on the system.*

This alternative statement of the principle of linear momentum is particularly useful; it reduces the determination of the motion of the mass center of any system under known external forces to a problem in particle dynamics. As illustrations, we may consider the motion of a high-explosive shell or of the earth in its orbit round the sun. To determine the motion of the mass center of the shell, we need know only the sum of the forces exerted by the air on the elements of its surface and, of course, the weight of the shell. Similarly, in the case of the earth, its mass center moves like a particle subject to the gravitational fields of the sun, moon, and other bodies in the solar system.

Principle of angular momentum.

By (11.502), the angular momentum of a system of particles about a point O is

$$(12.204) \qquad \mathbf{h} = \sum_{i=1}^{n} (\mathbf{r}_i \times m_i \mathbf{q}_i).$$

Here m_i = mass of ith particle,
$\mathbf{r}_i$ = position vector of ith particle relative to O,
$\mathbf{q}_i$ = velocity of ith particle relative to O,
n = number of particles in system.

In what follows, we shall consider O to be either a fixed point in a Newtonian frame of reference or the mass center of the system.

The rate of change of $\mathbf{h}$ is

$$\dot{\mathbf{h}} = \sum_{i=1}^{n} (\dot{\mathbf{r}}_i \times m_i \mathbf{q}_i + \mathbf{r}_i \times m_i \dot{\mathbf{q}}_i).$$

Since $\dot{\mathbf{r}}_i = \mathbf{q}_i$, the first vector product vanishes. Thus we have

$$(12.205) \qquad \dot{\mathbf{h}} = \sum_{i=1}^{n} (\mathbf{r}_i \times m_i \mathbf{f}_i),$$

where $\mathbf{f}_i$ is the acceleration of the ith particle relative to O.

If O is a fixed point, then $\mathbf{f}_i$ is acceleration relative to a Newtonian frame, and so

$$m_i \mathbf{f}_i = \mathbf{P}_i + \mathbf{P}'_i,$$

where $\mathbf{P}_i$, $\mathbf{P}'_i$ are, respectively, the external and internal forces on the ith particle. Hence, by (12.205),

$$(12.206) \qquad \dot{\mathbf{h}} = \sum_{i=1}^{n} \mathbf{r}_i \times \mathbf{P}_i + \sum_{i=1}^{n} \mathbf{r}_i \times \mathbf{P}'_i.$$

The second summation vanishes, since the internal forces have no moment about any point (cf. Sec. 10.2). Hence,

$$(12.207) \qquad \dot{\mathbf{h}} = \mathbf{G},$$

where $\mathbf{G}$ is the total moment of the external forces about the fixed point O.

If O is the mass center, the acceleration of the ith particle relative to a Newtonian frame S is

$$\mathbf{f}_0 + \mathbf{f}_i,$$

where $\mathbf{f}_0$ is the acceleration of O relative to S [cf. (11.108)]. Hence, the equation of motion of the ith particle is

$$m_i(\mathbf{f}_0 + \mathbf{f}_i) = \mathbf{P}_i + \mathbf{P}'_i.$$

Substitution for $m_i\mathbf{f}_i$ in (12.205) gives

$$(12.208) \quad \dot{\mathbf{h}} = \sum_{i=1}^{n} \mathbf{r}_i \times \mathbf{P}_i + \sum_{i=1}^{n} \mathbf{r}_i \times \mathbf{P}'_i - \left(\sum_{i=1}^{n} m_i\mathbf{r}_i\right) \times \mathbf{f}_0.$$

The second summation vanishes as before, and the last vanishes since $\sum_{i=1}^{n} m_i\mathbf{r}_i = 0$. Hence, we obtain again an equation of the form (12.207), where $\mathbf{G}$ is now the total moment of the external forces about the mass center.

We may sum up the principle of angular momentum as follows: *The rate of change of the angular momentum of a system about a point, either fixed or moving with the mass center, is equal to the total moment of the external forces about that point; in symbols,*

$$(12.209) \qquad\qquad \dot{\mathbf{h}} = \mathbf{G}.$$

The equations (12.203) and (12.209) are fundamental in dynamics and, indeed, in statics as well. Like the general conditions of equilibrium $\mathbf{F} = 0$, $\mathbf{G} = 0$, they hold for any system—it may be the whole, or any part, of a given distribution of matter. When the system is a single rigid body, (12.203) and (12.209) provide two vector equations for $\mathbf{q}_0$ and $\boldsymbol{\omega}$, the velocity of a base point (the mass center) and the angular velocity of the body (cf. Sec. 11.2). Moreover, when applied to a system in equilibrium, for which $\dot{\mathbf{q}}_0$ and $\dot{\mathbf{h}}$ vanish, they reduce to the conditions (10.207), the basic equations in statics.

Example. As a simple illustration, let us consider a cylinder rolling down an inclined plane. The mass center moves in a vertical plane, and so the vectors $\dot{\mathbf{q}}_0$ and $\mathbf{F}$ lie in this plane. Resolving them along and perpendicular to the inclined plane, we obtain the first two equations in (7.312). The angular velocity $\boldsymbol{\omega}$ is parallel to the axis of the cylinder, and the angular momentum about the mass center is

$$\mathbf{h} = I\boldsymbol{\omega},$$

where I is the moment of inertia about the axis of the cylinder. Since $\mathbf{h}$ has a fixed direction, (12.209) gives a single scalar equation—the third and last of the equations (7.312).

Principle of energy.

In addition to the principles of linear and angular momentum, there is a third general principle—the principle of energy. This principle, established in Sec. 5.2, is very useful when the working forces are conservative. Then it leads to the *law of conservation of energy*,

$$(12.210) \qquad T + V = E,$$

where T and V are the kinetic and potential energies and E is the constant total energy.

The two most common systems in mechanics are the particle and the rigid body. For each of these systems, the principle of energy is not independent of the principles of linear and angular momentum; it may, however, be used in place of any one of the scalar equations deduced from (12.203) and (12.209) by resolution of vectors. When it is used in this way, the value of the law of conservation of energy lies in its simplicity; it involves only positions and velocities, not accelerations.

Exercise. A rigid body turns about a fixed axis with constant kinetic energy. Show that the magnitude of the angular momentum $\mathbf{h}$ (about a point on the axis) is also constant. Is the direction of $\mathbf{h}$ necessarily fixed?

12.3. MOVING FRAMES OF REFERENCE

In Sec. 5.3 the question was raised: If the laws governing the motion of a body in a Newtonian frame of reference are known, how does it move when viewed from a frame of reference moving relative to the Newtonian frame? This question has been answered for a particle moving in a plane; we shall now consider three-dimensional motion.

Frame of reference with translational motion.

Let S be a Newtonian frame of reference and S' a frame of reference which has, relative to S, a motion of translation only. For a moving particle, we have, as in (11.108),

$$(12.301) \qquad \mathbf{f} = \mathbf{f}_0 + \mathbf{f}',$$

where $\mathbf{f}_0$ is the acceleration of S' relative to S. Since S is Newtonian, the law of motion is

$$m\mathbf{f} = \mathbf{P},$$

where m is the mass of the particle and $\mathbf{P}$ the force acting on it. In S' the law of motion is, by (12 301),

(12.302) $$m\mathbf{f}' = \mathbf{P} - m\mathbf{f}_0.$$

Thus the motion of S' gives rise to the fictitious force $-m\mathbf{f}_0$. This means that we can regard S' as Newtonian, provided we add to the actual forces a fictitious force $-m\mathbf{f}_0$ on each particle.

Rotating frames; rate of change of a vector.

Let $\mathbf{i}, \mathbf{j}, \mathbf{k}$ be a triad of unit orthogonal vectors in a frame of reference S', which rotates with angular velocity $\mathbf{\Omega}$ relative to a Newtonian frame S. Any vector $\mathbf{P}$ may be expressed in the form

(12.303) $$\mathbf{P} = P_1\mathbf{i} + P_2\mathbf{j} + P_3\mathbf{k}.$$

We shall now calculate the rate of change of $\mathbf{P}$ as estimated by an observer in S.

In calculating $d\mathbf{P}/dt$, we must remember that not only do P_1, P_2, P_3 vary, but also the vectors $\mathbf{i}, \mathbf{j}, \mathbf{k}$. Straightforward differentiation of (12.303) gives

(12 304) $$\frac{d\mathbf{P}}{dt} = \frac{dP_1}{dt}\mathbf{i} + \frac{dP_2}{dt}\mathbf{j} + \frac{dP_3}{dt}\mathbf{k} + P_1\frac{d\mathbf{i}}{dt} + P_2\frac{d\mathbf{j}}{dt} + P_3\frac{d\mathbf{k}}{dt}.$$

Now $\mathbf{i}$ is a vector fixed in a rigid body (S'), which rotates with angular velocity $\mathbf{\Omega}$. We may think of $\mathbf{i}$ as the position vector of a particle B of this body relative to a base point A, the origin of $\mathbf{i}$. Then $d\mathbf{i}/dt$ is the velocity of B relative to A; and so, by (11.203), $d\mathbf{i}/dt = \mathbf{\Omega} \times \mathbf{i}$. The same reasoning applies to $\mathbf{j}$ and $\mathbf{k}$; thus we have

(12.305) $$\frac{d\mathbf{i}}{dt} = \mathbf{\Omega} \times \mathbf{i}, \qquad \frac{d\mathbf{j}}{dt} = \mathbf{\Omega} \times \mathbf{j}, \qquad \frac{d\mathbf{k}}{dt} = \mathbf{\Omega} \times \mathbf{k}.$$

Substituting these results in (12.304), we obtain

(12.306) $$\frac{d\mathbf{P}}{dt} = \frac{\delta \mathbf{P}}{\delta t} + \mathbf{\Omega} \times \mathbf{P},$$

where

(12.307) $$\frac{\delta \mathbf{P}}{\delta t} = \frac{dP_1}{dt}\mathbf{i} + \frac{dP_2}{dt}\mathbf{j} + \frac{dP_3}{dt}\mathbf{k}.$$

We use the symbol $\delta/\delta t$ to denote a partial differentiation which $\mathbf{i}, \mathbf{j}, \mathbf{k}$ are held fixed.

We note that $d\mathbf{P}/dt$ consists of two parts. The first pa $\delta \mathbf{P}/\delta t$, is the rate of change of $\mathbf{P}$ as measured by an observ moving with S'; it may be called the *rate of growth*, since, calculating it, we think of the vector $\mathbf{P}$ as changing or growin whereas $\mathbf{i}, \mathbf{j}, \mathbf{k}$ remain constant. The second part of $d\mathbf{P}/dt$, vi $\mathbf{\Omega} \times \mathbf{P}$, is due to the rotation of the triad $\mathbf{i}, \mathbf{j}, \mathbf{k}$; it may be call the *rate of transport*. Thus, for a rotating frame, *the rate change of a vector equals rate of growth plus rate of transport.*

Motion of a particle relative to a rotating frame.

Let S' be a frame of reference which rotates with angu velocity $\mathbf{\Omega}$ about a point O, fixed in a Newtonian frame Relative to S, the velocity $\mathbf{q}$ of a moving particle A is, by (12.30

(12.308) $$\mathbf{q} = \frac{d\mathbf{r}}{dt} = \frac{\delta \mathbf{r}}{\delta t} + \mathbf{\Omega} \times \mathbf{r},$$

where $\mathbf{r} = \overrightarrow{OA}$. The acceleration is

(12.309) $$\mathbf{f} = \frac{d\mathbf{q}}{dt} = \frac{\delta \mathbf{q}}{\delta t} + \mathbf{\Omega} \times \mathbf{q}.$$

Substitution from (12.308) gives

(12.310) $$\mathbf{f} = \frac{\delta^2 \mathbf{r}}{\delta t^2} + \frac{\delta \mathbf{\Omega}}{\delta t} \times \mathbf{r} + \mathbf{\Omega} \times \frac{\delta \mathbf{r}}{\delta t} + \mathbf{\Omega} \times \left(\frac{\delta \mathbf{r}}{\delta t} + \mathbf{\Omega} \times \mathbf{r}\right)$$
$$= \frac{\delta^2 \mathbf{r}}{\delta t^2} + \frac{\delta \mathbf{\Omega}}{\delta t} \times \mathbf{r} + \mathbf{\Omega} \times (\mathbf{\Omega} \times \mathbf{r}) + 2\mathbf{\Omega} \times \frac{\delta \mathbf{r}}{\delta t}.$$

Let $\mathbf{q}'$ and $\mathbf{f}'$ denote, respectively, the velocity and accelerati of the particle relative to S', so that

(12.311) $$\mathbf{q}' = \frac{\delta \mathbf{r}}{\delta t}, \qquad \mathbf{f}' = \frac{\delta^2 \mathbf{r}}{\delta t^2}.$$

Now,

(12.312) $$\begin{cases} \frac{d\mathbf{\Omega}}{dt} = \frac{\delta \mathbf{\Omega}}{\delta t} + \mathbf{\Omega} \times \mathbf{\Omega} = \frac{\delta \mathbf{\Omega}}{\delta t}, \\ \mathbf{\Omega} \times (\mathbf{\Omega} \times \mathbf{r}) = \mathbf{\Omega}(\mathbf{\Omega} \cdot \mathbf{r}) - \mathbf{r}\Omega^2, \end{cases}$$

and so (12.310) may be written

(12.313) $$\mathbf{f} = \mathbf{f}' + \mathbf{f}_t + \mathbf{f}_c,$$

where

(12.314) $$\mathbf{f}_t = \frac{d\mathbf{\Omega}}{dt} \times \mathbf{r} + \mathbf{\Omega}(\mathbf{\Omega} \cdot \mathbf{r}) - \mathbf{r}\Omega^2, \qquad \mathbf{f}_c = 2\mathbf{\Omega} \times \mathbf{q}'.$$

For a particle fixed in S', $\mathbf{q}' = 0$; then $\mathbf{f}' = 0$ and $\mathbf{f}_c = 0$, so that $\mathbf{f}$ reduces to $\mathbf{f}_t$. For this reason $\mathbf{f}_t$ may, in the general case, be called the *acceleration of transport*. The acceleration $\mathbf{f}_c$ is called the *complementary acceleration* or *acceleration of Coriolis*. We note that the acceleration of Coriolis is perpendicular to both $\mathbf{\Omega}$ and $\mathbf{q}'$.

For a particle of mass m acted on by a force $\mathbf{P}$, the law of motion in S is

$$m\mathbf{f} = \mathbf{P};$$

in S', the law of motion is

(12.315) $$m\mathbf{f}' = \mathbf{P} - m\mathbf{f}_t - m\mathbf{f}_c.$$

Thus the rotation of S' gives rise to two fictitious forces, $-m\mathbf{f}_t$ and $-m\mathbf{f}_c$. The last of these is the *Coriolis force*; the first is intimately related to the force usually known as *centrifugal force*. When these two forces are added to the actual force $\mathbf{P}$, the law of motion of a particle in S' is precisely the Newtonian law—we say that S' is *reduced to rest* by the introduction of these fictitious forces.

Frames with constant angular velocity.

Let us now consider the case where the angular velocity of the rotating frame S' is constant. Since $\mathbf{\Omega}$ is a constant vector, it determines a fixed axis of rotation through O. Let AN be the perpendicular from the position of the particle A to this axis (Fig. 127). Then

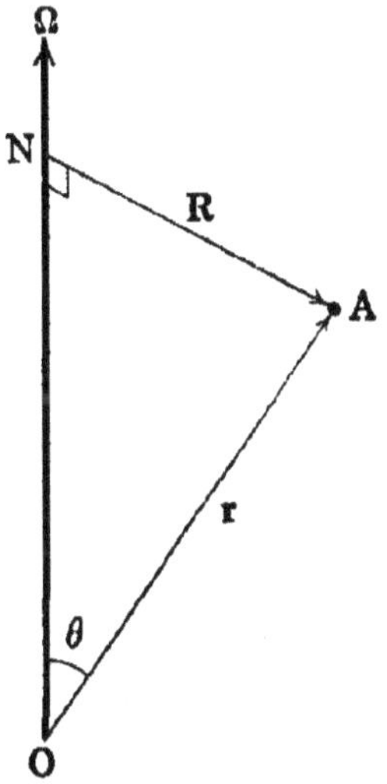

$$\mathbf{\Omega} \cdot \mathbf{r} = \Omega r \cos \theta,$$

Fig. 127.—The vectors **R** and **r** for a particle A.

where θ is the angle AON. The acceleration of transport is, therefore,

$$f_t = \Omega\Omega r \cos\theta - r\Omega^2$$
$$= \overrightarrow{ON}\Omega^2 - (\overrightarrow{ON} + \overrightarrow{NA})\Omega^2$$
$$= -\mathbf{R}\Omega^2,$$

where $\mathbf{R} = \overrightarrow{NA}$. In this case the equation (12.315) becomes

(12.316) $\qquad m\mathbf{f'} = \mathbf{P} + m\mathbf{R}\Omega^2 - 2m\mathbf{\Omega} \times \mathbf{q'}$;

the fictitious force $m\mathbf{R}\Omega^2$ is the centrifugal force, as ordinari[ly] understood.

For a particle at rest in S', $\mathbf{q'} = 0$, and so the only for[ce] required to reduce S' to rest is the centrifugal force. The cond[i]tion for relative equilibrium is

(12.317) $\qquad \mathbf{P} + m\mathbf{R}\Omega^2 = \mathbf{0}.$

This is actually the condition used in Sec. 5.3, in discussing t[he] equilibrium of a particle on or near the earth's surface.

Exercise. Show that in a frame with constant angular velocity reduced to rest, the centrifugal force per unit mass is $-\operatorname{grad} V$, whe[re] $V = -\tfrac{1}{2}\Omega^2 R^2$

Frames of reference in general motion.

The above results have been obtained on the supposition th[at] the point O is fixed in a Newtonian frame of reference If O [is] moving, the formulas (12.308) and (12.309) for $\mathbf{q}$ and $\mathbf{f}$ give mere[ly] the velocity and acceleration of A relative to O. The comple[te] expressions for velocity and acceleration are obtained by addi[ng] the velocity $\mathbf{q}_0$ and the acceleration $\mathbf{f}_0$ of O to these expressio[ns] for $\mathbf{q}$ and $\mathbf{f}$, respectively.

Thus, relative to a frame S' moving in a general manner, t[he] motion of a particle takes place in accordance with the equati[on]

(12.318) $\qquad m\mathbf{f'} = \mathbf{P} - m\mathbf{f}_0 - m\mathbf{f}_t - m\mathbf{f}_c,$

where $\mathbf{f'}$ = acceleration of particle relative to S',
$\mathbf{P}$ = force applied to particle,
$\mathbf{f}_0$ = acceleration of base point in S' (relative to a Ne[w]tonian frame),
$\mathbf{f}_t, \mathbf{f}_c$ = acceleration of transport and acceleration of Coriol[is] [cf. (12.314)].

For slow-moving frames, for which $\mathbf{f}_0$ and the angular velocity are small, the fictitious forces $-m\mathbf{f}_0$, $-m\mathbf{f}_t$, $-m\mathbf{f}_c$ may not [be]

noticeable. However, as remarked in Sec. 5.3, they become important for an airplane making a sharp turn or pulling out of a power dive; the formula (12.318) enables us to estimate the force which interferes with the motion of the pilot's hands in manipulating the controls.

12.4. MOTION OF A RIGID BODY

The general principles of Sec. 12 2 govern the motion of any system. In this section, they are used to find explicit equations of motion for a rigid body

Rigid body with a fixed point.

Consider a rigid body constrained to rotate about a fixed point O. By (11.509), the angular momentum about O is

(12 401) $\qquad \mathbf{h} = A\omega_1\mathbf{i} + B\omega_2\mathbf{j} + C\omega_3\mathbf{k},$

where $\mathbf{i}, \mathbf{j}, \mathbf{k}$ = unit vectors in the directions of principal axes of inertia at O,
$\quad A, B, C$ = principal moments of inertia at O,
$\quad \omega_1, \omega_2, \omega_3$ = components of the angular velocity ω of the body in the directions $\mathbf{i}, \mathbf{j}, \mathbf{k}$

As pointed out in Sec 11.4, in general the principal axes at O are fixed in the body, in that case the triad $\mathbf{i}, \mathbf{j}, \mathbf{k}$ has the angular velocity ω. But if A, B, C are not all different, we may use a principal triad which is fixed neither in the body nor in space. To allow for all possibilities, we shall denote the angular velocity of the triad by Ω, noting that $\Omega = \omega$ if the triad is fixed in the body.

Writing

$$\Omega = \Omega_1\mathbf{i} + \Omega_2\mathbf{j} + \Omega_3\mathbf{k},$$

we apply (12.306) and obtain

(12.402) $\quad \dot{\mathbf{h}} = \dfrac{\delta \mathbf{h}}{\delta t} + \Omega \times \mathbf{h}$
$\qquad = A\dot\omega_1\mathbf{i} + B\dot\omega_2\mathbf{j} + C\dot\omega_3\mathbf{k} + (\Omega_1\mathbf{i} + \Omega_2\mathbf{j} + \Omega_3\mathbf{k})$
$\qquad \qquad \times (A\omega_1\mathbf{i} + B\omega_2\mathbf{j} + C\omega_3\mathbf{k})$
$\qquad = (A\dot\omega_1 - B\omega_2\Omega_3 + C\omega_3\Omega_2)\mathbf{i}$
$\qquad \quad + (B\dot\omega_2 - C\omega_3\Omega_1 + A\omega_1\Omega_3)\mathbf{j}$
$\qquad \qquad + (C\dot\omega_3 - A\omega_1\Omega_2 + B\omega_2\Omega_1)\mathbf{k}.$

Now, by (12.209),
$$\dot{\mathbf{h}} = \mathbf{G},$$

where $\mathbf{G}$ is the total moment of the external forces about O; hence (12.402) gives, as the *equations of motion of a rigid body with a fixed point*,

(12.403) $\quad\begin{cases} A\dot{\omega}_1 - B\omega_2\Omega_3 + C\omega_3\Omega_2 = G_1, \\ B\dot{\omega}_2 - C\omega_3\Omega_1 + A\omega_1\Omega_3 = G_2, \\ C\dot{\omega}_3 - A\omega_1\Omega_2 + B\omega_2\Omega_1 = G_3, \end{cases}$

where G_1, G_2, G_3 are the components of $\mathbf{G}$ along $\mathbf{i}, \mathbf{j}, \mathbf{k}$.

If $\mathbf{i}, \mathbf{j}, \mathbf{k}$ are fixed in the body, so that $\boldsymbol{\Omega} = \boldsymbol{\omega}$, the equations (12.403) become

(12.404) $\quad\begin{cases} A\dot{\omega}_1 - (B - C)\omega_2\omega_3 = G_1, \\ B\dot{\omega}_2 - (C - A)\omega_3\omega_1 = G_2, \\ C\dot{\omega}_3 - (A - B)\omega_1\omega_2 = G_3. \end{cases}$

These are *Euler's equations of motion for a rigid body with a fixed point.*

When the working forces are conservative, we can use, in place of any one of the three equations in (12.403) or (12.404), the following equation, deduced from the principle of energy (12.210):

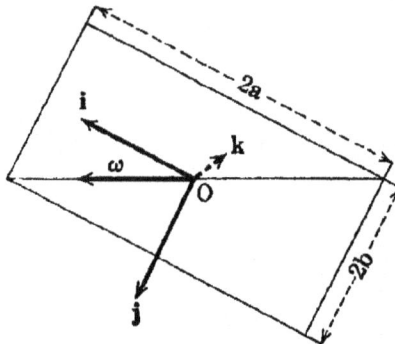

(12.405) $\quad \frac{1}{2}(A\omega_1^2 + B\omega_2^2 + C\omega_3^2) + V = E.$

Fig. 128.—A rectangular plate spinning about a diagonal.

Example 1. A rectangular plate spins with constant angular velocity ω about a diagonal. Find the couple which must act on the plate in order to maintain this motion.

In Fig. 128, O is the mass center of the plate and $\mathbf{i}, \mathbf{j}, \mathbf{k}$ are unit vectors along the principal axes of inertia at O, $\mathbf{k}$ is normal to the plate, and $\mathbf{i}$ and $\mathbf{j}$ lie in its plane, $\mathbf{i}$ being parallel to the length. The principal moments of inertia at O are

(12.406) $\quad A = \tfrac{1}{3}mb^2, \quad B = \tfrac{1}{3}ma^2, \quad C = \tfrac{1}{3}m(a^2 + b^2),$

where m is the mass of the plate, $2a$ its length, and $2b$ its breadth.

If α is the angle between $\mathbf{i}$ and the axis of rotation, so that $\tan \alpha = b/a$, the angular velocity of the plate is

$$\boldsymbol{\omega} = \omega \cos \alpha \, \mathbf{i} + \omega \sin \alpha \, \mathbf{j}.$$

Sec. 12 4]   *METHODS OF DYNAMICS IN SPACE*   353

The components of ω in the directions $\mathbf{i}$, $\mathbf{j}$, $\mathbf{k}$ are, therefore,

$$\omega_1 = \omega \cos \alpha, \qquad \omega_2 = \omega \sin \alpha, \qquad \omega_3 = 0$$

Substituting these values of ω_1, ω_2, ω_3 and the values of A, B, C from (12.406) in the equations (12 404), we get

(12.407) $\quad G_1 = 0, \qquad G_2 = 0, \qquad G_3 = \tfrac{1}{3}m(a^2 - b^2)\omega^2 \sin \alpha \cos \alpha$
$$= \tfrac{1}{3}m\omega^2 ab\, \frac{a^2 - b^2}{a^2 + b^2}$$

These are the components of the couple G which must act on the plate, we observe that the axis of the couple is normal to the plate and turns with it

If we suppose the plate to turn in bearings at the ends of the fixed diagonal and to be subject only to the reactions at these bearings, then clearly it is these reactions which supply the couple G Each reaction lies in the plane of the plate and is of magnitude

$$\tfrac{1}{6}m\omega^2 ab\, \frac{a^2 - b^2}{(a^2 + b^2)^{\frac{1}{2}}}$$

As the plate turns, these reactions turn with it.

Fluctuating reactions of this sort must be avoided in the case of flywheels and rotors   It is not enough to make sure that the mass center lies on the axis of rotation   The rotating body must be balanced so that the axis of rotation is a principal axis of inertia. It is left to the reader to prove, by means of (12.404), that the fluctuating reactions vanish for any rotating body if, and only if, this condition is satisfied.

Example 2   A circular disk of radius a and mass m is supported on a needle point at its center; it is set spinning with angular velocity ω_0 about a line making an angle α with the normal to the disk Find the angular velocity of the disk at any subsequent time.

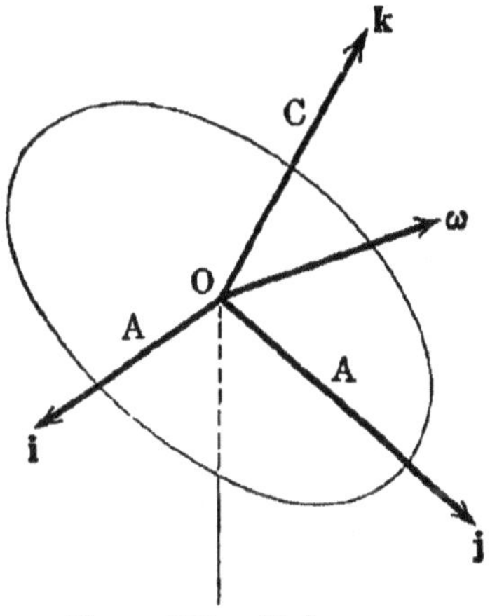

In Fig 129, $\mathbf{k}$ is a unit vector normal to the disk at the center O, and $\mathbf{i}$, $\mathbf{j}$ are fixed in the plane of the disk; we suppose $\mathbf{j}$ chosen so that the initial angular velocity lies in the plane of $\mathbf{k}$ and $\mathbf{j}$ The angular velocity of the disk at any time is

$$\omega = \omega_1 \mathbf{i} + \omega_2 \mathbf{j} + \omega_3 \mathbf{k};$$

at $t = 0$,

$$\omega_1 = 0, \qquad \omega_2 = \omega_0 \sin \alpha, \qquad \omega_3 = \omega_0 \cos \alpha.$$

The principal moments of inertia at O are

$$A = B = \tfrac{1}{4}ma^2, \qquad C = \tfrac{1}{2}ma^2.$$

Fig 129 —Disk spinning about its center, $\mathbf{i}$ and $\mathbf{j}$ fixed in the disk

Since the external forces (the reaction at O and the weight of the disk) have no moment about O, the equations (12.404) give

(12.408)
$$\begin{cases} A\dot\omega_1 - (A-C)\omega_2\omega_3 = 0, \\ A\dot\omega_2 - (C-A)\omega_3\omega_1 = 0, \\ C\dot\omega_3 = 0. \end{cases}$$

From the last of these equations it follows that ω_3 is constant; hence, $\omega_3 = \omega_0 \cos \alpha$. Multiplying the second equation in (12.408) by $i(=\sqrt{-1})$ and adding the result to the first of these equations, we get

$$A\dot\xi - i(C-A)\omega_0 \cos \alpha\, \xi = 0,$$

where $\xi = \omega_1 + i\omega_2$. Since $C = 2A$, this equation can be written

$$\dot\xi - i\omega_0 \cos \alpha\, \xi = 0;$$

the general solution is

$$\xi = \xi_0 e^{i\omega_0 t \cos \alpha},$$

where ξ_0 is a constant. From the initial conditions, we have

$$\xi_0 = i\omega_0 \sin \alpha,$$

and hence

(12.409) $\quad \omega_1 = -\omega_0 \sin \alpha \sin(\omega_0 t \cos \alpha), \quad \omega_2 = \omega_0 \sin \alpha \cos(\omega_0 t \cos \alpha),$

$$\omega_3 = \omega_0 \cos \alpha.$$

This is the solution of the problem as stated, but it does not tell us at once how the disk moves in space. To find this, we must either introduce the Eulerian angles defining the positions of i, j, k relative to fixed axes, or use a different method.

Example 3. *Find the motion in space of the disk considered in Example 2.*

In Fig. 130, h is the angular momentum vector, ω the angular velocity vector, and k a unit vector normal to the disk as before, i and j are unit vectors in the plane of the disk, but not fixed in it. The vector j is taken in the plane determined by h and k. We note the following facts:

(i) Since the external forces have no moment about O, then, by (12.209), h is a constant vector—it has a fixed direction in space determined by the initial conditions.

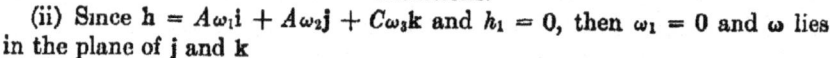

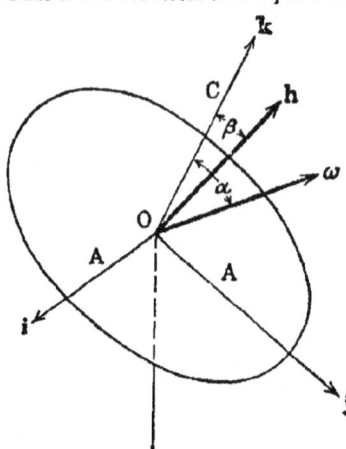

Fig. 130.—Disk spinning about its center; j coplanar with h and k.

(ii) Since $\mathbf{h} = A\omega_1\mathbf{i} + A\omega_2\mathbf{j} + C\omega_3\mathbf{k}$ and $h_1 = 0$, then $\omega_1 = 0$ and ω lies in the plane of j and k.

(iii) Since the triad i, j, k is not fixed in the disk, its angular velocity $\mathbf{\Omega}$ is different from ω. However, k is fixed both in the triad and in the disk. As

Sec. 12.4] *METHODS OF DYNAMICS IN SPACE* 355

a point of the triad, the extremity of **k** has velocity $\mathbf{\Omega} \times \mathbf{k}$; as a point of the disk, it has velocity $\boldsymbol{\omega} \times \mathbf{k}$. Hence,

$$(\Omega_1 \mathbf{i} + \Omega_2 \mathbf{j} + \Omega_3 \mathbf{k}) \times \mathbf{k} = (\omega_1 \mathbf{i} + \omega_2 \mathbf{j} + \omega_3 \mathbf{k}) \times \mathbf{k},$$

and so $\Omega_1 = \omega_1$, $\Omega_2 = \omega_2$. Since $\omega_1 = 0$, we have $\Omega_1 = 0$.

Applying the general equations (12.403) and making use of the above facts, we get

$$-A\omega_2 \Omega_3 + C\omega_3 \omega_2 = 0,$$
$$A\dot{\omega}_2 = 0,$$
$$C\dot{\omega}_3 = 0$$

Thus, ω_2, ω_3, h_2, h_3 are constants, and $\Omega_3/\Omega_2 = \Omega_3/\omega_2 = C\omega_3/A\omega_2 = h_3/h_2$, the angular velocity $\mathbf{\Omega}$ of the triad has constant magnitude and lies along the fixed direction **h**. The following facts concerning the motion are now obvious:

(i) The disk spins about its normal **k** at a constant rate ω_3.

(ii) The angle β between **k** and **h**, given by $h \cos \beta = h_3$, is constant; the normal to the disk moves on a cone with axis **h**, turning about **h** at the constant rate Ω.

(iii) The angle α between $\boldsymbol{\omega}$ and **k**, given by $\omega \cos \alpha = \omega_3$, is constant; the angular velocity vector $\boldsymbol{\omega}$ describes a cone about the normal to the disk. This is the body cone (cf. Sec. 11.2). The angle $\alpha - \beta$ between $\boldsymbol{\omega}$ and **h** is also constant, and so the space cone has constant semivertical angle $\alpha - \beta$ and axis **h**; it lies inside the body cone.

The above problem is a special case of the motion of a rigid body with a fixed point under no forces, considered in Chap. XIV.

General motion of a rigid body.

We now consider a rigid body moving quite generally. Let **F** denote the total external force and **G** the total moment of the external forces about the mass center. By (12.203), the acceleration **f** of the mass center (relative to a Newtonian frame) is given by*

(12.410) $$m\mathbf{f} = \mathbf{F},$$

where m is the mass of the body. For the motion relative to the mass center we have, by (12.209),

(12.411) $$\dot{\mathbf{h}} = \mathbf{G},$$

where **h** is the angular momentum about the mass center. This last equation is exactly the same as if the mass center were fixed, and so can be treated by the methods given above.

* For simplicity, we drop the subscripts from $\mathbf{q}_0$ and $\mathbf{f}_0$, the velocity and acceleration of the mass center.

Let us resolve the vectors $\mathbf{f}$, $\mathbf{F}$, $\mathbf{h}$, $\mathbf{G}$ along a principal triad $\mathbf{i}$, $\mathbf{j}$, $\mathbf{k}$ at the mass center. As before, this triad is supposed to be permanently a principal triad. Its angular velocity will be denoted by $\mathbf{\Omega}$; if the triad is fixed in the body, $\mathbf{\Omega} = \boldsymbol{\omega}$, the angular velocity of the body. Now, by (12.306),

$$\mathbf{f} = \frac{\delta \mathbf{q}}{\delta t} + \mathbf{\Omega} \times \mathbf{q},$$

where

$$\mathbf{q} = u\mathbf{i} + v\mathbf{j} + w\mathbf{k}$$

is the velocity of the mass center. Substituting for $\mathbf{f}$ in (12.410) and noting that (12.411) leads to equations of the form (12.403), we obtain the following scalar equations of motion:

(12.412)
$$\begin{cases} m(\dot{u} - v\Omega_3 + w\Omega_2) = F_1, \\ m(\dot{v} - w\Omega_1 + u\Omega_3) = F_2, \\ m(\dot{w} - u\Omega_2 + v\Omega_1) = F_3, \\ A\dot{\omega}_1 - B\omega_2\Omega_3 + C\omega_3\Omega_2 = G_1, \\ B\dot{\omega}_2 - C\omega_3\Omega_1 + A\omega_1\Omega_3 = G_2, \\ C\dot{\omega}_3 - A\omega_1\Omega_2 + B\omega_2\Omega_1 = G_3. \end{cases}$$

Here the constants A, B, C are the principal moments of inertia at the mass center.

The equations (12.412) are six equations for the components of velocity of the mass center and the components of angular velocity of the body. For any one of these six equations, we can substitute the law of conservation of energy,

(12.413) $$T + V = E,$$

provided the external forces are conservative. In a more explicit form, (12.413) reads

(12.414) $\quad \tfrac{1}{2}m(u^2 + v^2 + w^2) + \tfrac{1}{2}(A\omega_1^2 + B\omega_2^2 + C\omega_3^2) + V = E.$

Exercise. From the basic equations (12.410) and (12.411), deduce the principle of energy for a rigid body in the form

$$\dot{T} = \mathbf{F} \cdot \mathbf{q} + \mathbf{G} \cdot \boldsymbol{\omega}.$$

12.5. IMPULSIVE MOTION

The principles of dynamics, thus far considered in this chapter, deal with ordinary or continuous motion. By this we mean that the forces acting, and the accelerations produced, are finite.

Sometimes we have to deal with problems in which sudden changes in velocity occur. For two-dimensional problems of this type, we use the methods of Chap. VIII; similar methods for motion in three dimensions will now be developed.

General equations of impulsive motion.

Integration of the equations (12.203) and (12.209) from time t_0 to time t_1 gives*

(12.501) $\quad \Delta(m\mathbf{q}) = \int_{t_0}^{t_1} \mathbf{F}\, dt, \qquad \Delta\mathbf{h} = \int_{t_0}^{t_1} \mathbf{G}\, dt,$

where Δ denotes an increment in the time interval $t_1 - t_0$. These equations express the principles of linear and angular momentum in integrated form. In words, they read as follows:

(i) the increment in the linear momentum of a system is equal to the *total impulse* of the external forces;

(ii) the increment in the angular momentum about a point O (either a fixed point in a Newtonian frame or the mass center of the system in question) is equal to the time integral of the total moment about O of the external forces, i.e., the *total angular impulse* about O.

In this form the principles of linear and angular momentum can easily be applied to problems where sudden changes in velocity occur. The method of procedure is essentially that given in Chap. VIII, and so we shall give only a brief outline here.

The very short time interval $t_1 - t_0$ in which the changes occur is regarded an infinitesimal. Any finite force will then contribute nothing to the *total impulsive force*

$$\hat{\mathbf{F}} = \lim_{t_1 \to t_0} \int_{t_0}^{t_1} \mathbf{F}\, dt.$$

On the other hand, a force $\mathbf{P}$, for which

$$\hat{\mathbf{P}} = \lim_{t_1 \to t_0} \int_{t_0}^{t_1} \mathbf{P}\, dt$$

is finite, contributes the *impulsive force* $\hat{\mathbf{P}}$ to $\hat{\mathbf{F}}$. If $\mathbf{r}$ denotes the position vector of the point of application of such a force $\mathbf{P}$

---

* For simplicity, we drop the subscript from $\mathbf{q}_0$, the velocity of the mass center

(the position vector being relative to the point O about which the angular momentum is calculated), then $\mathbf{r}$ does not change by a finite amount in the infinitesimal time $t_1 - t_0$. Hence,

$$\lim_{t_1 \to t_0} \int_{t_0}^{t_1} (\mathbf{r} \times \mathbf{P})\, dt = \mathbf{r} \times \lim_{t_1 \to t_0} \int_{t_0}^{t_1} \mathbf{P}\, dt = \mathbf{r} \times \hat{\mathbf{P}},$$

and the force $\mathbf{P}$ contributes the *impulsive moment* $\mathbf{r} \times \hat{\mathbf{P}}$ to the *total impulsive moment*

$$\hat{\mathbf{G}} = \lim_{t_1 \to t_0} \int_{t_0}^{t_1} \mathbf{G}\, dt.$$

Then, from (12.501), we have

(12.502) $$\Delta(m\mathbf{q}) = \hat{\mathbf{F}}, \qquad \Delta \mathbf{h} = \hat{\mathbf{G}},$$

where $\hat{\mathbf{F}}$ = total impulsive force = vector sum of external impulsive forces,
$\hat{\mathbf{G}}$ = total impulsive moment = total moment of external impulsive forces.

These are the general equations of impulsive motion.

For a rigid body in general motion, the first of the above equations gives the change in the velocity of the mass center; the second gives the change in the angular momentum (and hence the change in angular velocity) about the mass center. For a rigid body with a fixed point, the second equation in (12.502) alone suffices to determine the change in angular velocity.

Example. A square plate, of mass m and edge $2a$, is suspended from one corner O. It is struck at a corner in a horizontal direction perpendicular to the plane of the plate. About what line does the plate begin to turn?

Let $\mathbf{i}, \mathbf{j}, \mathbf{k}$ be the principal triad of inertia at O (Fig. 131); $\mathbf{i}$ points upward along the diagonal through O, and $\mathbf{j}$ is a horizontal vector in the plane of the plate.

Before the plate is struck, the angular momentum about O is zero; immediately afterward, it is

$$\mathbf{h} = A\omega_1 \mathbf{i} + B\omega_2 \mathbf{j} + C\omega_3 \mathbf{k},$$

where $\omega_1, \omega_2, \omega_3$ are the components of angular velocity and A, B, C the principal moments of inertia at O. If $\hat{P}$ is the magnitude of the blow, the external impulsive forces are $\hat{P}\mathbf{k}$ at the point

$$\mathbf{r} = -a\sqrt{2}\,(\mathbf{i} + \mathbf{j}),$$

Sec. 12.5]   METHODS OF DYNAMICS IN SPACE   359

and an impulsive reaction $\hat{Q}$ at O. Since $\hat{Q}$ has no moment about O, the second of the equations (12.502) gives

$$A\omega_1 \mathbf{i} + B\omega_2 \mathbf{j} + C\omega_3 \mathbf{k} = -a\sqrt{2}\,(\mathbf{i} + \mathbf{j}) \times \hat{P}\mathbf{k}$$
$$= a\sqrt{2}\cdot\hat{P}(\mathbf{j} - \mathbf{i}).$$

Hence,

$$\omega_1 = -\frac{a\sqrt{2}\cdot\hat{P}}{A}, \qquad \omega_2 = \frac{a\sqrt{2}\cdot\hat{P}}{B}, \qquad \omega_3 = 0,$$

the plate begins to turn about a line in its plane passing through O. The angle θ, between $\mathbf{i}$ and this axis of rotation, is given by

$$\tan \theta = \frac{\omega_2}{\omega_1} = -\frac{A}{B}$$

Since

$$A = \tfrac{1}{3}ma^2,$$
$$B = \tfrac{1}{3}ma^2 + 2ma^2 = \tfrac{7}{3}ma^2,$$

we find

$$\tan \theta = -\tfrac{1}{7}.$$

the axis of rotation is indicated in Fig 131 by the vector ω

The impulsive reaction $\hat{Q}$ at O is easily found The velocity of the mass center, immediately after the plate has been hit, is

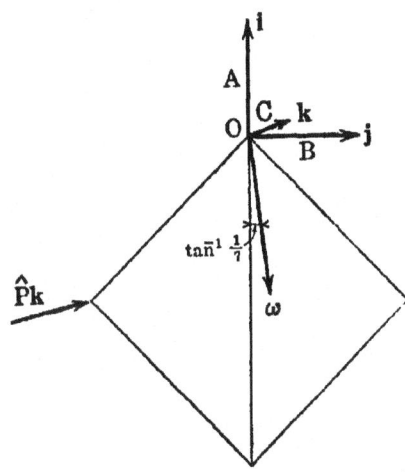

Fig. 131.—Square plate, suspended from O and struck by a blow $\hat{P}\mathbf{k}$.

$$\mathbf{q} = \boldsymbol{\omega} \times (-a\sqrt{2}\,\mathbf{i}) = \frac{2a^2\hat{P}}{B}\mathbf{k}.$$

Thus, from the first of (12.502), we get

$$\frac{2ma^2\hat{P}}{B}\mathbf{k} = \hat{P}\mathbf{k} + \hat{Q},$$

and so

$$\hat{Q} = -\tfrac{1}{7}\hat{P}\mathbf{k}.$$

12.6. SUMMARY OF METHODS OF DYNAMICS IN SPACE
I. Motion of a particle.
(a) Equations of motion:

(12.601) $\qquad m\mathbf{f} = \mathbf{P} \qquad$ (vector form);

(12.602) $\quad m\ddot{x} = X, \quad m\ddot{y} = Y, \quad m\ddot{z} = Z$
$\qquad\qquad\qquad\qquad\qquad$ (Cartesian coordinates),

(12.603) $\quad m\ddot{s} = P_1, \quad m\dfrac{\dot{s}^2}{\rho} = P_2, \quad 0 = P_3$
$\qquad\qquad\qquad\qquad\qquad$ (intrinsic equations).

(b) Principle of angular momentum:

(12.604) $\qquad \dot{\mathbf{h}} = \mathbf{r} \times \mathbf{P}.$

(c) Principle of energy:

(12.605) $\qquad \dot{T} = \dot{W}, \quad (T = \tfrac{1}{2}mq^2, W = \text{work done});$
(12.606) $\qquad T + V = E \quad$ (conservation of energy).

II. Motion of a system.
(a) Principle of linear momentum:

(12.607) $\qquad \dot{\mathbf{M}} = \mathbf{F}, \quad \left(\mathbf{M} = \sum_{i=1}^{n} m_i \mathbf{q}_i\right);$

(12.608) $\qquad m\dot{\mathbf{q}} = \mathbf{F} \quad$ (motion of mass center)

(b) Principle of angular momentum:

(12.609) $\qquad \dot{\mathbf{h}} = \mathbf{G} \quad$ (fixed point or mass center).

(c) Principle of energy:

(12.610) $\qquad \dot{T} = \dot{W};$
(12.611) $\qquad T + V = E \quad$ (conservation of energy).

III. Motion of a rigid body.
(a) Rigid body with a fixed point:

(12.612) $\qquad \dot{\mathbf{h}} = \dfrac{\delta \mathbf{h}}{\delta t} + \boldsymbol{\Omega} \times \mathbf{h} = \mathbf{G};$

(12.613) $\quad \begin{cases} A\dot{\omega}_1 - (B - C)\omega_2\omega_3 = G_1, \\ B\dot{\omega}_2 - (C - A)\omega_3\omega_1 = G_2, \\ C\dot{\omega}_3 - (A - B)\omega_1\omega_2 = G_3; \end{cases}$

(12.614) $\quad \tfrac{1}{2}(A\omega_1^2 + B\omega_2^2 + C\omega_3^2) + V = E$
$\qquad\qquad\qquad\qquad\qquad$ (conservative forces).

(b) Rigid body in general:

(12.615) $$\begin{cases} m\mathbf{f} = \mathbf{F} & \text{(motion of mass center)}, \\ \dot{\mathbf{h}} = \mathbf{G} & \text{(motion relative to mass center)}; \end{cases}$$

(12.616) $\tfrac{1}{2}mq^2 + \tfrac{1}{2}(A\omega_1^2 + B\omega_2^2 + C\omega_3^2) + V = E$

(conservative forces).

IV. Rotating frame of reference.

Rate of change of any vector:

(12.617) $$\frac{d\mathbf{P}}{dt} = \frac{\delta \mathbf{P}}{\delta t} + \boldsymbol{\Omega} \times \mathbf{P}.$$

V. Impulsive motion.

General equations:

(12.618) $$\Delta(m\mathbf{q}) = \hat{\mathbf{F}}, \qquad \Delta \mathbf{h} = \hat{\mathbf{G}}$$

EXERCISES XII

1. A heavy particle moves on a smooth surface. Show that its speed is the same whenever its path cuts a given horizontal curve on the surface.

2. Show directly from Euler's equations (12.404) that, if $\mathbf{G} = 0$ and $A = B$, then ω is constant.

3. A particle is attracted toward a fixed line by a force, perpendicular to the line and varying as the distance from the line. Show that its path is a curve traced on an elliptical cylinder.

4. A solid of revolution rotates with constant angular velocity ω about a fixed axis which passes through its mass center and is inclined to the axis of symmetry at an angle α. Prove that the reactions of the axis on the solid are equipollent to a couple of magnitude

$$\pm (C - A)\omega^2 \sin \alpha \cos \alpha,$$

where C is the moment of inertia about the axis of symmetry and A the other principal moment of inertia at the mass center.

5. Explain how a man, standing on a smooth sheet of ice, can turn round by moving his arms.

6. A bar of length $2a$ is fitted at its middle point with a nut which moves without friction on a fixed vertical screw of pitch p; the bar remains horizontal and turns with the nut. Find the acceleration of the nut.

7. Two particles, of masses m, m', attract one another according to the inverse square law. At time $t = 0$, m is at the origin and has a velocity u along the x-axis, and m' is at the point (a, b, c) and has velocity components (u', v', w'). Determine

(i) the coordinates of the mass center at time t,

(ii) the constant areal velocity of the motion of m' relative to m,

(iii) the constant areal velocity of the motion of m relative to m'.

8. Two men support a uniform pole of mass m and length $2a$ in a horizontal position. They wish to change ends without changing their positions

on the ground, by throwing the pole into the air and catching it. If the pole is to remain horizontal throughout its flight and the magnitude of the impulsive force applied by each man is to be a minimum, find the magnitudes and directions of the impulsive forces.

9. An equilateral triangle is formed of three rods, each of mass m and length $2a$. It hangs from one vertex, about which it is free to turn. A blow $\hat{P}$ is struck on one of the lower vertices in a direction perpendicular to the plane of the triangle. Prove that the impulsive reaction on the point of support has a magnitude $\tfrac{1}{2}\hat{P}$.

10. A solid homogeneous ellipsoid of mass m and semiaxes a, b, c spins with constant angular velocity ω about an axis which is fixed in space and makes constant angles α, β, γ with the axes of the ellipsoid. Show that the components (along the axes of the ellipsoid) of the couple that must act on it in order to maintain this motion are

$$\tfrac{1}{5}m\omega^2(b^2 - c^2)\cos\beta\cos\gamma$$

and two similar expressions

11. A particle of mass m moves in a plane under the action of two forces. One force is an attraction $mk^2 r$ toward the origin; the other is perpendicular to the velocity q and has magnitude $mk'q$. Show that the motion is given by an equation of the form

$$x + iy = e^{\frac{1}{2}ik't}(Ae^{ict} + Be^{-ict}).$$

How many arbitrary constants (to fit initial conditions) are present in this solution?

12. An insect runs with constant relative speed v round the rim of a wheel of radius a which rolls along a straight road with uniform velocity V. Find the magnitude and direction of (i) the acceleration relative to the wheel, (ii) the acceleration of transport, and (iii) the Coriolis acceleration. Indicate these accelerations in a diagram.

13. A free rigid body is at rest. Find three linear scalar equations to determine the components of an impulsive force which, applied at an assigned point of the body, imparts to that point an assigned velocity. Solve these equations in the case where the assigned point lies on one of the principal axes of inertia at the mass center.

14. A thin rod of mass m and length $2a$ is made to rotate with constant angular velocity ω about an axis which passes through one end of the rod and cuts it at a constant angle α. Reduce the force system exerted by the axis on the rod to a force at the fixed end and a couple

15. A rigid triangular target is fixed at the corners, and a bullet is fired normally into it. Find the region in which the bullet must strike in order that no support may experience an impulsive reaction normal to the target greater than half the momentum of the bullet.

16. A uniform circular disk of mass M and radius a is so mounted that it can turn freely about its center, which is fixed. It is spinning with angular velocity ω about the perpendicular to its plane at the center, the plane being horizontal. A particle of mass m, falling vertically, hits the disk near the

edge and adheres to it. Prove that immediately afterward the particle is moving in a direction inclined to the horizontal at an angle α, given by

$$\tan \alpha = 4 \frac{m(M + 2m)}{M(M + 4m)} \cdot \frac{v}{a\omega},$$

where v is the speed of the particle just before impact.

17. A homogeneous ellipsoid of semiaxes

$$a, b, c, \quad (a > b > c)$$

is to be mounted on a horizontal axis L in such a way that it may oscillate as a compound pendulum with the smallest possible periodic time. What position of L relative to the axes of the ellipsoid should be selected?

18. A crankshaft of mass m, in the form of a letter S formed out of two semicircles, each of radius a, spins with angular velocity ω in bearings at its ends. Find the magnitudes of the reactions exerted on the bearings, and show the directions of these reactions in a diagram.

19. A system is set in motion by impulsive forces applied to certain prescribed particles. If $\hat{\mathbf{P}}$ is the external impulsive force on a typical particle, $\mathbf{q}$ its velocity, and $\delta \mathbf{r}$ an arbitrary infinitesimal displacement consistent with the constraints (assumed workless), show that

$$\Sigma(m\mathbf{q} \cdot \delta \mathbf{r}) = \Sigma(\hat{\mathbf{P}} \cdot \delta \mathbf{r}),$$

where the summation on the left extends over all particles of the system and the summation on the right over the prescribed particles.

Let T be the kinetic energy of the actual motion and T' that of any other motion ($\mathbf{q}'$) consistent with the constraints and making $\mathbf{q}' = \mathbf{q}$ for the prescribed particles; prove that $T < T'$ (Kelvin's theorem).

20. A rhombus $ABCD$ is formed of four uniform rods, each of mass m and length $2a$, smoothly jointed at the vertices. Prove that if the rhombus is in motion in its plane, in such a way that A and C are moving along the diagonal AC, the kinetic energy may be expressed in the form

$$T = 2m(v - 2a\omega \sin \theta)^2 + \tfrac{8}{3}ma^2\omega^2,$$

where v is the velocity of A, ω the angular velocity of AB, and θ the inclination of AC to AB.

Hence, prove by Kelvin's theorem (see Exercise 19) that, if the rhombus is at rest in the form of a square and is jerked into motion by an impulsive force applied at A in the direction AC, then the angular velocity imparted to the rods is

$$\frac{3\sqrt{2}}{10} \cdot \frac{v}{a},$$

where v is the velocity imparted to A.

CHAPTER XIII

APPLICATIONS IN DYNAMICS IN SPACE—MOTION OF A PARTICLE

13.1. NOTE ON JACOBIAN ELLIPTIC FUNCTIONS

So far, we have used only the elementary functions, alone or in combination—polynomial, trigonometrical, exponential, and logarithmic. We now find it necessary to introduce the *elliptic function*.

Definition of a function by means of a differential equation.

A variable y is said to be a function of x when to values of x there correspond values of y. In fact, a function is determined by a *rule* which assigns y when x is given. Usually this rule is a formula admitting direct calculation of y (e.g., x^2, $3 \sin 2x$), but we may also use a differential equation to define a function; we must, however, assign initial conditions to make the solution unique.

Consider, for example, the differential equation

$$\frac{d^2y}{dx^2} + y = 0,$$

with the conditions $y = 0$, $dy/dx = 1$ for $x = 0$. If we had never previously heard of the function $\sin x$, this equation and the initial conditions would serve to define it. Another way of defining $\sin x$ is by the differential equation

$$(13.101) \qquad \left(\frac{dy}{dx}\right)^2 = 1 - y^2,$$

with the conditions

$$(13.102) \qquad y = 0, \quad \frac{dy}{dx} > 0, \quad \text{for } x = 0.$$

A type of differential equation with periodic solutions.

In connection with elliptic functions, we have to study the differential equation

(13 103) $$\left(\frac{dy}{dx}\right)^2 = (1 - y^2)(1 - k^2y^2),$$

where k is a constant such that $0 < k < 1$. It is really simpler, however, to take a more general point of view and study first the differential equation

(13 104) $$\left(\frac{dy}{dx}\right)^2 = f(y),$$

where $f(y)$ is a general function. We can find out a surprising amount about the solutions of this equation without specifying the function $f(y)$. We shall, however, assume that $f(y)$ is continuous; that it vanishes for $y = a$ and $y = b$ ($a < b$), but its derivative does not vanish for either of these values; and finally that $f(y) > 0$ for $a < y < b$. (The right-hand side of (13.103) has these properties, if we take $a = -1$, $b = 1$.)

Let us take a geometrical point of view, regarding x and y as rectangular Cartesian coordinates in a plane. The equation (13.104) is then a relation between the slope and the ordinate on a curve, and a solution, or integral curve, is a curve for which this relation is satisfied.

A number of statements can be made regarding the integral curves of (13 104). These will now be given, followed by their proofs.

(A) If we know an integral curve, then that curve translated through any distance parallel to the x-axis is also an integral curve.

(B) If an integral curve starts in the fundamental strip $a \leq y \leq b$, it cannot pass out of that strip.

(C) Every integral curve in the fundamental strip touches the bounding lines $y = a$, $y = b$ and has at no other point a tangent parallel to the x-axis.

(D) There is one, and only one, integral curve touching a bounding line at a given point.*

(E) All integral curves may be obtained from one integral curve by translation parallel to the x-axis.

(F) An integral curve is symmetric with respect to its normal at a point of contact with a bounding line.

* The bounding lines $y = a$, $y = b$ satisfy (13.104), but we do not regard them as integral curves. They are singular solutions.

(G) The x-distance between successive contacts of an integral curve with the bounding lines is

$$(13.105) \qquad P = \int_a^b \frac{dy}{\sqrt{f(y)}}.$$

(H) Any solution of (13.104), $y = \phi(x)$, is a periodic function with period $2P$, where P is given by (13.105); this means that

$$(13.106) \qquad \phi(x + 2P) = \phi(x),$$

for all values of x.

(I) If $y = \phi(x)$ is any one solution of (13.104), then the general solution is $y = \phi(x + c)$, where c is an arbitrary constant.

Some of these properties are shown in Fig. 132.

Proofs:

(A) Neither slope nor ordinate is changed by the translation; if the relation (13.104) is satisfied by the curve before translation, it will be satisfied after translation.

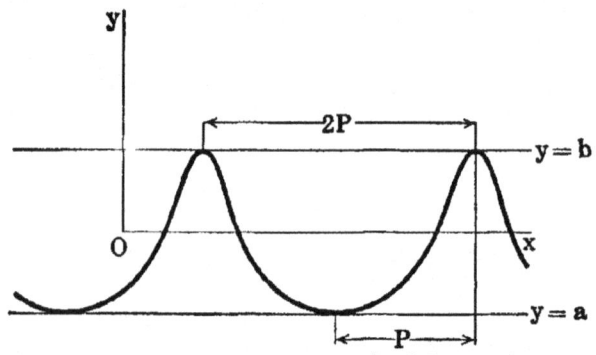

Fig. 132.—General character of a solution of the differential equation (13.104)

(B) If the curve passed out of the strip, $f(y)$ would become negative and dy/dx imaginary.

(C) By hypothesis, $f(a) = f(b) = 0$; hence, $dy/dx = 0$ on the bounding lines. Further, $f(y) > 0$ for $a < y < b$, and so dy/dx cannot vanish between the bounding lines.

(D) Let $x = x_0$, $y = a$ be a point on a bounding line. If we invert (13.104), take the square root, and integrate, we get

$$(13.107) \qquad x - x_0 = -\int_a^y \frac{d\eta}{\sqrt{f(\eta)}}, \qquad x - x_0 = \int_a^y \frac{d\eta}{\sqrt{f(\eta)}},$$

Sec 13.1]   MOTION OF A PARTICLE   367

according as $dy/dx < 0$ or $dy/dx > 0$. These two equations together give (in the neighborhood of $x = x_0$) the unique integral curve satisfying the condition of tangency.

(E) Let C and C' be any two integral curves. We have to show that C' may be made to coincide with C by a translation. Let C touch $y = a$ at $x = x_0$. Translate C' until it also touches $y = a$ at $x = x_0$. By (A), it is still an integral curve after translation; by (D), it coincides with C.

(F) The two equations (13.107) give the two parts of an integral curve, meeting at a point of tangency with $y = a$. To a given y, there correspond equal values of $x - x_0$, except for sign This establishes the symmetry for the parts of the curve running up from $y = a$ to $y = b$. But there is the same symmetry with respect to the normal at a contact with $y = b$ It is not difficult to see that this implies symmetry of the whole curve with respect to the normal at any point of contact with a bounding line. If the part of the curve to the right of such a normal is folded over the normal, it will coincide with the part of the curve on the left.

(G) This is obvious from (13.107).

(H) This follows from (G) and the symmetry of the curve.

(I) This merely expresses (E) in analytic form Since the differential equation is of the first order, we expect just one constant of integration.

The Jacobian elliptic functions.

Let us now apply our general results to the differential equation

(13.108) $$\left(\frac{dy}{dx}\right)^2 = (1 - y^2)(1 - k^2 y^2), \qquad (0 < k < 1).$$

The fundamental strip is $-1 \leq y \leq 1$. We define the *Jacobian elliptic function* sn x to be that solution of (13.108) which satisfies the conditions

(13.109) $$y = 0, \quad \frac{dy}{dx} > 0, \quad \text{for } x = 0.$$

It is evident that sn x depends on the value of k, which is called the *modulus* of the function, and we may write it sn (x, k); but it is usual to suppress the explicit dependence on k. (In speaking of the function, we call it "ess-en-ex.") .

From the result (I), stated on page 366, we know that the most general solution of (13 108) is

$$y = \operatorname{sn}(x + c),$$

where c is an arbitrary constant. Further, by (H), we know that sn x is a periodic function. Thus,

(13.110) $$\operatorname{sn}(x + 4K) = \operatorname{sn} x,$$

where K is the *elliptic integral*

(13.111) $$K = \tfrac{1}{2} \int_{-1}^{1} \frac{dy}{\sqrt{(1-y^2)(1-k^2y^2)}}$$
$$= \int_{0}^{1} \frac{dy}{\sqrt{(1-y^2)(1-k^2y^2)}};$$

K is, of course, a function of k.

By (F) the graph of the function sn x has symmetry with respect to each normal at a contact with the lines $y = \pm 1$. But, since the right-hand side of (13.108) is an even function of y, the graph has a further symmetry. The equation (13.108) and the conditions (13.109) are unchanged when we change x into $-x$ and y into $-y$, and so the curve is unaltered by a reflection in the origin. For the general case, shown in Fig. 132, the whole curve can be constructed by means of the symmetry when we know a half wave, running from $y = a$ to $y = b$. In the case of sn x, we need merely know the curve from $y = 0$ to $y = 1$ or, equivalently, from $x = 0$ to $x = K$.

The properties of sn x may be summed up as follows·

(13 112) $$\begin{cases} \left(\dfrac{d}{dx} \operatorname{sn} x\right)^2 = (1 - \operatorname{sn}^2 x)(1 - k^2 \operatorname{sn}^2 x), \\ \qquad\qquad\qquad\qquad\qquad\qquad (0 < k < 1), \\ \operatorname{sn} 0 = 0, \quad \left(\dfrac{d}{dx} \operatorname{sn} x\right)_{x=0} = 1, \\ \operatorname{sn}(x + 4K) = \operatorname{sn} x. \end{cases}$$

We now define other elliptic functions, cn x and dn x, by the equations

(13 113) $$\begin{cases} \operatorname{cn}^2 x = 1 - \operatorname{sn}^2 x, & \operatorname{cn} 0 = 1, \\ \operatorname{dn}^2 x = 1 - k^2 \operatorname{sn}^2 x, & \operatorname{dn} 0 = 1, \end{cases}$$

SEC. 13.1]　　MOTION OF A PARTICLE

with the further condition that the functions and their derivatives shall be continuous. Since $k < 1$, dn x is always positive It is clear that cn x has the period $4K$ and dn x the period $2K$.

If we take the square roots of the two sides of the first equation in (13.112), we get an ambiguous sign. However, for continuity, one sign must be taken throughout, and that sign is fixed by considering $x = 0$. Thus we find

(13 114) $\quad \dfrac{d}{dx} \text{sn } x = \text{cn } x \text{ dn } x.$

Differentiation of (13.113) gives

$$\text{cn } x \dfrac{d}{dx} \text{cn } x = -\text{sn } x \dfrac{d}{dx} \text{sn } x$$
$$= -\text{sn } x \text{ cn } x \text{ dn } x,$$

and so

(13 115) $\quad \dfrac{d}{dx} \text{cn } x = -\text{sn } x \text{ dn } x.$

Similarly,

(13 116) $\quad \dfrac{d}{dx} \text{dn } x = -k^2 \text{sn } x \text{ cn } x$

Just as (13 108) is a generalization of (13 101) and reduces to it if $k = 0$, so the elliptic functions are generalizations of the trigonometric functions. In fact, if $k = 0$, we have

(13.117) $\quad \begin{cases} \text{sn } x = \sin x, \\ \text{cn } x = \cos x, \\ \text{dn } x = 1, \\ K = \tfrac{1}{2}\pi, \end{cases}$

and (13.114), (13.115) reduce to familiar formulas.

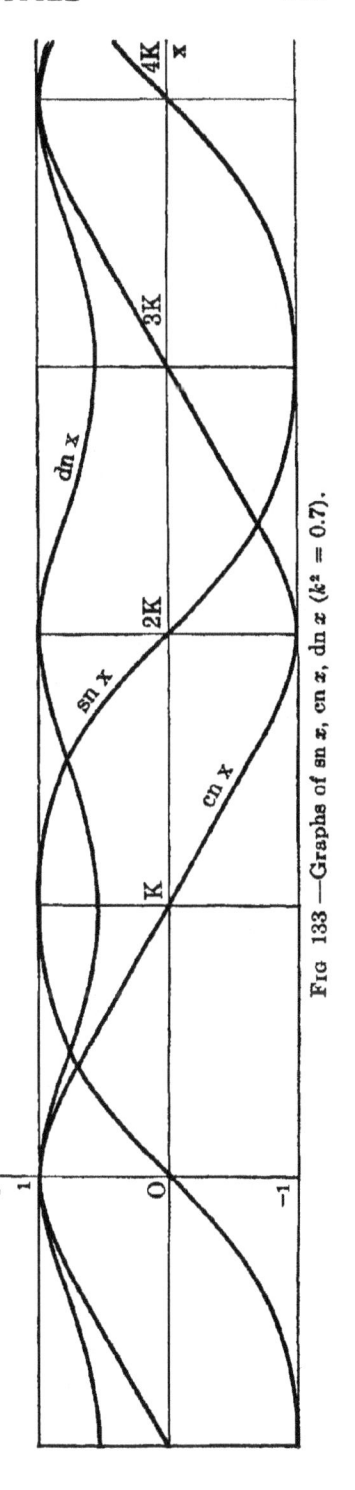

FIG 133 —Graphs of sn x, cn x, dn x ($k^2 = 0.7$).

The theory of elliptic functions is extensive, but this very brief presentation contains enough to enable us to solve certain dynamical problems. For numerical tables of the functions sn x, cn x, dn x, see L. M. Milne-Thomson, Die elliptischen Funktionen von Jacobi (Verlag Julius Springer, Berlin, 1931) Tables of elliptic integrals may also be used to find the elliptic functions; cf. J. B Dale, Five Figure Tables of Mathematical Functions (Edward Arnold, London, 1903), or E. Jahnke and F. Emde, Tables of Functions (B. G. Teubner, Leipzig, 1938) Figure 133 shows graphs of the functions, drawn for $k^2 = 0.7$; this makes $K = 2.07536$.

Exercise. Show that, in the limit $k = 1$, we get

$$\text{sn } x = \tanh x, \quad \text{cn } x = \text{dn } x = \text{sech } x.$$

13.2. THE SIMPLE PENDULUM

The motion in terms of elliptic functions.

We can now give the exact solution for the motion of a simple pendulum in terms of elliptic functions * Let m be the mass of the bob and a the length of the pendulum. The equation of energy (12.111) gives

(13.201) $$\tfrac{1}{2}ma^2\dot\theta^2 - mga \cos \theta = E,$$

where θ is the inclination of the string to the downward vertical, and E the constant total energy. We shall suppose the motion to be oscillatory with amplitude α, so that $\dot\theta = 0$ for $\theta = \pm\alpha$ Then $E = -mga \cos \alpha$, and (13.201) may be written

(13 202) $$\dot\theta^2 = 2p^2 (\cos \theta - \cos \alpha) = 4p^2 (\sin^2 \tfrac{1}{2}\alpha - \sin^2 \tfrac{1}{2}\theta),$$

where $p^2 = g/a$.

Let us define ϕ by

(13 203) $$\sin \tfrac{1}{2}\theta = \sin \tfrac{1}{2}\alpha \sin \phi,$$

so that

$$\tfrac{1}{2} \cos \tfrac{1}{2}\theta \, \dot\theta = \sin \tfrac{1}{2}\alpha \cos \phi \, \dot\phi.$$

---

* Since the motion of a compound pendulum is identical with that of the equivalent simple pendulum (cf Sec 7.2), the solution now given applies also to the compound pendulum; in (13 202) and the subsequent equations, we are to put $p^2 = ga/k^2$, where a is the distance of the mass center from the axis of suspension and k the radius of gyration about that axis.

[Sec. 13.2] MOTION OF A PARTICLE

Multiplying (13.202) by $\frac{1}{4}\cos^2 \frac{1}{2}\theta$, we get

$$\sin^2 \tfrac{1}{2}\alpha \cos^2 \phi \, \dot\phi^2 = p^2 \sin^2 \tfrac{1}{2}\alpha \cos^2 \phi \cos^2 \tfrac{1}{2}\theta,$$

or

(13.204) $$\dot\phi^2 = p^2(1 - \sin^2 \tfrac{1}{2}\alpha \sin^2 \phi)$$

If we multiply this equation by $\cos^2 \phi$ and put

(13.205) $$y = \sin \phi = \frac{\sin \tfrac{1}{2}\theta}{\sin \tfrac{1}{2}\alpha}, \qquad k = \sin \tfrac{1}{2}\alpha,$$

we get

(13.206) $$\dot y^2 = p^2(1 - y^2)(1 - k^2 y^2)$$

Except for the constant p^2 on the right, this has the form of the equation (13.108) To get the exact form, we define a new independent variable by

(13.207) $$x = pt$$

and obtain

(13.208) $$\left(\frac{dy}{dx}\right)^2 = (1 - y^2)(1 - k^2 y^2).$$

The general solution of this equation is

(13.209) $$y = \operatorname{sn}(x + c),$$

where c is a constant of integration Hence, we have the following result: *The general oscillatory motion of a simple pendulum, with amplitude α, is given by*

(13.210) $$\sin \tfrac{1}{2}\theta = \sin \tfrac{1}{2}\alpha \operatorname{sn}[p(t - t_0)],$$

where t_0 is a constant of integration, $p^2 = g/a$, and the modulus of the elliptic function is $k = \sin \tfrac{1}{2}\alpha$.

We usually find in dynamical problems that, if sn appears, the other elliptic functions cn, dn have simple physical meanings. From (13.210) we get at once, by (13.113),

(13.211) $$\cos \tfrac{1}{2}\theta = \operatorname{dn}[p(t - t_0)],$$

and differentiation of (13.210) gives

(13.212) $$\dot\theta = 2p \sin \tfrac{1}{2}\alpha \operatorname{cn}[p(t - t_0)].$$

The periodic time.

As we have seen, the periods of sn x and cn x are $4K$. Thus, by (13.210) and (13.212), the motion repeats itself after a time $4K/p$, and so the periodic time of the pendulum is

$$(13.213) \qquad \tau = \frac{4K}{p} = \frac{4}{p}\int_0^1 \frac{dy}{\sqrt{(1-y^2)(1-k^2y^2)}}.$$

Putting $y = \sin\phi$, we get

$$(13.214) \qquad \tau = \frac{4}{p}\int_0^{\frac{1}{2}\pi} \frac{d\phi}{\sqrt{1-k^2\sin^2\phi}}$$

$$= \frac{4}{p}\int_0^{\frac{1}{2}\pi}\left(1 + \frac{1}{2}k^2\sin^2\phi + \frac{1\cdot 3}{2\cdot 4}k^4\sin^4\phi + \cdots\right)d\phi.$$

Now,

$$\int_0^{\frac{1}{2}\pi} d\phi = \frac{\pi}{2}, \qquad \int_0^{\frac{1}{2}\pi} \sin^2\phi\, d\phi = \frac{\pi}{2}\cdot\frac{1}{2},$$

$$\int_0^{\frac{1}{2}\pi} \sin^4\phi\, d\phi = \frac{\pi}{2}\cdot\frac{1\cdot 3}{2\cdot 4}, \cdots,$$

and so we have the following infinite series for the periodic time of the pendulum:

$$(13.215) \qquad \tau = \frac{2\pi}{p}\left[1 + \left(\frac{1}{2}\right)^2 k^2 + \left(\frac{1\cdot 3}{2\cdot 4}\right)^2 k^4 + \cdots\right],$$

$$p^2 = \frac{g}{a}, \qquad k = \sin \tfrac{1}{2}\alpha.$$

For very small amplitude α, we get, as a first approximation,

$$\tau = 2\pi\sqrt{\frac{a}{g}},$$

agreeing with (6.307), where l was used to denote the length. The next approximation is

$$(13.216) \qquad \tau = 2\pi\sqrt{\frac{a}{g}}\left(1 + \frac{\alpha^2}{16}\right).$$

It is evident from (13.215) that the periodic time increases steadily with the amplitude.

13.3. THE SPHERICAL PENDULUM

A particle of mass m is attached to a fixed point by a light string or rod of length a and oscillates under the action of gravity. Since the particle is thus constrained to move on a sphere, this system is called a *spherical pendulum*. Under special initial conditions, a spherical pendulum will move in a vertical plane; then the motion is that of a simple pendulum, discussed in Sec. 13.2.

Although we shall be able to determine the general motion of a spherical pendulum in terms of elliptic functions, there are two particular motions which can be discussed quite simply. The first is a motion in which the particle performs small oscillations near the lowest point of the sphere, and the second is motion in a horizontal circle.

Fig 134.—Spherical pendulum

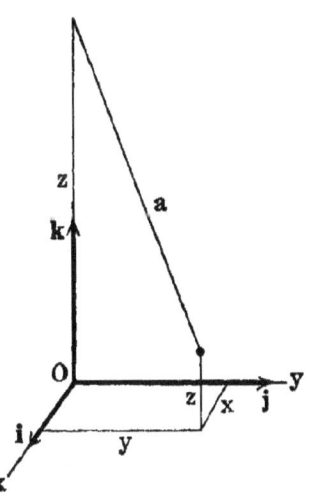

Small oscillations (first approximation).

Let $Oxyz$ be rectangular axes, O being at the lowest point of the sphere and Oz being directed vertically upward (Fig 134) If $\mathbf{i}, \mathbf{j}, \mathbf{k}$ is a unit orthogonal triad along the axes, the position vector of the particle is

(13.301) $$\mathbf{r} = x\mathbf{i} + y\mathbf{j} + z\mathbf{k}.$$

The force $\mathbf{P}$ on the particle is made up of gravity and the tension (S) in the string. Now the direction cosines of the string (running from the particle to the point of support) are

$$-\frac{x}{a}, \quad -\frac{y}{a}, \quad \frac{a-z}{a},$$

and so

(13.302) $$\mathbf{P} = -mg\mathbf{k} - [x\mathbf{i} + y\mathbf{j} + (z-a)\mathbf{k}]\frac{S}{a}.$$

So far the expressions are exact. But if x and y are small, z is a small quantity of the second order, since the plane $z = 0$ touches the sphere. Hence, we have as equation of motion,

omitting small quantities of the second order,

(13.303) $\quad m(\ddot{x}\mathbf{i} + \ddot{y}\mathbf{j}) = -\dfrac{xS}{a}\mathbf{i} - \dfrac{yS}{a}\mathbf{j} + (S - mg)\mathbf{k}.$

Comparing the coefficients, we see that $S = mg$, and

(13.304) $\qquad \ddot{x} + p^2 x = 0, \qquad \ddot{y} + p^2 y = 0, \qquad \left(p^2 = \dfrac{g}{a}\right).$

These are simple harmonic equations, as in (6.403). As far as its projection on the horizontal plane is concerned, the bob of the pendulum moves like a particle attracted toward O by a force proportional to the distance from O. As shown in Sec. 6.4, the path is an ellipse with center at O. (When the ellipse degenerates to a straight line, we get the motion of a simple pendulum, performing small oscillations.)

We have idealized the problem by leaving out all consideration of frictional resistance. The effect of this is to cause the bob of the pendulum to spiral in toward O, instead of continuing for ever in the elliptical path. However, the approximation (neglect of z) is perhaps a more serious oversimplification. We shall see the effect of this later, when we consider the second approximation.

The conical pendulum.

Any prescribed motion of a particle will take place under the action of a suitable force, namely, a force equal to the acceleration multiplied by the mass of the particle. Thus the bob of a spherical pendulum may be made to move in any way on the sphere defined by the length of the pendulum; to produce this motion, it is in general necessary to add a suitable force to the weight of the bob and the tension in the string. But if we can find a motion in which no such additional force is required, then that motion is a possible motion of the pendulum under weight and tension alone.

Consider a motion in a horizontal circle of radius R at constant speed q. The acceleration is of constant magnitude q^2/R and is directed in along the radius of the circular path. Resolving along this radius, along the tangent to the circular path, and vertically, we find that no additional force is required provided that

$$S \sin \theta = \frac{mq^2}{R}, \qquad S \cos \theta = mg,$$

where m is the mass of the bob, S the tension, and θ the inclination of the string to the downward vertical (Fig. 135). Since $\sin \theta = R/a$, elimination of S gives

(13.305) $$q^2 = \frac{gR^2}{\sqrt{a^2 - R^2}}.$$

If b denotes the depth of the horizontal circle below the center of the sphere, so that $b^2 = a^2 - R^2$, we have

(13.306) $$q^2 = \frac{g(a^2 - b^2)}{b}$$

This gives the speed q at which a horizontal circle at depth b may be described by the bob of the pendulum. When behaving in this way, the pendulum is called a *conical pendulum*, since the string describes a right circular cone.

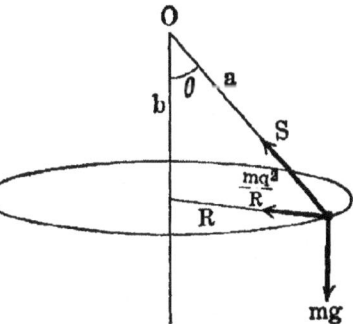

Fig. 135 —Conical pendulum

Exercise Find the tension in the string of a conical pendulum moving at a depth b. Examine the limits $b \to a$, $b \to 0$.

The general motion of a spherical pendulum.

To investigate the general motion of a spherical pendulum, we take cylindrical coordinates R, ϕ, z, the origin O being at the center of the sphere and the axis of z directed vertically upward. We have already obtained the equations of motion in (12.114) and (12.115); they may be written

(13.307) $$(a^2 - z^2)\dot\phi = h,$$
(13.308) $$\dot z^2 = f(z),$$

where

(13.309) $$f(z) = \frac{2g}{a^2}\left[(z^2 - a^2)\left(z - \frac{E}{g}\right) - \frac{h^2}{2g}\right].$$

We recall that a is the length of the string (i.e., the radius of the sphere on which the particle moves), and h and E are constants, the values of which depend on the initial conditions. We shall, for definiteness, assume h positive, so that ϕ increases; there is no loss of generality here, since we can reverse at will the sense in which ϕ is measured.

Our plan is to solve (13.308) for z as a function of t; then (13.307) will give ϕ by a quadrature.

We note that $f(z)$ is a cubic. It is positive for large positive values of z; it is negative for $z = \pm a$; it is positive for values of z occurring during the motion, as we see from (13.308) These last values must of course lie in the range $(-a, a)$. Since a cubic cannot have more than three changes of sign, it follows that

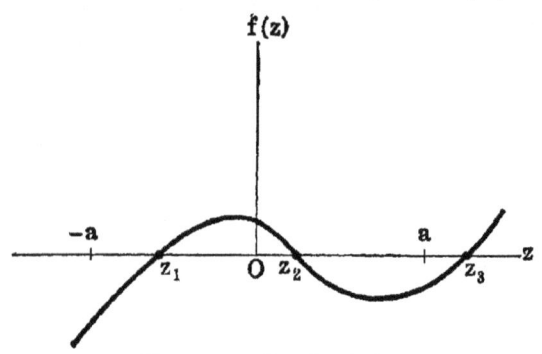

Fig. 136.—Graph of $f(z)$.

the graph of $f(z)$ is of the general nature shown in Fig. 136; the function $f(z)$ has *three real zeros*, z_1, z_2, z_3, such that

$$(13.310) \qquad -a < z_1 < z_2 < a < z_3$$

(In exceptional cases, we may have one or more signs of equality instead of inequality.) Since $f(z)$ cannot be negative during the motion, we see that z oscillates between the values z_1, z_2. We note that the equation (13.308) is of the type (13.104), so that all the general results established for (13.104) apply to (13.308).

To obtain z as a function of t, we proceed as follows: Since z_1, z_2, z_3 are the zeros of $f(z)$, we have

$$(13.311) \qquad f(z) = \frac{2g}{a^2}(z - z_1)(z - z_2)(z - z_3).$$

Let us define $u = \sqrt{z - z_1}$, so that $\dot{z} = 2u\dot{u}$. Then (13.308) gives

$$(13.312) \qquad \dot{u}^2 = \frac{g}{2a^2}(z_2 - z_1 - u^2)(z_3 - z_1 - u^2).$$

This suggests the differential equation (13.108) for the elliptic function sn. Let us define

(13.313)
$$\begin{cases} v = \dfrac{u}{\sqrt{z_2 - z_1}} = \sqrt{\dfrac{z - z_1}{z_2 - z_1}}, \\ k = \sqrt{\dfrac{z_2 - z_1}{z_3 - z_1}}, \quad p = \sqrt{\dfrac{g(z_3 - z_1)}{2a^2}}. \end{cases}$$

Then (13.312) may be written

(13.314) $$v^2 = p^2(1 - v^2)(1 - k^2 v^2),$$

and so

(13.315) $$v = \operatorname{sn}[p(t - t_0)],$$

where t_0 is a constant of integration. Hence we have

(13.316)
$$\begin{cases} z - z_1 = (z_2 - z_1)\,\operatorname{sn}^2[p(t - t_0)], \\ z_2 - z = (z_2 - z_1)\,\operatorname{cn}^2[p(t - t_0)], \\ z_3 - z = (z_3 - z_1)\,\operatorname{dn}^2[p(t - t_0)]. \end{cases}$$

Any one of these three equations gives z as a function of t. We note that z has the period

(13.317) $$\tau = \frac{2K}{p},$$

where K is as in (13.111). Since, by (13.307), ϕ increases steadily throughout the motion, the path of the particle on the sphere is as shown in Fig. 137

We have already seen that the particle oscillates between the two levels $z = z_1$ and $z = z_2$. We shall now show that the arithmetic mean of these levels lies below the center of the sphere, this statement being equivalent to

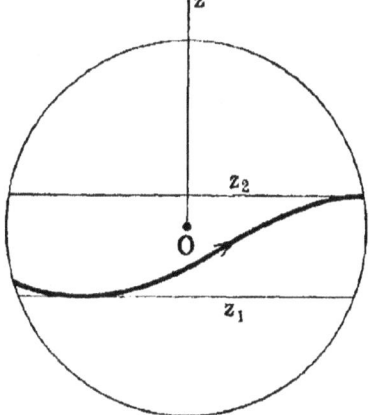

Fig. 137.—The path of the bob of a spherical pendulum.

(13.318) $$z_1 + z_2 < 0.$$

We have two different expressions for $f(z)$, (13.309) and (13.311); they must, of course, be identically equal, and therefore

(13.319) $$z_1 + z_2 + z_3 = \frac{E}{g}, \qquad z_2 z_3 + z_3 z_1 + z_1 z_2 = -a^2,$$

$$z_1 z_2 z_3 = \frac{h^2 - 2a^2 E}{2g}.$$

From the second of these, we have

$$(13.320) \qquad z_1 + z_2 = -\frac{a^2 + z_1 z_2}{z_3}.$$

Since z_1 and z_2 are each less than a in absolute value and z_3 is positive, (13.318) follows at once.

The path on the sphere is represented analytically by a relation connecting z and ϕ. Elimination of t from (13.307) and (13.308) gives the required relation in the form of a differential equation

$$(13.321) \qquad \left(\frac{d\phi}{dz}\right)^2 = \frac{h^2}{(a^2 - z^2)^2 f(z)}.$$

If we look down on the pendulum from a great distance above, the bob appears to describe a plane curve, with R and ϕ as polar coordinates. The motion resembles that of a particle attracted toward a center of force, the areal velocity ($\frac{1}{2}R^2\dot\phi$) being a constant for both motions. Just as we considered the apsides of the orbit of a particle in a plane, so we can consider the apsides of the horizontal projection of the path of the spherical pendulum. These points correspond to stationary values of R, i.e., to $\dot R = 0$. Hence $\dot z = 0$ at these points, since $R^2 + z^2 = a^2$. As the actual path oscillates between the circles at heights $z = z_1$, $z = z_2$ on the sphere, so the horizontal projection of the path oscillates between circles of radii $\sqrt{a^2 - z_1^2}$ and $\sqrt{a^2 - z_2^2}$.

The apsidal angle α is the increment in ϕ corresponding to the passage from $z = z_1$ to $z = z_2$. Thus, by (13.321),

$$(13.322) \qquad \alpha = h \int_{z_1}^{z_2} \frac{dz}{(a^2 - z^2) \sqrt{f(z)}}$$
$$= \frac{ha}{\sqrt{2g}} \int_{z_1}^{z_2} \frac{dz}{(a^2 - z^2) \sqrt{(z - z_1)(z - z_2)(z - z_3)}}.$$

Exercise. Find z_1, z_2, z_3 for a conical pendulum with the bob at a depth b below the center of the sphere.

Small oscillations (second approximation).

The expression (13.322) is too complicated as it stands to be of much interest. But it yields a definite simple result when we suppose the oscillations to be small. The reasoning is delicate, because, as z_1 and z_2 tend to $-a$ (the lowest point on the sphere), the extent of the range of integration tends to zero, and the

SEC. 13 3]   MOTION OF A PARTICLE   379

integrand tends to infinity. The method of approximation is important; the same method may be used in finding the rotation of the perihelion of Mercury in the general theory of relativity.

Before making any approximation, however, we shall first put (13 322) into a form in which a, z_1, z_2 are the only constants occurring explicitly. To do this, we refer to (13.319) We have

$$\frac{h^2}{2g} = z_1 z_2 z_3 + a^2(z_1 + z_2 + z_3), \qquad z_3 = -\frac{a^2 + z_1 z_2}{z_1 + z_2};$$

if we eliminate z_3 from these two equations and subtract z from the second equation, we obtain

(13.323)
$$\begin{cases} \dfrac{h}{\sqrt{2g}} = \dfrac{SD}{\sqrt{-(z_1 + z_2)}}, \\ z_3 - z = -\dfrac{1}{z_1 + z_2}[z(z_1 + z_2) + a^2 + z_1 z_2], \end{cases}$$

where

(13.324) $S = \sqrt{(a + z_1)(a + z_2)}, \qquad D = \sqrt{(a - z_1)(a - z_2)}$

Substitution in (13 322) gives for the apsidal angle the required expression

(13 325) $$\alpha = aSD \int_{z_1}^{z_2} F(z)\,dz,$$

where

$$F(z) = \frac{1}{(a^2 - z^2)\sqrt{(z_2 - z)(z - z_1)}[z(z_1 + z_2) + a^2 + z_1 z_2]}.$$

We cannot use the binomial theorem to expand negative powers of terms which vanish when z, z_1, z_2 tend to $-a$. However the term in the square bracket remains finite, and we may expand a negative power of it. Putting

(13.326) $$z = -a + \zeta,$$

where ζ is small, we get approximately, i.e., neglecting ζ^2,

$$\frac{1}{\sqrt{z(z_1 + z_2) + a^2 + z_1 z_2}} = \frac{1}{\sqrt{D^2 + \zeta(z_1 + z_2)}}$$
$$= \frac{1}{D}\left[1 - \tfrac{1}{2}\frac{\zeta}{D^2}(z_1 + z_2)\right].$$

Hence, we can write

(13.327) $$\alpha = aSI - \tfrac{1}{2}\frac{aS}{D^2}(z_1 + z_2)J,$$

where

(13.328) $$\begin{cases} I = \int_{z_1}^{z_2} \dfrac{dz}{(a^2 - z^2)\sqrt{(z_2 - z)(z - z_1)}}, \\ J = \int_{z_1}^{z_2} \dfrac{dz}{(a - z)\sqrt{(z_2 - z)(z - z_1)}}. \end{cases}$$

These integrals are evaluated without difficulty by means of the substitution

$$z = z_2 \sin^2 \theta + z_1 \cos^2 \theta,$$

and we find

(13.329) $$I = \frac{\pi}{2a}\left(\frac{1}{S} + \frac{1}{D}\right), \qquad J = \frac{\pi}{D}.$$

Substitution in (13.327) gives

(13.330) $$\alpha = \tfrac{1}{2}\pi\left[1 + SD\frac{D^2 - a(z_1 + z_2)}{D^4}\right].$$

It is evident from (13.324) that S is small, thus the last term is small, and we introduce only a negligible error (of the second order) if we substitute in the fraction

$$D = 2a, \qquad z_1 + z_2 = -2a.$$

This gives

(13.331) $$\alpha = \tfrac{1}{2}\pi\left(1 + SD \cdot \frac{3}{8a^2}\right).$$

Now if R_1, R_2 are the distances from the central vertical to the apsides, we have accurately

$$R_1^2 = a^2 - z_1^2, \qquad R_2^2 = a^2 - z_2^2, \qquad SD = R_1 R_2,$$

and so the approximate formula (13.331) becomes

(13.332) $$\alpha = \tfrac{1}{2}\pi\left(1 + \frac{3R_1 R_2}{8a^2}\right).$$

We saw, in connection with the equations (13.304), that in the first approximation the path of the particle is a central ellipse.

For that curve the apsidal angle is $\frac{1}{2}\pi$. Now we see, from (13.332), that the apsidal angle is a little greater than $\frac{1}{2}\pi$. This means that the apse advances; the path is approximately a central ellipse, but *this ellipse turns slowly forward* (i e , in the same sense as that in which the particle describes the path). In one rotation of the particle, the apse advances through an angle

$$(13.333) \qquad 4\alpha - 2\pi = \frac{3\pi R_1 R_2}{4a^2} = \frac{3A}{4a^2},$$

where A is the area of the ellipse. The advance disappears when $A = 0$, i.e., when the orbit is flattened into the track of a simple pendulum

This advance of the apse can be shown by fitting a light writing device to the bob of the pendulum. This traces the rotating elliptical path on a sheet of paper, placed underneath

13.4. THE MOTION OF A CHARGED PARTICLE IN AN ELECTROMAGNETIC FIELD

Much of our knowledge of the structure of matter is derived from the study of the motion of charged particles (electrons or ionized atoms) in electromagnetic fields. Further interest has been added to the problem by the invention of the electron microscope and other devices, in which streams of electrons produce images in much the same way as images are formed by rays of light in an optical instrument

Electrostatic and magnetostatic fields.

We shall consider only statical fields, i e., fields which do not change with time. Such fields are produced by electric charges at rest in condensers or by steady currents; permanent magnets may also be used.

In an electrostatic field, there exists at each point of space an *electric vector* **E**. It is the negative of the gradient of an *electric potential* V, so that

$$(13.401) \qquad \mathbf{E} = -\text{grad } V.$$

The potential V cannot take arbitrary values throughout space; it must satisfy Laplace's partial differential equation

$$(13.402) \qquad \frac{\partial^2 V}{\partial x^2} + \frac{\partial^2 V}{\partial y^2} + \frac{\partial^2 V}{\partial z^2} = 0.$$

Similarly, in a magnetostatic field there is at each point of space a *magnetic vector* **H**, such that

(13.403) $$\mathbf{H} = -\operatorname{grad} \Omega;$$

Ω is the *magnetic potential*, and it also satisfies Laplace's equation

(13.404) $$\frac{\partial^2 \Omega}{\partial x^2} + \frac{\partial^2 \Omega}{\partial y^2} + \frac{\partial^2 \Omega}{\partial z^2} = 0.$$

Both fields may be present at the same time. The force exerted on a particle carrying an electric charge ϵ, moving with velocity **q**, is

(13.405) $$\mathbf{P} = \epsilon \mathbf{E} + \epsilon \mathbf{q} \times \mathbf{H},$$

if the units are suitably chosen.

We accept these basic formulas of electromagnetic theory as the foundation for our dynamical deductions.

Before proceeding to discuss special fields, we shall obtain an equation of energy from (13.405). If m is the mass of the particle, its equation of motion is*

(13.406) $$m\dot{\mathbf{q}} = \epsilon \mathbf{E} + \epsilon \mathbf{q} \times \mathbf{H}.$$

Taking the scalar product of each side with **q**, we get

$$\frac{d}{dt}(\tfrac{1}{2}mq^2) = m\dot{\mathbf{q}} \cdot \mathbf{q} = \epsilon \mathbf{E} \cdot \mathbf{q} = -\epsilon(\operatorname{grad} V) \cdot \mathbf{q} = -\epsilon \frac{dV}{dt}.$$

Hence, we have the *equation of energy*

(13.407) $$\tfrac{1}{2}mq^2 + \epsilon V = \text{constant}.$$

If the field is purely magnetic, so that V disappears, the speed of the particle remains constant.

Exercise. The potential due to a charge ϵ at the origin is $V = \epsilon/r$, where $r^2 = x^2 + y^2 + z^2$. Verify that this satisfies Laplace's equation, and show that the force between two charges at rest satisfies the inverse square law (6.502).

---

* This is the nonrelativistic equation of motion and is a good approximation if the velocity of the particle is small compared with the velocity of light. In the accurate relativistic equation, we replace the left-hand side of (13.406) by $\dfrac{d}{dt}\left(\dfrac{m_0 \mathbf{q}}{\sqrt{1 - q^2/c^2}}\right)$; see Chap XVI.

Motion in a uniform field.

A simple solution of (13 402) is
$$V = ax + by + cz + d,$$
where a, b, c, d are constants. This gives a uniform electric field, in which **E** is a constant vector. Similarly, we may have a uniform magnetic field, in which **H** is a constant vector.

Let us now suppose that a particle, of mass m and carrying a charge ϵ, moves in a uniform electric and magnetic field. If **r** is the position vector of the particle, we have as equation of motion

(13.408) $$m\ddot{\mathbf{r}} = \epsilon \mathbf{E} + \epsilon \dot{\mathbf{r}} \times \mathbf{H}$$

Let us now choose our axes so that Oz is parallel to **H**. The vector equation (13 408) gives the three scalar equations (with the usual notation for components)

(13.409) $$\begin{cases} \ddot{x} = \dfrac{\epsilon}{m} E_1 + \dfrac{\epsilon}{m} H \dot{y}, \\ \ddot{y} = \dfrac{\epsilon}{m} E_2 - \dfrac{\epsilon}{m} H \dot{x}, \\ \ddot{z} = \dfrac{\epsilon}{m} E_3. \end{cases}$$

To complete the solution most conveniently, we introduce the complex quantities
$$\zeta = x + iy, \qquad F = E_1 + iE_2.$$

Then the first two equations of (13.409) may be written together in the complex form

(13 410) $$\ddot{\zeta} + \frac{i\epsilon H}{m} \dot{\zeta} = \frac{\epsilon F}{m}$$

This is a differential equation with constant coefficients, and the characteristic equation for solutions of the form e^{nt} is

$$n\left(n + \frac{i\epsilon H}{m}\right) = 0$$

Thus the general solution of (13.409) is

(13.411) $$\begin{cases} x + iy = \zeta = A + Be^{-ipt} - \dfrac{iFt}{H}, \\ z = C + Dt + \dfrac{\epsilon E_3 t^2}{2m}, \end{cases}$$

where $p = \epsilon H/m$ and A, B, C, D are constants of integration; A and B are complex, whereas C and D are real. *These equations give the motion of a charged particle in a uniform electric and magnetic field.*

Let us examine this motion in the case where the electric and magnetic fields are perpendicular to one another. Then $E_3 = 0$ and the z-velocity is constant. Let us, for simplicity, assume that this component of velocity vanishes and that $z = 0$ throughout the motion. Then the trajectory is described by the complex position vector ζ, as given by the first of (13.411). Let us write this equation in the form

$$(13.412) \qquad \zeta - \left(A - \frac{iFt}{H} \right) = B e^{-ipt}.$$

We recall that any complex number Z may be written in the form

$$Z = |Z| e^{i \arg Z}.$$

If Z is a complex position vector, $|Z|$ is the radius vector, and $\arg Z$ the azimuthal angle. Equating moduli and arguments in (13.412), we have

$$(13.413) \qquad \begin{cases} \left| \zeta - \left(A - \frac{iFt}{H} \right) \right| = |B|, \\ \arg \left[\zeta - \left(A - \frac{iFt}{H} \right) \right] = \arg B - pt. \end{cases}$$

If F were zero, the first equation would indicate motion in a circle with center A and radius $|B|$, and the second equation would tell us that the circle is described with constant angular velocity $-p$. (The sign shows the sense.) The effect of the F-term is simply to impose an additional motion in which the center of the circle moves with constant complex velocity

$$(13.414) \qquad -\frac{iF}{H} = \frac{1}{H}(E_2 - iE_1).$$

This velocity is of magnitude E/H and is perpendicular to the electric vector.

We sum up our description of the motion of a charged particle in perpendicular uniform electric and magnetic fields as follows: *If started with a velocity perpendicular to* **H**, *the particle moves as if*

it were attached to the edge of a circular disk which moves in a plane perpendicular to **H**; the disk spins with constant angular velocity $-\epsilon H/m$, and its center has a constant velocity E/H perpendicular to **E** (Fig. 138). The surprising part of this result is that, on the whole, the particle does not move in the direction of the electric field, but perpendicular to it.

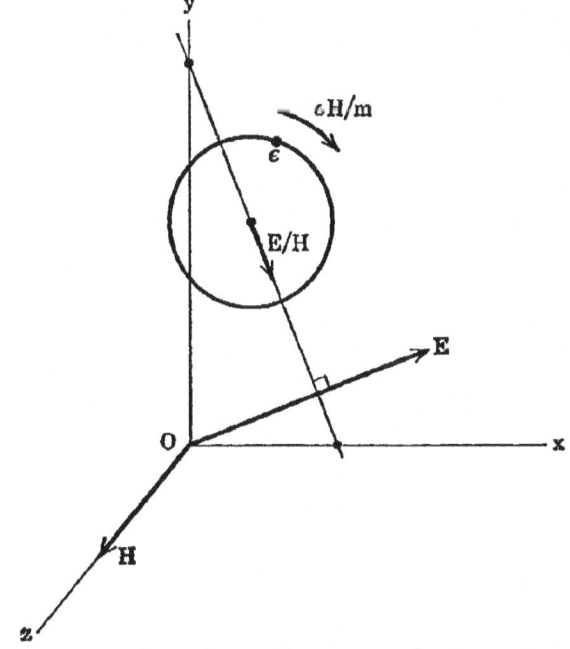

Fig. 138.— Motion of a charged particle in perpendicular uniform electric and magnetic fields

Exercise. Suppose the charged particle starts from rest at the origin at time $t = 0$. Starting from (13.412) prove the following facts concerning the motion:

(i) At time $t = 2\pi/p$, it will be at rest again at a distance $2\pi E/(pH)$ from the origin.

(ii) If H is very small, and if the particle is allowed to travel for a definite finite time t_1, then at $t = t_1$ its complex position is approximately $\frac{1}{2}\epsilon F t_1^2/m$, and its complex velocity is approximately $\epsilon F t_1/m$.

Motion in a purely electric field and in a purely magnetic field.

We have worked out (13.411) for the general case in which both electric and magnetic fields are present. In the case of a purely electric field ($H = 0$) we return to (13.408), which

becomes

(13.415)
$$m\ddot{\mathbf{r}} = \epsilon \mathbf{E}.$$

If the field is uniform, the acceleration is constant, and so the particle describes a parabolic trajectory like a projectile under gravity (cf. Sec. 6.1). The plane of the trajectory is determined by the vector $\mathbf{E}$ and the initial velocity.

In the case of a uniform purely magnetic field ($E = 0$), the equations (13.411) read

$$\zeta = A + Be^{-\imath pt}, \quad z = C + Dt, \quad \left(p = \frac{\epsilon H}{m}\right).$$

By moving the origin, we can make $A = C = 0$; then we have

(13.416)
$$\zeta = Be^{-\imath pt}, \quad z = Dt$$

Hence

$$|\zeta| = |B|, \quad \left|\frac{dz}{d\zeta}\right| = \left|\frac{D}{pB}\right|;$$

since these values are constant, it is clear that *the trajectory is a circular helix, with axis parallel to the magnetic field.* The azimuthal angular velocity is $-p = -\epsilon H/m$.

The simplest motion in a uniform magnetic field is one in which the initial velocity is perpendicular to the field. Then $D = 0$ in (13.416), and the trajectory is a circle described with constant speed.

The determination of the charge ϵ and the mass m of an electron is a problem of great physical interest. Let us see how the results we have established help in that determination. The first thing we notice is that ϵ and m appear in our equations only in the form ϵ/m, and therefore it is only this ratio that we can hope to find. It would seem a simple matter to find ϵ/m from the circular motion described in the preceding paragraph. The angular velocity is $-\epsilon H/m$, and so we have, on equating two different expressions for the angular velocity,

$$\frac{q^2}{R^2} = \frac{\epsilon^2 H^2}{m^2},$$

where q is the constant speed and R the radius of the circle. (We have squared the two expressions to avoid the question of sign, which is of no importance here.) If we could measure q, R, and H, we should at once have ϵ/m. Now R can be meas-

ured from a photograph of the track of the electron, and H can also be measured; but q presents a difficulty—electrons move too fast for us to find their speeds directly. We have therefore to find q indirectly. Before entering the magnetic field, the electron is accelerated from rest by an electric field. If it starts from rest at potential $V = V_0$ and enters the magnetic field with speed q at potential $V = V_1$, then

$$\tfrac{1}{2}mq^2 = \epsilon(V_0 - V_1)$$

by the principle of energy (13.407). Elimination of q between the two equations gives

$$\frac{\epsilon}{m} = \frac{2(V_0 - V_1)}{R^2 H^2}$$

This is a suitable expression for the determination of ϵ/m, since all the quantities on the right are measurable. This is the method of Kaufmann. The electromagnetic units are such that (13.405) holds.

Axially symmetric fields.

Let R, ϕ, z be cylindrical coordinates. A field is said to be *axially symmetric* with respect to the z-axis if the potential is a function of R and z only (i.e., independent of ϕ). An electric field of this type is produced by a system of charged plates perpendicular to the z-axis, a circular hole with center on the z-axis being cut from each plate. An axially symmetric magnetic field is produced by currents flowing in circular coils arranged in planes perpendicular to the z-axis, the centers of the coils being on the z-axis.

Let V be an axially symmetric electric potential. We assume that V can be expanded in a power series in x and y, the coefficients being functions of z. On account of the axial symmetry, x and y can be involved only in the form $x^2 + y^2 (= R^2)$, and so the expansion is of the form

(13.417) $\quad V = V_0(z) + \dfrac{R^2}{2!} V_1(z) + \dfrac{R^4}{4!} V_2(z) + \cdots$

Then, by an easy calculation,

(13.418) $\quad \dfrac{\partial^2 V}{\partial x^2} + \dfrac{\partial^2 V}{\partial y^2} + \dfrac{\partial^2 V}{\partial z^2} = [V_0''(z) + 2V_1(z)]$
$$+ R^2[\tfrac{1}{2}V_1''(z) + \tfrac{2}{3}V_2(z)] + \cdots$$

In order that Laplace's equation (13.402) may be satisfied, the functions $V_0, V_1, \cdots$ must satisfy the sequence of ordinary differential equations

(13.419) $\quad V_0''(z) + 2V_1(z) = 0, \qquad V_1''(z) + \tfrac{4}{3} V_2(z) = 0, \cdots$.

It is evident that $V_0(z)$ (the potential on the axis of symmetry) may be chosen arbitrarily, the burden of satisfying Laplace's equations being placed on $V_1(z), V_2(z), \cdots$.

We may treat an axially symmetric magnetic field in exactly the same way. Assuming for the magnetic potential an expansion of the form

$$(13.420) \quad \Omega = \Omega_0(z) + \frac{R^2}{2!} \Omega_1(z) + \frac{R^4}{4!} \Omega_2(z) + \cdots,$$

we deduce the relations

(13.421) $\quad \Omega_0''(z) + 2\Omega_1(z) = 0, \qquad \Omega_1''(z) + \tfrac{4}{3}\Omega_2(z) = 0, \cdots$

Motion of a charged particle near the axis of symmetry of an electromagnetic field.[*]

If we introduce the potentials from (13.401) and (13.403), the general equations of motion (13.406) read, when written out in full,

$$(13.422) \quad \begin{cases} \ddot{x} = k\left(\dfrac{\partial V}{\partial x} + \dot{y}\dfrac{\partial \Omega}{\partial z} - \dot{z}\dfrac{\partial \Omega}{\partial y}\right), \\ \ddot{y} = k\left(\dfrac{\partial V}{\partial y} + \dot{z}\dfrac{\partial \Omega}{\partial x} - \dot{x}\dfrac{\partial \Omega}{\partial z}\right), \\ \ddot{z} = k\left(\dfrac{\partial V}{\partial z} + \dot{x}\dfrac{\partial \Omega}{\partial y} - \dot{y}\dfrac{\partial \Omega}{\partial x}\right), \end{cases}$$

where $k = -\epsilon/m$. In the most interesting applications, the charged particle is an electron carrying a negative charge; in this case k is positive.

Let us assume that the electromagnetic field has the z-axis for axis of symmetry, so that we have the expansions (13.417) and (13.420) for V and Ω, respectively. We shall consider only motion near the axis of symmetry, so that x, y, and their derivatives are small. Then, neglecting terms of order higher than the

---

[*] Reference may be made to N. Chako and A. A. Blank, Supplementary Note No. I, in R. K. Luneberg, Mathematical Theory of Optics (Brown University, 1944)

first, we rewrite (13.422) in the form

(13.423) $$\begin{cases} \ddot{x} = k(xV_1 + \dot{y}\Omega_0' - \dot{z}y\Omega_1), \\ \ddot{y} = k(yV_1 + \dot{z}x\Omega_1 - \dot{x}\Omega_0'), \\ \ddot{z} = kV_0', \end{cases}$$

where the prime denotes d/dz. The last of these equations is equivalent, in our approximation, to the equation of energy (13.407), which may be written

(13.424) $$\dot{z}^2 = 2k(V_0 - C),$$

where C is a constant. This constant may be determined when the initial values of z and $\dot{z}$ are given.

We note that (13.424) determines $\dot{z}$ as a function of z, to within a sign. Let us assume that $\dot{z}$ is positive throughout the motion. Then we may write

(13.425) $$\dot{z} = w(z) > 0, \qquad w^2 = 2k(V_0 - C).$$

The function w is the axial component of velocity. Since we are neglecting $\dot{x}^2$ and $\dot{y}^2$, it is clear that, to our order of approximation, w also represents the magnitude of the velocity vector. By (13.419) and (13.421) we have

(13.426) $$\begin{cases} V_1 = -\tfrac{1}{2}V_0'' = -\dfrac{1}{4k}\dfrac{d^2}{dz^2}(w^2) = -\dfrac{1}{2k}(ww'' + w'^2), \\ \Omega_1 = -\tfrac{1}{2}\Omega_0''. \end{cases}$$

It is convenient to introduce complex notation, writing $\zeta = x + iy$. We multiply the second equation of (13.423) by i and add it to the first; this gives, on making use of (13.426),

(13.427) $$\ddot{\zeta} = -\tfrac{1}{2}(ww'' + w'^2)\zeta - ik\Omega_0'\dot{\zeta} - \tfrac{1}{2}ikw\Omega_0''\zeta.$$

We shall change the independent variable from t to z by the equations

(13.428) $$\dot{\zeta} = \zeta'\dot{z} = w\zeta', \qquad \ddot{\zeta} = w^2\zeta'' + ww'\zeta'.$$

Substitution in (13.427) gives

(13.429) $$\begin{cases} \zeta'' + P\zeta' + Q\zeta = 0, \\ P = \dfrac{w'}{w} + \dfrac{ik\Omega_0'}{w}, \qquad Q = \tfrac{1}{2}\left(\dfrac{w''}{w} + \dfrac{w'^2}{w^2}\right) + \dfrac{ik\Omega_0''}{2w}. \end{cases}$$

This is the differential equation from which the path of the particle is to be determined by finding ζ as a function of z.

The complex variable ζ represents the vector displacement of the particle perpendicular to the axis of symmetry (z-axis). The coefficients P and Q are functions of the independent variable z, and are determined by the axial potentials $V_0(z)$ and $\Omega_0(z)$ and by the initial conditions, which are needed to obtain the value of C in (13.425); we note that w depends on C.

In the case of an electrostatic field, we put $\Omega_0 = 0$; we note that then P and Q are real. In the case of a magnetostatic field, we put $V_0 = 0$; then, by (13.425), w is a constant and the terms in P and Q involving derivatives of w disappear, leaving purely imaginary expressions.

There is no simple general method of solving (13.429). However, the equation may be simplified by using a standard device to eliminate the first-order derivative by a change in the dependent variable. To carry this out, we substitute

(13.430) $$\zeta(z) = u(z)v(z)$$

in (13.429) and obtain

(13.431) $$u''v + u'(2v' + Pv) + u(v'' + Pv' + Qv) = 0.$$

We now choose v so as to make the coefficient of u' vanish. We do this by writing

(13.432) $$v = \exp\left[-\tfrac{1}{2}\int_{z_0}^{z} P(\xi)\,d\xi\right],$$

where z_0 is the initial value of z. When we substitute (13.432) in (13.431) we get, after some easy calculation,

(13.433) $$\begin{cases} u'' + S(z)u = 0, \\ S(z) = Q - \tfrac{1}{4}P^2 - \tfrac{1}{2}P'. \end{cases}$$

Also, by (13.430),

(13.434) $$\zeta = u\exp\left[-\tfrac{1}{2}\int_{z_0}^{z} P(\xi)\,d\xi\right].$$

When we substitute for P and Q the expressions given in (13.429), we obtain a much simpler expression for S than we might expect, and (13.433) reads

(13.435) $$u'' + S(z)u = 0, \qquad S(z) = \tfrac{3}{4}\frac{w'^2}{w^2} + \frac{k^2\Omega_0'^2}{4w^2}.$$

The relation between the actual displacement vector ζ and the

artificial displacement vector u is

(13.436) $\quad \zeta = u \sqrt{\dfrac{w_0}{w}} \exp\left[-\tfrac{1}{2}ik \int_{z_0}^{z} \dfrac{\Omega_0'(\xi)}{w(\xi)} d\xi\right],$

where w_0 is the value of w when $z = z_0$.

It may be convenient for reference to write the results separately for the cases of electrostatic and magnetostatic fields:

Electrostatic field:

(13.437) $\quad \begin{cases} u'' + S(z)u = 0, \qquad S(z) = \tfrac{3}{4}\dfrac{w'^2}{w^2} \\ \qquad\qquad\qquad\qquad\quad = \dfrac{3V_0'^2}{16\left(V_0 - V_{00} + \dfrac{w_0^2}{2k}\right)^2}, \\ w(z) = \sqrt{2k[V_0(z) - C]}, \qquad k = -\dfrac{\epsilon}{m}, \\ \qquad\qquad\qquad\qquad\qquad\qquad \zeta = u\sqrt{\dfrac{w_0}{w}}, \\ V_{00} = V_0(z_0), \qquad w_0 = w(z_0). \end{cases}$

Magnetostatic field:

(13.438) $\quad \begin{cases} u'' + S(z)u = 0, \qquad S(z) = \dfrac{k^2\Omega_0'^2}{4w_0^2}, \\ w_0 = \text{constant velocity}, \qquad k = -\dfrac{\epsilon}{m}, \\ \qquad\qquad\qquad\qquad \zeta = u \exp\left[\dfrac{ik}{2w_0}(\Omega_{00} - \Omega_0)\right], \\ \Omega_{00} = \Omega_0(z_0). \end{cases}$

There are some remarkable features in the preceding work. In (13.429) the coefficients P and Q were *complex;* but when we transform to (13.435), we get a *real* coefficient S. Not only is S real, it is also *positive,* this has an important bearing on the formation of "images" by an axially symmetric electromagnetic field, as we shall see later.

The mathematical difference between the electrostatic case and the magnetostatic case is less than we might expect. In each case the coefficient S is positive. The chief difference lies in the relation between ζ and u. In the electrostatic case, the connection is real, and the complex vector ζ has the same direction as the complex vector u. In the magnetostatic case the

connection is complex; the magnitudes of the two vectors are equal, and ζ is obtained from u by rotation through an angle

$$\frac{k}{2w_0}(\Omega_{00} - \Omega_0).$$

To sum up, in the general electromagnetic case, the determination of the path of the particle involves the solution of (13.435). As initial conditions, we may assume that the particle starts from the point (z_0, ζ_0) with velocity w_0 in a direction giving to ζ' the value ζ'_0. Thus, (13.435) is to be solved, with the initial conditions for $z = z_0$,

(13 439) $\quad u = \zeta_0, \quad u' = \zeta'_0 + \tfrac{1}{2}k\zeta_0\left(\dfrac{V'_{00}}{w_0^2} + \dfrac{i\Omega'_{00}}{w_0}\right),$

where
$$V'_{00} = V'_0(z_0), \qquad \Omega'_{00} = \Omega'_0(z_0).$$

In the electrostatic case, (13.437) replaces (13.435), and we put $\Omega'_{00} = 0$ in (13.439); in the magnetostatic case, (13.438) replaces (13.435), and we put $V'_{00} = 0$ in (13.439).

Exercise Show that the small angle between the initial velocity vector and the axis of symmetry is $|\zeta'_0|$.

The electromagnetic lens.

In an optical instrument, such as a microscope, camera, or telescope, rays of light are bent by a system of glass lenses, the system usually having an axis of symmetry. The function of the instrument is to produce an image, the rays from each point of the object being brought to a focus at an image point. In recent times, there has been a remarkable development of electromagnetic devices analogous to the image-forming optical instrument. Instead of rays of light bent by glass lenses, there are streams of electrons whose trajectories are curved by means of electromagnetic fields.* When an axially symmetric electromagnetic field is used, the equation (13.435) is the fundamental equation from which the trajectories of the electrons are determined.

Let Oz (Fig. 139) be the axis of symmetry of an electromagnetic field; let Π_0 be a plane perpendicular to this axis, with the equa-

---
* Cf L. M. Myers, Electron Optics (Chapman & Hall, Ltd., London, 1939), p. 100.

Sec. 13.4] MOTION OF A PARTICLE 393

tion $z = z_0$ Let P_0 be any point on Π_0 with a complex position vector $x + iy = \zeta_0$. We suppose that from the point P_0 there are projected a number of identical charged particles (electrons). Their velocities have a common magnitude w_0, but their directions are different; the directions are, however, nearly parallel to the axis of symmetry, so that our methods apply.

The trajectory of each electron satisfies (13.435). The function $w(z)$ is given by (13.425). Since all the electrons have the same charge ϵ, the same mass m, and the same initial velocity w_0,

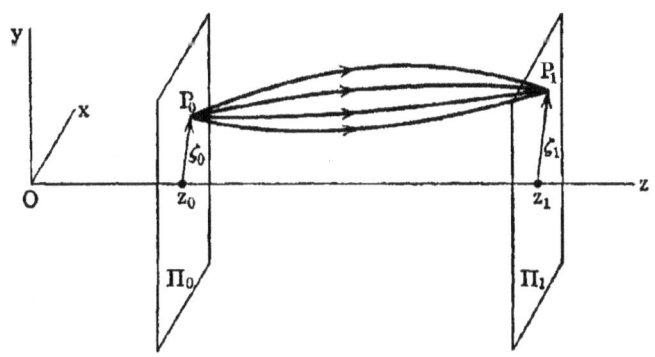

Fig 1.39—Formation of an image

the constant C has the same value for all the trajectories. Hence w [and consequently S in (13.435)] is the same for all the trajectories. This is, of course, a mathematical idealization. As far as we know, all electrons have the same charge and the same mass, but we cannot secure accurately a common initial velocity. Hence, in practice, the constant C and the functions w and S will not be quite the same for all the trajectories This leads to what is called, from the optical analogue, "chromatic aberration," the velocity of the electron corresponding to the color of the light. But for our purposes we shall neglect this effect and regard w and S as the same for all the trajectories.

We note that, from (13.439), for $z = z_0$ we have $u = \zeta_0$ for all the electrons; but the initial value of u' depends on the particular electron since ζ_0' is not the same for them all.

It is known from the theory of linear differential equations that the general solution of (13.435) is of the form*

(13.440) $$u = \alpha f(z) + \beta g(z),$$

* Cf. E L Ince, Ordinary Differential Equations (Longmans, Green & Co., Ltd., London, 1927), p 119.

where α, β are arbitrary constants of integration (which may be complex) and $f(z)$, $g(z)$ are independent particular solutions. Since the coefficient S in (13.435) is real, we can obtain two real independent particular solutions by taking the initial conditions

(13.441) $\quad f(z_0) = 0, \quad f'(z_0) = 1; \quad g(z_0) = 1, \quad g'(z_0) = 0.$

With this choice of f and g, it follows from (13.440) that

$$\alpha = u_0', \quad \beta = u_0,$$

where u_0, u_0' are the values of u, u' when $z = z_0$; then (13.440) may be written

(13.442) $\quad\quad\quad u = u_0' f(z) + u_0 g(z).$

Let u_1 be the value of u at the point where the trajectory cuts the plane $z = z_1$, then

(13.443) $\quad\quad\quad u_1 = u_0' f(z_1) + u_0 g(z_1).$

In the family of trajectories which we are considering, i.e., a family starting from a point (z_0, ζ_0), u_0 has a common value but u_0' changes from trajectory to trajectory. Thus, in general, (13.443) will give an *area* on the plane $z = z_1$ when we substitute the various values of u_0' corresponding to the various initial directions. The equation (13.443) will define a *single point* on the plane $z = z_1$ if, and only if,

(13.444) $\quad\quad\quad f(z_1) = 0.$

Let us recall that the function $f(z)$ is defined by the following differential equation and initial conditions:

(13.445) $\quad\begin{cases} f''(z) + S(z)f(z) = 0, \\ f(z_0) = 0, \quad f'(z_0) = 1. \end{cases}$

Can we find a plane $z = z_1$ (other than $z = z_0$) such that the whole family of trajectories cut it in a single point? This is equivalent to asking whether the equation (13.444) has a solution other than $z_1 = z_0$.

Although we cannot give a definite answer to this question in general, we can discuss it qualitatively. Consider the graph of $f(z)$. This graph starts from the z-axis at z_0, sloping up at 45°. Thus $f(z)$ is positive at first; hence by (13.445), since S is positive, $f''(z)$ is negative, and it remains negative as long as $f(z)$ is positive.

This means that the graph is convex when viewed from above Either of two things happens. The curve may turn down and cut the z-axis at some point z_1 (Fig. 140a); or it may turn so slowly that it reaches $z = \infty$ before coming down to the z-axis (Fig. 140b). In the former case, the equation (13 444) has a solution, in the latter case, it has no solution (at least not for values of z_1 greater than z_0, and we are interested only in such values). In general terms, we may say that the larger S is, the more chance there is that there will be a solution; because the larger S is, the more rapidly does the graph of $f(z)$ turn downward.

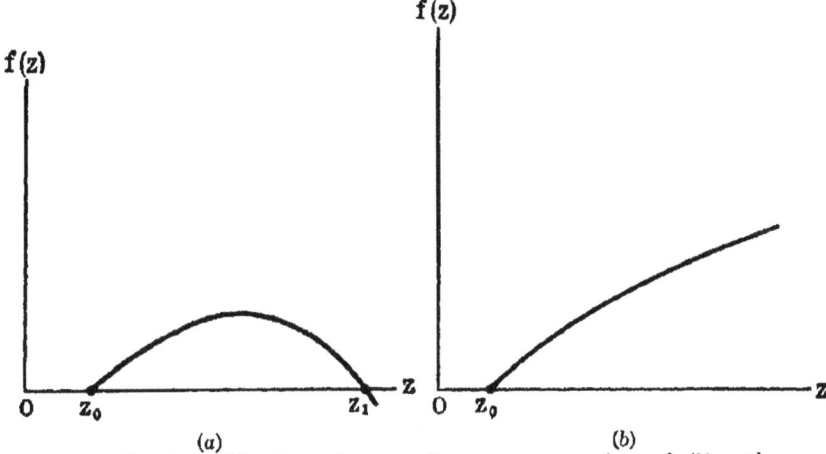

Fig 140.—Graph of $f(z)$. (a) in the case where an image is formed, (b) in the case where an image is not formed

If (13.444) has a solution, then the family of trajectories starting out from a point P_0 meet again in a point P_1, as shown in Fig. 139. Borrowing the language of optics, we may call P_0 the *object point* and P_1 the *image point*. In this sense, an *axially symmetric electromagnetic field may form images*. We might go further and say that it *will* form images if it is strong enough, because S is increased by an increase in the strength of the field.

It will be noted that the equation (13.444), which determines the plane Π_1 on which the image is formed, does not involve ζ_0. Consequently we may state the following important result: *If an object point P_0 on the plane Π_0 has an image P_1 on the plane Π_1, then every object point on the plane Π_0 (near the axis of symmetry, to make the approximate method valid) has an image on the plane Π_1.* In fact, we have an *object plane* and an *image plane*, just as in the

optics of a lens. Hence, by analogy, we may speak of an axially symmetric electromagnetic field as an *electromagnetic lens*.

Suppose that on the object plane Π_0 there is some minute structure which we wish to photograph. We set up a photographic plate at the plane Π_1 and bombard the plane Π_0 from the left with a stream of electrons. Each point of Π_0 becomes a source of electrons travelling on towards Π_1 and converging to an image point on Π_1. Thus the structure on Π_0 is reproduced point for point on Π_1. A point on Π_0 transparent to electrons gives a "bright" point on Π_1, and a point on Π_0 opaque to electrons gives a "dark" point on Π_1. Essentially, this is how an electron microscope works. Since magnification is the most important function of a microscope, let us now look into the question of the *magnification* m produced by an electromagnetic lens.

The image of a point (z_0, ζ_0) is (z_1, ζ_1), where z_1 is given by (13.444) and ζ_1 by (13.436) and (13.443); we have

(13.446) $$u_1 = u_0 g(z_1) = \zeta_0 g(z_1),$$

and

(13.447) $$\zeta_1 = \zeta_0 g(z_1) \sqrt{\frac{w_0}{w_1}} \exp\left[-\tfrac{1}{2} ik \int_{z_0}^{z_1} \frac{\Omega_0'(\xi)}{w(\xi)} d\xi\right],$$

where $w_1 = w(z_1)$. Magnification is defined by

(13.448) $$m = \left|\frac{\zeta_1}{\zeta_0}\right|,$$

and so, by (13.447), the magnification of an electromagnetic lens is

(13.449) $$m = |g(z_1)| \sqrt{\frac{w_0}{w_1}}.$$

We recall that $g(z)$ is defined by the following differential equation and initial conditions:

(13.450) $$\begin{cases} g''(z) + S(z)g(z) = 0, \\ g(z_0) = 1, \quad g'(z_0) = 0. \end{cases}$$

It is a real function, since S is real; and the modulus sign in (13.449) is needed only to take care of the possibility that $g(z_1)$ is negative.

In the case of an *electrostatic* field, the exponential disappears from (13.447); the vector ζ_1 has the same direction as ζ_0 or the

opposite direction, according as $g(z_1)$ is positive or negative. In the case of a *magnetostatic* field, (13.447) reads

$$(13.451) \qquad \zeta_1 = \zeta_0 g(z_1) \exp\left[\frac{ik}{2w_0}(\Omega_{00} - \Omega_{01})\right],$$

where Ω_{01} is the value of Ω_0 at $z = z_1$. The magnification is $m = |g(z_1)|$. The image vector ζ_1 is obtained by first applying this magnification to the object vector ζ_0 and then rotating it about the z-axis through an angle

$$(13.452) \qquad \alpha = \frac{k}{2w_0}(\Omega_{00} - \Omega_{01}).$$

Figures 141a and b show the projections of object point P_0, image point P_1, and trajectories on the plane $z = 0$. They are drawn for $m = 2$ and $\alpha = \pi/4$. In actual electron microscopes the magnification may be as high as 200,000

Approximations for electromagnetic lenses.

The determination of the focal properties of an electromagnetic lens depends, as we have seen, on the solution of the differential equation

$$(13.453) \qquad f''(z) + S(z)f(z) = 0,$$

with the initial conditions, as in (13.441),

$$(13.454) \qquad f(z_0) = 0, \qquad f'(z_0) = 1.$$

There is no simple way of solving this equation, and we have to fall back on approximate methods. We shall consider the case where the electromagnetic field is concentrated on a short length of the z-axis, so that there is practically no field outside this short range. Making a mathematical idealization, we shall assume that there is a field for $-h < z < h$ and no field outside that range.

In the absence of electric field, the axial potential V_0 is constant, and so, by (13.425), w is constant and $w' = 0$. In the absence of magnetic field, the axial potential Ω_0 is constant and $\Omega_0' = 0$. Thus, by (13.435), $S = 0$ for that range of values of z for which the electromagnetic field vanishes. By hypothesis, this is the case outside the range $-h < z < h$, and then the differential equation (13.453) becomes very simple: $f''(z) = 0$.

398 *MECHANICS IN SPACE* [SEC. 13.4

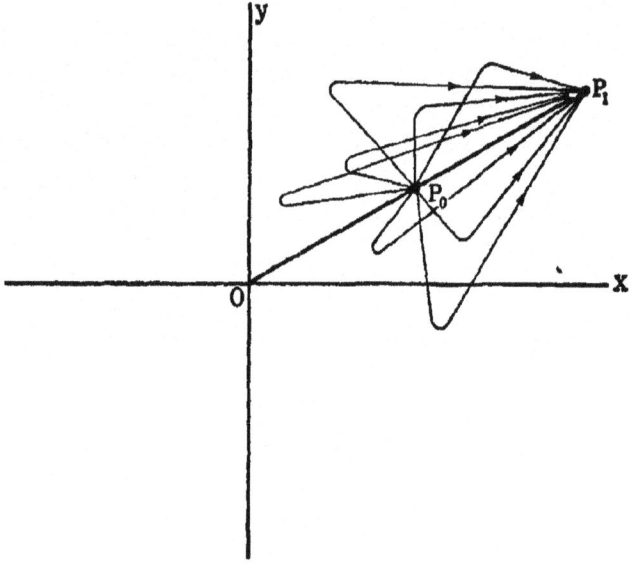

FIG. 141a.—Formation of an image by an electrostatic lens

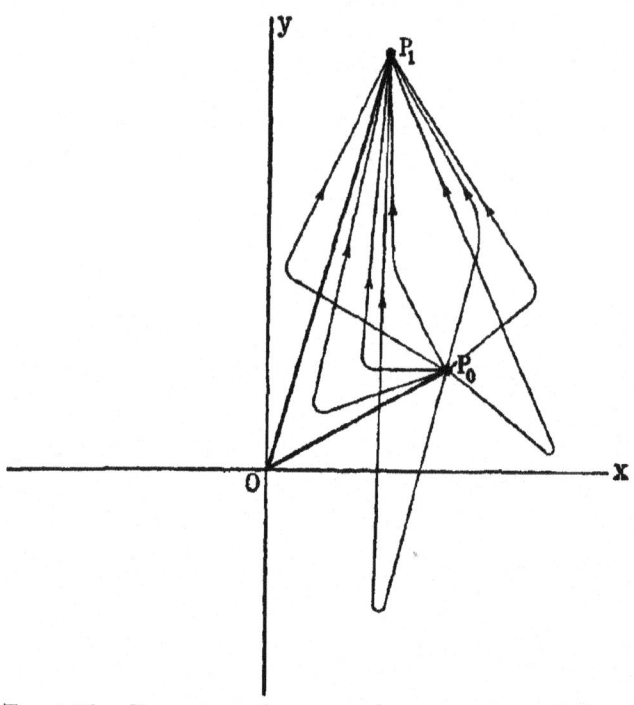

FIG. 141b.—Formation of an image by a magnetostatic lens.

The function $f(z)$ is therefore a linear function of z. This corresponds to the fact that, in the absence of electromagnetic field, an electron travels in a straight line with constant velocity. The projections of trajectories in Figs. 141a and b are drawn for such a case; each projection consists of two straight lines, connected by a curve. The curve is produced by the action of a concentrated electromagnetic field. If the field extended

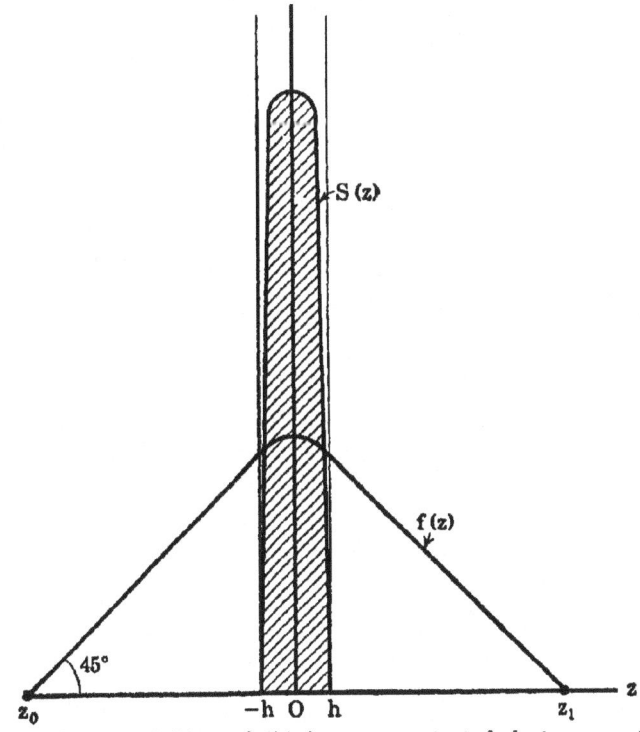

FIG. 142.—Graphs of $S(z)$ and $f(z)$ for a concentrated electromagnetic field

from z_0 to z_1, the projections of the trajectories would be curved all the way.

Figure 142 shows graphs of $S(z)$ and $f(z)$ for the case of a concentrated electromagnetic field, drawn on the assumption that $f(z)$ vanishes for some value z_1 of z, so that an image is formed.

Combining the initial conditions (13.454) with the fact that $f(z)$ is linear for $z < -h$, we obtain

(13.455) $\quad f(-h) = -h - z_0, \quad f'(-h) = 1.$

Thus we know the value of f and its first derivative on entering

the concentrated field. We now try to find out what happens as we go through the field.

Transferring the second term of (13.453) to the right-hand side and integrating from $-h$ to z, we get, remembering (13.455),

$$(13.456) \qquad f'(z) = 1 - \int_{-h}^{z} S(\xi)f(\xi)\,d\xi.$$

Another integration gives

$$(13.457) \qquad f(z) = z - z_0 - \int_{-h}^{z} d\eta \int_{-h}^{\eta} S(\xi)f(\xi)\,d\xi.$$

Putting $z = h$ in these two equations, we obtain

$$(13.458) \qquad \begin{cases} f(h) = h - z_0 - \int_{-h}^{h} d\eta \int_{-h}^{\eta} S(\xi)f(\xi)\,d\xi, \\ f'(h) = 1 - \int_{-h}^{h} S(\xi)f(\xi)\,d\xi. \end{cases}$$

At first sight it may appear that we have found the values of f and its derivative on leaving the field, but of course this is illusory, because we do not know the function f occurring in the integrals. However, we can use the above equations as a basis for approximation

If $S(z)$ is finite and h is small, it is evident from (13.458) that the changes in f and f' in passing from $z = -h$ to $z = h$ are small But to get an image, the graph of f must be bent through an angle of more than 45° on passing through the field. In fact, there must be a finite change in f', and consequently we must use a strong field It is clear that $S(z)$ must be large of the order h^{-1}. Then the integral in the second of (13.458) is finite; the double integral in the first of (13.458) is small of order h, showing that although the change in f' is finite, the change in f is small.

Before introducing the approximation, let us get an expression for z_1, the coordinate of the image point. From the linearity of the graph of f outside the field, we have

$$(13.459) \qquad f'(h) = -\frac{f(h)}{z_1 - h},$$

or

$$(13.460) \qquad \frac{1}{z_1 - h} = -\frac{f'(h)}{f(h)}.$$

This will give us z_1 if we can evaluate $f(h)$ and $f'(h)$ from (13.458).

We now take up the method of approximate solution by the method of iteration. The key equation is (13.457). For f under

Sec. 13 4] MOTION OF A PARTICLE 401

the sign of integration, we substitute f as given by the equation itself. This does not get rid of f on the right-hand side, but it pushes it under more signs of integration and thus reduces its importance. This procedure gives

$$(13.461) \quad f(z) = z - z_0 - \int_{-h}^{z} d\eta \int_{-h}^{\eta} S(\xi) \, d\xi \Big[\xi - z_0 \\ - \int_{-h}^{\xi} dq \int_{-h}^{q} S(p) f(p) \, dp \Big].$$

The multiple integrals are to be evaluated starting from the right-hand side. We can rewrite this in the form

$$(13.462) \quad f(z) = z - z_0 + z_0 \int_{-h}^{z} d\eta \int_{-h}^{\eta} S(\xi) \, d\xi \\ - \int_{-h}^{z} d\eta \int_{-h}^{\eta} \xi S(\xi) \, d\xi + \int_{-h}^{z} d\eta \int_{-h}^{\eta} S(\xi) \, d\xi \int_{-h}^{\xi} dq \int_{-h}^{q} S(p) f(p) \, dp.$$

This expression is accurate. For z in the range $-h < z < h$, the first integral is small of order h, and the remaining integrals are small of order h^2. Differentiation of (13 462) gives

$$(13.463) \quad f'(z) = 1 + z_0 \int_{-h}^{z} S(\xi) \, d\xi - \int_{-h}^{z} \xi S(\xi) \, d\xi \\ + \int_{-h}^{z} S(\xi) \, d\xi \int_{-h}^{\xi} dq \int_{-h}^{q} S(p) f(p) \, dp.$$

Here the first integral is finite, and the remaining integrals small, of order h. We observe that in (13.462) and (13.463), only the last integrals are unknown.

If we required a higher approximation, we could substitute again for f under the sign of integration; then the integrals containing f would be small of order h^3 in the expression for $f(z)$, and small of order h^2 in the expression for $f'(z)$. This process could be continued indefinitely.

Let us, however, content ourselves with approximations for $f(h)$ and $f'(h)$ which retain terms of order h but reject terms of order h^2. We shall commit an error only of order h^2 if we substitute $f(p) = -z_0$ in the last integral in (13.463). Accordingly, putting $z = h$, we get the following approximate expressions:

$$(13.464) \quad \begin{cases} f(h) = h - z_0 + z_0 \int_{-h}^{h} d\eta \int_{-h}^{\eta} S(\xi) \, d\xi, \\ f'(h) = 1 + z_0 \int_{-h}^{h} S(\xi) \, d\xi - \int_{-h}^{h} \xi S(\xi) \, d\xi \\ \qquad - z_0 \int_{-h}^{h} S(\xi) \, d\xi \int_{-h}^{\xi} dq \int_{-h}^{q} S(p) \, dp \end{cases}$$

To write these results more neatly, we introduce the finite constants

(13.465)
$$\begin{cases} A = \int_{-h}^{h} S(\xi)\, d\xi, & B = h^{-1} \int_{-h}^{h} \xi S(\xi)\, d\xi, \\ D = h^{-1} \int_{-h}^{h} S(\xi)\, d\xi \int_{-h}^{\xi} (\xi - \eta) S(\eta)\, d\eta. \end{cases}$$

We note that, by inversion of order of integration,

(13.466)
$$\begin{cases} \int_{-h}^{h} d\eta \int_{-h}^{\eta} S(\xi)\, d\xi = \int_{-h}^{h} (h - \xi) S(\xi)\, d\xi = h(A - B), \\ \int_{-h}^{h} S(\xi)\, d\xi \int_{-h}^{\xi} dq \int_{-h}^{q} S(p)\, dp \\ \qquad = \int_{-h}^{h} S(\xi)\, d\xi \int_{-h}^{\xi} (\xi - p) S(p)\, dp = hD. \end{cases}$$

Consequently, (13.464) read

(13.467)
$$\begin{cases} f(h) = -z_0 + h[1 + (A - B)z_0], \\ f'(h) = 1 + z_0 A - h(B + Dz_0). \end{cases}$$

The constants A, B, D may be evaluated numerically if the field is given, it should be noted however that they involve also the initial velocity w_0, since S involves w_0 (cf. equation (13.435)).

Exercise 1 Show that if $S = K/h$, a constant, for $-h < z < h$, then
$$A = 2K, \quad B = 0, \quad D = \tfrac{2}{3}K^2.$$

Exercise 2. Evaluate $A, B,$ and D, if, for $-h < z < h$,
$$S(z) = ah^{-1} \cos^2 \frac{\pi z}{2h},$$
where a is a constant.

Using (13.467) in (13.460), the image z_1 corresponding to an object z_0 is given by

(13.468)
$$\frac{1}{z_1 - h} = \frac{1 + z_0 A - h(B + Dz_0)}{z_0 - h[1 + (A - B)z_0]},$$

or more symmetrically, to the same order of approximation (i.e neglecting h^2),

(13.469)
$$\frac{1}{z_1} - \frac{1}{z_0} - A = -h\left(\frac{B}{z_1} + \frac{B}{z_0} + D\right).$$

If we let $z_0 \to -\infty$, we get

(13.470)
$$\frac{1}{z_1} - A = -h\left(\frac{B}{z_1} + D\right)$$

The value of z_1 so obtained gives the image of an object at infinity.

If we are satisfied with the rougher approximation in which h is neglected, (13.469) becomes

$$(13.471) \qquad \frac{1}{z_1} - \frac{1}{z_0} = A.$$

If we let $z_0 \to -\infty$, the corresponding value of z_1 is called the *focal length* F of the electromagnetic lens; by (13.471), we have

$$(13.472) \qquad \frac{1}{F} = A = \int_{-h}^{h} S(z)\, dz.$$

Exercise. Show that in the roughest approximation, the focal length of a concentrated electric lens is given by

$$(13.473) \qquad \frac{1}{F} = \tfrac{3}{16} \int_{-h}^{h} \frac{V_0'^2}{\left(V_0 - V_{00} - \dfrac{mu_0^2}{2\epsilon}\right)^2}\, dz$$

and the focal length of a concentrated magnetic lens by

$$(13.474) \qquad \frac{1}{F} = \left(\frac{\epsilon}{2mw_0}\right)^2 \int_{-h}^{h} H^2\, dz,$$

where H is the magnitude of the magnetic vector on the axis of symmetry ($H = |\Omega_0'|$).

13.5. EFFECTS OF THE EARTH'S ROTATION

The effect of the earth's rotation on a plumb line was found in Sec. 5.3. This is a statical phenomenon relative to the rotating earth, and only the centrifugal force is involved. In dynamical problems on the rotating earth the Coriolis force also enters, and the effects are hard to predict without a careful mathematical analysis.

Equations of motion of a particle relative to the earth's surface.

We accept the model of the earth used in Sec. 5.3—an oblate spheroid turning about its axis of symmetry with constant angular velocity Ω. The axis is supposed fixed in a Newtonian frame of reference. The vertical at any point on the earth's surface is defined by the plumb line, and the horizontal plane is perpendicular to the vertical. The latitude λ is the angle of elevation of the earth's axis above the horizontal plane.

In Fig. 143, SN is the earth's axis, drawn from south to north; O is a point on or near the earth's surface, and B the foot of the perpendicular dropped from O on SN; $\mathbf{I}$ is a unit vector along BO and $\mathbf{K}$ a unit vector parallel to SN. The triad of unit vectors $\mathbf{i}, \mathbf{j}, \mathbf{k}$ is fixed relative to the earth and directed as follows:

$\mathbf{i}$ is horizontal and points south;
$\mathbf{j}$ is horizontal and points east;
$\mathbf{k}$ is vertical and points upward.

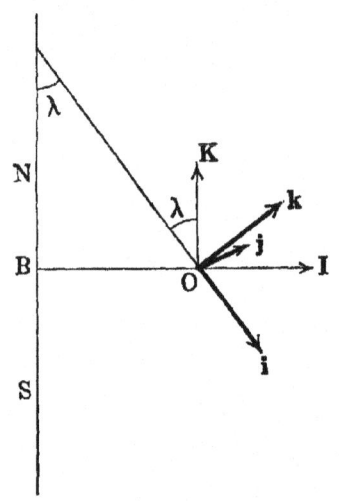

Fig. 143.—Vectors used in discussing the effects of the earth's rotation.

Let us put $\overrightarrow{BO} = \mathbf{a}$ and denote by $\mathbf{r}$ the position vector of a moving particle relative to O. Then the position vector of the particle relative to B is

(13.501) $$\mathbf{r}_B = \mathbf{a} + \mathbf{r}.$$

Since B is a fixed point in a Newtonian frame of reference, the absolute acceleration of the particle is

(13.502) $$\ddot{\mathbf{r}}_B = \ddot{\mathbf{a}} + \ddot{\mathbf{r}}.$$

Here $\ddot{\mathbf{a}}$ is the acceleration of O; since O moves in a circle with constant angular velocity Ω, we have

(13.503) $$\ddot{\mathbf{a}} = -a\Omega^2 \mathbf{I} = -a\Omega^2 (\sin \lambda\, \mathbf{i} + \cos \lambda\, \mathbf{k}).$$

Let m be the mass of the particle. The force of gravity is proportional to m and may be written $m\mathbf{F}$. We denote by $\mathbf{P}$

the resultant of all other forces The equation of motion is

(13 504) $$m\ddot{\mathbf{r}}_B = m\mathbf{F} + \mathbf{P},$$

or, by (13.502) and (13.503),

(13 505) $$m\ddot{\mathbf{r}} = m\mathbf{F} + \mathbf{P} + ma\Omega^2(\sin\lambda\,\mathbf{i} + \cos\lambda\,\mathbf{k}).$$

Let us apply this equation to a plumb line, hanging in equilibrium with the bob at O. Then $\mathbf{P}$ is the tension in the plumb line and points in the direction $\mathbf{k}$. As in Sec. 5 3, we define g to be this tension, divided by the mass of the bob, so that

$$\mathbf{P} = mg\mathbf{k}.$$

Since $\mathbf{r} = \mathbf{0}$, (13.505) gives

(13.506) $$\mathbf{F}_0 + a\Omega^2(\sin\lambda\,\mathbf{i} + \cos\lambda\,\mathbf{k}) = -g\mathbf{k},$$

where $\mathbf{F}_0$ is the force of gravity per unit mass at O.

Now $\mathbf{F}$ in the general equation (13 505) and $\mathbf{F}_0$ in (13.506) are not equal vectors unless the particle is at O, for the earth's gravitational field changes from point to point. But we shall assume that the particle always stays so close to O that variations in the earth's field are negligible. So we introduce our first approximation, putting

(13.507) $$\mathbf{F} = \mathbf{F}_0$$

in the equation of motion (13 505) When, further, we substitute for $\mathbf{F}_0$ from (13.506), we get for any moving particle

(13 508) $$m\ddot{\mathbf{r}} = \mathbf{P} - mg\mathbf{k}.$$

Our next task is to resolve this equation into components along $\mathbf{i}$, $\mathbf{j}$, $\mathbf{k}$. This triad turns with a constant angular velocity

(13.509) $$\boldsymbol{\Omega} = \Omega\mathbf{K} = -\Omega\cos\lambda\,\mathbf{i} + \Omega\sin\lambda\,\mathbf{k},$$

and so, by (12 310),

(13 510) $$\ddot{\mathbf{r}} = \frac{\delta^2 \mathbf{r}}{\delta t^2} + 2\boldsymbol{\Omega}\times\frac{\delta \mathbf{r}}{\delta t} + \boldsymbol{\Omega}\times(\boldsymbol{\Omega}\times\mathbf{r}).$$

We now introduce a second approximation, dropping the last term on account of the smallness of Ω. Substitution from (13.510) in (13.508) gives the *vector form of the equations of motion relative to the earth's surface*,

$$(13.511) \quad m\frac{\delta^2 \mathbf{r}}{\delta t^2} = \mathbf{P} - mg\mathbf{k} - 2m\boldsymbol{\Omega} \times \frac{\delta \mathbf{r}}{\delta t}.$$

Here $\delta^2\mathbf{r}/\delta t^2$ and $\delta\mathbf{r}/\delta t$ are, respectively, the relative acceleration and velocity, the last term is the Coriolis force. The centrifugal force has been eliminated in two steps, first by (13.506) and secondly by neglect of the last term in (13.510). It will be noticed that (13.511) is essentially the same differential equation as (13.406) or (13.408)—the equation of motion of a charged particle in an electromagnetic field.

Let us now introduce axes $Oxyz$ coincident in direction with $(\mathbf{i}, \mathbf{j}, \mathbf{k})$, so that Ox points south and Oy east. Let X, Y, Z be the components along these axes of the force $\mathbf{P}$, which, it will be remembered, is the force other than gravity. Since Ω is given by (13.509), we get from (13.511) the *scalar form of the equations of motion*,

$$(13.512) \quad \begin{cases} m\ddot{x} = X + 2m\Omega \sin \lambda \cdot \dot{y}, \\ m\ddot{y} = Y - 2m\Omega(\sin \lambda \cdot \dot{x} + \cos \lambda \cdot \dot{z}), \\ m\ddot{z} = Z - mg + 2m\Omega \cos \lambda \cdot \dot{y} \end{cases}$$

Motion of a free particle.

By a "free particle" we mean here a particle on which there acts no force but gravity. As remarked in Sec 6.1, this is an idealization difficult to approach in practice. The resistance of the air is always present and produces discrepancies between mathematical predictions and observed motions. It is therefore not surprising that the minute effects due to the earth's rotation are hard to detect.

For a free particle, we put $X = Y = Z = 0$ in (13.512). The resulting equations are easy to integrate, especially as further approximations, based on the smallness of Ω, are permissible. The equations now read

$$(13.513) \quad \begin{cases} \ddot{x} = 2\Omega \sin \lambda \cdot \dot{y}, \\ \ddot{y} = -2\Omega(\sin \lambda \cdot \dot{x} + \cos \lambda \cdot \dot{z}), \\ \ddot{z} = -g + 2\Omega \cos \lambda \cdot \dot{y}. \end{cases}$$

Each of these equations can be integrated once. Without loss of generality, we may suppose that the particle starts from the origin at $t = 0$ with velocity (u_0, v_0, w_0), and so we get

(13.514) $$\begin{cases} \dot{x} = 2\Omega \sin \lambda \cdot y + u_0, \\ \dot{y} = -2\Omega(\sin \lambda \cdot x + \cos \lambda \cdot z) + v_0, \\ \dot{z} = -gt + 2\Omega \cos \lambda \cdot y + w_0. \end{cases}$$

If we substitute from the first and third of these equations in the second of (13.513) and neglect Ω^2, we obtain

(13.515) $\quad \ddot{y} = -2\Omega(u_0 \sin \lambda + w_0 \cos \lambda - gt \cos \lambda),$

and hence, by integration,

(13.516) $\quad y = v_0 t - \Omega t^2 (u_0 \sin \lambda + w_0 \cos \lambda) + \tfrac{1}{3}\Omega g t^3 \cos \lambda.$

Then the first and third equations of (13.514) give, on neglecting Ω^2,

(13.517) $$\begin{cases} x = u_0 t + \Omega v_0 t^2 \sin \lambda, \\ z = w_0 t - \tfrac{1}{2} g t^2 + \Omega v_0 t^2 \cos \lambda \end{cases}$$

Two cases are of particular interest, a particle dropped from rest, and a particle representing a projectile fired with high velocity in a flat trajectory.

In the case of a particle dropped from rest, we put

$$u_0 = v_0 = w_0 = 0,$$

and get

(13.518) $\quad x = 0, \quad y = \tfrac{1}{3}\Omega g t^3 \cos \lambda, \quad z = -\tfrac{1}{2} g t^2.$

The path is a semicubical parabola in the east-west vertical plane,

(13.519) $$y^2 = -\frac{8}{9} \cdot \frac{\Omega^2 \cos^2 \lambda}{g} \cdot z^3.$$

It is evident from (13.518) that *the deviation from the vertical is toward the east.* From (13.519), the deviation for fall from a height h is

$$\tfrac{1}{3}\Omega \cos \lambda \cdot 2h \sqrt{\frac{2h}{g}}.$$

This is zero at the poles ($\lambda = \pm \tfrac{1}{2}\pi$), as we should expect.

For a projectile with large u_0 and v_0, we neglect the term in w_0 and also the last term in (13.516). Thus the projection of the trajectory on the horizontal plane has the equations

(13.520) $\quad x = u_0 t + \Omega v_0 t^2 \sin \lambda, \quad y = v_0 t - \Omega u_0 t^2 \sin \lambda.$

These may be expressed in complex form in the single equation

(13.521) $\quad x + iy = (u_0 + iv_0)(t - i\Omega t^2 \sin \lambda).$

Let us put

$$x + iy = Re^{i\phi}, \qquad u_0 + iv_0 = q_0 e^{i\alpha}$$

and write, as we may since Ω is small,

$$1 - i\Omega t \sin \lambda = \exp(-i\Omega t \sin \lambda).$$

Then (13.521) takes the form

$$Re^{i\phi} = q_0 t \exp(i\alpha - i\Omega t \sin \lambda),$$

and so

(13.522) $\quad R = q_0 t, \qquad \phi = \alpha - \Omega t \sin \lambda.$

The magnitude of the position vector grows at a constant rate q_0, and at the same time the vector turns at a constant rate $-\Omega \sin \lambda$ In the Northern Hemisphere, λ is positive and this rotation is clockwise when viewed from above; in the Southern Hemisphere, it is counterclockwise. This means that the projectile experiences, on account of the earth's rotation, a slight deviation—to the right in the Northern Hemisphere, and to the left in the Southern Hemisphere. This is known as *Ferel's law*.

Foucault's pendulum.

Let us suppose a pendulum set up at the North Pole If started properly, it may vibrate as a simple pendulum in a vertical plane which is fixed in the Newtonian frame of reference. As the earth turns under the pendulum with angular velocity Ω, the plane of vibration of the pendulum appears to an observer on the earth to turn with an angular velocity $-\Omega$. Foucault was the first to point out that a pendulum could be used to demonstrate the earth's rotation. It is not necessary that the pendulum should be situated at one of the earth's poles; an apparent rotation, due to the rotation of the earth, may be observed at any latitude except on the equator.

We shall now apply (13.512) to the motion of a pendulum. The pendulum consists of a particle of mass m attached by a light string of length a to a point with coordinates $(0, 0, a)$. Thus, in equilibrium the particle rests at the origin We shall discuss small oscillations about this position, a problem already

Sec. 13.5]   MOTION OF A PARTICLE   409

solved [cf (13.304)] for the case $\Omega = 0$. The question of interest now is to find how the simple motion there described is modified by the rotation of the earth.

We recall that X, Y, Z are the components of force other than gravity. For the pendulum, this consists of the tension S in the string; as in (13.302) the components are

$$(13.523) \quad X = -\frac{x}{a} S, \quad Y = -\frac{y}{a} S, \quad Z = \frac{a-z}{a} S.$$

We have to take care of two separate approximations. The first, based on the smallness of Ω, has already been used in obtaining (13.512); it consists in neglecting Ω^2. The second approximation is that arising from the smallness of the oscillations. This means that x, y, and their derivatives are small; z and its derivatives are therefore small of the second order and consequently will be neglected.

The last equation of (13.512) gives, since $Z = S$ approximately,

$$(13.524) \quad S = mg - 2m\Omega \cos \lambda \cdot \dot{y},$$

and so the first two equations become

$$(13.525) \quad \begin{cases} \ddot{x} - 2\Omega \sin \lambda \cdot \dot{y} + p^2 x = 0, \\ \ddot{y} + 2\Omega \sin \lambda \cdot \dot{x} + p^2 y = 0, \end{cases}$$

where $p^2 = g/a$. Multiplying the second equation by i and adding it to the first, we get the single complex equation

$$(13.526) \quad \ddot{\zeta} + 2i\Omega \sin \lambda \cdot \dot{\zeta} + p^2 \zeta = 0, \quad (\zeta = x + iy).$$

The general solution is

$$(13.527) \quad \zeta = A e^{n_1 t} + B e^{n_2 t},$$

where A and B are complex constants depending on the initial conditions and n_1, n_2 are the roots of the equation

$$(13.528) \quad n^2 + 2i\Omega \sin \lambda \cdot n + p^2 = 0.$$

These roots are

$$n_1, n_2 = -i\Omega \sin \lambda \pm i \sqrt{\Omega^2 \sin^2 \lambda + p^2}.$$

Neglecting Ω^2, we may write (13.527) in the form

$$(13.529) \quad \zeta = \zeta_1 \exp(-i\Omega t \sin \lambda),$$

where

(13.530) $$\zeta_1 = Ae^{ipt} + Be^{-ipt}.$$

To interpret this result, we suppose for the moment that $\Omega = 0$, so that $\zeta = \zeta_1$. On separation of the real and imaginary parts, it is easily seen that the path is an ellipse with center at the origin—the motion being a composition of perpendicular simple harmonic motions [cf. (6.405) and (13.304)]. The effect of the second factor in (13.529) is to rotate the complex vector ζ_1 through an angle $-\Omega t \sin \lambda$, proportional to the time. We may sum up our result as follows: *The effect of the earth's rotation on the elliptical path of a spherical pendulum is to cause the ellipse to rotate with an angular velocity* $-\Omega \sin \lambda$. *This rotation is clockwise in the Northern Hemisphere and counterclockwise in the Southern Hemisphere.* If we put $\lambda = \frac{1}{2}\pi$, so that the pendulum is at the North Pole, the angular velocity becomes $-\Omega$ and may be regarded as due directly to the earth's rotation beneath the pendulum.

When we discussed the spherical pendulum in Sec. 13.3, without taking the earth's rotation into consideration, we started with a first approximation and obtained an elliptical orbit from equations (13.304). We then proceeded to a second approximation and found, in (13.333), an expression for the rate at which the elliptical orbit advances. In the case of Foucault's pendulum, the situation is more involved. In the first place, the angular velocity Ω of the earth is small (cf. page 143), and that fact was used in obtaining (13.512). Secondly, we have considered only small oscillations (first approximation). If we were to proceed to a second approximation, we would find two superimposed rotations of the elliptical orbit—one depending, as in (13.333), on the area of the orbit (area effect), and the other an angular velocity $-\Omega \sin \lambda$ due to the earth's rotation (Foucault effect). Unless special precautions are taken, the area effect is likely to be much larger than the Foucault effect and to conceal it. To prevent this, it is usual to draw the pendulum aside with a thread and start the motion by burning the thread. This means that, for $t = 0$, we have $\zeta = 0$ and $\zeta = \zeta_0$ (say). Then, by (13.529),

(13.531) $\quad A + B = \zeta_0, \quad p(A - B) - (A + B)\Omega \sin \lambda = 0.$

Now (13.530) may be written

(13.532) $\quad \zeta_1 = (A + B) \cos pt + i(A - B) \sin pt,$

or, by (13.531),

(13.533) $\quad \zeta_1 = \zeta_0 (\cos pt + i \sin pt \ \Omega \sin \lambda/p).$

It is easy to see that this represents motion in an ellipse with semiaxes $|\zeta_0|$ and $|\zeta_0|\Omega \sin \lambda/p$. For an ellipse with these semiaxes, described in a Newtonian frame of reference, the advance of the apse in one period ($2\pi/p$) is, by (13.333),

(13.534) $\quad \dfrac{3\pi}{4a^2 p} |\zeta_0|^2 \Omega \sin \lambda,$

and so the angular velocity of the ellipse due to the area effect is

(13.535) $\quad \dfrac{3|\zeta_0|^2}{8a^2} \Omega \sin \lambda.$

Since $|\zeta_0|/a$ is small, this angular velocity is much smaller than the Foucault angular velocity $-\Omega \sin \lambda$ and may be regarded as negligible. Hence, if the pendulum is started by burning a thread, the rotation of the orbit may be regarded as due to the Foucault effect alone.

It should be noted that, for any small elliptical orbit, there is a distinction between the area effect and the Foucault effect. The area effect is always a rotation in the sense in which the ellipse is described and reverses when that sense is reversed, but the Foucault rotation takes place in a definite sense (clockwise in the Northern Hemisphere and counterclockwise in the Southern).

13.6. SUMMARY OF APPLICATIONS IN DYNAMICS IN SPACE—MOTION OF A PARTICLE

I. **Jacobian elliptic functions.**

(a) Differential equation:

(13.601) $\quad \left(\dfrac{dy}{dx}\right)^2 = (1 - y^2)(1 - k^2 y^2), \quad (0 < k < 1).$

(b) General solution:

(13.602) $\quad y = \operatorname{sn}(x + c).$

(c) Other elliptic functions.

(13.603) $\quad \operatorname{cn}^2 x = 1 - \operatorname{sn}^2 x, \quad \operatorname{dn}^2 x = 1 - k^2 \operatorname{sn}^2 x;$

(13.604) $\quad \dfrac{d}{dx} \operatorname{sn} x = \operatorname{cn} x \operatorname{dn} x, \quad \dfrac{d}{dx} \operatorname{cn} x = - \operatorname{sn} x \operatorname{dn} x,$

$$\dfrac{d}{dx} \operatorname{dn} x = -k^2 \operatorname{sn} x \operatorname{cn} x.$$

(d) Periodicity:

(13.605) $\quad \operatorname{sn}(x + 4K) = \operatorname{sn} x, \quad \operatorname{cn}(x + 4K) = \operatorname{cn} x,$
$$\operatorname{dn}(x + 2K) = \operatorname{dn} x;$$

(13.606) $\quad K = \displaystyle\int_0^1 \dfrac{dy}{\sqrt{(1-y^2)(1-k^2 y^2)}} = \int_0^{\frac{1}{2}\pi} \dfrac{d\phi}{\sqrt{1-k^2 \sin^2 \phi}}.$

II. Simple pendulum.

(a) Motion:

(13.607) $\quad \begin{cases} \sin \tfrac{1}{2}\theta = \sin \tfrac{1}{2}\alpha \operatorname{sn} [p(t - t_0)], \\ p^2 = \dfrac{g}{a}, \quad k = \sin \tfrac{1}{2}\alpha. \end{cases}$

(b) Periodic time:

(13.608) $\quad \tau = \dfrac{4}{p} \displaystyle\int_0^{\frac{1}{2}\pi} \dfrac{d\phi}{\sqrt{1-k^2 \sin^2 \phi}}$

$$= 2\pi \sqrt{\dfrac{a}{g}} (1 + \tfrac{1}{16}\alpha^2), \text{ approximately.}$$

III. Spherical pendulum.

(a) General motion: the pendulum oscillates between two levels, found by solving a cubic equation; the analytical solution is

(13.609) $\quad \begin{cases} z - z_1 = (z_2 - z_1) \operatorname{sn}^2 [p(t - t_0)], \\ p^2 = \dfrac{g}{a}, \quad k^2 = \dfrac{z_2 - z_1}{z_3 - z_1}. \end{cases}$

(b) Small oscillations: in the first approximation the path is an ellipse; in the second approximation the ellipse turns at a rate proportional to its area.

IV. Motion of a charged particle in an electromagnetic field.

(a) Uniform electric field: the trajectory is a parabola.
(b) Uniform magnetic field: the trajectory is a helix.

(c) Axially symmetric electromagnetic field: the trajectory satisfies

$$(13.610)\begin{cases} u'' + S(z)u = 0, \\ S(z) = \tfrac{3}{4}\dfrac{w'^2}{w^2} + \dfrac{k^2\Omega_0'^2}{4w^2} = \dfrac{3V_0'^2}{16\left(V_0 - V_{00} + \dfrac{w_0^2}{2k}\right)^2} \\ \qquad\qquad + \dfrac{k\Omega_0'^2}{8\left(V_0 - V_{00} + \dfrac{w_0^2}{2k}\right)}, \\ \zeta = x + iy = u\sqrt{\dfrac{w_0}{w}}\exp\left(-\tfrac{1}{2}ik\int_{z_0}^{z}\dfrac{\Omega_0'(\xi)}{w(\xi)}d\xi\right), \\ w = \text{speed of particle} = \sqrt{2k\left(V_0 - V_{00} + \dfrac{w_0^2}{2k}\right)}, \\ w_0 = w(z_0), \qquad k = -\dfrac{\epsilon}{m}, \\ V_0 = \text{axial electric potential,} \quad V_{00} = V_0(z_0), \\ \Omega_0 = \text{axial magnetic potential,} \\ \text{Prime indicates } d/dz. \end{cases}$$

(d) Electromagnetic lens.

(i) Image plane $z = z_1$ of object plane $z = z_0$ determined by

$$(13.611)\begin{cases} f(z_1) = 0, \\ f''(z) + S(z)f(z) = 0, \\ f(z_0) = 0, \qquad f'(z_0) = 1; \end{cases}$$

(ii) Magnification given by

$$(13.612)\begin{cases} m = |g(z_1)|\sqrt{\dfrac{w_0}{w_1}}, \\ g''(z) + S(z)g(z) = 0, \\ g(z_0) = 1, \qquad g'(z_0) = 0, \\ w_1^2 = w_0^2 + 2k[V_0(z_1) - V_0(z_0)]. \end{cases}$$

(e) Magnetostatic lens: rotation of image given by

$$(13.613)\qquad \alpha = \dfrac{k}{2w_0}[\Omega_0(z_0) - \Omega_0(z_1)].$$

V. Effects of the earth's rotation.

(a) Equations of motion:

(13.614)
$$\begin{cases} m\ddot{x} = X + 2m\Omega \sin \lambda \cdot \dot{y}, \\ m\ddot{y} = Y - 2m\Omega(\sin \lambda \cdot \dot{x} + \cos \lambda \cdot \dot{z}), \\ m\ddot{z} = Z - mg + 2m\Omega \cos \lambda \cdot \dot{y}, \\ X, Y, Z = \text{force other than gravity}, \\ \lambda = \text{latitude}. \end{cases}$$

(b) A falling body deviates to the east.

(c) A projectile deviates to the right in the Northern Hemisphere.

(d) Foucault's pendulum turns with angular velocity $-\Omega \sin \lambda$, clockwise in the Northern Hemisphere.

EXERCISES XIII

1. A simple pendulum of mass m and length a performs finite oscillations, the greatest inclination of the string to the vertical being 30°. Find the tension in the string when the bob is in its highest position.

2. The string of a spherical pendulum is held out horizontally and the bob started with a horizontal velocity perpendicular to the string. Find to the nearest foot per second the magnitude of this velocity if the minimum inclination of the string to the vertical in the subsequent motion is 45°. The length of the string is 54 inches.

3. A particle carrying a charge ϵ is projected from the origin with a velocity u_0 in the direction of the x-axis. There is a uniform magnetic field of strength H parallel to the z-axis. If the particle crosses the plane $x = 0$ at a distance a from the origin, find its mass. (Isotopes are separated in a mass spectroscope by a method such as this.)

4. A heavy bead is free to move on a smooth circular wire of radius a, which rotates with constant angular velocity Ω about a fixed vertical diameter. Find the possible positions of relative equilibrium. If $\Omega^2 > g/a$, find the period of small oscillations about a position of stable equilibrium.

5. A stone is thrown straight up, rises to a height of 100 ft., and falls to earth. Estimate the deviation due to the rotation of earth, the latitude of the place being 45° North. (Neglect air resistance.)

6. A particle moves under gravity on a smooth surface of revolution with axis vertical. The equation of the surface in cylindrical coordinates is given in the form $R = F(z)$. If the velocity is horizontal and of magnitude q_1 at a height z_1, and again horizontal and of magnitude q_2 at a height z_2, determine q_1 and q_2 in terms of z_1 and z_2. (Use the principles of energy and angular momentum.)

7. In a simple pendulum the bob is connected by a light string of length a to the fixed point of support. The bob starts in the lowest position with speed q_0. Show that if

$$2ga < q_0^2 < 5ga,$$

the string will slacken during the motion, so that the bob falls inward from the circular path.

8. Show that, on account of the rotation of the earth, a train traveling south exerts a slight sideways force on the western rail of the track. Give an approximate expression for this force in terms of the mass of the train, its speed, the latitude, and the angular velocity of the earth.

9. A particle moves on a smooth surface of revolution with axis vertical. The equation of the surface in cylindrical coordinates is $R = F(z)$. Use the principles of angular momentum and energy to show that

$$R^2\dot\phi = h,$$
$$\tfrac{1}{2}(\dot z^2 + \dot R^2 + R^2\dot\phi^2) + gz = E,$$

where h and E are constants. Deduce that z satisfies a differential equation of the form

$$\dot z^2 = f(z).$$

10. A particle slides on a smooth cycloid in a vertical plane, the cusps of the cycloid being upward. Show that the periodic time of oscillations under gravity is independent of the amplitude.

11. A spherical pendulum of length a and mass m oscillates between two levels which are at heights b and c above the lowest point of the sphere. Express its constant total energy in terms of m, a, b, c, and g, taking the zero of potential energy at the lowest point of the sphere. Check your answer by putting $b = c$.

12. A charged particle moves in a uniform electric and magnetic field, the electric and magnetic vectors being perpendicular to one another. Show that, if properly projected, the path of the particle is a cycloid.

13. The bob of a spherical pendulum, 10 feet long, just clears the ground. A peg is set up 1 foot due south from the equilibrium position of the bob, and the bob is drawn out to the east through a distance of 2 feet. Find (approximately) the direction and magnitude of the velocity with which the bob should be started from this position, in order to hit the peg and make it fall over toward the west.

14. For a simple pendulum of length a making complete revolutions, show that the periodic time is

$$\tau = \frac{4a}{q_0}\int_0^1 \frac{dy}{\sqrt{(1-y^2)(1-y^2/k^2)}},$$

where q_0 is the speed at the lowest position and $k^2 = q_0^2/4ga$.

15. A smooth cup is formed by revolution of the parabola $z^2 = 4ax$ about the axis of z, which is vertical. A particle is projected horizontally on the inner surface at a height z_0 with a speed $\sqrt{2kgz_0}$. Prove that, if $k = \tfrac{1}{4}$, the particle will describe a horizontal circle; also that, if $k = \tfrac{1}{50}$, its path will lie between two planes $z = z_0$ and $z = \tfrac{1}{2}z_0$.

16. A spherical pendulum of length a is held out horizontally, and the bob is started with a great horizontal velocity q_0. Show that it falls to a depth below its initial position given approximately by $2ga^2/q_0^2$.

17. A particle moves on smooth surface of revolution, the axis of symmetry being vertical. Show that motion in a horizontal circle of radius R is stable if

$$\frac{d^2z}{dR^2} + \frac{3}{R}\frac{dz}{dR} > 0,$$

where $z = z(R)$ is the equation of the surface in cylindrical coordinates. Deduce that the motion of a conical pendulum is stable.

18. A particle moves under gravity on a rough vertical circle. It starts from rest at one end of the horizontal diameter and comes to rest at the lowest point of the circle. Find an equation to determine the coefficient of friction.

19. A heavy bead starts from rest at a point A and slides down a smooth wire in the form of a helix having the parametric equations

$$x = a\cos\theta, \quad y = a\sin\theta, \quad z = a\theta\tan\alpha,$$

the axis of z being vertical. When it is vertically under A, a second bead starts from rest at A. Show that the tangential acceleration of each bead is $g\sin\alpha$, and deduce a formula determining all the subsequent instants at which one bead is vertically underneath the other.

20. A heavy particle is constrained to move on the inner surface of a smooth right circular cone of semivertical angle α, the axis of the cone being vertical and the vertex down. The particle is in steady motion in a circle at height b above the vertex. Find the periodic time for small oscillations about this steady motion.

21. A particle slides in a smooth straight tube which rotates with constant angular velocity ω about a vertical axis which does not intersect the tube. The tube is inclined at an angle α to the vertical. Initially the particle is projected upward along the tube with speed q_0, relative to the tube, from the point where the shortest distance between the axis and the tube meets the tube. Show that, no matter what the length of the tube may be, the particle will escape at the upper end provided

$$q_0 > \frac{g}{\omega\tan\alpha}$$

22. Consider an axially symmetric electric field in which the axial potential is of the form $V_0 = az + b$. Show that the field is uniform throughout space and parallel to the z-axis. Verify directly from (13.429) that the trajectory of a charged particle is parabolic.

Consider also the case of an axially symmetric magnetic field with the axial potential of the form $\Omega_0 = az + b$. Verify from (13.438) that the trajectory is a helix.

23. A particle moves under gravity on a smooth surface, the principal radii of curvature at its lowest point being a, b ($a > b$). The surface rotates with constant angular velocity ω about the normal at the lowest point. Show that, if Oxy are horizontal axes attached to the surface at the lowest point and directed along the lines of curvature at that point, then the equa-

tion of motion for small vibrations near the lowest point are

$$\frac{d^2x}{dt^2} - 2\omega \frac{dy}{dt} + \left(\frac{g}{a} - \omega^2\right) x = 0,$$
$$\frac{d^2y}{dt^2} + 2\omega \frac{dx}{dt} + \left(\frac{g}{b} - \omega^2\right) y = 0.$$

Considering solutions of the form $x = Ae^{nt}$, $y = Be^{nt}$, deduce that there will be instability if ω^2 lies between g/a and g/b.

24. If in a magnetostatic lens the axial component H of the magnetic vector is constant, show that an object point on the axis at $z = 0$ will give an image at

$$z = \frac{2\pi m w_0}{eH},$$

where w_0 is the initial velocity

25. For a magnetostatic lens, with the field concentrated in $-h < z < h$, prove that, to the order h inclusive, the magnification of an object in the plane $z = z_0$ is

$$|1 + Az_0 - h(B + Dz_0)|^{-1},$$

where A, B, D are constants defined by (13 465)   Evaluate explicitly, if the axial component of magnetic field H is constant in $-h < z < h$.

CHAPTER XIV

APPLICATIONS IN DYNAMICS IN SPACE—MOTION OF A RIGID BODY

14.1. MOTION OF A RIGID BODY WITH A FIXED POINT UNDER NO FORCES

If a rigid body is constrained to turn about a smooth fixed axis, under no forces other than the reaction of the axis, the motion is extremely simple: the body spins with constant angular velocity. But if, instead of fixing a *line* in the body, we fix one *point* only, the motion under no forces is much more complicated. The problem of finding this motion is of wider interest than might appear at first sight, for the motion of a rigid body relative to its mass center is the same as if the mass center were fixed (cf. Sec 12.4).

The mounting of a body so as to fix only one point is much more complicated than that required to give it a fixed line. It may be done by an arrangement of light rings, known as "Cardan's suspension" (Fig. 144). The body is represented by the inner circle. The points A, B are fixed. Rotation of the ring R_1 about AB gives one degree of freedom. Rotation of the ring R_2 about CD gives a second degree of freedom. Rotation of the body itself about EF gives the third. The body can take up all positions in which the point O of the body is fixed in space, O being the common intersection of AB, CD, and EF. All the apparatus, except the body itself, is to be regarded as massless in the mathematical theory; this cannot, of course, be achieved in practice, but the masses of R_1 and R_2 are made as small as possible compared with the mass of the body.

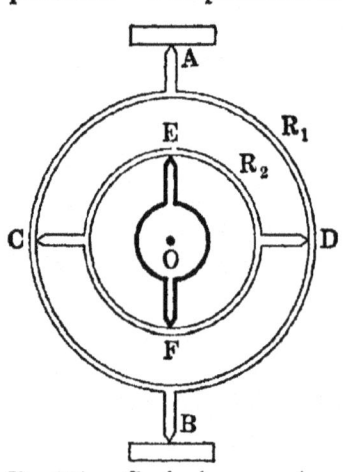

FIG. 144.—Cardan's suspension.

SEC. 14.1] MOTION OF A RIGID BODY 419

There are two ways of treating the problem of the motion of a body with a fixed point under no forces—the descriptive and the analytic. The descriptive method, or *method of Poinsot*, gives a good qualitative idea of the motion. In the case where the body has an axis of dynamical symmetry, the description is particularly simple; we shall consider that case in detail later.

The method of Poinsot.

Let O be the fixed point in the body, and A, B, C the principal moments of inertia at O. Let $\mathbf{i}, \mathbf{j}, \mathbf{k}$ be unit vectors fixed in the body and directed along the principal axes at O. For the angular velocity and angular momentum we have, by (11.509),

(14.101) $\quad \boldsymbol{\omega} = \omega_1 \mathbf{i} + \omega_2 \mathbf{j} + \omega_3 \mathbf{k}, \quad \mathbf{h} = A\omega_1 \mathbf{i} + B\omega_2 \mathbf{j} + C\omega_3 \mathbf{k}.$

When we say that the body is under no forces, we mean more precisely that the forces acting on the body have no moment about O (Thus our argument applies to a heavy body under the action of gravity, provided that O is the center of gravity) Since the external forces do no work and have no moment about O, we have the following facts to assist us in discussing the motion:

(i) the kinetic energy T is constant;

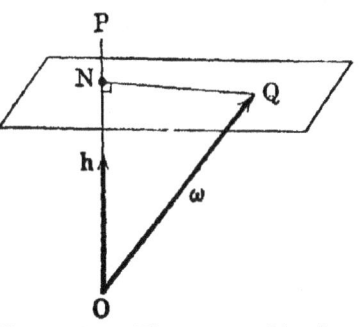

FIG. 145—The invariable line and the invariable plane.

(ii) the angular momentum $\mathbf{h}$ is a constant vector.

From the first of these we have, by (11.404),

(14.102) $\quad A\omega_1^2 + B\omega_2^2 + C\omega_3^2 = 2T = $ constant;

from the second, we know that $\mathbf{h}$ has a direction fixed in space and also a constant magnitude, so that

(14.103) $\quad A^2\omega_1^2 + B^2\omega_2^2 + C^2\omega_3^2 = h^2 = $ constant.

Let us draw through O a line OP in the fixed direction of $\mathbf{h}$ (Fig. 145); this is called the *invariable line*. Let OQ represent the angular velocity $\boldsymbol{\omega}$ at any instant. Drop the perpendicular QN on OP; then $ON = \boldsymbol{\omega} \cdot \mathbf{h}/h$. But, by (14.101) and (14.102),

(14.104) $\quad\quad\quad\quad \boldsymbol{\omega} \cdot \mathbf{h} = 2T,$

and so

(14.105) $$ON = \frac{2T}{h} = \text{constant}.$$

Thus N is a fixed point during the motion, and so the plane through N, perpendicular to the invariable line OP, is a fixed plane; it is called the *invariable plane*. The extremity Q of the angular velocity vector ω moves on the invariable plane.

Let us now take the point of view of an observer who moves with the body. (This is what we do in our daily lives, for we live on a rotating earth but regard a point on the earth's surface as "fixed.") To such an observer, the vectors **i**, **j**, **k** are fixed, but *both* the vectors **h** and ω are changing. If **i**, **j**, **k** are taken as coordinate axes and the extremity of the vector ω is given coordinates x, y, z, then

$$x = \omega_1, \qquad y = \omega_2, \qquad z = \omega_3.$$

By virtue of (14.102) and (14.103), we have

(14.106) $$Ax^2 + By^2 + Cz^2 = 2T, \qquad A^2x^2 + B^2y^2 + C^2z^2 = h^2.$$

In fact, *to an observer moving with the body, the extremity Q of the angular velocity vector ω describes a curve which is the intersection of the two ellipsoids (14.106), fixed in the body.*

The first of these two ellipsoids is similar to the momental ellipsoid and has the same axes; it is called the *Poinsot ellipsoid*.

The invariable plane is fixed in space, but to the observer moving with the body it is a moving plane. It touches a sphere of radius ON, but it has another remarkable property: *the invariable plane touches the Poinsot ellipsoid at the extremity of the angular velocity vector.*

To see this, we note that the tangent plane to the Poinsot ellipsoid at the point $(\omega_1, \omega_2, \omega_3)$ is

(14.107) $$A\omega_1 x + B\omega_2 y + C\omega_3 z = 2T.$$

So the direction ratios of the normal to the ellipsoid at this point are

$$A\omega_1, \qquad B\omega_2, \qquad C\omega_3.$$

But these are precisely the components of angular momentum; hence the normal to the Poinsot ellipsoid at the extremity of the angular velocity vector is parallel to the angular momentum vector, i.e., parallel to OP. This proves the result.

Sec. 14.1]   MOTION OF A RIGID BODY   421

As we have indicated, there are two different points of view:
(i) the point of view of an observer S fixed in space;
(ii) the point of view of an observer S' fixed in the body.

It is confusing to try to look at things simultaneously from the two points of view. We shall clarify the situation by taking them up separately.

The observer S, fixed in space, cuts away (in his imagination) all the body except an ellipsoid—the Poinsot ellipsoid. He fixes his attention on this moving ellipsoid and on a fixed plane (the invariable plane). As the body moves, the ellipsoid always touches the plane. It actually *rolls* on the plane, since it has an angular velocity vector which passes through the point of contact of the ellipsoid and the plane. This is a fairly complicated type of motion; it becomes quite simple, however, when the Poinsot ellipsoid is a surface of revolution, as we shall see later. But it may in any case be visualized by thinking of the invariable plane as a sheet of paper and the Poinsot ellipsoid as an inked surface. In the course of the motion a curve is thus drawn in ink on the invariable plane. On joining the fixed point O to the points on this curve, we get the *space cone* (cf. Sec. 11.2).

On the other hand, the observer S', fixed in the body, turns his attention to the two ellipsoids (14.106), fixed as far as he is concerned, and in particular to their curve of intersection. The angular velocity vector traces out a cone (the *body cone*), formed by joining the fixed point O to this curve.

The two points of view are brought into contact by the general result: the body cone rolls on the space cone The difference between the two is this: S regards the space cone as fixed, but S' regards the body cone as fixed.

The above method gives a qualitative, rather than a quantitative, description of the motion. For a quantitative description, we must use an analytic method.

The case of a general body; analytic method.

Since the external forces have no moment about O, Euler's equations (12.404) give

(14.108)
$$\begin{cases} A\dot{\omega}_1 - (B - C)\omega_2\omega_3 = 0, \\ B\dot{\omega}_2 - (C - A)\omega_3\omega_1 = 0, \\ C\dot{\omega}_3 - (A - B)\omega_1\omega_2 = 0. \end{cases}$$

We have also, as in (14.102) and (14.103),

(14.109) $$\begin{cases} A\omega_1^2 + B\omega_2^2 + C\omega_3^2 = 2T, \\ A^2\omega_1^2 + B^2\omega_2^2 + C^2\omega_3^2 = h^2, \end{cases}$$

where T and h are constants, which may be found by inserting the values of $\omega_1, \omega_2, \omega_3$ at $t = 0$. [The equations (14.109) may be deduced from (14.108) directly.]

We shall assume that A, B, C are all distinct. We may suppose the triad $\mathbf{i}, \mathbf{j}, \mathbf{k}$ chosen so that $A > B > C$. Then it follows from (14.109) that

$$2AT - h^2 > 0, \qquad 2CT - h^2 < 0.$$

There are three very simple particular solutions of (14.108). These are

$$\omega_1 = \text{constant}, \qquad \omega_2 = 0, \qquad \omega_3 = 0,$$
$$\omega_2 = \text{constant}, \qquad \omega_3 = 0, \qquad \omega_1 = 0,$$
$$\omega_3 = \text{constant}, \qquad \omega_1 = 0, \qquad \omega_2 = 0.$$

These three solutions correspond to steady rotations about the three principal axes of inertia. It is a remarkable fact that these are the only axes about which the body will spin steadily under no forces; the equations (14.108) are satisfied by constant values of $\omega_1, \omega_2, \omega_3$ only if two of these constant values are zero.

Turning now to the problem of finding the most general solution of (14.108), we must first eliminate two of the unknowns, so as to get a differential equation involving just one unknown. It proves best to concentrate our attention on ω_2. We solve (14.109) for ω_1^2, ω_3^2, obtaining

(14.110) $$\omega_1^2 = P - Q\omega_2^2, \qquad \omega_3^2 = R - S\omega_2^2,$$

where P, Q, R, S are positive expressions involving A, B, C, T, h. Substitution in the second equation of (14.108) gives

(14.111) $$\dot{\omega}_2^2 = \left(\frac{C-A}{B}\right)^2 (P - Q\omega_2^2)(R - S\omega_2^2).$$

This equation is of the same form as (13.312) and may be treated in the same way. Thus, from (14.111), we get

(14.112) $$\left(\frac{d\xi}{d\tau}\right)^2 = (1 - \xi^2)(1 - k^2\xi^2),$$

where

(14.113) $$\xi = \frac{\omega_2}{\beta}, \qquad \tau = pt,$$

the constants β, p, k being positive functions of A, B, C, T, h, with $k < 1$. Hence,

$$(14.114) \qquad \omega_2 = \beta \text{ sn } [p(t - t_0)],$$

where t_0 is a constant of integration. Substitution in (14.110) gives either

$$(14.115a) \quad \omega_1 = \alpha \text{ dn } [p(t - t_0)], \qquad \omega_3 = \gamma \text{ cn } [p(t - t_0)],$$

or

$$(14.115b) \quad \omega_1 = \alpha \text{ cn } [p(t - t_0)], \qquad \omega_3 = \gamma \text{ dn } [p(t - t_0)],$$

where α and γ are functions of A, B, C, T, h, determined except for sign. When we substitute in (14.108), we find that $\alpha\beta\gamma$ is negative. For definiteness, we may make α positive by suitable choice of the sense of the vector $\mathbf{i}$; then γ is negative.

That is the outline of the method of finding $\omega_1, \omega_2, \omega_3$ as functions of t. The completion of the argument consists in filling in the algebraic details. Care must be taken in selecting the constants β, p, k, so that k is less than unity; it becomes necessary to distinguish between the two cases (a) $h^2 > 2BT$, and (b) $h^2 < 2BT$. In the former case, we arrive at (14.115a), in the latter at (14.115b). We leave it to the reader to verify the following results.

CASE (a): $h^2 > 2BT$.

$$(14.116a) \quad \begin{cases} \alpha = \sqrt{\dfrac{h^2 - 2CT}{A(A - C)}}, \\ \beta = \sqrt{\dfrac{2AT - h^2}{B(A - B)}}, \\ \gamma = -\sqrt{\dfrac{2AT - h^2}{C(A - C)}}, \end{cases} \quad p = \sqrt{\dfrac{(h^2 - 2CT)(A - B)}{ABC}}, \quad k = \sqrt{\dfrac{B - C}{A - B} \cdot \dfrac{2AT - h^2}{h^2 - 2CT}}$$

CASE (b): $h^2 < 2BT$.

$$(14.116b) \quad \begin{cases} \alpha = \sqrt{\dfrac{h^2 - 2CT}{A(A - C)}}, \\ \beta = \sqrt{\dfrac{h^2 - 2CT}{B(B - C)}}, \\ \gamma = -\sqrt{\dfrac{2AT - h^2}{C(A - C)}}, \end{cases} \quad p = \sqrt{\dfrac{(2AT - h^2)(B - C)}{ABC}}, \quad k = \sqrt{\dfrac{A - B}{B - C} \cdot \dfrac{h^2 - 2CT}{2AT - h^2}}.$$

In establishing these results, the following identity is useful:

(14.117) $(B - C)(h^2 - 2AT) + (C - A)(h^2 - 2BT)$
$$+ (A - B)(h^2 - 2CT) = 0.$$

But the determination of $\omega_1, \omega_2, \omega_3$ as functions of t does not complete the solution of the problem. We should be able to tell, from given initial conditions, the position of the body at any time. To do this, we specify the directions of the triad **i, j, k**, relative to a triad **I, J, K**, fixed in space, by means of the Eulerian angles θ, ϕ, ψ. Then, by (11.202),

(14.118) $$\begin{cases} \omega_1 = \sin\psi\,\dot\theta - \sin\theta\cos\psi\,\dot\phi, \\ \omega_2 = \cos\psi\,\dot\theta + \sin\theta\sin\psi\,\dot\phi, \\ \omega_3 = \cos\theta\,\dot\phi + \dot\psi. \end{cases}$$

If we substitute for $\omega_1, \omega_2, \omega_3$ from (14.114) and (14.115), we obtain three differential equations for θ, ϕ, ψ. The solution of these equations in this general form presents a formidable problem. It is greatly simplified if we choose the vector **K** in the direction of the invariable line, defined by the constant vector **h**. Then the components of **h** along **i, j, k** are found by multiplying h by the direction cosines of **K** relative to **i, j, k**. These direction cosines are easily found (cf. Fig. 118, page 289) by projecting **K** on **i, j, k**, they are

$$-\sin\theta\cos\psi, \quad \sin\theta\sin\psi, \quad \cos\theta.$$

Hence,

(14.119) $$\begin{cases} A\omega_1 = -h\sin\theta\cos\psi, \\ B\omega_2 = h\sin\theta\sin\psi, \\ C\omega_3 = h\cos\theta. \end{cases}$$

From these equations, we get θ and ψ as functions of t without any integration, thus:

(14.120) $$\cos\theta = \frac{C\omega_3}{h}, \quad \tan\psi = -\frac{B\omega_2}{A\omega_1}.$$

To find ϕ, we deduce, from the first two of (14.118),

(14.121) $$\sin\theta\,\dot\phi = \omega_2\sin\psi - \omega_1\cos\psi,$$

and so ϕ is obtained by a quadrature, since $\theta, \psi, \omega_1, \omega_2$ are already known as functions of t.

From the periodic property of the elliptic functions, we see that θ, $\sin \psi$, $\cos \psi$, ϕ are periodic functions of t; in general, ϕ does not increase by a multiple of 2π in a period, and the motion as a whole is not periodic.

The case of a body with an axis of symmetry.

When the momental ellipsoid at the fixed point O has an axis of symmetry, two of the three moments of inertia A, B, C become equal to one another. This will be the case if the body is a solid of revolution of uniform density, but all that is actually required is the symmetry of the momental ellipsoid. The motion of the body under no forces is then greatly simplified. In fact, the simplification is so great that it is easier to discuss the problem afresh, rather than to apply the formulas of the general case. The motion can be determined, both qualitatively and quantitatively, by the method of Poinsot.

Let us denote the principal moments of inertia at O by A and C, C being the *axial moment of inertia* and A the *transverse moment of inertia*. (This means that C is the moment of inertia about the axis of symmetry and A the moment of inertia about any perpendicular line through O.) The cases $A > C$ and $A < C$ differ in some respects, but for the present we may treat them together.

The Poinsot ellipsoid is of revolution. Since its center is fixed and it rolls on the invariable plane, the following facts are obvious:

(i) The body cone and the space cone are both right circular cones.

(ii) The angular velocity vector is of constant magnitude ($\omega = OQ$) and makes a constant angle with the invariable line OP (cf Fig 145).

(iii) The invariable line, the angular velocity vector, and the axis of symmetry are coplanar at every instant.

(iv) The axis of symmetry makes a constant angle (α) with the angular velocity vector and a constant angle (β) with the invariable line.

To get a clear idea of the behavior of the body, let us start at the instant $t = 0$ with the body in some definite position and with some definite angular velocity ω, say $\overrightarrow{OQ_0}$. Let OR_0 be the initial position of the axis of symmetry. Then $\alpha = R_0\hat{O}Q_0$.

Let OS_0 be perpendicular to OR_0 in the plane R_0OQ_0. We resolve ω along OR_0 and OS_0, obtaining components $\omega \cos \alpha$ and $\omega \sin \alpha$. Since these are principal axes, the angular momentum vector **h** has components $C\omega \cos \alpha$ along OR_0 and $A\omega \sin \alpha$ along OS_0; it has, of course, no component perpendicular to the plane R_0OQ_0. We are now in a position to construct **h**, and hence the invariable line OP. The angle β ($= R_0\widehat{O}P$) is given by

$$(14.122) \qquad \tan \beta = \frac{A}{C} \tan \alpha.$$

We have now to distinguish two cases, as shown in Figs. 146a and b

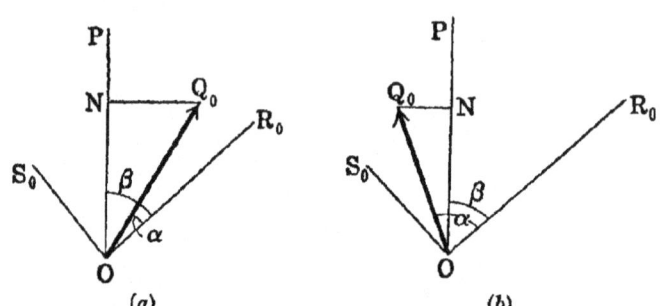

FIG. 146.—(a) The case where $A > C$. (b) The case where $A < C$.

CASE (a): $A > C$ (as in the case of a rod). Here $\beta > \alpha$; the angular velocity vector lies between the axis of symmetry and the invariable line.

CASE (b): $A < C$ (as in the case of a flat disk). Here $\beta < \alpha$; the invariable line lies between the axis of symmetry and the angular velocity vector.

We have spoken of the instant $t = 0$. But a similar construction may be made at any instant, and, as we have seen, the angles α and β, and the magnitude of the angular velocity ω are constants. So the figures we have constructed represent the state of affairs at any instant, the plane containing the figure rotating about the invariable line OP. This rotation is due to an angular velocity ω of constant magnitude, inclined to OP at a constant angle; hence the plane containing the axis of symmetry and the angular velocity vector rotates about OP with a constant angular velocity. We shall denote this angular velocity by Ω.

There is one more constant of importance. It is the angular velocity of the instantaneous axis about the axis of symmetry, as

Sec. 14.1]   MOTION OF A RIGID BODY   427

judged by an observer moving with the body. We shall denote this angular velocity by n.

We have, in all, the following constants:

$$\alpha, \beta, \omega, \Omega, n.$$

Of these, α and ω are determined by initial conditions; β is given by (14.122). We shall now set up equations to find Ω and n, and at the same time get a clear picture of the motion by considering the space and body cones (Figs. 147a and b). OP is the invariable line, OQ the instantaneous axis, OR the axis of symmetry, and QN, QM are drawn perpendicular to OP, OR, respectively. In each case the space cone is fixed, and the body cone rolls on

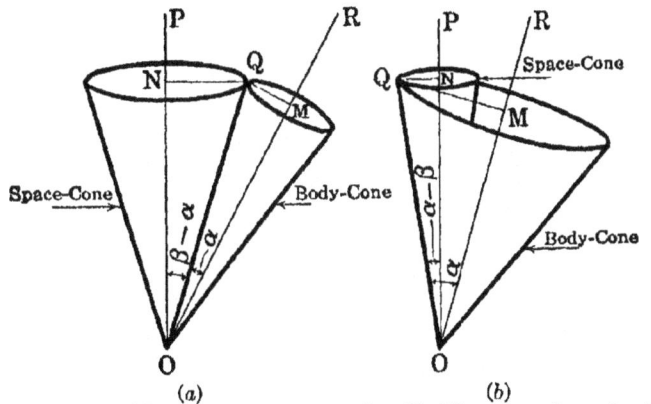

Fig. 147.—(a) The case where $A > C$ (b) The case where $A < C$.

it. This motion is easy to follow in Fig. 147a. The motion in Fig. 147b may be understood by thinking of what the motion looks like from above, or by making a simple model out of thick paper and working the cones through the fingers in order to reproduce the condition of rolling.

Case (a): $A > C$. The line OR turns about OP with angular velocity Ω. Thus, in time dt, the point M receives a displacement

$$OM \sin \beta \, \Omega \, dt = \cos \alpha \sin \beta \, OQ \, \Omega \, dt,$$

perpendicular to the plane POR. But M is a point fixed in the body cone, which is turning about OQ with angular velocity ω. Hence the displacement of M is also

$$QM \cos \alpha \, \omega \, dt = \cos \alpha \sin \alpha \, OQ \, \omega \, dt,$$

since $QM \cos \alpha$ is the perpendicular distance of M from OQ. Equating the two expressions, we obtain

$$(14.123) \qquad \Omega = \frac{\sin \alpha}{\sin \beta} \omega,$$

or, by (14.122),

$$(14.124) \qquad \Omega = \omega \sqrt{\sin^2 \alpha + \frac{C^2}{A^2} \cos^2 \alpha}.$$

To find n, we note that, in time dt, Q travels a distance $QN \Omega \, dt$ on the space cone. But, from the definition of n, in the same time Q travels a distance $QMn \, dt$ on the body cone. From the condition of rolling, these distances are equal to one another, and so

$$QMn = QN\Omega,$$

or

$$(14.125) \qquad n = \Omega \frac{\sin (\beta - \alpha)}{\sin \alpha} = \omega \frac{\sin (\beta - \alpha)}{\sin \beta}.$$

In terms of the basic constants, we have

$$(14.126a) \qquad n = \frac{A - C}{A} \omega \cos \alpha.$$

The sense of this rotation n is obviously retrograde, when compared with ω.

CASE (b): $A < C$. The reasoning in this case follows the same lines, and we get the same formula (14.124) for Ω, while

$$(14.126b) \qquad n = \frac{C - A}{A} \omega \cos \alpha.$$

The sense of this rotation n is direct, when compared with ω

In the case of the earth, which is slightly flattened from the spherical form, we have $A < C$, and the ratio $(C - A)/A$ is small. Thus, case (b) applies, but in an extreme form, since the instantaneous axis is close to the axis of symmetry and α is small. The angular velocity n represents the rate at which the celestial pole, or axis of rotation of the earth, moves round the earth's axis of symmetry. For the period, we have approximately

$$\frac{2\pi}{n} = \frac{A}{C - A} \cdot \frac{2\pi}{\omega}.$$

If the sidereal day is taken as unit of time, then $2\pi/\omega = 1$, and calculation gives the value 305 for the period. This prediction is in poor agreement with observation; for though a rotation of this sort is observed, its period is about 440 days.* The model used (a rigid body) proves at fault here, on account of the elasticity of the earth.

Exercise. A circular disk is mounted so that it can turn freely about its center. Its angular velocity vector makes an angle of 45° with its plane and has a magnitude of 20 revolutions per second. Make a rough sketch of the space and body cones, and find Ω and n.

14.2. THE SPINNING TOP

The spinning top is the most familiar example of a gyroscopic system. The word "gyroscope" was invented to denote an instrument in which the earth's rotation produced an effect which could be observed. But the word "gyroscope" (or "gyrostat") is now used for any system in which a rapidly rotating body is so mounted that it may change the direction of its angular velocity vector.

Why does a spinning top not fall down? How does its rapid rotation render it apparently immune to the force of gravity, which makes non-spinning bodies fall? It is difficult to give a simple answer to this question. The only way to explain the phenomenon is to construct the mathematical theory of the top. For our purposes, we shall understand a "top" to mean a rigid body with an axis of symmetry, acted on by the force of gravity. A point on the axis of symmetry is fixed. Thus we idealize the ordinary top by supposing it to terminate in a sharp point (or vertex) and to spin on a floor rough enough to prevent slipping.

Steady precession of a top.

The motion of any rigid body with a fixed point O satisfies the equation

(14.201) $$\dot{\mathbf{h}} = \mathbf{G},$$

where $\mathbf{h}$ is the angular momentum about O and $\mathbf{G}$ the moment of the external forces about O. In most dynamical problems, we

---

* Cf. H. N. Russel, R. S. Dugan, and J. Q. Stewart, Astronomy (Ginn and Company, Boston, 1945), Vol. I, pp. 118, 131–132. The section of the body cone by the earth's surface is a circle with a diameter of about 26 feet.

430   MECHANICS IN SPACE   [SEC. 14.2

think of the forces as given and the motion as unknown; in that case, G is given and h is to be found. But we can look at (14.201) the other way round. We may regard the motion as prescribed, so that h is known as a vector function of the time. Then (14.201) shows directly the moment G which must be applied to the body in order to give this motion.

Let us now describe a simple motion of a top, called *steady precession*, and inquire what forces must act on the top in order that this motion may take place.

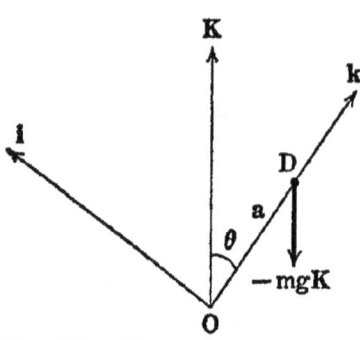

FIG. 148.— Vector diagram for top in steady precession.

In steady precession, the axis of symmetry of the top describes with constant angular velocity a right circular cone with the vertical for axis. At the same time the top spins about its axis of symmetry with constant angular velocity.

We shall use the following notation (Fig. 148):

 a = distance of mass center D from fixed vertex O,
 m = mass of top,
 A = transverse moment of inertia at O,
 C = axial moment of inertia at O,
 $\mathbf{K}$ = unit vector directed vertically upward,
 $(\mathbf{i}, \mathbf{j}, \mathbf{k})$ = unit orthogonal triad, with $\mathbf{k}$ along OD and $\mathbf{i}$ in the plane of $\mathbf{k}$ and $\mathbf{K}$,
 θ = inclination of OD to the vertical.

We note that

(14.202) $$\mathbf{K} = \sin\theta\, \mathbf{i} + \cos\theta\, \mathbf{k}.$$

The angular velocity vector ω of the top lies in the plane $(\mathbf{k}, \mathbf{K})$. It can be resolved along $\mathbf{i}$ and $\mathbf{k}$; we shall write

(14.203) $$\omega = \omega_1 \mathbf{i} + s\mathbf{k}$$

and call s the *spin* of the top. The velocity of the point D is

$$\omega \times a\mathbf{k} = (\omega_1 \mathbf{i} + s\mathbf{k}) \times a\mathbf{k} = -\omega_1 a \mathbf{j}.$$

We understand by the *precession* p the angular velocity with

which OD rotates about $\mathbf{K}$. The velocity of D is then

$$p\mathbf{K} \times a\mathbf{k} = -pa \sin \theta \, \mathbf{j}$$

Equating the two expressions for the velocity of D, we have

(14.204) $\qquad \omega_1 = p \sin \theta.$

In the steady precession θ, s, and p are constants.

The angular momentum is

(14.205) $\qquad \begin{aligned}\mathbf{h} &= A\omega_1 \mathbf{i} + Cs\mathbf{k} \\ &= Ap \sin \theta \, \mathbf{i} + Cs\mathbf{k}.\end{aligned}$

This vector lies in the plane $(\mathbf{k}, \mathbf{K})$, and rotates rigidly with it. Thus $\dot{\mathbf{h}}$ is the velocity of a point with position vector $\mathbf{h}$ in a rigid body which turns with angular velocity $p\mathbf{K}$. Therefore,

(14.206) $\qquad \begin{aligned}\dot{\mathbf{h}} &= p\mathbf{K} \times \mathbf{h} \\ &= p(\sin \theta \, \mathbf{i} + \cos \theta \, \mathbf{k}) \times (Ap \sin \theta \, \mathbf{i} + Cs\mathbf{k}) \\ &= p \sin \theta (Ap \cos \theta - Cs)\mathbf{j}.\end{aligned}$

The steady precession takes place, with assigned values of θ, p, and s, provided that the moment about O of all forces (including gravity) is

(14.207) $\qquad \mathbf{G} = p \sin \theta (Ap \cos \theta - Cs)\mathbf{j}.$

Now the weight of the top is a force $-mg\mathbf{K}$ at D and so has a moment

$$a\mathbf{k} \times (-mg\mathbf{K}) = -mga \sin \theta \, \mathbf{j}$$

about O. If this is equal to $\mathbf{G}$, as given by (14.207), no force other than the weight of the top is required to maintain the motion. Thus *the steady precession takes place under gravity alone if*

(14.208) $\qquad p(Cs - Ap \cos \theta) = mga.$

This is a single equation connecting the three constants θ, p, s. There is, therefore, a doubly infinite set of steady precessions corresponding to arbitrary values of two out of the three constants. It is not, however, possible to assign completely arbitrary values of two of the constants, these values must be such that (14.208) yields a real value for the third constant.

If we see a top spinning, θ and p are easy to observe In terms of them, s is given by

$$(14.209) \qquad s = \frac{mga}{Cp} + \frac{Ap \cos \theta}{C}.$$

We note that, if the precession is small, the spin is great and is given approximately by

$$(14.210) \qquad s = \frac{mga}{Cp}.$$

This is a very simple and useful formula.

Exercise. A disk, 6 inches in diameter, is mounted on the end of a light rod 1 inch long and spins rapidly It precesses once in 15 seconds Find approximately the spin, in revolutions per second, and the velocity of a point on the edge of the disk

General motion of a top.

To discuss the general motion of a top, we shall use the same notation for the constants of the top as that used above.

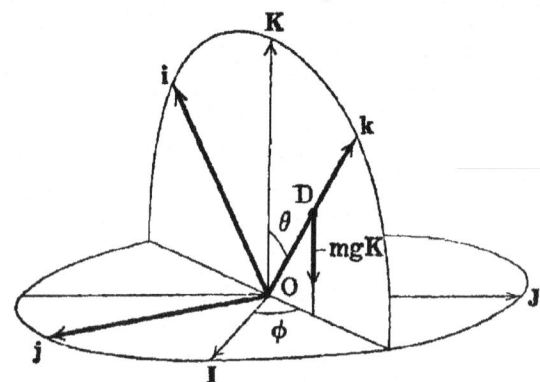

Fig. 149.—Vector diagram for top in general motion.

Let I, J, K (Fig. 149) be a fixed orthogonal triad, K being directed vertically upward. Let i, j, k be an orthogonal triad, with k pointing along OD, the axis of symmetry of the top, and i coplanar with k and K; thus j is horizontal. The triad i, j, k is fixed neither in space nor in the top, but k is fixed in the top.

Let θ, ϕ be the usual polar angles of k relative to the fixed triad. Variations in θ are referred to as *nutation*, and variations in ϕ as *precession*.

Let

$$(14.211) \qquad \omega = \omega_1 i + \omega_2 j + \omega_3 k$$

be the angular velocity of the top, and

(14.212) $$\mathbf{\Omega} = \Omega_1 \mathbf{i} + \Omega_2 \mathbf{j} + \Omega_3 \mathbf{k}$$

the angular velocity of the triad $\mathbf{i}, \mathbf{j}, \mathbf{k}$. It is easy to see that

(14.213) $\quad \Omega_1 = \sin\theta\, \dot\phi, \qquad \Omega_2 = -\dot\theta, \qquad \Omega_3 = \cos\theta\, \dot\phi.$

Now the relative motion of the top and the triad $\mathbf{i}, \mathbf{j}, \mathbf{k}$ consists only of a rotation about $\mathbf{k}$. Hence,

(14.214) $\quad \omega_1 = \Omega_1 = \sin\theta\, \dot\phi, \qquad \omega_2 = \Omega_2 = -\dot\theta.$

The angular momentum is

(14.215) $$\mathbf{h} = A\omega_1 \mathbf{i} + A\omega_2 \mathbf{j} + C\omega_3 \mathbf{k},$$

and its rate of change is, by (12.306),

(14.216) $$\dot{\mathbf{h}} = A\dot\omega_1 \mathbf{i} + A\dot\omega_2 \mathbf{j} + C\dot\omega_3 \mathbf{k} + \mathbf{\Omega} \times \mathbf{h}.$$

The moment about O of the weight of the top is

(14.217) $$\mathbf{G} = a\mathbf{k} \times (-mg\mathbf{K}) = -mga \sin\theta\, \mathbf{j}.$$

The motion of the top satisfies the fundamental equation

(14.218) $$\dot{\mathbf{h}} = \mathbf{G}$$

When we substitute the expressions given above, this vector equation gives three scalar equations for θ, ϕ, and ω_3. However, an indirect method of attack proves simpler, and we shall make direct use only of the third component of (14.218).

The component of (14.218) in the direction of $\mathbf{k}$ gives

$$C\dot\omega_3 = 0,$$

since, by (14.214) and (14.215), $\mathbf{\Omega} \times \mathbf{h}$ has no component in the direction $\mathbf{k}$. Hence

(14.219) $$\omega_3 = s,$$

a constant; *the spin of the top is a constant.* Further, since the weight of the top has no moment about $\mathbf{K}$, the component of angular momentum in this fixed direction is constant, and so

(14.220) $$\mathbf{h} \cdot \mathbf{K} = \alpha,$$

a constant. By (14.214) and (14.215), this gives immediately

(14.221) $$A\dot\phi \sin^2\theta + Cs \cos\theta = \alpha,$$

since $\mathbf{K} = \sin\theta\,\mathbf{i} + \cos\theta\,\mathbf{k}$. Finally, we have the equation of energy

(14.222) $$T + V = E,$$

or

(14.223) $$\tfrac{1}{2}A(\omega_1^2 + \omega_2^2) + \tfrac{1}{2}C\omega_3^2 + mga\cos\theta = E,$$

E being a constant. Substitution from (14.214) and (14.219) gives

(14.224) $$A(\dot\theta^2 + \dot\phi^2 \sin^2\theta) + Cs^2 = 2(E - mga\cos\theta).$$

We have in (14.221) and (14.224) two equations to determine θ and ϕ as functions of the time.

It is convenient to write $Cs = \beta$. Then our two equations read

(14.225) $$\begin{cases} A\dot\phi\sin^2\theta = \alpha - \beta\cos\theta \\ A(\dot\theta^2 + \dot\phi^2\sin^2\theta) + \dfrac{\beta^2}{C} = 2(E - mga\cos\theta). \end{cases}$$

The plan is now obvious. We are to substitute for $\dot\phi$ in the second equation from the first; this will give a differential equation for θ. When this is solved, the first equation will give ϕ by a quadrature.

Let us put $x = \cos\theta$. On multiplying the second equation in (14.225) by $\sin^2\theta$ and substituting for $\dot\phi$, we obtain for x the differential equation

(14.226) $$A\left[\dot x^2 + \frac{(\alpha - \beta x)^2}{A^2}\right] + \frac{\beta^2}{C}(1 - x^2) = 2(E - mgax)(1 - x^2).$$

This equation may be written

(14.227) $$\dot x^2 = f(x),$$

where

(14.228) $$f(x) = \frac{1}{A}\left(2E - \frac{\beta^2}{C} - 2mgax\right)(1 - x^2) - \frac{(\alpha - \beta x)^2}{A^2}.$$

This is a cubic in x, and, by the same form of argument as that used in Sec. 13.3 for the spherical pendulum, we see that it has a

graph of the general form shown in Fig. 150; the function $f(x)$ has three real zeros x_1, x_2, x_3, such that

$$-1 < x_1 < x_2 < 1 < x_3.$$

(In special cases, we may have one or more signs of equality instead of inequality.) Thus $f(x)$ may be written

(14.229) $$f(x) = \frac{2mga}{A}(x - x_1)(x - x_2)(x - x_3).$$

Again by the same argument as in Sec. 13.3, the solution of (14.227) is

(14.230) $$\cos \theta = x = x_1 + (x_2 - x_1) \operatorname{sn}^2 [p(t - t_0)],$$

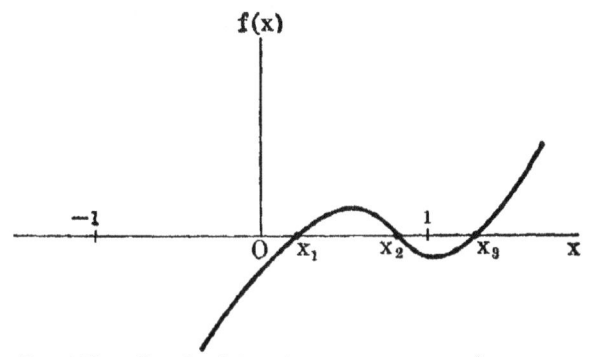

Fig. 150.—Graph of $f(x)$ for a top in general motion.

where p and the modulus k of the elliptic function are given by

(14.231) $$p^2 = \frac{mga(x_3 - x_1)}{2A}, \qquad k^2 = \frac{x_2 - x_1}{x_3 - x_1}.$$

The constants x_1, x_2, x_3 are functions of the constants occurring in (14.228), i.e., the constants of the top and α, β, E; the latter are known when the initial position and angular velocity of the top are given.

The complete solution for the motion of the axis of the top is given by (14.230) and

(14.232) $$\phi = \frac{\alpha - \beta x}{A(1 - x^2)}.$$

Since x is known as a function of t, this last equation gives ϕ by a quadrature.

This analytic solution does not immediately give a clear idea of the way in which the top behaves. However, we can

construct the essential features of the motion, by fixing our attention on the intersection of the axis of the top with a unit sphere having its center at O. It is interesting to compare the motion of this point with the motion of a spherical pendulum.

In the first place, it is clear from (14.230) that the representative point on the unit sphere oscillates between two levels $\theta = \theta_1$ and $\theta = \theta_2$, given by

$$\cos \theta_1 = x_1, \quad \cos \theta_2 = x_2$$

This behavior is like that of the spherical pendulum, but while the mean level for the spherical pendulum must lie below the center of sphere, that is no longer necessarily true for the top. There is, however, a more striking difference; in the case of the

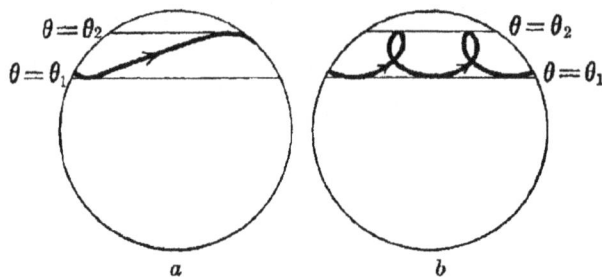

Fig. 151.—Motion of the axis of a top (a) without loops, (b) with loops

top, we may have loops on the curve. The absence of loops, as in Fig. 151a, or the presence of loops, as in Fig. 151b, depends on the way in which the motion is started, i.e., on the values of the constants α, β, E. The criterion for the existence of a loop is that ϕ should sometimes increase and sometimes decrease, and the condition for this is that $\dot\phi$ should vanish during the motion. By (14.232), $\dot\phi = 0$ when $x = \alpha/\beta$; since x oscillates between x_1 and x_2, it is just a question as to whether α/β lies in this range of oscillation. If it lies in the range, there are loops; if not, there are no loops.

Cuspidal motion of a top.

A particularly interesting case arises when the top is spinning with its axis fixed in position and then released. It starts to fall but recovers and rises to its former height, repeating this process over and over again.

This case can be discussed in terms of the theory just developed. The behavior of a top depends essentially on the cubic $f(x)$ of (14.228), and to it we must direct our attention.

First, let us note that initially $x = x_0$ (say), $\dot{x} = 0$, and $\phi = 0$. Hence, by (14.232), $\alpha = \beta x_0$; also, by (14.226),

$$E = \tfrac{1}{2}\frac{\beta^2}{C} + mgax_0.$$

Substitution in (14.228) gives

(14.233) $\quad f(x) = \dfrac{2mga}{A}(x_0 - x)(1 - x^2) - \dfrac{\beta^2}{A^2}(x_0 - x)^2.$

Obviously, one zero of $f(x)$ is $x = x_0$; but is this zero x_1 or x_2? Differentiation gives, for $x = x_0$,

$$f'(x_0) = -\frac{2mga}{A}(1 - x_0^2) < 0.$$

Since this value is negative, it is clear from Fig. 150 that $x_0 = x_2$, not x_1.

The oscillation of x is from x_1 to x_0 (or x_2), where x_1 is the smallest zero of $f(x)$. Putting

(14.234) $\quad \lambda = \dfrac{\beta^2}{4Amga} = \dfrac{C^2 s^2}{4Amga},$

we see that the three zeros of $f(x)$ are

(14.235) $\quad \begin{cases} x_1 = \lambda - \sqrt{\lambda^2 - 2\lambda x_0 + 1}, \\ x_2 = x_0, \\ x_3 = \lambda + \sqrt{\lambda^2 - 2\lambda x_0 + 1}. \end{cases}$

Thus the axis of the top falls down from an inclination θ_0 (where $\cos \theta_0 = x_0$) to an inclination θ_1, where

(14.236) $\quad \cos \theta_1 = x_1 = \lambda - \sqrt{\lambda^2 - 2\lambda x_0 + 1}.$

Then it starts to rise again and swings up to $\theta = \theta_0$, where the axis is again instantaneously at rest.

If λ is large, i.e., if the spin is great, binomial expansion of the radical in (14.236) gives approximately

$$\cos \theta_1 = \cos \theta_0 - \frac{\sin^2 \theta_0}{2\lambda}.$$

The difference $\theta_1 - \theta_0$ is small, and so we may use the approximation

$$\cos \theta_1 - \cos \theta_0 = -(\theta_1 - \theta_0) \sin \theta_0.$$

The axis falls only through the small angle

$$(14.237) \qquad \theta_1 - \theta_0 = \frac{2Amga}{C^2s^2} \sin \theta_0.$$

The differential equation of the path of the representative point on the unit sphere is

$$\frac{d\phi}{dx} = \frac{\dot\phi}{\dot x} = \frac{\beta(x_0 - x)}{\pm A(1 - x^2) \sqrt{f(x)}}.$$

Since $f(x)$ vanishes like $x - x_0$ as $x \to x_0$, it is clear that $d\phi/dx = 0$ at the highest positions of the axis. Hence the path of the representative point meets the circle $\theta = \theta_0$ at right angles; the path has cusps at these points, directed upward.

Stability of a sleeping top.

Anyone who has seen a top spinning is familiar with the general nature of the motions discussed above. Sometimes the top executes a motion of steady precession, and sometimes the more general motion in which the axis of the top nods up and down as it precesses. A third type of motion is often seen, in which the top spins with its axis vertical. The axis remains stationary and there is no apparent motion of the top as a whole—it is then said to be a *sleeping top*. A small disturbance of a sleeping top produces only a small oscillation when the spin is great; when the spin has been considerably reduced by frictional resistance, the top begins to wobble and ultimately falls down. We naturally ask: What is the critical value of the spin below which the motion of a sleeping top is unstable?

The answer is found by examining the cubic $f(x)$ given in (14.228). Since $\theta = \dot\theta = 0$ for a sleeping top, we have, by (14.221) and (14.224),

$$\alpha = \beta = Cs, \qquad E = \tfrac{1}{2}Cs^2 + mga;$$

hence, (14.228) gives

$$(14.238) \qquad f(x) = (1 - x)^2 \left[\frac{2mga}{A}(1 + x) - \frac{C^2s^2}{A^2} \right].$$

We observe that $x = 1$ is a double zero of $f(x)$. Two cases arise: either the third zero of $f(x)$ is greater than unity, or it is less than unity. The forms of the graph of $f(x)$ for these two

cases are shown in Figs. 152a and b; in terms of the notation used for the zeros of $f(x)$, Fig. 152a shows the case where the third zero is x_3, and Fig. 152b the case where it is x_1.

When the top suffers a small disturbance, the graph of $f(x)$ for the disturbed motion will not be the same as that for the

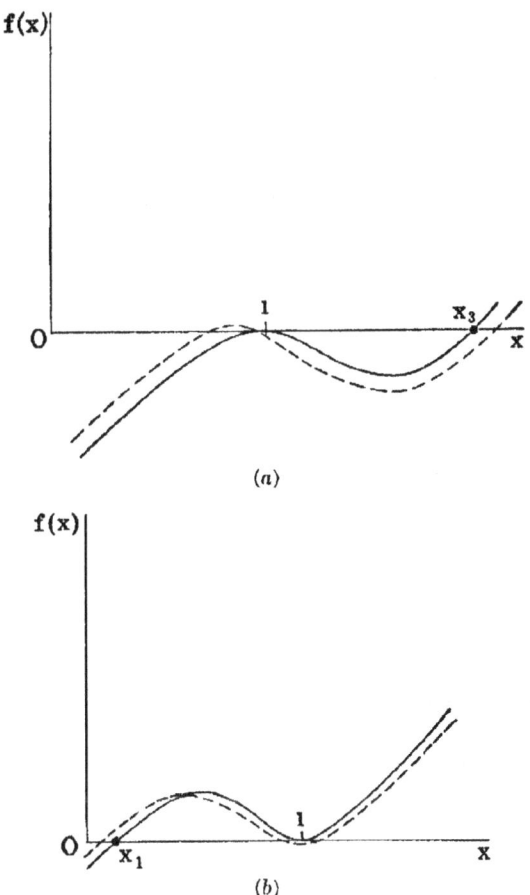

Fig. 152.— (a) Graph of $f(x)$ for a stable sleeping top (b) Graph of $f(x)$ for an unstable sleeping top. In each case, the broken curve is the graph for disturbed motion.

sleeping top. The difference will be small, however, since only small changes in the constants α, β, E can result from a small disturbance. The broken curves in Figs. 152a and b indicate the way in which the graphs of $f(x)$ are modified by a small disturbance. In general, the three zeros of $f(x)$ will become distinct—two of them must, of course, lie in the range $(-1, 1)$, and the third must exceed unity.

Since, in the disturbed motion, the value of x lies between the two smaller zeros of $f(x)$, it is clear that one or other of the following descriptions applies:

(i) The axis of the top, when disturbed, does not depart far from its original vertical position—the motion is stable. This corresponds to Fig. 152a.

(ii) The axis of the top falls to an inclination θ_1, where

$$\cos \theta_1 = x_1$$

—the motion is unstable. This corresponds to Fig. 152b.

To find the critical value of the spin s, it remains to distinguish the two cases analytically.

The two types of curve are distinguished by the sign of $f''(x)$ at $x = 1$; it is negative in Fig. 152a and positive in Fig. 152b. Differentiating (14.238), we find

$$f''(1) = 2\left(\frac{4mga}{A} - \frac{C^2 s^2}{A^2}\right);$$

this is negative and *the motion of a sleeping top is stable*, if

(14.239) $$s^2 > \frac{4Amga}{C^2}.$$

In the limiting case $s^2 = 4Amga/C^2$, it is easy to see that all three zeros of $f(x)$ coincide at $x = 1$, and the motion is stable.

Exercise. Show that, for a motion of steady precession, the cubic $f(x)$ has a double zero lying in the range $(-1, 1)$. Hence show that this type of steady motion is always stable.

Stability of a spinning projectile.

It is a well-known fact that an elongated projectile acquires *stability* from the spin imparted to it by the rifling in the gun. By this we mean that it does not turn broadside on to its direction of motion when in flight, nor does it tumble as a nonspinning projectile often does. We shall now use our theory of the motion of a top in an attempt to explain this spin stabilization.

In Sec. 6.2 we discussed the motion of a projectile in a resisting medium, the projectile being treated as a particle. The problem becomes much more complicated when the projectile is treated as a rigid solid of revolution, subject to gravity and to the aerodynamic force system due to the pressure of the air. We cannot

enter here into this general problem; instead, following the older writers on ballistics, we shall make some drastic simplifications.

Thus, we shall assume that the aerodynamic force system is equipollent to a single force (the drag) with fixed direction and constant magnitude (R), intersecting the axis of the projectile at a fixed point (the center of pressure). We can now use Fig. 149, with suitable changes, for the discussion of the motion of the projectile relative to its mass center. Let O be the mass center, $\mathbf{K}$ a fixed unit vector opposed to the direction of the drag, and $\mathbf{k}$ a unit vector along the axis of the projectile. The point D is taken to be the center of pressure; and the force at D, i.e., $-mg\mathbf{K}$ in the case of the top, is now to be replaced by $-R\mathbf{K}$. The weight of the projectile acts through O, and so the total moment about O is due to the aerodynamic forces alone; it is

$$(14.240) \qquad \mathbf{G} = -Ra \sin \theta \mathbf{j},$$

where a is the distance of the center of pressure in front of the mass center and θ the angle between the axis of the projectile and the direction of the drag reversed.

Since the fundamental equation (12.209) for motion relative to the mass center is of the same form as (14.218) and the expression (14.240) for $\mathbf{G}$ is of the same form as (14.217) with the constant mga changed to Ra, we can apply to the motion of the projectile the same mathematical analysis as we applied to the motion of the top. In particular, if the projectile is moving along its axis, the fixed direction of the drag will also lie on this line, and we have what is essentially a sleeping top. Then (14.239) yields the condition for stability of the spinning projectile, i.e., the condition that the projectile, if slightly disturbed, will not develop large oscillations. This condition is

$$(14.241) \qquad s^2 > \frac{4ARa}{C^2},$$

where s is the spin of the projectile, A the transverse moment of inertia at O (i.e., at the mass center), and C the axial moment of inertia.

14.3. GYROSCOPES

The stability of a gyroscope.

Let us suppose that a gyroscope (i.e., a rigid body with an axis of symmetry) is mounted in a Cardan's suspension (Fig. 144),

so that its mass center is fixed. It is set spinning about its axis of symmetry with a great angular velocity s. Now let an impulsive couple $\hat{G}$ be applied to the gyroscope. The instantaneous change in angular momentum is [cf. (12.502)]

(14.301) $$\Delta h = \hat{G}.$$

We have then a vector diagram as in Fig. 153. The vector $\overrightarrow{OA}$ is h, the angular momentum before the impulsive couple was

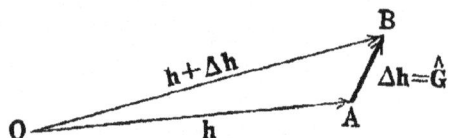

Fig. 153.—Change in angular momentum due to an impulsive couple

applied. It is made long, because s (and consequently h) is assumed to be large. The vector $\overrightarrow{AB}$ is Δh, and $\overrightarrow{OB}$ represents the final angular momentum. It is clear that the angle AOB is small; in fact, it tends to zero as s tends to infinity. Thus, the application of an impulsive couple to a rapidly spinning gyroscope makes only a small change in the direction of the angular momentum vector. It is easily seen that the corresponding change in the direction of the angular velocity vector is also small.

This simple result illustrates the stability which a rapid rotation imparts to a body. The gyroscope shows, as it were, an unwillingness to alter the direction of its axis. When it does yield, it does so in a manner which continues to cause surprise even to those familiar with the theory.

The gyroscopic couple.

In Fig. 154a, O is a fixed point on the axis of a gyroscope, and j a unit vector fixed in space. As pointed out earlier, any motion can be produced, provided suitable forces are applied. Let us demand that the gyroscope shall spin with constant angular speed s about its axis, and at the same time that the axis shall turn (or precess) with constant angular speed p in the plane perpendicular to j. If k is a unit vector along the axis of the gyroscope and i completes the triad, then the angular velocity of the gyroscope is

(14.302) $$\omega = pj + sk,$$

and the triad (**i**, **j**, **k**) has an angular velocity

(14.303) $$\mathbf{\Omega} = p\mathbf{j}.$$

If A and C are, respectively, the transverse and axial moments of inertia, the angular momentum is

(14.304) $$\mathbf{h} = Ap\mathbf{j} + Cs\mathbf{k},$$

and its rate of change is

(14.305) $$\dot{\mathbf{h}} = \mathbf{\Omega} \times \mathbf{h} = Csp\mathbf{i}.$$

Thus the *gyroscopic couple* **G** required to maintain this motion is

(14.306) $$\mathbf{G} = Csp\mathbf{i},$$

that is, a couple of magnitude Csp, produced by a pair of forces in the rotating plane of **j** and **k**.

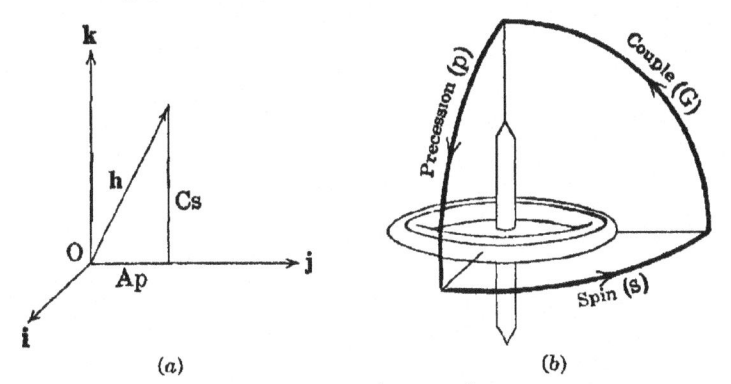

FIG 154.—(a) Angular momentum diagram for a precessing gyroscope
(b) Relations between couple, precession, and spin.

The relations between the couple, the precession, and the spin are shown in Fig 154b. It is more interesting here not to show the vectors in the usual way, but to represent them by arcs in the planes perpendicular to them. The curious fact, hard to understand intuitively, is that the plane of the couple does not coincide with the plane of the precession, but is perpendicular to it. Instead of yielding to the couple, the axis of the gyroscope turns at right angles to the plane of the couple.

It is evident from (14.306) that when the gyroscope spins rapidly, a very great couple is required to produce even a moderate rate of precession

Although the diagram of Fig. 154b shows only a simple gyro-

scopic phenomenon, it is very useful from a practical standpoint. We note that the three quadrants form a single closed curve. As we traverse it in the sense indicated by the arrows, we cover the following quadrants in order:

> Couple,
> Precession,
> Spin.

This is easy to remember, since the letters C, P, S are in alphabetical order.

Example. *An airplane has a rotary engine, which rotates in a clockwise direction when viewed from behind. The airplane makes a left turn. Does the gyroscopic effect of the rotating engine tend to make the nose rise or fall?*

First we suppose that the pilot sets the rudder and elevator in such a way that the nose goes neither up nor down. The mass center of the engine describes a circular arc C as the airplane turns (Fig. 155). The angular velocity of the engine is made up of a large component along the tangent to C and a small vertical component, due to the turning of the airplane as a whole. The quadrants of precession and spin are therefore as shown. Hence, by the rule of alphabetical order, the couple quadrant comes down in front. To maintain the motion described, the pilot must set the rudder and elevator in such a way that aerodynamic forces, acting on them, produce the required couple.

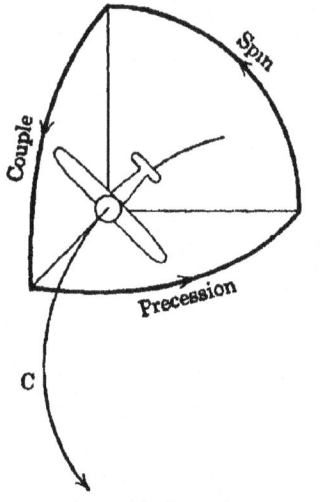

Fig. 155.—Airplane turning.

If the pilot flies the airplane with a rotary engine in the same way as he would fly a similar airplane with a stationary engine, the couple required to maintain the steady flight in a horizontal circle will not be present. Since the couple is one which tends to depress the nose, in its absence the nose will rise. What will happen after the initial lift takes place is a complicated question, not covered by the present simple theory.

The gyrocompass.

If the spinning of the earth on its axis were much faster than it actually is, it would be a simple matter to devise a mechanism by which the true north could be found on a ship at sea. However, the earth's rotation is so slow that an apparatus of great delicacy is required, in order that a minute effect may not be wiped out by frictional resistances. The modern gyrocompass

Sec. 14 3] MOTION OF A RIGID BODY 445

is such a piece of apparatus The simple system which we shall discuss is much less elaborate than the gyrocompass as it is actually constructed.* However, the basic fact that a spinning gyroscope enables us to find the north is demonstrated by a discussion of an ideally simple gyrocompass.

In Fig. 156, PQ is part of the earth's axis, drawn from south to north. The point O is on the earth's surface at latitude λ. Thus the horizontal line, drawn due north from O, is inclined to the earth's axis at an angle λ; this line is OQ in the diagram. The unit vector $\mathbf{K}$ is parallel to PQ.

A gyroscope is mounted in a Cardan's suspension (Fig. 144) so that its mass center lies at O. But it is not left free to turn about O; one pair of the bearings in the suspension is locked, so that the axis of the gyroscope can move only in the horizontal plane at O. The unit vector $\mathbf{k}$ lies along the axis of the gyroscope, making with OQ a variable angle θ, $\mathbf{i}$ is perpendicular to $\mathbf{k}$ in the horizontal plane, and $\mathbf{j}$ is vertical (i.e., coplanar with PQ, OQ and perpendicular to OQ). The gyroscope itself is not shown in the diagram; the curve is a unit circle in the horizontal plane.

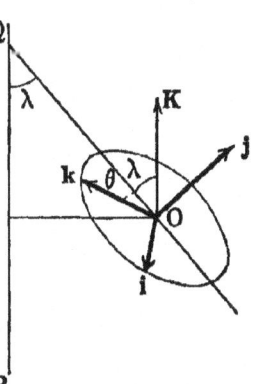

Fig 156.—Vector diagram for gyrocompass.

The angular velocity of the triad $(\mathbf{i}, \mathbf{j}, \mathbf{k})$ is made up of the angular velocity of the earth, which we may write $\Omega \mathbf{K}$, and an angular velocity due to change in θ, in fact, $\dot\theta \mathbf{j}$. Since

$$\mathbf{K} = -\sin\theta\cos\lambda\,\mathbf{i} + \sin\lambda\,\mathbf{j} + \cos\theta\cos\lambda\,\mathbf{k},$$

the angular velocity of the triad is

(14.307) $\quad \boldsymbol{\omega}' = -\Omega\sin\theta\cos\lambda\,\mathbf{i} + (\dot\theta + \Omega\sin\lambda)\mathbf{j}$
$\qquad\qquad + \Omega\cos\theta\cos\lambda\,\mathbf{k}.$

The angular velocity $\boldsymbol{\omega}$ of the gyroscope differs from this only in

---

* Cf. H. Lamb, Higher Mechanics (Cambridge University Press, 1929), p 144; R F Deimel, Mechanics of the Gyroscope (The Macmillan Company, New York, 1929), A L Rawlings, The Theory of the Gyroscopic Compass (The Macmillan Company, New York, 1929), E S Ferry, Applied Gyrodynamics (John Wiley & Sons, New York, 1932).

the third component; thus,

(14.308) $\quad \boldsymbol{\omega} = -\Omega \sin\theta \cos\lambda\, \mathbf{i} + (\dot\theta + \Omega \sin\lambda)\mathbf{j} + s\mathbf{k},$

where s is the axial spin, including a component of the earth's rotation. The angular momentum is

(14.309) $\quad \mathbf{h} = -A\Omega \sin\theta \cos\lambda\, \mathbf{i} + A(\dot\theta + \Omega \sin\lambda)\mathbf{j} + Cs\mathbf{k},$

where A and C are, respectively, the transverse and axial moments of inertia.

To keep the axis of the gyroscope in the horizontal plane, the bearings of the suspension must exert a couple $\mathbf{G}$ on it. Since the bearings are assumed to be smooth, no work is done by this couple in rotations about either $\mathbf{j}$ or $\mathbf{k}$. Hence, $\mathbf{G}$ is perpendicular to these vectors, and we may write

(14.310) $\quad\quad\quad\quad\quad \mathbf{G} = G\mathbf{i},$

where G may be either positive or negative.

The fundamental equation $\dot{\mathbf{h}} = \mathbf{G}$ gives

(14.311) $\quad -A\Omega \cos\theta \cos\lambda\, \dot\theta\mathbf{i} + A\ddot\theta\mathbf{j} + C\dot s\mathbf{k} + \boldsymbol{\omega}' \times \mathbf{h} = G\mathbf{i}.$

We now pick out the $\mathbf{j}$ and $\mathbf{k}$ components of this equation and so obtain two scalar equations for s and θ:

(14.312) $\quad \begin{cases} A\ddot\theta + Cs\Omega \cos\lambda \sin\theta - A\Omega^2 \sin\theta \cos\theta \cos^2\lambda = 0, \\ C\dot s = 0. \end{cases}$

The second equation shows that the spin s is constant. With Ω^2 neglected, the first equation may be written

(14.313) $\quad\quad\quad\quad \ddot\theta + n^2 \sin\theta = 0,$

where

(14.314) $\quad\quad\quad\quad n = \sqrt{\dfrac{Cs\Omega \cos\lambda}{A}}.$

Now (14.313) is the equation of motion of a simple pendulum. It is possible for the axis of the gyroscope to go right round the horizontal circle, but if the initial values of θ and $\dot\theta$ are small, the motion will be oscillatory. The important fact is this: *The axis of the gyroscope oscillates symmetrically about the direction $\theta = 0$.* Hence, by bisecting the angle of swing, we may find the north. The gyroscope therefore acts as a *gyrocompass*,

indicating the *true* north; the magnetic compass, of course, indicates the *magnetic* north

For small oscillations, the periodic time of swing for the gyrocompass is

(14.315) $$\tau = \frac{2\pi}{n} = 2\pi \sqrt{\frac{A}{Cs\Omega \cos \lambda}}.$$

Since Ω is so small (1 revolution per sidereal day = $2\pi/86{,}164$ radians per second), the spin of the gyroscope (s) must be given a large value in order to make τ reasonably small. If $\lambda = \pm \frac{1}{2}\pi$, the periodic time becomes infinite, and the gyrocompass fails to function; but that is only to be expected, for the points in question are the North and South Poles.

Exercise. Assuming the mass of the gyroscope concentrated in a thin ring, find the number of revolutions per second required for a periodic time of 10 seconds at latitude 45°.

14.4. GENERAL MOTION OF A RIGID BODY

The general motion of a rigid body consists of (i) motion of the mass center and (ii) motion relative to the mass center. The equations governing these have been given in Sec. 12.4. But it would be wrong to suppose that the determination of the general motion always splits into two parts—a problem in particle dynamics and a problem in the dynamics of a body with a fixed point. Constraints make the two problems interlock, and complications arise. We cannot give a general plan for the solution of all such problems but shall determine the motions of two systems as examples.

The motion of a billiard ball.

A billiard ball is struck by a cue. At time $t = 0$, we suppose that the ball is in contact with the table; its center has a horizontal velocity $\mathbf{q}_0$, and the ball has an angular velocity $\boldsymbol{\omega}_0$. We wish to find the subsequent motion of the ball.

If the table were perfectly smooth, the center of the ball would retain the velocity $\mathbf{q}_0$, and the angular velocity $\boldsymbol{\omega}_0$ would also be retained. But we shall assume the table to be rough, with a coefficient of kinetic friction μ.

At a general time t, the center O has a horizontal velocity $\mathbf{q}$, and the ball has an angular velocity $\boldsymbol{\omega}$. Let $\mathbf{K}$ be a unit vector

drawn vertically upward (Fig. 157). The reaction of the table on the ball at the point of contact P may be written

$$\mathbf{F} + R\mathbf{K},$$

where R is the magnitude of the normal reaction and $\mathbf{F}$ the force of friction, $\mathbf{F}$, of course, acts horizontally. The weight is $-mg\mathbf{K}$, where m is the mass of the ball. Thus the equation of motion of the center is, by (12.410),

(14.401) $\quad m\dot{\mathbf{q}} = \mathbf{F} + (R - mg)\mathbf{K}.$

But, since the ball remains in contact with the table, the acceleration of the center has no vertical component. Thus $R = mg$, and we have

(14.402) $\quad m\dot{\mathbf{q}} = \mathbf{F}.$

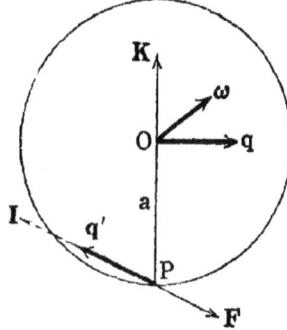

Fig. 157.—Ball slipping on a table

Since every axis at O is a principal axis of inertia, the angular momentum about O is $\mathbf{h} = mk^2\boldsymbol{\omega}$, where k is the radius of gyration about a diameter. Thus the equation for motion relative to O is, by (12.411),

(14.403) $\quad mk^2\dot{\boldsymbol{\omega}} = -a\mathbf{K} \times (\mathbf{F} + R\mathbf{K}) = -a\mathbf{K} \times \mathbf{F},$

where a is the radius of the ball.

In the vector equations (14.402) and (14.403), there are actually five scalar equations. There are seven unknowns, viz., two components of $\mathbf{q}$, three components of $\boldsymbol{\omega}$, and two components of $\mathbf{F}$. Thus, two more equations are required; they are furnished by the law of kinetic friction, as long as there is slipping between the ball and the table. This law tells us that $\mathbf{F}$ acts in a direction opposite to the velocity of the particle of the ball at P, and that

(14.404) $\quad\quad\quad\quad F = \mu R = \mu mg.$

Thus,

(14.405) $\quad\quad\quad\quad \mathbf{F} = -\mu mg \frac{\mathbf{q}'}{q'},$

where $\mathbf{q}'$ is the velocity of the particle at P, given by

(14.406) $\quad\quad\quad\quad \mathbf{q}' = \mathbf{q} + \boldsymbol{\omega} \times (-a\mathbf{K}).$

Hence, using (14.402) and (14.403), we get

(14.407) $$m\dot{\mathbf{q}}' = \mathbf{F} + \frac{a^2}{k^2}(\mathbf{K} \times \mathbf{F}) \times \mathbf{K}$$
$$= \left(1 + \frac{a^2}{k^2}\right)\mathbf{F},$$

since $\mathbf{K} \cdot \mathbf{F} = 0$. Thus, by (14.405) and (14.407), the derivative of $\mathbf{q}'$ has a direction opposed to $\mathbf{q}'$. This implies that, as long as slipping is taking place, the vector $\mathbf{q}'$ has a fixed direction.

Let $\mathbf{I}$ be a unit vector in this fixed direction. Then

(14.408) $$\mathbf{q}' = q'\mathbf{I}, \qquad \mathbf{F} = -\mu mg\mathbf{I},$$

and, by (14.407), the magnitude of $\mathbf{q}'$ changes according to the equation

(14.409) $$\dot{q}' = -\mu g\left(1 + \frac{a^2}{k^2}\right).$$

Hence,

(14.410) $$q' = q_0' - \mu g t\left(1 + \frac{a^2}{k^2}\right),$$

where q_0' is the magnitude of $\mathbf{q}_0'$, the initial velocity of slipping, viz.,

(14.411) $$\mathbf{q}_0' = \mathbf{q}_0 - a\boldsymbol{\omega}_0 \times \mathbf{K}.$$

By (14.410), we shall have $q' = 0$ when

(14.412) $$t = \frac{q_0'}{\mu g}\frac{k^2}{a^2 + k^2};$$

at this instant slipping ceases. It is easy to see that, once slipping ceases, the motion becomes a simple rolling in a straight line at constant speed, for (14.402) and (14.403) are satisfied by constant values of $\mathbf{q}$ and $\boldsymbol{\omega}$, with $\mathbf{F} = 0$.

There is a point of interest in connection with the motion of the center before slipping ceases. By (14.402) and (14.408), we have

(14.413) $$\dot{\mathbf{q}} = -\mu g\mathbf{I}.$$

This means that the acceleration of the center of the ball is constant in direction and magnitude, and so the center describes a parabolic path as long as slipping persists.

The above results hold for any ball in which there is a spherically symmetric distribution of matter. If the ball is solid and homogeneous, we put $k^2 = \tfrac{2}{5}a^2$.

The motion of a rolling disk.

Everyone knows that a child's hoop, or a rolling coin, acquires stability from its motion. If the hoop or coin rolls slowly, it will start to wobble violently, but if it rolls fast, it can pass over small obstacles without being upset. We shall now discuss such motions, idealizing for simplicity to the case where the body has a sharp rolling edge. We can treat the hoop and the coin (or indeed any body with a sharp circular edge, possessing an axis and a plane of symmetry) in a single argument by using general symbols for moments of inertia. For purposes of reference, however, we shall use the word "disk."

Figure 158 shows the disk in a general position; P is the point of contact with the ground, which we shall suppose rough enough to prevent slipping. Let θ be the inclination of the plane of the disk to the vertical, and ϕ the angle between a fixed horizontal direction and the tangent to the disk at P. Let $(\mathbf{i}, \mathbf{j}, \mathbf{k})$ be a unit orthogonal triad, $\mathbf{k}$ being perpendicular to the disk at its center O and $\mathbf{i}$ lying along the radius toward P; $\mathbf{j}$ is therefore horizontal and lies in the plane of the disk.

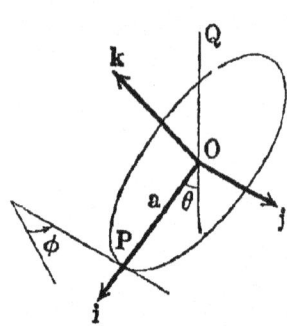

Fig. 158.—Disk rolling on a plane

For the velocity of the center and the angular velocity of the disk, we may write

$$\mathbf{q} = u\mathbf{i} + v\mathbf{j} + w\mathbf{k}, \qquad \boldsymbol{\omega} = \omega_1\mathbf{i} + \omega_2\mathbf{j} + \omega_3\mathbf{k}.$$

These two vectors are not independent, because the particle at P is instantaneously at rest. This gives the condition

$$\mathbf{q} + \boldsymbol{\omega} \times a\mathbf{i} = \mathbf{0},$$

where a is the radius of the disk; or, in scalar form,

(14.414) $\quad u = 0, \quad v + a\omega_3 = 0, \quad w - a\omega_2 = 0.$

These equations determine $\mathbf{q}$ when $\boldsymbol{\omega}$ is known.

Now the angular velocity $\boldsymbol{\Omega}$ of the triad arises solely from

Sec. 14.4] MOTION OF A RIGID BODY 451

changes in θ and ϕ. The former gives an angular velocity $-\dot\theta\mathbf{j}$, and the latter an angular velocity $\dot\phi$ about OQ, the vertical through O. Thus,

(14.415) $\qquad \boldsymbol{\Omega} = -\cos\theta\,\dot\phi\mathbf{i} - \dot\theta\mathbf{j} + \sin\theta\,\dot\phi\mathbf{k}.$

But the angular velocities of the disk and the triad differ only in the $\mathbf{k}$ component. Therefore

(14.416) $\qquad \omega_1 = -\cos\theta\,\dot\phi, \qquad \omega_2 = -\dot\theta.$

For the reaction of the ground, we write

(14.417) $\qquad \mathbf{R} = R_1\mathbf{i} + R_2\mathbf{j} + R_3\mathbf{k}.$

By (12.410) and (12.411), the two vector equations of motion are

(14.418) $\qquad \begin{cases} m\dot{\mathbf{q}} = \mathbf{R} + mg(\cos\theta\,\mathbf{i} - \sin\theta\,\mathbf{k}), \\ \dot{\mathbf{h}} = a\mathbf{i} \times \mathbf{R}, \end{cases}$

where m is the mass of the disk and $\mathbf{h}$ is the angular momentum about O; we have

$$\mathbf{h} = A\omega_1\mathbf{i} + A\omega_2\mathbf{j} + C\omega_3\mathbf{k},$$

A and C being transverse and axial moments of inertia at O.

Since, by (12.306),

(14.419) $\qquad \dot{\mathbf{q}} = u\mathbf{i} + v\mathbf{j} + w\mathbf{k} + \boldsymbol{\Omega} \times \mathbf{q},$

the first of (14.418) gives the three scalar equations

(14.420) $\qquad \begin{cases} m(\dot u - \dot\theta w - \sin\theta\,\dot\phi v) = R_1 + mg\cos\theta, \\ m(\dot v + \sin\theta\,\dot\phi u + \cos\theta\,\dot\phi w) = R_2, \\ m(\dot w - \cos\theta\,\dot\phi v + \dot\theta u) = R_3 - mg\sin\theta. \end{cases}$

By (14.414) and (14.416), we eliminate u, v, w and obtain

(14.421) $\qquad \begin{cases} ma(\dot\theta^2 + \sin\theta\,\dot\phi\omega_3) = R_1 + mg\cos\theta, \\ -ma(\dot\omega_3 + \cos\theta\,\dot\theta\dot\phi) = R_2, \\ -ma(\ddot\theta - \cos\theta\,\dot\phi\omega_3) = R_3 - mg\sin\theta. \end{cases}$

Turning now to the second of (14.418), we have

(14.422) $\qquad \dot{\mathbf{h}} = A\dot\omega_1\mathbf{i} + A\dot\omega_2\mathbf{j} + C\dot\omega_3\mathbf{k} + \boldsymbol{\Omega} \times \mathbf{h},$

and so we get the three scalar equations

(14.423) $\qquad \begin{cases} A\dot\omega_1 - C\dot\theta\omega_3 - A\sin\theta\,\dot\phi\omega_2 = 0, \\ A\dot\omega_2 + A\sin\theta\,\dot\phi\omega_1 + C\cos\theta\,\dot\phi\omega_3 = -aR_3, \\ C\dot\omega_3 - A\cos\theta\,\dot\phi\omega_2 + A\dot\theta\omega_1 = aR_2. \end{cases}$

By (14.416), these become

$$(14.424) \quad \begin{cases} A \dfrac{d}{dt}(\cos\theta\, \dot\phi) + C\dot\theta\omega_3 - A\sin\theta\, \dot\theta\dot\phi = 0, \\ A\ddot\theta + A\sin\theta\cos\theta\, \dot\phi^2 - C\cos\theta\, \dot\phi\omega_3 = aR_3, \\ C\dot\omega_3 = aR_2. \end{cases}$$

Associating these equations with (14.421), we have six equations for the six unknowns θ, ϕ, ω_3, R_1, R_2, R_3. They are the equations (12.412) applied to our special problem.

Before proceeding to discuss the stability of the disk rolling straight ahead, let us consider simple steady motions satisfying the equations (14.421) and (14.424).

The most obvious solution is

$$(14.425) \quad \begin{cases} \theta = 0, \quad \dot\phi = \text{constant}, \quad \omega_3 = \text{constant}, \\ R_1 = -mg, \quad R_2 = 0, \quad R_3 = 0. \end{cases}$$

This is the straight-ahead motion, in which the plane of the disk is vertical. Another simple motion is given by

$$(14.426) \quad \theta = \text{constant}, \quad \dot\phi = \text{constant}, \quad \omega_3 = \text{constant}.$$

The corresponding reactions are, by (14.421),

$$(14.427) \quad \begin{cases} R_1 = m(a\sin\theta\, \dot\phi\omega_3 - g\cos\theta), \\ R_2 = 0, \\ R_3 = m(a\cos\theta\, \dot\phi\omega_3 + g\sin\theta). \end{cases}$$

When we substitute in (14.424), the satisfaction of these equations requires

$$(14.428) \quad (C + ma^2)\cos\theta\, \dot\phi\omega_3 + mga\sin\theta = A\sin\theta\cos\theta\, \dot\phi^2;$$

this condition must be satisfied by the constant values of θ, $\dot\phi$, ω_3, in order that the steady motion may exist. It is, of course, a rolling in a circular path.

Exercise. If, in the motion given by (14.426), θ and $\dot\phi$ are small, show that the time taken to complete the circular path is approximately

$$2\pi\omega_3(C + ma^2)/(mga\theta).$$

Let us now discuss the stability of the rolling disk. We suppose the disk to be slightly disturbed from the steady motion given by (14.425). In the disturbed state the following quanti-

ties are assumed to be small, since they vanish in the steady motion:

(14.429) $\quad\theta, \dot{\theta}, \ddot{\theta}, \phi, \dot{\phi}, \dot{\omega}_3, R_1 + mg, R_2, R_3.$

With only first-order terms retained, (14.421) and (14.424) become

(14.430) $\quad\begin{cases} 0 = R_1 + mg, & A\dot{\phi} + C\theta\omega_3 = 0, \\ ma\dot{\omega}_3 = -R_2, & A\dot{\theta} - C\phi\omega_3 = aR_3, \\ ma\ddot{\theta} - ma\dot{\phi}\omega_3 = -R_3 + mg\theta, & C\omega_3 = aR_2. \end{cases}$

From the second and last equations we see that $\omega_3 =$ constant. Elimination of ϕ and R_3 from the other equations gives

(14.431) $\quad A(A + ma^2)\ddot{\theta} + [C(C + ma^2)\omega_3^2 - Amga]\theta = \alpha,$

where α is a constant of integration. Obviously the condition for stability is

(14.432) $$\omega_3^2 > \frac{Amga}{C(C + ma^2)}.$$

14.5. SUMMARY OF APPLICATIONS IN DYNAMICS IN SPACE—MOTION OF A RIGID BODY

I. Rigid body with fixed point under no forces.

(a) For a general body, the motion is given by rolling the Poinsot ellipsoid on the invariable plane; there is an analytic solution in terms of elliptic functions.

(b) For a body with an axis of symmetry, the Poinsot ellipsoid is of revolution, and the motion is given by rolling the right circular body cone on the right circular space cone at a constant rate.

II. The spinning top.

(a) Steady precession (p) with fast spin (s):

(14.501) $$s = \frac{mga}{Cp} \quad \text{(approximately).}$$

(b) General motion expressible in terms of elliptic functions.
(c) Sleeping top stable if

(14.502) $$s^2 > \frac{4Amga}{C^2}$$

III. Gyroscopes.

(a) A finite impulsive couple, applied to a fast-spinning gyroscope, alters the direction of the axis of rotation only slightly.

(b) Gyroscopic couple G required to maintain precession p:

(14.503)
$$G = Csp.$$
Couple → Precession → Spin.

(c) Gyrocompass

(14.504)
$$\tau = 2\pi \sqrt{\frac{A}{Cs\Omega \cos \lambda}}.$$

IV. General motion of a rigid body.

(a) Center of a slipping billiard ball describes a parabola.

(b) Rolling disk is stable if its angular velocity ω satisfies

(14.505)
$$\omega^2 > \frac{Amga}{C(C + ma^2)}$$

EXERCISES XIV

1. A circular disk, pivoted at its center, is set spinning with angular velocity ω about a line making an angle α with its axis. Find, in terms of ω and α, the time taken by the axis of the disk to describe a cone in space.

2. A gyroscope can turn freely about its mass center O which is fixed. Initially, it is set spinning about its axis, which is then struck perpendicularly. Find the angular velocity immediately after impact in terms of the initial spin, the moments of inertia, the magnitude of the impulsive force, and its distance from O. Draw a diagram showing the direction of the impulsive force, the angular velocity, and the angular momentum just after impact.

3. The center of a square plate is fixed. If at a certain instant the angular velocity vector makes an angle of 30° with the normal to the plate, find the inclination of the angular momentum vector to the normal.

4. A rigid body turns about a fixed point O under the action of a single force $\mathbf{F}$ (in addition to the reaction at the fixed point). If the extremity of the angular momentum vector, drawn from O, lies in a fixed plane P throughout the motion, show that $\mathbf{F}$ intersects or is parallel to the perpendicular dropped from O on P.

5. A heavy homogeneous right circular cone spins with its vertex fixed. The axis of the cone is 4 in. long, and the radius of the base is 2 in. The axis maintains a constant inclination to the vertical and completes a rotation about the vertical in 5 sec. Find approximately the number of revolutions per second of the cone about its axis.

6. A lamina turns freely under no forces in three-dimensional motion about its mass center, which is fixed. Use Euler's equations to prove that the component of angular velocity in the plane of the lamina is constant in magnitude.

7. A rigid body turns about a fixed point under no forces. The momental ellipsoid at the fixed point is of revolution, and the axial moment of inertia C is greater than the transverse moment of inertia A. Show that if α is the angle of inclination of the instantaneous axis to the axis of symmetry, then the semiangle of the space cone is

$$\tan^{-1}\frac{(C-A)\tan\alpha}{C+A\tan^2\alpha}.$$

Noting the inequality $C \leq A + B$, satisfied in general by moments of inertia, show that the semiangle of the space cone cannot exceed

$$\tan^{-1}\tfrac{1}{2}\sqrt{2}$$

8. Make a rough estimate of the speed at which a twenty-five-cent piece must roll in order that its motion may be stable.

9. A solid homogeneous cuboid of edges $2a, 2a, 4a$ can turn freely under no forces about its center, which is fixed. It is set spinning with angular velocity ω about a diagonal. Find the semivertical angle of the cone described in space by the line through the center parallel to the longer edges, and show that the time taken by this line to move once round the cone is $10\pi/(\omega\sqrt{11})$.

10. A circular disk of mass m and radius a is made to roll without slipping in steady motion on a rough horizontal plane, its plane being vertical and its track a circle of radius b. It completes a circuit in time τ. Reduce to a force at the center of the disk and a couple, the force system (including weight and the reaction of the plane) which must act on the disk in order that this motion may take place. The components of the force and the couple are to be expressed in terms of a, b, τ, m.

11. A rigid body with an axis of symmetry can turn about its mass center. There acts on it a frictional couple $-\lambda\omega$, where ω is the angular velocity vector and λ a positive constant. Show that the axial component of angular velocity is reduced to half its original value in a time $(C \log 2)/\lambda$, where C is the axial moment of inertia. If C exceeds the transverse moment of inertia A, show also that the semiangle of the body cone decreases steadily.

12. An egg-shaped solid of revolution rolls in steady motion on a rough horizontal plane, the axis of figure being horizontal. Establish the relation

$$(a^2 + k^2)ns = abn^2 + bg,$$

where a is the radius of the greatest circular section, b the distance of the mass center from this section, k the radius of gyration about the axis of figure, and n, s the vertical and horizontal components of angular velocity.

13. Prove that a top cannot move in steady precession with spin s and inclination θ to the vertical, unless

$$C^2s^2 \geq 4Amga\cos\theta$$

14. A solid cone of height b and semivertical angle α rolls in steady motion on a rough horizontal table, the line of contact rotating with angular velocity

Ω. Show that the reaction of the table on the cone is equipollent to a single force which cuts the generator of contact at a distance

$$\tfrac{3}{4}b \cos \alpha + \frac{k^2 \Omega^2}{g} \cot \alpha$$

from the vertex, where k is the radius of gyration of the cone about a generator. Deduce that the greatest possible value for Ω is

$$\frac{1}{2k} \frac{1}{\cos \alpha} [gb \sin \alpha (1 + 3 \sin^2 \alpha)]^{\frac{1}{2}},$$

as the cone would overturn if Ω exceeded this value.

15. A circular disk of radius a spins on a smooth table about a vertical diameter. Prove the motion is stable if the angular velocity exceeds $2\sqrt{g/a}$.

16. A circular disk of radius a rolls on a rough horizontal plane in steady motion. The speed of its center is q_0, and its plane is inclined to the vertical at a constant angle θ. Show that the radius r of the circle described by the center of the disk satisfies the equation

$$4gr^2 - 6q_0^2 r \cot \theta - q_0^2 a \cos \theta = 0;$$

deduce that, when θ is small,

$$r = \frac{3q_0^2}{2g\theta}, \text{ approximately.}$$

17. A rigid body can turn freely about a smooth axis, for which its moment of inertia is I. It is acted on by a couple of constant magnitude G, applied in such a way that, when the body has turned through an angle θ, the vector representing the couple makes an angle θ with the axis. If the body is initially at rest, find its angular velocity when it has turned through a right angle.

If the axis is an axis of symmetry of the body, find the reaction exerted by the body on the axis when it has turned through an angle θ.

18. A light axle L carries two gyroscopes, L is their common axis of symmetry, and they can turn freely about it. L is so mounted that it can turn freely about a fixed point on it, halfway between the mass centers of the gyroscopes. Find a quadratic equation to determine the angular velocities of steady precession under the action of gravity, in terms of the following constants.

m, m', the masses of the gyroscopes,
C, C', their axial moments of inertia,
A, A', their transverse moments of inertia at their mass centers,
s, s', their spins,
$2a$, the distance between their centers,
θ, the inclination of L to the vertical.

19. A rigid body turns about a fixed point under no forces. Show that, relative to the body, the extremity of the angular momentum vector **h** moves

on the curve of intersection of the sphere

$$x^2 + y^2 + z^2 = h^2$$

and the cone

$$x^2 \left(\frac{2T}{h^2} - \frac{1}{A}\right) + y^2 \left(\frac{2T}{h^2} - \frac{1}{B}\right) + z^2 \left(\frac{2T}{h^2} - \frac{1}{C}\right) = 0,$$

the axes being principal axes of inertia.

Sketch the curves, taking $A > B > C$ and considering all possible values of $2T/h^2$.

20. A top is spinning about its axis which is vertical. It is at the same time sliding over a smooth horizontal plane with velocity q_0. The vertex strikes a small smooth ridge on the plane, the direction of the motion being inclined at an angle α to the direction of the ridge. If the coefficient of restitution for the impact is e, find the angle at which the vertex rebounds from the ridge in terms of q_0, α, e, and the constants of the top. Find also the direction of motion of the mass center immediately after impact.

21. A thin elliptical plate of semiaxes a, b ($a > b$) can turn freely about its center, which is fixed; it is set in motion with an angular velocity n about an axis in its plane equally inclined to the axes of the ellipse. Show that the instantaneous axis will again be in the plane of the plate after a time

$$2 \int_0^\lambda (\lambda^4 - x^4)^{-\frac{1}{2}} dx,$$

where

$$\lambda^2 = \frac{n^2}{2} \frac{a^2 - b^2}{a^2 + b^2}$$

22. A thin hemispherical bowl of mass m and radius a stands on a smooth horizontal table. A horizontal impulsive force of magnitude $\hat{P}$ is applied along a tangent to the rim. Find the magnitude and direction of the velocity instantaneously imparted to the point of the bowl in contact with the table.

Show that, no matter how large $\hat{P}$ may be, the rim of the bowl will never come into contact with the table.

23. A rigid body with an axis of symmetry **k** is mounted so that it can turn freely about its mass center, which is fixed. To a given point on the axis of symmetry there is applied a force $F\mathbf{K}$, where **K** is a fixed unit vector and F a given function of the angle θ between **k** and **K**. Show that the system is conservative, and obtain equations analogous to (14.227) and (14.228). Show that **k** oscillates between two right circular cones having **K** for their common axis.

CHAPTER XV
LAGRANGE'S EQUATIONS

15.1. INTRODUCTION TO LAGRANGE'S EQUATIONS

The question must have occurred to many people: If science keeps on growing at its present rate, how are succeeding generations of students to keep up with it? We may find a partial answer by looking back at what has happened during the past two hundred years or so.

First, there has been the development of specialization—a broad specialization into subjects (pure mathematics, applied mathematics, astronomy, physics, chemistry), followed by a narrower specialization into branches (differential geometry, hydrodynamics, spectroscopy, to mention a few). Each branch is now big enough to provide work for a lifetime. A still narrower specialization is not a pleasant prospect, for intensive work in a restricted range becomes in time uninteresting and sterile.

But, side by side with the growth of specialization, we find an increasing tendency to use mathematical methods. Mathematics gives to science the power of abstraction and generalization, and a symbolism that says what it has to say with the greatest possible clarity and economy. The mathematician, penetrating deeply into the structure of theories, is often able to detect common features, not obvious on the surface. In this way, he breaks down the barriers between restricted fields and brings the specialists into contact with one another. Further, the mathematician can compress a mass of descriptive theory into a few differential equations and so greatly reduce the bulk of science.

Long before science reached its modern state of complexity, Lagrange invented a uniform method of approach for all dynamical problems. This method has formed the basis for nearly all work on the general theory of dynamics and is the foundation on which quantum mechanics is built. In the more elementary

Sec. 15.1] *LAGRANGE'S EQUATIONS* 459

parts of mechanics, it has not yet supplanted the more direct and physical approach, because its rather abstract and general character has made it appear difficult. However, it seems probable that as time passes the method of Lagrange will work its way from the end to the beginning of textbooks on mechanics The easier, but more cumbrous, methods are becoming a luxury for which we cannot afford the time.

Instead of proceeding at once to Lagrange's equations in their full generality, we shall start with the case of a particle in a plane. Much of the difficulty of understanding the method may be overcome by a study of this comparatively simple case.

Lagrange's equations for a particle in a plane.

Consider a particle of mass m, moving in a plane. Let Oxy be rectangular Cartesian axes, and let X, Y be the components of the force acting on the particle. The usual equations of motion are

$$(15.101) \qquad m\ddot{x} = X, \qquad m\ddot{y} = Y.$$

Now let q_1, q_2 be any curvilinear coordinates (e.g., polar coordinates). It will be possible to express x and y in terms of q_1 and q_2, and so we may write

$$(15.102) \qquad x = x(q_1, q_2), \qquad y = y(q_1, q_2).$$

These relations hold for all values of the time t, and so

$$(15.103) \quad \dot{x} = \frac{\partial x}{\partial q_1} \dot{q}_1 + \frac{\partial x}{\partial q_2} \dot{q}_2, \qquad \dot{y} = \frac{\partial y}{\partial q_1} \dot{q}_1 + \frac{\partial y}{\partial q_2} \dot{q}_2.$$

The partial derivatives occurring here are functions of q_1, q_2; we can calculate them when the functions (15.102) are given.

Looking at (15.103) in a formal way and forgetting that $\dot{q}_1$ is actually the derivative of q_1, we may regard them as equations expressing the two quantities $\dot{x}$, $\dot{y}$ as functions of the four quantities q_1, q_2, $\dot{q}_1$, $\dot{q}_2$; we may express this by writing

$$(15.104) \quad \dot{x} = f(q_1, q_2, \dot{q}_1, \dot{q}_2), \qquad \dot{y} = g(q_1, q_2, \dot{q}_1, \dot{q}_2).$$

If we speak of the partial derivatives

$$\frac{\partial \dot{x}}{\partial q_1}, \quad \frac{\partial \dot{x}}{\partial q_2}, \quad \frac{\partial \dot{x}}{\partial \dot{q}_1}, \quad \frac{\partial \dot{x}}{\partial \dot{q}_2}$$

or the corresponding derivatives of y, we understand that they are calculated from (15.104), all the quantities $q_1, q_2, \dot{q}_1, \dot{q}_2$ being treated as constants, except the one with respect to which we differentiate

But the functions in (15.104) are the same as those in (15.103), and so

$$(15.105) \quad \frac{\partial x}{\partial \dot{q}_1} = \frac{\partial x}{\partial q_1}, \quad \frac{\partial \dot{x}}{\partial \dot{q}_2} = \frac{\partial x}{\partial q_2}, \quad \frac{\partial \dot{y}}{\partial \dot{q}_1} = \frac{\partial y}{\partial q_1}, \quad \frac{\partial \dot{y}}{\partial \dot{q}_2} = \frac{\partial y}{\partial q_2}.$$

Furthermore, $\partial x/\partial q_1$ is a function of q_1, q_2; so, following the motion of the particle,

$$(15.106) \quad \frac{d}{dt}\frac{\partial x}{\partial q_1} = \frac{\partial^2 x}{\partial q_1^2}\dot{q}_1 + \frac{\partial^2 x}{\partial q_2\, \partial q_1}\dot{q}_2.$$

But, on the other hand, if we differentiate the first of (15.103) partially with respect to q_1, we get

$$(15.107) \quad \frac{\partial \dot{x}}{\partial q_1} = \frac{\partial^2 x}{\partial q_1^2}\dot{q}_1 + \frac{\partial^2 x}{\partial q_1\, \partial q_2}\dot{q}_2.$$

This is equal to the expression in (15.106). Hence, assembling this result with the other results obtained by using q_2 and y, we have

$$(15.108) \quad \begin{cases} \dfrac{d}{dt}\dfrac{\partial x}{\partial q_1} = \dfrac{\partial \dot{x}}{\partial q_1}, & \dfrac{d}{dt}\dfrac{\partial y}{\partial q_1} = \dfrac{\partial \dot{y}}{\partial q_1}, \\ \dfrac{d}{dt}\dfrac{\partial x}{\partial q_2} = \dfrac{\partial \dot{x}}{\partial q_2}, & \dfrac{d}{dt}\dfrac{\partial y}{\partial q_2} = \dfrac{\partial \dot{y}}{\partial q_2}. \end{cases}$$

The equations (15.105) and (15.108) are fundamental in the development of Lagrange's equations

The kinetic energy of the particle is

$$(15.109) \qquad T = \tfrac{1}{2}m(\dot{x}^2 + \dot{y}^2).$$

If we substitute for $\dot{x}$ and $\dot{y}$ from (15.103), we obtain a function of $q_1, q_2, \dot{q}_1, \dot{q}_2$,

$$(15.110) \qquad T = T(q_1, q_2, \dot{q}_1, \dot{q}_2).$$

Actually this function is of the form

$$(15.111) \qquad T = \tfrac{1}{2}(a\dot{q}_1^2 + 2h\dot{q}_1\dot{q}_2 + b\dot{q}_2^2),$$

where a, h, b are functions of q_1, q_2.

Sec. 15.1]   *LAGRANGE'S EQUATIONS*   461

Now, in (15.109), T is expressed as a function of $\dot{x}$, $\dot{y}$; by (15.103), $\dot{x}$, $\dot{y}$ are functions of q_1, q_2, $\dot{q}_1$, $\dot{q}_2$; hence we obtain, using (15.105),

$$(15.112) \qquad \frac{\partial T}{\partial \dot{q}_1} = \frac{\partial T}{\partial \dot{x}} \frac{\partial \dot{x}}{\partial \dot{q}_1} + \frac{\partial T}{\partial \dot{y}} \frac{\partial \dot{y}}{\partial \dot{q}_1}$$

$$= m\dot{x} \frac{\partial x}{\partial q_1} + m\dot{y} \frac{\partial y}{\partial q_1}.$$

Therefore, by (15.108) and (15.109), we have

$$(15.113) \quad \begin{cases} \dfrac{d}{dt}\dfrac{\partial T}{\partial \dot{q}_1} = m\ddot{x}\dfrac{\partial x}{\partial q_1} + m\ddot{y}\dfrac{\partial y}{\partial q_1} + m\dot{x}\dfrac{\partial \dot{x}}{\partial q_1} + m\dot{y}\dfrac{\partial \dot{y}}{\partial q_1}, \\[6pt] \dfrac{\partial T}{\partial q_1} = m\dot{x}\dfrac{\partial \dot{x}}{\partial q_1} + m\dot{y}\dfrac{\partial \dot{y}}{\partial q_1}. \end{cases}$$

Subtracting and using the equations of motion (15.101), we get

$$(15.114) \qquad \frac{d}{dt}\frac{\partial T}{\partial \dot{q}_1} - \frac{\partial T}{\partial q_1} = X\frac{\partial x}{\partial q_1} + Y\frac{\partial y}{\partial q_1}.$$

There is, of course, a similar equation with q_2 instead of q_1.

Any small virtual displacement* of the particle corresponds to increments δq_1, δq_2 in the coordinates q_1, q_2. The corresponding increments in x, y are

$$(15.115) \quad \delta x = \frac{\partial x}{\partial q_1}\delta q_1 + \frac{\partial x}{\partial q_2}\delta q_2, \qquad \delta y = \frac{\partial y}{\partial q_1}\delta q_1 + \frac{\partial y}{\partial q_2}\delta q_2.$$

The work done in this displacement is

$$(15.116) \qquad \delta W = X\,\delta x + Y\,\delta y,$$

or

$$(15.117) \qquad \delta W = Q_1\,\delta q_1 + Q_2\,\delta q_2,$$

where

$$(15.118) \quad Q_1 = X\frac{\partial x}{\partial q_1} + Y\frac{\partial y}{\partial q_1}, \qquad Q_2 = X\frac{\partial x}{\partial q_2} + Y\frac{\partial y}{\partial q_2}.$$

Hence, we have the following result *The motion of a particle in a plane satisfies the differential equations*

---

* It should be emphasized that this virtual displacement is arbitrary; it is not to be confused with the displacement actually occurring in the motion. If we want to refer to the latter, we write dx, dy, dq_1, dq_2.

$$(15.119) \quad \frac{d}{dt}\frac{\partial T}{\partial \dot{q}_1} - \frac{\partial T}{\partial q_1} = Q_1, \quad \frac{d}{dt}\frac{\partial T}{\partial \dot{q}_2} - \frac{\partial T}{\partial q_2} = Q_2,$$

where q_1, q_2 are any curvilinear coordinates, T is the kinetic energy (expressed as a function of q_1, q_2, $\dot{q}_1$, $\dot{q}_2$) and Q_1, Q_2 are obtained from the expression δW, as in (15.117), for the work done in an arbitrary small displacement.

These are *Lagrange's equations of motion*.

The curvilinear coordinates q_1, q_2 are, of course, *generalized coordinates*, as discussed in Sec. 10.6; the quantities Q_1, Q_2 are the *generalized forces* [cf. (10.708)].

It must be clearly understood that the Lagrangian method only provides the differential equations of motion; it does not *solve* them. It is true that the method does give some hints helpful for solution, but that is a matter into which we cannot go here.

Example Consider a particle of mass m moving in a plane, under an attractive force $\mu m/r^2$, directed to the origin of polar coordinates r, θ. If we take as generalized coordinates

$$q_1 = r, \quad q_2 = \theta,$$

and denote the generalized forces by R, Θ, the equations of motion (15.119) read

$$(15.120) \quad \frac{d}{dt}\frac{\partial T}{\partial \dot{r}} - \frac{\partial T}{\partial r} = R, \quad \frac{d}{dt}\frac{\partial T}{\partial \dot{\theta}} - \frac{\partial T}{\partial \theta} = \Theta$$

Now

$$T = \tfrac{1}{2}m(\dot{r}^2 + r^2\dot{\theta}^2),$$

and so

$$(15.121) \quad \frac{\partial T}{\partial \dot{r}} = m\dot{r}, \quad \frac{\partial T}{\partial r} = mr\dot{\theta}^2, \quad \frac{\partial T}{\partial \dot{\theta}} = mr^2\dot{\theta}, \quad \frac{\partial T}{\partial \theta} = 0$$

To find R and Θ, we have (for an arbitrary displacement δr, $\delta \theta$)

$$R\,\delta r + \Theta\,\delta\theta = \delta W = -\frac{\mu m}{r^2}\,\delta r,$$

and so

$$(15.122) \quad R = -\frac{\mu m}{r^2}, \quad \Theta = 0.$$

Substituting from (15.121) and (15.122) in (15.120), we get

$$(15.123) \quad m\ddot{r} - mr\dot{\theta}^2 = -\frac{\mu m}{r^2}, \quad \frac{d}{dt}(mr^2\dot{\theta}) = 0.$$

These equations are the same as (5.104); the present method of obtaining them is simpler than the method used earlier.

15.2. LAGRANGE'S EQUATIONS FOR A GENERAL SYSTEM

Lagrange's equations for a system with two degrees of freedom.

We pass now from a particle moving in a plane to any system with two degrees of freedom, with generalized coordinates q_1, q_2 (cf. Sec. 10.6). Let N be the number of particles forming the system, and let the Cartesian coordinates of a particle (of mass m_i) be x_i, y_i, z_i ($i = 1, 2, \cdots N$). Then x_i, y_i, z_i are functions of q_1, q_2, and we may write

$$(15\ 201) \quad x_i = x_i(q_1, q_2), \qquad y_i = y_i(q_1, q_2), \qquad z_i = z_i(q_1, q_2).$$

Here we have $3N$ equations like the two equations (15.102), and we obtain on differentiation $3N$ equations like (15 103),

$$(15.202) \quad \begin{cases} \dot{x}_i = \dfrac{\partial x_i}{\partial q_1} \dot{q}_1 + \dfrac{\partial x_i}{\partial q_2} \dot{q}_2, \\ \dot{y}_i = \dfrac{\partial y_i}{\partial q_1} \dot{q}_1 + \dfrac{\partial y_i}{\partial q_2} \dot{q}_2, \\ \dot{z}_i = \dfrac{\partial z_i}{\partial q_1} \dot{q}_1 + \dfrac{\partial z_i}{\partial q_2} \dot{q}_2 \end{cases}$$

As a matter of fact, the whole argument for a system with two degrees of freedom follows very closely the argument for a particle in a plane; the complication introduced by having $3N$ Cartesian coordinates, instead of only two, is not serious. Thus, if we use a symbol ξ to stand for any one of the coordinates x_i, y_i, z_i, we obtain, exactly as in (15.105) and (15.108), the following equations:

$$(15.203) \quad \frac{\partial \dot{\xi}}{\partial \dot{q}_1} = \frac{\partial \xi}{\partial q_1}, \qquad \frac{\partial \dot{\xi}}{\partial \dot{q}_2} = \frac{\partial \xi}{\partial q_2},$$

$$(15.204) \quad \frac{d}{dt} \frac{\partial \xi}{\partial q_1} = \frac{\partial \dot{\xi}}{\partial q_1}, \qquad \frac{d}{dt} \frac{\partial \xi}{\partial q_2} = \frac{\partial \dot{\xi}}{\partial q_2}.$$

The kinetic energy of the system is

$$(15.205) \quad T = \tfrac{1}{2} \sum_{i=1}^{N} m_i(\dot{x}_i^2 + \dot{y}_i^2 + \dot{z}_i^2),$$

and this is expressible in the form

$$(15.206) \quad T = T(q_1, q_2, \dot{q}_1, \dot{q}_2).$$

As in the case of the single particle, this is a quadratic expression

(15.207) $$T = \tfrac{1}{2}(a\dot{q}_1^2 + 2h\dot{q}_1\dot{q}_2 + b\dot{q}_2^2),$$

where a, h, b are functions of q_1, q_2

Then, by (15.203) and (15.205),

(15.208) $$\frac{\partial T}{\partial \dot{q}_1} = \sum_{i=1}^{N} \left(\frac{\partial T}{\partial \dot{x}_i} \frac{\partial \dot{x}_i}{\partial \dot{q}_1} + \frac{\partial T}{\partial \dot{y}_i} \frac{\partial \dot{y}_i}{\partial \dot{q}_1} + \frac{\partial T}{\partial \dot{z}_i} \frac{\partial \dot{z}_i}{\partial \dot{q}_1} \right)$$
$$= \sum_{i=1}^{N} m_i \left(\dot{x}_i \frac{\partial x_i}{\partial q_1} + \dot{y}_i \frac{\partial y_i}{\partial q_1} + \dot{z}_i \frac{\partial z_i}{\partial q_1} \right)$$

and so, by (15.204),

(15.209) $$\frac{d}{dt}\frac{\partial T}{\partial \dot{q}_1} = \sum_{i=1}^{N} m_i \left(\ddot{x}_i \frac{\partial x_i}{\partial q_1} + \ddot{y}_i \frac{\partial y_i}{\partial q_1} + \ddot{z}_i \frac{\partial z_i}{\partial q_1} \right)$$
$$+ \sum_{i=1}^{N} m_i \left(\dot{x}_i \frac{\partial \dot{x}_i}{\partial q_1} + \dot{y}_i \frac{\partial \dot{y}_i}{\partial q_1} + \dot{z}_i \frac{\partial \dot{z}_i}{\partial q_1} \right).$$

The last term on the right is $\partial T/\partial q_1$. Let X_i, Y_i, Z_i be the components of force (external and internal) acting on the ith particle, so that

(15.210) $$m_i \ddot{x}_i = X_i, \quad m\ddot{y}_i = Y_i, \quad m\ddot{z}_i = Z_i.$$

Then (15.209) may be written

(15.211) $$\frac{d}{dt}\frac{\partial T}{\partial \dot{q}_1} - \frac{\partial T}{\partial q_1} = \sum_{i=1}^{N} \left(X_i \frac{\partial x_i}{\partial q_1} + Y_i \frac{\partial y_i}{\partial q_1} + Z_i \frac{\partial z_i}{\partial q_1} \right).$$

Now, if Q_1, Q_2 are the generalized forces, so that the work done in a general displacement is

(15.212) $$\delta W = Q_1\, \delta q_1 + Q_2\, \delta q_2,$$

it is clear from (10.707) that the expression on the right-hand side of (15.211) is precisely the generalized force Q_1.

Thus, associating with (15.211) the companion equation in q_2, we have *Lagrange's equations of motion for a system with two degrees of freedom*,

(15.213) $$\frac{d}{dt}\frac{\partial T}{\partial \dot{q}_1} - \frac{\partial T}{\partial q_1} = Q_1, \quad \frac{d}{dt}\frac{\partial T}{\partial \dot{q}_2} - \frac{\partial T}{\partial q_2} = Q_2,$$
$$(\delta W = Q_1\, \delta q_1 + Q_2\, \delta q_2).$$

Sec. 15.2] *LAGRANGE'S EQUATIONS* 465

The form of these equations is precisely the same as for a particle in a plane; no additional complexity has been added by considering the general system with two degrees of freedom, of which a particle in a plane is, of course, a special case.

When the system is conservative, with potential energy $V(q_1, q_2)$, the generalized forces are connected with V by (10.712). Thus, (15.213) may be written

$$(15.214) \quad \frac{d}{dt}\frac{\partial T}{\partial \dot{q}_1} - \frac{\partial T}{\partial q_1} = -\frac{\partial V}{\partial q_1}, \quad \frac{d}{dt}\frac{\partial T}{\partial \dot{q}_2} - \frac{\partial T}{\partial q_2} = -\frac{\partial V}{\partial q_2}.$$

Example 1. We shall now find the equations of motion of a spherical pendulum. Let m be the mass of the particle and a the radius of the sphere on which the particle is constrained to move. We take as generalized coordinates

$$q_1 = \theta, \quad q_2 = \phi,$$

where θ is the angular distance from the highest point of the sphere and ϕ the azimuthal angle. Then,

$$T = \tfrac{1}{2}ma^2(\dot\theta^2 + \sin^2\theta\,\dot\phi^2), \quad V = mga\cos\theta,$$

and so

$$\frac{\partial T}{\partial \dot\theta} = ma^2\dot\theta, \quad \frac{\partial T}{\partial \theta} = ma^2\sin\theta\cos\theta\,\dot\phi^2, \quad \frac{\partial V}{\partial \theta} = -mga\sin\theta,$$

$$\frac{\partial T}{\partial \dot\phi} = ma^2\sin^2\theta\,\dot\phi, \quad \frac{\partial T}{\partial \phi} = 0, \quad \frac{\partial V}{\partial \phi} = 0.$$

Thus (15.214) give, as equations of motions of a spherical pendulum,

$$ma^2\ddot\theta - ma^2\sin\theta\cos\theta\,\dot\phi^2 = mga\sin\theta,$$

$$\frac{d}{dt}(ma^2\sin^2\theta\,\dot\phi) = 0.$$

Example 2. Consider a uniform bar hanging by one end from a smooth horizontal rail. It can move only in the vertical plane through the rail and is under the influence of gravity and a horizontal force X applied to its lowest point. Let us find the equations of motion.

For generalized coordinates, we take

q_1 = distance of point of suspension from some fixed point on rail,
q_2 = inclination of bar to vertical.

Then,

$$T = \tfrac{1}{2}m\left\{\left[\frac{d}{dt}(q_1 + a\sin q_2)\right]^2 + \left[\frac{d}{dt}(a\cos q_2)\right]^2\right\} + \tfrac{1}{2}mk^2\dot q_2^2,$$

where m = mass of bar,
    $2a$ = length of bar,
    k = radius of gyration about mass center.

The above expression reduces to
$$T = \tfrac{1}{2}m[\dot{q}_1^2 + 2a\cos q_2\, \dot{q}_1\dot{q}_2 + (a^2 + k^2)\dot{q}_2^2]$$

The generalized forces are given by
$$Q_1\, \delta q_1 + Q_2\, \delta q_2 = X\, \delta(q_1 + 2a \sin q_2) + mg\, \delta(a \cos q_2).$$

Thus
$$Q_1 = X, \qquad Q_2 = 2Xa \cos q_2 - mga \sin q_2,$$

and so the equations of motion are, by (15.213),

$$m\frac{d}{dt}(\dot{q}_1 + a \cos q_2\, \dot{q}_2) = X,$$

$$m\frac{d}{dt}[a \cos q_2\, \dot{q}_1 + (a^2 + k^2)\dot{q}_2] + ma \sin q_2\, \dot{q}_1\dot{q}_2 = 2Xa \cos q_2 - mga \sin q_2.$$

If the bar remains nearly vertical, so that q_2 is small, these equations simplify to the approximate form

$$\ddot{q}_1 + a\ddot{q}_2 = \frac{X}{m},$$

$$\ddot{q}_1 + \tfrac{4}{3}a\ddot{q}_2 + g q_2 = \frac{2X}{m}.$$

Lagrange's equations for a general system.

Consider a system with n degrees of freedom and generalized coordinates $q_1, q_2, \cdots q_n$. The method of finding Lagrange's equations in this general case differs from the method given above only in a slightly greater complexity, due to the n degrees of freedom. We shall give here an argument complete in essentials but omitting details which can be supplied by the type of argument used earlier.*

Let m_i, x_i, y_i, z_i ($i = 1, 2, \cdots N$) be the mass and coordinates of the ith particle. Then, for $r = 1, 2, \cdots n$,

$$\frac{\partial T}{\partial \dot{q}_r} = \sum_{i=1}^{N}\left(\frac{\partial T}{\partial \dot{x}_i}\frac{\partial \dot{x}_i}{\partial \dot{q}_r} + \frac{\partial T}{\partial \dot{y}_i}\frac{\partial \dot{y}_i}{\partial \dot{q}_r} + \frac{\partial T}{\partial \dot{z}_i}\frac{\partial \dot{z}_i}{\partial \dot{q}_r}\right)$$

$$= \sum_{i=1}^{N} m_i\left(\dot{x}_i\frac{\partial x_i}{\partial q_r} + \dot{y}_i\frac{\partial y_i}{\partial q_r} + \dot{z}_i\frac{\partial z_i}{\partial q_r}\right),$$

$$\frac{d}{dt}\frac{\partial T}{\partial \dot{q}_r} = \sum_{i=1}^{N} m_i\left(\ddot{x}_i\frac{\partial x_i}{\partial q_r} + \ddot{y}_i\frac{\partial y_i}{\partial q_r} + \ddot{z}_i\frac{\partial z_i}{\partial q_r}\right)$$

$$+ \sum_{i=1}^{N} m_i\left(\dot{x}_i\frac{\partial \dot{x}_i}{\partial q_r} + \dot{y}_i\frac{\partial \dot{y}_i}{\partial q_r} + \dot{z}_i\frac{\partial \dot{z}_i}{\partial q_r}\right).$$

* As in Sec. 10.6, non-holonomic systems will not be considered.

This last equation may be written in the form

$$\frac{d}{dt}\frac{\partial T}{\partial \dot q_r} - \frac{\partial T}{\partial q_r} = \sum_{i=1}^{N}\left(X_i\frac{\partial x_i}{\partial q_r} + Y_i\frac{\partial y_i}{\partial q_r} + Z_i\frac{\partial z_i}{\partial q_r}\right),$$

where X_i, Y_i, Z_i are the components of force acting on the ith particle.

Thus, by (10.707), we have *Lagrange's equations of motion for a system with n degrees of freedom,*

(15.215) $$\frac{d}{dt}\frac{\partial T}{\partial \dot q_r} - \frac{\partial T}{\partial q_r} = Q_r, \qquad (r = 1, 2, \cdots n),$$

where Q_r are the generalized forces, defined by the condition that the work done in a general displacement is

(15.216) $$\delta W = \sum_{r=1}^{n} Q_r\, \delta q_r.$$

If the system is conservative,

(15.217) $$Q_r = -\frac{\partial V}{\partial q_r}, \qquad (r = 1, 2, \cdots n).$$

Two features of Lagrange's equations should be emphasized. First, there is no unique set of generalized coordinates; however we choose them, the equations of motion always have the form (15.215). Secondly, since only working forces contribute to δW, reactions of constraint are automatically eliminated.*

15.3. APPLICATIONS

Components of acceleration in spherical polar coordinates.

Although the normal use of Lagrange's method is to obtain equations of motion, it may sometimes be used indirectly to give information not easy to obtain otherwise. Consider a particle moving in space. Let us take the spherical polar coordinates r, θ, ϕ as generalized coordinates q_1, q_2, q_3. Then, if the particle is of unit mass,

$$T = \tfrac{1}{2}(\dot r^2 + r^2\dot\theta^2 + r^2\sin^2\theta\,\dot\phi^2).$$

(To obtain this, we need only the components of velocity along the parametric lines.) If R, Θ, Φ are the generalized forces, the equations of motion are, by (15.215),

* Except where forces of friction do work.

$$\ddot{r} - r\dot{\theta}^2 - r\sin^2\theta\,\dot{\phi}^2 = R,$$

$$\frac{d}{dt}(r^2\dot{\theta}) - r^2\sin\theta\cos\theta\,\dot{\phi}^2 = \Theta,$$

$$\frac{d}{dt}(r^2\sin^2\theta\,\dot{\phi}) = \Phi.$$

Let f_r, f_θ, f_ϕ be the components of acceleration along the parametric lines. These are equal to the components of force in these directions. Hence, equating two different expressions for work done in an arbitrary displacement, we have

$$\delta W = f_r\,\delta r + f_\theta r\,\delta\theta + f_\phi r\sin\theta\,\delta\phi = R\,\delta r + \Theta\,\delta\theta + \Phi\,\delta\phi,$$

and so

(15.301) $\begin{cases} f_r = R = \ddot{r} - r\dot{\theta}^2 - r\sin^2\theta\,\dot{\phi}^2, \\ f_\theta = \dfrac{1}{r}\Theta = \dfrac{1}{r}\dfrac{d}{dt}(r^2\dot{\theta}) - r\sin\theta\cos\theta\,\dot{\phi}^2, \\ f_\phi = \dfrac{1}{r\sin\theta}\Phi = \dfrac{1}{r\sin\theta}\dfrac{d}{dt}(r^2\sin^2\theta\,\dot{\phi}) \end{cases}$

These are the components of acceleration along the parametric lines of spherical polar coordinates.

Normal frequencies of vibration of a system with two degrees of freedom.

Let C be a position of equilibrium of a conservative system with two degrees of freedom. Let us choose generalized coordinates such that $q_1 = q_2 = 0$ at C. The kinetic energy is expressible in the form

(15.302) $\qquad T = \tfrac{1}{2}(a\dot{q}_1^2 + 2h\dot{q}_1\dot{q}_2 + b\dot{q}_2^2),$

where a, h, b are functions of q_1, q_2. Let us, however, consider only *small* oscillations about C, so that q_1, q_2, $\dot{q}_1$, $\dot{q}_2$ are small. Then the principal part of T has the form (15.302), where a, h, b are constants, viz., the values of the coefficients for $q_1 = q_2 = 0$.

Consider now the potential energy V. We may choose C as standard configuration, so that $V = 0$ for $q_1 = q_2 = 0$. The expansion of V in a Taylor series reads

(15.303) $\quad V = \dfrac{\partial V}{\partial q_1}q_1 + \dfrac{\partial V}{\partial q_2}q_2$

$$+ \tfrac{1}{2}\left(\frac{\partial^2 V}{\partial q_1^2}q_1^2 + 2\frac{\partial^2 V}{\partial q_1\,\partial q_2}q_1 q_2 + \frac{\partial^2 V}{\partial q_2^2}q_2^2\right) + \cdots,$$

Sec. 15.3]   *LAGRANGE'S EQUATIONS*   469

where the partial derivatives are evaluated for $q_1 = q_2 = 0$. But, by the principle of virtual work (10.714),

$$\frac{\partial V}{\partial q_1} = 0, \qquad \frac{\partial V}{\partial q_2} = 0,$$

for $q_1 = q_2 = 0$. Hence the principal part of V is

(15.304) $\qquad V = \tfrac{1}{2}(A q_1^2 + 2H q_1 q_2 + B q_2^2),$

where A, H, B are constants. Thus, to our approximation, T and V are homogeneous quadratic forms with constant coefficients, T being quadratic in the velocities and V in the coordinates.

We have

$$\frac{\partial T}{\partial \dot{q}_1} = a\dot{q}_1 + h\dot{q}_2, \qquad \frac{\partial T}{\partial q_1} = 0, \qquad \frac{\partial V}{\partial q_1} = A q_1 + H q_2,$$

$$\frac{\partial T}{\partial \dot{q}_2} = h\dot{q}_1 + b\dot{q}_2, \qquad \frac{\partial T}{\partial q_2} = 0, \qquad \frac{\partial V}{\partial q_2} = H q_1 + B q_2,$$

and so Lagrange's equations read

(15.305) $\qquad \begin{cases} a\ddot{q}_1 + h\ddot{q}_2 = -(A q_1 + H q_2), \\ h\ddot{q}_1 + b\ddot{q}_2 = -(H q_1 + B q_2). \end{cases}$

We seek a solution of the form

$$q_1 = \alpha \cos (nt + \epsilon), \qquad q_2 = \beta \cos (nt + \epsilon).$$

When we substitute in (15.305) and eliminate α and β, we obtain for n the determinantal equation

(15.306) $\qquad \begin{vmatrix} an^2 - A & hn^2 - H \\ hn^2 - H & bn^2 - B \end{vmatrix} = 0$

If n_1, n_2 are the roots of this equation, the normal periods (cf. Sec. 7.4) are $2\pi/n_1$, $2\pi/n_2$, and the normal frequencies are $n_1/2\pi$, $n_2/2\pi$.

It is, of course, assumed that the equilibrium is stable. If it were not, we should discover the fact through the appearance of a zero or imaginary value for n.

The top.

Consider a top with fixed vertex O. The system has three degrees of freedom. For two generalized coordinates, we take θ, ϕ, the polar angles of the axis of the top, $\theta = 0$ being directed

vertically upward. For the third coordinate, we take the angle ψ between two planes, one fixed in the top and passing through its axis, and the other containing the vertical through O and the axis of the top. Then the angular velocity has components $\dot\theta$, $\sin\theta\,\dot\phi$, at right angles to one another and to the axis of the top, and a component $\dot\psi + \cos\theta\,\dot\phi$ along the axis. Thus the kinetic energy is

(15 307) $\quad T = \tfrac{1}{2}A(\dot\theta^2 + \sin^2\theta\,\dot\phi^2) + \tfrac{1}{2}C(\dot\psi + \cos\theta\,\dot\phi)^2,$

where A and C are the transverse and axial moments of inertia at the vertex. The potential energy is

(15.308) $\quad\quad\quad\quad V = mga\cos\theta,$

where a is the distance of the mass center from the vertex.

Lagrange's equations then read

(15.309) $\quad\begin{cases} A\ddot\theta - A\sin\theta\cos\theta\,\dot\phi^2 + C\sin\theta\,\dot\phi(\dot\psi + \cos\theta\,\dot\phi) \\ \quad\quad\quad\quad\quad\quad\quad\quad\quad\quad\quad\quad = mga\sin\theta, \\ \dfrac{d}{dt}[A\sin^2\theta\,\dot\phi + C\cos\theta(\dot\psi + \cos\theta\,\dot\phi)] = 0, \\ \dfrac{d}{dt}[C(\dot\psi + \cos\theta\,\dot\phi)] = 0. \end{cases}$

The last two equations give at once the first integrals

(15.310) $\quad\begin{cases} A\sin^2\theta\,\dot\phi + C\cos\theta(\dot\psi + \cos\theta\,\dot\phi) = \alpha, \\ C(\dot\psi + \cos\theta\,\dot\phi) = \beta, \end{cases}$

where α and β are constants. (These are actually integrals of angular momentum) When we substitute in the first of (15.309), we get a differential equation for θ

(15.311) $\quad \ddot\theta + \dfrac{(\alpha - \beta\cos\theta)(\beta - \alpha\cos\theta)}{A^2\sin^3\theta} = \dfrac{mga}{A}\sin\theta.$

If we multiply this equation by $\dot\theta$, integrate once, and put $\cos\theta = x$, we get (14.226). The detailed theory of the motion then proceeds as in Sec. 14.2.

Lagrange's equations for impulsive forces.

When impulsive forces act, there are instantaneous changes in velocity, without instantaneous changes in position. In terms of generalized coordinates q_r, there are instantaneous

Sec. 15.3] LAGRANGE'S EQUATIONS 471

changes in $\dot{q}_r$, but not in q_r. As usual, we approach impulsive forces by a limiting process, in which the forces tend to infinity and the interval during which they act tends to zero. We multiply (15.215) by dt and integrate over the interval (t_0, t_1). When $t_1 \to t_0$, the second term on the left disappears, and we have *Lagrange's equations for impulsive forces*,

$$(15.312) \qquad \Delta \frac{\partial T}{\partial \dot{q}_r} = \widehat{Q}_r, \qquad (r = 1, 2, \cdots n);$$

here Δ denotes a sudden increment and $\widehat{Q}_r$ are the *generalized impulsive forces* [cf. (8.112)]

$$(15.313) \qquad \widehat{Q}_r = \lim_{t_1 \to t_0} \int_{t_0}^{t_1} Q_r\, dt.$$

These may be calculated from a formula analogous to (15.216),

$$(15.314) \qquad \delta \widehat{W} = \sum_{r=1}^{n} \widehat{Q}_r\, \delta q_r,$$

where $\delta \widehat{W}$ is the work which would be done in a general displacement by the impulsive forces if they were ordinary forces.

The Lagrangian method is particularly useful for systems of linked rods, because the impulsive reactions are automatically eliminated. Thus, to take an example, consider the problem worked in Sec. 8.3 (Figs. 99a and 99b). As generalized coordinates we take x, y, the coordinates of the joint, and θ_1, θ_2, the inclinations of the rods to their initial line. Then, for the given position ($\theta_1 = \theta_2 = 0$),

$$T = \tfrac{1}{2} m[\dot{x}^2 + (\dot{y} - a\dot{\theta}_1)^2 + k^2 \dot{\theta}_1^2 + \dot{x}^2 + (\dot{y} + a\dot{\theta}_2)^2 + k^2 \dot{\theta}_2^2],$$

where k is the radius of gyration of a rod about its center. Now if $\widehat{X}, \widehat{Y}, \widehat{\Theta}_1, \widehat{\Theta}_2$ are the generalized impulsive forces, we have

$$\widehat{X}\, \delta x + \widehat{Y}\, \delta y + \widehat{\Theta}_1\, \delta\theta_1 + \widehat{\Theta}_2\, \delta\theta_2 = \widehat{P}(\delta y + 2a\, \delta\theta_2).$$

Thus

$$\widehat{X} = 0, \qquad \widehat{Y} = \widehat{P}, \qquad \widehat{\Theta}_1 = 0, \qquad \widehat{\Theta}_2 = 2a\widehat{P}.$$

Lagrange's equations give

$$2m\dot{x} = 0,$$
$$m(\dot{y} - a\dot{\theta}_1) + m(\dot{y} + a\dot{\theta}_2) = \widehat{P},$$
$$-ma(\dot{y} - a\dot{\theta}_1) + mk^2\dot{\theta}_1 = 0,$$
$$ma(\dot{y} + a\dot{\theta}_2) + mk^2\dot{\theta}_2 = 2a\widehat{P}.$$

Hence we obtain, with $k^2 = a^2/3$,

$$x = 0, \quad \dot{y} = -\frac{\widehat{P}}{m}, \quad \dot{\theta}_1 = -\tfrac{3}{4}\frac{\widehat{P}}{ma}, \quad \dot{\theta}_2 = \tfrac{9}{4}\frac{\widehat{P}}{ma}.$$

15.4. SUMMARY OF LAGRANGE'S EQUATIONS

I. Finite forces.

For system with kinetic energy T, expressed as function of $q_1, q_2, \cdots q_n, \dot{q}_1, \dot{q}_2, \cdots \dot{q}_n$:

(15.401) $$\frac{d}{dt}\frac{\partial T}{\partial \dot{q}_r} - \frac{\partial T}{\partial q_r} = Q_r, \quad (r = 1, 2, \cdots n).$$

(15.402) $$\delta W = \sum_{r=1}^{n} Q_r\, \delta q_r.$$

(15.403) $$Q_r = -\frac{\partial V}{\partial q_r}, \quad \text{for conservative system.}$$

II. Impulsive forces.

(15.404) $$\Delta \frac{\partial T}{\partial \dot{q}_r} = \widehat{Q}_r, \quad (r = 1, 2, \cdots n).$$

(15.405) $$\delta \widehat{W} = \sum_{r=1}^{n} \widehat{Q}_r\, \delta q_r.$$

EXERCISES XV

(To be done by Lagrange's equations)

1. Find the equation of motion of a simple pendulum, taking in turn the following generalized coordinates:
  (i) the angular displacement,
  (ii) the horizontal displacement,
  (iii) the vertical displacement.

2. Find the equation of motion of a sphere rolling down a rough inclined plane

3. Find the equations of motion of a spherical pendulum, taking as generalized coordinates the horizontal Cartesian coordinates of the bob. Reduce the equations to their principal parts for oscillations near the equilibrium position.

4. Four flywheels with moments of inertia I_1, I_2, I_3, I_4 are connected by light gearing so that their angular velocities are in fixed ratios $n_1:n_2:n_3:n_4$. Driving torques N_1, N_2, N_3, N_4 are applied to the flywheels. Find their angular accelerations.

5. Show that if a generalized coordinate (q_1) does not appear explicitly in either T or V, then $\partial T/\partial \dot{q}_1$ is constant throughout the motion.

A rod hangs by a universal joint from its upper end. For oscillations under gravity, use the above result and the equation of energy to find a differential equation of the first order for θ, the inclination of the rod to the vertical.

6. A pendulum consists of two equal bars AB, BC, smoothly jointed at B and suspended from A. The mass of each bar is m, and its length is $2a$. Find the normal periods for small oscillations in a vertical plane under gravity, in the form

$$2\pi\lambda\sqrt{\frac{a}{g}}$$

where λ is a numerical constant.

7. The pendulum described in Exercise 6 hangs at rest. A horizontal impulse $\hat{P}$ is applied at its lowest point. Find the angular velocities imparted to the bars.

8. The ends of a heavy uniform bar of mass 120 lb. are supported by springs of equal strength, the bar being horizontal. The strength of the springs is such that a weight W of 100 lb., placed gently at the middle point of the bar, causes it to descend 1 in. Find, to two significant figures, the normal frequencies of small vibrations of the bar (without the weight W), considering only vibrations in which the springs move vertically.

9. On a sphere, θ and ϕ are polar angles. A particle describes a small circle θ = constant with constant speed q_0. Find the generalized forces Θ, Φ consistent with this motion.

10. Consider a dynamical system with kinetic and potential energies

$$T = \tfrac{1}{2}(\dot{q}_1^2 + \dot{q}_2^2), \qquad V = f(q_1 - q_2),$$

where f is a given function. By choosing suitable new coordinates q_1', q_2', reduce the problem of determining the motion to the evaluation of an integral involving the function f. Determine q_1, q_2 as functions of t if $f(x) = x^2$.

11. A carriage has four wheels, each of which is a uniform disk of mass m. The mass of the carriage without the wheels is M. The carriage rolls without slipping down a plane slope inclined to the horizontal at an angle α, the floor of the carriage remaining parallel to the slope. A perfectly rough spherical ball of mass m' rolls on the floor of the carriage along a line parallel to a line of greatest slope. Show that the acceleration of the carriage down the plane is

$$\frac{7M + 28m + 2m'}{7M + 42m + 2m'}\ g\sin\alpha,$$

and find the acceleration of the ball.

12. A rhombus of equal rods, smoothly jointed, lies on a plane in the form of a square. An impulse is applied to one corner, along the diagonal through that corner. Find the angular velocities imparted to the rods, in terms of the impulse ($\hat{P}$), the mass (m) of a rod, and the length ($2a$) of a rod.

13. A smooth circular wire carries a bead. The wire is suspended from a point on it. Find the normal periods of small vibrations under gravity when the wire swings in its own plane and the bead slides on the wire. Show that, when the bead is fixed to the wire at its position of equilibrium when free to slide, the period coincides with one of these two normal periods.

14. Using the fact that T is a homogeneous quadratic expression in the generalized velocities $\dot{q}_r$, show that the integral of energy $T + V = $ constant may be proved as a mathematical deduction from Lagrange's equations. Note that, if f is a homogeneous function of degree m in $x_1, x_2, \cdots x_n$, then

$$mf = \sum_{r=1}^{n} x_r \frac{\partial f}{\partial x_r}.$$

15. A dynamical system has kinetic energy

$$T = \tfrac{1}{2}(a\dot{q}_1^2 + 2h\dot{q}_1\dot{q}_2 + b\dot{q}_2^2),$$

and potential energy

$$V = \tfrac{1}{2}(Aq_1^2 + 2Hq_1q_2 + Bq_2^2).$$

Additional generalized forces

$$Q_1 = -k_{11}\dot{q}_1 - k_{12}\dot{q}_2, \qquad Q_2 = -k_{21}\dot{q}_1 - k_{22}\dot{q}_2$$

are applied. All the coefficients a, h, b, A, H, B, and the k's are constants. Show that the energy sum $T + V$ decreases steadily during any motion, provided

$$k_{11} > 0, \qquad 4k_{11}k_{22} > (k_{12} + k_{21})^2.$$

16. A gyroscope is mounted in a light Cardan's suspension (Fig. 144). Take Eulerian angles simply related to the suspension, and find the equations of motion of the system under the action of a couple G applied to the outer ring, G being in the line of the outer bearings.

17. A system is said to have "moving constraints" when the configuration of the system is determined by the values of generalized coordinates $q_1, q_2, \cdots q_n$ and the value of the time t. Show that, for such a system, Lagrange's equations hold in the same form as when there are no moving constraints, but that the kinetic energy is no longer a homogeneous quadratic expression in $\dot{q}_1, \dot{q}_2, \cdots \dot{q}_n$.

Apply this result to find the equation of motion of a heavy bead on a smooth circular wire, the wire being made to rotate about the vertical diameter with constant angular velocity.

CHAPTER XVI

THE SPECIAL THEORY OF RELATIVITY

16.1. SOME FUNDAMENTAL CONCEPTS

The hardest part of a subject is the beginning. Once a certain stage is passed, we gain confidence and feel that, if need be, we could carry on by ourselves. The process of learning is very much the same whether in swimming or in mechanics—an initial feeling of insecurity is followed by a feeling of power.

The simple things that we learn first are the hardest to change later. Whether they are muscular actions or mental concepts, they are used again and again until they become part of us. Our bodies or minds have learned to follow a pattern, which can be broken only by a conscious effort.

Breaking up the Newtonian pattern.

We are now faced with the task of breaking up the pattern of Newtonian mechanics, to make way for the new pattern of relativity, which we owe to Einstein. This would be comparatively easy if it were merely a question of making changes in the later and more elaborate parts of the subject. But that is not the case. The change is to be made right down in the foundations—in our concept of time.

To show how fundamental the change is, we shall describe an imaginary experiment, putting into opposition the predictions that would be made by a follower of Newton on the one hand and a follower of Einstein on the other.

Two clocks stand side by side at a place P. They are of the very finest construction and identical with one another. Their readings are the same, and they continue to run in perfect unison as long as they stand side by side at P. One clock is left at P; the other is put in an airplane and flown with great speed on a long flight, being finally brought back to P and set up beside the clock that has stood there unmoved.

Will there then be any difference between the readings of the two clocks?

The practical physicist will, before answering, make inquiries as to the way in which the clock was treated on the flight—whether it was knocked about, whether it was subjected to extremes of heat and cold, and so on. Let us suppose that the greatest care has been taken, so that effects due to these accidental causes may be ruled out of consideration. Then the answers are as follows:

Newtonian theory: The clocks will show the same reading

Relativity theory: The readings will not be the same. The clock that has been on the flight will be slow in comparison with the clock that has stayed at home.

The follower of Newton reasons along these lines: A perfect clock registers *the* time. A flight in an airplane does not alter this fact, provided that proper precautions are taken. Since after the flight each clock registers *the* time, they must agree.

We cannot yet give the reasoning of the relativist; that will come later in the chapter. For the present, we must be satisfied with the words with which the relativist would begin his attack on the argument of the Newtonian: There is no such thing as *the* time, in any absolute sense.

It would be impossible to decide between the two predictions by carrying out the experiment we have described. The relativist would predict a difference between the two readings far too small to detect. The airplane would have to fly with a speed comparable with that of light before the effect would be noticeable. But it is the *principle* that is important. Other experiments can be carried out in which the predictions of the two theories are different and the difference is large enough to measure; in every case the relativistic prediction proves correct. There can be no doubt that the theory of relativity gives us a mathematical model closer to nature than the Newtonian model. We must therefore pay attention to the words: There is no such thing as *the* time, in any absolute sense. Once that point is conceded, the basis of the Newtonian pattern is broken, and the way is open for relativity.

The ingredients of relativity.

The theory of relativity is divided into two parts:
(i) the special theory;
(ii) the general theory.

The special theory deals with phenomena in which gravitational attraction plays no part, while the general theory might be called "Einstein's theory of gravitation." In this book, we shall be concerned solely with the special theory.

At this stage the reader should glance over Chap. I to concentrate his attention again on fundamental matters. Part, but not all, of the contents of that chapter will pass over into the theory of relativity, and we must understand clearly what passes over and what does not. Let us therefore start again with a blank sheet and put in, one by one, the ingredients of the theory of relativity.

First we introduce a *particle*, understood in the same sense as before. Next we introduce a *frame of reference* and an *observer* in it. The observer has a *measuring rod* with which he can measure the distances between the particles which form his frame of reference. If the distances between these particles remain constant, the observer declares that his frame of reference is a *rigid body*.

Now we provide the observer with a *clock* As in Chap. I, this is an apparatus in which the same process is repeated over and over again, the repetitions defining equal intervals of *time*. The actual mechanism of the clock does not matter We may think of it as an ordinary watch, driven by a spring and controlled by an escapement.

As we have indicated above, the transporting of a clock is an operation which may lead to curious consequences We shall therefore not expect the observer to carry his clock about but shall provide him with a great number of clocks, all of identical construction. These will be distributed throughout his frame of reference and kept fixed in it.

We must not overlook the fact that the *synchronization* of these clocks raises an important and difficult question. If there is no synchronization, the observer will note some strange things as he walks among his clocks. For example, he may start at 2:15 (by the local clock), walk a mile, and find that the time is 2:10 (by the local clock). Under such circumstances, in ordinary life, one would put a clock in his pocket and walk around, setting each local clock as he passed to agree with the clock in his pocket

But if our observer does this he finds the following strange result. The clocks which he synchronizes in walking out from

his base no longer agree with the clock in his pocket when he is walking back.

This is the same phenomenon as that described earlier in the case of the clock and the airplane, and the reason for it will be made clear later. The effects are so small as to be negligible in ordinary life, but our observer is expected to be mathematically accurate.

This description of the difficulties of synchronization may explain why the theory of relativity has had for the popular mind much the same appeal as Alice in Wonderland. Familiar ideas are turned upside down. Why does the observer not simply set all the clocks to show the *correct time?* The answer is: There is no such thing as the *correct time*.

We recall that, in Chap. I, we introduced the idea of an *event*—something happening suddenly at a point. We carry this idea over into relativity, where we shall make extensive use of it. Even though his clocks are not yet synchronized, the observer is prepared to describe any event by assigning four coordinates to it. Of these coordinates, three are spatial (x, y, z), and the fourth (t) is given by the local clock, i.e., the clock situated at the point where the event occurs.

Galilean frames of reference.

We have already seen in Newtonian mechanics the importance of making a proper choice of frame of reference. The laws of Newtonian mechanics take their simplest form only in certain special frames, which we called Newtonian. Similarly, in relativity there are frames of reference which are particularly convenient to use. These are called *Galilean frames of reference*.* They correspond in nature to rigid bodies situated in remote space, far from attracting matter, and without rotation relative to the stars as a whole.

We shall now make the following hypothesis regarding a Galilean frame of reference:

I. *A Galilean frame of reference is a rigid body, isotropic with respect to mechanical and optical experiments.*

---

* This is the usual name, and not a very good one, for Galileo lived before Newton and of course had no idea of the theory of relativity. "Einstein frame of reference" would be a better name.

To explain this, we note that "isotropic" means "the same in all directions." The neighborhood of the earth is not isotropic. If we drop a stone, it falls in a definite direction and the earth's rotation defines a direction which we can detect by means of a gyrocompass. However, in applying the theory of relativity, we may often regard the earth as a Galilean frame, for its gravitational attraction may be small compared with other forces involved and its rotation may be of no importance.

The assumption—that a rigid body in remote space is isotropic—is at least plausible. To assert that it was not isotropic would at once raise the question: Why should any one direction be privileged above another?

The hypothesis refers to mechanical and optical experiments. We must provide the observer with apparatus to perform these. We shall therefore give him mechanisms by which he can exert *forces*, and lamps and mirrors by which he can send out *flashes of light* and reflect them.

In Newtonian mechanics, we had no occasion to refer to light. Optics appeared to be a separate subject. In relativity, on the other hand, we have to discuss optics and mechanics together.

The synchronization of clocks.

Space does not permit us to attempt an axiomatic treatment of the theory of relativity. To reach the most interesting deductions quickly, we shall outline some steps in the development without proof.

Thus, we shall only sketch the method of synchronization of clocks in a Galilean frame of reference. The synchronization is done by means of light signals. Taking the clock at the origin O as master clock, the observer sends out flashes of light to the other clocks, from which they are reflected by mirrors back to O. Let t_1 and t_2 be the times (as given by the clock at O) at which a flash leaves O and returns to it after reflection at a point A. In ordinary life, we should reason in this way: If v is the velocity of light and r the distance OA, the light would take a time r/v to go and a time r/v to return. Thus $t_2 - t_1 = 2r/v$, and the time of arrival at A is

$$t = t_1 + r/v = t_1 + \tfrac{1}{2}(t_2 - t_1) = \tfrac{1}{2}(t_1 + t_2).$$

But we cannot use this argument, because velocity is a derived concept, depending on the measurement of both distance and

time. We should be arguing in a circle if we used velocity to define time. We shall merely adopt as definition of synchronization that the clock at A is synchronized when it is set to read $\frac{1}{2}(t_1 + t_2)$ at the instant when the flash strikes it. By this rule, all the clocks may be synchronized with the clock at O.

We ask the reader to accept the fact that, in consequence of the assumption of isotropy, this synchronization is satisfactory. That is, a repetition of the process, with another clock as master-clock, will find all clocks reading just what they ought to read, so that no change in the settings is necessary. This means that there is no confusion such as we predicted earlier, in the case where the synchronization was attempted by carrying a clock about.

The observer now has a serviceable time system. He can measure velocities, and in particular the velocity of light. By virtue of the assumed isotropy, this proves to be a constant, the same for all directions

Although we have met some new ideas in connection with synchronization, there is nothing new or strange about the final picture of a Galilean frame of reference and the time system we have set up in it. It differs in no essential way from the concept we have used in Newtonian mechanics. We do not encounter the real peculiarities of relativity until we consider *two* Galilean frames of reference and the relations between them

16.2. THE LORENTZ TRANSFORMATION

The principle of equivalence.

Let us suppose that we can shoot a rocket right out of the solar system. In this rocket we place an observer. When the rocket has passed far beyond the solar system, it forms a Galilean frame of reference. The observer has lost the sense of motion he had when rushing past the planets. He sees around him nothing but stars, and they are so far away that they appear fixed.

A second identical rocket is shot out with a greater speed and on such a track that it overtakes the first. In it there is also an observer. Now we have two Galilean frames of reference.

Imagine that the two observers leave their rockets and travel independently in space. One of them comes upon one of the rockets. How is he to tell whether it is the rocket he occupied

before or the other one? To answer this question, he is allowed to perform any mechanical or optical experiments he chooses

The same question in a different form occurred to the physicist Michelson in 1881. What he asked might be put thus. Is it possible to tell the season of the year (i.e., the position of the earth in its orbit round the sun) by means of optical experiments performed on a clouded earth? The earth at the two seasons corresponds to the two rockets (Galilean frames of reference). It was fully expected that the season could be determined in this way, for it was then believed that light was propagated in an "ether," and the difference between the velocities of the earth through the ether at the two seasons should be a measurable quantity.

The question was put to experimental test by Michelson and later by Michelson and Morley in 1887.* The expected result was not obtained. As far as this experiment was concerned, the two seasons (Galilean frames of reference) were indistinguishable.

Generalizing from the negative result of the Michelson-Morley experiment, we make the following sweeping hypothesis.

II. PRINCIPLE OF EQUIVALENCE. *Two Galilean frames of reference are completely equivalent for ALL physical experiments*

This gives the answer to the question raised earlier. The observer is *not* able to tell which rocket he has found. No experiment he can perform will tell him which it is—they are indistinguishable, like identical twins.

To the hypothesis already made we add another·

III. *Any two Galilean frames of reference have, relative to one another, a uniform velocity of translation. The relative velocity is less than the velocity of light.*

We may recall that, in Newtonian mechanics, two Newtonian frames of reference are similarly related, but in that case there is no restriction on the relative velocity. The assumption that the velocity of light is a limit which cannot be exceeded is something essentially new.

To sum up, we have made three hypotheses in all. The first deals with a single Galilean frame of reference; the last two concern the relations between two Galilean frames of reference.

* For an account of the Michelson-Morley experiment, see L. Silberstein, The Theory of Relativity (Macmillan Company, Ltd., London, 1924), p. 71.

The Lorentz transformation.

Let S and S' be two Galilean frames of reference. (We may without confusion also use these letters for observers in the two frames.) Consider any event, observed by both observers. To this event, S attaches coordinates (x, y, z, t), and S' attaches coordinates (x', y', z', t'). In doing this, each observer uses his own measuring rod and clocks. The event determines the coordinates, and conversely the coordinates determine the event. Thus, considering all possible events, four numbers (x, y, z, t) determine an event, and that in turn determines the four numbers (x', y', z', t'). The last four numbers are therefore functions of the first four, and we express this by writing

$$(16.201) \quad x' = f(x, y, z, t), \quad y' = g(x, y, z, t),$$
$$z' = h(x, y, z, t), \quad t' = l(x, y, z, t).$$

Such relations, connecting the coordinates of two Galilean observers, constitute a *Lorentz transformation*.

We have now to investigate the forms of these functions. We shall not, however, suppose that the axes $Oxyz$ and $O'x'y'z'$ are given arbitrary directions in the respective frames. We shall suppose them so chosen that Ox and $O'x'$ lie on a common line when viewed by either observer, this line being parallel to the relative velocity of either frame with respect to the other. We shall consider the Lorentz transformation only for events occurring on this common line. Thus $y = z = y' = z' = 0$, and the transformation is of the form

$$(16.202) \qquad x' = f(x, t), \qquad t' = l(x, t).$$

We must carefully avoid the idea that there is any "absolute" frame from which S and S' may be viewed. We must look at things either as they appear to S or as they appear to S'. First, S sees the particles of his own frame. They are fixed as far as he is concerned, and through them there pass the particles of the frame S'. These particles all move parallel to Ox with a constant speed V, the speed of S' relative to S. Similarly, to S' the particles of *his* frame appear fixed, and the particles of S pass with a speed V', directed in the negative sense of $O'x'$. To do justice to both observers, it is best to draw two diagrams, as in Figs. 159a and b. In Fig. 159a we take the view of S and

regard $Oxyz$ as stationary; in Fig. 159b we take the view of S' and regard $O'x'y'z'$ as stationary.

The two observers now fix their attention on a flash of light traveling along the common line Ox, $O'x'$. It will add to the complexity of our work if we assume that the units of space and time used by S and S' are completely independent. We shall therefore suppose that they have been supplied with measuring rods and clocks from a common stock. Then, by virtue of the principle of equivalence, the speed of light* has a common value in the two frames This common value we shall denote by c.

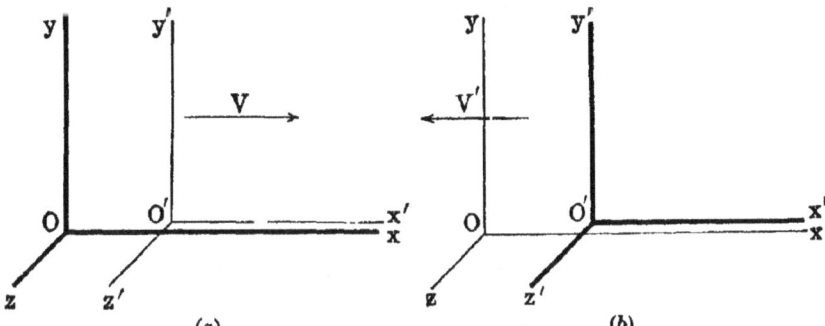

Fig. 159.—(a) The frame S' moving relative to the frame S. (b) The frame S moving relative to the frame S'.

As S observes the flash, he records the time t at which (by his local clock) the flash reaches the position x. Since the speed of light is c, x is a function of t satisfying

$$\left(\frac{dx}{dt}\right)^2 = c^2.$$

But similarly, for the observations of S',

$$\left(\frac{dx'}{dt'}\right)^2 = c^2.$$

Thus, for the sequence of events given by the passage of the flash, we have the two equations

$$dt^2 - dx^2/c^2 = 0, \quad dt'^2 - dx'^2/c^2 = 0.$$

Now a motion satisfying either of these equations represents the passage of a flash of light and therefore must satisfy the other

* 3.00×10^{10} cm sec^{-1} or 186,000 mile sec^{-1}

equation. Thus, if one of the equations is satisfied, so is the other, and therefore we have the identity

(16.203) $\qquad dt'^2 - dx'^2/c^2 \equiv k(dt^2 - dx^2/c^2),$

where k is some unknown factor. But by the principle of equivalence we must also have

(16.204) $\qquad dt^2 - dx^2/c^2 \equiv k(dt'^2 - dx'^2/c^2).$

Comparing these two identities, we see that $k^2 = 1$, and so $k = +1$ or -1. To see which value to take, we follow the particle O', fixed in S'. Then $dx' = 0$, and so, by (16.203), the history of O' satisfies

$$\left(\frac{dt'}{dt}\right)^2 = k\left[1 - \frac{1}{c^2}\left(\frac{dx}{dt}\right)^2\right].$$

But, by hypothesis III, $(dx/dt)^2 < c^2$; hence, $k = +1$. Accordingly,

(16.205) $\qquad dt'^2 - dx'^2/c^2 \equiv dt^2 - dx^2/c^2.$

The Lorentz transformation must be such that this identity holds.

We shall assume that the transformation is linear, and that the zeros of time are chosen so that $t = t' = 0$ when O' is passing through O. Thus we write, in place of (16.202),

(16.206) $\qquad x' = \alpha x + \beta t, \qquad t' = \alpha' x + \beta' t,$

where $\alpha, \beta, \alpha', \beta'$ are constants so connected that the identity (16.205) is satisfied. We have

(16.207) $\quad \begin{cases} dx' = \alpha\, dx + \beta\, dt, \qquad dt' = \alpha'\, dx + \beta'\, dt, \\ dt'^2 - dx'^2/c^2 = (\alpha'\, dx + \beta'\, dt)^2 - (\alpha\, dx + \beta\, dt)^2/c^2 \\ \qquad\qquad\qquad = dt^2 - dx^2/c^2, \end{cases}$

and so, equating the coefficients of dx^2, dt^2, and $dx\, dt$,

(16.208) $\quad \alpha^2 - c^2\alpha'^2 = 1, \qquad \beta^2 - c^2\beta'^2 = -c^2, \qquad \alpha\beta - c^2\alpha'\beta' = 0.$

Let us define ϕ, ϕ' by the equations

(16.209) $\qquad \sinh\phi = c\alpha', \qquad \sinh\phi' = \beta/c.$

Then, by the first two equations in (16.208), we have

$$\alpha = \cosh\phi, \qquad \beta' = \cosh\phi',$$

and the last of (16.208) gives
$$\sinh(\phi' - \phi) = 0.$$
Thus $\phi' = \phi$, and the transformation (16.206) is

(16.210) $$\begin{cases} x' = x \cosh \phi + ct \sinh \phi, \\ ct' = x \sinh \phi + ct \cosh \phi. \end{cases}$$

It is easy to verify directly that this transformation satisfies (16.205) for any constant ϕ.

To identify ϕ, we take the viewpoint of S and follow the particle O'. For O' we have $x' = 0$, $dx/dt = V$, and so differentiation of the first of (16.210) gives

(16.211) $$\tanh \phi = -V/c;$$

hence,

(16.212) $$\cosh \phi = \frac{1}{\sqrt{1 - V^2/c^2}}, \quad \sinh \phi = \frac{-V/c}{\sqrt{1 - V^2/c^2}}.$$

So we have the *Lorentz transformation*

(16.213) $$x' = \gamma(x - Vt), \quad t' = \gamma\left(t - \frac{Vx}{c^2}\right),$$
$$\gamma = \frac{1}{\sqrt{1 - V^2/c^2}}.$$

Solving for x, t, we get

(16.214) $$x = \gamma(x' + Vt'), \quad t = \gamma\left(t' + \frac{Vx'}{c^2}\right).$$

If we now take the viewpoint of S' and follow O, we have $x = 0$, $dx'/dt' = -V'$, where V' is the speed of S relative to S'. But when we put $x = 0$ in the first of (16.214) and differentiate, we obtain $dx'/dt' = -V$. Hence $V' = V$, as indeed we might have anticipated from the principle of equivalence.

Now we have the explanation why the theory of relativity did not force itself on the attention of mankind long ago. Apart from the high velocities of electrons, which were not observed until comparatively recent times, physicists and astronomers have had to deal only with relative velocities very small indeed compared with the velocity of light. If V/c is small, then γ is very

nearly unity; as $V/c \to 0$, the Lorentz transformation (16.213) tends to

(16.215) $$x' = x - Vt, \quad t' = t,$$

as in Newtonian mechanics (cf. Sec. 5.3).

Immediate consequences of the Lorentz transformation.

To a person accustomed to thinking in the Newtonian way, some of the predictions of the theory of relativity are startling. Outstanding among these are the contraction of a moving body and the slowing down of a moving clock. These apparently curious facts are consequences of the Lorentz transformation (16.213).

First, let us consider a measuring rod which S' lays down along his axis $O'x'$. To him it is a fixed measuring rod. If A, B are its ends, the history of A is a sequence of events for which $x' = (x')_A$, a constant, and the history of B is a sequence of events for which $x' = (x')_B$, also a constant; the length of the rod is

(16.216) $$L' = (x')_B - (x')_A.$$

Viewed by S, the rod is not fixed. An instantaneous picture, taken by S at time t, shows A at $(x)_A$, say, and B at $(x)_B$. If asked what is the *apparent* length of the rod, S naturally says that it is

(16.217) $$L = (x)_B - (x)_A.$$

Now, by the first equation of (16.213),

(16.218) $$\begin{cases} (x')_B = \gamma[(x)_B - Vt], \\ (x')_A = \gamma[(x)_A - Vt], \end{cases}$$

and subtraction gives, in view of (16.216) and (16.217),

$$L' = \gamma L,$$

or

(16.219) $$L = L'/\gamma = L'\sqrt{1 - V^2/c^2} < L'.$$

Thus L is less than L'; the rod appears to S to be contracted in the ratio $\sqrt{1 - V^2/c^2}:1$.

We might expect that, if S' viewed a rod fixed in S, he would see an expansion instead of a contraction. But if we carry out

the calculation, now using (16.214) instead of (16.213), we find the same contraction again. *Each observer considers that the measuring rod of the other is contracted.*

Now let us consider a clock carried along in S'. Let $(t')_A$, $(t')_B$ be two readings of the clock. These are two events, both with the same x', and with $t' = (t')_A$, $t' = (t')_B$, respectively. Viewed by S, the clock is moving; let the times of the two events be $(t)_A$, $(t)_B$, respectively, as measured in his time system. From the second equation of (16.214), we have

(16.220) $$\begin{cases} (t)_B = \gamma \left[(t')_B + \frac{Vx'}{c^2} \right], \\ (t)_A = \gamma \left[(t')_A + \frac{Vx'}{c^2} \right]. \end{cases}$$

By subtraction,
$$(t)_B - t_{(A)} = \gamma[(t')_B - (t')_A],$$
or

(16.221) $$T = \gamma T' = \frac{T'}{\sqrt{1 - V^2/c^2}} > T',$$

where T is the time interval recorded by S and T' the time interval recorded by S'. Since $T' < T$, the clock carried by S' appears to S to be running slow. Just as in the case of contraction of length, this result works both ways. *Each observer considers the clock of the other to be running slow.*

Space-time.

It does not seem possible at first sight to do justice simultaneously to each of two Galilean observers, for it appears necessary to take the point of view of either the one or the other. This difficulty is overcome by using a *space-time diagram*.

There is nothing peculiarly relativistic about a space-time diagram. We have used the idea in Newtonian mechanics, as in Fig. 78, when we plotted the position of a damped harmonic oscillator against the time. But it is in relativity that we get full advantage from this idea.

Consider first one Galilean observer S. Draw oblique Cartesian axes on a sheet of paper, and label them Ωx, Ωt (Fig. 160). (We use Ω instead of O for origin, to avoid confusion with the origin of the observer's axes.) Any event which happens on the

488 MECHANICS IN SPACE [Sec. 16.2

axis of Ox in the observer's frame will have attached to it values of x and t. It can then be represented by a point in Fig. 160, which is our space-time diagram. The history of a particle moving along Ox will appear as a curve C in the space-time diagram. If it moves with uniform velocity, dx/dt is a constant, and the curve becomes a straight line C_1.

Consider now a second Galilean observer S'. Instead of making a new space-time diagram for him, we superimpose his diagram on that of S. But we use new oblique axes $\Omega x't'$ (Fig. 161), so related to Ωxt that the geometrical law of transformation of coordinates in the plane is precisely the Lorentz transformation (16 213). Now any event E has, of course, two

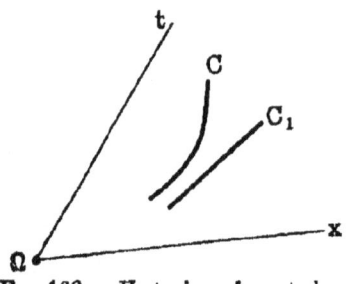

Fig 160.— Histories of particles in the space-time diagram.

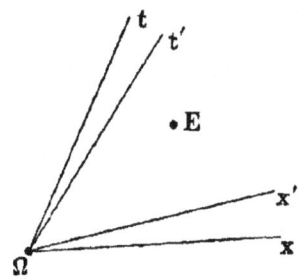

Fig 161 — An event E, and the space-time axes of two Galilean observers.

pairs of labels (x, t), (x', t'); but since these are connected by the Lorentz transformation, *E appears as a single point in the space-time diagram.*

In fact, the space-time diagram gives us a representation of events independent of the frame of reference. It is the same situation as we have in geometry. The sides of a polygon drawn on a plane have equations which depend on the choice of axes. The polygon itself is something absolute.

We must not, however, rush to the conclusion that the ordinary methods of geometry can be carried over completely into the plane of the space-time diagram. For example, in ordinary geometry we are accustomed to speak of the distance between two points as something independent of the axes used If we have two sets of rectangular axes Oxy, $Ox'y'$ in a plane, then the square of the distance between adjacent points is

(16.222) $$dx^2 + dy^2 = dx'^2 + dy'^2.$$

In fact, the quadratic expression $dx^2 + dy^2$ is an *invariant*.

But in the space-time diagram

$$dt^2 + dx^2 \neq dt'^2 + dx'^2.$$

The invariant quantity is, by (16.205),

(16.223) $\qquad dt^2 - dx^2/c^2 = dt'^2 - dx'^2/c^2.$

In geometry, we denote the invariant (16.222) by ds^2 and call ds the *distance* between two adjacent points in the plane. This suggests that we should give a name to the square root of (16.223). However, the minus sign introduces a complication, since the invariant may be negative, and hence its square root imaginary. So we put

(16.224) $\qquad \epsilon\, ds^2 = dt^2 - dx^2/c^2,$

where $\epsilon = +1$ or -1, according as the expression on the right is positive or negative. We call ds the *separation* between the events (x, t) and $(x + dx, t + dt)$.

In the case of two events which are not adjacent, we define the separation as $s = \int ds$, taken along the straight line joining the points in the space-time diagram which correspond to them. Since dx/dt is constant along a straight line, we easily find

(16.225) $\qquad \epsilon s^2 = (t_1 - t_2)^2 - (x_1 - x_2)^2/c^2,$

where the two events in question are (x_1, t_1) and (x_2, t_2). We note that, if the two events have the same x, the separation is simply the difference between the t's; if they have the same t, the separation is the difference between the x's, divided by c.

The lines in the space-time diagram satisfying one or other of the equations

(16.226) $\qquad dt = dx/c, \qquad dt = -dx/c,$

are called *null lines*, because the separation between any two points on such a line is zero. Clearly a null line represents the history of a flash of light traveling along the axis Ox of a Galilean frame, in one direction or the other.

So far we have made no hypothesis regarding the motion of a particle in a Galilean frame. We shall postpone the discussion of motion under a force to Sec 16.3, but now accept the law that *a free particle travels in a straight line with constant speed*, just as in

Newtonian mechanics. This means that a free particle traveling along Ox moves in accordance with

$$\frac{dx}{dt} = u,$$

where u is a constant. Its history appears in the space-time diagram as a straight line, with equation

(16.227) $$t - \frac{x}{u} = \text{constant}.$$

We shall now show how the contraction of a moving rod and the slowing down of a moving clock appear in the diagram.

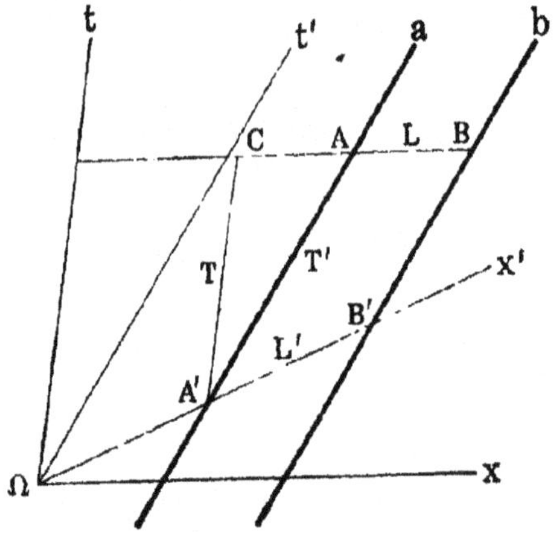

In Fig. 162 the lines a, b represent the histories of the ends of a measuring rod lying on Ox' and fixed in S'. These lines are drawn parallel to $\Omega t'$, because the x' of each end of the rod is a constant. The length L' (judged by S') is proportional to the separation $A'B'$. To get an instantaneous picture from the viewpoint of S, we draw a line parallel to Ωx (i.e., with t constant), cutting a, b at A, B, respectively. Then the length L (as judged by S) is proportional to the separation AB. That $L \neq L'$ is evident from the diagram.

Fig. 162.—Space-time diagram for the contraction of a moving rod and the slowing down of a moving clock.

The line a in Fig. 162 may also be regarded as the history of a clock fixed in S'. In its history, A', A are two events, and the time interval T' between them (as judged by S') is the separation $A'A$. As judged by S, however, the interval between these events is T, the increase in t in passing from A' to A; it is, in fact, the separation $A'C$, where $A'C$ is drawn parallel to Ωt. It is evident that $T' \neq T$.

There are some facts about the space-time diagram which we leave to the consideration of the reader. Why do the axes $\Omega x' t'$ not interlace with Ωxt? Why does T appear smaller than T' in Fig. 162, whereas we have proved the reverse in (6.221)?

Is it true, for a triangle in the space-time diagram, that the sum of the separations represented by two sides is greater than the separation represented by the third side?

16.3. KINEMATICS AND DYNAMICS OF A PARTICLE

Composition of velocities.

Let P, Q be two particles traveling with uniform velocities u_1, u_2 along the axis Ox of a Galilean frame of reference S. What is the relative velocity of the two particles? In Newtonian mechanics, we should answer: $u_2 - u_1$. In relativity, we say that this is only the *difference* between the velocities. The velocity of Q *relative* to P is the velocity of Q as estimated by a Galilean observer S' traveling along with P, i.e., using a Galilean frame of reference in which P is fixed.

Between S and S' we have the Lorentz transformation [cf. (16.213)]

$$(16.301) \qquad x' = \gamma_1(x - u_1 t), \qquad t' = \gamma_1\left(t - \frac{u_1 x}{c^2}\right),$$

$$\gamma_1 = \frac{1}{\sqrt{1 - u_1^2/c^2}}$$

Consider now the motion of Q; for it, $dx/dt = u_2$, and its velocity as estimated by S' is

$$(16.302) \qquad u' = \frac{dx'}{dt'} = \frac{dx - u_1\, dt}{dt - u_1\, dx/c^2} = \frac{u_2 - u_1}{1 - u_1 u_2/c^2}.$$

This is the law which replaces the Newtonian law,

$$(16.303) \qquad u' = u_2 - u_1.$$

We note that, if u_1 and u_2 are small compared with c, (16.302) differs very little from (16.303).

If we solve (16.302) for u_2 and then make a change in notation, we get the *relativistic law of composition of velocities*: If a particle moves with velocity u_1 in S', and S' has a velocity u_2 relative to S, then the velocity of the particle relative to S is

$$(16.304) \qquad \frac{u_1 + u_2}{1 + u_1 u_2/c^2}.$$

Proper time.

Let S be a Galilean frame of reference, and let P be a particle traveling along the axis Ox with uniform velocity u. It may be

regarded as a particle of a second Galilean frame S'. Consider two adjacent events in the history of P; the time interval dt' between them (as estimated by a clock carried with P) is, by (16.213),

$$dt' = \frac{dt - u\,dx/c^2}{\sqrt{1 - u^2/c^2}}.$$

But $dx/dt = u$, and so

$$dt' = dt\sqrt{1 - u^2/c^2} = \sqrt{dt^2 - dx^2/c^2} = ds,$$

where ds is the separation between the two events. Thus the separation equals the time interval, as measured by a clock carried with the particle.

Hitherto we have considered only particles with uniform velocities. We now think of a particle, traveling with *accelerated* motion. Its history appears in the space-time diagram as a curve. How does a clock behave if carried with the accelerated particle? Our previous hypotheses do not tell us; we must make a new assumption. This assumption is as follows: *The time interval between two adjacent events in the history of an accelerated clock is given by the separation between these events.*

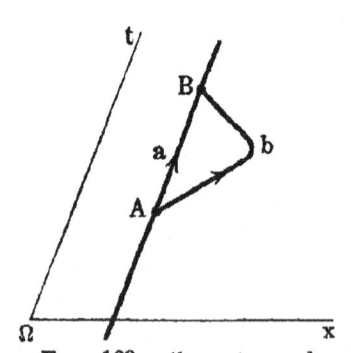

FIG. 163.—Space-time diagram of the histories of two clocks.

This separation is called the interval of *proper time* between the events. Thus the element of proper time for a particle moving along Ox with speed u is

(16.305) $$ds = dt/\gamma_u,$$

where

(16.306) $$\gamma_u = \frac{1}{\sqrt{1 - u^2/c^2}}.$$

Now we can give the explanation of the curious prediction made early in the chapter regarding the behavior of a clock taken on a flight. Figure 163 is a space-time diagram; a is the history of the clock that stayed at home. At the event $A(t = t_1)$ the

other clock left and described the space-time curve b, returning at the event $B(t = t_2)$. Suppose both clocks read zero at A. Then at B the clock that stayed at home reads (since $dx = 0$ throughout its history)

$$(16.307) \qquad T = \int_A^B ds \qquad \text{(along } a\text{)}$$
$$= \int_{t_1}^{t_2} dt$$
$$= t_2 - t_1.$$

The clock that flew reads

$$(16.308) \qquad T' = \int_A^B ds \qquad \text{(along } b\text{)}$$
$$= \int_{t_1}^{t_2} dt/\gamma_u$$
$$< t_2 - t_1.$$

Thus $T' < T$, which proves the validity of the prediction.

Equations of motion in absolute form.

It has been remarked that gravitation lies outside the scope of the special theory of relativity. But there are available other forces by means of which accelerated motion may be produced. What we shall have to say is theoretically applicable to the accelerated motions of ordinary life, but the differences between the relativistic and the Newtonian predictions are then far too small to measure. The differences become appreciable only in the dynamics of atomic particles accelerated by forces of electromagnetic origin. However, the same principle applies throughout, and we may understand it by thinking of any small body under the influence of any force.

We have accepted the hypothesis that all Galilean frames are equivalent. Thus, whatever form of equations of motion one Galilean observer adopts, a similar form must hold for any other Galilean observer In fact, *the equations of motion of a particle must be invariant under the Lorentz transformation.*

If we take the Newtonian equation

$$(16.309) \qquad m \frac{d^2x}{dt^2} = P$$

and apply the Lorentz transformation (16 213) to get an equation

in x' and t', we find an equation of quite different form. Thus (16.309) is *not* invariant under the Lorentz transformation.

To see what form of equation is suitable, we have to consider *space-time vectors*.

In Fig. 164, we have taken a point A in the space-time diagram and drawn a directed segment $\overrightarrow{\Omega A}$. This is a space-time vector; its components in the directions Ωx, Ωt are x, t, the space-time coordinates of A. If we use other axes $\Omega x' t'$, the *same* vector has different components. But between the two sets of components the Lorentz transformation holds.

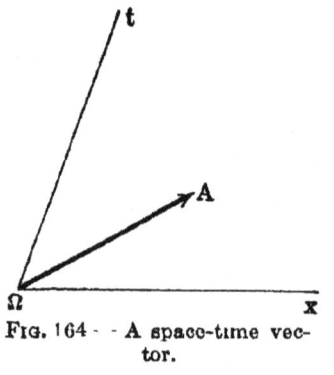

We define a space-time vector as a pair of quantities (ξ, τ) which transform, when we change axes in space-time, just like (x, t), i.e., according to

Fig. 164.—A space-time vector.

$$(16.310) \qquad \xi' = \gamma(\xi - V\tau), \qquad \tau' = \gamma\left(\tau - \frac{V\xi}{c^2}\right),$$

$$\gamma = \frac{1}{\sqrt{1 - V^2/c^2}}.$$

As we have stated, our problem is to build equations of motion invariant under a Lorentz transformation. The key to the solution is found in the idea of the space-time vector. *We shall form equations in which a space-time vector is equated to a space-time vector.*

Consider a particle moving along Ox with a general motion. This corresponds to some curve in space time. The proper time, measured from some initial point, may be taken as a parameter, and the equations of the curve written

$$x = x(s), \qquad t = t(s).$$

Since ds is an invariant, the pair of quantities $(dx/ds, dt/ds)$ is a space-time vector. We see this by differentiating (16.213). We call $(dx/ds, dt/ds)$ the *absolute velocity* of a particle. Explicitly we have, by (16.305),

$$(16.311) \qquad \frac{dx}{ds} = \gamma_u u, \qquad \frac{dt}{ds} = \gamma_u,$$

$$\gamma_u^{-2} = 1 - u^2/c^2,$$

where $u = dx/dt$, the velocity of the particle relative to the Galilean frame of reference S, corresponding to Ωxt. If the particle has a velocity small compared with that of light, so that u/c is small, the components of the absolute velocity are approximately $(u, 1)$.

Similarly, $(d^2x/ds^2, d^2t/ds^2)$ is a space-time vector. We call it the *absolute acceleration*.

We now accept, as satisfactory from the point of view of invariance under the Lorentz transformation, the following *equations of motion*:

$$(16.312) \qquad m_0 \frac{d^2x}{ds^2} = X, \qquad m_0 \frac{d^2t}{ds^2} = T,$$

where m_0 is a constant (the *proper mass* of the particle) and (X, T) is a space-time vector, called the *absolute force*.

In a different Galilean frame of reference S', with velocity V relative to S, these equations read

$$m_0 \frac{d^2x'}{ds^2} = X' \qquad m_0 \frac{d^2t'}{ds^2} = T',$$

where

$$(16.313) \qquad X' = \gamma(X - VT), \qquad T' = \gamma\left(T - \frac{VX}{c^2}\right),$$

$$\gamma = \frac{1}{\sqrt{1 - V^2/c^2}}.$$

This may be verified immediately by applying (16.213) to (16.312).

Equations of motion in relative form.

Let us now put the equations of motion (16.312) into another form in order to show the relation of relativistic to Newtonian mechanics. Since $ds = dt/\gamma_u$, these equations may be written

$$(16.314) \qquad \frac{d}{dt}(m_0\gamma_u u) = X/\gamma_u, \qquad \frac{d}{dt}(m_0\gamma_u) = T/\gamma_u.$$

Let us define some terms, as follows:

$$(16.315) \begin{cases} \text{Relative mass} = m = m_0\gamma_u = \dfrac{m_0}{\sqrt{1 - u^2/c^2}}. \\ \text{Relative momentum} = mu. \\ \text{Relative force} = P = X/\gamma_u = X\sqrt{1 - u^2/c^2}. \\ \text{Relative energy} = E = mc^2 = \dfrac{m_0 c^2}{\sqrt{1 - u^2/c^2}}. \end{cases}$$

Then the first of (16.314) may be written

(16.316) $$\frac{d}{dt}(mu) = P;$$

in words,

> rate of change of relative momentum = relative force.

This is the *equation of motion of a particle* moving on the x-axis under the influence of a force P. It is of the Newtonian *form*, but with a remarkable difference. The (relative) mass of a particle is *not* a constant; it varies with the speed of the particle according to (16.315).

If u/c is small, the variation of m from the value m_0 is insignificant, but on the other hand m tends to infinity as the speed of the particle (u) tends to that of light (c). No particle has ever been observed traveling with a speed equal to, or greater than, that of light. This physical fact agrees with the theory. If the speed of a particle were to increase up to and beyond the speed of light, the relative mass would become meaningless, passing through an infinite value to imaginary values.

To discuss the second equation of (16.314), let us first return to (16.224). This may be written

(16.317) $$\left(\frac{dt}{ds}\right)^2 - \frac{1}{c^2}\left(\frac{dx}{ds}\right)^2 = 1,$$

since $(dx/dt)^2 < c^2$ for a particle. Differentiation gives

(16.318) $$\frac{dt}{ds}\frac{d^2t}{ds^2} - \frac{1}{c^2}\frac{dx}{ds}\frac{d^2x}{ds^2} = 0$$

Thus, by (16.312),

(16.319) $$T\frac{dt}{ds} - \frac{1}{c^2}X\frac{dx}{ds} = 0,$$

or

(16.320) $$c^2T = Xu = Pu\gamma_u$$

In fact, the second component of absolute force is closely related to the first component.

If we multiply the second of (16.314) by c^2 and substitute from (16.315) and (16.320), we get

(16.321) $$\frac{dE}{dt} = Pu.$$

SEC. 16.3] THE SPECIAL THEORY OF RELATIVITY

This is the *equation of energy* and justifies the definition of relative energy as in (16.315). For (16.321) reads, in words,

rate of change of relative energy
$$= \text{rate of working of relative force.}$$

This has the Newtonian form, but the expression for energy (E) does not at first appear related to the Newtonian kinetic energy. However, if we expand by the binomial theorem, we obtain

$$(16.322) \quad E = \frac{m_0 c^2}{\sqrt{1 - u^2/c^2}} = m_0 c^2 \left(1 + \tfrac{1}{2} \frac{u^2}{c^2} + \tfrac{3}{8} \frac{u^4}{c^4} + \cdots \right);$$

and if u/c is small, we have approximately

$$(16.323) \quad E = m_0 c^2 + \tfrac{1}{2} m_0 u^2.$$

This differs from the Newtonian expression for kinetic energy only by the constant $m_0 c^2$, which is called the *rest energy* or *proper energy*.

The quantity $m_0 c^2$ appears of little importance here, because E is differentiated in (16.321), and so the constant disappears. The equation (16.321) would still hold if we had adopted the definition

$$(16.324) \quad E = \frac{m_0 c^2}{\sqrt{1 - u^2/c^2}} - m_0 c^2$$

for relative energy. There are, however, good reasons for preferring (16.322) to (16.324) as a definition of energy. Some of these are connected with the disintegration of atoms and their structure. The known atomic weights of the elements are consistent with the principle of energy only if (16.322) is regarded as the energy of a particle. In relativity, mass and energy are no longer distinct concepts. Even when a particle is at rest, it has energy $m_0 c^2$, and we cannot convert this energy into another form without destroying or altering the mass m_0.

Example Consider a particle moving on the x-axis under a constant relative force P, starting from rest at the origin at $t = 0$. By (16.316) the motion satisfies

$$(16.325) \quad \frac{d}{dt}\left(\frac{m_0 u}{\sqrt{1 - u^2/c^2}}\right) = P.$$

Hence,

(16.326) $$\frac{m_0 u}{\sqrt{1 - u^2/c^2}} = Pt.$$

Solving for u, we get

(16.327) $$u = \frac{cPt}{\sqrt{P^2 t^2 + m_0^2 c^2}}.$$

We note that u is less than c for all values of t and tends to the limiting value c as t tends to infinity. This behavior is, of course, quite different from the behavior of a particle under constant force in Newtonian mechanics.

Since $u = dx/dt$, (16.327) gives, on integration,

(16.328) $$x = \frac{m_0 c^2}{P}\left[\sqrt{1 + (P^2 t^2)/(m_0^2 c^2)} - 1\right].$$

If $m_0 c$ is large compared with Pt, this reduces approximately to

(16.329) $$x = \tfrac{1}{2}\frac{P}{m_0} t^2,$$

the familiar Newtonian formula.

16.4. SUMMARY OF THE SPECIAL THEORY OF RELATIVITY

I. There is no such thing as absolute time.

II. Lorentz transformation:

(16.401) $$x' = \gamma(x - Vt), \qquad t' = \gamma\left(t - \frac{Vx}{c^2}\right),$$

$$\gamma = \frac{1}{\sqrt{1 - V^2/c^2}}.$$

III. Space-time diagram.

(a) An event is represented by a point.

(b) The history of a free particle is represented by a straight line.

(c) The history of a flash of light is represented by a null line.

(d) The separation of two adjacent events is ds, where

(16.402) $$\epsilon\, ds^2 = dt^2 - dx^2/c^2 \qquad (\epsilon = \pm 1).$$

IV. Kinematics and dynamics of a particle.

(a) Element of proper time for moving particle:

(16.403) $$ds = dt\,\sqrt{1 - u^2/c^2}.$$

(b) Equation of motion.

(16.404) $$\frac{d}{dt}(m_0 \gamma_u u) = P, \qquad \gamma_u = \frac{1}{\sqrt{1 - u^2/c^2}}.$$

(c) Energy:

(16.405) $$E = m_0 \gamma_u c^2 = m_0 c^2 + \tfrac{1}{2} m_0 u^2, \qquad \text{approximately.}$$

(16.406) $$\frac{dE}{dt} = Pu.$$

EXERCISES XVI

1. An airplane sets out to fly at 500 miles per hour. Show that it would have to fly for more than a thousand years in order to make a difference of one one-hundredth of a second between the times recorded by a clock in the airplane and a clock on the ground.

2. Show that, if x/c and t are taken as coordinates in the space-time diagram, the history of a flash of light is equally inclined to the axes. Draw the history of a flash which passes to and fro between a mirror fixed at the origin and a mirror which moves along the observer's axis Ox with constant speed.

3. Prove directly from the formula (16.304) that, if the magnitudes of u_1 and u_2 are both less than c, the magnitude of the velocity relative to S is less than c.

4. Two electrons move toward one another, the speed of each being $0.9c$ in a Galilean frame of reference. What is their speed relative to one another?

5. For suitably chosen axes in two Galilean frames S and S', the complete Lorentz transformation is

$$x' = \gamma(x - Vt), \qquad y' = y, \qquad z' = z, \qquad t' = \gamma(t - Vx/c^2),$$
$$\gamma = (1 - V^2/c^2)^{-\frac{1}{2}},$$

where V is the relative velocity of S and S'.

A particle, as observed by S', describes a circle $x'^2 + y'^2 = a^2$, $z' = 0$, with constant speed. Show that to S the particle appears to move in an ellipse whose center moves with velocity V.

6. All electromagnetic waves travel with the fundamental velocity c in empty space. A radio station fixed in a Galilean frame of reference S sends out waves. Show that, to an observer in another Galilean frame S', these waves at any instant form a family of nonconcentric spheres. Is it possible that two of these spheres should intersect?

7. Show that the Lorentz transformation may be regarded as a rotation of axes through an imaginary angle.

8. The history of a moving particle is represented in the space-time diagram by the hyperbola

$$\frac{x^2}{c^2} - t^2 = \frac{1}{k^2}.$$

Show that

$$\frac{d^2x}{ds^2} = k^2 x, \qquad \frac{d^2t}{ds^2} = k^2 t.$$

9. Two particles, with proper masses m_1, m_2, move along the axis Ox of a Galilean frame with velocities u_1, u_2, respectively. They collide and coalesce to form a single particle. Assuming the laws of conservation of relativistic momentum and energy, prove that the proper mass m_3 and velocity u_3 of the resulting single particle are given by

$$m_3^2 = m_1^2 + m_2^2 + 2 m_1 m_2 \gamma_1 \gamma_2 \left(1 - \frac{u_1 u_2}{c^2}\right),$$

$$u_3 = \frac{m_1 \gamma_1 u_1 + m_2 \gamma_2 u_2}{m_1 \gamma_1 + m_2 \gamma_2},$$

where $\gamma_1^{-2} = 1 - u_1^2/c^2$, $\gamma_2^{-2} = 1 - u_2^2/c^2$.

10. A particle of proper mass m_0 moves on the axis Ox of a Galilean frame of reference, and is attracted to the origin O by a (relative) force $m_0 k^2 x$. It performs oscillations of amplitude a. Show that the periodic time of this relativistic harmonic oscillator is

$$\tau = \frac{4}{c} \int_0^a \frac{f\,dx}{\sqrt{f^2 - 1}},$$

where

$$f = 1 + \tfrac{1}{2} \frac{k^2}{c^2} (a^2 - x^2).$$

Verify that, if $c \to \infty$, $\tau \to 2\pi/k$ (the Newtonian result); and show that if ka/c is small,

$$\tau = \frac{2\pi}{k} \left(1 + \tfrac{3}{16} \frac{k^2 a^2}{c^2}\right), \qquad \text{approximately.}$$

APPENDIX

THE THEORY OF DIMENSIONS

Two physicists are shipwrecked on a desert island. After making qualitative observations of their surroundings, they wish to make measurements. But here a difficulty arises, for they have none of the usual apparatus of the laboratory—no meter scale, no set of weights, no clock.* Everything they require they must construct for themselves.

If they can agree on the length of a certain stick as unit of length, the mass of a certain stone as unit of mass, and the duration of some simple repeatable experiment as unit of time, all will be well; both experimenters will assign the same *number* to the same measurable quantity. But why choose one stick rather than another, one stone rather than another, one experiment rather than another? If the two physicists are obstinate, each in his own preference of units, there is no valid argument by which one can persuade the other to yield.

This disagreement concerns only physical measurements. In the realm of pure mathematics, there is complete accord; both agree, for example, that

(1) $\quad 2 + 2 = 4, \quad (x+1)(x-1) = x^2 - 1,$
$$\int_0^\infty e^{-x^2}\, dx = \tfrac{1}{2}\sqrt{\pi}.$$

But in the matter of the choice of units, we may well imagine that neither physicist will yield to the other. So they decide to work independently, each constructing his own apparatus, measuring quantities in the units he prefers, and developing his own results. If they wish to discuss their work, how is one to interpret the results of the other? How far do their individual efforts contribute to the construction of a common science, independent of the choice of units? These are questions which belong to the theory of dimensions.

---

* We may suppose the sky perpetually overcast, so that the rotation of the heavens cannot be used as a clock

It may appear strange that we have been able to postpone to an appendix the discussion of these important questions. The explanation is that the theory of dimensions becomes necessary only when we wish to compare results for two different systems of units. In our work, we have used arbitrary units and letters (algebra) instead of actual numbers (arithmetic). Our results are valid quite generally and can immediately be applied in any particular system of units.

Perhaps an analogy with analytical geometry will be helpful. We may develop results true for arbitrary Cartesian axes, e.g., properties of conics deduced from a general equation of the second degree. We meet the theory of transformations (the analogue of the theory of dimensions) only when we consider two different sets of axes at the same time. The invariants of analytical geometry are analogous to general physical laws, true for all systems of units.

Units and dimensions.

The theory of dimensions arises from the fact that units may be chosen arbitrarily. Instead of arguing over the respective merits of different systems of units (e.g., centimeter-gram-second and foot-pound-second), let us regard all systems as equally valid. Each physicist may select his own units. This means that he selects a piece of matter and says that its mass is unity, he selects a rigid bar and says that its length is unity, and he selects a repeatable experiment and says that its duration is unity. He can now measure masses, lengths, and times, and record them as so many units. To find a velocity, he measures distance traveled and time taken, and divides the one number by the other. He deals similarly with acceleration, moment of inertia, kinetic energy, and so on.

As for force, there are two possible plans: (i) he may use Newton's law of motion in the form $\mathbf{P} = mf$ to define force in terms of mass and acceleration, or (ii) he may use a separate arbitrary unit of force. The second plan is good in statics, but the first is far simpler in dynamics and may be used in statics also. We shall accept the first plan for the present discussion. With this understanding, all the quantities occurring in mechanics are built up out of mass, length, and time; the physicist can assign numerical values to them all, once he has selected his fundamental units of mass, length, and time.

Two physical quantities may have different numerical values and yet be of the same type. For example, the linear momenta of two particles may have different numerical values, but they are both built up out of mass, length, and time in the same definite way; in fact,

$$\text{(2)} \qquad \text{linear momentum} = \frac{\text{mass} \times \text{length}}{\text{time}}.$$

To express this more compactly, we introduce the symbols M, L, T for mass, length, and time, and write symbolically

$$\text{(3)} \qquad [\text{linear momentum}] = [MLT^{-1}].$$

The square brackets are to remind us that this is no ordinary equation connecting numbers but a symbolic shorthand to show how linear momentum involves the fundamental quantities. This is called the *dimensional* notation; we say that linear momentum "has the dimensions $[MLT^{-1}]$." All the quantities occurring in mechanics may be expressed dimensionally in the form

$$[M^\alpha L^\beta T^\gamma],$$

where α, β, γ are positive or negative powers, not necessarily integers. The following list of dimensions is easily verified:

$$\begin{aligned}
[\text{velocity}] &= [LT^{-1}], \\
[\text{acceleration}] &= [LT^{-2}], \\
[\text{force}] &= [MLT^{-2}], \\
[\text{moment of a force}] &= [ML^2T^{-2}], \\
[\text{linear momentum}] &= [MLT^{-1}], \\
[\text{angular momentum}] &= [ML^2T^{-1}], \\
[\text{energy}] &= [ML^2T^{-2}], \\
[\text{angular velocity}] &= [T^{-1}], \\
[\text{moment of inertia}] &= [ML^2].
\end{aligned}$$

In writing down the dimensions of a physical quantity, we pay no attention to numerical factors. Thus the dimensions of $\frac{1}{2}mq^2$ and mq^2 are the same, viz., $[ML^2T^{-2}]$.

We do not add or subtract quantities having different dimensions, but we frequently multiply such quantities by one another or divide them by one another. The rule by which we obtain the

dimensions of the product or quotient is obvious from the definition of dimensions. It is as follows:

Let Q_1 and Q_2 be physical quantities with dimensions

$$[Q_1] = [M^{\alpha_1} L^{\beta_1} T^{\gamma_1}], \qquad [Q_2] = [M^{\alpha_2} L^{\beta_2} T^{\gamma_2}];$$

then

$$[Q_1 Q_2] = [M^{\alpha_1+\alpha_2} L^{\beta_1+\beta_2} T^{\gamma_1+\gamma_2}],$$
$$\left[\frac{Q_1}{Q_2}\right] = [M^{\alpha_1-\alpha_2} L^{\beta_1-\beta_2} T^{\gamma_1-\gamma_2}].$$

If Q_1 and Q_2 have the same dimensions, then

$$\left[\frac{Q_1}{Q_2}\right] = [M^0 L^0 T^0],$$

and we say then that Q_1/Q_2 is *dimensionless*. For example, the circular measure of an angle is obtained by dividing a length (arc) by a length (radius), and so an angle is dimensionless. It is easy to verify that the following combinations are also dimensionless:

$$\frac{\text{force} \times \text{time}}{\text{linear momentum}},$$
$$\frac{\text{force} \times \text{length}}{\text{energy}},$$
$$\frac{\text{moment of inertia} \times \text{angular velocity}}{\text{angular momentum}}.$$

Exercise. Einstein's radiation formula is $E = h\nu$, where E is the energy of a photon, ν is its frequency, and h is Planck's constant. Show that Planck's constant has the dimensions of angular momentum.

Change of units. First method.

Let us now consider two physicists S_1 and S_2, who use different units of mass, length, and time. When they measure the same physical quantity, they record different results. But, as we shall now see, it is easy to pass from one numerical value to the other when we know the ratios of the two sets of units.

For symmetry, we introduce a third physicist S_0, using a third system of units; we shall call his units "absolute" for purposes of reference, without meaning to imply that they are in any way more fundamental than the units of S_1 or S_2. Let the units of S_1 contain m_1, l_1, and t_1, absolute units of mass, length,

and time, respectively; and let the units of S_2 contain m_2, l_2, and t_2 absolute units

Consider a physical quantity Q with dimensions $[M^\alpha L^\beta T^\gamma]$. This quantity is measured by S_0, S_1, and S_2, with numerical results as follows:

$$\begin{array}{ccc} S_0 & S_1 & S_2 \\ Q_0 & Q_1 & Q_2. \end{array}$$

Now every unit of mass recorded by S_1 corresponds to m_1 absolute units, and similarly for length and time. Hence, one S_1-unit of the quantity measured corresponds to $m_1^\alpha l_1^\beta t_1^\gamma$ absolute units, and Q_1 S_1-units correspond to $Q_1 m_1^\alpha l_1^\beta t_1^\gamma$ absolute units. But we know that Q_1 S_1-units correspond to Q_0 absolute units, and so

(4) $$Q_0 = Q_1 m_1^\alpha l_1^\beta t_1^\gamma,$$

similarly,

(5) $$Q_0 = Q_2 m_2^\alpha l_2^\beta t_2^\gamma.$$

Comparing (4) and (5), we see that the law of transformation connecting the results of S_1 and S_2 is

(6) $$Q_1 m_1^\alpha l_1^\beta t_1^\gamma = Q_2 m_2^\alpha l_2^\beta t_2^\gamma,$$

or

(7) $$\frac{Q_2}{Q_1} = \left(\frac{m_1}{m_2}\right)^\alpha \left(\frac{l_1}{l_2}\right)^\beta \left(\frac{t_1}{t_2}\right)^\gamma$$

If we identify the units of S_0 with those of S_1, so that the absolute units are now the S_1-units, we have

$$m_1 = 1, \quad l_1 = 1, \quad t_1 = 1,$$

and so

(8) $$Q_2 = \frac{Q_1}{m_2^\alpha l_2^\beta t_2^\gamma},$$

where m_2, l_2, t_2 are the numbers of S_1-units contained in the S_2-units. This formula gives the number Q_2 assigned by S_2 to a quantity, in terms of the number Q_1 assigned by S_1 to the same quantity and the ratios of the units.

Exercise An energy is 362 in c.g.s units. What is its numerical value in f.p.s units?

Change of units. Second method.

The above method is logical, but not good in practice. Conversion from one set of units to another is a process which we must be able to carry out quickly and accurately, and the rules should be simple and easy to remember. The formula (7) is bad because it involves a third system of units, and (8) is bad because it is unsymmetrical and hard to remember. The method we are about to describe is that in common use.

Compare the equations (1) with the following:

(9) 1 meter = 100 cm.,   1 lb. = 453.6 gm.,
        22 ft. per sec. = 15 miles per hr

These are true statements, but they differ from (1) in an important respect: the equations (1) involve only pure numbers, whereas (9) involve measurable physical quantities. To distinguish them, we may call (1) mathematicians' equations (or briefly *M-equations*) and (9) physicists' equations (or *P-equations*). We know what we can do with M-equations according to the methods of algebra and calculus. There are certain rules of manipulation, which we apply with confidence that we shall never reach a false conclusion. Let us boldly apply the rules of algebraic manipulation to P-equations, treating such words as meter, cm., lb. as if they were *ordinary algebraic symbols*. A word of warning, however—the signs =, +, and − are to be used to connect only quantities of the same type, i.e., of the same dimensions.

We think again of two physicists S_1 and S_2. Let S_1 name his units M_1, L_1, T_1; and let S_2 name his units M_2, L_2, T_2. These are *names* (like gm or cm.), not numbers. If S_1 measures a length, he records the result in the form

$$Q = Q_1 L_1;$$

this is a P-equation, in which Q stands for "the quantity which is measured," and Q_1 is a number. More generally, if S_1 measures a quantity with dimensions $[M^\alpha L^\beta T^\gamma]$, he records

(10) $$Q = Q_1 M_1^\alpha L_1^\beta T_1^\gamma,$$

where Q_1 is a number. If S_2 measures the same quantity, he records

(11) $$Q = Q_2 M_2^\alpha L_2^\beta T_2^\gamma.$$

There is nothing novel about this; it is what we do when we write

$$\text{acceleration due to gravity} = 32 \text{ ft. sec}^{-2}$$
$$\text{acceleration due to gravity} = 980 \text{ cm. sec.}^{-2}$$

Now we bring into operation our assumption that the P-equations (10) and (11) may be treated in the same way as we should treat M-equations. We get at once

(12) $$Q_1 M_1^\alpha L_1^\beta T_1^\gamma = Q_2 M_2^\alpha L_2^\beta T_2^\gamma,$$

and

(13) $$\frac{Q_2}{Q_1} = \left(\frac{M_1}{M_2}\right)^\alpha \left(\frac{L_1}{L_2}\right)^\beta \left(\frac{T_1}{T_2}\right)^\gamma.$$

If we interpret M_1/M_2 to mean the ratio of the unit M_1 to the unit M_2, then M_1/M_2 is a pure number—in fact, the measure of M_1 in terms of M_2. Since L_1/L_2 and T_1/T_2 may also be regarded as pure numbers, (13) is an M-equation, although (12) (from which it was obtained) is a P-equation.

Equation (13) is what we have been seeking—a formula to give Q_2 when Q_1 and the ratios of the units are known. If we lack confidence in it, because it has been obtained by a symbolic method, we can reassure ourselves by turning back to the first method; there only M-equations were used, and the deduction of (6) and (7) is logically sound. We see that (12) is merely the P-equation corresponding to the M-equation (6), and (13) is the same as (7)—both M-equations.

When we actually carry out a conversion from one system of units to another, it is the P-equation (12) rather than the M-equation (13) that we use. It would, however, be more correct to say that we use neither. Therein lies the simplicity of the symbolic method; we treat each problem on its merits, without having to remember anything, except that it is permissible to use the symbolic method, in which words are treated as algebraic symbols. The formulas (12) and (13) were obtained only for purposes of comparison with (6) and (7).

To show the symbolic method in action, let us convert an acceleration of 32 ft. sec.$^{-2}$ into mile hr.$^{-2}$* First we write down

---

* It is convenient to write each unit in the singular, to avoid waste of energy in deciding whether to use the singular or the plural. This is a mathematical symbolism, and in it simplicity is more important than grammar

so that
$$1 \text{ mile} = 5280 \text{ ft.}, \quad 1 \text{ hr.} = 3600 \text{ sec.},$$
$$1 \text{ ft.} = \frac{1}{5280} \text{ mile}, \quad 1 \text{ sec.} = \frac{1}{3600} \text{ hr.}$$

Then,
$$32 \text{ ft. sec.}^{-2} = 32 \frac{(1 \text{ ft.})}{(1 \text{ sec.})^2}$$
$$= 32 \frac{\left(\frac{1}{5280} \text{ mile}\right)}{\left(\frac{1}{3600} \text{ hr.}\right)^2}$$
$$= \frac{32 \times 3600 \times 3600}{5280} \text{ mile hr.}^{-2}$$
$$= 78{,}545 \tfrac{5}{11} \text{ mile hr.}^{-2}$$

A physicist would round off the result. For he would think of the number 32 as obtained by measurement carried out only to two-figure accuracy, and so he would prefer to write

$$32 \text{ ft. sec.}^{-2} = 79{,}000 \text{ mile hr.}^{-2}$$

This question of "significant figures" has nothing to do with the theory of dimensions, and we shall not pursue it further. The discrepancy between the two statements arises from the two ways of thinking—mathematical and physical—which we mentioned in Chap. I.

Exercise. Work out the exercise on page 505 by the above method.

Dimensionless quantities and physical laws.

If a quantity is dimensionless, then $\alpha = \beta = \gamma = 0$ in (13), and therefore $Q_1 = Q_2$. *A dimensionless quantity has a value independent of the system of units employed.* This fact makes such quantities particularly simple to handle, because any possible confusion regarding units is automatically eliminated. Any mathematical combination of dimensionless quantities is itself dimensionless.

We can now answer the questions raised in connection with the two shipwrecked physicists. The formulas given above enable the one to interpret the results of the other, i.e., to transform them into his own units. As for the second question—the building up of a common science independent of the choice of units—the

answer is to be found in the concept of the dimensionless quantity. *Any equation connecting dimensionless quantities is true in all systems of units, if true in one.*

Suppose, for example, that a physicist (prior to the time of Galileo) made measurements on a falling body, using some system of units of length and time. We assume that he was able to measure the height h from which the body fell, the speed q with which it struck the ground, and the time t it took to fall. Suppose he found

$$\frac{qt}{h} = 2,$$

for a whole set of experiments in which h was given different values. He would have been justified in regarding this as a result of great importance, because it holds in all systems of units, since qt/h and the pure number 2 are both dimensionless.

As shown above, any equation connecting dimensionless quantities is a *physical law*, in the sense that its truth is independent of the choice of units. However, it is not necessary to express a physical law in dimensionless form. It is merely necessary that the equation should be *dimensionally homogeneous;* i.e., the terms equated to one another must have the same dimensions. This will ensure that the law is true in **all** systems of units, if true in one.

The constants occurring in physical laws usually have dimensions. Consider the law of gravitational attraction (6.501)

$$P = \frac{Gmm'}{r^2},$$

where P is the magnitude of the force between particles of mass m, m' at a distance r apart. To make this dimensionally homogeneous, we must assign suitable dimensions to the constant G. This is easily done if we write the equation in the form

$$G = \frac{Pr^2}{mm'}.$$

We have then

$$[G] = \frac{[MLT^{-2}][L^2]}{[M^2]}$$
$$= [M^{-1}L^3T^{-2}].$$

In the c.g.s. system,

$$G = 6.67 \times 10^{-8} \text{ gm.}^{-1} \text{ cm.}^3 \text{ sec.}^{-2}$$

Exercise Form a dimensionless combination of the gravitational constant, density, and time

Applications.

Apart from its use in the change of units, the theory of dimensions has three important applications:

(i) It supplies us with a useful check against slips in calculation
(ii) It suggests forms of physical laws.
(iii) It enables us to predict the behavior of a full-scale system from the behavior of a model.

These applications will now be explained.

(i) Provided that we do not insert numerical values, the dimensions of every combination of symbols occurring in our work are obvious. For example, if a is the length of a pendulum and g the acceleration due to gravity, then

$$\left[\frac{a}{g}\right] = [T^2].$$

The basic law of motion (1.402) is dimensionally homogeneous, in the sense that both sides have the same dimensions, viz., $[MLT^{-2}]$. The operations we perform on this equation may change the dimensions of the two sides, but they are both changed in the same way. Thus, at all stages of our deductions we have dimensionally homogeneous equations. Indeed, it is inevitable that this should be so, since otherwise the two sides of an equation would change differently on change of units, and if true for one system of units would not be true for another. This gives a useful check. For example, suppose we are engaged in working out the formula for the periodic time of small oscillations of a simple pendulum. As a result of our work we arrive, perhaps, at the result

$$\tau = 2\pi \frac{a}{g}.$$

Dimensionally, this reads

$$[T] = [T^2],$$

which shows that the result is incorrect. Such a check will, of course, never be of any assistance as far as a numerical coefficient

is concerned; for example, the theory of dimensions alone cannot tell us that

$$\tau = \pi \sqrt{\frac{a}{g}}$$

is incorrect.

Exercise It is suggested that the equation of motion of a particle on a line is

$$\frac{d^2x}{dt^2} + a\frac{dx}{dt} + bx = 0,$$

where a has the dimensions $[L]$, and b the dimensions $[T^{-2}]$. Would you accept this equation as correct?

(ii) To see how the theory of dimensions suggests forms of physical laws, we shall consider the transverse vibrations of a heavy particle at the middle point of a stretched string. The quantities involved are

$$m = \text{mass of particle},$$
$$a = \text{length of string},$$
$$S = \text{tension},$$
$$\tau = \text{periodic time}.$$

The periodic time must be some function of the quantities m, a, S, and so we write

$$\tau = f(m, a, S).$$

The only combination of m, a, S having the dimensions $[T]$ is of the form $Cm^\alpha a^\beta S^\gamma$, where C, α, β, γ are pure numbers, at present unknown. Accordingly we assume

$$\tau = Cm^\alpha a^\beta S^\gamma$$

and obtain the dimensional equation

$$[T] = [M^\alpha][L^\beta][MLT^{-2}]^\gamma = [M^{\alpha+\gamma}L^{\beta+\gamma}T^{-2\gamma}].$$

Hence,
$$\alpha + \gamma = 0, \quad \beta + \gamma = 0, \quad -2\gamma = 1,$$
or
$$\alpha = \tfrac{1}{2}, \quad \beta = \tfrac{1}{2}, \quad \gamma = -\tfrac{1}{2};$$

and so our formula for τ is

$$\tau = C\sqrt{\frac{ma}{S}}.$$

512   PRINCIPLES OF MECHANICS

We cannot find the numerical factor C from the theory of dimensions. To obtain it theoretically, we must solve the differential equation of motion. But, if we are satisfied with an experimental result, one experiment will suffice to determine C.

This method is useful in the case of a complicated system, where the direct solution of the differential equations is difficult

Exercise Consider the transverse vibrations of a system consisting of 20 equal particles, equally spaced on a stretched string. Show that each of the twenty normal periods is of the form

$$\tau = C\sqrt{\frac{ma}{S}},$$

where m is the mass of each particle, a the length of the string, S the tension in it, and C a numerical constant which may depend on the particular normal mode.

(iii) To show how the theory of dimensions enables us to use a model to predict full-scale phenomena, let us consider the flow of air past the wing of an airplane. The lift Y on the wing obviously depends on the following quantities:

ρ = the density of the air,
U = the speed of the wing relative to the air,
l = a linear measurement of the wing (e.g., its width from back to front, at some definite position).

The lift depends, of course, on the shape of the wing; we shall consider only wings of one definite shape, transformed into one another by changing the length l.

The problem is to calculate the lift Y on the full-scale wing from the measurement of the lift Y' on a model. Now Y is a function of ρ, U, l; and Y' is the same function of ρ', U', l', where the accented quantities refer to the experiment on the model, the same units of mass, length, and time being used in both cases. So we write

$$Y = f(\rho, U, l), \qquad Y' = f(\rho', U', l').$$

As in the preceding example, we take

$$f(\rho, U, l) = C\rho^\alpha U^\beta l^\gamma,$$

where C is a pure number. Since $[\rho] = [ML^{-3}]$, $[U] = [LT^{-1}]$, $[l] = [L]$, and $[Y] = [MLT^{-2}]$, we easily find

$$Y = C\rho U^2 l^2, \qquad Y' = C\rho' U'^2 l'^2.$$

Hence the full-scale lift is
$$Y = Y' \frac{\rho U^2 l^2}{\rho' U'^2 l'^2}.$$

If the density of the air is the same for both cases, this becomes
$$Y = Y' \frac{U^2 l^2}{U'^2 l'^2}.$$

When we insert the numerical values for Y', U', l', obtained from experiment on a model in a wind tunnel, and the values of U and l appropriate to the full-scale wing in flight, we are able to read off the value of the lift Y.

Exercise. In order to study the deflections in an elastic beam with continuous and isolated loads (cf. Sec. 3 3), an engineer builds a model of the same material with a linear ratio 1 100. Show that, if the deflections in the model are to be one one-hundredth of the full-scale deflections, the continuous load per unit length in the model must be one one-hundredth of the full-scale load. In what ratio should the isolated loads be reduced?

INDEX

The numbers in heavy type refer to the Summaries at the ends of the chapters

A

Absolute equations of motion, 493–495
Absolute velocity, acceleration, and force, 494, 495
Acceleration, 27, 28, **36**, 305, **332**
  absolute, 495
  of automobile, 205, 206
  complementary, 349
  of Coriolis, 349
  in cylindrical coordinates, 306, 307
  due to gravity (see g)
  radial and transverse components, 120, **125**
  in relativity, 492, 493, 495
  in spherical polar coordinates, 467, 468
  tangential and normal components, 118, 119, **125**, 305, 306, **332**
  of transport, 349
Accelerations, composition of, 141, 307, 308
Action and reaction, law of, 32, **36**
Addition of vectors, 19–22, **35**
Air, resistance of, 151, 154–159, **184**
Airplane, 271, 272, 444, 512, 513
Ames, J S., 16
Amplitude of oscillations, 162
Angle of friction, 87, 88, **114**
Angular impulse, 357
Angular momentum, in impulsive motion, 229–231, **238**, 357, 358, **361**
  of particle, 128, 129, **146**, 329, **333**, 341, **360**

Angular momentum, relative to mass center, 135, 136, **147**, 330, 345, 355, **360, 361**
Angular momentum, of rigid body, 193, 194, 196, **222, 223**, 330–332, **333**
  of system, 134–136, **147**, 329, 330, 344, 345, **360**
Angular velocity, of the earth, 143
  of rigid body, 122, **125**, 308–311, **332**
Anomaly, 187
Aphelion, 180
Appell, P , xi
Applications, in dynamics in space, 364–**411–414**, 418–**453, 454**
  of Lagrange's equations, 467–472
  in plane dynamics, 151–**184–186**, 189–**222, 223**
  in plane statics, 74–**113–115**
  in statics in space, 275–278, 296–301
Applied force, 58, 295
Approximations for electromagnetic lenses, 397–403
Apse, 171–174, **185**
  advance of, for spherical pendulum, 381
Apsidal angle, 173, 174, 378–381
Archimedes, 82
Areal velocity, 170, 180, **185**
Associative property of vector addition, 22
Astatic center, 73
Astronomical frame of reference, 31, 33, 141, 143
Astronomical latitude, 145, 403

INDEX

Attraction, electrostatic, 176
    gravitational, 82–86, **114**, 144–146, 176, 177, 404, 405, 509
Automobile, 204–206
Axes of inertia, principal, 316–324, **333**
Axially symmetric electromagnetic field, 387–403, **413**
Axis, of rotation, instantaneous, 308
    of screw displacement, 285
    of symmetry, 78, 321, 322
    of wrench, 269, 270

B

Balancing, problems of, 219–222
Ball slipping on table, 447–450, **454**
Ballistic pendulum, **235**, 236
Ballistics, 151, **184**
    (See also Projectile)
Bars in frame, 106, 108
Base point, 61, 259, 280, 281
    change of, 260, 283, 284
Beam, internal reactions in, 92, 93, **114**, 272, 273
    thin, 92–98, **114**
Becker, K., 151
Bending moment, 92–98, **114**, 272, 273
Billiard ball, 447–450, **454**
Binormal, 264
Blank, A. A., 388
Body centrode, 124, **125**, 309
Body cone, 309, 421, 425, 427, **453**
Bound vector, 18, 19
Bridge, suspension, 100, **114**

C

Cable, flexible, 98–105, **114**, **115**
    in contact with curve, 104, 105, **115**
    in space, 265, 266
Cajori, F., 32
Calibration of spring, 17
Campbell, J. W., 103
Cardan's suspension, 418

Catenary, 100–104, **115**
Celestial pole, motion of, 428, 429
Center, astatic, 73
    of gravity, 84–86, **114**, 271
    instantaneous, 123–**125**
    of mass (see Mass center)
    of oscillation, 201
    of percussion, 239
    of system of parallel forces, 271
Centimeter, 13
Central force, general, 128, 168–176, **185**
    varying directly as distance, 168, 169, **185**
    varying as inverse square of distance, 176–184, **185**, 462
Central symmetry, 77
Centrifugal force, 143–145, **147**, 349, 350, 406
Centrode, 124, **125**, 309
Chain (see Cable)
Chako, N., 388
Change of base point, 260, 283, 284
    of units, 504–508
Charge on electron, 386, 387
Charged particle, in axially symmetric electromagnetic field, 388–403, **413**
    in electromagnetic field, 176, 381–403, **412**, **413**
    in uniform electromagnetic field, 383–387, **412**
Chasles' theorem, 303
Circular disk and cylinder, moments of inertia of, 190, 191, **222**, 324
Circular motion, 28
Circular orbit, stability of, 174–176
Clock, 12, 13, 501
    in relativity, 475–480, 482, 483, 487, 490, 492, 493
Clocks, synchronization of, 477–480
on x, 368, **412**
Coefficient, of friction, 87, 88, **114**
    of restitution, 232–234, **239**
Collar, A. R., 316
Collisions, 231–235, **239**

INDEX

Commutative property in vector operations, 19, 21, 246, **257**
Complementary acceleration, 349
Complex frame, 111, 112
Components of vector, 22–24, 32, **35, 36**, 245
(*See also* Acceleration; Velocity)
Composition, of accelerations, 141, 307, 308
  of couples, 268
  of finite rotations, 20, 282
  of infinitesimal displacements, 281–283, **302**
  of velocities, 140, 307, 308, 491
Compound pendulum, 198–201, **223**, 370
Compression, 233, 234
  modulus, 186
Cone, body or polhode, 309, 421, 425, 427, **453**
  of friction, 87
  space or herpolhode, 309, 421, 425, 427, **453**
Configuration of a system, 64, 286
Conical pendulum, 374, 375
Conjugate lines, 304
Conservation of energy, 130, 131, 137, **146, 147**, 196, 201, **223,** 231, 341, 346, 356, 360, **361**
Conservative field, 66
Conservative system, 65–67, 294, 295, **302**
Constant of gravitation (*see* Gravitational constant)
Constraints, 57–60, 285–292
  moving, 474
  workless, 54–57, **70**
Contact, rolling, 55–57, **70**, 123, 124
  rough, 86–88, **114**
  smooth, 54, 55, 57, **70**, 86
Continuity of bodies, 14, 15, 76
Contraction of moving rod, 486, 487, 490
Coordinate vectors, 23
Coordinates, cylindrical, 306, 307, 338
  generalized, 285–292, **302,** 462–**472**

Coordinates, spherical polar, 467
Coriolis, acceleration of, 349
  force, 143, 144, **147**, 349, 406
Coulomb's law, 176
Couple, 49
  gyroscopic, 442–444, **454**
  impulsive, 229
  moment of, 49, 50, 267
  twisting, in a beam, 272
  work done by, 64, 293
Couples, composition of, **268**
Courant, R., 320
Covering operation, 320
Cranz, C., 151
Critical form for a frame, 113
Cuboid, moment of inertia of, 324
Curvature, radius of, 119, **264**
Curves in space, 264, 265
Cuspidal motion of a top, 436–438
Cylinder, balancing problem for, 219–222
  moments of inertia of, 191, **222**, 324
  rolling down inclined plane, 202–204
Cylindrical coordinates, 306, 307, **338**

D

Dale, J. B., 370
D'Alembert's principle, 138, 139, **147**
Damped oscillations, 163–168, **185**
Deadbeat oscillations, 166, **185**
Decomposition, method of, 78, 79, **114**, 325
Decrement, logarithmic, 166
Degrees of freedom, 207, 208, 287
Deimel, R. F., 445
Density, 76, 77
Determination of past and future, 340, 341
Deviations due to earth's rotation, 145, 407, 408, **414**
Differentiation, used to find moments of inertia, 325, 326
  of vectors and their products, 24–26, **35**, 250, **257**

518 *INDEX*

Digonal symmetry, 321
Dimensional notation, 503
Dimensionless quantity, 504, 508
Dimensions, theory of, 501–513
Directed line, 22
Discontinuity in bodies, 14, 15
Discontinuous motion, 231
Disk, moment of inertia of, 190, **222**, 324
    rolling on plane, 450–453, **454**
Displacement, of rigid body, 61, 62, **70**, 278–285, 290, **301**, **302**
    reduced to translation and rotation, 61, 62, 280, 281, **302**
    screw, 284, 285
    virtual, 53, 58, 461
Distributive property of vector operations, 20, 246, 249
Disturbing force, 162, 163, 166–168, **184, 185**
dn x, 368, **412**
Drag, 272
Dugan, R. S., 13, 429
Duncan, W. J., 316
Dynamical unit of force, 34, 502
Dynamics, plane, applications in, 151–**184**–**186**, 189–**222**, **223**
    methods of, 127–**146**, **147**
    in relativity, 491–**498**, **499**
    in space, applications in, 364–411–**414**, 418–**453**, **454**
    methods of, 337–359, **360, 361**
      (*See also* Motion; Particle; Rigid body; System of particles)
Dyne, 34

E

Earth, angular velocity of, 143
    attraction of, 82, 84–86, 144–146, 404, 405
    models of, 5, 6, 84, 85, 144, 403, 428, 429
    rotation of, 13, 143–146, 403–411, **414**
Earth's axis, motion of, 428, 429

Eccentric anomaly, 187
Effective force, 138
Einstein, A., 7, 475, 477, 478
Elastic beam, 95–98, **114**
Elastic bodies in collision, 231–235, **239**
Electric field, axially symmetric, 387, 390–392, 396
    uniform, 383–386, **412**
Electric lens, focal length of, 403
    (*See also* Electrostatic lens)
Electric potential, 381
Electric vector, 381
Electromagnetic field, 381–403, **412, 413**
    axially symmetric, 387–403, **413**
    uniform, 383–387, **412**
Electromagnetic lens, 392–403, **413**
    approximations for, 397–403
    focal length of, 403
    magnification of, 396, **413**
Electron, determination of e/m for, 386, 387
Electron optics (*see* Charged particle)
Electrostatic attraction, 176
Electrostatic field, 381, 383–386, 387, 390–392, 396, **412**
    (*See also* Electric field)
Electrostatic lens, 398
Ellipse, momental, 322, 323
Ellipsoid, momental, 315–322, **333**
    moments of inertia of, 323–325
    of Poinsot, 420, 421, 425, **453**
Ellipsoidal shell, moments of inertia of, 326
Elliptic cylinder and plate, moments of inertia of, 324
Elliptic functions, 364–370, **411, 412**
Elliptic harmonic motion, 169, 374
Elliptic integral, 368
Elliptical orbit, 169, 179–182, **185**, 374
Emde, F., 370
Energy, principle of, 129–131, 136, **146, 147**, 196, 201, **223**, 231, 341, 342, 346, 352, 356, **360, 361**, 382, 495–497, **499**

INDEX

Energy in relativity, 495–497, **499**
  total, 130, 137, 341, 346
  (*See also* Kinetic energy; Potential energy)
Equation of the hodograph, 156, **184**
Equations of motion, impulsive, 229–231, **238**, 357, 358, **361**, **470–472**
  of charged particle, 382, 383, 386, 388, 389
  Lagrange's 458–**472**
  of particle, in cylindrical coordinates, 338
    in a plane, 127, 128, **146**, 461, 462
    relative to rotating earth, 403–406, **414**
    relative to rotating frame, 142, 348–350
    in relativity, 493–498, **499**
    in space, 337–342, **360**
  of rigid body, with fixed axis, 196, **223**
    with fixed point, 351, 352, **360**
    in general, 355, 356, **361**
    moving parallel to a plane, 202, **223**
Equilibrium, of particle, 39, 40, **69**, **70**, 262, **301**
  of rigid body, movable parallel to a fixed plane, 62–64, **70**
  in space, 273–278, **301**
  stability of, 214–222, **223**, 296
  of system of particles, 41–52, 261–266, 295–**301**
Equimomental systems, 326
Equipollent force systems, 47–52, **70**, 260, 261, 266–273, 293, **301**
Equivalence, of Galilean frames, 480, 481
  mechanical, 9, 10
Equivalent force systems, 47, 63, 64
Equivalent simple pendulum, 200, **223**
Erg, 54
Euler–Bernouilli, law, 96, **114**
  theory of beams, 95–98, **114**

Eulerian angles, 288–290
  angular velocity in terms of, **309**, 310
Euler's equations of motion, 352, **360**
Euler's theorem, 279, 280, **301**
Event, 11, 478, **498**
Ewald, P. P., 88
Extension, 96
External forces, 41, 42

F

Ferel's law, 408
Ferry, E. S., 445
Fictitious forces, 138, 139, 141–144, **147**, 347–351, 406
Field, scalar or vector, 28
Field of force, 66
  electromagnetic, 381–403, **412, 413**
  electrostatic, 381, 383–387, 390–392, 396, **412**
  gravitational, 82–86, 144, 405
  magnetostatic, 381, 382, 383–388, 390–392, 397, **412**
  uniform, 67
Finite displacement of rigid body, 278–282, **301, 302**
Flexible cable (*see* Cable)
Flywheel, 196–198
Focal length, of electromagnetic lens, 403
Foot, 13
Force, 15–17, **35**
  absolute, 495
  applied, 58, 295
  central, 128, 168–**185**, 462
  centrifugal, 143–**147**, 349, 350, 406
  on charged particle, 176, 382
  Coriolis, 143, 144, **147**, 349, 406
  effective, 138
  external and internal, 41, 42
  fictitious, 138, 139, 141–144, **147**, 347–351, 406
  field of, 66, 67
  of friction, 87, 88
  generalized, 293–301, **302**, 462, 464–467, **472**

Force of gravity, 82–86, 144–146, 404, 509
  impulsive, 228–**238**, 357–359, **361**, **470–472**
  in relativity, 479, 495–**499**
  reversed effective, 138, **147**
  shearing, 92–97, **114**, 272, 273
  total, 259, 285, **301**
  transmissibility of, 64
  unit of, 16, 34, 502
Force system, general, 259–261
  invariants of, 269, 270, 285
  reduction of, 50–52, **70**, 266–273, **301**
Force systems, equipollent, 47–52, **70**, 260, 261, 266–273, 293, **301**
  equivalent, 47, 63, 64
Forced oscillations, 166–168, **185**
Forces, parallelogram of, 32, 33, **36**
  polygon of, 40
  triangle of, 40
  which do no work, 54–57, **70**
Foucault's pendulum, 408–411, **414**
Foundations of mechanics, 3–**35**, **36**
Frame of reference, 11, 12, **35**, 477
  astronomical, 31, 33, 141, 143
  Galilean, 478, 479
  moving, 139–146, **147**, 346–351, **361**
  Newtonian, 32–34, 132, 134, **147**
  reduced to rest, 141–143, **147**, 347, 349, 350
  in relative motion in relativity, 480–491
  rotating, 142, 143, **147**, 347–351, **361**
Frames, 106–113, **115**
  analytical and graphical methods, 113
  critical forms, 113
  just-rigid and over-rigid, 106, 107
  simple and complex, 111, 112
  summary of methods, **115**
Frazer, R. A., 316
Free particle, in Newtonian mechanics, 32
  in relativity, 489, 490, **498**

Free vector, 18, 19
Freedom, degrees of, 207, 208, 287
Frenet-Serret formulas, 264
Frequencies, normal, 211–214, **223**, 468, 469
Frequency of harmonic oscillator, 162, 163
  (*See also* Periodic time)
Friction, 86–92, **114**
  angle of, 87, 88, **114**
  coefficient of, 87, 88, **114**
  cone of, 87
  limiting, 88
Function defined by differential equations, 364
Fundamental plane, 39
Future and past, determination of, 340, 341

G

g, 85, 86, **114**, 144–146, 405
Galilean frame of reference, 478, 479
General theory of relativity (*see* Relativity)
Generalized coordinates, 285–292, **302**, 462–**472**
Generalized forces, 293–301, **302**, 462, 464–467, **472**
Generalized impulsive forces, 470–**472**
Geodesic, 265, 266, 339
Gradient vector, 28–31, **35**, **36**
Gram, 13
Gravitation in relativity, 477
Gravitational attraction, 82–86, **114**, 144–146, 176–177, 404, 405, 509
Gravitational constant (G), 82–84, 176, 509, 510
Gravity, center of, 84–86, **114**, 271
Growth of vector, 348
Gyration, radius of, 189
Gyrocompass, 444–447, **454**
Gyroscope, 429, 441–447, **454**
Gyroscopic couple, 442–444, **454**
Gyroscopic effect of rotary engine, 444
Gyrostat (*see* Gyroscope)

H

Hamilton, W. R., 33
Harmonic oscillator, 159–168, **184, 185**
   with constant disturbing force, 162, **184**
   damped, 163–168, **185**
   forced oscillations of, 166–168, **185**
Hemisphere, mass center of, 78, 81
Hemispherical shell, mass center of, 81, 82
Herpolhode cone, 309
Heterogeneous body, 76
Hodograph, 120, 121, **125**, 156, **184**
Holonomic system, 287
Homogeneous body, 76
Hooke's joint, 297, 298
Hooke's law, 96, **114**
Hoop, moment of inertia of, 190, **222**
Horizontal plane, 85
   or rotating earth, 145, 403
Horsepower, 54
Hyperbolic orbit, 179, **185**

I

Image, formed by electromagnetic lens, 391, 395–403, **413**
Image plane, 395, **413**
Image point, 395
Impulse, 227, 357
Impulsive couple, 229
Impulsive force, 228–**238**, 357–359, **361**, 470–**472**
Impulsive moment, 230, 231, **238**, 358, **361**
Impulsive motion, 227–**238**, **239**, 356–359, **361**, 470–**472**
Ince, E. L., 393
Inclined plane, 202–204
Indeterminate problems, 68, 69, 90, 278
Inertia, moments of (see Moments of inertia)
   products of (see Products of inertia)

Infinitesimal displacement of rigid body, 61, 62, **70**, 281–285, **290, 302**
Ingredients, of mechanics, 8–17, **35**
   of relativity, 476–478
Instability (see Stability)
Instantaneous axis, 308
Instantaneous center, 123–**125**
Integration of equations of motion in power series, 339, 340
Intensity of wrench, 269
Internal forces, 41, 42
Internal reactions, in beam, 92, 93, 114, 272, 273
   in flexible cable, 98
   in rigid body, 56, 57, **70**, 206, 207
Intrinsic equation of catenary, 102
Intrinsic equations of motion, **338**
Invariable line, 419
Invariable plane, 420, **453**
Invariant element in space-time, 489
Invariants, of force system, 269, 270, 285
   of infinitesimal displacement, 285
Inverse square law, 176–**185**
Isotropy of Galilean frame, 478, 479

J

Jacobian elliptic functions, 364–370, **411, 412**
Jahnke, E., 370
Joints, in a frame, 106, 107
   method of, 108–110, **115**
Just-rigid frame, 106, 107

K

Kaufmann, method of, 387
Kelvin's theorem, 363
Kepler's laws, 181, 182
Kinematics, of particle, 118–121, **125**, 305–308, **332**
   in relativity, 485–495, **498**
   plane, 118–**125**
   of rigid body, 121–**125**, 308–313, **332**
   in space, 305–313, **332**

Kinetic energy, of mass center, 195
  of particle, 129, **146, 333**, 460
  of rigid body, 193–196, **222, 223**, 327–329, **333**
  of system, 136, 137, **147**, 463
König, theorem of, 195

L

Lagrange's equations, 458–**472**
  applications of, 467–472
  for general system, 466, 467, **472**
  for impulsive motion, 470–**472**
  for particle in a plane, 459–462
  for system with two degrees of freedom, 463–466
Lamb, H., 16, 113, 281, 445
Lamina, representative, 61
Lamy's theorem, 40
Laplace's equation, 381, 382
Latitude, astronomical, 145, 403
Law, of action and reaction, 32, **36**
  of motion, 32, 33, **36**, 140–143, **147**, 347, 349, 350
  of the inverse square, 176–**185**
  of the parallelogram of forces, 32, 33, **36**
Laws, of friction, 87, 88
  of Newtonian mechanics, 31–34, **36**
Left-handed triad, 247
Length, 11
  unit of, 11, 13, 14, 501, 502
Lens, electric, 403
  electromagnetic, 392–403, **413**
  magnetic, 403
  (*See also* Electrostatic lens; Magnetostatic lens)
Level surface, 29
Lift, 272, 512, 513
Light, in relativity, 479–481, 483, 485, 489, 496, **498**
  speed of, 27, 483
Limiting velocity, 159
Line density, 77
Linear moment, 74

Linear momentum, in impulsive motion, 229, 230, **238**, 357, 358, **361**
  of particle, 128, 337, 495, 496
  of system, 132–134, **146, 147**, 343, **360**
Linked rods, 236–238, 471, 472
Loaded string, vibrations of, 208–212, 511, 512
Logarithmic decrement, 166
Lorentz transformation, 480–491, **498**
Luneberg, R. K., 388

M

Mach, E., 16
Magnetic field, axially symmetric, 387, 388, 390–392, 397
  uniform, 383–387, **412**
Magnetic lens, focal length of, 403
  (*See also* Magnetostatic lens)
Magnetic potential, 382
Magnetic vector, 382
Magnetostatic field, 381–388, 390–392, 397, **412**
Magnetostatic lens, 398, **413**
Mass, 9, 10
  of electron, 386, 387
  in relativity, 495
  unit of, 10, 13, 14, 501, 502
Mass center, 74–82, **113, 114**
  angular momentum relative to, 135, 136, **147**, 330, 345, 355, **360, 361**
  found by integration, 77, 81, 82, **114**
  found by symmetry and decomposition, 77–79, **114**
  kinetic energy of, 195
  motion of, 132–134, **147**, 230, **238**, 343, **360, 361**
  motion relative to, 134–136, **147**, 234, 235, **238**, 344, 345, **360, 361**
  of solar system, 134
Mathematical models, 5, 6

Mathematical truth, 7
Mathematical way of thinking, 4, 5, 508
Mathematicians' equations, 506, 507
Matrix, 316
Mean anomaly, 187
Measuring rod or scale, 11, 477, 501, 502
   relativistic contraction of, 486, 487, 490
Mechanical equivalence of bodies, 9, 10
Mechanics, foundations of, 3-35, 36
Mercury, 7, 31, 379
Metacenter, 225
Methods, of dynamics in space, 337-359, **360, 361**
   of plane dynamics, 127-146, **147**
   of plane statics, 38-**69, 70**
Michelson, A. A., 481
Michelson-Morley experiment, 481
Milne-Thomson, L. M., 370
Minimum of potential energy, 214 220, **223**, 296
Mixed triple product, 250, 251, **257**
Model, mathematical, 5-7
   used for prediction of full-scale phenomena, 512, 513
Modes of vibration, normal, 207-214, **223**
Modulus, compression, 186
   of elliptic functions, 367
   Young's, 96, **114**
Moment, bending, 92-98, **114**, 272, 273
   of couple, 49, 50, 267
   impulsive, 230, 231, **238**, 358, **361**
   linear, 74
   of momentum, 128
   (*See also* Angular momentum)
   pitching, 272
   total, 259, 285, **301**
   of vector, about line, 43-45, 255-**257**
     in plane mechanics, 44, **70**
     about point, 252-255, **257**

Momental ellipse, **322, 323**
Momental ellipsoid, 315, 316, 318, 321, 322, **333**
Moments of inertia, 189-193, **222**, 313-326, **333**
   found by decomposition and differentiation, 325, 326
   principal, 316, 318-320, 322-325, **333**
   of simple bodies, 190-193, **222**, 323-325
Momentum (*see* Angular momentum, Linear momentum)
Morley, E. W., 481
Motion, defined, 14
   of charged particle, 381-403, **412, 413**
   impulsive (*see* Impulsive motion)
   of mass center, 132-134, **147**, 230, **238**, 343, **360, 361**
   of particle, under central force, 168-184, **185**, 462
     determined by initial conditions, 339, 340
     in plane, 118-121, **125**, 127-131, **146**, 151-**184-186**, 212-214, 459-462
     relative to moving frame of references, 139-143, **147**, 346-351
     in relativity, 489-**498, 499**
     in space, 305-308, 337-343, **360**, 364-**411-414**
   relative to mass center, 134-136, **147**, 234, 235, **238**, 344, 345, **360, 361**
   of rigid body, parallel to fixed plane, 121-124, **125**, 189-**222, 223**
     with fixed point, 308-310, **332**, 351-355, **360**, 418-444, **453, 454**
     general, 310-313, **332**, 355, 356, **361**, 447-453, **454**
   of system, 131-139, **146, 147**, 189-**222, 223**, 343-346, **360**
Moving constraints, 474

524 INDEX

Moving frames of reference, 139–146, **147**, 346–351, **361**
Moving rod, contraction of, 486, 487, 490
Multiplication, of vector and scalar, 19, 20
　of vectors, 245–**257**
Murnaghan, F. D., 16
Myers, L. M., 392

N

Necessary conditions of equilibrium, 39, 40, 42, 43, 45–47, 59, 60, **69, 70**, 262, 263, 273–275, 296, **301**
Neutral equilibrium, 216
Newton, I., 32, 82, 176, 475
Newtonian frame of reference, 32–34, 132, 134, **147**
Newtonian law of gravitational attraction, 82
Newtonian mechanics, laws of, 31–**35, 36**
Newtonian unit of time, 12
n-gonal symmetry, 322
Non-holonomic system, 287, 466
Normal components of velocity and acceleration, 118, 119, **125**, 305, 306, **332**
Normal frequencies and periods, 211–214, **223**, 468, 469
Normal modes of vibration, 207–214, **223**
Normal reaction, 87
Normal vector, principal, 264
Notation, dimensional, 503
　for vectors, 19
Null lines in space-time, 489
Null planes and lines in statics, 304
Nutation of top, 432

O

Object plane, 395
Object point, 395
Observer in relativity, 477
Optics, electron (*see* Charged particle)

Orbit, central, 166–184, **185, 186**
　circular, 174–176
　elliptical, 169, 179–182, **185**, 374
　　(*See also* Planetary orbit)
　hyperbolic or parabolic, 179, **185**
Ordered triad, 247
Orthogonal triad, 23
Oscillation, center of, 201
Oscillations, damped, 163–168, **185**
　deadbeat, 166, **185**
　forced, 166–168, **185**
　harmonic, 160–162, **184**
　　(*See also* Pendulum, Vibration)
Oscillator, harmonic, 159–168
Osculating plane, 264
Over-rigid frame, 106

P

Pappus, theorems of, 80, **114**
Parabola in suspension bridge, 100, **114**
Parabolic orbit, 179, **185**
Parabolic trajectory of projectile, 151–154, **184**
Parallel axes, theorem of, 191–193, **222**
Parallel forces, 270, 271
Parallelepiped (*see* Cuboid)
Parallelogram of forces, 32, 33, **36**
Parallelogram law, for couples, 268
　for infinitesimal rotations, 282
Particle, 8, 9, **35**
　angular momentum of, 128, 129, **146**, 329, **333**, 341, **360**
　under central force, 128, 168–184, **185**, 462
　charged, 176, 381–403, **412, 413**
　dynamics of, 127–131, **146**, 151–**184–186**, 212–214, 337–343, **360**, 364–**411–414**, 459–462, 491–**498, 499**
　equilibrium of, 39, 40, **69, 70**, 262, **301**
　free, 32, 489, 490, **498**
　kinematics of, 118–121, **125**, 305–308, **332**, 485–495, **498**

Particle, kinetic energy of, 129, **146, 333,** 460
  Lagrange's equations for, 459-462
  linear momentum of, 128, 337, 495, 496
  in a plane, 64-66, 118-121, **125,** 127-131, **146,** 151-**184**-**186,** 212-214, 217, 218, 370-372, 459-462
  potential energy of, 65-67
  principle of energy for, 129-131, **146,** 341, 342, **360,** 382, 496, 497, **499**
  in relativity, 477, 489-**498, 499**
  on rotating earth, 144-146, 403-411, **414**
  in rotating frame, 142, 143, **147,** 347-351, **361**
  in space, 305-308, 329, **332, 333,** 337-343, 346-351, **360,** 373-**411**-**414**
  on stretched string, 511
Particles, on stretched string, 208-212
  system of (see System of particles)
Past and future, determination of, 339, 340
Pendulum, ballistic, 235, 236
  compound, 198-201, **223,** 370
  conical, 374, 375
  equivalent simple, 200, **223**
  Foucault's, 408-411, **414**
  simple, 159-161, **184,** 370-372, **412**
  spherical, 373-381, **412**
Percussion, center of, 239
Perihelion, 180
Period (see Periodic time)
Periodic solutions of a differential equation, 364-367
Periodic time, 161
  of compound pendulum, 200, 201, **223,** 370
  of harmonic oscillator, 162, 163, 166, 168
  normal, 211-213, **223,** 468, 469
  of planet, 180-182, **185**

Periodic time of simple pendulum, 161, **184,** 372, **412**
Perpendicular axes, theorem of, 193, **222**
Phase of oscillator, 162
Philosophical ideas, 3-8
Physical laws and dimensions, 508-512
Physical truth, 7
Physical way of thinking, 3-5, 508
Physicists' equations, 506, 507
Pitch, of screw displacement, 284, 285
  of wrench, 269, 270, 285
Pitching moment, 272
Plane, fundamental, 39
  inclined, 202-204
  invariable, 420, **453**
  osculating, 264
  of symmetry, 78, 321
Plane dynamics, applications in, 151-**184**-**186,** 189-**222, 223**
  methods of, 127-**146, 147**
Plane equipollence, 48
Plane impulsive motion, 227-**238, 239**
Plane kinematics, 118-**125**
Plane mechanics defined, 39
Plane statics, applications in, 74-**113** 115
  methods of, 38-**69, 70**
Planetary orbit, 176-184, **185**
  constants of, 179, 180, **185**
  Kepler's laws for, 181, 182
  periodic time of, 180, 181, **185**
Plumb line on rotating earth, 145, 146, 403, 405
Poinsot, method of, 419-421, 425-429, **453**
Poinsot ellipsoid, 420, 421, 425, **453**
Polhode cone, 309
Polygon of forces, 40
Pöschl, Th., 88
Position vector, 24, **36,** 305
Positive rotation, 247
Potential, electric, 381
  gravitational, 83
  magnetic, 382

Potential energy, 64–67, 70, 85, **114**, 130, 294–297, 299, 300, **302**
   for inverse square law of attraction, 83, 178
   a minimum for stability, 214–221, **223**, 296
Pound, 13
Poundal, 34
Power, 54
Prandtl, L., 88
Precession, 429–432, 438, 442–444, **453**, **454**
Principal axes and moments of inertia, 316–326, **333**
Principal normal, 264
Principal planes of inertia, 318
Principle of angular momentum, in impulsive motion, 230, 231, **238**, 357, 358, **361**
   for particle, 128, 129, **146**, 341, **360**
   relative to mass center, 136, **147**, 202, **223**, 345, **360**, **361**
   for rigid body, 196, 202–204, **223**, 352, 355, **360**, **361**
   for system, 135, **147**, 344, 345, **360**
Principle of energy, for particle, 129–131, **146**, 341, 342, **360**, 382
   in relativity, 496, 497, **499**
   for rigid body, 196, 201, **223**, 352, 356, **360**, **361**
   for system, 136, 137, **147**, 346, **360**
Principle of equivalence, 480, 481
Principle of linear momentum, in impulsive motion, 229, 230, **238**, 357, 358, **361**
   for particle, 337, 496
   for system, 132, **146**, 343, **360**
Principle of virtual work, 57–60, 70, 295, 296, **301**
Procedure in theoretical mechanics, 6, 7
Products of inertia, 313–316, **333**
Products of vectors, 245–**257**
   mixed triple, 250, 251, **257**
   scalar, 245, 246, **257**
   vector, 247–250, **257**
   vector triple, 252, **257**

Projectile, with resistance, 154–159, **184**
   without resistance, 151–154, **184**
   on rotating earth, 407, 408, **414**
   stability of, 440, 441
Propeller, 312, 313, 321, 322
Proper energy, 497
Proper mass, 495
Proper time, 491, 492, **498**

Q

Quantum mechanics, 7, 8, 177, 340, 341

R

Radial components of velocity and acceleration, 120, **125**
Radius, of curvature, 119, 264
   of gyration, 189
   of torsion, 264
Range of projectile, 153, 154
Rate, of change of vector, 347, 348, **361**
   of growth, 348
   of transport, 348
Rawlings, A. L., 445
Reaction, in beam, 92–94, **114**, 272, 273
   normal, 87
   in rigid body, 56, 57, **70**
   in rotating rod, 206, 207
   at rough contact, 86–88, **114**
   at smooth contact, 54, 55, 57, **70**
   workless, 54–57, **70**
Reactions of constraint, 57–59, 295
Rectangular cuboid, moments of inertia of, 324
Rectangular plate, moments of inertia of, 190, **222**, 324
Reduction, of displacement, to screw, 284, 285
   to translation and rotation, 61, 62, 280, 281, **302**
   of general force system, 266–273, **301**

INDEX

Reduction, of plane force system, 50–52, **70**
   of system of parallel forces, 270, 271
Relative energy, 495, 497, **499**
Relative force, 495–**499**
Relative mass, 495
Relative momentum, 495, 496
Relativistic contraction of moving rod, 486, 487, 490
Relativistic slowing down of moving clock, 487, 490
Relativity, fundamental concepts of, 475–480
   general theory of, 7, 177, 476, 477
   measurement of time in, 475–480, 483, 487, 490, 492, 493, **498**
   motion of a particle in, 489–**498**, **499**
   special theory of, 475–**498**, **499**
Representative lamina, 61
Resistance of air, 151, 154–159, **184**
   varying as the square of the velocity, 157–159, **184**
   varying directly as the velocity, 159, **184**
Resonance, 163, 168
Rest, 14
Rest energy, 497
Restitution, 233, 234
   coefficient of, 232–234, **239**
Resultant, of finite rotations, 20, 282
   of forces, 32, **36**
   of infinitesimal displacements, 281–283, **302**
Reversed effective force, 138, **147**
Right-handed triad, 247
Rigid body, 10, 11, **35**
   angular momentum of, 193, 194, **222, 223**, 330–332, **333**
   angular velocity of, 122, **125**, 308–311, **332**
   displacement of, 61, 62, 70, 278–285, **301, 302**
   dynamics of, 189–207, 221–**223**, 351–356, **360, 361**, 418–**453, 454**

Rigid body, equilibrium of, 62–64, **70**, 273–278, **301**
   free, 290
   internal reactions in, 56, 57, 70, 206, 207
   kinematics of, 121–124, **125**, 308–313, **332**
   kinetic energy of, 193–196, **222, 223**, 327–329, **333**
   motion parallel to a plane, 121–124, **125**, 189–207, 221–**223**
   motion in space, 351–356, **360, 361**, 418–**453, 454**
   in relativity, 477
   rotating about fixed axis, 196–201, **223**
   work done by forces acting on, 63, **70**, 292, 293, **302**
Rigid body with a fixed point, angular momentum of, 330–**333**
   angular velocity of, 308–310, **332**
   displacement of, 279–282, 290, **301, 302**
   dynamics of, 351–355, **360**, 418–444, **453, 454**
   equations of motion of, 352, **360**
   Eulerian angles for, 288–290, 309, 310
   Euler's theorem for, 279, 280, **301**
   kinematics of, 308–310, **332**
   kinetic energy of, 327, 328, **333**
   mounting of, 418
   under no forces, 418–429, **453**
   (*See also* Gyroscope; Top)
Rod, moment of inertia of, 190, **222**
Rolling contact, 55–57, **70**, 123, 124
Rolling disk, 450–453, **454**
Rotating frame of reference, 142, 143, **147**, 347–351, **361**
Rotating rod, 206, 207
Rotation, of the earth, 13, 143–146, 403–411, **414**
   about fixed axis, 196–201, **223**
   about fixed point, 279–282, **301, 302**, 308–310, **332**
   instantaneous axis of, 308
   in a plane, 61, 62, 121–**125**

Rotation, positive, 247
Rotations, finite, resultant of, 20, 282
    infinitesimal, resultant of, 281, 282, **302**
Rough contact, 86-88, **114**
Routh's rule, 325
Russell, H. N., 13, 429

S

Scalar, 18
    multiplied by a vector, 19, 20
Scalar field, 28
Scalar product, 245, 246, 249, 250, **257**
Screw displacement, 284, 285
Second, 13, 14
Sections, method of, 110, 111, **115**
Semicircular plate and wire, mass centers of, 80
Separation in space-time, 489, **498**
Shearing force, 92-97, **114**, 272, 273
Shell (see Projectile)
Significant figures, 508
Silberstein, L., 481
Simple frame, 111
Simple harmonic motion, 160-162, **184**
Simple pendulum, equivalent, 200, **223**
    finite oscillations of, 161, 200, 370-372, **412**
    small oscillations of, 159-161, **184**
Sleeping top, 438-440, **453**
Sliding vector, 18
Slowing down of moving clock, 487, 490
Small displacement (see Infinitesimal displacement)
Smooth contact, 54, 55, 57, **70**
sn x, 367-370, **411, 412**
Solar system, dynamics of, 182
    mass center of, 134
Sommerville, D. M. Y., 320
Space centrode, 124, **125**, 309
Space cone, 309, 421, 425, 427, **453**
Space-time, 487-491, **498**
    vectors in, 494, 495

Special theory of relativity (see Relativity)
Speed, 27
    of approach, 232, 233, **239**
    of light, 27, 479-481, 483, 485, 496
    of separation, 232, 233, **239**
Sphere, mass center of, 78
    moment of inertia of, 191, **222**, 324
Spheres, collision of, 231-235
Spherical pendulum, 373-381, **412**
    apse of, 378-381
    general motion of, 375-378, **412**
    small oscillations of, 373, 374, 378-381, **412**
Spherical polar coordinates, 467, 468
Spherical shell, attraction of, 83, 84
    moment of inertia of, 326
Spin of top or gyroscope, 430, 433, 442-444, **453, 454**
Spinning top (see Top)
Stability, of circular orbit, 174-176
    of equilibrium, 214-221, **223**, 296
    of gyroscope, 441, 442, **454**
    of rolling disk, 450-453, **454**
    of sleeping top, 438-440, **453**
    of spinning projectile, 440, 441
Statically determinate problems for beams, 94, 95
Statically indeterminate problems, 68, 69, 90, 278
Statics, plane, applications in, 74-**113-115**
    methods of, 38-69, **70**
    in space, 259-**301, 302**
Stewart, J. Q., 13, 429
Stress, in bar of frame, 108
    in beam, 92, 93, **114**, 272, 273
String (see Cable)
Subtraction of vectors, 21
Sufficient conditions of equilibrium, 39, 40, 59, 60, 62, 63, **69, 70**, 273-275, **301**
Surface, level, 29
    rough, 86-88, **114**
    smooth, 54, 55, 57, **70**
Surface density, 77
Suspension bridge, 100, **114**

INDEX

Symmetry, axis of, 78, 321, 322
  central, 77
  of central orbit, 172, 173, **185**
  diagonal, trigonal, etc., 321
  plane of, 78, 321, 322
  used to find mass centers, 77, 78, **114**
  used to find principal axes, 320–323
Synchronization of clocks, 477–480
System of forces (*see* Force system)
System of particles, angular momentum of, 134, 136, **147**, **320**, 330, 344, 345, **360**
  dynamics of, 131–139, **146**, **147**, 189–222, **223**, 343–346, **360**
  equilibrium of, 41–52, 57–67, 70, 261–266, 295–**301**
  kinetic energy of, 136, 137, **147**, 463
  Lagrange's equations for, 463–**472**
  linear momentum of, 132–134, **146**, **147**, 343, **360**
  potential energy of, 64–67, 137, 294–297, 299, 300, **302**

T

Tangential components of velocity and acceleration, 118, 119, **125**, 305, 306, **332**
Tension, in bar of frame, 108
  in beam, 92–96, **114**, 272
  in cable, 98–105, **114**, **115**, 265, 266
Tensor, 316
Tetragonal symmetry, 321
Tetrahedron, mass center of, 79
Theory of dimensions, 501–513
Theory of relativity (*see* Relativity)
Thin beams, 92–98, **114**
Thrust, 108
Time, in Newtonian mechanics, 12, 13
  proper, 491, 492, **498**
  in relativity, 476–480, 483, 487, 490–493, **498**
  unit of, 12–14, 501, 502
Timoshenko, S., 113

Top, 429–441, **453**
  cuspidal motion of, 436–438
  general motion of, 432–436, **453**, 469, 470
  Lagrange's equations for, 469, 470
  sleeping, 438–440, **453**
  in steady precession, 429–432, **453**
Torque, 196
Torsion, radius of, 264
Total angular impulse, 357
Total energy, 130, 137, 341, 346
Total force, 259, 285, **301**
Total impulse, 357
Total impulsive force, 357
Total moment, 259, 285, **301**
Trajectory, of charged particle, 384, 386, 389–392, **412**, **413**
  of projectile, 151–159, **184**, 407, 408, **414**
Transformation, of axes in space–time, 488
  Lorentz, 480–491, **498**
  Newtonian, 486
  to principal axes of inertia, 318–320, 322, 323
Translation, 61, 279
Transmissibility of force, 64
Transport, acceleration of, 349
  of vector, 348
Transverse components of velocity and acceleration, 120, **125**
Triad, left-handed and right-handed, 247
  ordered, 247
  unit orthogonal, 23
Triangle of forces, 40
Triangular plate, mass center of, 79
Trigonal symmetry, 321
Triple products, 250–252, **257**
Trusses (*see* Frames)
Truth, mathematical and physical, 7
Twisting couple, 272
Two-body problem, 182–184, **186**

U

Uniform field of force, 67
  electromagnetic, 383–387, **412**

Unit coordinate vectors, 23, 247
Unit, of force, 16, 34, **35**, 502
    of length, 11, 13, 14, **35**, 501, 502
    of mass, 10, 13, 14, **35**, 501, 502
    of time, 12–14, **35**, 501, 502
Unit orthogonal triad, 23
Units, arbitrariness of, **35**, 502
    c.g.s and f.p.s., 13
    change of, 504–508

V

Varignon, theorem of, 44, 45, 255, 256
Vector, 17–19
    binormal, 264
    bound, 18, 19
    components of, 22–24, 32, **35**, **36**, 245
    differentiation of 24–26, **35**, 250
    electric, 381
    free, 18, 19
    gradient, 28–31, **35**, **36**
    magnetic, 382
    moment of, 43–45, **70**, 252–**257**
    multiplied by scalar, 19, 20
    notation for, 19
    position, 24, **36**, 305
    principal normal, 264
    rate of change of, 347, 348, **361**
    sliding, 18
    in space-time, 494, 495
    zero, 21
Vector field, 28
Vector function, 24–26
Vector product, 247–250, **257**
Vector triple product, 252, **257**
Vectors, addition of, 19–22, **35**
    coordinate, 23, 247
    products of, 245–**257**
    subtraction of, 21
Vehicle, self-propelled, 204–206
Velocities, composition of, 140, 307, 308, 491
Velocity, 26–28, **36**, 305
    absolute, 494
    angular, 122, **125**, 308–311, **332**

Velocity, areal, 170, 180, **185**
    in cylindrical coordinates, 306, 307
    of light, 27, 479–481, 483, 485, 496
    limiting, 159
    of particle of rigid body, 308–313, **332**
    radial and transverse components of, 120, **125**
    tangential component of, 118, **125**, 305, 306, **332**
Vertical, 85
    on rotating earth, 145, 403
Vibration, normal modes of, 207–214, **223**
    of particle in plane, 212–214
    of particle on stretched string, 511
    of two particles on stretched string, 208–212
    (*See also* Oscillations)
Virtual displacement, 53, 58, 60, 461
Virtual work, 57–60, **70**, 111, **115**, 295, 296, **301**

W

Ways of thinking, 3–5, 508
Weight, 17, 86
    on rotating earth, 145, 404, 405
Whittaker, E. T., xi, 16
Work, 53–67, **70**, 292–301, **302**
    done by couple, 64, 293
    done by force, 53, **70**
    done by forces on general system, 293, 294, **302**
    done by forces on rigid body, 62, 63, **70**, 292, 293, **302**
Work, virtual, 57–60, **70**, 111, **115**, 295, 296, **301**
Workless constraints, 54–55
Wrench, 269, 270, 285, **301**

Y

Young, D. H., 113
Young's modulus, 96, **114**

Z

Zero, force equipollent to, 48, 261
Zero vector, 21